The
COUNSELOR
and the
GROUP

The
COUNSELOR
and the
GROUP

Integrating Theory, Training, and Practice

Fourth Edition

JAMES P. TROTZER, Ph.D.

Routledge
Taylor & Francis Group
New York London

Routledge is an imprint of the
Taylor & Francis Group, an informa business

Published in 2006 by
Routledge
Taylor & Francis Group
711 Third Avenue
New York, NY 10017

Published in Great Britain by
Routledge
Taylor & Francis Group
2 Park Square
Milton Park, Abingdon
Oxon OX14 4RN

© 2006 by Taylor & Francis Group, LLC
Routledge is an imprint of Taylor & Francis Group
First issued in paperback 2013

International Standard Book Number-13: 978-0-415-95197-5 (Hardcover)
International Standard Book Number-13: 978-0-415-86117-5 (Softcover)
Library of Congress Card Number 2005028277

Library of Congress Cataloging-in-Publication Data

Trotzer, James P., 1943-
    The counselor and the group : integrating theory, training, and practice / James P. Trotzer.-- 4th ed.
        p. cm.
    Includes bibliographical references and index.
    ISBN 0-415-95197-6 (alk. paper)
    1. Group counseling. I. Title.

BF637.C6T68 2006
158'.35--dc22   2005028277

Taylor & Francis Group
is the Academic Division of Informa plc.

Visit the Taylor & Francis Web site at
http://www.taylorandfrancis.com

and the Routledge Web site at
http://www.routledge-ny.com

Contents

About the Author

James P. Trotzer is currently a consultant, counselor, coach, group facilitator, and trainer for ETC³ Professional Services and adjunct professor at Granite State College in New Hampshire and Framingham State College in Massachusetts. He received his M.A and Ph.D. degrees from the University of Colorado and completed a year of post-doctoral family therapy training in the Family Psychiatry Department of the Eastern Pennsylvania Psychiatric Institute. He is a Fellow, past President, and active member of the Association for Specialists in Group Work (ASGW) and is a member of the American Counseling Association (ACA), and the International Association of Marriage and Family Therapy (IAMFT).

Dr. Trotzer's professional writing includes twenty-two journal articles, two monographs, several books and book chapters, and a meditation series entitled "Renewing Your Mind: Meditations for Mental Health." His published books include *Marriage and Family: Better Ready than Not*, which he co-authored with his wife, Toni, and *The Counselor and The Group: Integrating Theory, Training, and Practice*, now in its fourth edition. He also serves on the editorial board of the *Journal for Psychology and Theology*. In addition, he has presented over 100 programs at national and international professional conferences.

Dr. Trotzer's clinical experience encompasses over 30 years as a counselor, psychologist, group therapist, marriage and family therapist, consultant, and clinical supervisor. He taught for 13 years as a counselor educator attaining the rank of Professor and for 10 years served as Executive Director of the Renew Counseling Center in Rye, New Hampshire, a nonprofit mental health agency. Additionally, he has over 20 years of experience in private practice. He has served as a visiting professor in Germany, Taiwan, and Japan and as an adjunct professor of counselor education at the Johns Hopkins University, Temple University, and the Rosemead School of Psychology at Biola University. He has been recognized professionally by ASGW, which awarded him its President's Award for Extraordinary Service in 1989 and 2001 and its Professional Practice Award in 1996. He served as President-Elect, President and Past-President of ASGW from 2003–2006.

A noted workshop leader, public speaker, and presenter, Dr. Trotzer has presented programs both nationally and internationally on topics such as "Treating Violence and Conflict in Families," "Counseling the Post-Divorce Family," "Family Therapy as a Group Resource," and "Problem-Solving (Solution-Focused and Brief) Group Counseling." Most recently Dr. Trotzer has developed and presented a training program for conducting crisis intervention discussion groups in the aftermath of local, national, or international traumas including human-made (e.g., September 11) and natural (e.g., tsunami, earthquakes, or hurricanes) disasters. This model is particularly designed for witnesses, bystanders, and those indirectly affected by the trauma as well as those who are directly involved. The training has been conducted in numerous sites in the United States and in Taiwan. Dr. Trotzer brings a wealth of knowledge, wisdom, and experience to his audiences, and his presentations are noted for their practicality, experiential involvement, and humor.

Dr. Trotzer is married to Toni and has three grown and married children. He enjoys biking, hiking and climbing the White Mountains of New Hampshire. He also works part time as a ski instructor and as a historical tour guide in Boston, Lexington and Concord focusing on the Colonial period and the American Revolution.

Preface

My understanding of the role and purpose of a Preface in a textbook is that it is 1) the least likely part of the book to be read or referred to, 2) essentially a place for the author to elaborate on the background dynamics and formulation forces that prompted the work as a sort of ritualistic, cathartic exercise before the book is published, and 3) the place where acknowledgments and appreciation are expressed to persons, places, events, and experiences that have contributed to the book's material and conceptual essence. I suspect that all three factors are accurate and in spite of the delimitation of the first factor, I make the following request of the reader (if noticed): *Please read the preface before reading any other portion of the book. It will provide the necessary perspective that will enhance the usefulness and your understanding of the group process as it is detailed in the text.*

I ask your indulgence regarding the boldness of the following statement, but it is my confirmed belief that the model of group process presented in this text is a model whose time has not only come, but is the very one that has the most relevance to the issues related to doing work in groups whether of a professional counseling or psychotherapy nature or in the context of group work in its many facets and forms that we as professionals participate in. Despite the fact that the model has been on the professional scene for about thirty years, it is in the context of contemporary pressures for efficiency, effectiveness and fiscal mandates for economy that the relevance and utility of the model as presented are realized in the therapeutic domain and in the community at large. Secondly, since the character and nature of group process are now recognized as essential components of all groups, whether therapeutic or task, the utility of the model presented is even more apparent. With that said, let me elaborate on the developmental dynamics of the current edition of *The Counselor and the Group: Integrating Theory, Training, and Practice.*

In writing this fourth edition I have made a concerted effort to maintain the integrity of the text as developed in the first three editions. The theme of integration, the purpose of practicality and the format combining explication and application have been sustained. As noted in the Preface of the first edition, group counseling is a helping process that is used increasingly in agencies, schools, inpatient settings, and private practice. As the viability of this means of helping people resolve their problems grew, so did the need for trained group leaders. This book continues to parallel and reflect that growth by providing information about group process, dynamics, skills, techniques, and experiences that knowledgeable leaders require in order to be effective. However, a concerted effort is also made in this edition to expand the utility of group dynamics and process to groups outside the mental health realm and into the work place and community with an emphasis on application of the model to task groups.

There are five prerequisites for an effective group leader: 1) cognitive knowledge about group process, 2) involvement as a participant in group interaction, 3) skills and techniques for use in the leadership capacity, 4) observation of both models of group leadership and process of group interaction, and 5) supervised experience in the leadership role. This text provides the means and direction for acquiring all five because it contains a wealth of information about *applying* knowledge to process.

This book is for persons in the helping professions who wish to develop or improve not only their understanding of the group process but also their leadership skills and the application of that process across a broad spectrum of groups including counseling/therapy groups, task groups, and other freestanding or temporary groups in which counselors lead or become members. The book specifically lends itself to use by counselor educators who teach group courses, students in training to become group workers, counselors in mental health agencies, private practices and schools that use groups, and consultants in group process in community organizations, business, and industry. Professionals who by the very nature of their professions may wish to enhance their group leadership capacities will find this book useful.

The format of this book is directed toward immediate integration of knowledge, experience, and application. Suggested activities are designed to demonstrate group concepts and provide first-hand involvement with the dynamics of the group process. In addition, most of the activities serve a dual purpose demonstrating cognitive components of the group process and providing prospective leaders with techniques to use in groups of their own. As such, this book is most appropriate for an initial group course and as a text to accompany a supervised group internship or practicum. It is also designed as a handbook for practitioners to use in developing and enhancing their group knowledge and skills and as a resource for understanding group dynamics and implementing group leadership methods and techniques.

Back in May 1985 a special issue of the *Journal for Specialists in Group Work* (Vol. 10, No. 2) entitled "Critical Issues in Group Work: Now and 2001" addressed the nature and prospects of group work in the 1980s and 1990s. A diverse group of contributors confirmed the presence and essence of group work and pronounced the group modality as a fundamentally sound professional tool in response to the therapeutic needs of our human environment. While endorsing the relevance of group work as a humanizing counter force in a society characterized by the dehumanizing forces of technology (information overload and interpersonal isolation), the inherent vulnerabilities of the group approach were also identified. In spite of an evolving history that had substantiated group work as effective across a wide range of helping disciplines, inherent weaknesses were noted that, if allowed to persist without remedy, would not only jeopardize the effectiveness of group work, but threaten its very existence. The weaknesses noted were encapsulated in three main categories: 1) inconsistent and insufficient training of group leaders, 2) need for a more substantial link between theory, research, and clinical practice, and 3) the necessity of integration in terms of theory, training, and practice across all therapeutic modalities (individual, group, couple, and family) and across disciplines. Since the publication of the third edition of this text, great strides have been made in improving the consistency of training and increasing the availability of advanced training in group work. The link between theory, research and practice has been made and is being nurtured and developed by a diverse group of researchers across a broad range of disciplines. And most of all, the centrality of group work within the full spectrum of therapeutic services has been solidified. Therefore, as this fourth edition is published, I am happy to report that this text along with the group work profession and professionals who enact group work have responded to that original mandate with aplomb. Now the task is to embellish and enhance the initiatives that have been launched and established while continuing to press the cutting edge of group work into a broader spectrum of applications so that the relevance of group work will be not only established but grow into a future that recognizes and uses its resourcefulness across disciplines and settings.

Modifications, additions, and revisions of the current edition reflect the progress that has been realized in group work, the contemporary status of group work, and the future prowess of the field. A substantive literature review of group articles published in the last five years served the purpose of updating both references and content to reflect the contemporary state of the field. Chapters solicited and developed for the last edition have been revised and updated along with the basic chapters that form the core of the text. All revisions were designed to emphasize and integrate contemporary issues and cutting edge trends into the text. Specifically chapters on best practices in group counseling and research in group work were revised by the original contributors and an additional colleague and the chapter on multicultural and diversity dynamics in group work was revised by a new contributor. Each of these chapters brings relevance, depth, and breadth to the text and incorporates cutting edge perspectives from the respective authors who are leaders in the group field and experts on their respective topics.

Lynn Rapin and Bob Conyne have once again collaborated in translating the ethics of group work into practice in the revision of their chapter entitled *Best Practices in Group Counseling* (Chapter 8). Lynn served as co-chair of the Association for Specialists in Group Work (ASGW) Ethics Committee that developed the Best Practices Guidelines adopted by ASGW in March, 1998 and has since co-chaired the Professional Standards Committee that along with the Ethics Committee is charged with transforming ASGW's Professional Standards in Group Work and Best Practices documents into group work training protocols. She is in private practice as a licensed psychologist and a counselor educator at the University of Cincinnati. Bob is widely published in the group literature, and is professionally acknowledged as a leading group expert. He has served in multiple leadership capacities in ASGW including President and Editor of the *Journal for Specialists in Group Work*. He is Professor of Counseling and Program Coordinator at Teachers College, University of Cincinnati, and recently received the Eminent Career Award from ASGW. Both Lynn and Bob have been acknowledged as ASGW Fellows.

Niloufer Merchant has written and presented extensively in the group work field and is recognized as a leader with respect to multicultural and diversity aspects of group work. She served as a consultant in the development of ASGW's Principles for Diversity-Competent Group Workers and is the Co-Chair of ASGW's Diversity and Human Rights Committee that is charged with translating the diversity principles document into a group work training protocol. She revised Chapter 9, *Multicultural Group Work*, which takes a pragmatic and realistic view of multicultural and diversity dynamics with respect to group process. Niloufer is a professor in the counselor education department of St. Cloud State University in Minnesota and has served as the Process Observer for the governing Council of the American Counseling Association and the ASGW Executive Board.

Rex Stockton and Paul Toth have been joined by D. Keith Morran in revising the chapter on group research. They have combined their many faceted talents in research, writing, teaching, and practice in the group field to reconstitute their vital and informative chapter bringing us up to date on the flourishing developments in group work research. They address a topic that is often under-emphasized or excluded in group texts. Their chapter 16, *The Case for Group Research: A Practitioner Friendly Proposition*, presents an informative, practical, and viable perspective for group practitioners relative to the vital link between research and practice. Rex is a recognized authority in group research, has served ASGW as President and in many other leadership roles and has an extensive record of publications in the group work field. Recently he was acknowledged as one of the first American Counseling Association Fellows. His research is the focus of a special edition of the *Journal for Specialists in Group Work* (Vol.

30(3), 197–298). He is Professor of Counselor Education at Indiana University. Paul, also a noted author and practitioner, is currently staff psychologist at the Indiana University Student Counseling Center, and Keith is widely published and a professor at Indiana University and Purdue University at Indianapolis. The three authors have collaborated in numerous group research endeavors and represent a research cohort in their own right.

Acknowledgments for this fourth edition span almost four decades of people, places, experiences, and events. Without them the cumulative result and continuing evolution of this text and my own experience and expertise would diminish. My interest and training in group work was initiated and nurtured into existence by Al Roark and Bill Sease, my mentors at the University of Colorado who gave me my first opportunities to study, research, and practice group work.

The extended group leadership experience that really taught me about group process, group dynamics, and therapeutic factors in groups occurred in the Intensive Treatment Unit of the Minnesota State Prison. I consider that experience as my experiential doctorate in group work. I am sure I learned more than the inmates benefitted, but I am deeply grateful to them. Combined with the many graduate student training group experiences and the groups I have been privileged to run in agencies, schools, churches and private practice, the debt to group members is only partially repaid by passing on what I have learned and taught. I have been fortunate to have had many perceptive and dedicated graduate students who have encouraged and many times forced me to grow and learn.

To Dr. C. S. Peng, former Chair of the Guidance Department at Taiwan Provincial College of Education (now National Changhua University of Education) I owe a special debt of gratitude for his role in motivating and encouraging me to write the first edition of this text during my tenure there as a visiting professor.

Professional colleagues during both my first and second "tour of duty" as a counselor educator have been and are stimulating contributors to the content and perspectives of the text. Wayne Kassera, Jim Lipsky, Dan Ficek, John Hamann among others at the University of Wisconsin-River Falls and Murray Finley at Rhode Island College are particular persons who merit acknowledgment. During the interim period of private practice and agency work, I am indebted to Ralph Fessler, Graduate Dean at The Johns Hopkins University and Fred Bemak (now at George Mason University) who made it possible for me to maintain my teaching orientation and formulate my conceptual framework while engaged in clinical practice by giving me the opportunity to teach group and family courses during summer sessions.

To Joe Hollis (now deceased) and his staff at Accelerated Development who assisted me in the renovation project that became the second edition of this text I owe a great deal of thanks. The input of their work and insight continues to reverberate in this edition. To the original Taylor & Francis staff that worked on the third edition, especially acquisitions editor Tim Julet, editorial assistant

Jill Osowa (now Jill Millard), and production editor Stephanie Weidel, I owe special thanks for the rigorous and stimulating process of refining that edition into reality. Finally a special note of thanks and appreciation to the staff at the Routledge, Taylor & Francis Group who did wonders in transforming the content of this edition into a streamlined and dynamic gem as a text and book that has appeal across the full gamut of professional readers, students, and practitioners alike. I especially thank George Zimmer and Brook Cosby who got the revision rolling and acquisitions editor Jay Whitney, his assistant Charlotte Roh, production editor Julie Spadaro, and Lynn Goeller and the staff of EvS for bringing it to fruition.

Finally, I wish to acknowledge my long term association with the group of dedicated and talented group work professionals who are the Association for Specialists in Group Work. Past, current, and ongoing relationships have immensely affected me personally and professionally, and activities engaged in under the auspices of the organization and its leaders and as President have contributed significantly to the content of this book. Special recognition goes to the following:

- Ben Cohn who initially provided me with a forum for developing and presenting my ideas about group work by including me in his team conducting group counseling workshops across the country.
- Marguerite "Peg" Carroll who as ASGW President recruited me to head up the ASGW Family Counseling Commission whose activities, presentations, and articles prompted much of the material for chapter 14 (*Family Theory as a Group Resource*) and who later as Director of the ASGW Training Institute Program enlisted my services as an Instructor.
- Bob Conyne who as editor of the *Journal for Specialists in Group Work* during my 3-year stint on the editorial board challenged and motivated me to think more seriously about writing and who as President continued to encourage and solicit my professional input.
- Diana Hulse-Killacky who as President literally propelled me into the group work spotlight and has subsequently been a supportive and stimulating colleague.
- Beverly Brown who offered me the opportunity to serve as Process Observer for the Executive Council during her term of office. That experience served to solidify and promote my interest and expertise in the process application of group dynamics to task and organizational groups and resulted in a series of articles on process observation that have been incorporated into this text.
- Michael Hutchins and Jeremiah Donigian who enlisted my services as co-coordinator of the ASGW Education and Training Cluster which gave me access to personnel and resources tapped for various aspects of this text.

- Andy Horne under whose tutelage I served as Co-Chair of the Professional Development Committee that in turn spawned ASGW's Advanced Group Training Institute that I have had the privilege to both develop, direct and participate in as an Instructor.
- Presidents Linda Keel, Lynn Rapin, Rod Merta and George Leddick kept me connected and involved professionally providing me with inspiration as well as encouragement to continue to develop the Professional Development thrust of ASGW that in effect led into my being elected President. The point of this recognition is that much of the professional development emphasis evident in this edition emerged under and in association with their leadership.

My current professional status relative to group work is directed toward training group workers encompassing undergraduates in groups dynamics, masters level graduate students in group and family counseling and group workers in clinical practice through the Advanced Group Training Institute. Specifically, I emphasize the adaptation of my model of group counseling to problem solving that is progressive, solution-focused and brief and can be utilized and applied in therapeutic, school, community, organizational, and work settings. I have extended the model's relevance to work and task groups and developed a highly effective crisis intervention group training model that trains leaders to run crisis groups in the aftermath of human-made, natural or accidental disasters at the local, national and international level. That focus is the subject of a new chapter on crisis intervention groups (see chapter 15). As a process consultant I am active in serving task/work and organizational groups as a process observer, trainer, and workshop leader. As a result of all the diverse settings and experiences that accompany my professional life, I have realized more than ever that, like the "Force" in the Star Wars saga, group process is always with you.

My experience in writing this fourth edition has been both a humbling and a growth experience. The humbling part emanates from the change in perspective that has evolved over the four editions. When I wrote the first edition I was in my thirties and the finished product represented everything I knew about groups. When in my forties I completed the second edition—which had expanded from 200 to 500 pages of text—I had the illusionary or delusionary feeling that it represented everything there was to know about groups. When I completed the third edition, I was in my fifties and was most impressed by how much I didn't know about groups and how much there was to know. That is the humbling part. Now that I am in my sixties the excitement of writing this edition, and what I consider to be the growth part, is that I am amazed, awed and deeply impressed with the wonderful work that is being done and published in the group work field. As I did the research for this edition I was struck with the high caliber of the up and coming group workers who, along with those who are the core and leaders of the field, as practitioners, educators, researchers, trainers or all of the above, are forging an impressive professional arena that I am proud to participate in and contribute to. Their extensive group work knowledge and ability nurtured and disseminated by the technological resources and demonstrated by research and practice exudes a prowess that has stimulated great excitement about the field of group work and affirmed my commitment to it.

My hope is that this fourth edition of *The Counselor and the Group* will continue to be a functional tool in the training process and practice of group work. Someone once compared teaching with doing and noted that doing is the humbler work. This book is thus dedicated to the doers, the group workers, in hopes that it will serve as a resource in the often difficult and thankless occupation of helping, leading and facilitating and the always challenging effort to interact effectively with people in groups whether they are clients, co-workers or colleagues, strangers, family or friends. In any case, it is great to know that group work is dynamic not static and as such is energizing in itself. Just as growth never stops, so the process of helping people grow must never stop—otherwise, we become impediments to growth and healing rather than facilitators or stimuli to them. Therefore I present this edition to you with the sincere desire that it will spur your professional development as group workers in a constructive and fulfilling manner just as preparing it has done for me.

And finally, (and this is really just for me) I want to express my appreciation and gratitude to my ever expanding primary group, my family, who have taught and continue to teach me about the joys and challenges of intimate group interaction, and who continue to encourage, demand, and invite me to grow as a person and a group member.

JIM TROTZER

Prologue

The emergence of the metaphor as a pragmatic and creative tool in the conduct of counseling and psychotherapy has provided clinicians with a resource that can be adapted to any client, context, and modality. A metaphor is a word, picture, object, story, or analogy that conveys information and meaning that has therapeutic impact cognitively, behaviorally, and affectively. Clinically, metaphors "represent words, analogies, non-verbal expressions and stories in which thoughts and feelings about an emotionally charged situation have been transferred to an analogical situation that preserves the original dynamics" (McClure, 1989, p. 239). As such, metaphors create analogies that substitute "a non-threatening external subject for a threatening internal one" enabling clients to experience affectively charged "worlds of meaning from a safe distance" (Rossel, 1981, p. 120). Gladding (1984, 1992a, & 1992b, 1998, 2002) explicated the metaphor as a particularly relevant tool in group work (Campbell, 1996), and the literature is replete with examples of how metaphors are utilized in groups (e.g., Carmichael, 2000; James & Martin, 2002; Mathis & Tanner, 2000).

Metaphors serve to enhance learning and therapeutic impact in many ways. They inform (establish meaning), amplify (expand meaning), illuminate (supply meaning), and provide material for interpretation (suggest meaning) (McClure, 1989). As such the metaphor has impressed me with its usefulness in both clinical practice and teaching. For many years now I have started each group class I have taught by developing and sharing a metaphor for group work. I have also incorporated these metaphors into the initial sessions of my counseling and therapy groups. The result has typically fostered engagement in the process and produced constructive results relative to learning and experience. So as we begin our journey together into this fourth edition of *The Counselor and the Group*, I would like to share the following metaphor for group work:

Group work is like a bird feeder
or
Everything I ever learned about group dynamics and process I learned by watching my bird feeder.

I have a couple of bird feeders in my back yard that I can observe while sitting at the kitchen table. One day as I watched the flurry of activity around the bird feeders, it occurred to me that the essence of group work is effectively reflected in the dynamics surrounding the bird feeder, hence the metaphor that follows.

Doing group work is like setting up and maintaining a bird feeder in your back yard. The bird feeder is not the bird's natural habitat and as such is an artificial intrusion in their lives, but birds are attracted to it, use it, accommodate to it, become attached to it, and benefit from it. This concept is particularly relevant to psychoeducational, counseling and therapy groups that are established to provide needed skills or information or on a need basis of client problems or personality issues. The leader is the person who determines what type of bird feeder to set up (type of group: boundaries, parameters, and purposes) and what kind of bird feed to put in it (style of leadership and content emphasized). The type of feeder and nature of the feed determines the birds that will show up to eat at the feeder (members of the group).

Like group members, there are many types of birds (small, medium sized, and large birds; different species of birds—Blue Jays, Cardinals, Morning Doves, Chickadees, Sparrows, Finches, Rose-Breasted Grossbeaks, Crows, Pigeons, and Seagulls; seasonal and year-round birds—short-term and long-term groups). The birds reflect both similarity and diversity, and at any one time the bird feeder may have homogeneous activity as flocks of the same species inhabit the feeder or heterogeneous activity with many species being represented. But in either case there is always uniqueness in how individual birds feed and react. Sometimes the birds get along together, cooperate, collaborate (help each other) and sometimes they fight (conflict), compete (challenge) and intimidate (apply peer pressure or bully). Some birds come in couples, some in flocks, and some alone (all reflective of how members show up and are selected to participate or elect to do so).

Birds have different styles of relating to both the feeder and each other. Some fly in and out grabbing a bit of food and then leaving, repeating this pattern until they are satisfied. Some claim and defend a perch until they are done eating. Others knock feed out of the feeder and on to the ground either for themselves, their companions or their offspring. In fact, sometimes they are amazingly "other-oriented," a trait we as human beings are wise to emulate in relationships and which is a useful commodity in effective groups.

The bird feeder experience is also fraught with dangers from both inside and out. Some birds like Blue Jays and Starlings are continually intimidating other birds and seem to have no ability to share the feeder. They are like members who endanger other group members or dominate to the detriment of the group. Other dangers come from outside the group like the squirrels who try to commandeer the feeder for their own use, and cats who stalk the feeder in hopes of making one of the birds their lunch. Like the tender of the bird feeder, the leader has to make the group safe (put up baffles to fend off the squirrels and scare off the cats). Groups, like bird feeders, must be safe places for the participants. That objective is one of the most important responsibilities of the leader and must be incorporated into the ground rules or norms of the group.

Some birds do not fit the bird feeder because they are too big or too heavy (bird feeders, like groups, are designed with different types of birds/members in mind). This relates to the screening mandate for group inclusion or exclusion. In addition, there are problem birds that must be dealt with by the other birds and in some cases by the tender of the bird feeder. In any event the activity of the bird feeder reflects the dynamic interaction between the birds (members), the bird feeder attendant (leader), and the bird feed (focus and purpose of the group). In many ways this book is a manual for setting up and attending to a bird feeder (i.e., establishing and leading groups of various types for a variety of members in a host of environments).

If you are using this book in a class, the bird feeder metaphor also has relevance. The class is the bird feeder. The instructor is the one who sets it up and fills it (syllabus, course outline, agenda, teaching style, and content). You are the birds (students/members) who choose to come to eat. Most likely you will also have the opportunity to tend the feeder (leadership opportunities) and observe the activity around the feeder (process observation). Like a bird feeder, the course is a temporary addition to your life that you can use to acquaint yourself with the essence of group work and engage in the process of developing your self as a group worker (leader, member, and process observer). You will use as much or as little of this book and course as you choose, and it will be up to you to decide what you will take away and what you will discard. My job is to create a manual that provides information, guidelines, and tools that will assist you in setting up your bird feeders (groups) and lays the foundation for effective group work. My hope is that you will enjoy your bird feeder experience and become fully immersed in group work as an integral part of your professional life.

Learning Activity

As you read this book, develop a metaphor that captures the essence of group work for you. Keep a log or journal with ideas and applications gleaned from your reading and experiences. As you read each chapter, develop the metaphor to incorporate key concepts that are presented. When you have finished the book, write a comprehensive explanation of your metaphor representing your understanding and perspective of group work. If you are in a class or group setting, share the metaphor with your colleagues in an interactive forum. If you are leading a group, share the metaphor with the group as a means of generating group process. I regularly assign the task of developing a group metaphor in the first class and have class members share their metaphors as a culminating experience in the final class session. This activity produces a wonderfully creative elaboration of each person's learning in the course and produces a fascinating interactive closing process to the class group experience. To assist you in your initial thinking about a metaphor read the following example as a resource to stimulate your creative thinking (Breier, 1997, p.12).

Group Counseling is Like . . .
by Christine A. Breier

. . . a track event because everyone can't go forward if there is a false start.

. . . a beard because it can get a little hairy at times.

. . . photography because you give it your best shot and see what develops.

. . . carbon monoxide because an unacknowledged presence in the room can be fatal if not caught in time.

. . . the deep south because sometimes you've got to take the heat.

. . . a ball point pen because sometimes it rolls and sometimes it doesn't.

. . . a side-view mirror because sometimes things are bigger than they appear.

. . . ironing because sometimes a little steam is necessary to work the wrinkles out.

. . . fishing because sometimes the fish are biting most when the surface is calm.

. . . a geode because there are many sparklies waiting to be found inside.

. . . e-mail because there's no communicating if the system crashes.

. . . a microwave because there's warmth created when lives touch and bounce off one another.

. . . a turtleneck because some people can feel warm while others feel choked.

. . . a smoke detector because it intermittently chirps loud when it needs more energy to do its work.

. . . an abacus because it can be counted on.

. . . a postage stamp because oftentimes the parts that are the most gluey stick best over the long haul.

. . . a washing machine because you might have to go around and around before you come clean.

. . . a computer keyboard because you have to enter and then return.

1
Introduction and Context

In our technologically sophisticated and media driven world, individuals are bombarded by default and by choice with more information in one day than our ancestors were exposed to in a lifetime. There is more information on the head of a pin (micro-chip) than is housed in a library. (Futurist quip)

Our Changing World

The evidence is overwhelming that the world around us is changing at an ever increasing rate and that we as individuals are faced with an ever more expansive and complex environment. We are constantly forced to adjust and adapt if we want to achieve our potential, individually and collectively. More than three decades ago Gazda (1971a) pointed out that "the world each of us personally inhabits grows steadily and rapidly larger. No (person) today has any choice but to be part of a greater and more diverse community" (p. 6). That observation has not only been realized, but accelerated by the technological advancements of the computer age.

The primary indicator of our expanding world is that we are inundated with the exponential development of new information often referred to as the knowledge explosion. Access to that new knowledge is promulgated by the perpetual evolution of the information superhighway that gives us rapid retrieval through computer technology, the internet, email, fax machines, instant messaging, and cellular phones. So sophisticated is consumer access to information that Waitley's (1978) observation that we are bombarded with eight times more information than our grandparents were exposed to in their lifetime is archaic. Futurists drumming the perspective of space age technology indicate there is no possibility of human beings keeping up with the development of new knowledge in any

1

discipline without the assistance or rather the necessity of computers. No wonder people who have not grown up with computers as their mode of communication feel completely overwhelmed. Even those with computer competence and allegiance have difficulty keeping pace with the rapid changes in the information industry. Such realities have prompted ethologists to muse about the impact of knowledge acquired technologically rather than through human intermediaries in the course of human evolution (Miller, 2001).

Information overload that encourages and demands dependence on technology not only overwhelms individuals but produces a byproduct of isolation (Klein, 1985). As individuals, our sense of identity is eroded as it becomes modified by and melded with the mechanics of knowledge rather than forged in the cauldron of human interaction. As this experience escalates, the seeds of dehumanization are planted, nurtured, and bloom into a world society where electronic interpersonal contact globally supercedes talking with your neighbor (Beebe, Beebe, & Redmond, 2005). It is more likely that you will communicate via e-mail with a business associate in another country or with a long lost friend who looked you up on the Internet rather than to spend a few minutes passing the time of day with your next door neighbor.

The problems of adjusting to such a world, however, are not the result of the essence or speed of change itself nor the nature or plethora of knowledge, but rather are the result of the conflict that is produced because individual adjustment to change is a slow process. C. Gilbert Wrenn (1962, 1971), one of the forefathers of the counseling movement and a great humanitarian, noted that the critical conflict of the human experience is associated with the discrepancy between what he called outer reality and inner reality. Outer reality—the world outside the boundaries of the individual person—changes very quickly. Inner reality—each person's personality, identity, values, attitudes, and perceptions—changes very slowly. Consequently, all human problems are essentially adjustment problems. The clash between these two realities sums up the basic stress we all experience and provides a context for the problems that confront us.

Since the pace of scientific and technological change far exceeds that of social change, each of us is confronted with the task of not only getting ourselves together but also developing the interpersonal skills necessary to meet our needs in a global, mobile, and changing society. This requires each individual to be strong, flexible, and able to act interdependently and collaboratively. Each of us must increase what Toffler (1970) called our "cope-ability" capacity defined as the speed and economy with which we adapt to change.

The personal consequences of change in our environment are readily evident. The individual is bombarded with the inconceivable nature of change, the futility of understanding or impeding it, and the inability to change quickly enough to adapt to it. "We have more knowledge than we know what to do with, more people than we know how to live with, more physical energy than we know how to cope with, and in all things a faster rate of change than we know how to keep up with" (Dyer, 1967, p. 4). The implications of these realizations on our existence have effected a massive shift in our patterns of life, our sense of security and our definitions of human functionality and mental health.

Life styles have paradoxically taken on characteristics of a global expansiveness communicationally while generating relational reclusiveness personally. A person can do business by fax, e-mail, cell phone, or the Internet all over the world but remain interpersonally isolated relying on technology to stay in contact rather than making a connection personally (Beebe, Beebe, & Redmond, 2005). In addition, physical mobility has produced life styles of a nomadic nature as opposed to a stationary one associated with a community. Career experts Tiedeman and Tiedeman's (1973) observation that "today we move more, change jobs more and ourselves more and rely on faster and more elaborate technology and communication" (p. 336) is both prophetic and understated. Technology has affected the very nature of occupation by causing many jobs to become archaic, creating jobs requiring different skills and functions, and making other jobs obsolete if not upgraded with computer capabilities and competencies. Without word processing skills and computer proficiency neither professors nor secretaries can function effectively in their respective capacities. Information processing capabilities have become more crucial than discipline specific productivity as a marketable career quality. This fact makes Katz's (1973) projection that the concept of "job" would be phased out in favor of a view of "occupation" that is more of an attitude toward learning short sighted. Now you do not necessarily have to know how to do things as long as you know how to outsource or access information and resources. In fact, a whole new approach to human development referred to as information processing theory has emerged as one of the most influential developmental psychologies (Miller, 2001).

Expanded communication capabilities expose us to problems and social concerns that intrude upon our lives and demand our attention. Wars, racism, sexism, terrorism, ageism, poverty, inflation, overpopulation, ecology, global warming, corruption, crime, and disasters of human and natural causality, locally, nationally, or globally, confront us each day. As a result, we can be assured that we will face the prospect of changing old relationships and beginning new relationships throughout our lives. We must learn the efficacy of saying goodbye to the old and hello to the new as part and parcel of daily life. But at the same time we must learn how to retain the positive and critical aspects of our past experience to assure our present and future growth. Change and retention are facets of life adjustment that must be balanced so that stability and progress are possible.

The Domain of Choice

What then are the implications for the child, the adolescent, and the adult whose personality and identity are constantly developing and emerging through the process of interaction between the self and the rapidly changing world they live in? Individuals must be prepared to engage in a continual process of decision making to maintain purposeful and responsible control over their own lives because of the ever-increasing variety of attitudes, values and life styles that are becoming part of the "domain of choice."

Children are more aware of the diverse elements of their environments than ever before. Mass media, computers, family mobility, and educational systems that stress exposure and experience all contribute to this awareness of an ever increasing range of possible behaviors and life styles. Pre-teenagers and adolescents are faced with choices earlier and in a more intense manner than ever before. Drugs, sex, morals, values, occupational choices, relationships, identity, and sexual orientation all must be grappled with. Neither is the adult freed from the necessity of choosing. Social awareness developed through education and the media impede acting in ignorance or irresponsibly. The economy, occupational evolution, increased leisure time, and value changes continually force adults to reassess themselves and their life style. Even the aging process is complicated by issues of quality of life, health choices, living wills, the prospect of living but being unable to care for oneself and the perplexing elements of the dying trajectory (DeSpelder & Strickland, 2005). Thus the domain of choice is not only larger but extends over a longer period of time as life span and life expectancy increases.

The common element needed for successful resolution in all these cases is the ability to make good decisions based on accurate self-knowledge and relevant knowledge of the environment. Victor Frankl (1984) once observed that "man has to make choices" and ultimately decides for himself. (p. 111). As such, education, counseling, therapy, or any learning experience must move human beings toward having proficiency in the "ability to decide." The parameters of that decisiveness encompass both the freedom to decide and the responsibility for deciding captured in Frankl's (1984) astute metaphorical assessment of the essence of freedom in our Western world view: "I recommend that the Statue of Liberty on the East Coast be supplemented by a Statue of Responsibility on the West Coast" (p. 134).

The development of decision-making skills including the processes of introspection, communication, and relationship formation are necessary because only through the experience of self-exploration and feedback from others can a person become fully aware of those options and consequences that must be considered in making the best decisions possible. In addition, ecologists, ethologists, and socioculturalists emphasize the critical importance of context in the decision-making process (Miller, 2001). Therefore, the acuity of contextual awareness and processing is also necessary as a harbinger of effective decision-making. By acquiring and internalizing these characteristics, skills, and perspectives, we as individuals, whatever our age or circumstance, can retain control over our lives and destinies in spite of pressures brought to bear on us by our changing world.

The Need for Group Counseling

Groups and group work are peculiarly and uniquely designed to address the problems of living in our contemporary society. Hulse (1985) stated that "against the backdrop of a complex and highly technological world and our own needs for connections and support, the group emerges as a potentially humanizing force" (p. 93). Dies (1985) elaborated noting that the

> heightened individualization of learning and sense of isolation … threatens to undermine the sense of personal relatedness that provides the foundation of human interaction. The feeling of universality and cohesiveness and the quality of interpersonal learning … of group experiences promise to be effective antidotes to counteract these depersonalizing forces. (p. 70)

He continued to state that groups "will be used to rehumanize the educational process for children … and revitalize adults who feel alienated in a technological society" (p. 71). Conyne, Dye, Gill, Leddick, Morran, and Ward (1985) concurred with this view and predicted that groups "will become major forces in combating the increasing depersonalization and anomie that are likely to accompany the computer and '"high tech' revolution" (p. 114).

Dye (DeLucia, 1991) pointedly states that "counseling groups are places where people exchange ideas and teach each other and learn from each other" (p. 68). In a practical sense, small groups in general and counseling, therapy and psychoeducational groups in particular are valuable tools in helping people improve their ability to make decisions and act in a manner that is personally meaningful, constructive, and socially relevant. The positive aspects of the helping process are incorporated into the group setting and facilitate the transfer of learning more readily to the ongoing life of the participant. For example, the group counseling process if properly constituted and led meets the demands of an effective learning environment because it is safe, understanding, participating, and approving (Ohlsen, 1977). In addition, the process is directed toward self exploration, encouraging introspection and feedback so that communication can occur and relationships can develop (Beebe, Beebe, & Redmond, 2005). Therefore, it establishes the fundamental basis needed to make good decisions. Consequently, "it is the content and process of group involvement that impacts the very essence of our lives and leads us to new possibilities" (Gladding, 1990, p. 130).

The group process is also a most appropriate means of meeting the personal needs of individuals who often feel isolated, alienated, confused, frustrated, or lost in a world characterized by change, bureaucracy, and bigness. The group supplies a personal touch to the individual's life, serving as an oasis in the wasteland of an impersonal existence that is often a byproduct of scientific and technological advancement. It is a means whereby we as individuals can reconstitute and revitalize the type of personal experience that gives meaning to human existence and generates the impetus to incorporate those experiences into our daily lives.

Group counseling has broad applicability, encompassing the needs of persons from a wide variety of backgrounds and age groups. For individuals who have identifiable problems that encumber their lives, group counseling and group therapy can help them resolve their concerns in a personally responsible and realistic manner. For individuals who do not have specified concerns, the group process can help them improve themselves developmentally and serve as a preventative measure to ensure continued growth, adjustment, and personal satisfaction in their lives.

The flexibility of group work and group counseling facilitates adaptability to a broad range of helping environments and programs. Groups are a relevant means of helping clientele in schools, mental health centers, correctional institutions, halfway houses, drug treatment programs, employment agencies, welfare programs, homeless shelters, and many other organizations whose purpose is to help people with their personal development and concerns. Group work is also an appropriate and effective modality in an organizational sense where the goals are improved productivity and more effective utilization of human resources (see Association for Specialists in Group Work, 1982).

However, the need for group work expertise generally and group counseling specifically extends beyond the persons and organizations served. A professional need exists to develop group work expertise as a core characteristic of counselors and as a vehicle for providing helping services to the counselor's clientele thereby expanding the counselor's effectiveness. In this age of accountability the counselor must be a visible professional who demonstrates group process expertise across varied venues and willingly demystifies the nature of the helping process (Ivey & Alschuler, 1973). Groups can be used to increase client-counselor contact and to extend the role of the counselor by providing services to larger numbers of persons in the schools and in the community (Cottingham, 1973). Group work expertise and the group process are the keys to providing the helping process in a manner that will best serve the interests of clients, the educational or therapeutic staff and setting, the community, business and industry, and the counseling profession. As Conyne and Bemak (2004) emphatically state: "Group work is not only a required area of training (for counselors), but a very important one. Tomorrow's counselors simply will be unable to function effectively and efficiently unless they can work with a range of people in groups of various kinds for various purposes" (p. 3).

The Need for Training

The success and impact of group work is primarily dependent on the ability of a competent leader. Most counselor training programs recognize the need to train future counselors in group procedures and incorporate at least one course in group process into their requirements (ASGW, 2000; Furr & Barrett, 2000; Hensley, 2002; Riva & Korinek, 2004). Professional standards developed by relevant professional organizations and their derivatives (e.g., American Counseling Association and their credentialing counterparts, Council for Accreditation of Counseling and Related Educational Programs [CACREP] and National Board of Certified Counselors [NBCC]) have all promoted the requirement of group work competency. The Association for Specialists in Group Work (ASGW) specifically emphasizes group work as a fundamental competency for all counselors (Conyne, 1996). ASGW (2000) recommends that core training of counselors should include "at least one graduate course in group work that addresses, but is not limited to scope of practice, types of group work, group development, group process and dynamics, group leadership and standards of training and practice for group workers" (p. 331). To support this emphasis ASGW has developed a trifecta of professional documents to guide the training of group workers including *ASGW Best Practice Guidelines* (ASGW, 1998), *ASGW Principles for Diversity-Competent Group Workers* (ASGW, 1999) and *Professional Standards for the Training of Group Workers* (ASGW, 1983, 1990, 2000). State licensing boards and certification agencies have followed suit by incorporating professional credentialing requirements or specifying their own stipulations relative to group work. However, most counselors complete their training at the master's degree level with only one or at most two group courses and possibly some supervised group experience during their practicum or internship (Huhn, Zimpfer, Waltman, & Williamson, 1985; Henseley, 2002). This factor prompted Stockton (Morran, 1992) to state, "I am often impressed with the large number of counselors who have graduated from training programs with solid individual counseling skills and minimal group counseling skills" (p. 7). Consequently, they venture forth to their jobs with a minimum of training and a maximum of timidity with respect to implementing group work. This reality has prompted group counselor educators and group professional organizations like ASGW to launch the initiative to make group work an "independent therapeutic discipline that 'stands alone'" (Bemak & Chung, 2004, p. 37) in order to narrow "the gap between the demand for group work and the supply of well-trained group workers within the socioecological context of contemporary society" (Conyne & Bemak, 2004, p 3).

Counselors who were trained prior to the 1980s and have not subsequently pursued specific additional training in group work also may lack the skill and possibly even the philosophical basis for group counseling. Group counseling demonstrations, continuing education presentations, and professional conference programs serve to promote the group modality as a viable procedure. At best the training value of these programs is important, but the impact is still sporadic. Counselors often come away from these programs with enthusiasm and some new techniques but without the depth necessary to develop functional and comprehensive group programs. For this reason ASGW has recently organized the Advanced Group Training Institute (see http://www.asgw.org) to fill the gap by providing advanced group training programs in geographically diverse areas in association with institutions of higher educations that will build upon the foundation of graduate courses and field experience and foster the professional development of group workers.

Professional literature back to the 1970s has posited the necessity for a group work foundation in training. Katz (1973) pointed out that an abundance of persons want to participate in experiential groups, but few persons are qualified to organize and lead them. Aubrey (1973), in discussing models to expand the effectiveness and role of the counselor, identified the group as the primary means of doing so. Carroll (1973) in her discussion of the "supracounselor" (a counselor who is expert as a helper and in training others to be helpers) also affirmed that perspective. However, Conyne et al. (1985) added that in spite of the growing need for groups in our society there is "a disappointingly insufficient supply of well trained group workers." They also cited poor leadership training as the "single weakest area in the group work field today" (p. 113).

A great need still exists for the development of training programs at graduate, postgraduate, continuing education, and inservice levels to prepare group leaders. Lifton (Christensen, 1990) opined, "We need trained group counselors to be counselor trainers, because counselors will find themselves in many settings where group skills will be needed, and the people won't know how to apply them or how to use them" (p. 138). Conyne, Harvill, Morganette, Moran, and Hulse-Killacky (1990) observed,

> In general, counseling graduates are moving into work sites with some knowledge of group counseling, a lesser amount of competency training in group membership and leadership and with severely limited supervised experience in actually leading groups. Group leadership effectiveness cannot be accomplished under these training conditions. (p. 31)

Conyne and Bemak (2004) recognized that "while demand for group work has grown, the need for group work to address modern day concerns and the supply of well-trained group workers are both lagging" (p. 3), and guest edited a special issue of the *Journal for Specialists in Group Work* (March, 2004) on the topic of "Teaching Group Work". They address the issues involved in developing training programs under the rubric of the ASGW professional documents mentioned above in order to upgrade counselors' professional competence in group work. However, much more is needed. Therefore, the purpose of this book is to train counselors as group workers thereby enabling them (1) to work effectively with their clients in group settings, (2) to share their expertise by training others to be effective group leaders, and (3) to emulate and express their group process expertise in all types of groups thus enhancing their consultative and resource roles in a wide variety of settings.

Basic Training Components

As stated in the Preface, the five basic training prerequisites for becoming an effective group worker and leader are:

1. Acquisition of cognitive knowledge and information about group process (academic component).
2. Experiential involvement as a participant in group process (experiential component).
3. Development of strategies, skills, and techniques to use in the leadership capacity, (skills component).
4. Observation of leadership models and group processes in a variety of venues (observation component).
5. Supervised experience in the leadership role (supervision component).

Barlow (2004) collapses these five dimensions into four, but puts them all under the umbrella of learning group skills. In other words, leadership skills can be learned via experiential, academic, observational, and supervision modalities.

Cognitive knowledge is necessary to provide the counselor with a philosophical, theoretical, and technical understanding of the group process. This information—encompassing group theory, dynamics, and process—serves the counselor well in terms of understanding and directing the group process and in describing its nature to others. Often cognitive awareness of the goals and dynamics of group work in its various forms is required by prospective group members and other significant persons before they will agree to participate in or support the group process as a helping procedure. Similarly, cognitive understanding of the group process and leadership role lays the foundation for self-confidence as a group leader. Reading, listening (class lectures, audio and video tapes, etc.), observing process, research projects, and class discussions can provide much of the needed intellectual basis for leading groups. Observation of professional leaders as role models complements the cognitive learning and is considered by Shapiro and Shapiro (1985) as an essential part of training. Tape series such as Carroll's (1986) *Group Work: Leading in the Here and Now* and Stockton's (1992) *Developmental Aspects of Group Counseling: Process, Leadership and Supervision* available from ASGW (http://www.asgw.org) through the American Counseling Association (http://www.counseling.org) are excellent learning tools. However, a cognitive understanding of the dynamics and process of group work in and of itself is insufficient (Akos, 2004; Riva & Korinek, 2004).

Prospective leaders must complement cognitive learning with *experiential involvement* in the group process. This involvement must occur on two levels. First is the personal involvement level where prospective leaders become members of an ongoing group process. The process of becoming an effective group leader begins within the realm of one's own experience. Personally participating in the group process enables the prospective leader to fully understand the impact of group pressures and dynamics and facilitates firsthand learning about the process intended for helping others (Kottler, 2004, 2001). Without this kind of experience group workers will lack the depth necessary to give their approach to leadership authenticity and personal integrity.

Two types of personal group experience are advisable. The first type is as a member of a process group composed of members drawn from a common context. This experience is typically obtained in graduate school as part of group classes where groups are formed consisting of graduate students who are peers. Many forms of this type of personal group experience are described in the literature involving formats related to personal growth, role playing, in vivo enactment, microlabs, inner circle–outer circle processing, the use of actors and others (Forrester-Miller & Duncan, 1990; Merta, Wolfgang, & McNeil, 1993; Brenner, 1999; Marotta, Peters, & Paliokas, 2000; Fall & Levitov, 2002; Hensley, 2002; Cox, Banez, Hawley, & Mostade, 2003; Davenport, 2004; Falco & Bauman, 2004; Akos, 2004; Akos, Goodnough, & Milsom, 2004). The second type of personal group experience is being in a group composed of members drawn from populations that are not relationally connected other than in the group. Shapiro and Shapiro (1985) identified personal group therapy as one of their core training components, and therapy groups are usually composed of members who have no other common relational context. These two types of experiences are recommended to acquaint potential group leaders with the dynamic differences that ensue when working with contextually related versus nonrelated group members.

The second level of experiential involvement is *experimental involvement*. This is necessary to help prospective leaders learn and understand the *concepts, skills,* and *techniques* associated with the group process. A laboratory milieu involving experiential learning centering on specific techniques is useful in complementing didactic learning about group process. These experiences help bridge gaps between the cognitive process and personal experience as a group member. They are important in initial training to help group workers enhance their leadership ability and develop a repertoire of methods, techniques, and activities for use in groups. They provide the foundational competencies for effective practice. Once the foundation has been laid, attending group workshops and group presentations at professional meetings and conventions is invaluable to the continued development of leadership competence.

The newest dimension of group work that has fully emerged as an integral part of group work training is *process observation*. This cutting edge entity encompasses all aspects of the training process and all forms of group work. It is critical to learning from both a leadership and a process perspective (Hulse-Killacky, Killacky, & Donigian, 2001). Trainees benefit from the opportunity to observe *leadership role models* both in and out of class and to observe *group process* in a variety of groups including the class group, training groups associated with the program and a variety of task and helping groups outside the training venue as well (Bieschke, Matthews, Wade, & Pricken, 1998; Hensley, 2002; Riva & Korinek, 2004;).

Finally, the old adage "there's no substitute for experience" applies to the group leader. Until the counselor has the opportunity to function in a leadership capacity and try out methods, skills, and techniques in actual situations, learning is incomplete. The process of obtaining leadership experience should begin in training under competent *supervision* in a group practicum or internship or as part of a general practicum or internship and then continue under supervision as group professionals enter the field (Linton, 2003; Rivera, Wilbur, Robert-Wilbur, Phan, Garrett, & Betz, 2004; Granello & Underfer-Babalis, 2004). All too often, however, counselors are left on their own to take care of this aspect of their development. This book will describe some possibilities for initial leadership experiences and will make additional suggestions for getting the necessary experience to become a competent group leader.

Book Format

The objective of this book is to provide the group leader with the first four prerequisites mentioned above and to initiate the process for realizing the fifth. Each chapter is composed of didactic discussion and experiential activities to complement the discussion. The information included was selected on the basis of its particular relevance to community, agency, private practice, and educational settings, although the appropriateness for other group oriented initiatives in business and industry environments is not excluded.

The second criterion in selecting material was practicality because my intent is that this book will have merit on the basis of its usefulness rather than its erudite scholarship or theoretical prowess. Techniques and exercises were chosen or developed on the basis of their applicability to learning and using the group process. Special attention was given to including activities that can be used in training *and* practice. The hallmark of any good technique is that it substantially aids the group process and at the same time teaches the group members about the group process (Trotzer, 2004). Therefore many of the techniques or adaptations of them will be useful to group leaders in conducting their own groups.

Finally, the information and activities can be used in total or in part since much of the emphasis in this book is directed toward utilization. The book is written so that selective usage or adaptation will not interfere with the fluidity of the presentation. Therefore readers are encouraged to complement, supplement, revise, delete, or adjust the concepts and activities of this book to meet their own group work needs.

Strategies for Obtaining Group Experience

Strategies for obtaining group experience (the second prerequisite) are included in this first chapter because cognitive learning and experiential learning need to proceed hand in hand. In this way prospective leaders are given the opportunity to approach their group experience with their own expectations rather than with expectations gleaned solely from reading or lectures. They also begin the process of testing knowledge against experience immediately. Strategies are broken down into two groups, the first directed toward counselor trainees and the second toward practicing counselors who wish to develop their group work skills.

Strategies for Counselor Trainees

Most group training work begins with a formal course in group process. For example, Hetzel, Stockton, and McDonnell (1994) found that an introductory group course was part of the curriculum in 98% of the counseling departments that responded to their survey. Merta, Wolfgang, and McNeil (1993) found that 88% of the counselor education programs they surveyed included experiential groups as a component of training in group practice. Corey and Corey (1992) have stipulated that group experience should be a requirement of an initial, or any, group counseling course. Therefore, the first strategies discussed are intended for incorporation into a class format. While the specific proportion of experiential versus didactic training varies, a reasonable balance is one-third to one-half experiential and the remainder didactic. Some programs have implemented experiential group process courses extending the requirements to a sequence of two courses, one focusing on cognitive learning and the other on experiential learning. The following strategies suggested will still apply but with the added adaptation and advantage that the group process course can be administratively recognized as part and parcel of an instructor's teaching load. The first step is to divide the class into counseling size groups (preferably eight members per group) and organize a schedule of meetings for the entire quarter or semester. A general guideline is to have at least one group meeting for each week of the term.

Extensive discussions of the nature of the experiential group requirement have occurred in the literature (Donigian, 1993; Forester-Miller & Duncan, 1990; Lloyd, 1990; Merta & Sisson, 1991; Williams, 1990; Davenport, 2004) and in the annals of professional organizations and credentialing agencies responsible for setting training standards and licensing/certification requirements (ASGW, 1991; CACREP, 1994). Primary concern has been to ensure both quality training *and* ethical practice relative to group work trainees. (Ethics in the form of Best Practices in group work will be discussed extensively by Rapin and Conyne in chapter 8.) The general consensus of that debate is that group experience should be a required dimension of group courses, but the experiential aspect itself should not be evaluated as a portion of the student's academic grade in the course. Pierce and Baldwin (1990) summarized the issue effectively as follows:

> In the context of training students to become group workers, students become clients whose welfare must be protected. This means that group leadership in a counselor education program must be fair, do no harm (non-maleficence), respect the individual's right as a free agent and yet at the same time, do them some good (beneficence) in being able to participate constructively and to use and control self disclosure effectively. (p. 149)

Therefore, the standard parameters for implementing any and all of the strategies are:

1. Required participation in experiential groups as part of graduate training group work is not to be evaluated as part of the student's grade.
2. The requirement of participation in experiential groups (however framed) is mandatory, *but* the depth of involvement and self-disclosure is the option of the student.

Note: Most training programs reserve the right to review a student's appropriateness for the program at any time which is different from the limitation with respect to group participation and grades (Sklare, Thomas, Williams, & Powers, 1996).

Group Strategy 1: Instructor as Group Leader

This approach requires the leader to wear two hats—instructor and group leader—and the students to wear two hats—student and group member. The advantage of this approach is that an immediate integration of the instructor's cognitive expertise and leadership style is realized. He or she becomes both expert and model, which provides the class members with an example of how the two fit together. The disadvantage is that one or the other of the roles or the dual role itself may be an inhibiting factor to class members' participation. Similarly, the leader may have difficulty switching hats and may experience added pressure if a discrepancy occurs between what he or she says and does.

Group Strategy 2: Outside Professional as Group Leader

This strategy involves the instructor enlisting the cooperation of trained leaders from among the counseling staff or faculty to lead the facilitated group experience part of the class. Sometimes instructors can trade services or responsibilities to facilitate this strategy. If the training program has a doctoral component, advanced degree students can also be utilized as group leaders. The advantage of this approach is that group members do not have to encounter the dilemma of the instructor being the leader and can experience the group in a more natural, autonomous manner. As such the experience tends to approximate the manner in which most groups are conducted in field settings where the counselor has no role in the lives of group members other than group leader. The disadvantages of this approach are that instructors lose the opportunity for more personal contact with students that takes place in the group and have more difficulty assessing student needs and thus planning their instruction accordingly. In addition, the mentoring dimension of instruction is limited.

Group Strategy 3: Outside Professional, Instructor-Observer

This strategy requires the cooperation of a trained leader and a facility that will allow for unobtrusive observation by the instructor (preferably a group room with a one-way mirror, audio system, and video taping capability). The distinct feature of this strategy is the incorporation of a feedback session in which the instructor-observer shares perceptions of the group interaction for purposes of educating members and elucidating group process. The feedback sessions are critical to this approach but can cause difficulties if comments are not made tentatively and supportively and time is not allowed for discussion and processing of the process observation.

With the advent of the process observer emphasis and orientation in group work (Bieschke, Matthews, & Wade, 1996; Hulse-Killacky, 1996), this particular strategy has almost unlimited potential. Using a micro-lab format and the inner circle–outer circle structure the instructor can divide the class into two groups and designate one as a process observation group while the other group is participating in an experiential group process. The process group can learn from the experiential group and contribute feedback thereby multiplying the learning potential of both group experiences. The student gains experience as a group member and as a process observer as each group alternately observes while the other experiences. A student leadership component can also be easily incorporated into this format. Leaders or coleaders from the process observer group can be assigned to facilitate the experiential group on a rotating basis adding a supervised leadership dimension to this framework. This format also stimulates professional growth in the leader and instructor who can try out new ideas and get immediate feedback as to their relevance and meaning.

Group Strategy 4: Leaderless Group, Instructor-Observer

The basic advantages of this method are that the instructor does not have to depend on outside help and that less time is involved since more than one group can be going at a time. The same types of facilities are necessary as for Strategy 3, but the group functions without a designated leader. Structuring or nonstructuring is the prerogative of the instructor. Feedback sessions at the end of each session or in separate sessions are also important. The instructor can keep pace with the group members' experiences, provide important insights, intervene when necessary, and structure teaching around group process. The disadvantage is that the group does not have a designated leader to provide a model or supply expertise to help develop the flow of group interaction. In addition, less similarity occurs to the nature of the groups used in professional settings that tend to follow a leader-member group model. The process observation group variation mentioned in Strategy 3 can also be incorporated into this option.

Group Strategy 5: Required Participation in an Outside Group

Basically this strategy requires class members to participate in a counseling/therapy or personal growth group experience outside of class as a supplement to their learning in the course. If this strategy is used, the instructor should screen and approve class members' choices to ensure greater relevance to the course. The instructor also may locate groups and then encourage or require class members to choose from an approved list. The advantage of this approach is that the range of class members' group experiences is broader, which leads to a very positive result if the instructor can facilitate discussion of these experiences within limits of confidentiality.

If this option is pursued, two guidelines are helpful and necessary for ethical purposes. First, members are required to inform their group that they are in a group class, are participating as a requirement of that class, will be processing their experience with their instructor as part of the learning experience, and need to obtain the group's permission to do so. Second, a ground rule is established that discussion will only pertain to the member's own experience and observations of the group process. In addition, it is usually beneficial to have members keep journals of their experiences and then discuss them with the instructor in light of the course content. Regardless of strategy chosen, the journal idea is a good one because it helps group members consolidate their experiences and integrate them with their cognitive learning (Cummings, 2001; Falco & Bauman, 2004). The disadvantage of this strategy is the complete lack of contact with the actual experience of the group members and that, even when the preceding guidelines are followed, the experiences chosen or obtained may not be relevant. Opportunity to mentor and model is again limited.

Group Strategy 6: Designated Leader, Instructor-Observer

The format of this strategy entails designating leaders from among the group trainees as an added dimension to their experiential learning. As designated leaders for one or more sessions (coleaders can also be used), trainees obtain firsthand experience in the leadership role whetting their appetites for further experience and initiating the process of deciphering differences between member and leader roles in the group. The instructor observes incorporating feedback to the designated leader(s) and the group as part of a follow-up session. Leaders can be video taped and review their work with the instructor and other students to enhance the learning experience.

Whitman, Morgan, and Alfred (1996) describe a coleading training experience that pairs a student with a senior therapist. Their model could be adapted to an introductory course. However, since coleadership adds another process variable to the group dynamics, their model may be more appropriate for more advanced courses where students have more experience and training before they move into a coleader position.

The disadvantages of this strategy are that the group process may become disjointed as leadership is rotated and members do not get an experienced leader as a role model. These disadvantages tend to be outweighed by the advantage of providing a brief leadership experience for trainees. (A variation combining, aspects of Strategies 3, 4, and 6 using fishbowl methodology is described by Kane [1995]).

Group Strategy 7: Structured Versus Nonstructured Group Leadership

This strategy is more of a modification of Strategy 1 (Instructor as Group Leader) than an alternative. The group process is divided into two parts, the first in which the leader takes a facilitative, nondirective role and the second in which the leader structures group interaction using communication exercises and directed focus activities to generate group interaction. This strategy gives members a sense of where they function best relative to the structure/nonstructure continuum both as individuals/members and as potential group leaders. The disadvantages are those of administration and orchestration rather than experience. Some instructors, including the author, resolve this dilemma by incorporating structured activities into the cognitive portion of the course using experiential activities to demonstrate group concepts, process, and dynamics.

Additional Considerations Whenever the group experience is organized around subgroups of an entire class, the very nature of group experience can cause factionalism, coalitions, and polarization. The instructor when approaching the class must take this into account and organize class experiences that tend to offset the tendency toward group cliques and subgroup coalitions. These issues can usually be resolved by structurally rotating subgroup membership across different activities and using purposeful subgrouping interventions such as team building activities to off-set the impact of default subgrouping. Changing the physical environment also may be a useful intervention in organizing group experiences. Sometimes changing rooms for class and group experiences helps ease the transition from one experience to the other.

Strategies for Practicing Counselors

Practicing counselors who wish to develop their expertise in leading groups sometimes have a difficult time arranging learning experiences due to lack of time in their own schedules and lack of opportunities in their immediate environment. The first possibility is to take a graduate level advanced group course, either by audit or on a credit basis. Prior to enrolling the counselor should check with the instructor to determine the amount and types of experiences expected.

Group courses can be selected from a variety of professional fields including counselor education, psychology, social work, human relations, or communications programs. When group process courses are selected from fields outside of counselor education, counselors may have to rely on their own professional experiences and previous training for adapting and applying the course material to their own settings and use. The advantage of selecting courses from counseling related fields is that counselors may be able to apply credits earned toward an advanced degree, meet professional continuing education requirements for licensure or certification, or realize increments on a salary schedule while at the same time improving their professional skills. The advantage of a counselor education group course is the direct relationship the course has to the counselor's role in the agency, school, or private practice setting in which he or she works. It provides the opportunity for the immediate integration of training and practice. ASGW's Advanced Group Training Institutes are designed to provide professional development training in group work as just described in an effort to provide group practitioners with the proverbial second course in group work.

Many counselors choose to pursue group training in noneducational settings such as private, profit and nonprofit organizations, professional associations, or training institutes that provide courses and programs on a per person cost basis. Examples of these programs are National Training Laboratories Institute (http://www.ntl.org), Esalen Institute (http://www.esalen.org) and Western Behavioral Science Institute (http://www.wbsi.org). In addition, a host of organizations have emerged in the wake of licensure/certification continuing education requirements that advertise and provide training in group work. Professional organizations such as the American Psychological Association (http://www.apa.org), Division 49 (Group Psychology and Group Psychotherapy), The American

Group Psychotherapy Association (http://www.apga.org) and the Association for Specialists in Group Work (http://www.asgw.org)a division of the American Counseling Association (http://www.counseling.org) sponsor regional and national training programs as part of their continuing education thrust. Some of these programs may lead to a credential in group leadership. Whenever one of these programs is selected, counselors should again determine the nature of the experience and assess its relevance to their own settings prior to becoming involved. This requires professional judgment as well as a cognitive grasp of the group process prior to investigating the various group programs.

Local continuing education or inservice training in group process may be the most viable and relevant means of obtaining group expertise. The counselor can organize a group of professionals interested in learning the group counseling process and then bring in an outside consultant who has the most appropriate credentials and experience to serve as group leader. The advantages of this approach are numerous. There is greater assurance that the desired experience and the resulting experience will be congruent because the counselor has input into the organization of the experience and the selection of the leader. Cooperation between the educational setting and the group leader's university or professional organization is facilitated, increasing the amount of input from outside experts and stimulating the professional life of the counselors and staff. Since the program is organized in a field setting, the time involved is reduced and attendance is more convenient. Administrators look favorably on programs such as this and may provide financial support for the group leaders and salary reinforcement to the participants. Such efforts may also qualify as peer supervision hours required by licensure and certification requirements. Inservice programs have some inherent disadvantages including lack of interest and motivation due to fatigue of the participants and difficulty in locating an expert who will be stimulating and relevant at an affordable price. Careful planning directed toward meeting the need for effective group training and wise selection of the consultant can overcome these difficulties.

The Mythical, Ideal, Ultimate, Basic Group Course

In spite of all the discussion and research in training group workers and the development of training and certification standards and requirements, the fact still remains that the vast majority of master's level counselors and clinicians will complete their training with only one group class and possibly some supervised group work experience in their practicum or internship. Consequently, I would like to conclude this chapter with a brief sketch of an ideal group course that identifies the components, experiences, and requirements necessary to provide a substantial and solid foundation for group work competence.

Class Format The class format should incorporate lecture/presentation, structured group activities for demonstration, process observation, leadership labs and facilitated group process for personal experience. By the end of the course student should have experienced the three primary roles related to group work: member, process observer, leader.

Academic Requirements Reading requirements should include an appropriate group text, supplemental reading and familiarization with the group work literature (professional journals and appropriate Internet resources). Writing projects should include a minimum of five projects identified as follows:

1. A research paper on the ethics of group work.
2. A research paper on a selected group topic using current professional group literature.
3. A group proposal or plan for a specific population, situation or setting using a specific type of group format (counseling, psychoeducational, therapy, task).
4. A task group process observation paper involving at least two small groups outside of class, one in which the student asked and received permission to observe and one where process observation was done without the knowledge of the participants. This nonpermission group usually entails attending a public meeting or a group the student is involved in and is reported anonymously (Hulse-Killacky, Killacky, & Donigian, 2001).
5. A group learning journal composed of entries derived from the entire fabric of the group course and experience.

Experiential Requirements The class framework should provide the following experiences as an integral dimension of the course:

1. A facilitated group experience (required but nongraded) of at least 10 sessions. This experience should be facilitated by a trained and experienced leader. A journal should be required but not read or evaluated by the instructor.
   Note: A follow up activity to the experiential group could involve the student writing a two to five page summation of their group experience to be discussed with the group instructor after the academic work is completed (grades are in) as part of an overall assessment of the student's learning, progress, and appropriateness for group work.
2. Each student should have the opportunity to serve as a process observer for at least one class session and have their process observation incorporated in the class process.

Note: Preparation for the process observer experience can involve required reading of material from the *Gleanings of a Process Observer* (Trotzer, 1997a,b,c) incorporated into chapter 6.

3. Each student should have one group leadership experience consisting of a minimum of 45–60 minutes in the leadership role (preferably video taped). Group composition is the class or subgroups of the class. The focus of the group can be getting a group started, demonstrating a structured group activity, or an evolving focus reflecting the development of the group process (stage related and class related). Feedback by the instructor and class members can be incorporated into the experience and the tape (if available) can be reviewed by the student individually, with peers, and by the instructor as a leadership learning experience.

Recommended Resources for Framing Your Ideal Course

Association for Specialists in Group Work (ASGW)(1998). ASGW best practice guidelines. *Journal for Specialists in Group Work, 23,* 237–244.

Association for Specialists in Group Work (ASGW)(1999). ASGW principles for diversity-competent group workers. *Journal for Specialists in Group Work, 24,* 7–14.

Association for Specialists in Group Work (ASGW)(2000). ASGW professional standards for the training of group workers. *Journal for Specialists in Group Work, 25,* 327–342

Conyne, R. K. & Bemak, F. (Guest Editors)(2004). Teaching Group Work. *Journal for Specialists in Group Work, 29*(1), 1–154.

Conyne, R., Wilson, F. R., & Ward, D. (1997). *Comprehensive group work: What it means & how to teach it.* Alexandria, VA: American Counseling Association.

DeLucia-Waack, J., Gerrity, D. A., Kalodner, C. R., & Riva, M. T. (2004). *Handbook of group counseling and psychotherapy.* Thousand Oaks, CA: Sage Publications, Inc.

2
Definitions and Distinctions

Groups are an integral part of our world. Our participation in groups encompasses all aspects of our life spanning involvement in family, work, social, and community group relationships. Without groups we would not know the full meaning of our humanity.

A Group Is A Group (Or Is It?)

Each one of us spends a significant portion of our lives in groups: family groups, work groups, neighborhood groups, church groups, social groups, internet groups, chat rooms, conference calls; the list could go on ad infinitum. Periodically, in the course of our interaction in these groups, we find ourselves sharing or disclosing personal information about our hopes or disappointments, joys or pain, problems or achievements. These disclosures may emanate from the turmoil or excitement within ourselves, from the perceived amenability to sharing observed or experienced in the nature of the group itself, or some combination of the two. What triggers these disclosures are the rudiments upon which group process as a significant force in interpersonal communication and the helping endeavor is built.

Vignettes of naturally occurring therapeutic group interactions abound:

Jane, a 31-year-old mother of two, discloses to three neighborhood women friends that she has discovered a lump in her breast and is scared to death to tell her husband or go to a doctor.

Bill, a 43-year-old middle manager, is noticeably angry as he gets into his office car pool Monday morning and proceeds to tell the passengers about an argument he and his wife had over the weekend that continued unresolved right up to the point he got into the car.

Diane, an executive secretary, gathers each day for a coffee break with other women in similar positions in the corporation. A main topic of conversation is female issues so they name this group "OVA" and make efforts to get together outside office hours.

Dierdre at age 16 talks enthusiastically and intensely about her new boyfriend with a group of three or four close friends.

Billy, age 4, tells his playmates at his preschool that his parents are getting a divorce.

Jim, 22 and in his first year of teaching, receives an offer for a three year doctoral fellowship and talks it over with fellow teachers in the teachers' lounge asking, "What should I do?"

Ben talks excitedly with a group of coworkers about the birth of his new daughter.

All these examples reflect the personal nature and helping capacity of groups, but what distinguishes a counseling or therapy group from these or any other personally meaningful group interactions? Answering that question is the focus of this chapter.

General Nature of Groups

The purpose of this chapter is to define the general and specific nature of groups and discuss the characteristics that distinguish them and give them identities of their own in the broad spectrum of group processes and group work. To accomplish this we first must look at the general nature of groups so we can develop some guidelines for delimiting the context in which we will consider the four primary types of groups that will be addressed in this text: psychoeducation, counseling, therapy, and task groups.

Slavson (1952) stated that a group consists of "at least three persons because it is the third and succeeding persons who introduce problems and stress that do not ordinarily exist in two person relationships" (p. 223). This definition denotes the minimum number of persons required for the group process to occur and distinguishes a group from a dyadic relationship (e.g., individual counseling or a marriage) based on the inclusion of group dynamics in addition to personality dynamics. With three or more persons new forces and pressures are introduced into the group as members attempt to relate, communicate, and achieve objectives. The interaction becomes more complex, communication is more difficult to follow, and control is less easily obtained.

Coalitions can now form that precipitate the creation of subgroups and member hierarchies are now possible. Additionally the emergence of multiple member roles can occur (e.g., in a three person interaction there can be a message-sender, a message-receiver, and an observer of the transaction). These dynamics escalate with expanding group size and necessitate the establishment of an optimal group size that constitutes a small group. This is a difficult task because no clear basis exists for determining a specific number above which a group becomes impersonal or nontherapeutic—a point beyond which an individual's identity is submerged or lost in the group.

Some guidelines are available to help us determine a general perspective on the optimal group size necessary to maintain personal and therapeutic group interaction. Homans (1950) defined a therapeutic group as a "number of persons who communicate with one another over a span of time and who are few enough so that each person is able to communicate with others, not at second hand through other people, but face to face" (p. 1). This definition stresses the importance of groups maintaining a size where members can communicate directly and personally with one another. A therapeutic group must be small enough so that the identity of the individual is preserved and each member has some degree of reciprocal influence on each other (Schmuck & Schmuck, 1971). When a group becomes so large or develops a style of communication that prohibits personal and direct contact between members, its therapeutic nature is severely restricted.

A maximum size limit depends, to some extent, on the purposes and type of group involved, the nature and maturity of the group members, and/or the experience and expertise of the group leader. However, once a group exceeds a range of 8 to 12 members, the therapeutic atmosphere and impact become proportionally less evident. A general guideline relative to an effective small group size is 5 to 12 members (Roark & Roark, 1979). Corey and Corey (2006) note that the appropriate size of a small group should be "big enough to give ample opportunity for interactions and small enough for everyone to be involved and to feel a sense of 'group'" (p. 117). Specifically by age group, recommended group size is:

1. elementary school age, 3 to 4 members;
2. middle school to junior high age, 4 to 6 members;
3. high school age, 6 to 8 members; and
4. young adult to adult age, 8 to 10 members.

Groups with the elderly vary in size depending on the interactive capabilities of the participants ranging from adult group size (8 to 12 members) to smaller groups of 3 to 6 members. In addition, psychoeducation or guidance groups may expand to 12 to 20 members depending on the structure and topic. Group size will be addressed more specifically in chapter 10, but in general we will be considering a group size of 3 to 12 members as the range within which the group process as discussed in this book operates.

Generic Definition of Group Work

A comprehensive and operational definition of group work must include comments on the following components: process, atmosphere (climate) of the group, purpose (focus), membership, and leadership. With these components in mind let's turn our attention to the definition of group work as it will be used throughout this book. This definition is designed to answer three basic questions with respect to small group organizational structures: What?, Who?, and Why? .

What?

Group work is the development of a face to face interpersonal network or system.

This network is what creates the atmosphere and milieu necessary for constructive interpersonal processes and allows the helping process to work. The ingredients that are essential to effective small group relationships that must be present in the interaction between the leader and group members include trust, acceptance, respect, warmth, communication, and understanding.

Trust is basically the experience of feeling safe and secure in sharing one's self, ideas, perceptions and feelings with others without fear of rejection or reprisal. It involves both trusting others and being trustworthy. The development of trust is the cement that respects privacy and secures confidentiality into place as the cornerstone of the group process.

Acceptance is the quality of being allowed to be freely yourself regardless of circumstances or problems you have in your life. Victor Hugo captured the essence of this characteristic when he stated that "the supreme happiness of life is the conviction that we are loved, loved for ourselves or rather, loved in spite of ourselves."

Respect is the quality of relating to one another based on the inherent worth and dignity of each person recognizing their uniqueness and diversity and affirming the commonality of humanness we all share. Yalom (1995) referred to this type of connectedness in human experience as the principle of "universality." The adage that "every person is in certain respects like all other persons, like some other persons, like no other person" also captures the essence of the this quality. John Ruskin, the English literary critic, accentuated the importance of respect for the worth of each person when he noted, "the weakest among us has a gift, however seemingly trivial, which is peculiar to him (her) and which worthily used will be a gift to his (her) race forever."

Warmth is the human capability that is best described as unconditional positive regard (Rogers, 1961). It combines the elements of caring, nonpossessive love, prizing, and liking and is difficult to measure except in terms of one's own experience and feelings. Its presence is completely dependent on the sensitivity of each person to recognize and receive it and the ability of each person to feel and express it. More recently, the concept of "immediacy" with its implications of being undistractedly present in relationships has been incorporated into the quality of warmth (Beebe, et al., 2005).

Communication is also a necessary relational factor in that it provides the means whereby meaningful interaction between persons is facilitated (Stewart, 2002). The type of communication referred to here is two-way communication in which all persons involved have the desire and ability to initiate, respond to, and receive the communication process (Johnson, 1972; Johnson & Johnson, 1997; Schmuck & Schmuck, 1971, Beebe, et al., 2005).

The final ingredient is *understanding*, referred to by Rogers (1961) as empathy, Truax and Carkhuff (1967) as accurate empathy, and Boszormenyi-Nagy (Boszormenyi-Nagy & Spark, 1973) as multi-directed partiality. Understanding is the ability to see things from the other person's frame of reference, to be able to step into another person's shoes but at the same time maintain your own identity and reality and to do so in the presence of others who may have a different viewpoint. It is the capacity to perceive another person's perspective or experience *as if* you were that person but without losing the "as if" quality. Rogers (1952) believed that the ability to "listen with understanding" removes barriers in communication that often develop from our tendency to evaluate communications we receive.

If we are successful in creating relationships within the group characterized by these qualities, a constructive or therapeutic atmosphere will be the end product.

Who?

Through which a counselor and several members come into contact.

(Leadership in groups will be addressed from the perspective of the professional counselor in this text.)

This aspect of our definition gives the principals involved in the process. The counselor is a person with professional training in group work and group process and who has specific competence as a group leader (Cohn, 1967). In this sense, he or she is the "more knowing" person (from a group process perspective) who combines professional expertise and personal commitment to help the members and the group engage in an effective small group interaction. The members are considered "less knowing" relative to group process, but have the capacity to engage in, learn from, and contribute to effective small group participation. In counseling and therapy groups, members may also be considered "less knowing" because they are experiencing problems and concerns that, for reasons known or unknown to them, they have not been able to resolve on their own which has prompted their participation in the group. These feelings of being unable to cope or at least the discomfort of having problems they cannot resolve supply the impetus for attending a group with a trained leader (Trotzer, 1975).

Ultimate responsibility for the group process rests on the shoulders of the counselor, although each counselor's personality, training, and experience will determine the nature or style of leadership and the amount of responsibility shared by group members. Counselors have responsibility *to* members in that they use their expertise, knowledge, and personality to facilitate the group process, help members whenever possible, and protect or defend members' well being if that becomes necessary. However, the counselor is not responsible *for* members since the members are individually responsible for decisions, actions, and changes in their own lives. (The exception to this perspective, otherwise known as the free agency of the client, involves clear and present danger situations and duty to warn provisions of ethical and legal codes that govern the practice of professional counselors.)

Why?

In order to help each other address the purposes of the group and discover, understand, and implement ways of accomplishing the objectives inherent in the group's formation and purpose.

The focus of group work is on process in relationship to purpose (Hulse-Killacky, et al., 2001). It is oriented toward helping members express themselves and relate as they address the topic/focus of the group. The objective is to mobilize the group resources with regard to the group's purpose thereby integrating process and purpose. This integration of process and purpose is a prominent element in our definition. Process involves two basic phases. The first is characterized by relationship development that emanates from and leads to self-disclosure and understanding of one's role and presence in the group, and the second is associated with action directed toward contributing to the purpose and work of the group. For example, in a counseling group clients express and explore their difficulties in an effort to mobilize group resources to find ways of overcoming their problems and live more fulfilled and satisfying lives. Each client uses the group to help him or her examine their problem, discover problem-solving alternatives, evaluate their implications and probabilities of success, and decide on an action plan. The client then practices, implements the plan, and reports results to the group. Thus, the purpose of group counseling, to address client problems, concerns, and dissatisfactions in an effort to remove them as factors impeding the client's growth, development, and personal fulfillment, is achieved. In this particular case the unique benefit of the "helping each other" process is realized in the individual lives of the members, a point that will be discussed in greater depth a little later in this chapter.

So let's apply our generic definition to group counseling, the central theme of this text.

Consequently:

Group work—the development of a face to face interpersonal network or system characterized by trust, acceptance, respect, warmth, communication, and understanding through which a counselor and several members come into contact in order to help each other address the purposes of the group and discover, understand, and implement ways of accomplishing the objectives inherent in the group's formation and purpose.

Becomes:

Group counseling—the development of a face to face interpersonal network characterized by trust, acceptance, respect, warmth, communication, and understanding through which a counselor and several clients come in contact in order to help each other confront unsatisfactory or problem areas in the clients' lives and discover, understand, and implement ways of resolving those problems and dissatisfactions (Trotzer, 1972).

This definition differentiates counseling or therapy groups from other small group experiences or interactions based on the mobilization of interpersonal human resources in relation to a helping objective that is realized in the individual lives of the group members rather than a group product or the accomplishment of a task. As such several key points are emphasized. First, as an interpersonal network the counseling group represents a human process reflective of the domain of human relationships in which members are experiencing their problems.

Second, the traits of that therapeutic network only have meaning in a relational context. Trust, acceptance, respect, warmth, communication, and understanding can only be experienced if interpersonal relationships are present. Third, there is a built-in interpersonal growth dynamic in that the purpose depends on members helping each other. And finally, the focus and purpose of the group are explicit. Counseling groups are initiated for the purpose of problem solving. As such the counseling group represents a temporary interventive modality in each group member's life, the therapeutic impact and duration of which is governed by the intention on the part of both leaders and members to dissolve the group by resolving the problems (Trotzer, 1985).

Advantages of Group Work

Advantages of group work as defined above can be considered from several perspectives. The first is in contrast to dyadic relationships such as individual counseling, noting those helping characteristics the group can provide that are not readily available to the counselor in one-to-one relationships. Second is the perspective that views group work as an entity in and of itself with its own merit and advantageous characteristics. Third is the viewpoint that presents advantages of group work but takes particular care to define the qualifications and conditions under which they operate and limits that must be observed to prevent an asset from becoming a liability. A fourth perspective projects constructive assets and qualities of group dynamics beyond the therapeutic setting. These dynamics are called process dynamics and reflect generic qualities endemic to all group work. All four of these vantage points will be incorporated into our succeeding discussion with particular emphasis on the counseling group.

The reader should keep in mind that different group approaches may emphasize different positive qualities of the group process. It is possible for all advantages to be evident at some time during the group process. However, it is more likely that only a few will be consistently prominent. The following list of advantages/assets is comprehensive in nature encompassing a broad spectrum of approaches rather than a definitive list of advantages characterizing every group approach.

Safety Factors in Groups

Groups have the capacity to grant a sense of safety and security to members that is not as readily available in one-to one-relationships.

For example, group counseling provides group members with an automatic camouflage if they desire to use it. Due to the fact that each member of the group is a client, an initial feeling of safety exists because the probability of being the center of attention decreases in direct proportion to the size of the group. In addition, the feeling that there is strength in numbers also is present. These assumptions may be enough to encourage group members to embark on the journey toward working on their problems in the group. Members often are more willing to discuss feelings, concerns, attitudes, and beliefs in groups of peers than in individual counseling (Dinkmeyer & Muro, 1971). In fact, Ohlsen (1970) pointed out that "some clients find it easier to discuss difficult subjects in group counseling" than in one-to-one counseling (p. 5).

The climate of the group generated by the relationships formed is also a factor in members feeling safe. In the first place, relationships are developed in an atmosphere of controlled intimacy, which reduces the risk in forming relationships and the contingent obligations that usually result from them (Mahler, 1969). Dynamics related to transference and counter transference are also reduced enabling members to learn from the face value of their interactions with others. Second, members have a natural feeling that fellow clients will accept them and empathize with them, which makes facing up to problems and weaknesses safer (Ohlsen, 1977).

Problems can result from these safety factors. Individual members can successfully lose themselves in the group and never have to confront their problems. When this occurs the safety in numbers influence undermines the helping process. Another problem results when the group becomes so safe that nothing is risked and, therefore, no action toward resolving problems is taken (Vorrath, n.d.). When either of these two situations arises the group leader must take steps to create tension in the group or confront the group to activate the helping process once again.

Sense of Belonging

Groups have the capacity to extend the experience of belonging to members.

> We are not only gregarious animals liking to be in sight of our fellows, but we have an innate propensity to get ourselves noticed, and noticed favorably, by our kind. No more fiendish punishment could be devised were such a thing physically possible, than one should be turned loose in society and remain absolutely unnoticed by all the members thereof. (William James, 1890, p. 293)

The enticement of group counseling is that it spawns the conditions that enable both the *noticing* to occur and the *ignoring* to be avoided. Lakin (n.d.) pointed out that one of the key distinctions between individual and group psychotherapy is that the group has the capacity to provide members with an experience of belongingness. Thus the group member has the opportunity to feel a part of a social group, one of our essential needs as human beings. While deep intimacy and closeness are still the bailiwick of the dyadic relationship, the group can provide social support in the form of group membership, which can never be an element of the one-to-one relationship. When members experience acceptance, understanding, and cohesiveness in the group, they begin to realize they are important and worthwhile. They feel they need the group and are wanted by the group, which is the essence of belonging. The key dynamic operating here is that (1) groups help individuals create their personal identity, and (2) individuals influence the traits that groups exemplify. The interaction of these two processes helps members find belongingness, which provides them with the support they need to work on improving themselves and contributing constructively to the group's purpose.

The problem presented by the group's belongingness factor is that members may lose sight of the fact that the counseling group is intended to be transitional in nature rather than permanent. In other words, group counseling is not a process designed to give group members a permanent social group within which to operate and meet their needs. Rather, the group is a temporary stopping-off place where members can reconstruct themselves for the purpose of living more effective lives in their regular environments. The element of belonging is only useful as it aids the member in achieving a better life outside the group. A derivative of this same problem is that the sense of belonging may also be a manipulative tool in the hands of the members or leader prompting individual members to defer or suppress their free agency or the group to distort reality, i.e., to produce the phenomena of "group think." Careful attention must be given to whether its impact is constructive or simply a power play used by the group to dominate, control, or manipulate individual members.

Social Value of Group Counseling

Groups by their very nature reflect, represent, and contribute social value.

In the literature there is clear consensus that group work in its various forms has definite social qualities that make it particularly relevant for helping people solve their problems (Yalom, 1995). Barlow, Fuhriman, and Burlingame (2004), in tracing the history of group counseling, affirm the social value of groups stating that "humans gather together to give and receive help, both formally and informally" and when that "human group phenomena" is labeled "group counseling or psychotherapy," research substantiates positive outcomes (p. 18). Groups by their very nature tend to take on social characteristics representing the environment in which they are formed. Individual members through their input into the group represent the broader society in which their learnings and experiences have occurred (Trotzer, 1975). Gazda (1968) referred to this phenomenon when he stated that the group is "a microcosm of social reality" (p. 1). Dinkmeyer and Muro (1971) called the group a "reflection of society as a whole" (p. 60). Hinckley and Herman (1951) commented that the group resembles "true-life situations" where dependence and independence are constantly interchanging, and Vorrath (n.d.) stressed the role of the group as an "ongoing community." Matthews (1992) has noted that people in society dance to the oscillating dynamic described as a conflict between responsibility to self versus responsibility to the group. Counseling and "therapy conducted in groups has the advantage of treating the members in the context of this fundamental dance of life" (p. 162). In all cases the affirmation is that groups are mini-societies that reflect to some degree the reality of the outside world.

Very early in my work as an individual therapist, I realized a major discrepancy existed between what happened in the counselor's office and the client's life. The best laid plans tended to go awry once the client encountered the expectational pressures of their real world. Consequently, the necessity of upgrading the transferability potential in counseling became paramount. The social environment of the small group does just that. There is an inherent transitional value that bolsters the probability of successful implementation of change outside the group. This transferability dynamic is a major therapeutic asset.

The group is a valuable tool in the hands of a trained counselor because it is a social laboratory where results obtained have transitional properties to implement in real life. The group has the advantage of being a laboratory where individuals are able to understand the social meaning of thoughts, feelings, and behaviors because they are being reviewed and experienced in a social context (Dinkmeyer & Muro, 1971). Since we as human beings are social by nature, to fully understand our actions is difficult if we divorce them from the social milieu and the systems in which we function. The group can retain this dimension, while individual counseling must depend almost entirely on verbal description (a second hand account) to account for it. The group atmosphere provides the opportunity for members to learn more about themselves because it gives them a more comprehensive social mirror to look into than individual counseling. In fact, individual change may actually be an easier process in groups. Kurt Lewin once observed that "it is easier to change individuals formed into a group than to change any of them separately" (Maples, 1992, p. 145).

The group is an arena where social comparisons can be made and evaluated. Members have the advantage of practicing behavioral and attitudinal changes prior to attempting them in real life situations. This process, called reality testing, is a major ingredient in the successful resolution of problems. Members can assess the probability of success by using the group as a sounding board in formulating, developing, and evaluating alternatives. By using the group in this way members also can develop the self-confidence needed to implement the changes outside the group.

The extent to which groups are representative of society is difficult to determine and for this reason must be carefully considered in the interaction of any group. Lakin (n.d.) warns that groups are not only capable of defining social reality but are capable of defining it in such a way that it is distorted. When this occurs, the resulting perceptions and changes may in fact be detrimental to problem resolution rather than therapeutic.

An example of reality distortion occurred in an adolescent girls' counseling group where group members, in response to one girl's disclosure of her loneliness and desire to have a boyfriend, coerced a boy to invite her to a dance. This was done outside the group without the knowledge of the group leaders. The girl was noticeably overweight, and when the two appeared at the dance, the boy became subject to cat calls and snide remarks with negative innuendos. He became embarrassed and angry and made an impulsive decision to leave the girl standing alone in the middle of the dance floor, thus devastating her already fragile sense of self-esteem. The group had failed to consider social reality factors in attempting to respond helpfully to the girl's problem as they perceived it. Leaders are responsible for preventing the distortion of social reality whenever possible and must be willing to bear the negative reactions of members when they intervene to maintain a realistic focus in the group.

Group as Power

Groups have power that can influence members constructively or destructively.

The aspect of group process that triggers the most varied and intense reaction is its power. Agreement is plentiful that the group process is powerful, however, no end is in sight regarding the controversy as to if and how that power should be used to change individual lives. To review this subject is beyond the scope of this book, therefore, we will turn our attention to the issue of power in the context of group counseling. Suffice it to say that the influence of groups and group dynamics is inevitable in each of our lives, and our task is to define those elements that make the group counseling process a beneficial tool in the hands of the counselor.

The power of the small group centers around peer group pressure and influence. One of the most important aspects in the development of every person is the reaction of those persons in his or her peer group. This is particularly true during adolescence but is no small matter in the lives of children and adults—from young adults to the elderly. Group counseling harnesses this power of the peer group in an effort to make it a constructive influence in helping group members resolve their problems. One of the most surprising revelations that occurs again and again as one works with groups is that individuals in many cases know what they want to do or should do to better themselves but will not act on that knowledge until they feel it is acceptable and valued by their peer group.

The power of the peer group is revealed in the natural tendencies of the group to influence individuals in terms of conformity, identity, reward and punishment, and social controls. In each of these cases, the counseling group uses peer group dynamics to help individual members contribute appropriately to the group, live satisfying lives in a personal and community sense and act constructively in resolving problems or accomplishing tasks. As a result, the counselor has available vastly expanded resources that can be used in counseling. Individual counseling does not have these resources directly available since the counselor is usually not a member of the client's peer group and is not in a position to engage significant peers in the counseling process. Peer influence therefore becomes a primary factor of change in the group counseling process. Vorrath (n.d.) felt this was such an important aspect of the group process that he built his entire approach to working with adolescent delinquents around it.

In addition to the forces already mentioned, the use of peer group dynamics provides a buffer zone between the adult world and the child or adolescent. Ohlsen (1974) gave a brief description of how this works:

> When some members of the group fail to act, other members can put pressure on reluctant actors without arousing the defensiveness that results when parents and teachers pressure adolescents to behave differently. (p. 144)

This process helps bridge the generation gap by improving communication. Group members can say the same things and demand or urge the same things that adults would but without the contingent emotional resistance. Among adults this same phenomenon can be observed based on the distinction of emotional involvement. The same input that would be resisted or rejected out of hand when given by spouses, bosses, close friends, or parents of adult children is received as revelation, insight, or helpful when obtained from a noninvolved third party of the same age or role category.

As with any source of power the group's power also can be abusive and destructive. If peer pressure is directed toward achieving unrealistic goals or used to force individuals into actions detrimental to themselves or others, the group leader must take steps to intervene. Group pressure is only beneficial if it facilitates the process of self-development on the part of individual group members. Its influence should not become the all consuming power in the client's life. As in the case of belongingness, the group must exert its power to get the most out of group members in the group and in the case of group counseling to get members out of the group via successful resolution of problems rather than totally immersing them in a process that is an end in and of itself.

Helping and Being Helped

Groups extend dual role opportunities that enable members to give and receive in the context of the group process.

Group counseling provides members with the opportunity to both help and be helped. Lakin (n.d.) credited the availability of this option in the group to the group's capacity to redistribute power. The counselor is not the only one who can aid members and indeed should not be since the members are invaluable resources in the helping process. That is why Conyne (Ward, 1993) called members "the most important resource in the whole group" (p. 103). More than any other this characteristic of mutual help contributes to the appeal of group counseling. In individual counseling, clients seldom if ever have the opportunity to help the counselor. They are always in the position of being the ones with the problems who are being helped. In the group they can still get the help they need but in addition they can maintain and build their self-respect and self-worth by assisting others with their problems. Vorrath (n.d.) stressed this concept of "doing things to help one another" as the key therapeutic element in the group process. The impact of this dynamic creates a spiral effect in the group. As members see help being given or give help, they become more willing to ask for and accept help for themselves. As more members ask for help, a greater opportunity exists to be helpful, and so on. Ohlsen (1970) observed that when members discover others struggling with similar problems, their own problems become more acceptable.

Seeing others learn to cope with their problems is encouraging and helps them increase their sense of self-respect. "Thus group counseling...enables them (the members) to satisfy some of their strongest needs, especially in providing real assistance to peers while obtaining assistance from them" (Ohlsen, 1970, p. 206).

The only problems with this small group dynamic are associated with the manner and content of the help that is given. In most cases members provide assistance in the form of feedback and alternatives that are realistic and relevant to the concerns of the members being helped. In giving assistance, however, the one being helped must retain the right to weigh and select the alternatives and perceptions that he or she views as most helpful. In that way ultimate responsibility for change is on the shoulders of the member not the group. Also, the leader is responsible for making sure the help given is realistic and that all members have equal access to the group's assistance, intervening when individual members become dominant or isolated with respect to obtaining help in the group. Extremes of members being too needy, too eager or too withdrawn regarding the helping and being helped process must be addressed as it can negatively affect the productivity of the group.

Self-Correcting Group Dynamics

Groups have inherent self-correcting dynamics that serve the purpose of internally mediating group process.

Small interactive groups have certain inherent self-monitoring and self-correcting tendencies. These tendencies are resources that are naturally available and are mobilized as the flow of the group interaction evolves. However, these dynamics are not absolute and can be obliterated or negated by circumstances, events, and conditions that occur in the group. The most prominent of these tendencies is the dual dynamic of countering ostracism and enmeshment in the group. The best illustration of this dynamic is your hand. Physically attempt to disassociate one finger from the rest of your fingers. As you do so you will feel a natural resistance and a pressure to pull that finger back in thereby reducing the tension. The same phenomenon occurs in groups when one member or several members become peripheral or ostracized. The group finds ways of pulling the detaching or isolated members back in by shifting focus or attention or by siding with and defending extruded members.

Now, clench your hand into a fist asserting all the pressure you can to hold it closed. Note that tension once again is evident precipitating an impulse to relax the hand thereby separating its members (the fingers) from such close proximity. The same dynamic occurs in groups when intensity becomes overwhelming. A natural tendency exists on the part of individuals and the group to lighten up.

This may be done through humor, a shift in focus, or a direct confrontation of the fact that things are too tight. Members may even suggest physical activities to relieve the stress of becoming so embroiled in the group.

Another self-correcting group trait is *centering* where group members act to draw the group back from tangents or distractions to a theme or focus of personal or practical relevance. Frustration, enthusiasm, and the desire to get something out of the group or to get something done in the group are motivators for members to get the group to center. These self-correcting traits are unique to group counseling, not being available at all in individual counseling, and being superseded by homeostatic forces in family counseling. However, they are not sufficient to insure that groups will function therapeutically. Group leaders may rely upon them as the first line of defense against excesses or distortions, but must be ready to intervene if the group does not mobilize them. Donigian and Malnati (1997) make the further point that these same self-regulating processes function to maintain the status quo or homeostasis and as such may represent resistance. Consequently, the leader may have to intervene to generate tension so that the group and its members can move ahead with the change process. Also, one of the reasons leaderless groups are vulnerable to nontherapeutic interactions is that the group process can generate dynamics that exhaust or mitigate against these natural helping and healing properties of the group substituting negative dynamic processes that proceed unchecked.

Curative Factors in Groups

Groups have an intricate fabric of qualitative properties that commend the process relative to constructive productivity.

Yalom (1975) coined the term curative factors to describe components of the group process that account for the therapeutic impact of group process. He considers these factors to have a common manifestation across the "entire spectrum of therapeutic groups among a wide variety of populations" (MacDevitt, 1987, p. 76). Based on a foundation of research, clinical practice and theoretical conceptualization, Yalom (1995) identified the following components that characterize therapeutic groups:

1. *Altruism*: the process of helping others.
2. *Cohesion*: feeling that one truly belongs to the group.
3. *Catharsis*: being able to express feeling and concerns to others.
4. *Insight*: Acquiring self-knowledge or self-understanding.
5. *Interpersonal learning-input*: receiving feedback from other members.
6. *Interpersonal learning-output*: acquiring interpersonal skills.
7. *Guidance*: receiving advice and suggestions.

8. *Family reenactment*: experiencing and learning from the group as if it were one's family, i.e., recapitulization of family dynamics.
9. *Instillation of hope*: being encouraged by seeing that others have solved or are solving their problems.
10. *Universality*: realizing that one is not so different from others.
11. *Identification*: modeling oneself after another member or the therapist.
12. *Existential factors*: realizing important, painful truths about life (MacDevitt, 1987, pp. 76–77).

Together these factors interrelate in such a way to both create conditions for change and generate change. They are interdependent but have properties that allow them to be identified and specified for conceptualization purposes. As such they account for the distinctive nature of group counseling/therapy and are the assets that advocate the use of groups as practical and effective in helping clients.

Donigian and Malnati (1997) contribute four additional factors to the above list. In their system the group processes of contagion, conflict, anxiety, and consensual validation are therapeutic factors that make change possible in groups. *Contagion* occurs when one member's actions or expressions create ramifications that impact the group generating a kind of ripple effect. *Conflict* is the dynamic that provides focus and focal direction in the group and raises issues that become the work of the group. *Anxiety* is the tension or fuel that drives the group. It reflects both past conflicts (e.g., unresolved family of origin issues) and present manifestations of conflict from past and/or current (ingroup) sources. *Consensual Validation* is the opportunity for group members to check out their behavior with other members and receive feedback.

Bemak and Epp (1996) have proposed nonsexual love as another curative factor in groups. They describe love as a unique characteristic of therapeutic groups that is not accessible in such a potent form in any other counseling modality. Due to the fact that American pop culture has distorted love by entangling it with eroticism, sensuality, and sexuality, counseling theorists have had to "intellectually disguise love's positive non-erotic role in the therapeutic process" (p. 119). Consequently terms such as "unconditional positive regard," "positive reinforcement," "transference," "countertransference," and "positive strokes" have been devised as "love's euphemistic disguises" (p. 120). The fact that groups can provide these powerful nurturing dynamics definitely has curative implications. Even Freud noted the propensity for group members desperate for nurturing "to find someone to hate so they could band together in love" (Bemak & Epp, 1996, p. 123). As such, love qualifies as a potent asset in groups, a fact echoed by Gawrys and Brown's (1963) observation that being accepted and understood by a counselor is a satisfying experience but being accepted, understood, and cared for by a group is profound.

Spectator Therapy

Groups provide an ideal arena for observational learning.

A derivative of the social laboratory characteristic of group work is what Dinkmeyer and Muro (1971) called "spectator therapy." For example, in counseling groups members have the opportunity to observe others talk about and work through problems in the group. Whether those topics are similar to or different from their own, the member engages in observational learning. Thus members can experience the benefits of the group without revealing their own problems. This is certainly not a characteristic of individual counseling and therefore is unique to the group process. The inherent weakness of this trait is an obvious one—if everyone observes and no one works, nothing will be learned by being a spectator.

Feedback for Growth

Groups provide a unique setting for giving and receiving feedback.

The nature of communication in group work is special because of the opportunity for members to give and receive multiple feedback (Bednar & Kaul, 1994; Morran, Stockton, & Teed, 1998). While individual counseling enables the client to receive feedback from an understanding, supportive and helpful expert, the group incorporates both that feedback and feedback from peers. Paraphrasing Cohn (1967) the impact of this process is as follows:

> When persons are placed within the context of a group they cannot continue to rely only upon their own perceptions for a view of themselves. Through the process of group interaction each person comes in contact with the group's perception of what he or she is or what he or she purports to be. Thus it is within the context of the group that each person gains greater self-awareness. (p. 1)

For example, group counseling effectiveness is directly related to the quantity and quality of the feedback (Morran, Stockton, & Teed, 1998). As members receive feedback about their actions, feelings, thoughts, and problems, they become more clearly aware of the impact of their behavior on others and others' problems and concerns. In addition, they find out more about themselves, which gives them a stronger basis on which to make decisions beneficial to their lives. Research links feedback in groups to "increased motivation for change, greater insight into how one's behavior affects others, increased comfort with taking interpersonal risks, higher ratings of satisfaction with the group experience and increased capacity for intimacy" (Widra & Amidon, 1987, cited in Burlingame, Fuhriman, & Johnson, 2004, p. 55).

Groups must guard against using feedback in a destructive, perjorative, or personally damaging manner. When used for the purpose of ostracizing, scapegoating, or criticizing or with no positive purpose in mind, the person and the group process are damaged. Groups must establish guidelines for feedback (see Guidelines for Feedback, below), and the leader must act to facilitate positive use of feedback while safeguarding individuals and the group from using it negatively.

Guidelines for Feedback

Feedback is a way of helping others to consider changing their behaviors. It is communication to a person (or a group) that gives that person information about how he or she affects others. Like a guided-missile system, feedback helps individuals keep behavior on target and thus achieve their goals. It is a shared corrective mechanism for the individual who wants to learn how well behavior matches intentions. The following guidelines were listed by David W. Johnson (1972) in his book entitled *Reaching Out: Interpersonal Effectiveness and Self-Actualization* on pages 16–17.

1. Focus feedback on behavior rather than on the person.
2. Focus feedback on observations rather than on inferences.
3. Focus feedback on description rather than judgment.
4. Focus feedback on descriptions of behavior that are in terms of "more or less" rather than in terms of "either-or."
5. Focus feedback on behavior related to a specific situation, preferably to the "here and now," rather than on behavior in the abstract, or in the "there and then."
6. Focus feedback on the sharing of ideas and information rather than on giving advice.
7. Focus feedback on exploring alternatives rather than on giving advice.
8. Focus feedback on the value it may have to the receiver, not on the value of release that it provides the person giving the feedback.
9. Focus feedback on the amount of information that the person receiving it can use rather than on the amount that you have and would like to give.
10. Focus feedback on time and place so that personal data can be shared at appropriate times.
11. Focus feedback on what is said rather than on why it is said.

Personalizing the Learning Process

Groups personalize the learning process.

The group process by its very nature enhances the learning process (Hulse-Killacky, 1986). Therefore, group counseling is especially helpful in educational settings because it contributes to the personalization of the learning process by providing an environment in which members can discuss their unique and common problems (Akos, 2000; 2004). It has all the properties of an ideal learning environment in the sense that it has a trained leader, involves peer group dynamics, and takes into account individual differences of the group members. The focus is personal and problem oriented, and members are given the opportunity to deal responsibly with themselves and their concerns (Trotzer, 1972). Immediate integration occurs with the education process because members are encouraged to discover more effective methods of living their lives.

Group counseling presents a helpful alternative to students who have difficulty functioning in the less personal environment of the classroom or who shy away from the intensity of individual counseling or psychotherapy. By working on problems in a group setting, individuals realize the school or the community has resources for helping them and has a personal interest in them (Akos, 2004). This creates a greater personal commitment to the school and the educational process in general. Thus group counseling is a means of maximizing the educational process by making contact with the personal lives of students in a manner that is meaningful to both parties in the learning enterprise—the student and the school.

Hulse-Killacky (1996) has posited even broader relevance to this personalization of the educational process. "As group work is recognized more and more as a broad methodology, there will be new and rich opportunities to link group work with teacher education, special education and educational leadership programs" (p. 166). Thus the reality of group work in educational settings personalizing the learning process is validated and the potential is unlimited (Killacky & Hulse-Killacky, 2004). However, the personalization of learning in groups extends beyond the educational domain. Groups conducted in agencies and private practice settings provide participants with a host of opportunities for personalized learning about themselves and their problems. A growing trend in business and industry is to use groups called quality circles and focus groups to enhance productivity, generate strategy and direction, improve efficiency, and boost morale. These formats essentially use groups to mobilize worker input, facilitate employee involvement, and stimulate a process whereby workers share their knowledge and experience in an atmosphere where they collaborate with each other—all in the best interest of the company or corporation. In a sense, there is no limit to the applicability of group process to enhance personal and interpersonal learning regardless of purpose or setting.

Increasing Counselor Contact

Groups provide counselors with leadership opportunities that expand their role and share their expertise.

Since its inception, group work has always been promoted as a means of increasing the amount of counselor-client contact time and thereby expanding the impact of the counselor's professional role. The only logical conclusion is that if a counselor effectively spends one hour per week with eight clients in a group as opposed to one hour per week with each of those clients individually, he or she will choose the group approach. That decision makes for the most efficient use of counselor time.

Strangely enough, though, group work still does not have the unequivocal support from counselors, administrators, counselor educators, and consumers that individual counseling does. Part of the reason for this is the lack of training and training programs (Carroll, 1985; Conyne, et al., 1985; Shapiro & Shapiro, 1985). But the more important reason seems to be a complex problem of hesitancy regarding the group process and lack of motivation to try it on the part of counselors. As Dansby (1996) indicated "there is evidence that the belief in the importance of group far exceeds the actual practice" (p. 232). Inevitably, actual priorities in guidance, counseling, and psychotherapy programs place group work low on the list regardless of its position idealistically. However, the recent emergence of cost consciousness promulgated by insurance companies and managed care in the private practice domain and budget restraints in educational domains has once again raised the cost effectiveness benefit of group work. This time, however, it is also supported by distinctive efforts by group counselor educators and group work organizations to supply the needed training to support the growth of group work (see Conyne & Bemak, 2004a, pp. 1–154). Consequently, professional counselors are being encouraged and prepared to use group work in their settings and job descriptions and are doing so effectively. The fact that this trend is pragmatic from an expediency perspective (read business, budget, or profit motivation) as opposed to a concern for people is moot. The benefits of group work are relevant regardless of motive. As this trend continues advantages of greater counselor-client contact and expanded counselor role will be realized.

The Group Work Umbrella

The field of group work has expanded and developed to a point where an umbrella construct encompassing a veritable rainbow of group modalities and processes has emerged. (The "Group Work Rainbow" was conceptualized by Dr. Robert K. Conyne and promulgated during his tenure as president of ASGW, 1995–96.) The Association for Specialists in Group Work has developed Professional Standards

I. Task/Work Groups

The task/work group specialization refers to the utilization of group dynamics, organizational development, and team building to enhance group members' skills in task accomplishment and group maintenance. The focus is on the application of group process skills, principles, and dynamics to improve, practice, and achieve realization of identified work goals. The scope of practice for task/work group specialists includes normally functioning individuals who are members of naturally occurring task or work groups typically operating in organizational settings such as businesses, industries, schools, health care environments, institutions of higher learning, or religious organizations (see Hulse-Killacky, Killacky, & Donigian ,2001).

II. Guidance/Psychoeducation Groups

The guidance/psychoeducation group specialization refers to the utilization of the group modality for educative and preventive purposes. The guidance/psychoeducation specialist uses the group medium to educate and assist group participants who are at risk for, but presently unaffected by, environmental threats (e.g., AIDS), who are approaching a developmental transition point (e.g., preparing for college), or who are embroiled in the turmoil of coping with a life crisis (e.g., suicide of a loved one). The overarching goals of guidance/psychoeducation groups are to assist members in present adjustment and prevent future development of debilitating dysfunction while strengthening coping skills and self-esteem. The scope of guidance/psychoeducation group practice is essentially normally functioning individuals who are in need of information, skills, and guidance in a wide range of settings (see Brown, 2004).

III. Counseling/Interpersonal Problem Solving Groups

The counseling\interpersonal problem solving group specialization addresses the task of helping group participants resolve the usual, yet often difficult, problems of living through interpersonal support and group problem solving. Group counselors help participants develop their existing interpersonal problem solving competencies so that they can resolve current problems and be better able to handle future problems of a similar nature. The scope of group counseling practice includes individuals who are experiencing nonsevere career, educational, personal, social, and developmental concerns.

(Continued)

IV. Psychotherapy/Personality Reconstruction Groups

The group psychotherapy specialization addresses the concerns of individuals who are in need of reconstructive or remedial psychological treatment. Group psychotherapy is focused on helping individuals with acute or chronic mental or emotional disorders evidenced by marked distress or impairment in functioning for the purpose of generating major personality change.

Compiled from: Association for Specialists in Group Work: Professional Standards for the Training of Group Workers (Association for Specialists in Group Work, 1992, p. 13; Conyne, 1996, pp. 157–158).

---

for the Training of Group Workers (ASGW, 1991) that delineate four specific arenas of group practice. The box above presents a brief summary of the four specializations. The discussion that follows has been subsumed by the umbrella, but has also served as its inception and impetus when the first edition of this text was published (Trotzer, 1977). Appropriate adaptations have been made, but the wheel has not been reinvented or relabeled since the ASGW standards and the material that follows are quite compatible.

Group work with regard to the helping professional would not be complete without a consideration of the relationship between task, guidance/psychoeducation, counseling and therapy groups. Figure 2.1 presents a graphic illustration of the relationship among three of these group processes and details the essential characteristics of each one. You will notice overlap between group guidance/ psychoeducation groups and group counseling and between group counseling and group psychotherapy. These processes are not mutually exclusive entities but are on a continuum. Although we can identify specific characteristics that generally apply to each process, in practice some degree of commonality does exist. The group leader, therefore, must maintain a flexible attitude in working with these processes and recognize that their characteristics are fluid rather than rigid.

Group guidance/psychoeducation groups involve the process of providing personally relevant information of a developmental nature to group members. This information may be in terms of facts and figures, procedures, requirements, or skills necessary to help them in their lives. The focus of the process is decidedly cognitive in nature with emphasis on environmental factors, content, and topics and the format is typically structured with regard to both process and content. Methods are usually centered on presentation and discussion with the leader taking the primary responsibility for organizing and directing the group and

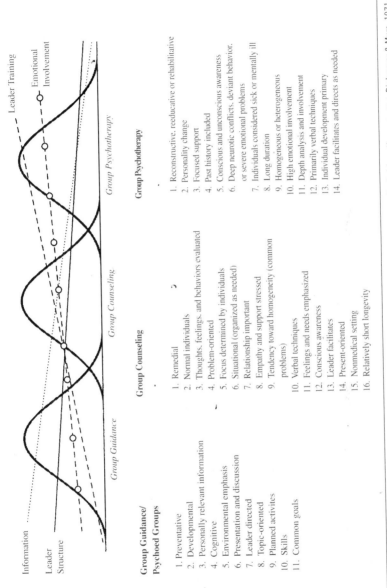

Information ....
Leader Structure
Leader Training — — —
Emotional Involvement

Group Guidance   *Group Counseling*   *Group Psychotherapy*

Group Guidance/ Psychoed Groups

1. Preventative
2. Developmental
3. Personally relevant information
4. Cognitive
5. Environmental emphasis
6. Presentation and discussion
7. Leader directed
8. Topic-oriented
9. Planned activities
10. Skills
11. Common goals

Group Counseling

1. Remedial
2. Normal individuals
3. Thoughts, feelings, and behaviors evaluated
4. Problem-oriented
5. Focus determined by individuals
6. Situational (organized as needed)
7. Relationship important
8. Empathy and support stressed
9. Tendency toward homogeneity (common problems)
10. Verbal techniques
11. Feelings and needs emphasized
12. Conscious awareness
13. Leader facilitates
14. Present-oriented
15. Nonmedical setting
16. Relatively short longevity

Group Psychotherapy

1. Reconstructive, reeducative or rehabilitative
2. Personality change
3. Focused support
4. Past history included
5. Conscious and unconscious awareness
6. Deep neurotic conflicts, deviant behavior, or severe emotional problems
7. Individuals considered sick or mentally ill
8. Long duration
9. Homogeneous or heterogeneous
10. High emotional involvement
11. Depth analysis and involvement
12. Primarily verbal techniques
13. Individual development primary
14. Leader facilitates and directs as needed

Figure 2.1 Group guidance, group counseling, and group psychotherapy. (Material for this diagram was collected from these sources: Dinkmeyer & Muro, 1971; Gazda, Duncan, & Meadows, 1967; Goldman, 1962; Mahler, 1969; Ohlsen, 1970, 1974; Schmidt, n.d.; Trotzer, 1975. Partially adapted from L. M. Brammer & E. L. Shostrom, 1976, *Therapeutic Psychology: Fundamentals of Counseling and Psychotherapy* (3rd ed.). Reprinted by permission.)

engaging the members in interactive processing. Although members may collaborate in selecting topics that are in line with their interests and needs, Mahler (1969) pointed our that "in schools group guidance is usually oriented toward telling students what adults think the youngsters should know about themselves" (p. 11). The most common themes involve teaching coping skills and supplying information that facilitates decision-making, understanding of self, others, and the environment in order to enhance the prospect of effective adjustment in group members and to help individuals more fully realize and apply their human potential (Robinson, 1980). (See special issues of The Journal for Specialists in Group Work on "Psychoeducational group work" (2000), 25(1) and "Use of groups for prevention" (2001), 26(3) for examples and formats.)

The main emphasis in guidance/psychoeducation groups is dealing with people on the basis of their developmental status in life. As such the process takes on dimensions of being preventative and facilitative in nature. Group members often know what they want to do but do not know how to do it. Efforts are directed toward supplying members with essential skills and information that will enable them to address current developmental tasks and prevent or circumvent problems in the future (Owens & Kulic, 2001). The primary byproduct of such groups is effective decision-making based on relevant knowledge of one's self and one's environment. The different types of guidance/psychoeducation groups are discussed in detail in chapter 10, and more specific examples are included there.

In contrast to guidance/psychoeducation groups, group counseling is primarily remedial and interventive in nature and focuses on problem-solving. It deals with normal individuals who are experiencing problems that are interfering in some respect with their lives. As a result, the development of a group relationship characterized by empathy and support is stressed where members can evaluate their thoughts, feelings, and behaviors in a safe yet social environment. Counseling groups are formed in light of certain personal and interpersonal problems and therefore tend to be homogeneous in nature. Members are organized into groups that discuss problems with which they can identify, at least to some extent. Groups meet until the problems are solved for the most part and tend to be organized in a time limited manner of relatively short duration (e.g., 10–20 weekly group sessions). Counseling groups tend to mirror quarter or semester time frames in schools and extend three to nine months in other settings depending on their purposes and organizational formats. Members are encouraged to work toward dissolving the group by resolving their problems.

Because of the emphasis on personal problems, the focus of the group is determined by the members, and a contingent emphasis on feeling is due to the emotional involvement required to engage in self-disclosure and feedback. The leader is primarily a facilitator who uses verbal techniques, stresses conscious awareness, and keeps the group oriented to the here and now problems of group interaction and member concerns (Carroll, 1986; Carroll & Wiggins, 1997). These groups are usually conducted in nonmedical settings, such as schools, agencies, private practices, and other helping institutions serving clients who have not been diagnosed with a mental disorder.

The distinction between group counseling and group psychotherapy is associated more with the type of clients than the process itself. *Group psychotherapy* is utilized to work with clients who are dysfunctional, or psychiatrically impaired in some respect, and are typically labeled with a DSM-IV (Diagnostic and Statistical Manual of Mental Disorders, fourth edition) diagnosis of a mental disorder. They may be considered sick, mentally ill, or emotionally disturbed, have psychotic traits, tendencies, or deep neurotic conflicts, or engage in deviant behavior. In any event, the causes of the problems are related to personality dynamics and development. Therefore, the purpose is to effect personality change with group effort directed toward reconstructing, reeducating, or rehabilitating individual members relative to personality characteristics that are creating problems in their lives. In addition, psychotherapy groups may be utilized to help members maintain functional lifestyles in spite of psychiatric maladies and support independent living of members who might otherwise require institutional care. Since the focus is on personality, the process tends to be quite long in duration because personality patterns develop over a long period of time and are therefore resistant to change. Support is necessary to the process in the sense of (1) providing it when clients are working on their issues and patterns and (2) when they need therapeutic intervention to circumvent relapses or to maintain functionality. Often clients in group therapy try to avoid working on their problems because of the effort required to change. If the group supports members' actions that are not associated with the task of changing personality or maintaining functionality, the whole process is undermined. Therefore, support is used as a reinforcement that focuses on encouraging and promoting individual efforts toward resolving personality problems and maintaining accountable functionality.

Group psychotherapy may be composed of either homogeneous or heterogeneous members and is characterized by a high degree of emotional involvement. The leader facilitates or directs as is necessary and uses primarily verbal techniques. Conscious and unconscious awareness, a concern for the past history of the client, and depth analysis and exploration may be involved in the process with the expertise of the leader being essential to the constructive use of these procedures. Groups are organized in medical or institutional settings on an inpatient basis or in private practices, mental health clinics, counseling centers, or agencies where referred clients (including self-referred ones) are treated as outpatients.

General trends evident on a continuum from group guidance/psychoeducation groups to group psychotherapy are that the role of cognitive information and the amount of leader structure decreases while the degree of emotional involvement (affect) and required leadership training and expertise increase. In addition, elements of guidance and counseling groups may be integrated into psychotherapy groups; and counseling groups often include guidance or psychoeducational dimensions. However, when individuals present issues or problems in guidance or counseling groups that significantly derail or distract the intended process, referral to the appropriate therapeutic entity is in order.

Relating Focus and Process

Figure 2.2 illustrates the relationship among group guidance/psychoeducation groups, group counseling, and group psychotherapy with the basic focus of each process. The essence of every person's identity is the result of continual interaction between personality, thoughts, feelings, behaviors, and environment. Personality is that aspect of a person that develops over time and is characterized by a consistency that gives each person a uniqueness unparalleled by any other human being. Personality is composed of the patterns and characteristics that are generally stable and that change at an increasingly slower rate as one matures and grows older. These patterns and traits dictate each person's adjustment to life and the concomitant satisfaction or dissatisfaction that he or she experiences. When a person develops characteristics that consistently and continually create frustration, anxiety, problems, and dissatisfactions, efforts must be made to change those traits and develop different or revised characteristics to facilitate satisfactory adjustment. The process of group psychotherapy is directed to that end.

Thoughts, feelings, and behaviors are the three components of one's experience that have the dual role of expressing personality and affecting personality. The characteristic that distinguishes these components from personality is their tendency to fluctuate according to situations and experiences one is exposed to or solicits. A person often shows markedly different behavior at a party than on the

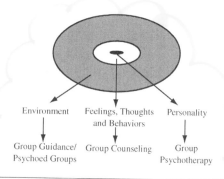

Figure 2.2 Relating process and focus in groups.

job. Similarly, a person's feelings sometimes change very rapidly with the advent of an unexpected gift or visit from an important person in one's life.

The whole process of education is such that a person often has learning experiences that change their thinking in a very short period of time. In any case, the changes occur quickly and can be accounted for by any number of reasons including role demands, expectations, events, circumstances, or inner turmoil. Attesting to the importance of these components as the moderators between one's personality and one's environment is the fact that theories of counseling and psychotherapy focus on them as channels for instituting change in a person's life. For example, Carl Rogers' (1951) Person-Centered Therapy focuses on feelings, William Glasser's (1965) Reality Therapy, and Albert Ellis' (1971) Rational-Emotive Therapy emphasize thinking and cognitions while social learning theorists such as John Krumboltz and Carl Thoreson (1976) zero in on behavior.

Problems occur in people's lives when they cannot adjust to changes in any or all of the three areas. The problems may be the result of a change that occurs too quickly (traumatic events), or is too intense (crisis situations), or is so divergent and varied as to become unsettling to the person.

When individuals cannot understand, cope, or deal adequately with their thoughts, feelings, or behaviors and feel something must be done to rectify the situation, they may look outside themselves for a source of help. Group counseling is one process that can effectively provide the help in a meaningful and constructive manner. Its focus is on evaluating thoughts, feelings, and actions of normal human beings for the purpose of helping them adjust adequately, cope effectively, grow developmentally, and live more satisfying and productive lives.

Each person lives in an environment or life space that provides experiences, opportunities, and pressures or stresses that must be dealt with to achieve personal fulfillment. To do that, individuals must implement decisions based on their knowledge of that environment and the interaction of their own selves within it. Decisions that are based on accurate information about one's self and one's world and include steps to develop the personal skill necessary to carry out those decisions are by far the most rewarding. They accelerate one's progress and achievement and create a more satisfying lifestyle. The process of group guidance and psychoeducation groups is directed at providing the information and skills that are personally relevant and that facilitate the decision-making process in the manner just described.

Learning Activities

The Nature of Group

The following activities can be used in classes or groups to help members assess the characteristics of groups and the group process. Since their purpose is to integrate experience and cognition, these activities require both involvement and observation on the part of each participant.

The Ball Game

I have been using the following activity to introduce group dynamics and group process in my undergraduate group dynamics class for the past few years. It is adapted from Halbur (2002, pp. 45–46) and effectively stimulates experience and discussion of the developmental stages of the group process.

Instructions:
1. Divide the class into subgroups of four to eight (depending on class size) and have them sit in a circle.
2. Place a ball (nerf basketball, football, soccer balls work very well) in the center of each group.
3. Tell the group: "Your task is to use this ball to invent, organize, and play a game in the next 15 minutes. You will receive no outside assistance from the instructor in regard to this task."
4. When the time is up, process the experience using the following questions:
   a. How did the group begin?
   b. What struggles did you have as a group?
   c. How did you address the task?
   d. What was the experience like for you?
   e. Who took the leadership role?
   f. What did you like/dislike about the experience?
   g. Who was glad the activity was over? Why?
   h. Who wanted to continue? Why?
   i. How is this activity like a group experience?
   j. Compare and contrast the manner in which the different subgroups addressed the task.

Building Blocks Dyads (Option 1)

This technique is particularly useful in the beginning stages of group development since it encourages group members to get to know one another, and, at the same time, demonstrates some of the peculiar properties that differentiate group and dyadic (one-to-one) relationships.

Have class members pair off with a person they do not know or know least well in the group. Give them 5 to 10 minutes to get to know each other as best they can. About half way through the time allotted, stop the discussion and have each partner write down an initial impression of their partner. Then allow the conversation to continue to the end of the stated time period. At the end of the time period form the dyads into groups of four (two dyads to a group) and have the dyad members introduce their partners and give their initial impressions. After each member has been introduced, each group can proceed to get better acquainted. At the end of about 10 minutes form the groups of four into groups of eight and instruct them to get to know each other without any specific directions. After 15 minutes of discussion, form the groups of eight into groups of 16 (or some number larger than eight depending on class size), and once again give them about 15 minutes to get to know each other. The total time involve should be about 45 to 60 minutes.

Discuss the experience in terms of the purpose (getting to know one another) and the characteristics revealed about groups and group process. What differences were noted between one-to-one and group relationships? What impact did the size of the group have on the nature of the discussion? Did dyads and subgroups retain their identity when merged into a large group? What happened to communication and to the influence of the individual as groups changed in size?

Building Blocks Dyads (Option 2)

A variation of the technique just described is to divide the class in half. In one group, follow the procedures described above starting with dyads and then proceeding to four and eight and so on up to the total size of subgroup. With the other half of the group, reverse the procedure moving from the large group by one-halves down to two persons (dyads). For example, if there are 16 people in the subgroup, your groups would start with 16. Then they would divide into eight, four, and two, in that order. At each level, give the members of both sections a personal sharing task to perform. Examples that could be used follow:

1. Share a meaningful experience you have had recently.
2. Share one thing about your personality that you feel is a positive attribute.
3. Share one thing about yourself that you would like to change.
4. Share a problem in your life right now that you have not been able to deal with satisfactorily.
5. Share one negative and one positive thing about your _____ (job, family, school, etc.) that you are aware of right now.

(These types of personal sharing tasks are also useful in group counseling as initiating procedures that help group members interact and get material to be worked with out on the table.)

Allot an appropriate amount of time at each level of interaction so that members have sufficient time to discuss the personal sharing tasks in some depth.

After all steps have been completed, conduct a follow-up discussion based on the processes and reactions of members in the various sized groups. Contrast the experience of moving from the large group to dyads and from dyads to the large group.

Dyads versus Groups (Option 1)

To compare the process of individual counseling with group counseling more directly, try the following exercise. Using the personal sharing tasks previously listed or similar ones, have members of the class pair off and discuss the chosen task in detail. Then divide the class into small groups (six to eight members) and repeat the process using a different personal sharing task. It is not necessary that persons who were partners in the one-to-one sharing be in the same group. In fact, it is usually a good idea to split them up. Allot plenty of time for discussion in each exercise and then process it in terms of similarities and differences between the two experiences.

Dyads versus Groups (Option 2)

Using the same format as that just described, we can add the dimension of process observation. In the first phase, use triads (groups of three) instead of dyads. Two persons interact using one of the personal sharing tasks and the third person observes. After an appropriate length of time (5–10 minutes) the observers give feedback to the two persons who participated in the sharing. This procedure is repeated three times with three different personal sharing tasks until each person has had the opportunity to be the observer. After each round of sharing (three in all), have the process observer rotate to the next triad and reassign a new process observer before the next sharing task is given. That way the composition of the groups will change and class members will get to interact with more members of the class.

For the group phase, use the fish bowl approach. Divide the class into subgroups large enough for each one to be subdivided into two smaller groups of three to five members each. One small group sits in an inner circle and proceeds to discuss one of the personal sharing tasks. The other small group sits in an outer circle observing the interaction of the inner. Each member in the outer circle should be assigned one person in the inner circle to observe in addition to the group process. At the end of the discussion, each observer sits down with the person he or she was observing and gives feedback on his or her participation and reactions in the group. During the feedback session, the person receiving the feedback initially is not allowed to comment until the observer finishes. After the feedback is completed, discussion can ensue. After individual feedback has been given and discussed, the outer circle members convene as an inner circle to discuss together their observations of the inner group process while the original inner group listens. Repeat the whole process reversing the inner and outer circles and making sure each person in the observer circle is assigned a different person to observe than the one who observed her or him in the first round. On completion of both phases hold a general discussion comparing and contrasting the dyadic and group processes.

Consensus

The consensus exercise entitled "Agree-Disagree," described in the box on the next page, is another useful method of learning about group process. This exercise has a great deal of flexibility and can be utilized effectively in a variety of group situations that require group decision making. The statements used for generating discussion can be varied to fit the situation, the nature of the group members, and the purpose for which the group was formed. After completing the exercise, discuss the factors involved in reaching consensus as the group became larger.

Starting a Group From Scratch

This activity is particularly effective if utilized at the very inception of a class or group experience since it reduces social stimuli to a minimum and accentuates the dynamics that individuals experience as they encounter the task of becoming part of a group process. The following sequence of steps is suggested:

1. Blindfold each group member as they arrive and lead them to a seat in a circle of chairs set up beforehand. (An alternative method is to let members sit in the circle upon arrival, give them a blindfold, and instruct them to blindfold themselves.)

2. When all members are blindfolded and seated, explain that the group has begun and that the first part of the experience will be nonverbal. Have group members stand and begin to mill around within the perimeter of the chairs (as the leader you can direct people back into the group if they wander out). While milling, they are to make physical contact with other members making an effort to greet each person with whom they come in contact. (This is to be done completely without talking.)

3. Each group member is to make contact with at least five different people during the milling. When a member makes contact with the sixth person, they are to nonverbally signal that person that they want to be their partner. If that person has made contact with five other people already, they signal agreement. If they have not connected with five other people, they must refuse the invitation (nonverbally) and both continue to mill in search of a partner.

Agree–Disagree Activity

Directions

1. Read each statement individually and decide whether you agree or disagree with it.
2. Select another person, and the two of you come to agreement on each of the statements. Words may be changed or added in order to come to an agreement. If you don't agree with the statement as it stands, you must come up with a revision that each person agrees with at each level.
3. After each statement has been discussed and agreement reached, select two other people who have reached agreement. The four of you now go through the process of reaching agreement on each of the statements.
4. After the four of you have reached agreement, select another foursome and the eight of you try to come to an agreement.

Sample Statements

1. Sex education is the responsibility of the family; the schools should not become involved.
2. Learning disabled children are basically mean spirited kids who don't listen and are lazy.
3. Students should not be allowed to have a voice in school administration or curriculum matters.
4. People of Color have less ability than Whites and should be treated accordingly.
5. No prison inmate or ex-convict should ever be trusted.
6. Law and order is the cure for our social problems today.
7. The red states and the blue states are a suitable metaphor for depicting the political nature of our society.
8. Individual freedom should be guaranteed at all costs.
9. The role of the U.S. military as a police force is vital to the stability of our global society and the perpetuation and protection of democracy.
10. Self-examination and self-disclosure are necessary prerequisites for effective training and development as a professional counselor.
11. HIV/AIDS is receiving sufficient attention from both the public and private sectors of our society.
12. Create your own stimulus statements!

Note: An effective adaptation of this activity for strategic planning in groups is to have each person write a statement describing a major objective, purpose or program that represents their perspective of the focus of the group. Then proceed through the consensus process as described until full group consensus has been achieved. In this case, statements can be accumulated at each level rather than simply merged into one thereby producing a list of group strategies or purposes that has the support of the entire group.

4. When all group members have found a partner based on the five contacts criteria, the leader assists each dyad to find seats for the next phase which is getting acquainted (both remain blindfolded). Have partners get to know each other in two ways. First, by using the question "Who are you?" and, second, by sculpting. Partners alternate asking "Who are you?" repeatedly with the **requirement** that *each answer must be different* and the **limitation** that *neither party may give his or her name*. Allow three to four minutes for the "Who are you?" repetitions, and then instruct the partners to sculpt each other's head to get a sense of their partner's physical features. Be sure to obtain prior consent for the sculpting activity in order to adapt the activity in consideration of individual members' cultural or religious beliefs that may mitigate against physical contact.

5. When the sculpting is completed, the leader separates the partners and forms two lines of chairs which are back to back so that partners will have restricted visual access to each other when the blindfolds are removed.

6. Give each member an 8½ × 11 (or larger) sheet of paper and a magic marker. Remove the blindfolds and instruct each person to create a "Wanted" poster by drawing a picture or caricature of their partner's head or face on the top half of the sheet and describing them with identifying data on the bottom half.

7. When the "Wanted" posters are complete, use masking tape to post them on a wall for all to see. Give each member another sheet of paper and have them number the sheet from 1 through X (number of people in the group). Number the posters 1 through X and have group members independently match posters and people, writing down the correct name next to the appropriate number on their sheets.

8. When most or all have been identified, review the posters as a group and place the members' names on each poster.

9. Process the activity in light of individual member's feelings and experiences and in terms of group process dynamics.

An alternative to the poster procedure (steps six to eight) is to separate partners in step five and place them in separated places in the circle. Remove the blindfolds and complete the identification phase verbally by having each person describe their partner and attempt to identify them in the group.

Group Counseling Definition and Advantages

A Cognitive Exercise

Have each class member write his or her own definition of counseling or psychotherapy (e.g., counseling/psychotherapy is...). Encourage members to use their own words and to focus on aspects particularly meaningful to them. The definition need not be comprehensive, but it should reflect the unique perception of each class member. Discuss the definitions in class, noting on the board the different characteristics pointed out by class members. Then have the sub-groups of 3–4 class members write out definitions of group counseling or group psychotherapy following the same guidelines of using their own words and focusing on aspects each person deems important. Discuss these definitions in the same manner as before, and then compare the two in an effort to identify similarities between them and differences that can be attributed to the special qualities of the group process.

"Ask the Expert" Activity

(Adapted from Crowley, 1989, pp. 173–75.) Follow the sequence of steps below.

1. Divide the class into subgroups of three to four members and instruct them to come up with three questions they want to ask the expert (i.e., the instructor) about group counseling or group work.
2. Each subgroup presents their questions to the class (list on the board).
3. The subgroups are then redirected to come up with an answer to one of their own questions.
4. Each subgroup presents their answer to the class.
5. Process follow-up: The instructor can (a) facilitate a follow-up discussion bringing out the group's expertise, and/or adding/sharing her or his expertise, or (b) use the material presented by the subgroups as a springboard into appropriate lecture or presentation material related to the course outline or agenda.

Curative Factor Activity (Option 1)

This activity (adapted from Sklare, Thomas, Williams, & Powers, 1996, p. 268) is based on Yalom's 12 curative factors listed earlier in this chapter. It has most relevance after the class or group has had a number of sessions to generate experiences for the class members to draw upon.

1. Divide the class in into triads. Each member of the triad is asked to share a personal group experience related to one of the therapeutic factors in groups. (A total of three different experiences will be shared by the end of the activity.)
2. Rotate triad group membership and repeat the sharing two more times.
3. The instructor then introduces the 12 (or more) curative factors in group counseling and facilitates a discussion of the class members' group experience relative to the factors.

Curative Factors Activity (Option 2)

Devise a set of Q Sort cards for each class member composed of the curative factors or advantageous characteristics described previously in this chapter (adapted from Hetzel, Barton, & Davenport, 1994, pp. 58–59)

Following a group process experience in class (e.g., personal sharing task), have members sort the cards based on their experience in the group. Process the group experience by: (1) identifying the top ranked curative factors and noting common and divergent member perceptions of the group process, and (2) noting present and absent therapeutic factors as indicated by the rankings. This activity can be used periodically or routinely as a process activity to accentuate learning of the curative factors in group process.

Group Dynamics

The following activities can be used to illustrate some of the various characteristics unique to the group process described in this chapter. Many similar activities can be found in the books listed in the references (Bates, Johnson, & Blake, 1982; Corey, Corey, Callanan, & Russell, 1992; DeLucia-Waack, Bridbord, & Kleiner, 2002; Hamachek, 1971; Johnson, 1972; Johnson & Johnson, 1997; Katz, 1973; Moustakas, 1972; Pfeiffer & Jones, 1969–85; Rosenthal, 1998; Schutz, 1967; Stevens, 1971). The examples included here were selected because they involve a physical dimension and demonstrate a psychological concept. Using techniques of this nature may be particularly effective with certain populations (e.g., adolescents or young adults) in certain settings (e.g., adventure learning or outward bound programs) and can help facilitate clearer understanding of group dynamics while at the same time adding diversity and variety to the group process experience. However, as with any activity involving physical contact, appropriate precautions must be followed and informed consent obtained before engaging group members in them.

Breaking Out

Place one member in the center of the group and have other members form a tight ring around him or her. The person in the center is instructed to try to get out of the group in any way possible without resorting to physical violence. The group is instructed to impede such an escape. The leader should keep close control over the action to prevent excesses that might cause physical harm, and members should be cautioned not to exert themselves if they have some physical problem that might be aggravated. This exercise should seek its own level of time and participation.

Follow-up discussion should center around the member's experience and the implications of the exercise relative to group process characteristics and the power of the group. Emotions elicited and strategies used to escape from or conform to group pressure in the exercise tend to reflect the actual feelings and reactions of members regarding group pressure toward conformity, identity, and loss of individual uniqueness. (This exercise may also be useful in group counseling when individual members are dealing with problems of dependency or lack of individual initiative.)

Breaking In

This exercise is the converse of the previous one. One member is placed outside the group, and the other group members form a tight circle that the outsider is instructed to try to get into. The same precautions relative to control of excesses and limiting participation in case of physical disabilities should be followed. This exercise has relevance for demonstrating the group's capacity for cohesiveness and members' needs for belongingness that the group can meet. It also demonstrates the power of the group in preventing members from joining. The appeal of group membership must be grappled with by the outsider and involves making decisions as to the amount of personal effort that will be exerted to get into the group. Time involved and participation again are dependent on the situation.

Discussion should relate to members' experiences and eventually move into the domain of relating the exercise to the power of the group and its dynamics. In group counseling, this exercise is sometimes used to help members who feel isolated or lack commitment to the group understand their feelings and behavior more clearly.

Behind-the-Back Technique

This technique developed by Corsini (1968) demonstrates the intense power of the group process when used in the manner described by its creator. Corsini developed the method in his work with prison inmates and used the negative feedback of the group to break down the personality attributes of individual members that were creating problems for them. A greatly modified version can be useful in group counseling or psychotherapy.

One member of the group is asked to sit with his or her back to the group. He or she is instructed to listen and at no point is allowed to respond or react until the feedback is completed. The rest of the group proceeds to discuss their perceptions and feelings about the person relating both negative and positive reactions. It is necessary to let this activity proceed for an extended period of time for its full impact to be realized.

On completion of the feedback, the member turns into the group and shares the feelings experienced during the feedback session. She or he should be encouraged to comment on the accuracy of the group's response from a personal point of view, and group discussion should attempt to clarify misunderstanding and mediate possible differences of perception. The feelings experienced by members usually reflect the helplessness people often feel in the face of group pressure and the fear that the group will respond negatively. Follow-up discussion should make members aware of using feedback and the group's power in a therapeutic manner. Efforts should be made to help the member receiving the feedback make constructive use of relevant material and discard the rest. In psychotherapy groups more intense focus may be placed on the feedback itself since personality traits are at stake.

3
Rationale for Group Counseling

Group work is a Bowl of P's, and doing group work is a matter of "minding your P's." It involves a leader who has a *Philosophy* that values groups, a *Personality* that thrives in groups and a *Perspective* that promotes groups; a *Psychological Rationale* the must account for the *Persons* who make up the group, the *Process* that occurs in the group and the *Purpose* for which the group is convened; a *Protocol* that includes *Planning, Performing*, and *Processing*; and, a *Practice Paradigm* that utilizes *Procedures* all of which are validated by *Process Observation*.

The Development of a Psychological Framework

Group work has relevance and meaning only if it is understood and applied in the psychological context of human growth and development. A psychological framework is needed to guide the process, evaluate its impact, and provide a rationale for its use. However, while such a framework is a necessity, Jourard (1968) pointed out that to simply imitate someone else's theory or rationale is not sufficient. Each helping person must develop his or her own theoretical viewpoint to be truly effective in helping others. The development of a personal approach is necessary for a counselor to make the best use of the resources available in providing leadership and therapeutic help to other people. Major resources include the counselor's philosophy, personality, knowledge, perspective, and training. These resources combined with each leadership and helping experience enable the counselor's theoretical approach to come to fruition.

The general impact of training and practice on the development of one's own approach to group work is illustrated in Figure 3.1. In training, the counselor is given an overview of the group process, which is implemented from a variety of

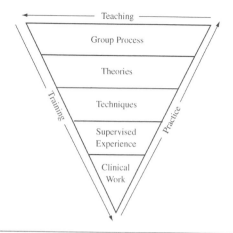

Figure 3.1 A model relating training and practice.

theoretical perspectives. Each of the theories utilizes certain procedures, methods and techniques that can be learned and applied in the group setting. Once a counselor has an understanding of the process, an initial commitment to a theoretical model that is congruent with her or his personality, and has acquired techniques relevant to that theory, then she or he is ready to apply that learning in a supervised setting.

The practice vector functions in the opposite direction of training, helping counselors develop their own rationales and approaches to group work. From their very first experience as group leaders, counselors begin to evaluate their knowledge and skills relative to the group process. They develop, adapt, revise, and delete methods and techniques to improve effectiveness. They weigh the theoretical concepts they have learned, affirming some and refuting others, reorganizing, refining, or rejuvenating still others, and discovering new ones that fit the reality of their experiences in group work. It is at this point that each counselor develops a personal conceptualization of the total group process. Thus individual personality, training, and experience have become intertwined in a dynamic relationship that will continue to develop throughout a professional career.

Keep this conception of the relationship between training and practice in mind while I present the psychological rationale for group work that will be used in this book. Remember that my perspective and subsequent framework is the result of the interacting forces of my training, group membership, leadership experience, and teaching. All of these factors inform my understanding of the group process, influence how I operate as a group leader, and impact how I teach that process to prospective group leaders.

Psychological Rationale for Group Work

The psychological rationale for group work entails the dynamic interaction of three generic psychological components (Trotzer, 1997d). The nature and substance of every group construed under the group work umbrella described in the last chapter results from the interaction of *persons, process,* and *purpose.* First of all, every group is composed of individuals, each of whom brings with him or her needs, abilities, expectations, and experiences. These persons provide the resources and raw materials out of which the group emerges. As individuals interact, process is conceived. Process refers to the relationship that eventuates between members over the course of the group's life. This relationship is critical to the impact and results of the group experience. As Gladding (Campbell, 1996) observed, "process truly drives content, . . . relationships between members . . . either (make) or (unmake) the productivity in groups" (p. 74).

The impetus for process that brings individuals (persons) together in groups is the reason for which the group is formed. Consequently, purpose is the final component that supplies the nature and character of the group. It contributes the overall identity of the group. For example, guidance/psychoeducation groups are formed to educate or inform, counseling groups to solve problems, therapy groups to change personality, and work groups to accomplish the task or mission for which it was convened.

In this chapter the person component will be presented in terms of Maslow's (1970) hierarchy of human needs. The process component will be addressed utilizing an adaptation of Luft and Ingham's (Luft, 1984) Johari Window, and the purpose component will incorporate a generic problem solving model for group counseling and a variety of purpose factors related to other types of groups especially task groups. Subsequently, the psychological rationale for group work presented in this book can be summarized by the following formula:

Individual Needs + Relationship Development + Group Purpose = Group Work
(Person Component) (Process Component) (Purpose Component)

In other words, individual members motivated by their respective needs interact in a group milieu to develop a relationship or system in which they work to address the task or purpose for which the group was formed.

The Person Component

The basic supposition of the person component of my rationale is that each person has certain human needs that are met primarily through social interaction with other human beings. The extent to which our needs are met is dependent on the type and quality of interpersonal relationships we have with others. The manner in which we meet our needs supplies the foundation of our life styles, and the relationships we develop influence the nature of our personality and form the bulwark of our identity. Our needs are the motivators of our behavior and are hierarchical in nature. Our environment and heredity provide us with opportunities we can utilize in meeting our needs (Jourard, 1968), but we basically depend on our interpersonal relationships to determine how. The ordering of our needs reflects the developmental process of the group within which the relationships formed provide the means by which the group addresses its purposes.

Basic Human Needs

Maslow (1943, 1954, 1962) developed the hierarchical conceptualization of human needs that is used as the basis for our discussion of the person component. Figure 3.2 presents an adapted and embellished version of Maslow's original hierarchy. Maslow contended that people have certain basic needs that motivate them to behave in a manner to satisfy those needs. Our needs are differentiated and

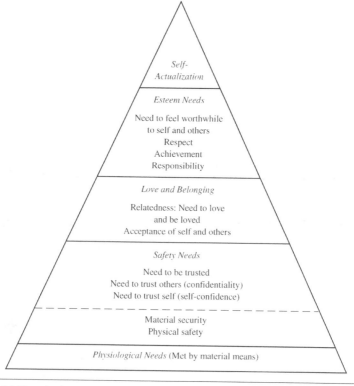

Figure 3.2 Hierarchy of Human Needs. (Data for diagram based on Hierarcy of Needs in "A Theory of Human motivation" in *Motivation and Personlity*, 2nd edition. Abraham H. Maslow [1970]. Use by permission.)

have prepotent qualities that influence which need is going to be called into play as predominant and which need will emerge upon satisfaction of a prior need. Maslow postulated five basic needs including (in order of priority): physical needs, safety, love and belonging, esteem, and self-actualization. He stressed, however, that the individual should be viewed as a total person and that any motivated behavior can satisfy several needs at the same time. His main thrust was that human beings are dominated by wants and not by satisfactions because once a need is satisfied or even partially satisfied, other needs emerge that must be dealt with. Carroll (1969) noted that this situation usually results in people being "partially unsatisfied in all (their) needs," which he called "a normal state of affairs to which a person learns to adjust" (p. 27). In addition, Laird and Laird (1967) in discussing the relationship among our different needs observed that under stress the higher order needs (called "wants" in their terminology) tend to peel off. This creates a situation where due to stress individuals are prompted to operate on a less sophisticated level until they can once again proceed up the hierarchy.

Besides the priority aspect of our needs, Maslow noted an important distinction between our lowest order physiological needs (food, clothing, and so on) and the progressively higher order needs of safety, love and belonging, esteem, and self-actualization. Physiological needs are meant to be gratified and not deprived so that the higher order needs and their goal directed behaviors can emerge. These higher order needs are social needs, and an individual's drive to satisfy them is much more critical in human motivation than is physical need gratification. This is particularly true in our society, where for all practical purposes most people have access to the means of satisfying their physiological needs.

The needs hierarchy and the physical-social need distinction have direct application to counseling. If our clients are experiencing deprivation in any of these areas, that area most likely will be the focus of or at least an impediment to the counseling process. An overall goal of group counseling is to help clients meet their lower order needs in a consistent manner, which will enable them to progress toward self-actualization. In addition, the social nature of the higher order needs suggests that the group work and group process are plausible means of helping members meet these needs. Let's turn our attention then to a specific discussion of each of these needs and consider their implications for group work.

Physiological Needs

All of us have experienced being too tired, too cold, or too thirsty to think about anything other than alleviating that sensation. Deprivation of our physical needs alters our perceptions drastically and effectively distorts our view of human nature and life (Maslow, 1943). Tolerance levels naturally vary and can be substantially altered in some cases, but ultimately failure to meet these needs is self-destructive. Our most basic drive, self-preservation, usually takes the form of making sure we have sufficient food, clothing, and shelter to sustain life. However, even in a society with an adequate level of material wealth, often cases of deprivation interfere with learning and the process of self-development. Students in a classroom who have not had sufficient rest the night before are difficult to motivate. People who have missed breakfast or lunch often find it difficult to concentrate on their jobs. Teachers who must participate in inservice meetings at the end of a teaching day may lack alertness due to fatigue. Group members who should be interacting may be distracted by such physical discomforts as a chilly room or uncomfortable seating. Group leaders who have physical ailments such as a cold or headache may be inattentive or distracted. In any case physiological needs can create havoc with our concentration and make it difficult to utilize our abilities to their fullest potential.

Physiological need fulfillment is a prerequisite for everything, including functioning effectively in task groups or getting the most out of group counseling. The group process specifically—and human relationships generally—cannot directly reduce that need. An effective group process depends on having members at a point where they are ready to work on meeting their higher order needs. Physiological deprivation of members may pose insurmountable barriers to the group process. A group leader should be aware of this possibility, both in the obvious sense (members dozing or inattentive) and in the subtle sense (pride may prevent acknowledgement of hunger caused by poverty or parental neglect). This second case is sometimes manifested in hostile or antagonistic behavior on the part of the member who for fear of losing esteem in the group's eyes will not admit to the lack of physiological requirements. For example, a 12-year-old inner city youth from an economically deprived family consistently acted out during mid-morning group sessions at a child guidance center. When the group leader, in consultation with a social worker, discovered that the boy seldom ate breakfast or even dinner, she instituted a snack at the beginning of each group session, which substantially reduced the boy's disruptive behavior. Leaders therefore must try to identify physiological needs when they account for unusual member actions and suggest activities and make arrangements that will alleviate those needs if members cannot do so on their own.

In contrast, however, group leaders also must be alert to group members using physiological need ploys to resist involvement in or to obstruct the group process. In my work with inmates in a prison setting one of their biggest complaints was that the physical environment was not conducive to group therapy and the therapeutic process. Another group of educators at a weekend inservice program conducted in a hotel setting raised such a fuss about the physical conditions that we spent the first day in search of an appropriate setting moving from auditorium to secluded lobby to a hotel room to a member's home who lived nearby and finally in frustration disbanded to a lounge. The second day we reconvened in the original location with the group rule of "no moves" and the group finally formed and started to work.

Safety Needs

The desire for safety is basic to every human being. Our greatest frustrations are most often associated with our fear of the unknown, in social as well as physical situations. When we lack knowledge or commitments on which we can depend, we lose touch with our sense of confidence. That in turn gives rise to anxiety and the urge to protect ourselves.

The need for safety is related to the essential nature of trust, which is the ability to and experience of depending on something or someone other than ourselves as the stabilizing force in our lives. Franz Kafka acknowledged the importance of this need when he wrote that "man cannot live without a lasting trust in something indestructible within him, but both his trust and its indestructible object can remain forever concealed from him." Maslow (1943) has indicated that the safety need is the driving force behind our preference for routine, our withdrawal from the unfamiliar, and our mobilization of resources in times of emergency. Adler (Carroll, 1969) was even more emphatic, calling security the basic drive of human beings and adding that "it is the feeling of inferiority, inadequacy, insecurity, which determines the goal of an individual's existence" (p. 25). The emphasis on this need for security places it near the very core of human existence and demands our active attention to satisfy it.

In Figure 3.2 are indications that safety needs are manifested in five specific ways. The desire for physical safety is foremost, although individuals often risk endangering their bodies to achieve certain valued objectives. Individuals may choose to endanger their physical well being in exchange for thrills or a sense of accomplishment when they engage in certain activities such as rock climbing, stock car racing, or contact sports. Or, they may choose occupations that have high physical risk integrated into the performance of their job. Generally, however, people are cautious and concerned about protecting themselves from physical harm.

The guarantee of physical safety to members while in groups is a standard requirement. Ethical principles of group practice dictate that groups be conducted in a manner such that clients never feel physically endangered or intimidated; members should not be forced to risk physical harm doing group activities (Corey, Corey, & Callahan, 1993). The group has no control over outside dangers other than to help members develop precautionary guidelines if they are concerned about situations in which they may experience physical harm. However, the group leader has an ethical responsibility and a legal obligation (duty to warn) to invoke interventive action if a clear and present danger situation in a group member's life surfaces in the course of group interaction. This duty to warn mandate applies to both ingroup and out of group situations the leader becomes aware of.

The need for material security is also a concern of most people, especially where value systems and life styles are based on material acquisition and monetary self-sufficiency. The terminology of economics and the banking industry clearly reflect this need, with words such as "trust fund," "securities," and "low risk investments." This need becomes increasingly important as one grows older. Retirement benefits are always a key concern in labor negotiations and in occupational choices. Some people spend their entire work lives preparing for a retirement in which they will be financially solvent.

The material aspect of the safety need can be met by the process of attaining financial security in the form of secure employment, well paying jobs, insurance policies, retirement programs, bank accounts, debt free possessions, investments, and the like. But group work or group counseling has little direct relationship to meeting this need. The group can help individuals develop and understand their values with respect to material acquisitions. It can also help members develop self-knowledge relative to educational and vocational planning, that contribute to meeting the need for material security. Some groups for the elderly are formed for the specific purpose of helping members deal with problems of physical and material security that often face them in their older years. Counseling groups for workers who are within a few years of retirement are becoming more prevalent in business and industry. However, groups of this nature often move from a materialistic emphasis to a consideration of the higher order needs, which must be dealt with to develop a personally meaningful existence in retirement and old age.

The other three aspects of safety needs are person oriented and relational in nature and are set apart from physical and material security by a broken line in Figure 3.2. We all have the need to trust ourselves, to trust others, and to be trusted by others. The need to trust ourselves, to have self-confidence, is perhaps the most elusive personal characteristic we attempt to establish. We strive to build a sense of personal security in an ever increasing number of situations as we mature. We tend to become involved when we feel sure of ourselves, and we tend to avoid or resist becoming involved in situations in which we lack confidence. Even as experience positively affects our self-confidence, we need to continually reaffirm it. Most people experience frustration with regard to self-confidence, feeling they never have enough. Although some people may be accused of being overly self-confident, in many cases their behavior is an overreaction to their lack of self-confidence. Even people who appear to have a healthy self-assurance report they experience doubts and anxieties about their ability to trust themselves. Only as we meet this need can we experience any satisfaction in our growth and accomplishments, and only on the basis of self-confidence can we build a predictable stability to pave the way for personal fulfillment in social situations.

For example, the need for self-confidence is typically associated with the problems of most members in a counseling group. Either lack of self-confidence or ostentatious self-assurance used to defend against one's fears is common. The group therefore must provide an atmosphere where threat to one's personal security is minimal and where members can develop the ability to trust themselves. This ability is particularly important at the point of implementing change. The group is only the testing ground, and it depends on the individual to determine whether change will materialize. Thus the amount of confidence individuals feel in themselves is directly related to the probability of successful change.

The needs to trust others and to be trusted by others are the foundation of our social relationships and are essential therapeutic elements in the group process. We can only meet these two needs through our personal contacts with others, and in most cases they have a reciprocal effect. The need to trust others is our desire to place ourselves or some aspect of ourselves in the confidence of another person. This need is the foundation dynamic of confidentiality in groups. May (1953) had the idea that each person has a natural thrust beyond himself or herself toward others, and this is partly manifested in the need to trust others. Johnson (1981) has indicated that human beings have a relationship imperative that motivates them to reach out in confidence to others. However, a subtle but critical relational counterpart to that thrust in each of us is needed. An ancient Chinese proverb declares, "A sure way to help someone is to let them help you." When we confide in (trust) another person we invoke the self-confidence in that person and invite reciprocity. This precipitates bonding in the relationship while enhancing the security of the individual. Our need to trust propels us to overcome our aloneness and sets the stage for deeper emotional attachment to others. Our need to trust generates opportunities to rely on other people as resources in our growth and development and in problem solving. That need to trust is a motivating force in the group counseling process that enables self-disclosure to occur and gives psychological credence to sharing.

The need to be trusted by others promotes the group process of identity formation and opens the door for constructive feedback in our relationships. Our need to be trustworthy is evident in our desire for relationships that result in increased self-respect and self-confidence. As others share themselves with us, we perceive ourselves as important and capable of caring and respect. The need to be trusted enables our social interaction to become a dynamic growth process, giving us both the capacity to depend on others and to be depended on by others. In the group process the need to be trusted encourages members to supply therapeutic help to their fellow members. It motivates them to demonstrate their trustworthiness by their care, concern, and resourcefulness, which is reflected in their feedback. This trustworthiness is a vital personality trait that forms the basis for positive interpersonal relationships. It acts as a lubricant reducing the social friction created by group dynamics and pressures and ameliorates the defensive posture of individuals that produces resistance to both the group process and individual change.

Love and Belonging

Some years ago I came across a quotation by John E. Largients, which expresses emphatically the nature of the need for love and belonging. He wrote, "Not many men may be willing to die for love these days. But you can't escape the fact that millions are dying daily for lack of it." Maslow (1943) pointed out that we all have a desire for accepting and affectionate relations with people and for a place in a group. The absence of these relationships with family, friends, or people in general results in loneliness and social isolation. Glasser (1965) affirmed that the need for relatedness or the need to love and be loved is basic to human beings. Dinkmeyer and Muro (1971) stated that people have affection needs that are expressed in their desire to belong, help, and be helped. Common agreement is that every human being experiences an essential necessity for love and that our need for love is not one-sided. To give love to others is equally important as to receive it from others. Stendhal summarized this quality of love when he said that "love is a well from which we can drink only as much as we put in."

Many levels of this need for love and belonging exist, ranging from simple acceptance to the complex intimacy of a love relationship with an intimate partner or in a marriage or family. Our need for love is initially exhibited in social situations by our desire for acceptance by individuals or groups that are attractive to us. When we experience acceptance by others, we experience fulfillment and a sense of belonging. This leads to an association with the person or group who accepted us, thus contributing to our identity. This experience of acceptance by others is a reflection of their own acceptance of themselves. We not only have a need to be accepted by others, but we also have a need to accept ourselves. The relationship between acceptance of self and the ability to accept others is pointed out in the Judeo-Christian commandment "love your neighbor as yourself." If we have little love for ourselves, then only little love can be shown to those around us. Wrenn (1971) related this idea to counselors when he wrote that the amount of caring counselors can show their clients can be measured by the amount of caring they show for themselves.

For example, in counseling groups members usually are struggling with this need for acceptance in some way. They may be experiencing problems in their social relationships that make them feel isolated from and unaccepted by others. They may have negative feelings about their own selves, not liking who they are and therefore being unable to accept themselves. Their behavior may be such that they experience rejection from others, including their families. The group process therefore must take the need for love and belonging into account. An atmosphere must be created in the group where the members feel accepted and free to share their true selves with others, thus resulting in greater self-acceptance. If the need for acceptance is not met in the group, members will use their energies to defend themselves and resist the process. Whereas trust is the foundation of the

Trust is the foundation.
Acceptance is the framework.
Rationale for Group Counseling • **69**

group process, acceptance is the framework around which it is built. If members can feel accepted even though they have unresolved problems and difficulties, facing up to the task of change is less threatening.

Esteem

The need for esteem is unique because it possesses a quality that can drive people to make extreme sacrifices in its pursuit. We can find many examples of people who have severely taxed their minds and bodies, sacrificed values, and renounced friends and family to attain the fame, fortune, or status they feel will give them esteem. However, in such efforts the meaning of esteem is frequently lost or confused. Maslow's (1943) idea of esteem centers around seeking recognition from others and from oneself as a worthwhile person. This need is satisfied when one experiences feelings of worth, strength, usefulness, and confidence. Unfortunately, the need for esteem has too often been associated with financial success, social position, role attainment, material acquisition, and accomplishments. This has caused confusion leading to the simplistic notion that achievement equals esteem, which is inaccurate.

The need for esteem is very complex and involves an integration of the elements of worth, respect, achievement, and responsibility. Glasser (1965) stated that the second basic human need is the need for respect or the need to feel worthwhile to self and others. In his description we have the essence of esteem. It is a human feeling that can only be transmitted on an interpersonal basis. The meaning of esteem comes from within oneself and from others. It does not come from achievements, position, or money, although these things can be used to command the attention that relates to esteem. Without the psychological reaction of self-respect or self-esteem generated by one's accomplishments, the accomplishment is personally meaningless. Without the respect communicated by other people, position or wealth fails to give us feelings of worth. In other words, the esteem need can only be met through a reciprocal interaction with other human beings who value us in conjunction with our own inner perception of our self as worthwhile.

Another characteristic of the esteem need that is overlooked at times is its relationship to responsibility. We can only experience feelings of worth to ourselves and others if we act in a responsible manner. The relationship between responsibility, achievement, and respect is cyclical. To achieve something we must take responsibility. Once we have taken responsibility and realized an accomplishment, respect is generated both from ourselves and from others. To maintain this respect, we must continue to be responsible, and so on. The amount of responsibility we assume is directly related to what we accomplish and the amount of respect we experience. The reverse of this relationship is equally valid.

Let's apply this idea to a counseling group. Low self-esteem and feelings of worthlessness are common in counseling group members. As individuals experience problems they cannot resolve themselves, the natural tendency is to think less of themselves and to feel that others think less of them. This downward spiral must be broken by the group process. Within the group the client should be able to realize feelings of worth. The climate should be characterized by a positive attitude that takes into account the strengths of individual members as well as their weaknesses. The group can meet client needs for esteem initially by focusing on individual assets. By allowing members to experience responsibility for themselves and by encouraging them to help one another, the group can facilitate the process of solving individual member problems while at the same time meeting the need for respect.

Self-Actualization

We must distinguish between self-actualization and the need for self-actualization. The former is a state of being, and the latter is a motivating force that influences our actions. Although the tendency is to relate self-actualization to a utopian life style devoid of stress and full of peace, fulfillment, and satisfaction, a more realistic perspective is to view it as a state in which all of one's energy can be mobilized to achieve one's potential. This definition has potent import, because one goal of the group process is to help individuals utilize all their resources in the context of the group and its purpose.

Many descriptions of a self-actualized person can be given, all of which reveal the positive quality of the state. Gilmer (1970) described self-actualized people as fully functioning; they think well of themselves and others and view relationships with others as important investments and as opportunities for developing their own selves. The self-actualized person according to Johnson (1972) is "time competent, that is (one) having the ability to tie the past and the future to the present in a meaningful continuity while fully living in the present" (p. 2). Hesse (1971) captures this conception of self-actualization in his discourse on the river. The following excerpts are examples.

Today he saw one of the river's secrets, one that gripped his soul. He saw that the water continually flowed and flowed and yet it was always there; it was always the same and yet every moment it was new. (p. 102)

The river is everywhere at the same time, at the source and at the mouth, at the waterfall, at the ferry. In the ocean and in the mountains, everywhere and . . . The present only exists for it, not the shadow of the past, nor the shadow of the future. (p. 107)

Finally, Carroll (1969) summarized the characteristics of self-actualized, persons in practical and specific terms. They are spontaneous and feel free to be themselves because they have confidence in and acceptance of themselves. They are self-sufficient but have feelings for mankind. They have a strong desire to help others, have a good social conscience, are creative, natural, and flexible. They are problem-centered rather than self-centered and are able to tolerate ambiguity. The have the particular capacity to be "other oriented" in their social relationships (Beebe, Beebe, & Redmond, 2005).

Although describing a self-actualized person is relatively easy, being one is much more difficult. The experience of being self-actualized is difficult to identify because when one is in that state it is not necessary to think about being self-actualized. In fact, one of the cues that a person is no longer self-actualized or has not yet become so is when he or she is concerned about being self-actualized. Self-actualization is therefore a transient state for most people that is moved into and out of with the flow of life experiences and relationships with others. One is aware of it as a goal to be strived for or an identifiable condition that has passed. The more critical consideration then is the drive to become self-actualized, which has relevance to group dynamics and process.

Maslow (1954) ascribed the need for self-actualization to a human being's "desire for self-fulfillment; namely to the tendency for him (her) to become actualized in what he (she) is potentially" (pp. 91–92). Combs and Snygg (1959) called self-actualization humanity's basic need and describe it as "that great, driving, striving force in each of us by which we are continually seeking to make ourselves more adequate to cope with life" (p. 46). The desire to realize our potential is the motivating force that drives all of us to attempt to remove obstacles from our lives and is the therapeutic generator of efforts made by group counseling members to resolve their problems. Even though we can never completely fulfill our potential, the striving to do so is the self-actualization process. The concept of self-actualization is not a static state that, once attained, can be maintained indefinitely. Rather it embodies a continual growth process, which is characterized by momentary peak experiences and plateaus of satisfactory fulfillment but which pushes us toward continual self-development and growth throughout our lives.

Bach (1970) presented this perspective of the continuous self-actualizing process in his book *Jonathan Livingston Seagull: A Story*. The excerpt that follows points out the unceasing nature of the drive toward fulfillment of one's potential (Jonathan Livingston Seagull is speaking to his protégé Fletcher Seagull as he is about to send him out into the world on his own):

> You don't need me any longer. You need to keep finding yourself, a little more each day, that real unlimited Fletcher Seagull. He's your instructor. You need to understand him and to practice him. (p. 92)

As applied to a counseling group, the need for self-actualization has several dimensions. As group members' needs for safety, love, and esteem are met, they have access to those resources of energy that had previously been used to meet those needs. The need to actualize oneself emerges as the important motivator in clients' lives through which they not only gain a greater awareness of their potential but also find ways of using it to improve their lives. *Growth groups* are formed for the express purpose of helping members expand their awareness and utilize their potential more fully. These groups use encounter or T-group methods and are designed to help adequately functioning people become even more effective. In counseling groups, however, as lower order needs are met in the group, clients can focus attention more intensively on their problems and a work oriented atmosphere develops. Group members can attack their difficulties in a pragmatic manner without the emotional overtones usually associated with confronting personal problems. In accord with the idea that self-actualized people are not devoid of problems, the group members not only learn how to solve specific problems but learn general problem-solving skills that will be useful to them in the future.

Needs and Relationships: Formation of the Self/Viewing Human Beings in a Social Context

The philosophical pursuit of an explanation to the nature of our humanity always leads to an answer that construes human beings in some social context. Whether given extensive or minimal credit, the interpersonal environment must always be accounted for. William James (1890) observation that "no more fiendish punishment could be devised, were such a thing physically possible, than that one should be turned loose in society and remain absolutely unnoticed by all the members thereof" (p. 293) underscores the crucial relevance of our interpersonal network—without it we simply would not be. Johnson (1981) pointed out that human beings "desire and seek out relationships with others" and "have personal needs that can be satisfied only through interacting with other humans" (p. 1).

Interpersonal relationships are extremely important in meeting our basic human needs. Relationships with others are required to adequately satisfy our needs for safety, love and belonging, and esteem. Having positive relationships with others is a key quality of a self-actualized person. Because of this basic dependence on human relationships, people are primarily social in nature. Interpersonal contacts not only meet our needs but also develop the qualities that make us uniquely human. As I have noted elsewhere:

> In the development of our personhood, individual needs prompt interaction with and response from people in our environment. As a consequence of that interchange over time, we develop our individuality and our sociability. Subsequently, any (constructive and) interventive group process must reflect dynamics of that primary interaction for (a) therapeutic effect to be realized. (Trotzer, 2001, p 503)

Therefore we need to look intensely at interpersonal relationships to determine their impact on the human growth process and their relevance to group work.

The Process Component

Schmuck and Schmuck (1971) stated that "human beings develop in a sequential and systematic manner, not because of the gradual unfolding of instinctual tendencies, but because they experience a regular sequence of interpersonal interactions in their lives" (pp. 11–12). Gazda (1971b) added that "it is primarily through people that we grow into what we are today, and it is primarily through our relationships that we grow into what we will be tomorrow" (p. 1). Vygotsky (1978) noted that the human mind is inherently social, and that the path from object to child in the learning and enculturation process always proceeds through another person. In fact, sociocultural psychologists assert that no knowledge is acquired without the involvement of interpersonal process (Miller, 2002). The importance of the group process stems from the fact that we are social beings who develop through adequate and meaningful exposure to social situations and relationships. Clearly, we can neither meet our needs nor develop our humanness in isolation. We must have contact with others, and these contacts must qualify as relationships for their influence to be realized.

Our relationships have a socializing effect on our lives, not only shaping our behavior to conform to the standards of society, but also having a differentiating impact that enables each person to develop a unique personality, self-concept, and identity. Johnson (1981) stated that "our identity is built out of our relationships with other people. As we interact with others we note their responses to us, and we learn to view ourselves as they view us" (p. 2). In fact, he went so far as to state that our "psychological health depends almost entirely on our relationships with other people. The ability to build and maintain cooperative, interdependent relationships with other people is often cited as a primary manifestation of psychological health" (p. 3).

Combs and Snygg (1959) stipulated that our self is basically a social product that arises out of our experience with other human beings. Self-image and the self-system acquired through social contact are built on experiences of approval or disapproval and are called *reflected appraisals* by Sullivan (1953a). In other words, the essence of a person's identity depends on social interactions, that help the person differentiate himself or herself from the environment and others, and to be a person in his or her own right (Allport, 1960).

Our interpersonal relationships form the learning environment in which we acquire self-knowledge. "We learn about ourselves not only by experiencing our own actions, but also by experiencing the action of others, who serve as both mirrors and models for imitation" (Carroll, 1969, p. 270). Sullivan (1953b) contended that personality is almost entirely the product of interaction with other significant human beings. Who we are is forged in the cauldron of our human relationships. Carl Rogers' (1951) self-theory acknowledges the impact of interpersonal relationships. One of his 19 propositions states: "As a result of interaction with the environment and *particularly, as a result of interactions with others,* one's picture of oneself is formed" (italics added) (p. 483). The importance of this self-knowledge was underscored by Kubie (1958) as the key to effective maturation and development: "Without self-knowledge in depth ... we can have no adults, but only aging children who are armed with words and paint and clay and atomic weapons, none of which they understand" (p. 133).

The group is one of the primary vehicles that provides us with self-knowledge. Family, peer group, school group, occupational group, religious affiliation or church fellowship, neighborhood, community, and social set supply us with the interactions and experiences whereby we learn about ourselves. Mahler (1969) effectively tied this influence of groups to the group counseling process when he stated:

> A major goal of group counseling is to develop a relationship which will enable the counselor to meet the important developmental needs of (clients) and to help them with the identity-seeking process. Group counseling provides an opportunity for (clients) to examine in a friendly and permissive atmosphere their feelings and attitudes and the ideas they have about themselves and the world. (p. 141)

Group work such as group counseling has process merit for another reason. Although our relationships are the key to meeting our needs and developing our personality, they also are the core of most of the problems we experience. Dinkmeyer and Muro (1971) said that "all human problems are primarily social" (p. 9). Gazda (1971b) noted that "Many of our real problems in living are interpersonal in nature. Therefore it seems reasonable to help (clients) develop skills necessary for establishing and maintaining effective interpersonal relationships ... We must help (clients) become socially competent" (pp. 6–7). Mahler (1969) added that "the major concerns people bring to group counseling focus around the basic socialization process" (p. 11). Therefore the social milieu of the counseling group is conducive to helping members deal effectively with their concerns because it stresses effective relationship development as a means of learning about oneself and finding socially relevant solutions to personal problems. The nature of interpersonal relationships and interpersonal communication are thus vital to the essence of group work (Beebe, Beebe, & Redmond, 2005; Stewart, 2002).

The Johari Window

Since relationships are the key to meeting many basic needs and are also the means by which we develop personality, identity and self-concept, the nature

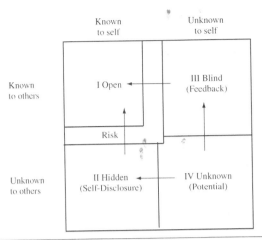

Figure 3.3 Johari window. From *Group Processes: An Introduction to Group Dynamics*, Joseph Luft. Reprinted by permission.

of our relationships takes on strategic value in our growth and development. To understand how relationships develop and how positive ones differ from negative ones is imperative. This understanding is necessary from a psychological standpoint and a group process frame of reference. In this regard Luft and Ingham (Luft, 1984) designed a relationship development model called the Johari Window to explain the process of relationship development. Figure 3.3 presents an adapted form of their basic model.

Relationships develop as a result of interaction between people in which information is exchanged. The extent to which a relationship develops depends on the intensity of the interaction involved and the nature and depth of the information shared.

In any relationship, two person components—self and others—and two information components—known and unknown—exist. Juxtaposed to one another, a grid of four quadrants is created that can be used to graphically illustrate the nature of all relationships from initial contacts or acquaintances to our most deeply intimate associations. By modifying the size of the various quadrants, we can graphically illustrate the nature of all relationships from superficial (small open area) to deeply intimate (large open area). No intrinsic value orientation is implied in the model to infer that all our relationships should be characterized by a certain degree of openness. Rather, the model is a descriptive tool for studying relationships, and it provides a basis for assessing their nature and development. Typically, our relationships run the full gamut on the openness continuum from small open area to extensive open area. However, no human relationship can be characterized as being completely open. Construing any relationship as totally open would extinguish individuality by default and eliminate the growth dynamic in relationships.

Quadrant I is called the *open* area and represents all information that is mutually accessible to all participants in the relationship. This information may range from the mere exchange of names with a first time acquaintance to a deep sharing of our innermost thoughts and feelings with an intimate partner. As relationships develop and grow, the open area expands. Note that we have relationships of all degrees of openness, and that the open quadrant increases in size as a result of interactions where information drawn from the other quadrants of the grid is exchanged in the relationship.

Quadrant II is called the *hidden* area and represents information known to the self but not shared with others. This quadrant encompasses all our self-knowledge accrued through personal experience and learning. This area is the domain which houses the real you. Only when you want others to know this information does it pass into the open quadrant through a process known as self-disclosure. The important characteristic of this area is that you control the nature and amount of information that is disclosed. You usually make the decision as to when to share and what to disclose based on the level of trust and acceptance sensed in the relationship. Any time you choose to self-disclose you take a risk because now others have access to the information and as such you lose control of it. John Powell (1969) in his book *Why Am I Afraid to Tell You Who I Am?*, discussed many of the barriers that hinder us in telling others about ourselves. However, the more we do disclose, the greater the likelihood that others will know us as we really are.

Quadrant III is called the *blind* area. This area contains information, i.e., knowledge and perceptions, others know about us but have not shared with us. Each of us develops impressions of those to whom we relate. However, until we tell them what our perceptions are, that information remains part of the blind area in the relationship. The only way to remove this barrier in a relationship is through the communication mechanism of giving feedback. However, feedback involves risk just as self-disclosure does. Therefore, we usually hold back giving feedback until (1) we are sure that the relationship will not be jeopardized, (2) we feel the relationship will improve because of it, or (3) the need to express it exceeds the concern for its impact on the relationship.

Quadrant IV is called the *unknown* area and represents the potential for growth that is a part of all relationships. Information from this quadrant materializes as a relationship progresses through its various stages of development (Beebe et al., 2005). For example, we all have the capacity to love. However, until we become involved in a relationship where we experience loving and being loved, that information is an unknown entity. Similarly, as we relate to others over time, aspects of ourselves emerge (a process referred to as co-construction) that neither we nor our partners knew existed. Information seldom moves directly from the unknown to the open; it usually follows a route through either the hidden or blind quadrants into the open area.

The factor governing the amount of self-disclosure and feedback that occurs in relationships is *risk.* As human beings, we are endowed with self-protective defense mechanisms that intercede whenever we sense we are vulnerable to reprisal or rejection. Consequently, we do not unleash overly personal, positive, or negative information unless we are somewhat assured that we will not be punished or hurt or that the relationship will be able to stand it.

Very little risk occurs in disclosing something about yourself that is already obvious or in giving feedback that a person is familiar with already. However, as the material shared becomes more personal in nature, the element of risk increases. Risk involves taking the chance that others will reject us or that we will experience some form of reprisal as a result of what we share. For this reason we tend to guard against letting others know us or sharing our perceptions of others until we are reasonably sure that such action will be received in a nonthreatening manner or will accomplish a desired result. However, a certain degree of risk taking must occur for any relationship to grow. Benjamin Franklin's old adage, "nothing ventured, nothing gained," is applicable to the arena of relationships. Generally speaking, when we risk self-disclosure or feedback and experience positive results, we become more willing to do so again. Thus a positive growth cycle is initiated in the relationship (relational escalation). On the other hand, if we experience negative consequences, we are less likely to risk again which inevitably results in relational stagnation, deterioration, or termination (relational de-escalation).

In relationships generally and in group work particularly, risk is reduced when trust, acceptance, respect, communication, and understanding characterize our interpersonal contacts. Self-disclosure and feedback can then operate freely, generating more opportunities for productivity, personal learning and growth. In addition, a reciprocal effect occurs: as conditions suitable for personal sharing improve the quantity and quality of self-disclosure and feedback increase, and as more self-disclosing and feedback occur, the conditions for doing so improve. In conducting groups then, the leader must help develop a climate where members can take risks, thereby enabling the mechanisms of self-disclosure and feedback to function in a constructive manner.

Putting it All Together

Figure 3.4 illustrates the development of personality, identity, and self-concept based on the interaction between basic human needs and relationships with others. Personality is the behavioral dimension of our self that develops over time and is manifested in the manner in which we relate to the world around us. It includes our traits, habits, and basic tendencies that characterize us over time and across circumstances. Identity is the cognitive component of our self and encompasses all information that we perceive to pertain directly and indi-

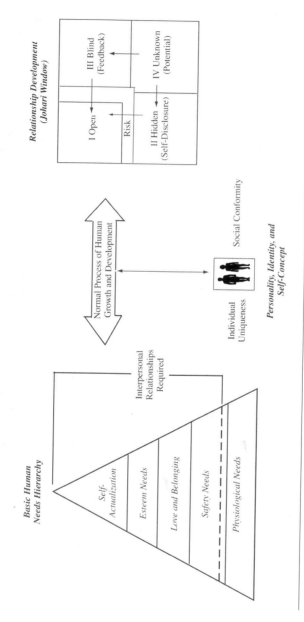

Figure 3.4 Needs, relationships, and personal development.

rectly to answering the question "Who am I?" for ourselves. Self-concept is the affective element of the self that contains our subjective evaluative conclusions of how we feel about our self at any point in time. Our self-esteem may be positive or negative, high or low depending on circumstances and situations. But the composite of all evaluations in both a contemporary and longitudinal sense forms our self-concept.

Glasser (1965) pointed out that our needs can only be met through involvement with other human beings. Relationships with others help us develop our individual uniqueness and adapt to societal standards. White (1966) indicated that one primary growth trend is that of developing better interpersonal relationships to improve our lives. In this case our needs motivate us to form relationships that will help us achieve our potential and in that manner improve our lives. The overall result of this interactive process is the personhood of each human being. It must be noted that this illustration is an oversimplification of a very complex process, the dynamics of which affect the development of each person throughout life.

The Purpose Component

The representation in Figure 3.5 depicts the overall relationship between the psychological framework discussed in this chapter and the group counseling process. The normal process of growth and development entails the interaction between our needs and our relationships and results in the nature of our personal identity. However, within that process obstacles in the form of problems occur that impede our growth. These problems generally fall into two generic categories: problems in meeting our individual needs and problems in social relationships. These categories are certainly not mutually exclusive but each has one basic distinguishing characteristic. Needs problems tend to be *intrapersonal* in nature, while social problems are *interpersonal.* The problems have a symbiotic relationship to each other in the sense that problem resolution is contingent on the interaction of needs with relationships.

In some ways these two problem categories are reciprocal (i.e., unmet individual needs will contribute to relationship problems, and relationship problems present obstacles to getting personal needs met). In most instances, an interpersonal component to all human problems must be addressed when presented in counseling (Trotzer, 1985). Yalom (1995) confirmed this view noting that in therapy goals often shift from relief of suffering (intrapersonal) to goals that have relational implications (interpersonal). Patients who come into therapy desiring release from anxiety or depression move to wanting to improve communications, develop relationships, learn to trust others, love, or be honest in their relating. This interpersonal factor in and of itself commends group counseling/therapy as a more comprehensive therapeutic modality. Consequently, the group counseling

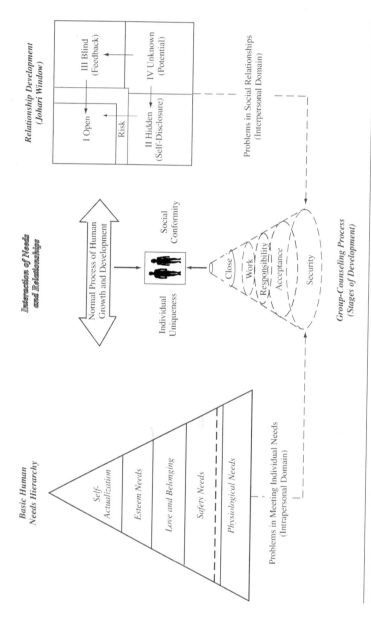

Figure 3.5 The psychological rationale and the group counseling process.

process must account for the needs of the individuals and the social relationships required to meet those needs. This creates a climate conducive to helping clients resolve problems in their lives and thus validates the purpose for forming groups as a helping modality. In the broader group work perspective similar dynamics are involved. The group process in task groups for example must account for individual needs in the context of the relational milieu that develops in order for the individual member and the group to contribute most effectively to productivity and accomplishment of the group's purpose.

The problem-solving process itself contributes merit to the purpose dynamic in group counseling. When faced with issues or problems one cannot resolve on her or his own, turning to others for assistance is a common option. For that option to be effective a set of typical steps is usually involved. These basic elements of problem-solving are:

1. Identifying a safe context (relationship) in which to talk about, share and address the problem.
2. Accepting the problem as part of one's self, i.e., perceiving the problem as ego syntonic rather than ego dystonic.
3. Owning responsibility for the problem, i.e., acknowledging an internal locus of control rather than an external locus of control.
4. Devising a means to resolve the problem that involves the following:
   a. Identifying alternative ways of viewing the problem and/or alternative solutions to resolving it, i.e., using the brainstorming capacity of divergent thinking to assess the problem and identify possible means of resolving it.
   b. Evaluating alternatives to establish the most relevant perspective of the problem and most plausible solution, i.e., using the mental capacity of convergent thinking to specify a focus and direction.
   c. Making a decision, i.e., choosing an alternative to apply to the problem.
   d. Planning a course of action.
   e. Practicing the alternative if possible (as in a group setting).
   f. Implementing the plan.
   g. Evaluating whether the problem is solved.

Group counseling provides a context where these steps can be experienced and implemented.

Relating the Rationale to the Group Counseling Process

The developmental sequence of the group counseling process falls into a series of stages that reflect the *person* component (basic human needs), the *process* component (relationship development generating qualities amenable to self-disclosure and feedback), and the *purpose* component (e.g., resolving intrapersonal and interpersonal problems). As indicated in Figure 3.5, the sequence includes the following stages in order of occurrence: *Security, Acceptance, Responsibility, Work,* and *Closing.* The characteristics and dynamics of each of these stages and their corresponding developmental tasks will be discussed in the following chapters. Application to the various forms of group work including task groups will be integrated into that discussion.

Learning Activities

The learning activities selected for this chapter relate to the basic needs hierarchy and relationship development pertaining to self-disclosure and feedback. In most cases the exercises are very flexible in terms of purpose; therefore, follow-up discussion may result in widely varied reactions. Each exercise has relevance to the group process from both a teaching and a practicing perspective.

Needs and Groups: A Self-Assessment Exercise

The purpose of this exercise is to demonstrate the relationship between our needs and relationships with respect to identity development. It is useful as an assessment tool for the purpose of setting interpersonal and personal growth goals in groups. Each person completes the exercise individually as a prerequisite to group interaction.

Instructions:

1. Make an exhaustive list of all the groups of which you are a member.
2. Identify those groups which meet the needs listed below and place them in the appropriate column.

SECURITY	LOVE AND BELONGING	ESTEEM

Using only your group memberships as material write a one-paragraph description of your identity.

Identity Self-Assessment

1. List those groups that you value highly and which contribute positively to your identity.
2. List those groups you think contribute negatively to your identity.
3. List groups with whom you would like to disassociate yourself.
4. List groups with whom you would like to join or increase your participation.
5. Based on your entries in b, c, and d, set goals for yourself to work toward.

Coming to Life Activities

Physiological needs, particularly those associated with fatigue, boredom, and tension can be effectively dealt with through the use of physical activities that stimulate physical and mental alertness and relieve tension and anxiety. The following are examples of activities that can be done individually, in dyads, or in groups. An excellent sequence to follow in a group situation is to select one activity from each category and build from individuals to dyads to groups. These activities are most useful as icebreakers at the start of group sessions or energizers when group members indicate a need for a physical break from the psychological stress of group interaction (Kassera & Kassera, 1979).

Individual Activities

Deep Breathing Disperse group members around the room. Have each group member take three deep breaths, increasing the volume of air intake with each successive breath. Have members follow your example so that everyone is doing the same thing. Then have members inhale and hold their breath for 15 seconds. At the end of 15 seconds, have them exhale forcefully making their own personal sound in unison with the group. Take several easy breaths to relax. Have them repeat the breath holding sequence, this time for 20 seconds. Once again breathe easily to relax. Repeat a third time for 25 seconds. (Note: You may vary the amount of time your clients spend holding their breath up to as much as 45–60 seconds.) At the end of this exercise members should experience rapid heartbeats. Relax with easy breathing and move on to the next activity

Isometrics Isometrics utilize mental imagery as the means of simulating physical exertion thereby stimulating physical alertness. Have group members stand with hands extended slightly above their heads. Tell them to imagine that a 2-ton elevator is descending on them and at your signal they must hold the elevator up to prevent being crushed. Signal the members to start, allowing them to exert themselves for 15 seconds. Repeat this process three times, allowing time for members to relax and breathe easily between each effort. Encourage members to put their whole bodies into the effort. Repeat this same sequence using the concept of two walls closing in a la a *Star Wars* trash compactor. The members must hold the walls off by extending their hands out from their sides. On the third trial of each isometric sequence have group members succeed, i.e., tell them to push the elevator up or the walls out as far as they can.

Dyad Activities

Mirroring Pair group members off and have them face each other. Appoint one as the actor and one as the mirror. The objective is for the mirror to imitate all motions and actions of the actor. Have the actor begin slowly and gradually, quicken the pace to a point where it is impossible for the mirror to follow, and then gradually slow down again. Reverse roles and repeat the exercise. You also may want to have your clients switch partners several times or form an inner and outer circle of partners and then rotate one of the circles.

Hand Dancing Have partners face each other and place their hands, palms extended, approximately 1 inch from each other. Have one partner begin to move his or her hands slowly. The other partner is to follow the actions of the first pair of hands maintaining the 1-inch distance and not touching. Tell your clients to speed up the process to the point where following is impossible and then slow down. Reverse roles, and repeat the same process.

An alternative form of hand dancing that can be used to help group members focus on the nature of relationships and communication in a three-step sequence that uses three different versions of hand dancing. First, have members do the hand dancing activity as previously described but with hands about 6 inches apart. Second, have members clasp hands (i.e., lock fingers). Use the same leader-follower instructions, but at some point add an instruction for the follower to resist following. Third, have partners touch hands (palms and fingers). Repeat leader-follower and resister instructions. Upon completion of the sequence, process the activity in light of members' experiences and relate these experiences to the nature and effectiveness of communication in relationships.

Back Breakers Have partners stand back to back locking their arms at the elbow. Instruct them to cooperate in turning side to side and stretching each other's arm and shoulder muscles. Then have one partner bend over slowly pulling the other on to his or her back, holding the person there for a short time (*Note*: the emphasis is on stretching not lifting). Have partners reverse the process and repeat the exercise three or four times. This exercise should be done slowly and carefully so the participants can feel the stretching; they should not overdo either the lifting or the strain of being stretched.

An added task can be to have partners work together to sit down on the floor and get back to their feet while retaining their back to back, arms locked position.

Trust Walk The concept of trust in our lives is sometimes easier to grasp if we can experience it physically. The trust walk is one example of a concrete experience that can be used to understand the abstract concept of trust. Pair group members off and designate one or the other of the partners as blind. You may wish to use blindfolds to prevent peeking but simply having the partner close his or her eyes is sufficient. In fact, not using artificial means of blinding puts added pressure on the blind partner. The seeing partners are then directed to take their blind partners on a walk, giving them as many experiences as possible but always maintaining responsibility for their safety. The entire exercise should be conducted without words. Partners must work out their own strategies for nonverbal communication. After a designated period of time (10 minutes or more), reverse the roles and repeat the exercise. Follow-up discussion should relate the members' experiences to trusting oneself, trusting others, and being trustworthy. The discussion can easily be directed to a consideration of the security factor in group dynamics.

Note: It is often appropriate to demonstrate several versions of leading and following as part of the introduction to the activity. This tends to alleviate some of the anxiety associated with touch and introduces modeling as a legitimate learning tool in the group.

An alternative version of the trust walk format is to start with the "touch but no talk format" and then alter the instructions to a "talk but no touch" format for the second experience. In the first version, the pairs must figure out a physical means of communication since no words can be used and in the second they must rely on words since no physical direction (touch) can be used.

Trust Fall Another way of demonstrating the concept of trust physically is using the trust fall, which is usually more threatening than the trust walk. Have each dyad move to an area free of objects and with sufficient room to conduct the exercise. Have one partner stand facing away from the other partner with feet together, eyes closed, and body rigid. Simply instruct the person to fall backward when ready. The other partner is instructed beforehand to catch the person. Demonstration is recommended prior to activation in order to demonstrate to group members how to catch their partners and to model how to engage in the falling-catching sequence by degree. Persons with physical problems, such as bad backs, should be cautioned before becoming involved. An additional precaution is to match partners according to size for the sake of physical compatibility. After several falls, reverse positions and repeat the exercise. Discussion can be much the same as with the preceding exercise, but you may wish to add the dimension of relating the trust-falling experience to sharing personal problems with other people you do not know or trust.

Group Activities

Human Machine Have one member of the group begin a motion of some kind. A second member attaches physically to the first, adding another motion but keeping in tune with the first. The rest of the members attach themselves one at a time until the whole group is functioning as a machine. Once the whole group is involved, moderate the motion by directive, speeding up and slowing down. At least once, accelerate to the point of disintegration to demonstrate the importance of group coordination and teamwork.

Circle Massage Have group members stand in a circle shoulder to shoulder. Have them take a right face, form cupped hands, and begin to beat on the back of the person in front of them in a rapid staccato manner moving all around the person's back. Have them switch to a neck and shoulder massage after about 30 seconds. The circle will often begin to move around of its own volition. After a suitable time period have the group do an about face and repeat the same process.

Group Hop Form the group into a circle standing shoulder to shoulder. Have the group make a right face placing their left hand on the left shoulder of the person in front of them and reaching down with the right hand to pick up that person's right ankle. When the group is steady, instruct them to hop forward and then backward. Next, instruct the group to make an about face and repeat the activity using right hands on shoulders and left hands holding ankles.

Dr. Untangle Have group members (at least six) stand in a circle. Number off the group 1–X (number in the group). Have them raise their arms over their heads and clasp hands as follows:

1. In even numbered groups, have the odd numbered persons grasp the left hand of the next highest even numbered person with their right hand. (Each person in the circle should have one free hand remaining.)
2. Instruct group members to grasp the free hand of another person in the group who is NOT standing immediately to their right or left.

    In odd numbered groups, the last odd numbered person must grasp the respective hands of the last highest even numbered person and the number one person, i.e., the last odd numbered person must take the hand of the person on each side of him or her.
3. Once all members are appropriately clasped, instruct them to untangle themselves without letting go of their hands. (Properly completed the result will be a full circle with members holding hands.)

The Knot Another version of the untangling task is to have members stand in a line holding hands. As leader, grasp the hand of the person at one end of the line and proceed to weave, snakelike in and out of the line with members following your lead as best they can. When you have the group sufficiently tangled up, connect the person's hand you are holding to the free hand of the last person in the line. Instruct the group to untangle the knot without letting go of hands. The successful result will be a connected circle.

Coin on the Forehead With group members standing in a circle, place a coin (quarter or nickel) on the forehead of one member. Instruct the group to pass the coin forehead to forehead without using their hands to touch the coin. Group members may assist each dyad making the pass as long as they do not touch the coin with their hands.

Trust Ring A group version of the trust fall is to have group members form a ring around one person who stands erect, feet together, arms folded across their chest, and eyes closed. Upon a signal (verbal or a slight push from the leader) the center person falls toward the ring, which is then responsible for catching and moving the person around while maintaining responsibility for his or her safety.

In this activity an important procedure is for the leader to demonstrate appropriate ways of catching and touching especially for female members. Females can fold their arms over their breasts and catchers from the front can be directed to arms and shoulders rather than the chest area. This activity demonstrates the dynamic of group trust especially in regard to the individual-group interaction. In fact, this activity can be helpful in assisting individual members who are hesitant to place their confidence in the group. Once they experience the group's capability relative to their physical safety, they may be more confident that the group also can be trusted with their psychological safety.

Three Secrets This exercise gets at the importance of safety and security on a more personal and psychological level. Have each group member write three secrets that they would not tell the group under any circumstances at this point in time. Assure them that they will not have to share their secrets, that no tricks are involved and that they will not be manipulated into disclosure. On completion of the writing, have members put the secrets away for safe keeping, and conduct a discussion centered around why they would not want to share their secrets in the group. Focus attention on the need for developing trusting relationships and confidentiality in the group. Help members come to grips with the threat involved in sharing their private world with others. The information written in this exercise often surfaces later voluntarily when members feel the group can be trusted. Members who decide to share their secrets will usually preface or follow their self-disclosure by telling the group that they would not have been able to do so before. This tends to bolster the morale of the group and serves as an indication that a trusting climate is developing. This activity, developed by Dr. Dan Ficek of the University of Wisconsin-River Falls Student Counseling Center, also serves to demonstrate that boundaries will be respected in the group relative to a member's privacy.

Will and Won't Cards This activity extends the boundary setting process from a non-disclosure focus to a disclosure focus. Members are given two 3×5 cards and asked to write three things they "will not talk about in the group" (Won't Card) on one card and three things they "will talk about in the group" (Will Card) on the other. The Won't Cards are discarded and the Will Cards are shared in a go-round format to introduce the self-disclosure process and the voluntary nature of the sharing process (Trotzer, 2001). Process the activity in terms of ground rules that affirm the individual member's right to determine what to share and what not to share emphasizing that the "right to pass" or refuse will be respected in the group as a viable option relative to disclosure.

Self-Collage Self-knowledge, self-disclosure, and self-acceptance are intricately inter-woven in the fabric of our identity. This exercise ties these threads together in a manner that is useful in the group counseling process. Have each person develop a collage using magazines, newspapers, photos, and so on, centered around the question "Who am I?" Have each person share his or her collage with the group and describe the connection between the items included and his or her personality and life style. On completion of the descriptions, have group members comment on aspects of the collage that stand out for them and that they identify with or admire. The focus of this feedback should be on appreciation and affirmation (rather than analysis or criticism) as a means of identifying and valuing similarities and differences among group members. In the follow-up discussion, relate the experiences in this exercise to the process of self-disclosure and self-acceptance.

A Symbol of You This exercise has merit because it encourages self-disclosure in initial group sessions. Have each person bring to the group a material object that represents something meaningful in his or her life. Each person in turn presents their object to the group and describes what it is, what it symbolizes, and why it was chosen. A variation of this activity is to have group members go outside and find some object of nature that represents who they are or how they feel. When they return ask each person to show their object and describe its meaning.

One Thing You Value The concept of acceptance is sometimes difficult to comprehend. This activity can serve the purpose of more clearly differentiating between acceptance and judgment. Have the members think of something they value deeply as a part of themselves. It can be an attitude, belief, characteristic, or possession, but it must be something they hold dearly. Form dyads and have the partners in turn describe their valued entity. Instruct the listener to help the speaker explain what they value by reflecting or asking questions, but under no circumstances must the listener make an evaluation of any kind. Stress this last point emphatically. After both parties have had the opportunity to be speaker and listener, discuss the experience. Ask if the members followed the rules or if some made evaluations in their minds like that's "like me" or "not like me" or, "I believe that, too." Most likely all group members broke the rule because it is impossible to keep if you become at all involved in the other person's sharing. Point out that acceptance does not mean evaluation is absent, but it does mean that judgments are not passed. Acceptance is also distinct from condoning, because the latter implies a choice not to act on a judgment that has already been made.

What's Your Bag? (or Pushing the Envelope) The following activity is an excellent advance organizer for discussion of the Johari Window and relationship development. Pass out crayons or magic markers and brown paper lunch bags (You can use grocery bags if you want this to be a big production, or envelopes and pens or pencils can be substituted.). Have members decorate the outside of the bag with their name and words, symbols, and pictures that portray things about themselves that they would share easily with other people. Once the bag is completed, pass out three blank slips of paper and ask them to write three things about themselves they do not easily share with others. Have them fold each slip and place it inside the bag. Assure group members that they will not be required to share what is on the slips of paper inside the bag. Finally, pass out a fourth slip and ask them to write one thing they absolutely would not share with the group. Place that slip inside the bag also. (You may want to color code the final slip.) Have members close their bags or seal their envelopes. Process the activity as follows:

1. Have group members share the outside of their bags with the group one at a time.
2. When all have shared the outside of their bag *invite* members to share one item from inside the bag. Indicate that each person may choose to decline the invitation.
3. When all have either shared or declined, process the activity in light of self-disclosure relating it to the hidden and open quadrants of the Johari Window model of relationship development.

Circles of Relationships Have each group member create a relationship map using the diagram in Figure 3.6. In each circle have members identify by first name or initials, persons in their life who fit in each of the circles. In addition, have them use arrows to represent persons who are moving away or toward them. Solid arrows can be used to designate movement they actually perceive is occurring and dash line arrows can be used to designate persons they would like to move toward or away from. As an indicator of group development, have members place group members in their relationship maps. Use the maps as a springboard to discuss characteristics of relationships, identify relationship problems, and assess the current status of relationship development in the group. This activity is an excellent means of helping group members discuss the ethical issues of contact between members outside the group and maintaining

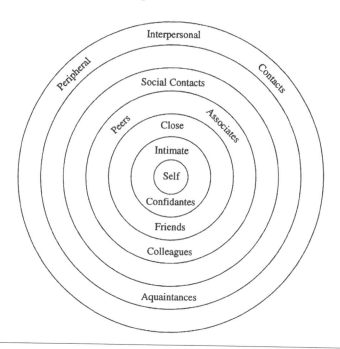

Figure 3.6 Relationship map. (Trotzer & Trotzer, 1986)

boundaries that differentiate membership in a counseling/therapy group from other relationships.

Road of Life A person's life story is sometimes more readily told as a series of critical incidents that stand out in memory. This exercise can be used to effect self-disclosure through the process of describing key experiences in the life of each group member. On a blank sheet of paper, have each person place a dot on the left hand side of the sheet representing birth and a dot on the right hand side representing death. Have them draw a curvy road representing life's ups and downs between the two dots. Designate a point on the road as the present. Using symbols such as balloons or clouds attached to the road, have each person indicate past, present, and anticipated future experiences (critical or important incidents or events) that are meaningful to them. Then have each person share their road with the group. Group discussion can revolve around similarities and differences between members and stress the uniqueness of each person as well as the mutuality of human experience.

Impression-Go-Round This simple activity is effective in demonstrating the feedback mechanism in group work. Have each person in the group give their impression of every other person in the group. This can be handled in one of two ways. The first is to have one person at a time give their impression of every other member. When that person has completed the impression-go-round, the next person does the same and so on. The second method is to have one member be the focal point and the other members in turn give their impressions. When all members have given their impression of the spotlighted member another member gets the limelight, and the process is repeated until each person has received feedback from all the others. Variations of this impression-go-round include using animals or colors that represent each member's impression of each of the other members of the group. The members in turn share their choices and explain why they chose them.

Self-Actualization (Cognitive Exercise) Because the nature of self-actualization is very complex and frequently confusing, this exercise can serve to help clarify its meaning. Have each class member write down a personal definition of self-actualization. The definition need not be comprehensive but should reflect the most important aspects of the term in each member's mind. Discuss the definitions, listing on the board the various characteristics. Then divide the class into small groups of four to eight, and have them develop a comprehensive definition of self-actualization.

4
Group Process
A Developmental Perspective

Effective group process is the practice of organizing systemic chaos into collaborative productivity while stimulating creativity, affirming individuality and respecting human dignity and diversity.

Background

Group theory, research, and practice have all provided evidence to substantiate the premise that small groups in the form of therapeutic, learning or task groups evolve through a developmental process characterized by identifiable phases that are recognizable, verifiable, and consistent within and across groups (Trotzer, 1985, p. 94). These phases may vary in number and nomenclature according to author but have a generic commonality that gives them concurrent relevance across perspectives and theoretical models.

Cohn (Osborne, 1990) pointed out that "in group counseling there is a testing period, then a working through period followed by an analyzing period and finally a follow-up period" (p. 5). These process components are often consolidated into stages and labeled. For example, Tuckman (Tuckman, 1965; Tuckman & Jensen, 1977) identified five stages using the dynamic descriptors of forming, storming, norming, performing, and adjourning to depict the group process. Corey (1995) describes the stages more generally as initial, transition, working, and termination. Clark (1992) used broader strokes to delineate group development as three stages: relationship, integration, and accomplishment. And Anderson (1984) coined the rubric TACIT to emphasize the group process: Trust, Acceptance, Closeness, Interdependence, and Termination. Hulse-Killacky, Killacky, and Donigian (2001) describe task group process in three stages identified as warm-up, action, and closure. A simple perusal of these varied process descriptions reveals the correlational affinity of the distinctive labels to the generic process.

The process of group work presented in this chapter has emerged from experience in a variety of settings and with a wide range of clients and age groups. Contributing to this model have been my involvement and leadership experience in schools with middle, junior high, and senior high students; at the Minnesota State Prison doing group therapy with inmates and group training with staff; at the university level working with graduate students in counselor education programs, in numerous human relations workshops with a variety of educators; in church related youth retreat groups; in interracial and multicultural groups; and in other diverse community and business settings as a consultant. Recently, leading and supervising counseling and therapy groups in both private practice and at a mental health agency and as a consultant conducting leadership training groups in a variety of higher education, business, and community settings has further helped me develop and refine this model. Finally, teaching an undergraduate small group communication class serving as a general education requirement for business, behavioral science, and liberal arts majors has contributed to the development of this process model as described in this chapter.

Contrary to what might be expected from reading the previous chapter, the basic framework of this process model was developed first (Trotzer, 1972), and the rationale supplied later. The model is experience based rather than theory based and is rooted in observation of actual group interaction rather than in empirical assessment of hypothetical constructs. However, the theoretical, training, and research literature of the group field has consensually validated its process components as relevant and applicable in the practice of group work (Conyne, 1985; Corey, 1995; Gazda, 1984a; Johnson & Johnson, 1997; Rogers, 1970; Yalom, 1995).

Nature of the Process

The model described presents a developmental perspective of group dynamics that is intended for use as an aid in understanding, directing and explicating the group process and as a framework for many different theoretical approaches and techniques. The group process itself is divided into five stages. However, the stages are not autonomous or independent of each other. Each stage has certain characteristics that distinguish it, but their meaning and impact are obtained only within the context of the total group process. The duration of each stage is dependent on the nature of the leader and group members and the interaction between them (Donigian & Malnati, 1997). In some cases, the stages turn over very rapidly; in some, the stages overlap and are almost concurrent; and in others, a particular stage may continue for a long period of time and can lead to stagnation in the group process, especially if this occurs early.

Rogers' (1967) description of the group process correlates well with this idea of stages emerging and submerging in group interaction: "The interaction is best thought of, I believe, as a varied tapestry, differing from group to group, yet with certain kinds of trends evident in most of these intensive encounters and certain patterns tending to precede and others to follow" (p. 263). Each stage of the group is like a wave in the sea that has a momentary identity as it crests but whose beginning and demise are swallowed up in the constant movement of the water as the tide like the group ebbs and flows.

Group Process and Problem Solving

The stage cycle of the group process reflects characteristics of our basic human needs and depicts the essential qualities of good interpersonal relationships. In therapeutic groups the model also mirrors a basic pattern for successful personal problem solving while in task or work groups the model reflects the process involved in group problem solving related to strategic planning, action plans and programs or products that address the purpose of the group. The integration of the stages (see Figure 3.5) into a conceptualization of a method for resolving problems and addressing group tasks is readily evident. The stages of security, acceptance, responsibility, work, and closing (Termination) are easily translated into a step-by-step procedure for resolving personal concerns (see Table 4.1) and participating in a work group.

Therapeutic Groups and Personal Problem Solving

First of all, on the personal level, as we experience problems we cannot solve, a natural tendency is to hide or deny them because we do not want negative repercussions in our self-image or in reactions of others around us. Problems threaten our security as persons and our relationships with others. Therefore, problems are only shared with others if an atmosphere of safety is part of our relationship with them. The first step is *security*. Feelings of trust and confidence reduce resistance and risk and facilitate our sharing of personal concerns with others. The amount of trust necessary for disclosing our problems is a product of the combined emotional seriousness of the problem and the quality of our relationships. Some problems we experience force us to use disclosure as a means of developing a trusting climate. For example, a client who has recently undergone a traumatic experience (e.g., a close friend was injured while riding in a car the client was driving) may be motivated by intense emotional feelings to share the problem without first determining if the atmosphere is safe. Such risks are sometimes taken without a foreknowledge of trust in the relationship. However, other problems may have emotional or social overtones or undercurrents that demand an atmosphere of confidentiality before any self-disclosure follows. Examples of these kinds of problems include mental health problems (anxiety, depression), sexual problems, drug or alcohol problems,

TABLE 4.1 Group Process and Problem Solving.

Process (Group Dynamics)	Content (Problem Solving)
I. Security Stage: Develop a psychologically safe environment in which each member can feel secure and free to talk about themselves and their problems.	1. Find a person or place where it is safe to admit to and talk about problems.
Individual Need: Security *Relationship Trait: Trust*	
II. Acceptance Stage: Form a milieu in which members experience a sense of belongingness and acceptance as a person and as a member with and in spite of problems or issues they are dealing with.	2. Accept problems as part of one's self.
Individual Need: Love and Belonging *Relationship Trait: Acceptance*	
III. Responsibility Stage: Develop an atmosphere that emphasizes individuality in a group context and develop a norm of owning responsibility for one's self and one's problems.	3. Take responsibility for one's own problems and commit to resolving them.
Individual Need: Esteem *Relationship Trait: Differentiation and Accountability*	
IV. Work Stage: Develop a collaborative culture where group members work together to help each other deal with their issues and solve their problems.	4. Identify, clarify, understand the problem and work to resolve it, i.e. develop a solution-focused plan, practice, implementation, and evaluation.
Individual Need: Self-Actualization *Relationship Trait: Cooperation*	
V. Closing Stage: Formulate closure with an emphasis on transfer of learning, internalization of change, affirmation, and confirmation.	5. Problem is solved and problem-solving process is learned.

and difficulties in relationships with significant others such as bosses, coworkers, parents, teachers, or an intimate partner. In any event, step one in resolving our problems is to find a safe place physically, psychologically, and relationally where we can talk about them.

The second step is associated with *acceptance*. Although the term acceptance encompasses a broad range of concepts, such as acceptance of self, acceptance of others, and acceptance by others, a key point in solving a problem is to accept that problem as a part of our self. Until we recognize that the problems we experience are part of us, we cannot act constructively to resolve them. Denial and unwillingness to face our problems are the biggest deterrents to their resolution. The old adage "a problem faced is a problem half solved" expresses the importance of this step. In order to accept our problems, we need to know that recognition of them as our own will not be devastating to ourselves or to our relationships with others.

In other words, our own acceptance of our problems is contingent to a large degree on the reactions or the perceived reactions of others. If we sense we are accepted by others as persons with and in spite of our problems; if we feel we can let them see who we are including our problems and be received with empathy, we are more willing to identify, share, and acknowledge our problems. In addition, acceptance of the problem as our own shifts our perception of the problem from being "ego dystonic" (outside of our control) to being "ego syntonic" (within our control). In Covey's (1989) terminology, such a change moves the problem from the "circle of concern" controlled by forces outside our selves to the "circle of influence" controlled by forces within our selves. This lays the foundation for the next step in the problem solving process.

Taking *responsibility* is the third step in the problem solving process. After we acknowledge our problems, we also must admit to our part in their cause and shoulder the responsibility to act positively to resolve them. Responsibility brings into focus the action phase of problem solving. The realization that problem solving is an active process and that the individual with the problem is primarily responsible for that action is a difficult but necessary step toward resolution. Clients often hope that once they have admitted to, identified, or accepted their problems something almost magical will occur and the problem will be resolved. They sometimes feel that because they have made the courageous effort to reveal themselves, their reward should be instant resolution, or at least that the counselor should take over. Therefore, the process of getting clients to take responsibility for themselves is another key step in successful resolution. Doing so shifts the solution process from an external locus of control (something others must do) to an internal locus of control (something the client must do).

The fourth step is to *work* out the means whereby the problem can be solved. This involves understanding the problem, identifying alternative solutions, evaluating them, planning and practicing new attitudes or behaviors, and trying them out in the real world. The helping relationship at this point is a working relationship in which all parties exert energy and intelligence toward helping the individual find and implement a successful solution.

The final step is to *terminate* the helping relationship when clients begin to experience success more than failure in their attempts to implement and integrate changes into their lives. In terminating, clients should not only realize problem resolution but should also have learned the problem solving process and increased their confidence in using it.

Group Process and Problem Solving: The Broader Contemporary Perspective

In accord with the purpose of this volume to present a broader more applicable view of the utility of group process in the hands of a professional counselor, the importance of problem solving is presented as a key element for bridging the differences reflected in the various types of small group across a variety of settings.

Problem solving is integral to group work in whatever form it assumes. In counseling and therapy groups, members address personal and interpersonal issues in the context of a collaborative milieu for the purpose of enhancing their developmental well-being or restructuring personality patterns that persistently result in dysfunctional behavior. In work or task groups members interact and engage in problem solving in order to produce programs, policies, or products that are endemic to the nature of the group's existence. Consequently, the more knowledgeable and skilled the group leader is in using problem-solving methods and skills in a group context, the more effective the group will be in accomplishing its objectives, the more satisfied the members will be with their participation, contribution and achievements, and the more successful the leader will be in overseeing, guiding, and facilitating the group enterprise (Trotzer, 2000, p. 10).

Group Work is a Bowl of P's

Effective group work generically requires that group leaders operate from a rationale and perspective that is founded upon a conceptual paradigm and practice model. My particular view of this requirement as noted in the opening quotation of chapter 3 includes a number of elements that all happen to begin with the letter **P**, hence the metaphor, "Group Work is a Bowl of P's." I have a **P**hilosophy of treatment that values group interaction as a primary resource of our humanity. I have developed a **P**sychological rationale that accounts for the fact that groups are comprised of **P**ersons who have needs that both prompt interpersonal dynamics and must be addressed by the group **P**rocess in order for the **P**urposes of the group to be realized and for members to benefit individually and collectively. In addition, ASGW's (1998) *Best Practice Guidelines* inform professional group leaders that effective practice and leadership requires attention to **P**lanning, **P**erforming and **P**rocessing. Consequently, I utilize a **P**ractice **P**aradigm (Figure 4.1 Box Inset) that combines personality dynamics, group dynamics and systemic dynamics to generate interaction that respects the person, mobilizes the resources of the group and addresses the purpose for which the group is convened. In that context I have developed methods for introducing **P**roblem solving as both a **P**rocess and **P**roduct dimension of the group. This conceptual **P**erspective will be integrated into the framework of this and succeeding chapters (Trotzer, 2000, p. 10).

Adaptation to Task Group Process

In work groups the process model generalizes to group problem solving in the form of mobilizing individual members to become part of a team that collaborates to address the task of the group or generate a product. Hulse-Killacky, et al., 2001) refer to this approach in the form of five questions that parallel the steps of the problem-solving process in a group context. Three of the questions relate to the process of the group and two relate to the content, and all five relate to the five stages of our model.

Question one is "**Who am I?**" which relates to the fact that each group member brings their individuality to the group and must find the internal motivation to share that uniqueness in the climate of the group. This process relates to the security stage and involves both knowing the answer and sharing the answer in a manner that is relevant to the group context. In other words, the member must experience a sense of safety to let others in the group know who they are.

Question two is "**Who am I with you?**" This question relates to the acceptance stage in that each member engages in a coconstructive interpersonal process with other group members that results in each person to being themselves in the group, and being part of the group.

Question three is "**Who are we together?**" This question relates to the process of creating a group identity in which the individual member is both differentiated in the context of the group and a contributor as a member of the group. As such the issue of responsibility is addressed as each member is a resource as a person and a contributor as a member. These three questions together form the process components of the work or task group.

Questions four and five relate to the work stage of the group process and construe the content of the group's interaction. "**What do we have to do?**" relates to identifying and accepting the group purpose which in turn produces a strategic plan, and "**What do we need to do to accomplish our goals?**" (or "**How are we going to do it?**") relates to the action plan for accomplishing the group's job.

The final question (added by me) is "**How will we know when we are done?**" This relates to the closing stage and identifies the criteria for knowing when the job is done both in terms of a quantitative result (product) and qualitative result (level of performance). Answering the six questions therefore provides a paradigm for group problem solving in work groups.

The following discussion will describe the life cycle of a group in which the problem solving characteristics just detailed will be related to the group process. Each stage will be discussed separately, considering factors such as major identifying characteristics, focus, leader role, and resulting impact. The ABCs of group dynamics will be incorporated into the description of each stage from both the member and leader perspective. *A* stands for the *A*ffective component and represents emotions and feelings experienced in the group. *B* is the *B*ehavioral dimension that indicates how participants act or behave, and *C* is the *C*ognitive aspect of group experience that identifies how participants think and perceive.

The Security Stage

The initial stage of the group process is characterized by tentativeness, ambiguity, anxiety, suspicion, resistance, discomfort, and other such emotional reactions on the part of both the members and the leader. Members experience these reactions because they are entering a new social situation in which they cannot predict what will occur and they are not confident of their ability to be in control of themselves or relate well to the group. Even though orientation procedures may be used, once the group comes together and interaction begins, the cognitive preparation gives way to the normal emotional reactions experienced in new social situations. In therapeutic groups uncomfortable feelings also arise because each member is aware that he or she is in counseling and has personal concerns that are not easily shared under any circumstances. In work groups questions of fitting in and being an effective performer generate the same feelings.

An example of the inner turmoil a group member experiences was demonstrated by a young woman who requested admittance to a therapy group at a university counseling center. During the first session she paced and stood outside the room, struggling with the decision of whether to enter or not. The group leader, aware of her fears and misgivings about the group, left the door open and indicated to her that she could come in when she was ready. Toward the end of the session she entered the room and stood against the wall but did not join the group until the second session. So extensive was her discomfort that she did not participate until the fourth session and did not risk disclosing anything about herself until much later. Although most group members do not experience reactions to that extent, feelings of discomfort in the early sessions are typically prevalent.

The security stage is a period of testing for group members. Much of this testing can be categorized as resistance (Schneider-Corey & Corey, 2006) and is displayed in the form of passivity, withdrawal, distractibility, uncooperativeness, or hostility. Bonney (1969) pointed out that "resistance and hostility toward the leader and conflict among group members are... expected outgrowths of the basic insecurity of procedural direction and uncertainty concerning the capacity of the group to achieve its proposed aims" (p. 165). The testing takes many forms and is aimed in many directions but the most common challenges are leveled at leader competency, ground rules, and other members' actions. Rogers (1967) felt that negative expressions are a way of testing the trustworthiness and freedom of the group. All persons in the group experience some form of nervousness that generates defending types of behaviors rather than the authentic sharing of feelings and thoughts. As such, the normality and commonality of the experience justifies some counselors' view that resistance in an inappropriate term to use (Schneider-Corey & Corey, 2006).

Therefore, the focus during this initial period must take into account these insecure feelings of members. Underlying concerns that brought the members to the group or that members bring with them should be set aside for the moment, and the here and now discomfort facing the group should be worked with. Some leaders like to use group warm-ups to help members express and work through these initial feelings and to establish a comfortable rapport within the group. The individual problems or insecurities of members, though they may be categorically similar, are most likely quite dissimilar in the perception of each member at this point. Thus an important procedure in the forming stage of a group is to establish a common ground so that members can make contact with each other, get acquainted, and open lines of communication.

Since each member is preoccupied with dissatisfactions in his or her own life or worried about their fitting in, an immediate focus on any one problem or emphasizing these underlying conerns can lead to a rather disjointed process or generate a high risk of losing the involvement and cooperation of all the members. This type of emphasis might also allow some members to go too deep too quickly and scare off others. Cohn (1973) warned leaders to avoid this possibility and stressed that one essential feature of the group process is that members must be moved to deeper levels of interaction together. In a sense, the first and most important task of a group leader is to get all the members on the same page. By initially focusing on the discomfort that all are experiencing, a common ground is established that moves the group toward more cohesiveness. This identification with one another helps members to overcome feelings of isolation and lays the foundation for the development of trust (Trotzer, 1972).

A significant aspect of the security stage is the leader's part in sharing the discomfort. Seldom will a leader enter a group without some feelings of uneasiness and hesitancy. These feelings do not necessarily reflect the skill, experience, and expertise of the counselor but rather are indicative of the effort involved in working toward closeness between people, helping people with problems and helping groups be successful. If leaders do not enter groups with some of these feelings, they are probably not prepared to become involved in the very personal worlds of the members.

The leader's role in the security stage is to perform what Lifton (1966) called *security-giving operations*. Leaders must be able to gain the confidence of the members, display warmth and understanding, provide for the various needs of members, and create and maintain a friendly and safe atmosphere in the group. Sensitivity, awareness, and an ability to communicate feelings and observations to the group without dominating it are important qualities of group leadership at this stage of the group's development.

As the group resolves the discomfort of the artificial and/or new social situation, members can begin delving into the problems in their lives or get about the business of the group. As members share their common feelings and perceptions, trust develops. Cohn (1964) emphasized this concept of trust, suggesting that once group members trust and are trusted the groundwork is laid for making the effort needed to improve their real life situations. Rogers (1967) stated that the "individual will gradually feel safe enough to drop some of his(her) defenses and facades" (p. 8). The members will become more willing to show their inner selves rather than just their outer selves. They will begin to direct energy toward *expression*—communication that allows oneself to be known to others authentically and transparently - rather than *impression*—communication that involves putting on a face in order to attract others (Schmuck & Schmuck, 1971).

Ohlsen (1970) also described the impact of the security stage: "When clients come to feel reasonably secure within their counseling group, they can be themselves, discuss the problems that bother them, accept others' frank reactions to them and express their own genuine feelings toward others" (p. 91). In other words, the development of trust provides the basis for getting down to the business of working on one's problems. Vorrath and Brendtro (1974) added that the most dynamic experience members gain from the group is learning to trust people. Therefore, "group leaders need to work on not taking the lack of trust personally while at the same time, helping members experience being able to trust in the group" (McBride & Emerson, 1989, p. 29). As such, trust has a process dimension and an outcome dimension that give it a two-fold impact in the group process. During the security stage the development of a trusting, nonthreatening atmosphere is the primary objective. This objective is in accord with each member's basic human need for security. As trust increases, the willingness for personal involvement and commitment increases. Members are more likely to risk letting themselves and their problems, frustrations, joys, and successes be known. Because of the atmosphere created by the movement toward trust, the individual members feel freer to be themselves. When this occurs the transition into the second stage of the group process takes place.

From the leader perspective, the affective dynamics tend to be a modified, mirror image of members' feelings. Whereas, members may be uneasy, resistant, anxious, and filled with self-doubt, leaders typically experience similar feelings in the form of performance anxiety, anticipatory nervousness, and doubts relative to self-confidence and leadership competence. In the cognitive realm, leader and member expectations may be slightly or greatly incongruent. Member expectations (cognitions relative to how they perceive the group) are influenced by past group experiences, pregroup orientation (if used) or how the group is introduced, and what they have heard or read about group process. Leader expectations tend to be based on their conception of what the group is for and where he or she would like it to go in a general sense. This variation in perception contributes to the ambiguity and lack of clarity as to group purpose and focus. Leader-member cognitive disparity combined with emotional uneasiness produces behavioral activity in the group that validates the underlying discomfort. Nervous gestures and person specific, social idiosyncrasies occur. Over-talking or under-talking coupled with nonverbal cues and messages that are noted but not acknowledged verbally, pursued interactionally, or clarified communicationally typify early group interaction.

Leader preparation for the security stage involves pregroup consideration of the following questions:

1. Why is the group being called into existence and what implication does that have relative to process dynamics?
2. What do you want the group to accomplish (goals/objectives)?
3. How will you help the group accomplish the goals for which it was formed?
4. How will you set parameters and ground rules and clarify expectations?
5. How will you proceed in your first session?

Mental imaging is a useful tool in the consideration of all these questions. At the security stage, the leader must be willing to participate in the affective discomfort of the group, have cognitive clarity about a direction for the group, and have a behavioral repertoire of responses to model, generate, and facilitate effective adjustment in the group. The interaction of these three elements creates a sense of security in the group that leads to a basic trust level that will enable the group to make the transition to the acceptance stage.

The Acceptance Stage

The acceptance stage is directly related to our need for love and belonging and therefore has many derivatives that influence the direction of the group process. Generally, this stage is characterized by a movement away from resistance and toward cooperation on the part of group members. As members begin to overcome the discomfort and threat of the group, grounds for their fears dissipate and they become more accepting of the group situation. As they become more familiar with the group's atmosphere, procedures, leader(s), and members, they become more comfortable and secure in the group setting. They accept the group structure and the leader's role. This acceptance does not necessarily mean the purpose of the group is clear to members, but it does mean they are accepting the method. For example, the meaning and purpose of a counseling group must be derived from the group members not from the group structure.

Inherent in the group members' acceptance of the group as a vehicle for their interaction is their need to belong and the need for relatedness. The members' desire to be part of the group emerges as an important motivating factor. This desire is inwardly evident to the individual from the outset of the group. But at first it is stifled for fear of acting in a manner that might ultimately jeopardize that belonging. However, with the foundation of trust established, the members are more willing to be their real selves and risk being known for the sake of being accepted. A journal entry of a 34-year-old Vietnam veteran who exercised a sentencing option choosing an alcohol treatment center rather than jail effectively depicts the acceptance stage of the group process:

At first there was no way I was going to admit to being an alcoholic or even that I had a drinking problem. But as I listened to the other guys talk about booze in their lives, I began to realize they were all talking about many of the same experiences I had. The first thought that came to me was "Hey, you can't fool these cats because they've been there." I felt lots of pressure to 'fess up' but still held back because I wasn't sure how they (the group) would take me nor was I sure I could stomach myself if I did. I finally decided to share my drinking problems when I saw the group treat another Nam vet in a sensitive way, giving him support and help with a problem I thought was even worse than mine. When I did admit I had a drinking problem, the group seemed to open up to me and let me in, and I also liked myself better.

As acceptance is experienced, relationships grow and cohesiveness develops. Cohesiveness is important to the group process because it makes group members more susceptible to the influence of each other and the group. It also provides the impetus for group productivity. It is a key factor in the helping process in groups because "those who are to be changed and those who influence change must sense a strong feeling of belonging in the same group" (Ohlsen, 1970, p. 88). Thus group cohesiveness meets the members' needs to belong, provides them with a temporary protective shield from the outside world, and is a potent therapeutic factor in the change process.

The therapeutic influence of cohesiveness makes use of peer group dynamics as its key resource in the group. As members experience genuine acceptance by fellow members, self-esteem is enhanced, ego is strengthened, self-confidence is bolstered, and they develop more courage in facing up to their problems or contributing to the group tasks. The impact of feeling accepted by a group of one's peers was stated succinctly by Gawrys and Brown (1963): "To be accepted and understood by the counselor is a satisfying experience; to be accepted and understood by a number of individuals is profound" (p. 106). Within this context, then, potential peer group influence can be mobilized in a positive manner by the counselor. The group leader's role in this stage is no small factor in generating an accepting atmosphere in the group and contributing directly to the individual members' experiences of feeling accepted. Leaders must be models of acceptance from the onset of the total group process. They must demonstrate a genuine caring for each of the group members. Their leadership must be characterized by acceptance of each person regardless of the differences or characteristics each person presents or the behaviors he or she exhibits inside or outside the group. The process of acceptance is initiated by leaders who practice Rogers' (1962) concept of unconditional positive regard and who value diversity whether of a volitional (individual beliefs, values, or choices) or predetermined (race, culture, or ethnicity) variety. Two basic leadership skills are essential at this stage of the group. The first is "active listening" (see pages 283–285) where leaders communicate empathic understanding to each group member. The second is "multi-directed partiality" (Boszormenyi-Nagy & Krasner, 1986) where leaders communicate partiality (i.e., side with or demonstrate empathy for each member in the presence of the other members in spite of acknowledged differences). This skill creates a context in which members experience acceptance while at the same time establishing the basis for dialogue as a resource for acknowledging, valuing, and resolving differences. As members experience acceptance from the leader, they feel more accepting of themselves and follow the leader's model in their actions toward one another. As members feel more accepting of themselves and other members, an atmosphere of acceptance as a norm is created.

This brings us to the primary objective of the acceptance stage from a problem solving perspective—developing acceptance of self. For members' problems to surface in the group they must feel free to truly be themselves without fear of rejection or reprisal. As already stated, members cannot deal effectively with their problems without recognition that the problems are a part of their personhood. Further, they must know that even though they have problems, they are still persons of worth and importance. All people have the desire to like and accept themselves and to be liked and accepted by others. This desire is what the group utilizes in helping members deal with their problems. When each member can accept feelings, thoughts, and behaviors, whether positive or negative, as part of self and still feel accepted as a person, a big step has been taken in the helping process of the group.

The focus during the acceptance stage should be on the whole person and not just on isolated problem areas. In order to attain self-acceptance and acceptance of others, members must work with the total picture of themselves and others. Getting to know oneself and each other, and engaging in "Who am I?" and "Who are you?" activities, serve to promote self-disclosure. As individuals share themselves and describe their problems, accepting problems as part of themselves occurs more naturally and is less threatening. Many leaders like to integrate the first two stages of security and acceptance, using structured, personal sharing activities and techniques. In this way sharing promotes trust, and trust encourages sharing. Members find that many of their concerns are similar to those of other members if not in content at least on an affective level. This similarity among members leads to identification with each other and facilitates openness. As members can speak more freely about their problems, they find they can embrace these problems without losing self-esteem or position in the group; this experience paves the way for the more individualistic stage of responsibility.

The acceptance agenda of the second stage represents a big order to fill in a re-lational, practical, and conceptual sense. However, results, when attained, unleash acceptance as a powerful force in facilitating the problem solving process. When established, acceptance removes many of the roadblocks in the change process.

It enables the group to begin constructive individual help. The development of acceptance accomplishes three main objectives (Trotzer, 1972).

1. It aids the group in becoming cohesive and connected thus meeting Gendlin and Beebe's (1968) guideline that *closeness must precede unmasking* and supports the supposition in task groups that *connectedness precedes contribution.*
2. It helps each individual feel accepted as a person of worth even though life is not satisfactory at the moment. This meets Gendlin and Beebe's (1968) guideline of putting *people before purpose.* It releases the potential of peer-group influence to be used in a positive rather than negative manner.

The affective dynamics of the acceptance stage place leaders in somewhat of an emotional quandary as they grapple with their role in the group. As members feel more comfortable and experience a growing sense of camaraderie and belonging, leaders feel a sense of being in between. Issues such as, "Am I part of this group or not part of this group?", and "How much should I be a leader, and how much should I be a person?" emerge to create mixed emotions that pull leaders into the group and push them out at the same time. Feelings of wanting to be more personal contrast with the desire to maintain an emotional objectivity or detachment.

In the cognitive domain the leader is aware of the need for personally relevant topics and information to be shared and that a total person emphasis needs to be maintained to give the group balance and stability as the relational bonding occurs. Norms are forming that will provide the group with security and predictability. The leader is responsible for seeing that these norms are dynamic and therapeutic and not forged at the expense of differences.

Behaviorally, the leader notices that self-disclosure increases and that feedback is given on an experimental basis. He or she sees members exhibit the rudiments of helping behaviors and realizes more dramatically the importance of leadership in generating, modeling, and facilitating appropriate group actions. Content of the group interaction addresses the purposes and problems that called the group into existence, and the leader must act to meld the relational and helping dynamics to key the transition to responsibility.

The following are questions leaders ask and answer at the acceptance stage:

1. What is my relationship as a person and a professional in the group?
2. How can I best assist the bonding process of the group?
3. What norms are forming in the group, and are these norms conducive to therapeutic impact?
4. How does the content being shared relate to the purposes of the group?

5. What can I do to merge the relationship development process and the problem solving process?

As the leader addresses these questions in a framework of developing a group identity and building cohesiveness, the groundwork is laid for movement into the responsibility stage of the group process.

The Responsibility Stage

The third stage of the group process is characterized by a movement on the part of group members from acceptance of self and others to responsibility for self and to others. A subtle but distinct difference exists between acceptance of and responsibility for self. Acceptance helps members realize and admit that problems are a part of their selves. However, acceptance alone leaves members with an avenue of retreat away from taking responsibility for working on their problems or owning a role in causing or contributing to them. Members can say, "Yes, that's the way I am" or "All right, that's my problem" but can disclaim any part in its cause or rectification. Acceptance alone allows members to claim no fault and negates any responsibility for doing anything about resolving, changing or taking initiative. The inclusion of responsibility, however, moves members toward resolution. The combination of acceptance and responsibility encourages members to state "Yes, that's my problem, and I have to do something about it." It activates the change vector in Covey's (1989) "circle of influence" and places it directly in the hands of the member and not some outside person or force. The ground is thus made fertile for constructive change to take place.

A divorced mother with two children shared her problems and frustrations in a women's counseling group at a mental health center. Her story exemplifies the difference between acceptance and responsibility. During the fourth group meeting, she talked extensively about the pain of her divorce and the subsequent difficulties of trying to raise her children alone. She became very emotional at times, and the group facilitated catharsis in a very sensitive, empathic, and supportive manner. At the end of the session, the group leader helped the woman put herself back together emotionally and solicited feedback from the group couched in terms of support. During the following session, she was again the focus of attention, but this time members began to suggest alternatives that could possibly help her cope better and improve her life. To each alternative she responded by saying, "I already tried that" or "I don't think that would work." After several attempts to get her to consider alternatives failed, one member observed that maybe she really did not want to do anything different in her life to overcome the problems. The woman denied that but soon afterward asked that the focus of the group attention be directed elsewhere. During the following sessions this woman's situation was brought up several times by herself, other group members, or the leader, but the discussion always stalemated at the point of her taking any responsibility for the problems or for initiating changes either behaviorally or attitudinally. At one point, a member made the astute observation that "in life, sooner or later it is wise to give up the hope of a better past." This seemed to pinpoint the issue for this woman. However, eventually she told the group that she felt her problems were the result of others being unfair and insensitive to her and that she was a victim and not a cause in her situation. Soon afterward she left the group. She was willing to share her problems in the group but was not able to see herself as a contributor or take the initiative to work toward resolving them.

The issue of responsibility in the group emanates from both our needs as human beings and the nature of the problem solving process. Members can only meet their need for esteem and respect through actions and achievements that require the person to take responsibility. If members feel causes are external, they will also feel the cures must come from sources external to themselves and not from their own efforts, resources, and initiatives. Both differentiation and empowerment are critical to the responsibility stage. Members need to differentiate as individuals within the group and experience the sense of empowerment necessary to take ownership and responsibility for themselves and their issues.

Our needs are reflected in the pressure of the group to move on in its developmental life cycle. The social aspect of cohesiveness developed in the acceptance stage wears thin after a while, and a natural tendency toward getting down to the business for which the group was created emerges. This tendency, according to Bonney (1969), is a mark of group maturity in that group members begin to accept responsibility for the management of the group and exert their energies to the task of problem solving. As members take increased responsibility for themselves and the therapeutic process, their chances for growth within the group improve. In fact, Lindt (1958) found that only those who accepted responsibility in the helping process of the group benefited from their experience. Riva, Wachtel, and Lasky (2004) concluded that one of the components of effective group leadership is enabling members to both develop cohesion (acceptance) and take over management of the group (responsibility).

During the early stages of the group process the task is to develop trust and acceptance by focusing on similarities among members and identifying and accepting differences between members. This process universalizes. It helps members recognize that their problems are experienced by others (universality), even though individual differences are apparent (Dinkmeyer & Muro, 1979; Yalom, 1995). During the responsibility stage the focus changes to individualization and differentiation based on each person's uniqueness and responsibility. The atmosphere of the group provides for considerable personal freedom with the implication that members have permission to (1) explore their weaknesses, strengths, and potentialities; (2) determine a way of working on problems; and (3) express feelings. The here and now emphasis is a key component in the responsibility stage, but it takes on a broader, problem oriented perspective. During the early stages of the group the here and now is directed to present feelings about the group and one's part in it. At this point, however, the focus expands to the individual lives of the members and helps them to focus on their here and now problems outside the group as well. This can be done in a step by step process in which expression of feelings is the starting point. For example, the expression of personal feelings and perceptions about one's self and others is one basis for learning responsibility in the group. To emphasize taking responsibility for what one thinks and feels, leaders can ask members to state their own perceptions or feelings and to tack on the statement "and I take responsibility for that." In this manner members learn to take responsibility for expressing anger and caring and can offer constructive criticism without the threat and risk usually associated with the expression of such feelings or observations.

As the members learn to accept responsibility for their personal feelings and perceptions, accepting responsibility for their actions, and eventually their problems, becomes easier. These steps must be taken if the counselor and the group are to have any significant impact on the individual member's life. Mahler (1969) emphasized the importance of responsibility for oneself: "Counselees must realize the importance of being responsible for their own lives, behavior, and actions, making their own decisions and learning to stand on their own perceptions" (p. 140). He added that "People need opportunities to learn that only by taking actions, making decisions, and accepting responsibility for their own lives can they become adults in the full sense of the word" (p. 141). Effective group process provides that opportunity.

The leader's role during this stage centers around helping members realize self-responsibility. Lakin (1969), Glasser (1965), Kottler (2001), and Riva and Korinek (2004) all stress the modeling nature of the leader role in which the counselor's actions must depict the proper attitude toward responsibility. Glasser (1965) believes that responsibility can only be learned through involvement with responsible people. Therefore, the member's primary example to follow in the group is the leader. The leader must help members maintain a focus on themselves and their problems rather than on events, people, or situations external to the group and beyond its influence. The group can only affect people and situations through its effect on the person in the immediate presence of the group. The counselor must stress an internal frame of reference rather than an external one. The question that ultimately must be faced is not "What can others do?" but "What can I do?"

The leader faces a crucial issue during the responsibility stage, and a word of caution is apropos. In our concern for our clients to make it on their own, we often see opportunities in the group process that could be used to *make* members be responsible. This situation must be handled carefully. For group members to become responsible they must experience responsibility, not be told about it or forced into it. At times, the issue of responsibility can be appropriately brought up and addressed as a topic in a teachable moment. At other times, confrontation may need to be used with members who have not recognized their responsibilities. Regardless of other actions, the choice to be responsible is best left to members. Mahler (1969) went so far as to state that "counselors who teach in group counseling violate the concept that basic responsibility for management of one's own life is up to the individual" (p. 103). Therefore, leadership should be directed toward helping members feel accepted and responsible without domination. When successful, members will feel a more personal, individual responsibility, experience empowerment, and exhibit less dependency.

The responsibility stage sets the tone for the remainder of the group work process. Once members realize their responsibility for themselves and understand that while the leader and the group will hold them accountable neither will infringe upon this responsibility, they can direct their entire attention to problem solving or the task agenda of the group. The responsibility stage affirms the inherent worth of members, assures them of respect as human beings, and points out qualities necessary to enhance self-worth, resolve problems, and become viable, contributing group members. Those qualities are self-assessment, congruence, honesty, responsibility, initiative, and commitment. When the members willingly engage in the introspective process, self-disclose, demonstrate their acceptance of others and willingness to help others, and—with very little or no help from the leader—take responsibility, the work stage of the group process is imminent.

The affective dimension of leadership experience is a useful gauge reflecting the process dynamics in the responsibility stage. As members struggle emotionally with responsibility and commitment the leader experiences a greater sense of clarity as to his or her role in the group. A sense of confidence evolves that facilitates ease of movement as a leader and enables him or her to be resourceful and maneuver effectively using a variety of appropriate roles. Leaders begin to trust their intuitions and impulses in this particular group and feel more capable in the leadership position.

In the cognitive domain, the leader consciously shifts focus from a "forest-trees" point of view to a "trees-forest" perspective. Whereas, in the earlier stages leader emphasis is given to context (forming the group out of individual components), the focus now changes to components (differentiating individuals in the group context). The uniqueness of each person and each person's role becomes important and the goal evolves from giving members an "I belong" experience to giving them an "I contribute" experience as they transition from being part of to taking part in the group.

Leaders also notice significant behavior changes in the group. Members begin to use more "I" language increasing their reliance on and utilization of first and second person pronouns rather than third person referents in their interaction with each other. Concreteness and specificity increases in member disclosures. Members are more prone to describe their actions in specific terms rather than using general descriptions, jargon, or colloquial aphorisms. Finally, more confrontations and conflicts begin to arise drawing the leader into a mediating role.

While the responsibility stage is the most difficult to delineate as a stage, it is of crucial importance to the group process because of its impact on the group's ability to engage in critical thinking which is so essential to problem solving. Janis (1971; 1972) identified and researched the phenomenon of *groupthink,* a process that cohesive and bonded groups substitute for critical thinking. He stated: "the more amiability and esprit de corps there is among members of a policy-making ingroup, the greater the danger that independent critical thinking will be replaced by groupthink, which is likely to result in irrational and dehumanizing actions directed against outgroups" (p. 44). Applied to the group counseling process, this means that groups that develop through the security and acceptance stages but do not move into responsibility will introduce interactive mechanisms and behaviors that will undermine and subvert critical thinking, distort reality, suppress individuality, fail to acknowledge and account for diversity and generally detract from therapeutic problem solving. Consequently, leaders must be especially sensitive to danger signals that come not only from individuals (members who resist being responsible for their own lives) but from the group as well.

McClure (1990) characterized groups that stagnate prior to the responsibility stage as *regressive.* These groups put forth a demeanor that creates a harmony illusion. "The group creates a public myth that there are no conflicts or intellectual differences among group members" (p. 161). Furthermore, these groups consciously and unconsciously avoid conflict, abdicate responsibility, and experience psychic numbing. These dynamics in turn lead to scapegoating, group narcissism, suppression of divergent thinking, inability to resolve internal group conflict, and self-interest. Subsequently, one of the critical channels through which individuation and productive group development occurs—the emergence and resolution of conflict—is stymied.

McRoy and Brown (1996) have stipulated that "conflict in small groups is inevitable, and...without conflict development into a productive group may be impaired" (p. 12). They point out that theorists and researchers concur that "groups develop in stages and conflict occurs naturally as the group strives to reach a productive or problem-solving stage" (p. 12). Therefore, one of the traits that may signal the emergence of the responsibility stage is conflict. To respond effectively the leader must be cognizant of the contest between the dynamics of suppression that may emanate from the cohesiveness of the acceptance stage and the growth oriented dynamics of expressiveness that propel the group into the productivity of the work stage.

The following are key leadership questions for the responsibility stage:

1. What can I do to enhance the emergence of each member's individual identity in the group?
2. How can I facilitate individual responsibility for self and problem ownership as a group norm?
3. Is the dual commitment of taking from the group (group as a resource for individual problem solving) and giving to the group (being a resource to other members or group problem solving) emerging?
4. Are the interactions and perspectives emerging in the group in touch with reality in spite of the supportive bonding in the group?
5. What obstacles (resistances) stand in the way of the problem solving process, and how can they be addressed?

As noted, the responsibility stage is the least definitive process-wise, but the most critical progress-wise, so answering these questions will prepare the way for therapeutic and constructive group work.

The Work Stage

The character of the work stage organizes itself around the individual problems and concerns of group members and the purposes for which the group was formed. In therapeutic groups as trust, acceptance, and responsibility are experienced and learned, what becomes increasingly evident is that some areas in each member's life are not satisfactory and could benefit from change. When these areas are pinpointed and discussed specifically, the work stage goes into full operation. Vorrath and Brendtro (1974) felt that the core of the group process is reached at this point because the goal of any counseling or therapy group is to work on problems and get them solved.

The work stage of the group process is exemplified by the interaction of a human relations group designed to improve communication and relationships between racial groups in a large urban high school. The members decided that the basic problem was "not knowing how to approach students who were racially different from themselves." They tended to be hesitant, fearing overtones of prejudice or racism might be communicated. To work on this problem, the leader first had racially similar members discuss their perceptions of themselves and racially different groups and then make suggestions that they felt would facilitate better relationships. After each subgroup had discussed their perceptions and made their suggestions, a comprehensive list of suggestions was developed in terms of skills. The leader then formed racially mixed dyads to try out the suggestions. During the work stage, partners were rotated periodically to give members the experience of trying out alternatives and building their skills and confidence with all racial groups represented.

The basic purposes of the work stage are to give group members the opportunity to (1) examine personal problems and issues closely in an environment free of threat, (2) explore alternatives and suggestions for resolving the problems, and (3) try out new behaviors or attitudes in a safe setting prior to risking changes outside the group (Trotzer, 1972). The energy of the group is concentrated on accomplishing these three purposes through the use of clarification, feedback, support, encouragement, information giving, skills training (Gazda & Brooks, 1985), strategic planning, and in vivo practice. Once in motion the productivity of the group is quite amazing and at times needs to be held in check because of the tendency to begin to solve problems before they are fully understood.

The leader role in the work stage is extremely vital from two perspectives. Leaders must be both facilitator and expert. They must be able to facilitate the discussion of problems, bringing out as many facets as possible, and create an atmosphere where alternatives can be suggested. These two processes entail mustering the total perceptual and experiential resources of the group. After a particular problem has been discussed and alternative solutions suggested, leaders must use their expertise to provide vehicles for examining the consequences of the suggestions as a means of aiding the decision making process. These activities can take the form of role playing, sociodramas, communication exercises, or discussion. In this way, alternatives can be assessed and evaluated, thus avoiding shot-in-the-dark failures. This type of reality testing in the group provides the group member with an idea of both the feasibility of a specific alternative and the effort involved in using it to resolve the problem. It also provides the member with an opportunity to develop self-confidence before attempting to make any specific changes in the less receptive and more threatening world outside the group.

Another important facet of the group process that surfaces during the work stage is the dual role of the group member as both the helper and the helped. When any one member of the group is working on a particular problem, the other members provide help through their feedback, sharing, suggestions, discussion, and participation in group activities. The experience of being in the helper role increases members' feelings of self-worth because now they are in the position of giving rather than receiving. The ancient oriental proverb that says "The best way to help a person is to let him or her help you" captures the impact of the helper role in groups. The giving of assistance to others raises ones self-esteem and also produces a more congenial attitude toward receiving assistance from others. The two-way process of helping and being helped is thus established. This process makes good use of members' altruistic tendencies and allows them to engage in *spectator therapy* where they benefit from watching others work out their problems.

During this stage, the group also represents *society in microcosm* (Gazda, 1968); that is, group members represent, as best they can, the forces, attitudes, reactions, and ideas of the world outside the group. Through the process of feedback, the group helps each member develop realistic alternatives to problems that can reasonably be applied in their lives outside the group. This mini-society, laboratory function is important because of its transitional value in preparing members for the task of implementing changes. The greater the approximation of societal or community reality, the greater the probability of effective change or resolution.

The *healing capacity* (Rogers, 1967) of the group emerges in the work stage, and the specific goals and objectives of the counseling group are addressed. Each group has different objectives based on the diversity of the group membership and the setting in which the group is formed. However, since most counseling/therapy groups are usually organized to deal with specific problems or mental health conditions, this is the point in the group process where efforts are focused on resolving them. The work stage prepares members for reentry into the world where they are experiencing their problems. They are armed with a well-conceived and evaluated plan, and self-confidence has been shored up through practice, personal encouragement and supportive accountability. However, individuals do not have to make the changes and implement their plans without some form of social support which the group provides until such time as termination is appropriate.

The approach-avoidance dynamics of initiating change and resisting change that emerge in the work stage can be emotionally draining. Leaders often experience this stage as a combination of excitement and frustration. As members mobilize around the motivation provided by their need to actualize their potential, they run smack into resistances that hinder their growth and development. Their resulting frustration may be shared by the leader who has become personally attached in some degree to each group member and the process of problem solving each person is experiencing. When added to the leader's professional commitment to being personally effective, a sense of challenge may emerge that entices leaders to overstep boundaries of responsibility and try to do too much for their clients. This emotional bonding is indicative of effective process dynamics, but must be kept in balance by parallel dynamics in the cognitive domain.

Leaders are cognitively aware that the norm of problem solving is operationalized and they must keep in mind the parameters that will most effectively ensure that both the process and product are personally relevant to each group member. So, while being emotionally supportive, leaders must actively remind themselves of their role in being a reality check to the group process and its members. In addition, maintaining a clear conceptual perspective of the fundamentals of effective problem solving is essential. This awareness produces leader behavior that facilitates helper-helpee role reciprocity by members and enables the leader to act as a resource in problem solving. Behaviors that present the process expertise of the leader emerge as he or she provides tools and vehicles (e.g., initiates activities such as role playing) to help group members address their problems.

The more capable leaders are of monitoring their own affect, cognition, and behavior, and the more successful they are in maintaining a balance between support for and perception of group members, the more effective their actions will be in the work stage. Following are questions that help leaders apprize their role at this stage:

1. What is my relationship to each group member? (How do I see each person and the problem(s) each is addressing?)
2. What resources do I have that can be mobilized to guide, direct and assist the problem solving process?
3. How can I most effectively carry out my role with respect to the relationship between group process and social reality?
4. How can I most effectively mobilize group resources in doing therapeutic work?
5. How can I best serve the individual members and the group with respect to the purpose of the group?

As each of these questions is answered, the resulting success in problem solving will naturally raise the issue of termination for individual members and/or the group as a whole.

The Closing Stage

The final stage of the group process is mainly supportive in nature and is characterized by feedback, encouragement, perseverance, accountability, and acknowledgement. Although group members may successfully work through their problems within the group, they still face the difficult task of modifying their behavior and attitudes outside the group. The expectations of significant others outside the group are still based on past experience with the group member, thus making it difficult to give encouragement or reinforcement to the member for acting in new or different ways. The group is a place where members can share their frustrations, successes, and failures and also reassess their actions for possible changes that will increase their effectiveness. Without a source of support, the potential for regression to old ways is greater.

The group also serves as a motivator. Part of this function entails rejecting excuses and confronting members with their own lack of commitment and effort if need be. Sometimes members need to be pushed out into the real world when they cannot venture forth on their own. The group has uncanny competence in assessing whether members are authentic in their efforts and whether they have performed up to their capability. During this stage the group can provide both a sounding board function and an accountability function.

Group support facilitates the integration of change into the client's life. Efforts to change and the change process itself are supported until internalization of change takes place individually and reinforcement occurs in members' lives outside the group. As changes become a more natural part of their lifestyles, the difficulty of adapting new behaviors, feelings, and attitudes decreases. The support of the group is only necessary until the balance between ease and difficulty in implementing change swings to the ease side of the scale.

The focus of the group thus turns to members' behaviors and experiences outside the group and deals with the progress they are making. The leader helps members discuss their experiences and feelings and offers support, understanding, and encouragement. The leader also helps members begin to take credit for their own changes instead of giving credit to the group or the counselor. In this way the individual members can integrate their new behaviors and attitudes into their everyday lives and can feel reinforcement from within themselves rather than from the group.

The closing stage for individuals may take many different forms. For example, a student who had been a member of a therapy group at a college counseling center for three years began to miss group meetings, showing up periodically but with longer time lapses between attendance. As he entered the final semester of his senior year, he relied less and less on the group for feedback and support and took more and more responsibility for himself. His need for the group and his involvement in the group lessened, with termination coinciding with graduation.

Another example of the closing stage is the standard procedure used at an alcohol treatment center when individual patients are preparing to leave treatment. The patient's group holds a graduation ceremony for the departing member during which that person makes a commencement address reviewing and summarizing their treatment and describing goals and objectives for the future. The group then engages in a serenity prayer during which group members give support, feedback, and encouragement to the graduating member. The person is then presented with a coin that has a missing piece symbolizing the unending process involved in rehabilitation and growth. The ceremony thus serves to summarize and reinforce changes that have occurred but also prepares the person for the rigors of adjusting to life outside the treatment center.

The point at which a group or individual member should terminate is sometimes difficult to determine. For this reason groups are often terminated on the basis of a preset time schedule, for example, after 10 sessions or at the end of a semester. However, ending a group is also appropriate when group members experience more success than frustration in solving their problems and feel intrinsic rather than extrinsic reinforcement for their actions in doing so. As members become more autonomous, they lose their dependence on the group. As they resolve their problems and learn how to solve problems, they no longer need the group. When any of these situations occur the group has run its course and should be disbanded.

The leader's affective experience of the closing stage typically includes ambivalence. Personally, a certain amount of over-involvement may have occurred that mitigates against members terminating. Professionally, the realization that the effort expended to make this group work will have to be repeated with another group may produce feelings of resistance relative to closure. The natural inclination to desire affirmation as a person and professional may produce feelings of incompleteness or even insecurity if such feedback is not forthcoming. Consequently, for leaders to have emotional approach-avoidance tussles with respect to closing is not unusual.

Cognitively, the purposes of termination are quite clear:

1. to translate closing into commencement;
2. to continue the impetus of the change process beyond the life of the group;
3. to ensure that closure does not disrupt or undermine growth or generate regression;
4. to provide a therapeutic exodus from the group for each participant, including the leader; and
5. to enable group members to assume credit and responsibility for their own changes.

These purposes can be addressed through behaviors that incorporate a process and product review regarding the history of the group and each of its members. Using self-disclosure and feedback tools, specific marker events, successes, failures, and the nature of the experience can be shared. Looking ahead to future goals and anticipating potential predicaments is also common in the closing stage. Sometimes members, out of a sense of nostalgia or simply to hang on, will manufacture problems or recycle old problems to keep the group going. This tends to be rather short lived, however, since the momentum to get on with life already has set the disbanding process in motion. Celebratory and symbolic termination gestures reflecting individual personalities and the group milieu emerge enabling members and leader(s) to say goodbye.

The following are questions leaders need to address in the closing stage of the group process:

1. How can I assist members in detaching and/or the group in disbanding in a therapeutic manner?
2. What is the degree of my investment in the group, and what do I need to do to detach effectively?

3. How can I facilitate closing so that it preserves progress and serves as a commencement to continued growth?
4. What resistances to closing are evident, and how can they be reframed into initiatives for ending?

With termination, the history of the group as an entity is complete. However, the impact of the group may carry beyond the life of the group itself involving the leader in individual member's lives either by choice (follow-up) or circumstance. Either way, the closing stage may include some spillover dynamics that will persist even though for all intents and purposes, the group officially ends with the last meeting.

Parallel Process in Task Groups

Hulse-Killacky, et al. (2001) have identified a list of traits that characterize successful task groups and that effectively parallel and reflect the themes of the group process developmental life cycle just described. Each trait is a theme both within the stages and across stages that make the group process model applicable to task as well as helping groups. They note that in effective task group members (stage relationship in parentheses):

- Feel listened to (Security and all other stages).
- Are accepted for their individuality (Acceptance and all other stages).
- Have a voice (Responsibility and all other stages).
- Are part of a climate in which leaders and members acknowledge and appreciate varied perspectives, needs, and concerns (Responsibility and all other stages).
- Understand and support the purpose of the group (Work stage).
- Have the opportunity to contribute to the accomplishment of particular tasks (Work stage) (Hulse-Killacky, et al, 2001, p. 6).

You will note that the first four traits relate to the process of the group and the interpersonal dynamics that create the culture of the group and the last two traits relate to the content of the group representing the interactive and collaborative nature of the group as it addresses its purpose.

A Precautionary Note

Viewing group counseling as a developmental sequence of a set number of stages raises the possibility of unnecessary and undesirable rigidity in conceptualizing the group process. To circumvent this and maintain flexibility in this group model, it is necessary to remember that within each stage there can be many levels. Different degrees of trust, acceptance, and responsibility are reached by the group and its members at different times. Some problems, topics, or issues discussed in the group require less trust than others. At other times recycling the process may be necessary to develop deeper levels of trust, acceptance, or responsibility in order to deal with a particular problem, topic, or issue. Bonney (1969) labeled this phenomena *retransition* referring to the tendency of groups to go back through the early phases of group development before proceeding to a deeper level. At any one time and with any one problem, topic or person the group may have to retreat to a previous stage before it can move to the next one. In fact, all stages may recur several times before the group has run its course.

The recycling of stages is particularly evident in open ended groups where individual members terminate and other members join, all in the course of the ongoing group life. Each exit and entrance sets off dynamics that are the impetus for recycling elements of earlier group stages so as to reform the group into a therapeutic entity consisting of the current participants.

Another consideration is that components of two or more stages may be prominent in the group at the same time. The group may be learning trust, acceptance, and responsibility while working on a particular problem. The group does not develop in a lock-step manner even though general trends can be noted and specific characteristics consistently appear at certain points in the group's development. Neither can the group process be forced to conform to an external standard or model. Rather, it is a responsive and flexible process that is influenced by the leader's personality, differences between people and their problems, nature of the group's purpose and variations in the rate at which different people develop relationships, work out individual change and become team players.

Concluding Comments

Group work and group process bring into perspective the relationship between psychological needs and the socialization process, whereby human learning, problem solving and task achievement occur through interpersonal interaction. Group process accentuates the social learning process by focusing on the dynamics of the group itself rather than on some environmental context. That focus is informed by ecological considerations and the context in which the group is formed (Conyne & Bemak, 2004), but the emphasis is on the group dynamics not the environment. Group members are given the opportunity to learn how they function individually and socially. They can do this because the leader and other members have created a climate or atmosphere characterized by psychological safety and acceptance where they can take responsibility for their own lives. In such a situation members can experience the healthy attributes of individuality or uniqueness and relatedness or conformity. They learn and express both autonomy and interdependence.

Members can express themselves freely and engage in open and honest interaction with other members without the fear of rejection or reprisal that so often tempers interaction in one's environment. Within the group, members can experience and learn responsibility. They can confront problems, issues, differences, and conflicts openly, knowing they will obtain support and assistance as needed. In therapeutic groups members experience the interchanging role of being the helper and the helped as they work on their own problems and assist others with theirs. The member can discover and evaluate alternative solutions to personal concerns while at the same time building self-confidence and personal security, that serve as enabling factors in implementing change outside the group. Thus group work as presented provides both a setting and a process whereby the basic objectives of counseling and therapy can be attained and the tasks of a work group can be accomplished.

Learning Activities

Activities presented here are organized in sequence to relate to the stages of group development discussed in this chapter. Although the primary characteristic and use of each activity is stage related, each can be used for many other purposes. These activities are versatile and adaptable, depending on the leader's approach and the nature of the group.

Trust Ring

Option 1 This activity is useful in demonstrating the characteristics of trust and confidentiality that are necessary for a group to work effectively. Have all group members stand in a circle in an area that is free of material objects such as chairs or tables. Have group members join hands strongly gripping the hand or wrist of the persons standing beside them. Members should have a strong grip on each of their partners' hands or wrists. Then have the group extend out as far as possible forming a taut circle. Instruct all members to lean back exerting pressure on the circle and slowly move their feet toward the center of the circle creating a centrifugal pressure on the group. Have the group move in a clockwise direction maintaining this centrifugal pressure. After a few moments, reverse the direction. Follow the activity with a discussion of each person's reaction in terms of the amount of pressure he or she was personally willing exert on or in the group circle and feelings regarding the partners on either side and the total group. Stress the importance of the whole group going to the aid of individuals who were slipping in order to protect them and maintain solidarity in the group. Discussion also can focus on the amount of pressure the group as a whole exerted relating it to risk taking in self-disclosure and feedback.

Option 2 A variation of this exercise is to have members stand in a circle shoulder to shoulder. Instruct members to interlock their arms around the back or waist of the persons beside them. Then have group members lean inward and slowly move their feet away from the center of the group creating a centripetal force on the group. Have the group move alternately in a clockwise and counter clockwise manner. At the conclusion of the exercise have the group members retain their interlocking positions in the circle and discuss the reactions in the same manner as described in Option 1. An added feature of this discussion can be the impact of closeness created by the "arms around each other" dimension, relating it to the effect of warmth and closeness in developing cohesiveness and trust in the group.

The Trust Ring exercises of Options 1 and 2 were developed by Jim Ross and demonstrated in my group counseling class at the University of Wisconsin-River Falls.

Closed Fist

This activity lends itself to a consideration of strategies used by people in negotiating trust in human relationships. It is particularly applicable to group counseling because of the risk intrinsic to the process of sharing. Break the group down into dyads. Ask partners to exchange some material object that they value (such as a ring, a picture, or a wallet). Have each partner put the object away out of sight for the time being. Then instruct members to think of something that is extremely valuable to them, something they would not wish to give up under any circumstances. This may be a material object or a conceptual object. Give the group a few moments to choose something. Then ask one of the partners to figuratively place the visualized item of value in a closed fist without telling their partner what it is. Instruct the other partner to try to get it. Allow this process to proceed for a time without any intervention. Then ask for an account of what happened, noting the different strategies that were used to obtain the object and pointing out their relevance to the group process. After this discussion, ask members to negotiate retrieval of the actual objects they exchanged initially.

Important factors to consider in this activity are the type of exchange strategies that produce competitiveness, cooperation, collaboration, ill will, intimidation, and positive interpersonal feelings. Strategies that are conducive to positive relationships are recommended for use in the group. Also, note that the value of the objects exchanged reflects the amount of commitment and trust in the relationship. Members will share more willingly and at a deeper level if other members share reciprocally.

This exercise was demonstrated by Dr. Dan Ficek in a Human Relations Workshop he and I led in Red Wing, Minnesota.

Life Story

Vorrath and Brendtro (1974) used this technique to introduce new members into the group. It is especially appropriate for ongoing counseling groups that experience member turnover. New members after a brief period of time in the group are asked to tell their life stories as completely and as accurately as they possibly can. The life stories should include a description of problems that brought the new people into the group. The other group members have the responsibility of facilitating the new member's efforts. Under no circumstances should views of the person be challenged at this point. After the story is completed the group can begin to work with discrepancies or other factors that might relate to examining and resolving the member's problems. The main impact of this technique is that members realize their side of the story is going to be heard first. They receive guarantees that their frame of reference and perspective is important and will be considered by the group. They experience acceptance and find the group is a safe place to air their problems.

Poem of Self

This activity helps establish a minimum level of self-acceptance for each group member and helps the group become involved in introspection and self-disclosure essential to the group process. Use the following directions in carrying out the exercise.

1. List four adjectives that describe what you look like.
2. List four adjectives that describe what you act like (personality).
3. List five words ending in "ing" that describe things you like to do (if you like to read, put reading). Words may be created by adding "ing" to any word that represents an activity, e.g., tennis-ing.
4. List six things (nouns) that would remind people of you (e.g., possessions, such as a guitar, or roles you play, such as a student).
5. List four places you would like to be.
6. On a sheet of paper draw the following diagram or hand out a copy of the diagram (Figure 4.1).
7. On the first line of the diagram write your full given name.
8. Choose one word from list 1 (what you look like) and one word from list 2 (what you act like) and place them in the blanks on line 2 in any order you choose.
9. Choose three words from list 3 (things you like to do) and insert them in the blanks on line 3 in any order you choose.
10. Choose four words from list 4 (things that remind people of you) and write them in the blanks on line 4 in any order you choose.

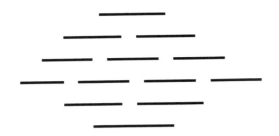

Figure 4.1 Diagram.

11. Choose two words form list 5 (places) and write them in the blanks on line 5 in any order you choose.
12. On the bottom line write a nickname or any name by which you are called other than your given name. (This may be a derivative of your given name, such as "Toni" for Antoinette.)

Have each member read his or her poem to the group twice, the first time quickly with rhythm and poetic expression and the second time slowly so that they can catch all the words. After everyone has read and explained the meaning of the words in their poems, discuss how the activity contributed to getting to know one another.

Coat of Arms

The coat of arms has more depth to it than the poem of self and can be used in conjunction with it. This activity gets at more varied aspects of each person's life and provides a good beginning for the actual counseling process. It also combines

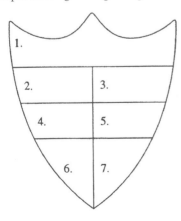

Figure 4.2 Personal coat of arms diagram.

the medium of illustration with verbal description, which makes sharing an easier process. Give each person a sheet of paper with the Alternative Instructions diagram below on it or have the people draw it. Then have them fill in the numbered sections of the shield according to the following instructions.

1. In the section numbered 1, write a motto or phrase that describes how you feel about life or that is a guide to your life style. (Some people create their own; others use slogans, proverbs, quotations, poems, or Bible verses.)
2. In section 2, draw a picture that represents your greatest achievement or accomplishment to this point in your life (no words).
3. In section 3, draw a picture that represents something other people could do to make you happy (no words).
4. In section 4, draw a picture that represents a past failure or disappointment in your life (no words).
5. In section 5, draw a picture that represents the most significant goal in your life right now (no words).
6. In section 6, draw a picture that represents a problem you would like to work on in this group (no words).
7. In section 7, write three things you would like people to say about you if you died today (or write your epitaph).

After all the members have completed the shield, have each member share it with the group and explain the meaning of each section. This exercise has the positive impact of acceptance since it deals with each person's strengths, weaknesses, goals, relationships with others, and problems. The instructions for the various parts can be changed to meet the demands of the situation and the needs of the members, thus making this activity a flexible and effective tool in the hands of the group leader.

Alternative Instructions:
Draw a picture that represents:
      A talent, ability, or gift you have.
      An important person in your life.
      An important decision you have made.
      A special interest, hobby, or recreational pursuit.
      Write your pet peeve.

Gestalt Interventions

One of the ways we avoid being responsible for ourselves and in control of our own lives is through the words we use in communication (Stevens, 1971). The following intervention techniques drawn from the Gestalt approach to group therapy can be used to help group members take responsibility for their own thoughts, feelings, and behaviors and, ultimately, for their problems.

Questions or Statements

Many questions that group members ask are really camouflaged statements. Before responding with an answer, ask the questioner to change the question into a statement that expresses personal perceptions, observations, or feelings. For example, a question like "What are you going to do about that conflict with your boss?" can be restated as "I'm wondering what you are going to do about that conflict with your boss." This expresses the perspective of the speaker, but leaves the option of responding up to the person to whom the statement is referring.

I Can't/I Won't Statements Members often use the words "I can't" in discussing problem situations, giving the impression that control is really outside of themselves. When you hear an "I can't" statement ask the member to repeat the statement using "I won't," to convey the message that the person has a choice in the matter. "I just can't talk to my father" changes to "I just won't talk to my father."

I Have to/I Choose to Statements Have group members make a list of "I have to" statements describing all the things in their lives they feel they have to do. Have them share their lists in the group. Then have them change "have" to "choose" and discuss the difference such a change makes in their perception of their list. Discussion usually pinpoints quite clearly the issue of personal responsibility and choice. As a group leader you also can ask members to substitute "I choose to" for "I have to" during group discussions. In doing this the members realize that they are responsible, and that they do have a choice.

I Need/I Want Statements Group members often express desires as needs, creating the impression that severe personal consequences will result if needs are not met. They say "I need" which depicts whatever it is as essential to their well being. To define more accurately what really is and isn't needed, have members change "I need" statements to "I want" statements and discuss which is more appropriate and accurate. Incorporate feedback from other members as to the validity of the statement.

Strength Bombardment

Otto (1967) first posited the idea that problems could be solved by starting with people's strengths and then focusing on their weaknesses. That premise is particularly relevant to the responsibility stage of group development. One means of helping group members accept responsibility for themselves is to approach it from a perspective of strengths, assets, and accomplishments of which the member is already aware. This activity uses the processes of self-disclosure and feedback to help members take responsibility for their behavior.

First, have each group member develop a list of personal accomplishments or achievements. Define accomplishments as "anything you think is an accomplishment." Encourage the members to feel completely free in forming the list drawing from any time or period of life. Expressly instruct them not to think about the criteria or reactions of others or about the ego related emotional connotations such a request usually conjures up. Upon completion of the list, have the members write a paragraph, starting with "I am," that describes only their positive qualities (provide a 3 × 5 card for this activity). Assure them that no one else will see the paragraph, but indicate that they should include only positive qualities and not put in any negative ones. When the paragraph is completed have members put the card away, stating that they can do what they want with it, possibly keeping it tucked away to pull out for a rainy day ego boost. Now have the members share their initial list of accomplishments with the group. Then place two chairs facing each other in the center of the circle. Ask one member to volunteer to take one of the chairs in order to receive positive feedback from the other members. When one person has taken a chair, each other person in turn gets up, sits in the opposite chair and gives the first person only positive feedback. There should be no "I would like you if…" or "I like you but…" comments, and the person receiving the feedback can only respond with expressions of appreciation, not with denials or counter remarks. This process continues until each person has received positive feedback from every other person in the group. On completion of the activity, relate the experience to the issue of responsibility and discuss how one's positive qualities can be used as resources to help overcome one's negative qualities and problems. This activity is useful as a springboard to the work stage of the group process.

Awareness and Responsibility

This technique was developed out of the Gestalt approach to group therapy and combines the concepts of personal awareness and individual responsibility. It has relevance to therapeutic groups and task groups because it clarifies where members are personally and helps them take responsibility for their own thoughts, feelings, and behaviors in the group. Each group member is asked to share with the group thoughts, feelings, and perceptions or observations using the format: "Right now I am aware…" (members complete the statement describing what they are aware of)… and then add "and I take responsibility for that awareness." The last part of the statement is added to get individuals to affirm their own part in feeling, acting, or thinking the way they do and to prevent them from putting responsibility on others. A leader can effectively use the last part of the statement by simply asking members to add it to any statement involving a personal emotion, assertion, interpretation, or perception. In this way, the impact of the statement becomes just one person's frame of reference and allows other members the freedom to respond as they see fit without feeling threatened by the imposition of another person's point of view on them.

Problem Identification and Rating

The work stage is the point in the group process at which problems should be dealt with directly. This activity pinpoints problems that are pertinent to individual members and are relevant to other members' lives as well. Give each member a 3 × 5 card to anonymously write a description of a problem he or she would be willing to discuss with the group. Stress the "willing to discuss" aspect. When the descriptions are finished, collect the cards and read them one by one to the group. After each problem is read, ask members to individually rate it on a 1 to 5 scale (5 is high and 1 is low), showing their **interest** in discussing the problem, their perception of its **importance**, and their **identification** with it. Record each individual rating on each card (remember, this is a rating not a ranking). After reading and rating all the problems, add up the total ratings on each card. A hierarchy of problems develops based on the scores. Reread the highest rated problem and ask the person who wrote it to own and describe it in detail. The group can then work with that specific person and problem.

This procedure results in a hierarchical agenda, but if the group is particularly effective in helping the first person, other members may decide to reveal deeper problems with which they want help. The problem agenda and hierarchy should be adhered to only if it is in the best interests of the group. Rigid structuring of the group focus based on the ratings could deter progress if flexibility is not incorporated into the processing.

Behavioral Problem Solving

Many times group members have difficulty resolving their problems because they lack specificity. Have members write down and then briefly describe to the group three personal concerns with which they are struggling. Then have each member select one of his or her concerns and describe it in detail following the four basic behavioral steps:

1. Describe in behavioral terms what you do not like or what is wrong (*problem*).
2. Describe in behavioral terms what you would like to change or how you would like to be (*goal*).

3. Discuss with the group how you might be able to accomplish your goal and develop a strategy for doing so (*plan*).
4. Try out the plan and report back to the group on your progress (*evaluation*).

For the last two steps a contract system (Dustin & George, 1973) is helpful where the group member writes the plan in the form of a contract. He or she signs it in the presence of witnesses, which increases the individual's commitment and gives the group a solid basis for follow-up, reinforcement, accountability, encouragement, and evaluation of progress. Some groups use *Goal-Boards* to keep the group cognizant of each person's goal and progress. A check-in system is then used each session to chart the change process. Some groups also incorporate the use of accountability partners to assist in the implementation of the plan. These relationships are usually defined with parameters that may include only in group contacts or both in and out of group contacts. It is important to have the dimension of contact specified for both ethical and practical reasons.

Go-Round

One of the simplest and yet most versatile and effective exercises that can be used in group work is the go-round. Jacobs, Masson, and Harvill (2002) condensed the title of this technique to "rounds" and have demonstrated the latitude of its use in broadly diverse groups and circumstances from training to practice to supervision. As the name implies, this technique involves going around the group person by person, giving each a specific opportunity to respond. This technique has many variations and purposes and fits at any stage of group development. For instance, a go-round is a good way to begin a group to find out what everyone is thinking or feeling and to get some cues about how to proceed. A go-round when a group ends gives members the opportunity to say what they have not had a chance to say and is a good way to tie up loose ends. During the group sessions, go-rounds immediately following critical incidents are useful to air feelings and release tension, as well as to move the group on to the next phase of the process.

Feelings Face

This activity is a useful tool for ending an individual group session or an overall group experience. Have group members draw a caricature of a face that represents their feelings about the group experience on an 8 × 11 sheet of paper. On each corner of the paper have members write a different word or phrase describing their experience in the group. When completed, have them fold the corners of the page back so only the face is showing. Instruct the group to mill around the room showing their faces to other members on a one to one basis. Members are to guess what the other person's face is portraying. After guessing, each shares one of the words or phrases written on a corner explaining the reasons for their feelings. When each group member has shared all their corners (four in all), they turn their faces in to the group leader who holds the faces up one at a time in the group as a stimulus for discussion and closing feedback.

An alternative mode for processing the feelings face is to share the faces and the feelings directly in the group. The leader also can have each member share the face and feelings with him or her as an exit visa from the group.

Feelings Doodles

A modification of the previous activity is to have members create an eyes-closed doodle attempting to portray their feelings. The same format can be used to process the doodle as is described in the Feeling Face activity. Or, the created doodles can be used as a kind of group Rorschach activity. Have members pass their doodles to you as leader without any identification. Show the doodles to the group one at a time and ask for projective feedback responses. Questions like, "What do you see in this doodle?" can be used to elicit input. Once the group has responded to the doodle, the person who drew it can be asked to identify himself or herself and respond to the group's perceptions. Projected feelings as perceived by the group and acknowledged feelings of the person can be discussed as a processing activity.

Appleton and Dykeman (1996) have noted that this activity has cultural relevance when working in groups with Native Americans. The shapes, symbolism, and images facilitate expressiveness and communication from a cultural heritage that has long used and valued symbols.

5
Process to Practice

Group work practice combines personality dynamics, group dynamics and systemic dynamics to generate interaction that respects the person, mobilizes the resources of the group and addresses the purpose for which the group is convened (Trotzer, 2000, p. 10).

Turning Group Dynamics into Form and Function

Developmental psychology's most significant contribution to our knowledge of human beings emanates from the basic premise that by understanding normal functionality, we are able to facilitate and enhance normality as well as accommodate to and correct abnormality. Its methodology entails studying organism change phenomena and identifying sequences of events that constitute normal growth and development over the organism's life cycle. Once clarified, these sequences or stages serve as the reference base when any individual unit of the organism is encountered. Consequently, development principles are relevant to any organism or organization that evolves through developmental phases that have sequential and life cycle dimensions. Individuals, relationships, systems, and groups all qualify as being developmental in nature. As we have seen in the previous chapter, the group process is a specific example of the developmental psychology perspective.

Developmental Perspective

Simply understanding the development of a particular type of group is insufficient since the utility of that process only has meaning if transformed into a pragmatic application that helps people change and gets work accomplished. In other words, process dynamics must be translated into form and function as well as serve as our evaluative criteria for determining if the process is evolving appropriately. This chapter is designed to bridge the gap between process and practice. The developmental concept most relevant to this chapter is that given typical conditions, growth or change in any organism unfolds predictably in a sequence of stages each of which involves certain developmental tasks (Havighurst & Neugarten, 1968). These tasks must be addressed for successful completion of a particular stage to occur and serve as the foundation for proceeding to the next stage. These stages are the building blocks of the organism's growth and development. How they are addressed determines how a particular organism will adjust and function. Over time, how these tasks are handled will indicate where the organism will fall on the continuums of normality and functionality and whether it will be typical or atypical. The stages of the group process contain such developmental tasks. They are embedded in the interactional dynamics of the ongoing process. The purpose of this chapter is to identify those tasks and demonstrate their relevance to the structure and utility of the group as a therapeutic change agent or productive work setting. Each group stage will be deconstructed in terms of specific developmental tasks. Implications for using the tasks as a basis for structuring the group process will be discussed. The phases of an individual group session which generally reflect process dynamics and developmental tasks in prototypical form will also be described. The chapter will conclude with a set of task related group activities.

Developmental Tasks: Seeds of Form and Function

Every group has a structure that develops and evolves during the course of the group forming and interacting through its life cycle. Landreth (1973) has pointed out that the question is not whether structure exists in groups but rather what kind of structure exists and how it is generated. Impetus for structure emanates from any number of sources alone or in combination.

> Leader personality, training and theoretical orientation, the focus and purpose of the group and the individual and collective nature of the group members all affect group structure. In addition, contemporary group process has been influenced by the evolution of group techniques and activities that are being used as structuring tools to implement and facilitate the group process. (Trotzer, 1979, p. 177)

These structural agents, however, require material to respond to for their impact to be realized in the group. That material is supplied by group dynamics of which developmental tasks are an integral part. Each stage of the group process has inherent tasks that depict the sequential nature of the group's development.

A developmental task is an objective, need, or responsibility that must be addressed in the group in order to insure therapeutic and constructive progress. As these tasks are dealt with effectively, the result is a stronger foundation for group interaction and an achieved readiness to continue the group process through closure. If inappropriately handled or ignored, these tasks can present obstacles that disrupt the group or become the basis for resistance that is detrimental to group development. Thus effective group interaction is contingent upon a structure that considers the developmental tasks as the group moves through its life cycle (Trotzer, 1979, pp. 179–80).

The interface between the structuring agents and the developmental tasks creates the actual form of the group and produces the function that the group serves in the lives of its members. The tasks are guideposts to which structural factors can relate in guiding, stimulating, and facilitating the group.

The developmental tasks corresponding to each group stage will now be described. Figure 5.1 graphically depicts the relationship among stages and tasks. A brief summary of each stage will precede explication of its developmental tasks (see also Table 4.1 Group Process and Problem Solving, p. 96 and Figure 10.1 Group guidance: Program development format, p. 367).

Group Process Stages				
Security	Acceptance	Responsibility	Work	Closing

```
D       S1. Getting Acquainted            ─────────────────────►
E       S2. Interpersonal Warm-Up          ─────────────────────►
V       S3. Setting Boundaries             ─────────────────────►
E       S4. Building Trust                 ─────────────────────►
L            A1. Personal Sharing          ─────────────────────►
O            A2. Giving Feedback           ─────────────────────►
P            A3. Building Group Cohesiveness ────────────────────►
M            A4. Accepting Self            ─────────────────────►
E            A5. Accepting Others          ─────────────────────►
N                 R1. Self-Assessment       ─────────────────────►
T                 R2. Recognizing Ownership ─────────────────────►
A                 R3. Building Responsibility ───────────────────►
L                 R4. Giving Respect        ─────────────────────►
                  R5. Doing a Fair Share    ─────────────────────►
                       W1. Problem Solving   ─────────────────────►
T                      W2. Mobilizing Group Resources ────────────►
A                      W3. Reality Testing   ─────────────────────►
S                           C1. Giving Support ──────────────────►
K                           C2. Addressing Unfinished Business ───►
S                           C3. Affirming and Confirming Growth ──►
                            C4. Saying Goodbye ────────────────────►
                            C5. Follow-Up     ─────────────────────►
```

Figure 5.1 Group process: Stages and development tasks.

As described in chapters 3 and 4 the group process is composed of five stages that reflect characteristics of our basic human needs, qualities of therapeutic and effective interpersonal relationships, and dynamics of problem solving. Each stage has certain traits that distinguish it, but its meaning and impact are evident only in terms of the total group process. Although leadership style, techniques, group purpose, and membership vary, these stages tend to emerge and evolve as part and parcel of most small group interactions (Trotzer, 1985).

Security Stage

The initial stage of the group process is characterized by feelings of discomfort common to forming interpersonal relationships in a new social environment. Group members are reluctant to interact because their presence in the group is contingent on some recognized purpose that requires personal vulnerability or accountability. The purpose of this stage is to develop an atmosphere in which members can relate without hesitancy and where discomfort is alleviated as trust develops. This stage is referred to as the security stage because it must account for each group member's need for psychological safety and initiate trust which is essential to therapeutic and constructive interaction and necessary for members to disclose personal problems or assets and become meaningful contributors.

The developmental tasks of the security stage collectively combine to accomplish the objectives of getting the group started, generating forming dynamics, and laying a foundation of trust which can be broadened and deepened as the group interacts. Four developmental tasks are identified for the security stage.

Task S1: Getting Acquainted

The goal of this task is to help group members make initial contact with one another and exchange basic information about each other. This task is particularly important when convening groups composed of members who do not know each other. Getting acquainted breaks the social ice of new relationships and provides a means by which members can begin to move toward one another in their relationships. It also enables members to begin to find their place in the group and alleviates some of the ambiguity associated with possessing little knowledge of the people with whom the individual member is interacting. As members become acquainted with each other, an important security plank is laid for relationship development between members.

Task S2: Interpersonal Warm-Up

This task relates to the period of time at the beginning of each group session that group members need to warm-up to one another and addresses the interpersonal stiffness that commonly pervades the reconnecting experience in groups. As such, its goal is similar to getting acquainted with more far reaching implications. Group members have social muscles that need to be warmed-up each time the group reconvenes. Group members need to have time to focus - to move from their lives outside the group to their experience in the group. Interpersonal warm-up enables them to do that. Group participants must be helped to get totally into the group in a way that does not precipitate undue stress and that alleviates the problems of jumping in too fast. Effective interpersonal warm-up allows members to get in touch with themselves, the group, and their confidence in the group and is essential to developing a sense of security.

Task S3: Setting Boundaries

Boundaries or ground rules serve an important security-giving function for members. By establishing guidelines under which the group will operate, members sense limits and expectations that remove much of the ambiguity associated with beginning groups. Boundaries also help the group members get a grasp on where they are, how they are expected to fit in, and what they can expect. The group environment becomes more predictable and thus more within the member's control. Boundaries also provide a focus for testing—sometimes producing storming dynamics and resistance—which in turn further clarifies the arena of interaction for members. Boundary formation may be addressed in several ways. Leaders may determine the ground rules and inform group members of them during pregroup screening and orientation interviews or during the initial group session. Or, leaders may give the group the task of developing the boundaries and ground rules for the group in the first group session. Some leaders use a combination of these two approaches identifying one or two critical boundaries and then relying on the group to flesh out the rest. A final method used most typically in growth, sensitivity, or encounter groups is to convene group interaction and address the task of boundary setting as the need arises. Whether group rules are established by the leader, developed by the group, or invoked as the need arises, they facilitate trust by providing members with concrete guidelines to govern their interaction. They are a form of protection and insurance against personal harm in the group, and they are the seeds from which group norms develop (see below for examples of counseling and therapy group ground rules).

Guidelines for Group Members

1. Let others know what your ideas are. What every member has to say is important. Sharing your thoughts and reactions with the group will stimu-

late other members and will help them to share what they are thinking about.

2. Ask questions. If you have a question or there is something you want to know more about, ask. There is no such thing as a stupid question in this group. Several other members probably want to know the same thing.

3. Don't do all the talking. Others want to participate also and they can't if you take too long to express your ideas.

4. Help other members participate. If someone looks as though he wants to say something but hasn't, encourage him or her to do so. You could say, "Joe, you look as though you'd like to say something." Silent members may especially need your support and encouragement to participate verbally. Don't overdo it. A member doesn't have to talk to be involved in what is going on.

5. Listen carefully to other members. Try to listen so intently that you could repeat what the other member has said to his or her satisfaction. You aren't listening effectively if you are thinking about what you are going to say when you get the chance. Give the other person's ideas a chance and try to understand what he or she is saying. Listen to him or her the way you would want him or her to listen to you.

6. Group members are here to help. Problems can be solved by working cooperatively together. In the process of helping others, you can help yourself. The information you have can be helpful to others. Suggesting alternatives or causes can help other members to make better decisions.

7. Be willing to accept another point of view. Don't insist that you are right and everyone else is wrong. The other person just might be thinking the same thing. Try to help other members understand you rather than trying to make them understand.

8. Keep up with the discussion. If the discussion is confusing to you, say so.

9. In this group it is okay to talk about your feelings and reactions.

From "Group Counseling: To Structure or Not to Structure," G. L. Landreth, *The School Counselor* (1973). Reprinted by permission.

Ground Rules for Group Sessions

1. Everyone who is here belongs here because he or she is here, and for no other reason. (This is our top rule. It depends on nothing else. Nothing changes it.)

2. For each person what is true is determined by what is in him or her, what he or she directly feels and finds making sense in him or herself and the way he or she lives inside him or herself.

3. Our first purpose is to make contact with each other; everything else we might want or need comes second.
4. We try to be as honest as possible and to express ourselves as we really are and really feel just as much as we can.
5. We listen for the person living and feeling inside.
6. We listen to everyone.
7. The group leader is responsible for two things only: he or she protects the belonging of every member, and he or she protects their being heard if that is getting lost.
8. Realism: if we know things are a certain way, we do not pretend they are not that way.
9. What we say here is confidential; no one will repeat anything said here outside the group, unless it concerns only him or herself. This applies not just to obviously private things but to everything. After all, if the individual wants others to know something, he or she can always tell them him or herself.
10. Decisions made by the group need everyone taking part in some way.
11. New members become members because they walk in and remain. Whoever is here belongs.

From "An Experiential Approach to Group Therapy," E. T. Gendlin and J. Beebe, *Journal of Research and Development In Education* (1968). Reprinted by permission.

How to Get the Most Out of Group

1. No matter how hard it may be for you, participate. You cannot make progress unless you get involved and allow yourself to experience your true feelings and reactions to others in the group. Question, challenge, say what you feel. Try to be as open and honest with yourself and others as you possibly can.
2. Make the group part of your life. In other words, don't think of group as something that happens one day and then forget about it until the next day. After the group session, think over what happened. What feelings did you feel when you talked about yourself? You may feel depressed or happy after group. Try to figure out why you are feeling this way. Take a few minutes to write these things down. Discuss it next group.
3. You are not in group to be tactful or popular. Be yourself whatever that takes. Show the group all sides of your personality.
4. Don't wait for a golden opportunity before you start talking or getting into your feelings. Make your own openings. Likewise, if you feel bored and think that the person who holds the floor is going nowhere, tell him or her so!

5. This is your group. If it is not moving in the direction you would like it to move, say so!

6. Try to move into areas that are emotionally uncomfortable to you, both inside and outside the group. You grow in your treatment only by going beyond the limits you have set for yourself in the past.

7. Experiment in and outside the group with new forms of behavior. Unless you start to act differently and take some risks, you will not change!

Therapy Group Ground Rules

1. Confidentiality: Everything shared and discussed in group remains in the group. Do not discuss content, observations, or reactions outside the group. Any discussion outside the group should pertain only to your self. All other discussions outside the group are breaches of confidentiality.

2. Contact Between Group Members: There is to be no contact in person or by telephone (or other electronic communication device, e.g., e-mail, voice mail, or Fax) between members outside the group. Any inadvertent or informal or formal contact must be reported to the group. Note: This ground rule pertains unless formally modified by the group and leader in the group

3. Purpose of the Group: Each person has been selected and invited to be a member of this group because he or she has both assets and issues. The intent of the group is to work on your issues and use your assets to help yourself and each other.

4. Content of the Group: Issues and content that brought you into this group may derive from the past, present, or future of your life, but will be addressed in a here and now context for the purpose of resolution, personal empowerment, and growth.

5. Group Attendance: Members must commit to a minimum of __#__ sessions and must make every effort to attend each session. In the event of an emergency that interferes with attendance, please call to inform the leader of your absence.

6. Charge for the Group: The charge for each group session is $_____. You may pay in advance or at each group session. Place your check or cash (clipped with your name) into the envelope that will be passed at the beginning of each session. No group time will be used to collect fees.

7. Group Time Frame: Each group session will be one and one-half hours (90 minutes) in length beginning at_____ and ending at_____ on _____ (day). Please plan to arrive a few minutes early so the group can begin promptly.

8. Responsibility of Group Members: It is the responsibility of each group member to participate in the group on the basis of awareness in the following areas:

a. Awareness of what you bring with you to the group.
b. Awareness of what is going on in you while in the group.
c. Awareness of what is going on with each group member as they share in the group; and
d. Awareness of what is going on in the group.
Participation is primarily through the vehicles of self-disclosure (personal sharing) and giving feedback.

9. Commitment of the Group Members: Each member is committed to interact as openly and honestly as possible in a context where each person's dignity, worth, and personal boundaries are respected.

I have read the above ground rules and agree to them as the basis for my participation in this therapy group conducted by (leader's name).

Signature_____

Task S4: Building Trust

The goal of this task is to help group members deal with the dynamic of trust in the group. It involves both experiencing and understanding trust as it pertains to interpersonal relationships in the group. Members must confront what is meant by trusting themselves and others and come to grips with where they are as both trusting and trustworthy individuals within the group. Members need to realize and be open to the developmental nature of trust as the foundation upon which risk taking in the group is based. Trust building, once initiated, is an ongoing task that, by necessity, must be continually responded to if the group is to develop an in depth personal quality to its interaction.

Acceptance Stage

The acceptance stage of the group process focuses on the development of group cohesiveness that is an outgrowth of our psychological need to belong. Caring and being cared about are essential therapeutic qualities in this stage because members need to experience acceptance as a total person before they are willing to disclose those parts of themselves that require change. As group cohesiveness develops, a supportive milieu is formed in which the norm of personal sharing is reinforced and where disclosing problems is an integral part of a total person perspective. The tasks associated with the acceptance stage are directed toward pulling the group together as a unit in which communication channels are opened and where members are experiencing belongingness, warmth and acceptance.

Task A1: Personal Sharing

The goal of this task is to establish self-disclosure as one of the primary means of interacting in the group. Personal sharing involves learning the skill of self-disclosing and the presentation of self as a total person including assets and liabilities. Individuals make choices to disclose or share either by invitation or personal initiative and that begins the process of letting the group know who they are. The information shared is that which they are in control of and generally involves some risk taking. Luft (1970) refers to this information as the *hidden* area of the person that in a relational context is subject only to that person's recall and choice relative to disclosure. This task is essential because it provides the main communication channel by which the group can come to know and understand its members. It is also the major means available to members to let others know who they are. Personal sharing is progressive in nature because the degree of self-disclosure increases within the context of group interaction provided conditions are supportive. Personal sharing opens the door for potential connectedness and closeness in the group, and paves the way for personal vulnerabilities and resources to emerge.

Task A2: Giving Feedback

The task of giving feedback is essential to the group process because it provides the communication channel whereby members can disclose their perceptions and observations about each other. It is also crucial to problem solving in the group context. Members need to learn the skill and precautions giving feedback (see Guidelines for Feedback, p. 38). Feedback is a means of increasing members' awareness and self-knowledge in that it taps into what Luft (1970) referred to as the *blind* area or things others know about us that we do not know. Like personal sharing, giving feedback involves risk taking and is progressive in nature as facilitated by conditions in the group. Giving feedback provides another major communication channel in the group that is necessary for a therapeutic or collaborative atmosphere to be realized and the group's resources to be mobilized in a constructive manner.

Task A3: Building Cohesiveness and Closeness

This task develops a positive relationship between group members by harnessing the power of peer influence to generate group cohesiveness. The goal is to achieve togetherness and identification with the group thus providing members with a sense of belongingness. It is based on helping members recognize similarities and common characteristics and falls in line with Gendlin and Beebe's (1968) concept that closeness must precede unmasking and the task group aphorism that connectedness precedes contribution. It is intended to help the group realize their relatedness and experience working together under the common bond of their group experience.

Task A4: Learning to Accept Self

The main point of this task is to help group members learn to accept themselves more readily through expression of their identity and characteristics in an atmosphere of support. As group members experience the acceptance of the group, they become more cognizant of their own selves and their own needs to accept themselves. This results in a greater feeling of self-confidence and self-worth and provides a stimulus to treat others in a like manner. It also makes members more open to considering vulnerabilities and looking at those aspects of self that are not as desirable with the intention of initiating a serious effort toward change.

Task A5: Learning to Accept Others

This task is important to the development of awareness and sensitivity among group members. Through the process of supportive listening, observing leader and member acceptance models, and risking one's own self through self-disclosure, members find their own feelings of worth are enhanced because others treasure and desire their acceptance. As members risk being open to and accepting of other members who are different from themselves, they realize the value of difference and diversity and the merit of differentiation.

In reality, these last two tasks are reciprocal in nature. Either can be the initial thrust but once in motion, the two become self-perpetuating. Therefore, groups often move quickly to a cohesive state once these two tasks have been addressed.

Responsibility Stage

The responsibility stage of the group process emerges from our psychological need for esteem (respect) that is acquired through responsible individual action and experiences in therapeutic relationships where individuals are perceived as worthwhile. Members move from an emphasis on acceptance of self and others to evaluating self and others in terms of ownership of behaviors, feelings, and thoughts and taking responsibility for one's own part in them. The problem-solving process is contingent on individuals recognizing responsibility for their own problems and group members making a commitment to help each other work to resolve them. As this occurs, the group moves into the working phase of the group process.

The responsibility stage tasks seek to generate individual commitment to the group in terms of willingness to be accountable for one's own behavior and to contribute responsibly to the group process.

Task R1: Self-Assessment

The focus of this task is to give members an opportunity to engage in self-evaluation as a means of identifying their own uniqueness, determining their assets and liabilities and defining their role in what ever issues they may have. The thrust of self-assessment is to focus on individualization and differentiation between members and to get members to view responsibility from an internal perspective. Members must realize that looking at oneself realistically is essential and that engaging in constructive self-criticism is healthy. In doing so, the foundation for responsible action is laid.

Task R2: Recognizing Ownership

Part of being responsible for self includes taking ownership of thoughts, feelings, and behaviors. The goal of this task is to help members adopt an internal frame of reference (i.e., internal locus of control) with respect to claiming their own actions. This is especially important in group problem solving because if members do not perceive themselves as contributors to their concerns and problems or resources to accomplishing the group's task, they will not view themselves as responsible for changing to resolve them or becoming contributing team members. If causes are viewed as external (someone else's fault), then cures will be perceived in the same manner.

Task R3: Experiencing and Building Responsibility

The main purpose of this task is to help members engage in actions that enable them take the initiative in being responsible as opposed to just telling them to be responsible. Since responsibility is so closely tied to self-worth, this task purports to enhance self-worth by helping members put themselves directly on the line relative to their interaction in and out of the group.

Task R4: Giving Respect

This task presents a balance to the self-oriented thrust of the responsibility stage. It is important as a means of checking the tendency of the group to encourage individuals to do their own thing even to the detriment of others. Giving respect entails recognizing other people's needs and rights in the process of attempting to meet one's own needs and claim one's own rights. This task asserts that mutual respect is an essential entity if different individuals are to grow in different directions with each other's help. Glasser (1965) has noted that the mark of a responsible person is being able to meet one's needs without depriving others of meeting their needs. This task assists members in their growth toward being responsible people.

Task R5: Doing a Fair Share

The goal of this task is to attain and actualize a commitment from individual members to help one another by serving as a constructive resource when another member is working on a problem or concern and by carrying a fair share of the responsibility in a work group. This task also provides a balancing effect that enables group members to continue to contribute their fair share to the therapeutic endeavors of others regardless of their own status at the time. This task has special impact because it teaches interdependency and collaboration and helps members realize a necessary balance between self-interest and social responsibility.

Work Stage

The purposes for which the group was formed, the relevance of the group to individual members and the relationship of individual members to the group task emerge as focal points in the work stage of the group process. In counseling and therapy groups the atmosphere and relationships in the group are such that individuals can examine personal concerns without fear of reprisal or rejection, explore alternatives for resolving problems, and experiment with new behaviors in a safe environment prior to risking changes in the outside world. Members participate in the interaction as both helpers and helpees and have the opportunity to engage in spectator therapy as they observe other members working on concerns that may be similar to their own. The leader, as both expert and facilitator, contributes to the process by encouraging members to be resources to persons working on their problems and by keeping the group in touch with reality. The work stage prepares group members for reentry into the world outside the group by arming them with well thought through plans, plausible skills or behaviors, and bolstered self-confidence. Emphasis is on implementation and integration of change, but not without the continued support of the group.

The primary purpose of the tasks in the work stage is to put the group to work on the collective and individual issues that brought the group into being.

Task W1: Problem Solving

The major goal of this task in therapeutic groups is to help members learn and experience the problem solving process. This process includes:

1. Identifying, clarifying, and understanding the problem;
2. Generating alternatives to resolving the problem (divergent thought processes, creative thinking, and brainstorming);
3. Evaluating alternatives (convergent thought processes, critical thinking, and reality testing);
4. Decision making (choosing a viable alternative);
5. Planning (developing a strategy for implementation);
6. Practice (trying out new behaviors in the social laboratory of the group);
7. Implementing (introducing changes into the world outside the group and reporting results and experiences to the group); and
8. Evaluating (determining if changes have resolved the presenting problem).

Task W2: Decision Making

This task is pivotal to the problem solving process because it transfers responsibility for initiative from the group to the individual in therapeutic groups and prompts a consensual process and product in task groups where individuals must contribute to the group's choice or strategy. The decision-making task provides opportunity for members to make decisions in their lives individually thereby facilitating empowerment and enables members to contribute to the synergy of group decision making. In one case, (therapeutic groups) the task translates group dynamics into personality dynamics (personal problem solving) and in the other (work groups) personality dynamics are translated into group dynamics (group problem solving).

Task W3: Learning and Applying Information and Skills to Personal Life

This task represents the practical, technical aspect of the group process wherein members acquire information and skills that relate to their personal lives or their role in the group as a team member. It is a particular emphasis in psychoeducation or guidance groups and has pragmatic relevance in training groups.

Task W4: Mobilizing Group Resources

The ultimate effectiveness of a group is determined by the extent to which resources of that group are utilized to achieve the best possible solution relative to individual needs and problems and the most efficient and effective strategy to accomplishing the purpose of the work group. The purpose of this task is to facilitate, mobilize and utilize the helper or resource role of group members making good use of their assets and expertise that encompass a broad range of life experiences, diversity, knowledge, wisdom and skills. Mobilizing group resources extends the helping potential of the group and is a means of enhancing the self-esteem of group members who realize their own value through giving assistance to others or contributing to the group's achievements.

Task W5: Reality Testing

The goal of this task is to make sure that the group engages in interaction that results in a realistic understanding of problems and their solutions. The importance of this task is tied to the fact that members must function effectively outside the group. Therefore, to promote the mental health of members, to increase the probability of constructive change occurring in their lives, and to come up with the most realistic approach to achieving the group's purpose, the group must act responsibly in terms of providing realistic feedback, alternatives, and information. If group members do not embrace this responsibility, they are acting in a manner detrimental to the therapeutic process and risk making decisions, formulating plans, or developing products that are destined to fail.

Closing Stage

Since the overriding objective of any therapeutic group experience is ultimately to dissolve the group by resolving the presenting concerns for which the group was organized, the closing stage serves a valuable transitional function. It is characterized by members actively pursuing change in their lives outside the group while still experiencing the support, encouragement, and accountability of the group. The members use the group as a sounding board and the group acts as a reinforcing and motivating agent. Once the individual has begun to experience success, either through external or internal means, and has begun to take credit for the change, termination is appropriate. Closure brings the group experience to an end by enabling members to be responsible for themselves, reinforcing changes that have occurred, and giving members help in moving smoothly back into the mainstream of their own lives. The basic objective of the closing stage tasks is to help members effectively conclude their group experience.

In task groups closure is signaled by the achievement of the purposes for which the group was formed either precipitating disbanding of the group or prompting it to formulate a new vision or purpose in the context of the organization in which it exists. Continuity is facilitated via a closure process that recognizes achievements, celebrates accomplishments, validates group members and the group and uses the closure process as a transition to springboard to the next project.

Task C1: Giving Support

In therapeutic groups the goal of this task is to give members psychological and emotional support during the period of time when they are implementing changes in their lives outside the group. This support may take the form of encouragement, reinforcement, or confrontation designed to foster positive action by members in their own environments. The intent is to provide support without creating dependency so that members can learn to function effectively on their own. Part of this task may include revising, substituting, or refining action plans to facilitate effective change in the member's life. The provision of support is necessary only until members have integrated the changes into their lives to the point of experiencing internal reinforcement and positive recognition from their environment. In task groups giving support refers to banding together to carry out strategic and action plans formulated in the group and holding one another accountable to follow though with assigned tasks.

Task C2: Addressing Unfinished Business

As groups move toward termination, unfinished business may emerge as a critical component of the ending process. Unfinished business issues may stem from a variety of sources, and how they are addressed carries significant weight in the overall effectiveness of the group. Notice that the unfinished business task is process oriented (*addressing*) rather than product oriented (*finishing*). It is generally improbable and unfeasible that all issues can be resolved before a group terminates but a valid and serious effort needs to be made to address them. This is particularly true of on-going task groups where carry-over of unfinished business can impede progress relative to the next project.

The source of unfinished business may be individual group members or the group process. Individuals may feel they still have unidentified issues on which to work or that their concerns have not been completely resolved. Interpersonal interactions within the group may produce unresolved relational issues and un-settling or uncomfortable events in the group's history may still need processing before the group can effectively end or move on.

The goal of this task is to allot time and energy to address unfinished busi-ness—whatever its source—as a means of clearing the way for termination.

Task C3: Affirming and Confirming Growth

The goal of this task is to review, summarize, and reinforce what has been learned and experienced through the process of group interaction. It builds self-confidence in members and generates a dependence on self rather than the group. Affirming growth relates to each member's self-disclosures of learning and change that have occurred as a result of group involvement. Confirming growth relates to group feedback acknowledging change in or contributions of individual members thus giving credence and value to the process of change and the result.

Task C4: Saying Goodbye

The goal of this task is to provide an opportunity for members to terminate their group experience. Saying goodbye provides a stepping off point at a time when ending may be difficult due to relational bonds forged in the group, time restrictions, or the particular focus of interactions in the group. It precipitates closure to the group experience when an individual leaves, a group session ends, or a group disperses and eases the transition of members back into their ongoing life experiences or the group into the next phase of its history.

Task C5: Follow-Up

This particular task is sometimes difficult to address effectively but is important if the impact of the group is to be minimally sustained. The goal is to make provision for post-group contact with group members for purposes of assessing whether changes that have been realized continue to be an integral part of group members' lives. Another feature of follow-up is as a stimulus to rekindle motivation to change and growth that may have receded since the group disbanded.

Structural Dynamics

The relationship between group process and group structure becomes clearer in the context of developmental tasks which elucidate the life cycle of a group. These tasks both substantiate and facilitate the group process and provide a focal point for the various factors that constitute structure. As groups proceed through the tasks of various stages, structural dynamics are revealed in different ways.

One or all of the structural dynamics noted may be operational in a group at any particular time. However, whether their impetus is purposes, leader, activities, members, or any combinations thereof, stage related developmental tasks provide a concrete conceptual basis for construing group process.

Natural Progression: Purpose Prompts Progression

Groups that have clearly defined and consensually agreed upon purposes move naturally through the various developmental tasks and stages en route to achieving their objectives. The impetus for this progression is the group's *purpose* but since groups have an inherent life cycle, the group interaction accounts for the tasks thus making both the process and the outcome therapeutic or constructive. In other words, purposes impose a structure that process carries out in order for those purposes to be effectively realized.

Note the Obstacles: Leader Prompts Progression

Impediments to developmental progress evident in a group at any one time are usually indicative of the stage the group is in and pinpoint tasks that need to be addressed to move the group forward. Identification of impasses, barriers, and resistances and initiating appropriate action to overcome them are the bailiwick of the group *leader*. For example, if the group is characterized by anxiety, suspicion and distrust, the leader might initiate or facilitate a focus on the developmental tasks of the security stage. If the group is grappling with pejorative dynamics, relational distancing or interpersonal friction, the leader might use the acceptance stage tasks as a basis for intervention. On the other hand, if the group has become too safe or to cohesive (i.e., no intrapersonal or interpersonal risks are being taken that might upset the equilibrium of the group or no effort is being made to address differences or underlying conflict), then the leader would be wise to introduce a focus based on the responsibility stage tasks. In the performance or action stage the group may stall in the planning or implementation phases thus prompting the leader to introduce interventions that relate to problem solving or work stage tasks. And finally, if the group is dragging its feet trying to hang on rather than move on to transition or dissolution, leader prompts related to the closure stage tasks are appropriate. Thus the leader's impact on structure materializes.

Structuring the Group Process: Tools/Techniques Prompt Progression

Group leaders can control or influence the sequence and flow of group interaction by using the developmental tasks as the basis for selecting group *activities*. These activities are incorporated directly into the group process and create a structure that has conceptual validity. Chapter 13 on using communication activities in groups goes into detail relative to this particular focus emphasizing how structured exercises can be used to initiate, facilitate and culminate progress in groups.

Member Motivation: Members Prompt Progression

Each individual group member's drive toward self-enhancement or desire for accomplishment often surfaces as the motivating force to move the group along in the developmental process. Boredom or frustration among members stuck in one place in the group process, pain of individual problems that need attention, individual enthusiasm to grow and learn or simple dedication to getting the job done will stimulate *members* to press the issue of structure in order to deal with appropriate developmental tasks that will help the group progress. In this case the impetus for developmental progress will come from the members who assert their energy to address the process and content issues of the group.

Individual Group Sessions

Each individual group session represents in prototypical fashion the overall group process and elements of developmental tasks that pertain to the stage of development the group is in as well as certain tasks that pervade the entire group process. As such, each session is a picture in miniature of the total process. At the same time it is a step in the evolution of that process. Just as the life cycle of a group has stages, a group session has sequential phases that are distinguishable. These phases evolve and merge as the group interacts, but in most cases they are evident to some degree in each session. Acknowledging, understanding, and accounting for these phases will enhance the group process and facilitate the most effective interactive pathway for the group to follow. The basic phases of each session are as follows:

1. Energizing phase;
2. Advance organizing phase;
3. Working phase;
4. Processing phase; and
5. Closing phase.

Each will be elaborated upon identifying key characteristics and developmental tasks that pertain to each phase and its role, purpose, and focus relative to the group process (Trotzer, 1980).

The phases of a group session as described in this section can be used as a cognitive overlay for groups at any point in the group process. Doing so enables the group leader to maintain a balanced perspective of both the overall group process and the specific events of a particular session. This produces a flexibility and dynamism that avoids the errors of not seeing the forest for the trees (getting myopic with regard to a specific group session) and not seeing the trees for the forest (missing the specificity and importance of individual group sessions in the overall process). Thinking of a group meeting in terms of phases also assists the group leader in planning group sessions.

Energizing Phase: Mobilizing Group Energy

The energizing phase is the period of time at the beginning of each group meeting that is used to get members *connected or reconnected* to each other and the group. It is the timeframe during which group members shift focus from their lives outside the group to their experience in the group. During the early stages of the group process, this phase is closely related to the Getting Acquainted task but throughout the group process it is related to the Interpersonal Warm-Up task and serves the purpose of mobilizing group member energy.

The transition from outside the group to inside the group is always an important issue each time a group assembles. Kassera and Kassera (1979) pointed out that leaders can facilitate more effective beginnings if they make an effort to recognize and respond to the dynamics involved in initiating a group interaction. For example, activities called *energizers* can be used to facilitate contact between group members and prepare them for interacting with one another and tuning in to the focus of the group session. Research supports the idea of using energizing activities in the early stages of group development and the beginning phase of group sessions (McMillon, 1994; Hetzel, Barton, & Davenport, 1994; Stockton, Rohde, & Haughey, 1994; Schechtman, 2001; Conyne & Horne, 2001).

The key goals of the energizing phase are to stimulate a here and now perspective and generate a present oriented readiness to concentrate on the tasks and experiences of the group session. This phase is primarily one in which members clear their minds of distractions and attain an ingroup focus laying the groundwork for the advance organizing phase. Initially, and at certain resistance points in the group process, the energizing phase may be extended to as long as 15 to 30 minutes but once the group is formed beyond the security stage, the time needed for members to clear their minds and connect with each other is generally reduced to 5 to 10 minutes.

Advance Organizing Phase: Directing Group Energy

The initial struggle of any learning effort is to connect the attention of the learner to the material to be learned. This is particularly crucial to the personal learning involved in therapeutic or psychoeducation groups and the corporate agenda in work groups. If something can be done to trigger curiosity, invoke relevance, stimulate interest, or enhance motivation, the whole process of learning is accelerated and becomes more exciting and engaging. The advance organizing phase of a group session is the period of time during which the group moves from being in the group to being *involved* in the group. While the energizing phase serves to energize individual members and connect them with the group and each other, the advance organizing phase serves to direct that energy and connect the group to the focus for which the group was convened.

The advance organizing phase is an ingroup transition phase in which members' interests are aroused and connected to the theme, purposes, and business of the group. Advance organizers designed to prepare members for involvement or set a group agenda are helpful in this phase. For example, many groups use go-rounds to identify topics, problems and issues that members wish to discuss during the session as a means of planning the agenda for the session and allocating time.

Developmental tasks of the various stages often surface as content areas during the advance organizing phase. Issues such as trust, cohesiveness, or accountability/responsibility may be raised as the group works on making itself a more therapeutic or collaborative environment. Once the group is fully operational, however, the tasks of the work stage tend to predominate as members focus on problem solving or accomplishing the objectives of the group.

Except for periods when the group is at an impasse or when resistance emerges either in the form of process obstacles or member's obstructing their own progress, the advance organizing phase of a group session tends to be brief and concrete, signaling the group to get down to business. Consequently, the tasks of the responsibility stage are often reflected in this phase of the group session.

Working Phase: Activating Group Energy

The working phase is the heart of a group session. Whether the work is process work (dealing with the forming process of the group) or content work (dealing with the purposes for which the group was formed and problems of individual members), this phase carries the most weight both in terms of time and effort. Here again, the developmental tasks of the stage the group is in are reflected in the work being done. The members are *activated to and engaged in* addressing the agenda items created in the advance organizing phase and the group uses its energy to do the therapeutic work or task work it was formed to do. In counseling groups, members work on problems, try out solutions, practice skills, and generally use the group as a social laboratory for problem solving. In task groups, members apply themselves to the strategic or action plans regarding the group's objectives and set about directing the program or developing the product for which the group is responsible. Or, they may focus on themselves as persons or the group as an entity as in the case of training workshops that are integrated into the life of the group to enhance its productivity and improve its process. Either way, the group is activated in the working phase, and the tasks of the work stage are typically reflected.

Processing Phase: Recycling Group Energy

The processing phase of a group session is complementary to but distinct from the working phase. It has meaning because of what occurs in the working phase, but adds an invaluable dimension to the work because it *consolidates, validates,* and *integrates* the learning that has taken place. The processing phase is the time period near the end of each session in which the group reviews or reflects back on what occurred in the session. It recycles the energy of the group by shifting emphasis from the hands on, experiential work of the session with its affective nature and pragmatic emphasis to the integrative work with its cognitive bearing. Processing may be directed at either the group's functioning or the individual members' efforts or both. In other words, it may focus on content or process or both. The closing stage tasks of giving support, unfinished business, and affirming and confirming growth are reflected in the processing phase.

The processing phase is a first step in detaching from the group experience as the group and its members step back to look at themselves and their efforts. As they do so, a shift occurs from being experientially engaged to being cognitively engaged. Processing is essential because it helps members summarize, personalize, and generalize what they have learned about the group, each other, and themselves. During this phase members synthesize and apply their group experience making it a more integral part of their lives and become more invested in the group.

A typical tool of the processing phase is the *go-round* in which members share their reactions, insights, and perspectives on the group experience. The timeframe tends to be relatively brief, normally 5 to 15 minutes, but under certain circumstances this can be extended. Certain events in the group or particularly crucial incidents may require extensive processing for the group or certain individuals. Under such circumstances processing may dominate a significant portion of the session. In more structured groups where agenda items direct the work phase, processing may be interspersed during the course of the session after each item on the agenda has been addressed. However, the typical case is for processing to be relatively brief serving as a springboard for the closing phase of a session.

Closing Phase: Redirecting Group Energy

The closing phase deals with the dynamics of leaving a group session. Just as starting is an issue at the beginning of a session, closing is an issue at the end. The closing phase should provide a meaningful transition from the world inside the group to the world outside the group by winding down the group energy and *redirecting* individual member energy to their life beyond the group. It should aid and facilitate leaving, opening the door for members to reconnect with their world outside the group, but should also project their thoughts toward the next session. As such, closing is a delicate process because it is done under time constraints (most groups have a scheduled ending time), but it must account for the past, present, and future in some way. Helping members reconnect with their lives without carrying disturbing unfinished business from the group and positively anticipating the next session is no small assignment. Yet, the closing phase is designed to do just that. One of the biggest mistakes made by group leaders is to not plan for or not set time aside for closing. Allowing time constraints, agenda pressures, or individual member schedules to dictate closing undermines the valuable role that the closing phase plays in the effective and efficient continuity of the group.

The developmental tasks of the closing stage (such as saying goodbye) are activated in this phase. Although closing tends to be brief, it is significant. Left unattended or mishandled, it can seriously jeopardize therapeutic or constructive progress. Structured activities and closing rituals are helpful in handling this phase. In addition, some leaders add a feedback or evaluation component to closing to assist them in thinking about and planning future group sessions.

Learning Activities

In this section learning activities are organized sequentially with regard to developmental tasks of the group process described in this chapter. Activities have been related to each task or to a group of tasks to exemplify how structured activities can be used to address specific group tasks. However, remember that activities themselves may be utilized flexibly and related to other tasks as well. In addition, keep in mind that other structuring agents (leaders, purposes, members, etc.) may address the tasks without using structured activities.

Learning Activities for Security Stage

Task S1: Getting Acquainted

Personality Profile Pass out a 3 × 5 card and pencil to each group member informing them that this is their personality profile. Ask members to congregate in the center of the room with their cards and pencils. Explain that they will have to make a series of choices that will reflect the characteristics of their personality. They are to first make their choice by physically moving to one side of the room or the other as traits are identified and then record their choice on the card. Present the following (or other) polarity choices to the group using the directive: "If you are more like (insert word) move to the right side of the room, and if you are more like (insert word) move to the left side of the room."
    Ground rules:

1. A choice must be made (no middle ground).
2. All choices are final.
    Polarity samples:

flower—rock	heart—brain
night—day	work—play
steak—hamburger	mountain—valley
think—feel	push—pull
anger—hurt	thunder—lightning
lake—river	together—alone
talk—listen	early—late
lead—follow	spontaneous—deliberate
hug—handshake	mall—mail order catalog
Internet—cell phone	L.L. Bean—Victoria's Secret

(Use at least 10 varied polarity choices to create a profile of traits)

After the choices have been made, instruct members to circle the five choices most descriptive of their personality. Have them study their own profiles for a minute or two and then write a narrative personality description on the back of the 3 × 5 card.

Have group members share the five choices and their reasons for selecting them as a way of getting acquainted with each other. (If the group is large, this can be done in subgroups of three to four members). Close the sharing by having each person read their personality statement.

Name Saying Split the group in half forming two concentric circles facing each other. Using the statement, "My name is _____," have the outer circle members rotate around inner circle members introducing themselves to each other. Repeat this rotation four times alternating, having the outer circle move and the inner circle move. Each time, create a different demeanor for presenting the introduction.

Examples: Introduce yourself by expressing the introductory statement:

1. Casually (laid back)
2. Very formally (formal occasion like meeting the President of the United States)
3. Lovingly (like you want to sweep the person off his or her feet)
4. Angrily (like you are irritated or angry at the person)

This activity is useful for groups who have never met before and tends to be a tension breaker as well as starts the process of getting to know each other's names.

Task S2: Interpersonal Warm-up

Balloon Game Assemble the group in a circle holding hands. Present them with the task of keeping a balloon aloft without letting go of each other's hands and without letting the balloon hit the floor or get away from the group. Once they seem to be mastering the task, add a second, third, and fourth balloon until the group is in chaos. Process the activity in light of group dynamics. This activity not only warms people up, but accentuates the working together dimension of the group and serves as a metaphor for the complications of dealing with the varied concerns of the group members or multiple tasks that work groups must address.

Place and Space Activity As an initiating activity, have group members mill around the room without talking, trying to find a comfortable place in the room in relation to the other members. Allow enough time for members to experiment with different places and spaces. Once the group has formed up in a solidified manner, have members explain how they arrived at their place and space. Reassemble the group and process the activity in light of group dynamics.

Task S3: Setting Boundaries

List of Group Rules Activity Have each group member create a list of rules they think are important/necessary for the group to be effective. Have them place a star by those rules that they believe are a necessity for them to feel at ease in the group. Have members share their lists and personal requirements as a means of addressing the formation of ground rules for the group.

Create Your Own Ground Rules Present the group with the task of devising a set of ground rules for the group. This activity is best conducted over two sessions where the first produces the basic rules and the second refines, redefines, adds, or deletes rules so that the group has a set of workable guidelines. The rules generated also may be periodically reviewed as a means of evaluating the group atmosphere and keeping the group on target therapeutically and constructively.

Task S4: Building Trust

Anonymity Bag One of the reasons people keep things inside is because they don't know how people will respond to what they think or feel. Therefore, they choose not to say anything because they would be personally accountable and possibly vulnerable. This activity is designed to provide an anonymity cushion so members can get a sense of how the group will respond to their input without having to directly risk putting themselves on the line.

Have group members write down anonymous statements about what they think, feel, and believe about themselves, the group, someone else in the group, the leader or the group's task. These statements are placed in a bag. The statements can be processed in one of two ways.

> *Leader Processing*: The leader selects a statement from the bag, reads it to the group and facilitates a discussion regarding the statement.
> *Member Processing*: The bag is passed around and each member draws out a statement making sure it is not his or her own. In turn, each member reads the statement to the group and gives his or her reaction or opinion as to its meaning and relevance. This process continues until all statements have been discussed.

I Can Hardly Believe It Using the stimulus statement, "Something I find hard to believe about myself is_____," invite group members to disclose elements of themselves that (1) they are not really sure are a part of their person, and (2) they would not usually risk saying are a part of who they are. Create a risk inviting atmosphere by making the activity light, experimental, and fun. Encourage the sharing idea of ideals, fantasies, and exaggerations about themselves that members often toy with in their minds, but tend not to disclose. After sharing, process the information in relation to each person's goals, problems, desires for change, or role in the group.

Learning Activities for Acceptance Stage

Task A1: Personal Sharing

Who Am I Hierarchy Pass out five 3 × 5 cards to each group member. On each card members are to write different responses to complete the statement, "I am a person who _____." Once they have the five cards completed, have them rank the cards based on the importance of each statement to them as persons (1 = most important, 5 = least important). Process the activity in the group by having each member share their statements starting with number five and working up to number one. They are to share the statement and then comment on, "What life would be like if that statement was not part of who I am." This activity serves as a means of identifying and appreciating qualities in a person relative to resources they bring to the group and pinpointing areas that may benefit from work in the group.

5 × 8 Sharing Pass out 5 × 8 cards to each member. Have them draw a diamond in the center of the card dividing it into four corner sections. Have them write their name in the center of the diamond. Then have them complete the following statements in each of the areas of the card designated by the instructions:

> Upper left corner: I am . . .
> Upper right corner: I worry about . . .
> Lower left corner: I am here because . . .
> Lower right corner: By the end of the group I will . . .

When the task is completed have group members share their statements either sequentially using one stem at a time or by having each member share their entire card. Process relative to the dynamics and purpose of the group.

Task A2: Giving Feedback

OTINAY and MIOYI Introduce this activity by writing one of the above combinations of letters (acronyms) on the board explaining that it stands for an ancient oriental ritual that is eminently growth producing. The letters stand for one of the following phrases:

"*O*ne *T*hing *I* *N*oticed *A*bout *Y*ou..." and
"*M*y *I*mpression *O*f *Y*ou *I*s..."

Using one of these statements, have group members engage in a feedback activity either by designating one person at a time to be the focal point or doing it spontaneously until all members have given and received feedback. These terms sometimes become symbolic and members may ask for feedback or for permission to give feedback by referring to OTINAY or MIOYI at any point in the group process.

Making The Shoe Fit Have group members remove one of their shoes and place it in a pile in the center of the group. Each member selects a shoe other than their own and puts it on (actually or symbolically). Their task is to explain what they perceive it is like to be the person whose shoe they have on.

A variation of this activity is to have members remove both shoes and exchange them with another group member. This activity called *Walk a mile in my shoes* requires that each person become the person whose shoes they are wearing for a significant amount of time. This activity is very useful as a feedback exercise after the group members have gotten to know each other fairly well and can carry out the other person's role in the group in a realistic manner for a reasonable period of time.

Task A3: Building Cohesiveness and Closeness

2-Foot Square This energizer draws attention to the importance of cohesiveness and closeness with respect to working together effectively as a group. Using masking tape or chalk, mark out a square on the floor that is smaller than a group can easily fit into (a 2-foot square is an approximate size for a six to eight person group). Inform the group that their task is to get everyone inside the square with no physical part touching the floor outside the designated area. If the group is outdoors, a stump or stone can be used for the same purpose. Tell the group you will not help them in any way, but you will determine if and when they have succeeded. Give the group sufficient time to accomplish the task and then process it in light of the group dynamics involved in completing the task and generalizing to the developmental dynamics of the group.

Group Recipe Have each group member write two ingredients (on separate slips) that they believe they contribute to the group. Place these ingredients in a bag. Process this activity in two steps:

1. Draw out the slips ingredient by ingredient writing them on a white board or newsprint. As each ingredient is drawn, the group gives feedback on why that ingredient is important to a group. Optional: The group may also guess who supplied the ingredient as a means of affirming the person who contributed it.

2. When all the ingredients are listed, have the group discuss what the result of their group recipe is. Members can be asked to write a summary description of the group as a means of initiating discussion, as a home work task to be read the next session as a group opener or as a closing group summary.

Task A4 and A5: Learning to Accept Self and Others

Attitudes Toward Self and Others Activity The following activity combines the acceptance of self and others tasks and uses self-disclosure as the interactive mechanism. Pass out an 8½×11 sheet of paper and pencil to each group member. Divide the sheet into two columns labeling them *self* and *others*. Further divide each column in half to create four quadrants. Finally, divide the upper quadrant of each column into two columns so the sheet of paper looks like the example shown in Figure 5.2 (this activity is facilitated if a prepared sheet containing the design and information is passed out to the group).

In the two columns under *self* place the stems "I like these things about me..." and "I dislike these things about me..." Have group members list those things they like and dislike about themselves in the respective columns.

In the two columns under *others* write the stems "I am attracted to people when..." and "I am turned off to people when..." Have group members list those things that attract them to people and turn them off to people in their respective columns.

In the bottom quadrant of each column have the group members write two paragraphs. Under the *self* column they are to start the paragraph with "I am a person who..." and use all the information from the like and dislike lists. Under the *others* column they are to start their paragraphs with "My attitude toward others is..." and use all the information from the attracted to and turned off lists.

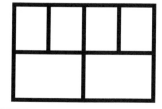

Figure 5.2

When the members have completed their lists and paragraphs, have them share their observations about themselves and others by reading their paragraphs. Start with the *self* paragraphs and then move on to the *others* paragraphs. Facilitate interaction using their self-disclosures to further address the acceptance tasks in the group process.

Learning Activities for Responsibility Stage

Task R1: Self-Assessment

Creating Your Own Birthday Celebration One of the ways to teach and experience the task of self-assessment is to provide group members with choices they have to prioritize according to their own interests, values, and inclinations. (This activity was demonstrated by Sydney Simon in a values clarification workshop attended by the author.) Pass out two sheets of 8½ ×11 paper to each person. Have them fold the two sheets so that each sheet has 12 sections (fold in half then in half again to produce quarters. Fold quarter size sections into thirds so that when you open the sheets you will have 12 sections). Direct members to number the sections consecutively 1–12 on one sheet and then tear or use a scissors to cut the second sheet into 12 separate sections. Introduce the activity with the following instructions:

> You are going to have a birthday and you must decide what you want to do to celebrate it. I will give you your choices one at a time. Write a key word or phrase on one of your 12 slips and place it on your numbered sheet starting with number one. As each choice is given you may rearrange your choices.

Present the following presents or activities the person could choose for their birthday (key word or phase is in italics):

1. Have someone write a *poem* in honor of your birthday.
2. Receive an *expensive necessity* as a present.
3. Have a number of people give you *precious validations* confirming your importance and worth as an individual.
4. Slips of paper with *personal messages* hidden around the house (one for every year of your life).
5. Gifts of *socks* and *underwear* or *panties* and *pantyhose*.
6. Receive *homemade gifts*.
7. Have your *birthday ignored*.
8. *Cake, ice cream,* and *candles* to celebrate.
9. *Surprise party.*
10. *Coupons of Time*: someone gives you coupons that you can redeem for extra time when you need it.

11. Have a *week-long celebration*.
12. Gift of a *body tattoo or piercing*.

Optional Item: *Write your own* (have each person write their own idea for how they would celebrate).

When members have completed their prioritizing, have them share and explain their top three or four choices.

This activity can be adapted to any group situation where priorities are involved. Simply construct 11 items that fit the situation and present them one at a time and add a "write your own" item. It can be helpful in assessing motivational factors, (why people want to be in a group, part of a program, or picked for a position), identifying problems and planning agendas (what should be addressed first), and identifying key functions or roles that are part of a job description.

Tasks R2 Through R5: Responsibility Stage Tasks

One activity can often be designed to address more than one developmental task. In fact, structured activities by their very nature tend to incorporate more than one task. The following example is an activity that addresses all the developmental tasks of the responsibility stage in the context of one structured experience.

Diamond and 4 Activity or Boxed In Instructions for members (Trotzer, 2001):

1. Draw a large diamond in the center of an 8½ × 11 sheet of paper or pass out the design (shown in Figure 5.3).
2. In the diamond or box, write a brief description of a problem you have been unable to resolve or something you have always wanted to do, but haven't been able to.
3. On each side of the diamond write a brief description of an obstacle or barrier that has stood in the way of solving your problem or doing what you want to do (identify four barriers or obstacles).

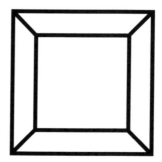

Figure 5.3

4. Divide the group into subgroups of at least four members. (If the group is small enough and time allows, the following steps can be completed using the entire group.)
5. Processing the material (this is a timed activity).
   a. Member 1: Spend 60 seconds describing to the group the problem and the obstacles. (1 minute)
   b. Group members: Member #1 turns his or her back to the group and listens as the remaining group members discuss the problem or situation and seek to identify ways of overcoming the obstacles or barriers. (2 minutes)
   c. Member/group interaction: The member and the group discuss the ideas that have been generated relative to the problem. (3 minutes)
   d. Repeat the sequence with each member in the group.

Evidence of the responsibility stage developmental tasks are as follows:

Instructions 1 through 3: Self-Assessment (R1)
Instruction 5: Recognizing Ownership (R2), Giving Respect (R4) and Doing a Fair Share (R5)
Instructions 1 through 5: Experiencing and Building Responsibility (R3)

The *strength bombardment activity* described in chapter 4, pages 125–126, is another activity that lends itself well to integrating the tasks of the responsibility stage.

Concentric Contributions This activity explores the personality factors that individual members bring to the group enabling them to self-assess and recognize ownership of traits and also informs the group of the traits that are operational in the group. (This activity is adapted from Guth, 2001.)
Instructions:
Create a design of four concentric circles (see Figure 5.4) using masking tape or drawing on the ground if conducted outdoors. Provide each person with a 3 × 5 card on which to write the trait and the degree of identification with it (e.g., 4, 3, 2, 1, etc.).

Figure 5.4

1. Have the group members stand around the outside of the circles.
2. One by one provide the stimulus word trait and have each person locate himself/herself relative to that trait by moving into the circle to the degree that he/she believes it represents who he/she is (e.g., 4 - outer circle to 1 – inner circle). After writing the trait and the degree of identification on the 3 × 5 card, each person returns to the outer circle before the next stimulus is given.

List of Traits (Use for therapeutic or task groups)

Extrovert	Introvert	Planner	Feeling oriented
Collaborative	Independent	Adaptable	Thought oriented
Perceptive	Bossy	Sociable	Self-confident
Responsible	Energetic	Calm	Achievement driven
Dependable	Enthusiastic	Direct	Supportive

As a group process the experience in terms of individual perceptions and perception of the group.

Learning Activities for Work Stage

Tasks W1 through W3

Reality Therapy Problem Solving Glasser's (1965; Glasser & Wubbolding, 1995; Wubbolding, 1991) reality therapy approach translates into six basic steps that adapt nicely to the developmental tasks of the work stage. The following steps can be taught to the group and used as an agenda for personal problem solving.

1. *Wants (W)*: What do you want? The group member describes generally and specifically what he or she wants in life immediately and long term.
2. *Direction and Doing (D)*: What are you doing? The group member describes what he or she is doing in a particular circumstance or relationship and how he or she acts.
3. *Evaluation (E)*: Is what you are doing helping or hurting you? The group member evaluates whether or not what they are doing is resulting in the kind of experience desired. (If yes, stop or start over; if no, go on to Step 4.)
4. *Planning (P)*: Can we work out a plan to make your life more successful? Focus group resources on helping the group member develop a plan that will successfully resolve his or her problem.
5. *Commitment*: Will you commit to the plan? Obtain a personal commitment from the group member to carry out the plan.

6. *Persistence*: No excuses; no punishment; no withdrawal. Hold the person accountable to their commitment, revising the plan if necessary to ensure success. Respect the person's efforts but accept no excuses for not following through on the commitment.

All work stage developmental tasks are addressed in the context of this activity format. A method of problem solving is taught and used by group members. The *WDEP* steps directly mobilize group resources and reality testing is built into Step 3 (evaluation) and Step 4 (planning) via the criteria of improving one's life and making it more successful.

Learning Activities for Closing Stage

Task C1: Giving Support

Gift Giving As a closing activity inform group members they will be exchanging gifts as part of the last group session. Have them think of a gift they would like to give each group member as that person leaves the group and goes on with their life. Gifts may take any shape or form and may be concrete or abstract, but each gift should in some way be related to the work that person had done in the group.

Gifts may be exchanged either spontaneously with members picking individual gifts off their gift list until all gifts have been exchanged or one person at a time may be designated as the receiver or giver depending on the inclination of the group. Create a festive atmosphere for this activity.

Task C2: Addressing Unfinished Business

The Unfinished Business Card A tool to assist group members in addressing unfinished business that stems from interaction between individual members in the group is the Unfinished Business Card. Distribute the card (as depicted in Figure 5.5) to group members several sessions (two or three) prior to the group's designated termination session. Have them place the name of each member in the Group Member column and a brief description of any Unfinished Business they believe they have with any member. The Contact column refers to whether time and attention were devoted to the unfinished business, and the Status column indicates whether the unfinished business was completed or left incomplete as the group ends.

The card may be used solely to stimulate group members to think about unfinished business with the initiative to address the unfinished business left up to the members, or specific time can be allocated in the final sessions to deal with the input from the cards. Either way, do not expect that all unfinished business between members will be addressed before the group ends.

Group Member	Unfinished Business	Contact	Status	
			Complete	Incomplete
1.				
2.				
3.				
4.				
5.				
6.				
7.				
8.				
9.				
10.				
11.				
12.				

Figure 5.5 Unfinished business card.

Task C3: Affirming and Confirming Growth

Rock, Scissors, Paper (adapted) The old game of rock, scissors, paper involves two people who, on the count of three, flash a hand signal: fist for rock, flat hand for paper, and two fingers separated in a V for scissors. The sequence of ascendance is:

1. Paper covers rock,
2. Rock crushes scissors, and
3. Scissors cuts paper.

The winner gets rewarded. Using this game, have group members pair off for the purpose of disclosing what they have gained from or contributed to the group (affirming personal growth) and giving their partner feedback as to how he or she was perceived to grow or contribute in the group (confirming personal growth). The person who wins the game gets to go first disclosing their own growth or change and receiving feedback. Their partner goes second. Rotate partners until each group member has been paired with every other group member. Process the activity as a group focusing on how the group has impacted upon group members' lives.

Task C4: Saying Goodbye

Annual Signing Party As a closing activity, fashion booklets out of four sheets of 8½ × 11 paper cut in half lengthwise, folded, and stapled in the center. Each member is given a booklet and asked to design their own cover representing the group. Have each member place their name on the front of the booklet accompanying their designs. Booklets can then be exchanged for group members to write in, reflecting on their view of the person and the group experience. This activity works well if the group is inclined to close with a commencement atmosphere or celebration. Allot time for the members to write in each other's books as a lead in to closing.

Circle For Closure This activity is specifically designed as a final group experience. Have group members form a circle with arms locked around each other. Ask members to share brief thoughts about the group in either a go-round or spontaneous manner. When completed, have members silently make eye contact with each group member signaling acknowledgment and goodbye nonverbally. When eye contact has been made with each person, have members close their eyes. Using guided imagery, verbally instruct the group to visualize the group's history and their own part in it. Have them visualize each group member and think a specific thought about that person. Finally, have them think about themselves and their experience in the group.

At this point have the group drop their locked arms position (eyes still closed) and clasp hands. Introduce the idea of closure by informing the group the time has come for the group to end. Have members drop hands to their sides and take an about face. Instruct them to say goodbye to the group in their minds. Ask them to think about what is coming up for them in their lives in the next few days or weeks. Have them think specifically about what they will be doing next (after the group). Instruct them to take one step forward (away from the group circle), open their eyes and go about their business.

Task C5: Follow-Up

A Letter To Myself This terminating activity can be used to extend the impact of the group and serves to remind group members about changes they have made or plans they intend to carry out. During the last session of the group have members write letters to themselves in which they state where they would like to be with regard to their goals or problems at some future date (one month hence or six months, etc.). Then have group members address and seal envelops with their letters in them and turn them over to the group leader who serves as the sender. As a group agree on a sending date. Variations of this activity could involve follow up phone calls, individual interviews, or a reconvening of the group by the group leader.

6
Group Leader

The most important task of a group leader is to get all of the members on the same page. The second most important task is to keep them there. (Ben Cohn aphorism)

The objective of this chapter is to describe and delineate the qualities, skills, and functions of effective group leaders. The inherent difficulty in this task is related to the wide variety of characteristics that can be attributed to effective leadership. This variability is the result of differences in leader personalities as well as divergent training programs, philosophies, and theories. The diversity in member personalities and the varied purposes for which groups are formed also must be considered in discussing successful leadership. Therefore, any effort to describe the perfect leader would be a useless academic exercise and have little relevance because of its nearsightedness. Describing basic tendencies that seem to have commonality among effective leaders and discussing a broad range of leadership traits, skills, functions, and issues seems to be a more plausible manner of accomplishing the stated objective of this chapter. In this way, the prospective leader can assess the information in light of her or his own personality, theoretical convictions and philosophy of group work.

This chapter includes such topics as the personality of the group leader, training for group leadership, leader skills and functions, basic issues in group leadership, and special considerations for the group leader. It also includes suggested activities for obtaining supervised leadership experience that is so imperative in developing expertise in group work and concludes with learning activities that focus on leadership dynamics and characteristics.

Personality of the Group Leader

In any treatise on effective therapeutic intervention, whether in the form of psychiatry, psychotherapy, or counseling, with individuals or in groups, the one overriding characteristic that is discussed repeatedly is the personality of the individual who is cast in the helping role. This is only logical since the service performed is basically a human service and therefore remains just out of reach of empirical and laboratory controls that could mechanize the process. Although this is true, it raises some difficult problems in distinguishing who the most effective helpers are and what qualities describe them (Stockton & Morran, 1982; Stockton, Morran, & Velkoff, 1987). This same problem confronts leaders and trainers in group work.

The professional literature is replete with articles and books that stress personal characteristics as the most important aspect of a counselor's ability to perform professionally (Corey, 1995; Corey & Corey, 2002; Mahler, 1969; Yalom, 1995). Since each individual is unique, he or she brings to the counseling role his or her own particular capacities and incapacities that enhance or deter the therapeutic process. To know which traits are assets and which are liabilities the counselor must engage in an introspective process to attain the knowledge that will help him or her decide which qualities to use, which to modify or develop, and which to circumvent. Therefore, the first characteristic of an effective leader is *self-awareness*. Self-awareness or self-knowledge is the very personal education that enables us as persons and leaders "to listen to almost anything without losing our temper or our self-confidence" (Robert Frost).

Self-awareness is important because the group leader influences the nature of the group. How the leader acts determines to a great extent how the group will respond. Leaders must know what qualities about themselves make them attractive to the group. They must know how they influence others and how others affect them. Mahler (1969) pointed out that awareness of one's self and one's personality must involve "knowing strengths, weaknesses, conflict areas, motivations and needs" (p. 170). Without this knowledge leaders not only open themselves up for potential problems in the group but also jeopardize their effectiveness in utilizing their own personal resources in directing the group.

Dustin and George (1973) stated that leaders' self-awareness must include a thorough knowledge of their own rewards in relating to others. Without knowing what personal attributes reinforce other people, the leader cannot be effective in helping members modify and change their behavior. Lakin (1969) went a step farther and stressed that group leaders must be clear about their own intentions and goals. Lack of such understanding can result in damaging indecisiveness on the leader's part. It can also subject the group to unnecessary pressure and lead to the use of unethical practices under the guise of leadership expertise.

Without self-awareness leaders may become subject to emotional responses emanating from their own issues without knowledge of their origins. As such, self-knowledge becomes a fundamental component of leadership relative to facilitation and intervention in groups. Kline (1990) stressed self-monitoring and conducting self-inventories as a routine practice for group leaders. He noted that "when leaders encounter their limitations or identify their own personal issues in others they are likely to respond emotionally" (p. 196). Such awareness behooves the leader to proceed carefully and take steps to clarify their interventions before responding. Yalom (Forrester-Miller, 1989) validated this point of view stating that "no one can effectively lead a group who is unwilling or unable to look at his or her own feelings and neurotic conflicts" (p. 199).

The counselor's *attitudes* also are important components of self-awareness. They will eventually become apparent to group members; therefore, counselors need to have a firm grasp on their values, beliefs and attitudes so that they can be as transparent to the group as possible. This enables them to interact with members more freely. One value of special import to the leader is that of valuing self-awareness since the whole group process tends to center around self-disclosure and feedback, which is designed to promote the members' self-knowledge and to help them use this knowledge to solve their problems and become contributing group members. Leaders who do not value self-knowledge for themselves can hardly expect group members to see it as important in their lives.

Leader *personality* is the core of leadership style, and if leaders do not know of what that core consists, they have nothing on which to build their approach nor can they authenticate their style. During the beginning stages of the group process, personality characteristics of the leader determine how quickly rapport is established. As the group develops, the counselor's personality is the factor that defines the ultimate limits of the group experience because anything considered is contingent on the value system of the leader. In fact, when problems or impasses arise in the group a good guideline is for leaders to first look at themselves before trying to determine if the causes come from sources in the group. Substantial self-knowledge is thus mandatory as a leader personality trait in successful group leadership.

Openness and *flexibility* are two personality characteristics that lend themselves well to effective group leadership. There is a direct positive correlation between the possession of these two qualities and the range of people with whom the counselor can effectively work. This is not to imply that counselors who set no limits or boundaries and make no demands are the most effective. Rather, these qualities help the leader develop parameters appropriate to the nature of clients and their problems. *Openness* is the quality that stems from a secure knowledge of one's self so that the ideas of others can be received without feeling personal threat. Leaders, because of their own self-knowledge, can open themselves to the exposés of their clients without using judgment as a protective device. Instead they communicate an *appreciation of diversity* which Hulse (1985) considered an essential attribute of effective group leaders. Clients experience this openness in the form of acceptance, which paves the way for further self-disclosure on their part.

Flexibility is an outgrowth of the leader's confidence and sensitivity to the needs of the clients. The less confidence leaders have in themselves the more rigid they tend to become. Dogmatic nonstructuring by a leader is an example of high rigidity rather than the ultimate in flexibility. Flexible people know their own boundaries but are willing to vary within those boundaries and are continually testing their limits to reaffirm their whereabouts. One error that group leaders often make is that they go through the limit-testing process once, define for themselves what the extremities of their effectiveness are, and then never test them again. This is a sure way to stifle growth because, as one's experience increases, *self-confidence* increases, and with added self-confidence, flexibility increases. However, if counselors lapse into rigid patterns of operation they will curtail their creativity and never realize the gain in flexibility.

Allied closely with openness and flexibility is *tolerance of ambiguity*. This term is often narrowly construed as the ability to keep quiet in silent periods. Although at times this is indeed an example of being tolerant of ambiguous circumstances, it is a shallow test in most cases because silence can be more a matter of resistance than constructive or therapeutic action. A more viable definition for the group counselor is *the ability to act constructively in the interest of the group in the absence of knowledge about what is in the minds of group members.* This may take the form of being silent and allowing the pressure of silence to produce meaningful disclosures by sharing or of breaking the silence to alleviate tension that is inhibiting interaction. In any event, the most effective leaders have personalities that can carry them through new and ambiguous situations without imposing their will on others simply to resolve their own discomfort. Or as Lao-Tse has noted, sometimes "a leader is best when people barely know he(she) exists."

Effective group leaders are essentially *positive individuals*. People who think positively about life tend to have a constructive influence on those around them. The positive person is also in a good position to see strengths in others. This is an important asset in groupwork because clients steeped in their own problems sometimes fail to see the positive aspects of their lives. There must be a diplomatic aspect to the leader's positivity, however, in order to make the best use of it as a resource. Members can be turned off by a "look at the good side" routine, and therefore the positive perspective must be tempered with sensitivity to the negative side of things so the clients are assured that their perspectives are valued also.

A number of leader personality traits can be grouped under the general heading of *human qualities*. These characteristics tend to encourage others to have good feelings about themselves and help in developing therapeutic relationships. They can be described as social interest traits and they give the counselor a good rapport with people. *A genuine and sincere interest in others* is one of these qualities. People who find other people interesting, intriguing, and exciting and can convey that enthusiasm in a nonthreatening manner make good group workers. This is especially true if that interest can be attached to the specific individual in the group as well as to the group as a whole. This interest, coupled with a *sensitivity to others* that allows the counselor to put members and their interests and problems first, is a potent force in a group setting. Some people have a natural *empathic ear* and others have to develop it, but the counselor who can tune in to the lives of others without disturbing or possessing them has the capability of being especially effective in group work.

Warmth and *caring* are also human qualities that effective group leaders tend to have. The impressive thing about these qualities is that they can be conveyed in innumerable ways. Some people do it by their effervescence and enthusiasm, others by their smiles or attention, and others use their seriousness or quietness to show their depth of concern. The means of expression are not limited to one style, and if warmth and caring are present, usually no confusion exists on the part of the message receiver. Being a caring person is a must for group leaders. It provides them with the necessary fortitude to deal with people who have problems. It gives them leverage in the group interaction because of its importance to group members. It provides a model for others to follow, and it lays the groundwork for strong mutual liking and respect in the group which is essential to success.

Birnbaum (1969) cited *human objectivity* as a necessary quality for persons engaged in the helping professions. This characteristic allows the counselor to be involved with others but at the same time be apart from them in order to assess things more rationally and objectively. It might be equated with the *as if* quality in Rogers' (1962) definition of empathy: understanding another person *as if* you were that person, but without losing the *as if* quality. In other words, the counselor is able to walk in their client's shoes and see things as they see them, but without losing their own personal identity and perspective in the process. People who are able to think clearly when emotionally involved and under pressure tend to function well as group leaders. People who can be receptive to others while functioning in accord with their own values, and maintaining a clear personal perspective while affirming the perspective of members, make good group leaders.

Finally, effective group workers are *mature* and *integrated* persons who identify with the struggles involved in the process of life and can appreciate the efforts of members who are working on personal problems. They are able and willing to share themselves if necessary and to work in the best interest of the group. They are not devoid of problems and concerns in their own lives, but are able to put them into proper perspective while working with group members. They have *integrity*, which carries them through their own personal struggles and facilitates their handling of problems in the group process. They are strong enough not to wield their power to direct and badger members and strong enough to admit their own weaknesses. They are true to themselves, their clients, and their professional responsibility. Effective group leaders are people who can deal successfully with life's tasks and who are able to function interdependently with others. They are active and growing human beings who are continually striving for self-actualization without depriving others of opportunities to do the same.

The personality characteristics described here may not be definitive, but they do provide a strong basis for effective leadership when combined with the unique therapeutic qualities of individuals and the philosophical, theoretical, and technical factors provided by training. Hogan, Curphy, and Hogan (1994) have identified the essential nature of effective leadership as a form of persuasion. Adapted to therapeutic group leadership the implication is that leaders are effective when members "willingly adopt, for a period of time, the goals of a group as their own" (p. 493). Leadership is not domination. "Persons who can require others to do their bidding because of their power are not leaders" (p. 493). Rather leadership involves persuading group members to work toward a common goal that is important to the welfare of the group while benefiting its individual members. Leaders who manifest the characteristics described above tend to be persuasive in a therapeutic manner.

Many individuals display the aforementioned qualities naturally but still may not know how to use them effectively in groups. Training, which is the topic of the next section, is the means whereby personality characteristics are translated into leadership skills that enhance the group process.

Training Group Workers

In 1985 Carroll (1985), Shapiro, and Shapiro (1985), and Conyne et al. (1985) all specified insufficient and inadequate training of group leaders as a major, critical issue for group work. In spite of significant efforts to address this problem, Riva, Wachtel, and Lasky (2004) and others (Fuhriman & Burlingame, 2001; Weinstein & Rossini, 1998) have asserted that training still receives less than adequate or sufficient attention to produce competent leaders. Yalom (1985) pinpointed the price that is paid for this deficiency noting that without constant and continual attention to training, group counseling and group therapy naturally decline toward a second rate status as helping modalities. The view of these experts is that even with the maturation of group work as a full fledged professional entity, we are continuing to turn out professional counselors who have some knowledge and interest in group work but who are lacking in the technical skills and experience needed to implement a group program on the job or in clinical practice. Thus, the process that for decades has been acclaimed as a potential means of solidifying and promoting the counselor role still receives but scant emphasis in comparison to its purported impact. Lakin (1969) alerted us to the prospects of this reality when he proffered the somber warning that if proper attention is not given to training, effective group leaders while promoting the group process as a viable means of helping people, we risk having "vast numbers of inadequate [leaders] who practice their newly discovered insights on others in the naive conviction that they have all but mastered the skills involved" (p. 927). Thus, we may have to face charges of incompetence leveled at group leaders who were inadequately trained and lack the skills to function effectively in group settings. As was pointed out in chapter 2, the group has unique characteristics that require knowledge and experience to handle appropriately, so the need for training is clearly obvious. But what should that training entail? Fortunately, significant efforts have been mobilized to address the training issue as will be noted below.

In addition, a major philosophical and perceptual issue has plagued the group work training process for some time. The underlying assumption that if counselors are competent in individual counseling they will also be proficient in groups is still embedded in the core of many training programs implicitly or explicitly. Long ago Mahler (1969) pointed out the fallacy of this assumption, arguing that the reverse is much more likely to be the case—a person who is effective in group work probably would also do well in individual counseling. Pearson (1981) noted that group skills tend to be viewed as extensions of one-to-one skills rather than having a separate differentiation and defined viability in their own right. Therefore, the focus in training tends to be on similarities rather than on the differences between group skills and basic individual counseling skills. Harvill (Conyne, Harvill, Morganette, Morran, & Hulse-Killacky, 1990) further noted that due to the emphasis on process training (learning about groups by experiencing groups) in most programs, teaching leadership facilitation via specific skills—the "how to" of group leadership—has been missing. The need then is for delimited programs, i.e., master's programs with highly structured degree and licensure/certification requirements, to emphasize a group focus that is separate from and in concert with the individual orientation that predominates if competent group leaders are to be prepared. Fortunately, this challenge has been addressed in the form of training protocols that specify concrete programs for training group leaders with specific group work competencies (Akos, Goodnough & Milson, 2004; Barlow, 2004; Conyne & Bemak, 2004; Gillam, 2004; Guth & McDonnell, 2004; Riva & Korinek, 2004; Smaby, Maddux, Torres-Rivera & Zimmick, 1999; Stockton & Toth, 1996; Toth, Stockton & Erwin, 1998; Wilson, Rapin & Haley-Banez, 2004; VanVelson, 2004).

As a final note on the importance of training competent group workers, Dinkmeyer and Muro (1971) were forward looking in affirming that the skill of utilizing group process must become the primary emphasis of training counselors. This is important according to their purview because counselors place their skills at the disposal of a vast range of clientele and significant others in their clients' lives. Without adequate group skills, counselors' direct and indirect service functions are severely curtailed because they have neither the time nor the tools to meet the needs of these people individually. Consequently, the contemporary emphasis on the broader domain of group work that is being promoted by professional organizations such as the Association for Specialists in Group Work is apropos.

Training Standards and Competencies

In response to the aforementioned concerns and issues, the Association for Specialists in Group Work developed and revised the Professional Standards for the Training of Group Workers (ASGW, 1983, 1990, 2000), The Best Practices in Group Work Guidelines (ASGW, 1998) and the Principles for Diversity-Competent Group Workers (ASGW, 1999) documents that now inform and advise group work training initiatives. In addition, these documents are currently being transformed into training protocols by the related ASGW Committees (Professional Standards, Ethics and Diversity) and are being presented at the ACA and ASGW National Conferences (Phan, Merchant, Salazar, Torres-Rivera, Banez, & Vasquez, 2005; Rapin, Wilson, & Newmeyer, 2005; Thomas, Pender, Brock, Gambino, Morrow, & Neill, 2005). The purposes of both the documents and the training protocols are to assist training programs in preparing group leaders while holding them accountable for quality preparation and competent performance (Conyne et al., 1992). These documents define group work and delineate its knowledge, skills and experiences into *core competencies, group work specializations, best practices and diversity competent principles*. All documents are available online at http://www.asgw.org. The expectation is that training programs in group work will provide the core group competencies as the minimum level of proficiency for entry into the field and advanced training to generate group work specialists in one or more of the four group work specialties. For example, masters level graduate programs—the programs that produce the majority of group practitioners in professional settings—are expected to provide the core group competencies with access to the specialization level in at least one type of group work. Currently, this expectation is still relegated to one, or at most two, required courses in group dynamics and process and sporadic attention in practicums or internships (Merta, Johnson, & McNeill, 1995; Robison, Jones, & Berglund, 1996; Wilson, Conyne, & Ward, 1994;).

In reality, the application and implementation of the training standards is a work in progress (Conyne, Wilson, Kline, Morran, & Ward, 1993). For specific examples of training models in each of the group specializations and for curricula in compliance with ASGW Professional Training Standards the reader is referred to Conyne, Wilson, and Ward (1997) *Comprehensive Group Work: What it Means and How to Teach It.*

Group textbooks, professional literature, and professional standards all emphasize four specific areas in the training and development of competent group leaders. The first is access to the vast body of knowledge associated with the group modality as an entity in and of itself (books, journals, online sources, videos, etc.). The second is concentrated involvement in groups—as members, process observers and leaders—to integrate knowledge and practice and to develop a conceptualized framework for working with groups. Third is supervised practice both as a graduate student in practica and internships and as an in the field group practitioner. And the fourth is professional commitment to continually update group work knowledge and skills concomitant with the practical experience of conducting groups on the job. In line with these four areas of concentration the following components are described as generic resources for the effective preparation of counselors to work in groups.

General Coursework

These courses should form a broad foundation for group counselor training, as well as providing supplemental knowledge about the group process. The basic requirements of most counselor education programs can supply this foundational aspect, and courses drawn from psychology, sociology, and human relations can provide the supplemental. Preference should be given to courses that use group process methods as part of their format (Hulse-Killacky, 1996; Killacky & Hulse-Killacky, 2004).

Group Coursework

Every group counselor should have the equivalent of two courses in group work, one that emphasizes group dynamics and process and one that involves theories, techniques, skills, and procedures—including training in at least one of the group work specializations (Conyne & Bemak; 2004; Guth & McDonnell, 2004; Wilson, Rapin, & Haley-Banez, 2004). These courses should be taken in the department that is most closely allied to the setting in which the counselor wishes to work. Although it might be advantageous to have more group course work, most programs do not have the resources or flexibility to provide them. Besides, once the basic coursework is taken, preference should be given to the experiential domain rather than the academic.

Membership Experience

Every group counselor should be required to participate in at least one intensive, ongoing group counseling experience (see chapter 1 for examples and details). The ongoing nature of the experience is stressed to ensure that synthesis of the cognitive and experiential learning processes takes place over time and has more opportunity to develop. One shot marathons or short term group experiences can certainly provide supplementary data but cannot substitute for the extended process of the typical therapeutic group.

Process Observer Experience

The value and skill of process observation is a critical tool in both the learning of group process and group work and the conducting of groups as a leader (Hensley, 2002; Ward & Litchy, 2004). Trainees should be introduced to process observation at the very inception of their learning about groups. This experience elaborated in detail later in this text should involve process observer experience in and out of class and across the wide varieties of groups that competent group workers will lead (therapeutic, psychoeducation, and task groups).

Practicum/Internship Group Experience

Specific requirements to engage in a variety of groups should be a part of the general field work for counselor trainees. Minimally the practicum student/intern should conduct an ongoing counseling/therapy group, a series of psycho-education/guidance groups and/or classroom meetings (in schools) or a series of structured preventive mental health groups (in agencies), in addition to the usual one-to-one counseling and other requirements. These experiences give potential group leaders the opportunity to develop expertise in groups on an equal footing with individual counseling.

Formal Group Practicum/Internship

This requirement needs to be added in most training programs. A specific field experience concentrating entirely on the development of the counselor's group leadership ability in a preferred setting is a necessity. Supervision should concentrate on the development of personal qualities and competence of the leader and provide technical skills for organizing and conducting group programs and developing one or more of the group work specializations.

On-the-Job Leadership Experience

No substitute exists for experience. Once counselors have completed their training and are out on the job, they should proceed immediately in getting groups started. Many counselors never use their group work training because they never get started—a reason not to always exists and plenty of other things can be found to do. Carroll (1985) has observed that the systemic expectations of the counselor role in schools often undermine implementation of group programs by school counselors. Yalom (1985) cited the old nemeses of groups being "second rate," "superficial or dangerous," and "only useful if individual counseling is not available as factors that impede group work" (p. 515). Nevertheless, group counselors must take the initiative, set and stick with priorities, and place groups at the head of their professional "to do" list.

Personal Reading

The professional journals are continually adding to the information in the field of group work, and group leaders should make every effort to keep themselves current. Three recommended journals that have stood the tests of time and relevance as to group work are the *Journal for Specialists in Group Work*, the *International Journal of Group Psychotherapy*, and *Small Group Research: An International Journal of Theory, Investigation*, and *Application*. New books and materials are also reviewed in these journals periodically, so there is no excuse for not keeping abreast of new ideas, research, and practices in the group domain. The very fact that the last 30 years have witnessed vast and penetrating changes in the area of group work should be reason enough to stay well read.

Professional Organizations, Workshops, and Meetings

Membership in professional organizations such as the Association for Specialists in Group Work (division of the American Counseling Association), Group Psychology and Group Psychotherapy (Division 49 of the American Psychological Association) and/or the American Group Psychotherapy Association is imperative. Such membership provides plenty of opportunities to participate in or observe group programs at professional meetings or conventions, in workshops, and in inservice situations. Counselors who lead groups should make a concentrated effort to attend these sessions and to contribute to them as well. Sharing experiences is an excellent way to develop new ideas and get feedback on your own.

If prospective group leaders can acquire training and experience in each of these categories, they will have a substantial basis on which to build an effective group leadership style that will be professionally competent, personally satisfying, meaningfully therapeutic and constructively productive in the lives of the group members with whom they work.

Specialized Training

Specialized training in the following areas will accentuate effectiveness and provide invaluable resources in leading counseling and therapy groups.

Assertiveness Training

Many client problems revolve around the issue of assertiveness. Realizing the need for and learning appropriate assertive behavior skills is one way of assisting group members in their relational dilemmas. Most assertiveness training programs utilize group process. For example, Lange and Jakubowski (1976) presented extensive structured exercises and illustrations depicting cognitive, affective, and behavioral procedures for increasing group members' responsible assertiveness. Alberti (1977) and Alberti and Emmons (1995a; 1995b) also are helpful resources with respect to assertiveness training.

Interpersonal Skills Training

Training in this area includes a wide range of skills encompassing communication, relationship development, self-awareness, social skills, and interpersonal problem solving. Interpersonal skills are the links that connect the individual and other people and determine the quality and satisfaction of our relationships. A major portion of those links involve communication. Satir (1972) wrote that once a human being has arrived on this earth, "communication is the single largest factor determining what kinds of relationships he (she) makes with others and what happens to him (her) in the world about him (her)" (p. 30). Miller, Nunnally, and Wackman (1975) added that "communication is both a vehicle for creating relationships and an index of relationships" (p. 279). Consequently knowing how to assist group members in acquiring interpersonal skills is vital. In fact, Yalom (1985) pointed out that socializing techniques are a component of the curative factors that operate in all helping groups.

Several sources for content and techniques in this area are Johnson (1981), Hamachek (1978), Miller, Nunnally, and Wackman (1975), Satir (1972), Tubbs and Moss (1978), and Platt and Spivak (1976). Two current texts with both conceptual and experiential resources are Beebe, Beebe, and Redmond (2004) and Stewart (2002).

Social Learning Techniques and Behavior Modification

A wide range of methods and techniques based on social learning theory and behavioral principles are applicable to personal problem solving. Techniques that stress imitative, cognitive, cognitive-behavioral, emotional, or operant learning all provide helpful tools to the group leader. Helpful resources in this area are Agras (1978), Bandura (1969; 1997), Krumboltz and Thoreson 1976), Kanfer and Goldstein (1975), Wolpe (1990), Beck and Weishaar (1995), and Meichanbaum (1977; 1985).

Marital and Family Processes and Dynamics

Many of the interpersonal concerns members bring to group emanate from their family relationships. Yalom (1970) even went so far as to say that "without exception patients enter group therapy with a history of highly unsatisfactory experience in their first and most important group—their primary family" (p. 12). Satir (1972) stated simply that "troubled families make troubled people" (p. 18). Seigelman (1983) said that the greatest interpersonal risks are related to marriage, separation, divorce, confronting family members, and raising children. Finally, Yalom (Forrester-Miller, 1989) noted emphatically "when you work with any patients who are having problems in living, everybody comes from a dysfunctional family" (p. 199). It stands to reason then that extensive knowledge and understanding of the dynamics of marital and family relations is vital in group counseling (Connors & Caple, 2005; Matthews, 1992). A background in family systems theory related to nuclear, single, blended, extended and alternative family development and interaction, understanding family constellation and ordinal position, and a myriad of other concepts drawn from marriage and family therapy are vital (Trotzer & Trotzer, 1986). More attention will be given to this area in chapter 14 in which we will focus on family theory as a group resource.

Conflict Resolution and Mediation

Conflict in relationships is inevitable and often surfaces as the focus of attention in many types of groups. Johnson (1981) pointed out that "an interpersonal conflict exists whenever an action by one person prevents, obstructs, or interferes with the actions of another person" (p. 195). Given the fact that conflict typically arises in groups (McClure, 1990), effective conflict resolution is a necessity. Conflict resolution is often the key to not only solving the presenting problem for members, but future problems as well (chapter 9 in Johnson, 1981 and chapter 8 in Beebe, et al. (2004) are excellent chapters on managing and resolving interpersonal conflicts). Developing expertise in teaching conflict resolution strategies is thus another valuable asset to the group leader.

Mediation training is also a valuable adjunctive resource for group leaders providing principles, formats, tools, and procedures that can be adapted for use in the group and taught to group members relative to conflict situations outside the group. Resources for mediation training include:

1. Association for Conflict Resolution
   1015 18th Street, NW, suite 1150
   Washington D.C. 20036
   http://www.acrnet.org

2. American Arbitration Association
   335 Madison Ave., Floor 10
   New York, NY 10017-4605
   http://www.adr.org
3. Society of Professionals in Dispute Resolution
   1527 New Hampshire Ave., NW. 3rd Floor
   Washington D.C. 20036
   (202) 667-9700

Values Clarification

Many interpersonal difficulties stem from a lack of understanding of one's values or from values conflicts. Knowing values clarification strategies and techniques will prove valuable in group work. Helpful sources include Harmin, Kirschenbaum, and Simon (1973); Kirschenbaum (1977); Raths, Harmin, and Simon (1966); and Simon, Howe, and Kirschenbaum (1972).

Violence and Abuse

Specific training for assessment, intervention, and treatment across the broad spectrum of violence and abuse is critical for group leaders. Training in the recognition and treatment of the following and other similar areas will enhance leader effectiveness:

1. Substance abuse.
2. Violence in its many aspects—family and intimate (domestic) relationships; community, workplace, and school locations; victim and perpetrator assistance; and prevention, intervention and treatment (Koss, Goodman, Fitzgerald, Russo, Kita, & Browne, 1994; Brown, 1991).
3. Sexual abuse in its various forms including assault, rape, sexual harassment, and incest (Rencken, 1989; Courtois, 1988).
4. Emotional abuse.
5. Posttraumatic stress disorders (full range and nature of PTSD syndromes).

Training and expertise in these areas provide a necessary background for the group leader who works extensively in schools, community agencies, or private practice and will help the leader anticipate the types of problems that will arise in clinical groups.

Group Leadership Skills

The function of training should be to help group practitioners develop the interpersonal skills that translate personality, academic, and theoretical factors into practical tools for use in group work. These designated leadership skills certainly are not an exhaustive list but they are representative of the wide range of skills recognized as valuable to group leaders. Pearson (1981) has divided leadership skills into the two basic categories of *teaching skills* and *group management skills*. Teaching skills include explicit teaching (e.g., information giving, skills training, mini-lecturing), implicit teaching (e.g., modeling, in vivo experiences), and process observation (e.g., intrapersonal, interpersonal and interactional reflections). Group management skills include convening, eliciting, channeling, limit-setting, and protection. Jacobs, Harvill, and Masson (1988) have identified 12 basic skills for group leaders, and Corey and Corey (2006) described 18. Morran, Stockton and Whittingham (2004) identified 10 specific groups of skills supported by research that reflect effective leadership. For our purposes group leadership skills will be discussed under the three major categories of reaction skills, interaction skills, and action skills.

Reaction skills are responsive in nature and aid the leader in being receptive to individuals and the group as a whole. *Interaction skills* serve a mediating/moderating function in the group. They provide the leader the wherewithal to control and guide the group interaction and they facilitate, therapeutic impact. *Action skills*, as their title implies, are vehicles that the leader can use to be proactive in promoting and directing the group process. They serve to increase the depth of group interaction and provide the means whereby leaders can assert their expertise for the good of certain individuals or the group.

The overarching nature of these skills is that they qualify as here and now intervention skills (Carroll & Wiggins, 1997) that experts in the field assert are essential for conducting the group process (Morran, et al, 2004; Toth & Stockton, 1996). The specific skills in each of these categories are listed and briefly described in this section.

Reaction Skills

Active Listening

The skill of active listening is the most important skill a group leader can develop. Listening is all too frequently taken for granted as a natural part of the communication process that occurs automatically. That assumption is exactly where the problem lies. Because of the emphasis on and need for verbal expression in most areas of our lives, we work very hard at developing our expressive abilities but do very little to improve our receptive abilities. Group leaders must develop their potential as listeners to ensure understanding of the members, their problems, and their communications in the group. The listening skill must be active and not passive in nature; its influence is only useful if counselors can put into words what they are hearing and sensing so that all can benefit from their understanding. In other words, what is received in the private domain of the counselor's person must be returned to the public domain of the group for best results.

Group leaders who listen actively communicate four very important therapeutic and validating qualities to the members of the group. They communicate *acceptance,* because they are willing to hear what members have to say in a responsive manner rather than in a judgmental or pejorative manner. They communicate *respect* by giving members the opportunity to express how they see things without demeaning them or their perceptions. They communicate empathic *understanding* through the process of returning to the client what they understand the client's words to mean. And they communicate *caring* because of their interest in the member's point of view. All the other skills discussed in this category are really subskills of active listening. When combined they communicate all four of these qualities in a manner that accentuates the helping process (see Beebe, Beebe, & Redmond (2005), chapter 5 for an excellent generic consideration of the nature and importance of effective listening).

In addition, active listening skills provide the means by which leaders determine what Makuch, Robison, and Stockton (1998) call the *focus of leader interventions* in their Leadership Characteristics Inventory. As such these skills provide a basis for assessing leadership style from a process perspective. Categories of style include:

1. *Individual-directed* intervention style.
2. *Group-directed* intervention style.
3. Focus on *thinking.*
4. Focus on *feelings.*
5. Group *process* focus.
6. Group *topic* focus.

Consequently, the content of a leader's active listening responses are critical to his or her influence in the group.

Restatement

Restatement is the skill of repeating the basic content of a member's communication using much the same language and syntax. Its main purpose is to convey to the speakers that they are being heard and that the leader is with them at the moment and following attentively in their discussion. This skill is relatively easy to develop but can become sterile and distracting if overused. It is mainly effective in the beginning stages of communication and loses some of its utility as the depth of conversation increases.

Member: I have to make a decision about college right away because my parents are getting impatient.

Leader: You must decide about college soon because your parents are losing their patience with you.

Reflection

Reflection is the skill of expressing the meaning of the members' communications, indicating that they are not only heard but understood. Reflections can focus on the content of the communication or on the feelings that constitute the member's affective stance in regard to the communication. Reflection is useful because it helps the leader tune in to the internal frame of reference of the group member and because it helps members express what they might not have been able to express under other circumstances or when left to their own resources. It also assists other members in developing empathy for the speaker and models effective receptive responses for them.

Reflection is a very complex skill because it encompasses both verbal and nonverbal communication and in its most sensitive form can penetrate to the very core of the client's being. As such it is also a potentially threatening mechanism that can frighten members if it is not adjusted to the level at which they are operating. Moving too quickly or too deeply in a reflective manner can create the impression that the leader is seeing right through the person. As one of my supervisors aptly warned: "Reflection is supposed to be a resource to the client in assisting them as they explain their life experience not a scalpel in the hands of the counselor to dissect it." Using reflection as a scalpel can interfere with the group's progress and create a barrier between the members and the leader.

Member: I have to make a decision about college right away because my parents are getting impatient.

Leader: It sounds like you are feeling a lot of pressure from your parents about college, but that you are still not sure what you want to do.

Clarifying

Clarifying is the skill of improving communication by responding to confusing and unclear aspects of a message in order to better understand it. Sometimes simply asking the member to say it again removes difficulties and clarifies the communication. At other times the leader may have to help members find the words necessary to relate their meaning. Clarification is used to consolidate and accentuate the key components of the speaker's statement so that the whole group is mutually cognizant of them. It is also useful in addressing process dynamics of the group that may be obscure but inhibiting or detrimental to group progress.

Member: I'm experiencing so much failure lately that I'm beginning to think there is no hope at all for me to be happy. My grades are all Ds, I flunked my driver's test, and my parents are breaking up. I guess I'll just have to roll with the punches.

Leader: Could you explain that to the group again. At the beginning it sounded like you were so discouraged that you were on the brink of giving up, but at the end you sounded more resilient.

Summarizing

Summarizing is the skill of pulling together the important elements of a particular conversation or a group session and presenting them in capsule form. Often summaries are offered in a concluding manner, but they also are useful for transitional purposes to stimulate further reactions on the part of the group members. However used, the tying together aspect of a summary is a very useful learning experience for members.

Leader: Our discussion so far seems to have centered on our difficulties in relating to teachers who have old fashioned ideas. It seems some of you like these teachers because you always know what's expected, but that the rest of you feel they're "out of it" and that they're poor teachers. It also seems like the problems you mentioned are those teachers' responsibilities. So I'm wondering what part, if any, you think you play in the problems.

Tracking

Tracking is the nonverbal prerequisite to verbal expression. The leader utilizes eye contact and attending behavior to demonstrate interest and attention in the member who is speaking and follows the verbal flow of the group as it moves from member to member. Tracking supplemented with preverbal acknowledgements (head nodding) and limited verbal notations (e.g., "uh-huh," "I see") demonstrates the leader's involvement in the group interaction and in each participant as their participation evolves. It provides the basis or stimulus for verbal expression using the skills previously mentioned.

Scanning

Scanning is the nonverbal counterpart to tracking that incorporates the non-speaking group members into the leader's purview. As one member is talking, sharing, or disclosing, the leader visually scans the rest of the group to observe their actions and reactions and notes their attentiveness. This skill provides valuable input to the leader relative to the interactive dynamics occurring in the group and helps the leader keep in touch with the other members while one member holds the focus. It serves as the means by which reaction skills can be extended to the group generally and, more often than not, provides the springboard for shifting into the use of the interaction and/or action skills described below.

Effective leaders maintain an equitable balance between tracking and scanning as the baseline for insuring their involvement with both the individual members and the group interaction.

Reframing

The skill of reframing emerged to prominence in family counseling and is especially useful in helping members broaden their perspective of an issue, topic or problem removing the restrictions that inhibit acquisition of new meanings, perceptions, or solutions (Coe & Zimpfer, 1996). Clark (1998) relates reframing to the "semantic aspect of interpretation as the meaning of a group member's experience is altered through a relabeling or reclassification procedure" (p. 67). As such reframing is a responsive tool in the hands of a group leader that helps members realize Yalom's (1995) "attribution of meaning" therapeutic factor. Once introduced into the group, members quickly resonate to the skill and use it to provide diverse viewpoints to each other in the course of group discussions and interactions. As such the members learn to "co-create new understandings through the interactive exchange of reframing" (Clark, 1998, p. 69). Clark (1998) provides the following example of effective reframing:

Member: "I have such difficulty in making my mind up about things, especially the more important decisions in my life."
Leader: "This is disturbing to you because you want to make sure that you are making choices that seem right to you. I am wondering though if it is possible for you to look at this in a different way. Perhaps what you are doing may also be considered being thoughtful and careful in your approach to solving problems." (p. 66)

Notice the tentative nature of the response that gives the member the option to consider and adapt the message rather than imposing it. This trait makes the response inviting and persuasive to the member rather than intrusive. It also lends credibility to the message in the eyes of other group members. This skill is particularly useful in the working phase of a group where members are addressing their own issues or attending to group problem solving.

Interaction Skills

Moderating

Moderating is a regulatory skill used by a leader to govern the group interaction, ensuring that all opinions, perceptions, thoughts, and feelings are aired. Moderating is also used to maintain a mode of discussion that's fair and equitable to all members. It requires an ethical objectivity on the part of the leader to perform so as not to be viewed as biased by members.

Leader: There seem to be two sides of this issue in our group. We just heard from those who are against any curfew. Now what about those of you who see a curfew as a positive thing.

Interpreting

Interpreting is the skill of relating material and feelings being discussed to an external criterion as a frame of reference to help members gain insight and understanding (Clark, 1993). In most cases the frame of reference is not cognizant to members and requires the leader's expertise to relate it to the situation being discussed. This skill is often used to introduce and teach theory to group members, a factor that is very helpful in providing a conceptual base to the work a leader does in groups. Any theory of counseling and development can be translated into a practical form and format, and interpretation is the means by which that transformation is validated (Jacobs, Masson, & Harvill, 2006). However, Morran, Stockton, and Whittingham (2004) point out that although interpreting promotes member insight and assists meaning attribution, it is also subject to over use, a tendency that elevates the leader to an expert role that precludes members from making their own interpretations. Consequently, interpreting should be used judiciously and tentatively to keep members in the processing loop rather than abdicating it to the leader.

Group interpretations—interpretations that focus on the functioning of the group rather than on an individual in the group—help the group readjust communication patterns in a manner beneficial to therapeutic growth.

Leader: The group is jumping from topic to topic and person to person so quickly today that it's difficult to follow. We might be using this scatter gun approach to avoid getting personal because we really don't trust each other.

Linking

Linking is the skill of tying together common elements in the communication of individual members to help them identify more closely with one another or to raise contrasting perspectives by juxtaposing one member's viewpoint with another's. It is a very useful tool in developing cohesiveness in the group and ferreting out differences that can lead to synergy and creativity. Linking also is used to pinpoint subgroups with different perceptions on the same issue or to give direction to the group relative to themes that have been considered over time (Morran, Stockton, & Whittingham, 2004). At times it is useful in bringing to the surface underlying dynamics occurring in the group among members, and is a means of making the implicit explicit by verbalizing the nonverbal signals that are evident in the group.

Leader: Bill and Cheryl seem to think alike on the idea that dating should be done in groups, while Mary and Frank seem to favor the individual couples approach.

Blocking

Blocking is the skill of stepping in to prevent the execution of an undesirable, unethical, or inappropriate action by the group or its members. This skill requires leaders to use their knowledge of the group process as well as their sensitivity to individual member's rights, needs, or values to intercept, divert, or stop group actions that are detrimental to the members or the group. It is imperative that the leader using this skill be warm but firm and not influenced by the emotional climate that may prevail in the group at the moment that may be prompting detrimental dynamics.

Member: Betty has missed one group session, has been late to the other two, and isn't here today. I don't think she cares about our group at all, and that we should just boot her out.
Members (chorus): (I agree)
Leader: I'm not sure why Betty has acted the way she has, but I think you should bring this up to her in the group. You can't just eliminate her without hearing her side of it.

Jacobs, Masson, and Harvill (2006) refer to this skill as "cutting off" and Morran, Stockton and Whittingham refer to it as one of the key skills needed to protect members and the group process and to promote safety. Jacobs (Jacobs et al, 2006) notes four situations in which "cutting off" is appropriate:

1. When the leader or situation call for a brief response and the member is elaborating.
2. When the member diverts attention away from the consideration of a topic or person that is valuable.

3. When one member attacks another or provides inaccurate information.
4. When a member is on focus but rambling.

When intervening to cut off, the leader has several options to choose from. The leader can (a) cut off but stay with the person, (b) cut off but stay with the topic, or (c) cut off and leave the person and the topic (Jacobs, et al., 2006). In any event the purpose of this skill is to curtail any individual or group activity that is not constructive to the members or the group process.

Supporting

Supporting is the skill of providing reinforcement, encouragement, and backing to group members in their efforts to interact in the group. It is most useful when members are risking involvement, disclosing difficult personal information or giving emotionally tinted feedback. It also is useful for drawing out quiet members and aiding shy individuals to express themselves. The giving of support also implies that it can be withdrawn and therefore it can be used as a means of modifying members' behavior in both a positive and negative sense.

Member: I guess what I have really been wanting to say but couldn't is that I would like the group's help in overcoming my shyness in relating to people.

Leader: John, you showed a lot of courage in sharing that, and maybe you have just taken an important first step in overcoming your fear of relating to other people.

The one caution that relates to this skill in to avoid "spotlighting" members as a means of giving them support. In most cases, support should follow or accompany member action not prompt it. If an invitation is extended to a member as a means of getting involved it should be couched in the context of others not just focused on the member. For example, it is better to state,

I have noticed that Don has been pretty quiet (pause for just a moment to see if Don will take up the invitation to speak and then continue) as have Matt and Sarah.

Rather than:

I have noticed that Don has been pretty quiet. Would you like to talk about what is going on?

Limiting

Limiting is the skill of defining boundaries to give structure or direction to the group. It provides the framework within which the group can interact and prevents excesses and deviations that will infringe on the rights of members or result in irresponsible actions in the group. It cuts two ways at once because it curtails harmful interaction from occurring while at the same time denoting guidelines for constructive interaction.

Leader: It's in the best interest of the group and of each of the members if we don't discuss with others what we talk about in here. That way we won't run into problems like gossiping or breaking confidences.

Protecting

Protecting is the skill of preventing individual members from being unduly criticized, scapegoated, or hurt in a nontherapeutic manner. This skill is essential in combating the overwhelming force of group pressure, which can become a problem at times or addressing the force of a particularly strong personality in the group who does not know how to use their power sensitively or constructively. Protecting may be used to defend individual members from the onslaught of the group, and to protect subgroups of members who are being treated unfairly or inappropriately. This skill demands the ultimate in sensitivity because the leader must be aware of the individual member's limits and ploys, the group's intentions, the possibility of protection coming from within the group, and personal responsibility for making the decision to protect. It is particularly relevant in regard to recognizing and respecting cultural characteristics and diversity factors represented in group members.

Leader: It seems like everyone in the group has had something to say about Joanna, but no one has mentioned anything positive. I feel she has held up very well under all that pressure, but now I think maybe we should look at the group's behavior for a while to find out what is happening to make us so caustic.

Protecting is generally associated with psychological risks though at times physical risk is also a prompt particularly if any member is prone to losing physical control in the group as in the case of anger management groups. Then protecting has to be both proactive relative to group boundaries and interactive relative to any here and now actions in the group. Morran, Stockton, and Whittingham (2004) note that protecting can also be indirect such as alerting or reminding members that they have the option to defer, stop or continue as a choice when involved in a process relative to disclosing personal information.

Consensus Taking

Consensus taking is the skill of finding out where members stand in their perceptions of the various topics and problems that are being considered in the group. It is of particular importance to tap all divergences of opinion in the group so that members clearly understand where they are in relation to each other. This skill is useful when topics of intense personal or emotional content are discussed and the conversation becomes heated and difficult to follow. It settles the group down and clears the air, making it possible to proceed with both better understanding and less affective interference. It is useful in processing group experiences and events facilitating integration and closure.

Leader: We have been hard at it for the last 15 minutes about how much commitment we really have to this group, and it has been heavy and a little difficult to come to grips with. Maybe we could do a go-around where each one of you speaks only for yourself, giving your own feeling of commitment. Anyone can start it off, and we can go around clockwise from there."

Action Skills

Questioning

Questioning, according to Benjamin (1987), is another of those natural tendencies that needs to be refined and developed before it has a positive impact on the group process, the helping initiative or the leadership role. Our automatic reliance on the question is a dependency that must be overcome if we are to be effective in groups. If we do not develop alternatives and vary the nature of our questioning we not only limit the effectiveness of the helping process but also model less effective questioning styles for group members to use in their interaction with each other. The negative effect is cumulative. With these reservations, the skill of questioning is still an important and highly relied on tool in the group process. Clark (1989) delineated the qualities of effective questioning into the following categories. Effective questions are:

1. *Supportive*: allow the respondent independence and latitude to reflect and respond;
2. *Relevant*: relate to the "immediate experience of the group member and lead to productive discussion."
3. *Regulated*: frequency and timing are critical and in the control of the group leader;
4. *Expansive*: enable or facilitate member expressiveness as opposed to closed questions which curtail response; and
5. *Open ended*: prompt members to generate material and expand expressiveness (pp. 121–122).

He also advocates the use of questions as processing tools in the group for purposes of assessing, convening, confronting, expanding, universalizing, linking, and controlling.

Questions can be used to help group members consider aspects of themselves and their concerns they haven't thought of before. Questions also can serve to transfer ambiguous silences into productive discussion. The types of questions used should typically open the door for further discussion. Closed ended or yes/no questions tend to create unbalanced conversation patterns and seldom result in spontaneous discussion. The exception, of course, is when a closed ended question is used to get a quick consensus of where members are or what they are thinking. Then a closed ended question is a prompt that can be followed up with a more direct inquiry based on the data collected.

Member: I'm afraid my parents no longer trust me, and that there's nothing I can do that will change their minds.

Leader: It sounds like you feel you might have violated their trust to a point where it's irreparable. But you seem to know what they do expect. Could you tell us what you think their standards of trust are for you?

Probing

Probing is the skill of helping group members go more deeply into themselves and their problems under the direction of an outside source such as the leader. Members often will not take responsibility upon themselves to go more deeply into their problems or perspectives but will consent to do so if the leader takes a more active role in the process. Effective probing requires the leader to be aware of the sensitive points in the client's frame of reference and the limits to which the client can be asked to go. Awareness of cultural and diversity factors is particularly relevant when probing is considered. Probing should be tentative, always leaving an avenue open for the client to stop or defer if the procedure gets too threatening. Probing is useful in helping members learn the process of introspection and can be an effective means gradually moving the group to deeper levels of interaction and problem or issue examination.

Member: I know I have some real feelings of anger inside me, but I don't really know where they come from.

Leader: So you know you feel angry but don't know why. I wonder, could you identify any situations where you feel more angry than in other situations?

Jacobs (Jacobs et al., 2006) refers to two elements of probing as "drawing out" and "going deeper." These two terms reflect the nature of the relationship between the leader and the member in the process. "Drawing out" implies a side by side type of assistance that the leader supplies to support, guide and assist the member in sharing who they are or what they think or feel. "Going deeper" is more of a process element that invites not only the member, but the whole group to engage in a more intense or serious (deeper) process. In either case, the leader's awareness, sensitivity and proficiency in probing as an active contribution to the group is critical. "Drawing out" is typically associated with the initial stages of the group process while "going deeper" has greater relevance in the work stage of the process.

Tone Setting

Tone setting is subtle but crucial to the atmosphere and attitude of the group. It is the process of establishing a qualitative standard the group can observe and to which it can respond. Leaders can establish the tone of the session in many ways, including the arrangement of the physical setting, the personal mood that they express to the group, the character of their actions in the leadership role, and the activities or suggestions they propose in the group. Tone setting is not only important in the initial moments of the group session, but also can be extremely useful when the group could benefit from a change in mood. For example, comic relief often serves the purpose of pulling the group out of extended discussions that have become emotionally draining or boring. Tone setting gives members a base rate to use in gauging their own behaviors, feelings, and thoughts and provides them with a means of determining how to respond appropriately.

Leader: We've been struggling along here talking about all the things we have to change about ourselves, so as a point of contrast lets have each person share a couple of things about themselves or their life that don't need changing.

Confronting

Confronting is the skill of getting individual members or the group to face things about themselves that they are blatantly or subtly attempting to avoid. The use of this skill can have potentially explosive repercussions, which may be detrimental to the group and its members if not handled appropriately and sensitively. In counseling and therapy groups, confrontation should generally be tentative and rather than forcing a member into a corner with no escape. This skill is most useful in helping the group deal with discrepancies and inconsistencies in individual and group behavior. It also is helpful in getting members to face responsibility in regard to their problems and behavior and to engage the group or individuals in reality testing.

Confrontation should typically be used after a foundation of trust and acceptance has been laid and when the dynamics in the group are cohesive in nature. With these safeguards the members realize that confrontation is directed at their actions, not their persons, and is motivated by intentions that are constructive rather than destructive.

Member: I am doing everything I possible can to fulfill my contract of studying one hour a day at home, but I just can't make it.

Leader: As you came in today, Jack, I heard you telling Sally you watched TV for three hours last night and never cracked a book. How do you explain that in connection with what you just said?

Personal Sharing

Personal sharing is the means by which leaders disclose themselves to the group. It is an important skill because any time leaders do give of themselves by sharing personal concerns or perceptions it usually has a significant effect on the group. Seldom is the impact neutral. For this reason the leader's personal self-disclosure can facilitate the group process as well as help him or her deal with what is going on inside. Of course, leaders must be sensitive to the amount and depth of personal revelation that is appropriate and that the group can handle. Personal sharing is useful in setting an example for group members and helps them see the leader as a fellow human being. It also serves the function of demonstrating that the leader is willing to engage in the same process in which the members are expected to become involved. The overriding purpose of personal sharing, however, should be for the benefit of the group and its members. If personal issues emanating from the group or the leader's life outside the group emerge and need attention, the more appropriate forum is consultation, supervision, or personal counseling. The two criteria that inform the decision to self disclose are: (1) Is it beneficial to the group and/or its members, and (2) Is it appropriate as a means of modeling effective or constructive personal or group behavior (e.g., for demonstration purposes). A third criterion as represented in the example that follows is to clear the air so the leader can concentrate more effectively in the group. In this case, the material disclosed should not have the propensity to become the focus of the group's discussion.

Leader: I guess I'm really not quite with it today. My mind keeps wandering ahead to next week when I'll be having surgery.

Member: I thought you were kind of daydreaming today, but I guess you're just a little uptight about your operation.

Modeling

Modeling is the skill of demonstrating by exemplary action the qualities, characteristics, and skills that members may need to learn to function effectively in the group and in their personal lives. Leaders are models whether they choose to be or not because of their position in the group. Therefore, leaders must make the best use of the situation rather than leaving their modeling impact to chance. Modeling is helpful in teaching members important interpersonal skills that will make communication and interaction in the group more effective. It also is useful in alleviating the problems of orientation in the group process. Members can take their cues from the leader and model their own behavior and involvement accordingly. Morran, Stockton, and Whittingham (2004) reviewed a number of studies that reported leader modeling is effective in prompting members to display appropriate interpersonal behaviors relative to feedback delivery, acceptance and here-and-now communications.

Leader: Today I would like to begin the session by having each of you describe yourself as if you were your own best friend. Use your first name and the third person at all times in describing yourself. I'll start with myself and you can see how it works. Jim is. . . .

Group Leadership Functions

Skills are only the building blocks that leaders use to perform their functions. The manner in which the leader uses his or her skills is determined by the leader's personality, theoretical orientation, and the nature of the group process. Which skills are used at what time and for what purpose depict *the functions of group leadership*. The generic functions of leaders in counseling and therapy groups include initiating and maintaining effective group process, helping members establish goals, protecting members from harm, and effecting appropriate termination (Kaplan & Saddock, 1993). The content of those functions outlined by Polcin (1991) include:

1. *emotional stimulation*: fostering expressions of feelings, values, beliefs, and emotional concerns;
2. *caring*: expressions of warmth, acceptance, concern, and genuineness;
3. *meaning attribution*: providing cognitive understanding to members, and
4. *executive leadership*: setting limits, suggesting norms, pacing, managing time, blocking, and interceding (p. 10).

Functions are also the means by which leaders help the group process develop in accord with the needs of the group members and the goals of the group.

Leader functions embody the essential components of a leader's group theory and approach. Although the manner of carrying out the various functions is influenced by training, theoretical orientation, and leader personality, their basic impact on the group remains much the same. The specific functions explicated below are not mutually exclusive, but they do tend to be relatively comprehensive and generically relevant to the group process.

Promoting Interaction

One of the primary functions of the group leader is to promote interaction in the group. An atmosphere of interaction accelerates group integration. Therefore, leaders must do their utmost to promote its development. This function is as much a contingency of what leaders do not do as it is of what they do. Leaders who dominate, sermonize, evaluate, teach, and moralize in their group leadership role tend to deter interaction rather than promote it. In fact, leaders who manifest aggressive leader attributes, are charismatic, or use the power of their personality or position to control are associated with negative outcomes in groups (Korda & Pancrazio, 1989). In contrast, leaders who are able to share leadership responsibility, relinquish the role of expert by encouraging members to help each other, and include all the group members in the discussion create conditions that are highly conducive to therapeutic group interaction and member involvement. Dye (DeLucia, 1991) emphasized that "leaders should be as active as they need to be to get those vital (group) processes going. Once they do get them going, it's time to get out of the way and let the people work things out on their own" (p. 68). In support of this view Conyne et. al. (1990) stipulated, "If group leaders can consistently exhibit high levels of facilitative responses, serve as a model to the group, function as a director of communication and be a catalyst to move the process, the consequences would be demonstrated by changes in member behavior, attitudes and/or affect" (p. 33).

Leaders also can promote interaction by the physical arrangements they set up in the group. Groups that meet in comfortable rooms and sit in a circle as opposed to a square or ellipse find it much easier to relate and communicate with one another. The use of a skill such as linking to promote member-to-member communication is very effective in carrying out this function. Another helpful technique is personal sharing. If leaders share their feelings and perceptions—especially early in the group's development—they will encourage members to interact with each other in much the same way. The overall purpose of this function is to create an atmosphere that encourages honest, spontaneous give-and-take discussion among members.

Facilitating Interaction

The facilitating function, though similar to the promoting function, has several unique qualities that merit its separate consideration. Lakin (n.d.) stated that one essential function of any group leader is to facilitate social interaction. Facilitation implies that action is taken to enhance interaction that is already occurring. In other words, facilitating is a responsive function. It depends on the group to provide the stimulus that propels it into action. The leader responds to the action by suggesting methods that make communication patterns more meaningful and effective. Facilitation is directly related to increasing understanding in the group. Its effective use is dependent on group leader's sensitivity and awareness and hinges on the ability to express one's self clearly to the group members. Stockton (Morran, 1992; Stockton & Toth, 1996) has broken down the facilitating function into component parts of perceiving what is occurring in the group, mentally devising or developing an appropriate leadership response, and expressing that response as an intervening activity. He noted that "the three components of perceiving, developing strategies, and intervention are inextricably intertwined" (Morran, 1992, p. 8). Chapter 13 includes a discussion of the use of communication exercises in performing the facilitating function.

Initiating Interaction

The initiating function refers to the leader's active role in structuring the interaction of the group. It can be utilized to generate interaction and determine what the focus of that interaction will be or how it will proceed. The action skills are very important in performing this function, as are activities designed to make things happen in the group. The effective use of this function depends on the leader's knowledge of the group process and his or her expertise in determining the needs of the group members. In most cases initiating is done to direct the group to considerations the leader deems beneficial to the members or the group process. The initiating function also is useful in alleviating anxieties caused by unstructured situations. Chapter 13 describes the use of communication exercises in carrying out the initiating function and gives more details as to its nature.

Guiding Interaction

The guiding function of the group leader has been alluded to in Hulse's (1950) description of the dynamics of group therapy. "Tension is the motor which keeps the therapeutic group going. Anxiety is the fuel that makes the motor run. The group therapist becomes the responsible conductor of this vehicle" (p. 834). The group, because of its complex and potentially destructive nature, needs someone to keep it goal oriented and to steer interaction into the most beneficial channels. Dinkmeyer and Muro (1971) stated that this guiding function helps the group move toward its accepted goals and is the "sum total of the counselor's efforts to utilize effectively the unique benefits of the group situation for personal growth"

(p. 118). Lakin (n.d.) refers to this function as the leader's role in "intermanaging interaction." The skills of most consequence in performing this function are the interaction skills, although other skills such as tone setting, drawing out, "going deeper," and questioning are also useful.

Some theorists stress the guiding function as primary and cast the leader in the role of a participant-observer who refrains from personal involvement, stepping in only to guide the group when it deviates from its set purpose and then stepping out again. Vorrath and Brentro's (1974) Positive Peer Culture Groups operate on this model. An important aspect of this function is the leader's ability to control the speed and depth of involvement and interaction. Leaders must be able to encourage members to recognize feelings and proceed to deeper levels and yet maintain a modulated pace that does not leave members behind or hanging. In either case, however, effective leadership requires "spontaneous and creative responses to complex, unrehearsed situations" (Conyne, et al., 1990, p. 33).

Intervening

The intervening function is used to protect group members and contain excesses in the group process. It is used to ensure that each member can exercise the right to be heard and retain the right to privacy. Intervening is necessary to counter the dangers of the group process. Groups may not give support when it is needed, may distort reality, or create pressures that lead to loss of control (Lakin, n.d.). If any of these situations becomes imminent, the leader must intervene to prevent them from damaging individuals or disrupting the group process. Dinkmeyer and Muro (1971) listed several instances in which leader intervention may be appropriate:

1. When individuals are victimized by group forces.
2. When groups create excessive anxieties or pressures for conformity.
3. When hostility is misdirected.
4. When the majority (consensus of opinion) may be incorrect.
5. When individuals are forced to accept group solutions.
6. When groups become too comfortable and no action toward resolving problems occurs.

Intervening may also entail keeping time limits, making sure time is allotted for closing, and bringing the group discussion back to its proper focus. Most of the interaction skills are useful in performing this function and the leader must be willing to take responsibility to preserve the psychological well being of members and the therapeutic intent of the group process. Hansen, Warner, and Smith (1980) referred to actions involved in intervening and the rules-keeping function described next as *executive functions*.

Rules-Keeping

Rules-keeping is one of the more technical but necessary functions the leader performs in the group. Its basic intent is to see that the group interaction stays within the framework of the guidelines established to govern that interaction. These guidelines or rules may be stipulated by the leader at the outset of the group (see pages 135–139), can be developed cooperatively between the leader and members, or can be allowed to evolve during the course of group interaction. In any event, the leader's function is to see that they are maintained and use the authority of the leader role to address any infractions that might develop. The performance of this function should not be arbitrary but should be solidly based on the leader's knowledge of what constitutes constructive group interaction and a sensitivity to member needs (Polcin, 1991).

Consolidating

The consolidating function of the leader is the action he or she takes to draw things together in a meaningful way so that group members can relate to them. It also may involve tying together numerous thoughts and feelings in a brief and coherent way. Leaders must be aware of the consensus in the group in order to perform this function effectively. They also must realize that differences of opinion will exist and use this function to help members communicate and understand their differences and similarities. Skills that facilitate this function are clarifying, summarizing, and linking. The main purposes of the consolidating function are to keep the group members at the same level of understanding as the group process unfolds and develops and to help them differentiate, acknowledge, and value diversity in the group.

Enhancing Communication

The function of enhancing communication serves to help group members express themselves more precisely and understand each other more accurately. The leader is able to perform this function by focusing attention on each client's needs and exhibiting genuine caring but at the same time maintaining a healthy separateness to allow for objectivity. Ohlsen (1970) described the nature of this function as follows: "When he (she) is at his (her) best, a counselor can feel deeply with a client without experiencing emotional reactions which are deleterious to the counseling relationship" (p. 2).

The leader who operates in this manner builds relationships in the group by being empathic. The skills of greatest use for enhancing communication are the reaction skills, all of which depend on the counselor's ability to listen actively and to understand members sensitively (Egan, 1986). Leaders must be aware of multiple levels in the member's verbalizations. They must be able to take words and actions at face value while at the same time realize that an underlying ambivalence may be in the message. The leader who can work to merge external expression with internal motivation in the member's communication will be making significant progress in securing a foundation of understanding in the group. The effectiveness of this function depends on the leader's ability to observe and deal with the impact of each member's communication on the rest of the group. Ohlsen (1974) stated that "While trying to detect the speaker's feelings, encouraging him (her) to act and reinforcing his (her) desired behaviors, the counselor also must note how the speaker's behavior is influencing others and how the behavior of others is influencing the speaker" (p. 144). In this way the leader can work with the total process—encompassing expression, reception, and response—and thus increase the influence of communication in the helping process.

The group leader can accelerate and enhance communication by encouraging members to speak directly to each other rather than to the leader (Yalom, 1985). Getting members to send "I messages," using first and second person pronouns (I, me, you), has a significant effect in drawing members together. This personalization of communication clarifies meaning and makes speakers more cognizant of their own motivations, thus improving the quality of their messages.

Resolving Conflicts

If one adage about the group process consistently holds true, it is that the course of group work in its various forms never runs smooth. Inevitably in the process of intense interpersonal interaction, conflicts will arise (McClure, 1990). Not only is conflict inevitable but how it is addressed is a crucial factor in the movement of the group toward productive results (Rybak & Brown, 1997). In a sense, conflict serves a functional purpose in groups since it represents both an enhanced level of relationship development and requires cooperation, collaboration and continued communication to resolve. If not resolved, groups can get stuck or side tracked. The group leader's task is to see that conflicts are addressed and resolved beneficially if not harmoniously for all parties involved. This function requires all the skill and sensitivity the counselor can muster to effect it constructively. It requires that the leader be aware of sources of conflict such as frustrated individual needs, conflicting goals, hidden agendas, disappointment with leader functioning, groping for structure, and anxiety over a new and novel situation. This function requires that leaders know how to implement strategies for conflict resolution. Rybak and Brown (1997) describe two perspectives for dealing with conflict: *conflict management* and *conflict resolution*. They note that "conflict can be destructive to a group, but as members experience satisfactory resolution of conflict, they learn to trust the constructive dialogue that led to resolution"

(p. 31). Conflict management takes into account the norms of the group in accordance with cultural and personal values regarding conflict (Merta, 1995). Conflict management relates to the manner in which conflict is addressed. When conflict emerges, leaders must know how to respond, when to step in, when to allow the group or the particular members to work it out. Most of all, they must be willing to acknowledge conflict and deal with it therapeutically, attempting to identify its roots and use it constructively in helping group members to grow and the group process to mature (McRoy & Brown, 1996).

Mobilizing Group Resources

This function more than any other determines the optimum level of a group's effectiveness. For example, a unique trait of group counseling is that it offers individual members many potential sources of help as opposed to just one. The effective group leader therefore is able to assess what the group resources are and mobilizes them for the benefit of the individual and the group. The more successful leaders are in performing this function, the less pressure and responsibility they will feel in being the expert in the group. The more adept they are at drawing upon group resources, the more self-esteem members will experience which in turn will improve the morale of the group. The purpose of this function is to get group members to help themselves by helping each other. Group leaders who function well in this way find that many of the other functions are no longer necessary because the group will take responsibility for performing them.

Most of the skills described earlier assist the group leader in performing this function but the key to its effectiveness is the leader's willingness to operate behind the scenes through group members rather than in a direct helping capacity. Leaders who actively share, redistribute, and defer power and use *contingent statements* rather than *direct approach statements* in responding to members (Rybak & Brown, 1997) are more successful in carrying out this function. Counselors who prefer to do the counseling themselves often do not utilize the group's helping potential to the fullest possible extent.

Process Observation:
The Group Leader's Resource and Reference

The Cutting Edge and Core of Group Work

Process observation has emerged as the single most dynamic factor in the group work field over the last two decades. As such, it has become both the cutting edge and the core of the field because of its inherent relevance to the productivity of the group and the nature of the group experience. Ward and Litchy (2004) in their extensive treatise of the history, nature, relevance, and potential of processing in groups state simply that "processing is critical to and synonymous with sophisticated modern group work" (p.115). This assertion is supported by ASGW training standards (2000) and ASGW Best Practice Guidelines (1998) that state:

> Group workers process the workings of the group with themselves, group members, supervisors, or other colleagues, as appropriate. This may include assessing progress in group and member goals, leader behavior and techniques, group dynamics and interventions, as well as developing understanding and acceptance of meaning. Processing may occur both within sessions and before and after each session, at time of termination and later follow-up, as appropriate. (p. 243)

This practice constitutes the *resource* dimension of process observation. ASGW Best Practice Guidelines (1998) also stipulate:

> Group workers attend to opportunities to synthesize theory and practice and to incorporate learning outcomes into ongoing groups. Group workers attend to session dynamics of members and their interactions and also attend to the relationship between session dynamics and leader values, cognition and affect. (p. 243)

This practice constitutes the *reference* dimension of process observation. Both of these practices are reflective in nature and together represent the two facets of processing referred to by Lynn Rapin and Bob Conyne in chapter 8 as "pragmatic" and "deep" processing, the former referring to the impact of process observation in relation to a particular group and the latter referring to the impact on leader expertise and growth across groups over time.

Consequently, the following section reviews the nature of process observation for the purpose of providing practical and concrete assistance to group leaders in incorporating it into their leadership role and orienting, teaching and modeling its relevance to group members. This section is written in a guidelines format to facilitate use of the information across all forms of group work and easily lends itself to replication in handout form to trainees and students learning the group process.

Guidelines for Process Observation in Educational, Task, Work, and Clinical Groups

In ancient times when grain was harvested by hand in the fields, it was common practice for villagers to follow the reapers and collect for themselves the remnants of the crop, a process called gleaning. In this way, members of the community benefited from the labor of the farmer and produce of the farm and the practice represented a form of sharing and caring. The purpose of this section of the chapter on group leadership is to share the gleanings of my work as a process observer in a wide range of groups including work groups, task groups, class groups, and clinical groups. These groups have been conducted in a wide variety of settings from the school to the community to the workplace and have encompassed educational, religious, mental health, business, profit and nonprofit enterprises. The intent is to provide rationale, guidelines, methods, perspectives and tools for process observation that leaders can use and adapt across the broad range of groups, they may lead. Material is framed in terms of the leader as a process observer and including process observers as resources in their groups. This material is an adaptation and modification of a series of four articles that first appeared as columns in the Association for Specialists in Group Work newsletter entitled Together (since retitled The Group Worker). Original articles appeared under the rubric "Gleanings of a Process Observer" and were published in volume 25, numbers 2 and 3 and volume 26, numbers 1 and 2 (1997–98).

The Process Observer: Gleanings as to Role and Function

The process observer is a catalytic agent who functions in a group for the specific purpose of enhancing process dynamics for the benefit of product results. Consequently, the guiding principle of process observation must be related to the purpose of the task rather than how it is carried out. The general objective of process observation is: *to make the Implicit Explicit so that group members have greater Choice-Ability.*

This principle relates to at least three domains of the group enterprise:

1. **The Intrapersonal Domain:** The personality dynamics of individual members in the group and what is happening within group members during the course of the group.
2. **The Interpersonal Domain:** The relationship dynamics that emerge between members in the process as the group evolves.
3. **The Interactional Domain:** The dynamics that emerge from the interaction between the content or focus of the group, the group process and the individual members.

Attending to these three arenas is intensely engaging, optimally energizing and critically helpful to the leader in carrying out the task of process observation, especially when the content focus of the group or emotional climate invites the leader to become personally involved thus usurping the catalytic quality of the role.

As a catalytic agent, process observation is partly like the gelling agent that stimulates jello to congeal and partly like the mold that shapes the jello into a pattern leaving its imprint on the jello but no part of the mold in it. Thus, the personality of the leader and his/her perspective of group process are critical. Just as no one group leader is exactly like another, no one process observer will have the same catalytic effect as another. This feature promotes autonomy and creativity in process observation while accommodating the personality variations of the leader.

The process observer function can be introduced in many ways, intentionally by initiative and responsively by invitation. For example, the leader as process observer may reflect on, monitor, facilitate, interrupt, analyze or confront the group. When these activities stimulate rather than deter progress, clarify rather than confuse or distort perception, improve rather than impede communication and help focus rather than distract the group, process observation is a resource or asset to the group. At other times process observation may seem neutral (have no immediate impact) or may even appear to be detrimental. However, input relative to process is seldom a liability and often has important influence over time.

Sometimes leaders call in process observers as an adjunct to the leadership role and group process or may appoint group members to take on the role of process observer in the group. Over time and across groups, it has become clear to me that the process observer role is a vital one in any small group and works best when instituted as a formally appointed position in the group rather than an informal adjunct to the group. For example, I now use process observers in all my classes rotating the position so that all class members have the experience and opportunity to learn and contribute to the group process in that way. As a defined position in a class, on an executive board or in a counseling group, the process observer is recognizable and accountable. These features give the person a sense of identity and value in the group. In that regard, groups that incorporate process observers into their structure demonstrate far-sighted leadership wisdom that recognizes the impact of effective group process in producing desirable group outcomes. From a training perspective serving as a process observer enhances the learning process for prospective group leaders (Hensley, 2002).

Gleanings as to Effective Group Process

As noted above, the objective of process observation in a group is "to make the implicit explicit so that group members have greater choice-ability." The implications of this objective manifest themselves in the functionality, productivity and atmosphere of the group and in the morale and experience of the group members. Group process either enhances or impedes a group's effectiveness and contributes to or detracts from a group member's satisfaction (Hulse-Killacky, Killacky, & Donigian, 2001). Therefore, it is important to note the various ways in which group process affects a group's interaction and results.

Group Process is Prophetic

The foundation for effective learning, decision making, problem solving, and conflict resolution in groups is effective group process. Groups have easier and more successful experiences dealing with concepts, policies, issues and problems when they put forth an early effort to attend to process. Destructive impasses, tension, conflicts, and polarization arise when group process is defective or ignored. These dynamics stall the group, undermine its morale and impede its efficiency and productivity. On the other hand, good group process facilitates the internalization of learning, stimulates cooperation, promotes problem resolution and enhances task accomplishment while valuing and affirming diversity and respecting individuality.

A potent indicator of poor process is the escalation of tension and anxiety over time rather than an ebb and flow in relationship to topics and issues pertinent to the group's content or task. Unattended, that anxiety and tension become part of the fabric and context of the group rather than companions to issues, topics and problems experienced in the normal course of addressing the group's agenda. Therefore, leaders and process observers must pay particular heed to the nature of the group's dynamics because they more than anything predict the group's final result.

Group Process is Prototype

From a systemic perspective, the nature of group process in the leadership group (team leaders, board, administrators) of an organization provides the prototype for the subgroups of the organization as a whole. Process-wise: as goes the leadership team, so goes the organization. If the leadership group process reflects collaboration, cooperation and communication, the organizational derivatives or subgroups will follow suit. If leadership group process models individual vs. group initiatives or adversarial or competitive dynamics, the organizational components will reflect that style of process in doing their work. Thus, leadership and group process dynamics permeate the structure of all subgroups thereby influencing their style of interaction and their productivity. If a process observer is operating in a leadership group, the systemic perspective must be incorporated into the process. In that way, the involvement of the process observer has ramifications beyond leadership to the subgroups of the organization and the organization as a whole.

Group Process is Perspective

The manner in which a group incorporates differences, diversity and multicultural characteristics of its members provides the perspective the group will hold and the attitude it will convey not only to its members but also to people outside the group. This perspective becomes the norm of the group as a whole and the model by which it functions. For example, a group that values difference, diversity, and multicultural complexity in its members and deliberations might ask the following catalytic questions at a process level: "Is diversity core and commonality context?" or "Is commonality core and diversity context?" Following either route for effective process can lead to productivity. However, ignoring the duality of core and context with respect to diversity and commonality may result in a form of "Groupthink" that produces results devoid of diversity and multicultural dynamics, reflecting overt or covert insensitivity or bias. Or just as problematic, such an oversight may create a mindset that consciously or unconsciously promotes a perspective that flaunts either diversity or commonality at the expense of the other. Process observers must be cognizant of the diversity dimension inherent in group members that can contribute to or disrupt group process and the ameliorating effect of group dynamics that can either promote difference as an asset or suppress difference to the detriment of the group (see chapter 9: Multicultural and Diversity Competent Group Work by Niloufer Merchant for more detail).

Group Process Has Power

Since the endemic nature of group process as manifested in any group is prophetic of the group's functionality, prototypical of the group's productivity and provocative of the group's perspective, the power of the group process is eminently evident. Therefore, it is essential that leaders work to make process awareness an integral part of member consciousness as they relate to each other and the topic, task, issue or problem that constitutes the purpose for the group's existence. The methods for doing so will be addressed next.

Methods of Process Observation

The methods used to raise group members' process awareness are the means through which process observation is integrated into the group interaction. They also formulate the role of the process observer and generate the specific impact of process observation. Several generic procedures are noted below.

Feedback By Invitation

The group leader or members of the group can solicit input from the process observer periodically during the course of a group session, at critical junctures or stuck points during interaction, or as part of closure or review of the group's work. In any case, the tenor of solicited feedback should balance credit and acknowledgement with constructive criticism or corrective inquiry. Presenting input in an observational manner tempered by tentativeness rather than absoluteness facilitates positive group functioning.

Taking Initiative to Intervene

The process observer's autonomy as a defined group position provides a springboard from which to make initiatives in the best interests of group productivity. Initiatives relative to group process are apropos when the group ignores process, engages in distracting or destructive process, or overlooks process resources in addressing their task or topic. The process observer's style of intervention may vary from "process bulldog" holding the group accountable for good process to "cuddly kitten," encouraging, supporting and smoothing to facilitate good group process. Leaders can incorporate this same dimension into their leadership protocol by specifically bringing the group's attention to process dynamics or events.

Getting the Group To Process Process

Soliciting process input and discussion from the group is a very effective way to generate effective process. This not only raises group member consciousness but their expertise as well and serves to soften the process observer's role boundaries helping to avoid the trap of being perceived as a process "expert" who is an adjunct to the group rather than as an integral part of the group. Leading questions or requests introduced by the leader or process observer such as, "I'm wondering what each of you is experiencing at this time given the intense interaction that just occurred?" or "Maybe we could take a few minutes to process what is going on inside and between us," can be useful in helping the group attend to its own process.

Physical Location and Process Perspective

The physical positioning of the leader or process observer affects both the group's interaction and the process observer's perspective. Location, in and of itself, has meaning (e.g., sitting in the circle vs. outside the circle, or sitting next to the leader vs. across from the leader). Changing location, periodically and strategically, varies the process observer's perspective. Modifying location (e.g., moving in and out of the group) is also useful to accentuate process dynamics. For a process observer, maintaining a mobile physical position in the group is generally advantageous to effective process observation.

Turning Process Observation into Group Development

The content of process input needs to account for and reflect the developmental dynamics of the process stage the group is in at the time it is delivered. Every group and every group session goes through a developmental process sequence characterized by a beginning, middle and ending stage. Generally, the early stage is associated with getting started, getting connected and getting tuned in to the topic, task or focus of the group. The middle or working stage is characterized by focused intensity as the group addresses its agenda in accord with its purpose, and the ending phase is devoted to summary, transition, closure and preparation for future meetings. An effective process observer is cognizant of these developmental differences and the corresponding tasks that must be addressed for the group to function effectively. Feedback presented is therefore commensurate with the phase of the group session (Warm-up, Action, or Close) and the stage of the group (Security, Acceptance, Responsibility, Work, or Closing) and thereby aids the transition and flow of the group accordingly. As process input is attuned to reflect, inform and facilitate the developmental level of the group, functionality is enhanced, leadership is solidified and the role of the process observer or process observation is secured as an asset to the group.

General Gleanings

The Presence and Expression of Leadership: A Process Within a Process

While group process is an integral dimension of every group, a parallel and equally inherent dimension is leadership. Every group that has a leader will experience the impact of leadership on group process both formally (specific roles and actions of the leader carried out in accord with the job description) and informally (personality and style of the leader as manifested in the group). Effective process observation will pay heed to the leader-group interaction and incorporate it into the context of the group dynamics and development. Leader role (job description) and leader personality are critical factors in the group process and need to be acknowledged for both good and ill if the group is to benefit from process observer input. Process observers who hesitate to include leader dynamics in their feedback and leaders who are not self-reflective in that regard curtail the impact of the catalytic role of process observation.

The Complexity of Group Process in a Technological World

The advent of the fax machine, e-mail, and cell phones has greatly modified and enhanced the process dimension of groups. The mere ease of access made possible by "techno-progress" impacts most groups. In groups where members utilize techno-process, information is rapidly and effectively exchanged while members are separate from one another thus affecting the face to face interactions in ways that are not readily accessible to process observation. The e-phenomenon (i.e., easy access of information) is definitely associated with the content and product dimensions of the group often prompting group activity and action without the benefit of group processing. Since the leader or process observer cannot possibly keep tabs on the e-ways, efforts must be made to help group members "talk to each other" rather than simply assume valid communication has occurred because contact was made via an e-device. Face to face interaction still holds the key to effective group process because it gives access to all the personal and interpersonal cues that are eliminated over the e-ways.

Effective Group Process Criteria:
Balancing Being and Belonging in the Course of Producing

In group process terms, *being* is associated with the expression of one's individuality, uniqueness and diversity in the face of group solidarity; and *belonging* relates to modifying one's individuality for the sake of cooperating, complementing, connecting and communicating in the course of group interaction. A critical question that emerges in most groups is: Can individual members be and belong in the course of doing the group's work? Leaders and process observers must keep a keen eye pealed to the delicate balance between these two entities and must make appropriate (well-timed) interventions to promote, facilitate and enhance being and belonging so that they complement each other rather than compete with each other. Generally speaking, groups that emphasize the balance between these two entities and stress their importance are more effective in addressing their tasks.

Process Observation in Practice

The noted advances in processing and process observation combined with the practical relevance of attending to process has prompted me to regularly include process observers and process observation in my group work. In classes and training, for example, the learning process is greatly enhanced and students resonate to being involved in the dynamics of the learning process. The learning environment is expanded, and I receive vital and necessary feedback that helps me modify my teaching, training, and leadership in ways that are beneficial to learning, the learners, and the learning context. Process observation as a leadership skill and the use of process observers whenever possible are critical dimensions of effective group work representing the "cutting edge" of the group work field and contributing to the ever increasing vitality of group process across groups and disciplines. For this reason processing has been acclaimed to have added significant power to the work of group specialists (Ward, 2003; Ward & Litchy, 2004).

Issues in Group Leadership

Leaders must grapple with several basic issues in developing their own approaches to group work. The manner in which they resolve these issues determines their leadership style. Although theories and training influence and guide the leader's development, the responsibility still remains for each person to decide how to function in the group. The purpose of this section is to elucidate those basic issues confronting all group leaders, the resolution of which affects the group process and molds the unique style of the leader's approach.

Responsibility

The issue of responsibility, while somewhat difficult to clarify, is crucial. It can be discussed on a philosophical level, looking at the interactive process and making corresponding assumptions about the basic nature of personhood. On the one hand, if people are viewed as incapable of directing themselves, then leadership must take responsibility to direct and influence them in order to help them accomplish their tasks or resolve their problems and live more satisfying and productive lives. On the other hand, if people are viewed as capable and having sufficient resources to direct themselves, leadership need only entail providing a set of conditions or an environment where those resources can emerge and be used by the individuals to resolve problems and enhance life adjustment or contribute to accomplishing the tasks of the group. In between these two extremes are a plethora of positions that different theories expound as the proper perspective on the responsibility issue in the leadership process. However, the transition from theory to practice is challenging and critical especially in clinical groups where the leader must cope with a wide variety of expectations and pressures from group members in addition to handling the responsibility issue in a professional manner.

Leader responsibility is a continuum issue, with one polarity stressing the leader as primarily responsible for the interaction and impact of the group and the other placing the primary responsibility on the group. Somewhere in between is Mahler's (1969) position, which states that "the main responsibility for growth of the group rests with members but the leader does all he (she) can to facilitate that process" (p. 194). Although these positions describe the relationship of leader responsibility to the group, they do not elaborate on how responsibility is actually manifested.

Leaders who assume primary responsibility take charge of the group experience and its members and operate in much the same manner as the director of a movie. They direct, maneuver, push, confront, structure, and demonstrate to bring out the best possible picture or result. Jacobs (Jacobs, Harvill, & Masson, 2006) promotes this type of active leadership in groups stipulating that "People don't mind being led when they are led well," and "A good group leader is creative, courageous, and makes sure the group is not boring" (personal communication). This type of leadership is designed to produce results that are in accord with individual needs and group goals but the nature of the group experience is mainly the responsibility of the leader. The liabilities of this type of leadership are much the same as those of autocratic leadership styles. Members may not learn to take responsibility for themselves. They may learn dependence rather than autonomy, and their needs and goals are met only to the extent that leaders personally can extend themselves and their expertise to encompass them. Since most group approaches aspire to increase individual responsibility rather than decrease it, this particular approach to leadership is seldom seen in total. Some leaders, however, begin by taking more comprehensive responsibility initially and gradually shift responsibility to the members as they see them develop the competence to handle it. This process of responsibility transfer is usually concurrent with the stages of group development and the typical steps of problem solving to be taken to move members from dependence on outside help at the beginning to independence to autonomy at the end of the group process.

Leaders who invest primary responsibility in the group tend to operate from a frame of reference that is based on confidence and trust in the members and the group to do what is best for their own growth. A common cliché, "Trust the process," supports this perspective. Leaders trust the group to monitor and address excesses and detrimental group actions as well as engage in constructive interpersonal interactions. Consequently, the group's ability to function in a responsible manner is often demonstrated by members stepping in to give support and assistance and diverting overly emotional or inappropriate feedback into more positive channels. Members in this type of group certainly learn responsibility but may at times mistake freedom for license. Because of the extensive pressure groups can exert; at times members become so embroiled in the interaction of the moment that they miss the cues that indicate destructive or unhelpful dynamics are occurring that could produce negative results. In these instances this style of leadership breaks down and could have adverse effects on the individual members and the total group process. However, most leaders who use this approach retain the option of stepping in to intervene if the group does not redirect itself to a more constructive course of action.

The key considerations in handling the responsibility issue relate to the general group goals of helping members learn individual responsibility, guaranteeing their personal well being in the group process while accomplishing the goals of the group. However the leader decides to operate, responsibility must always be evaluated in terms of its impact on the members' ability to function adequately on their own in the context of the group and outside its parameters. In therapeutic groups, if the leader's actions do not increase member independence and autonomy in resolving their personal concerns and problems, those actions are counter-productive. If, however, the leader's stand on responsibility accentuates member self-sufficiency and self-efficacy (Bandura, 1997) in a constructive and growth producing way, then those actions are congruent with the intent of the growth and change process.

Ethically and professionally the leader is always ultimately responsible for the well being of group members and for ensuring that the group interaction is constructive in nature (American Counseling Association, 1995; ASGW, 1998). In other words, leaders, because of their training and professionalism combined with legal and ethical obligations, are remiss if they do not exercise their responsibility to prevent negative consequences in the group. Leaders can share responsibility to a very large degree, but they can never abdicate their responsibility. Doing so jeopardizes the nature of the helping profession and is potentially detrimental to positive therapeutic intervention. Leaders must be willing to divert topic and conversational trends that seem to be shaping into negative and damaging content (Blaker & Samo, 1973). They must be willing to intervene to protect members and to serve as a reality check if the group does not do so. As Lakin (1969) noted, responsibility must be consciously exercised and modeled by the leader if the group is to qualify as a professional therapeutic venture. As Morran, Stockton, and Whittingham (2004) point out, effective leaders know how to promote member safety and protect group members from detrimental effects of the group process while energizing and involving them in the group process.

Many, if not most, of the following issues are contingent upon the position the group leader takes regarding responsibility. Leader decisions about structure and role are particularly related to responsibility.

Role of the Group Leader

The role of the group leader is not only a composite of skills and functions performed but a manifestation of the philosophical biases held. The role issue primarily concentrates on how leaders interact in the group in terms of behavior. In actuality, the leader role is a conglomeration of subroles that emerge in the interaction between the group leader's personality, philosophical orientation, training and the needs of group members and purposes of the group. The subroles that are most frequently used tend to form the character of the leader's style and influence the nature of the group process.

The most common subroles are those of director, facilitator, participator, observer, and expert. The *director* takes an active role in determining the nature and focus of group interaction; the *facilitator* is responsive to what is already occurring in the group; the *participator* operates on an equivalent level with the group members in the discussion; the *observer* stands apart from the interaction interjecting comments as they appear necessary or appropriate; and the *expert* is the source of knowledge, information, and wisdom that can be utilized to help members or improve the group process. These roles are not always separate entities, but they do involve significant identifiable characteristics that perpetuate the group process. Each will be discussed in turn.

The *director* role helps the group process by giving it structure and direction. It is closely aligned with the philosophy of active leadership that places responsibility in the hands of the leader. It enables group leaders to take an active part in prompting the group and to assert themselves in the group process and gives members respite from struggling with ambiguous circumstances. The use of the director role is appropriate to either meet individual needs in the group or initiate useful group interaction. Excessive dependence on this role reduces opportunities for group members to assert themselves and reduces flexibility in the group.

The *facilitator* role depends on the group for an impetus to action. It helps the group process develop by responding to the direction and goals initiated by the group. This role is related to the position where responsibility is placed in the hands of group members. Members feel more freedom to direct their own interactions but are also confident the leader will step in to make suggestions or help when appropriate. Total reliance on this role may create undue pressure and frustration in the group and may even lead to disenchantment with the group process as a whole. Mahler (1969) pointed out that some counselors confuse the facilitation role by combining it with a misconceived notion of permissiveness. "Some counselors appear to be comparable to indecisive and insecure parents; they hope that their 'permissiveness' will enable (clients) to find themselves. However, counselors must have a sense of purpose and direction or they will be able to accomplish very little" (p. 17). In other words, the facilitator role is enacted according to a specific purpose and is not just a matter of rolling with the tide of group interaction.

The *participator* role probably gives group leaders the most difficulty. Knowing when and how to participate with members is hard to determine. Sometimes members really do not want to know about the leader and prefer to have him or her to step forward only in times of crisis. Other times leaders may think they are participating on an equal level only to find they are being perceived as dominating. Of particular importance in this role is the amount and type of sharing the counselor does. The decision about how deeply counselors can or should go into their own lives and feelings is a difficult one. Mahler (1969) indicated that the participatory leader has the most positive impact on group morale and feelings. Through leader participation members come to see the leader as a real human being and do not feel that they are being forced to engage in things the leader is not willing to do. Dinkmeyer and Muro (1971) also pointed out that the effective group counselor is one who is viewed by group members as being with them, and for them, as individuals. Participating can contribute to that perception. An effective participator can usually be active in the group without creating the undesirable side effects usually associated with subroles that cast the leader in a more separated position from members. Participating is a good alternative to passive group leadership for those leaders who want to be active but do not want to dominate or take charge of the group process.

The *observer* role is one of the most flexible roles the leader can play because it can usually be combined with other roles (participant-observer, director-observer). In its more pure form leaders attempt to maintain an objective yet sensitive awareness of what is transpiring in the group. Bieschke, Matthews, Wade, and Pricken (1998) make a valid distinction between "observation" as a static activity where the observer is rarely involved in the group process and "process observation" as dynamic and leading to the observer being actively involved in the group process. The latter role is the one being addressed here. At times the observer role may rankle members because they feel they are being analyzed and watched. This reaction can cause rifts between the members and the leader. If, however, leaders attend to process and can parlay their observations into meaningful comments that are beneficial to individuals or the group process, the leader's role as observer will be validated and negative reactions curtailed.

The *expert* role of the counselor is potentially both the most problematic and most useful role the counselor can play in the group. The temptation to be the expert is one of the major pitfalls of many group leaders. As experts, leaders sometimes get themselves into an advice-giving bind or set a pattern of doing individual counseling in a group from which they have difficulty extricating themselves. Mahler (1969) stated the basic problem with leaders who are too quick to use their expertise: "A counselor is lacking in knowledge and understanding of how behavior is changed if he (she) is too eager to give answers, solutions to problems or advice instead of helping individuals discover answers and solutions for themselves" (p. 17). The counselor as expert is also a necessary and useful aspect of the group leadership role. Leader training, experience, and knowledge are invaluable assets in helping individuals with their problems and in developing a therapeutic group atmosphere. It is particularly helpful in teaching interpersonal skills and translating theory into practical problem-solving methods in the group. Striking a balance between using expertise and refusing to do so is a complex task for the group leader. One general guideline in determining whether the leader should opt for the role of expert or not is to assess the motivation for that action. If it is in the best interests of an individual or the group process, most likely the effect will be positive. If, however, it is motivated by self-gratification or ego reinforcement on the counselor's part, it should be used hesitantly. Since expertise inherently carries some residual effect of personal gratification, enhancing the group process and assisting individuals should predominate as the impetus for its use.

The interplay between these roles is of significant import to the group process. The leader must carefully assess their utility and influence in order to function in the most positive manner as a leader and develop professional competence as a group worker.

The Structure Dimension

The dynamic interplay of structured groups versus unstructured groups has been with us almost as long as the group movement itself (see *Journal for Specialists in Group Work*, 1979). Although some would argue that lack of structure by the group leader is in itself a form of structure, a semantic battle does little to help the group leader resolve this dilemma. Landreth (1973) zeroed in on this issue definitively when he wrote that "the basic question is not whether or not to structure but rather what kind of structuring is needed and how much to structure" (p. 371). Bednar and Langenbaum (1979) added that a linear polarity of structure to nonstructure does not exist because the nonimposition of expectations (ambiguity) is in and of itself a structure. From these premises then our discussion will derive.

Nonstructured groups basically mean that the leader does less to initiate group interaction and functions in the more responsive capacity of a facilitator a la Carl Rogers. *Structured groups* usually refer to groups that the leader actively directs in an initiating manner, often with the help of structured activities and with ostensible control over the interaction. In the former case, the leader's image is submerged in the group process to a point where his or her eminence as the titular head of the group is diffused. In the latter case, the leader is always an obviously significant person who seldom loses either position or influence as the leader of the group. Between these two points are many positions that reflect more or less the basic positions.

A perusal of the pros and cons of these basic positions on structuring reveals the surprisingly complementary nature of the two positions. What is an advantage to one side is a disadvantage to the other and vice versa. Thus when viewed through a flexible perspective, movement one way or the other on the structure continuum becomes less a liability and more an asset in making the group process effective. So we come full circle to Landreth's (1973) position.

The arguments for nonstructured groups revolve around the learning by experience philosophy. Group members, in struggling with the lack of structure, come to realize the need for and nature of positive structure and work to develop it. They learn personal responsibility and identify more closely with their work.

Less structure gives more opportunity for individual differences to be accounted for and provides members with more freedom to act constructively on their own behalf and in helping others. The leader in less structured groups needs to tolerate ambiguity and risk member dissatisfaction and negative feedback during the initial phases when members are grappling with the lack of leader direction. When successful, the less structured approach creates strong group cohesiveness, high morale, and a positive therapeutic milieu in which members can help and be helped without the prior sanction of the group leader to do so.

Arguments for the more *structured group* more than compensate for the drawbacks of the less structured approach, just as the strengths of the less structured approach counter the deficiencies of more structured groups. Dinkmeyer and Muro (1971) referred to structuring as programming: "To program a group means that the group counselor, the official group leader, chooses to initiate specific group behaviors of his (her) own choosing at some time in the group's life. Spontaneous interaction, of course, refers to behaviors that originate within the context of the group life itself" (p. 122). Bach (1954) enumerated several advantages to structuring. It enhances cooperation in early group life, decreases leader and member anxiety, enlarges weak minority participation, contrasts individual performance against group performance, differentiates group life from the outside world culture, and reduces emotional anxiety over free expression without altering the leader's role. Landreth (1973) added that structuring may help leaders approach the group with more self-confidence, a prerequisite to the development of a cohesive group. By structuring, group members know what is expected and can therefore concentrate their energies toward accomplishing the goals of the group and resolving their own problems.

Caple and Cox (1989) investigated the relationship between structure and the variables of cohesion and attraction in groups. They found that initial group sessions that were too ambiguous produced anxiety that was detrimental to self-disclosure and deterred both cohesion and attraction. On the other hand, "groups on which structure was imposed reported higher levels of attraction" (p. 22). In contrast, too much structure resulted in lower group cohesion. Over time, however, both structured and unstructured groups evened out relative to self-disclosure and subsequent levels of attraction and cohesion. These findings led them to recommend the use of structure initially to facilitate self-disclosure and thereby enhance the development of attraction and cohesion. Hetzel, Barton, and Davenport (1994) supported this finding and stipulated that structured activities are particularly relevant for initiating men's groups. Initial structuring reduces anxiety and improves communication which opens the way for group dynamics to develop.

The point of the matter is that the need for structure varies from group to group and leader to leader. Some groups do not need any help in structuring, while others need help because they will not, or do not know how to, assume responsibility for doing so. In addition, the purpose for which groups are formed greatly affects the need for structure. Thus the resolution of this issue is contingent on a variety of factors. The most important variable seems to be the leader's propensity to determine how much structure is needed and to act in accordance with that awareness.

Group Leadership: Art or Science?

Max DePree (1989) in his classic leadership primer entitled *Leadership is an Art* states the following:

> The first responsibility of a leader is to define reality. The last is to say thank you. In between the two, the leader must become a servant and a debtor, That sums up the progress of an artful leader (p. 11).

Although emanating from the world of business and Fortune 500 companies, there is a lot of wisdom to be gleaned from DePree's perspective in the field of human services—specifically group leadership. He emphasizes that the signs of outstanding leadership appear primarily among the followers, in this case members of the group. Are they "reaching their potential? Are they learning? Do they achieve required results? Do they change with grace? Manage conflict?" (DePree, 1989, p. 12). What better criteria to determine the merit of leadership in all forms of group related to this text.

The art versus science dilemma often is raised in the helping professions, particularly those which are concerned with helping people resolve psychological and personal-social problems. However, this issue need not force a group leader into a decision one way or the other since in all probability leading a group is a combination of both. Mahler (1969) described leadership as a science because its methods and procedures are exposed to objective assessment for validation (see DeLucia-Waak & Bridbord, 2004). Leadership is also an art because it depends on the "counselor's intuitive sensitivity in knowing when to make a suggestion or provide information, when and how to challenge clients to action, and when to support client efforts to face disturbing feelings" (Mahler, 1969, p. 12). Dinkmeyer and Muro (1971) stated that successful group counselors are an integrated blend of specialist and artist. Ohlsen, Horne, and Lawe (1988) referred to the leader as both a scientist and a practitioner.

Leaders must be scholars who keep themselves continually abreast of new knowledge pertaining to the field of group work. They must be scientists who use empirical methods to assess the impact of the group process and evaluate results. And they must be artists who can use their knowledge and the results of scientific inquiry to meet the needs of group members, develop the group milieu, help members resolve their problems, accomplish the group's tasks and guide the group process. Any time leaders lose sight of the personal element by attempting to conduct groups according to standardized scientific principles, they will become rigid and inflexible, jeopardizing the effectiveness of the group in helping individuals. Any time leaders rely only on their own personality and artistic/intuitive prowess in leading a group, they lose the perspective of objective evaluation and conceptual stability that is necessary to elicit the benefit and consistency of the group process in helping people resolve their problems and groups to accomplish their goals. To state it another way, a leader's style must be founded in theory and validated by research so that the creative and conceptual basis for leadership is balanced by the empirical evidence of effectiveness. So, the resolution to this whole issue is to develop a balance between leadership as an art—accounting for the subjective nature of human beings, their needs, differences, and uniqueness and the vitality of the group process—and leadership as a science—supplying structure and direction to the group process and objectivity to its impact. In this way the best qualities of both can be used to make group work a dynamic and viable method of helping people engage in personal change and to enhance productivity.

Rules for Group Interaction

One of the most important issues that demand the attention of the group leader is the development of agreed upon rules to govern the group's interaction. This issue has been referred to as a developmental task in groups (setting boundaries) and as a function of the group leader (rules-keeping) but needs to be reiterated here for emphasis. Burlingame, Fuhriman, and Johnson (2001) identified "defining group rules" as part of pre-group preparation which is one of six empirically supported principles that affirm the validity of the therapeutic relationships in groups.

Many strategies are available for handling the rules issue in groups. Some leaders prefer to establish a comprehensive set of ground rules, discussing them thoroughly with group members in screening interviews, pre-group preparation meetings or the first group session. If relegated to the first session, however, Jacobs (Jacobs et al., 2006) cautions leaders not to begin the session with rules as it may set a tone that neither the members nor the leader prefers. Other leaders present a skeleton list of basic rules and then rely on the group to develop additional rules relevant to that particular group. Still others make the development of guidelines to govern interaction a group task. Together with the leader the group works out the rules by which they will relate. Leaders who prefer this method praise it as an excellent means of developing cohesiveness and commitment to the rules and the group. A final strategy is to develop ground rules as the need arises. In this approach the guidelines take on a developmental perspective, since needed rules are invoked as the group moves from stage to stage in its life cycle. In all approaches are two main similarities: (1) the group needs to arrive at consensus regarding the rules and be willing to act in accord with them, and (2) the leader is responsible to see that they are sufficiently comprehensive, reasonable, and adhered to.

Ethical Practice

Certainly counselors who are group workers have a professional commitment to function in accordance with the ethical codes developed by the American Counseling Association (1995), the American Psychological Association (2002), and other professional organizations that devise ethical standards to govern professional conduct. In addition, acting in accordance with *Best Practices in Group Counseling* (chapter 8) and ASGW's Best Practice Guidelines (1998) is imperative. Beyond that the implications of many of the leader skills and functions already discussed that relate to protection of the individual, maintaining rules, and containing excesses are geared to helping group workers operate in an ethical manner. Leaders have a professional obligation to function in the best interests of group members, the setting in which they function, and the community to the maximum degree possible. Of course there will always be conflicts of interests, ambiguous situations, and crises in which counselors will have to make decisions based on their own professional judgment, their commitment to their clients, the purpose of the group and conformity to the legal and ethical standards that govern their profession. These decisions are not always easy, require careful consideration before acting, and are best made under the auspices of supervision or peer consultation. Ultimately, group leaders are always responsible for ethical practice in their leadership role. Dye (1981) defined ethical practice as the "consensus of judgment on the part of competent, experienced practitioners" (p. 234). As such, familiarity with ethical and legal parameters along with ongoing consultation, supervision, and keeping abreast of current developments in the profession provide the leader with the necessary background for making judgments in any particular group situation. For licensed professionals, continuing education requirements are designed to help professional group workers stay current often stipulating that ethics continuing education hours be completed annually.

One pitfall that needs to be specifically mentioned about ethical practice relates to depending on group approval as a means of deciding whether a particular experience, method, or technique is ethical or not. Leaders must always be aware of their own professional responsibility and the variety of personality and cultural differences among group members. The simple fact that professional people advocate an experience, or that members involved agree to an experience, does not necessarily justify those experiences as ethically defensible, culturally appropriate, or psychologically sound. Any experiences, interactions, or activities of a questionable nature in the group require the maximum use of counselor competence and resources to support their inclusion. Sensitivity to and resolution of ethical dilemmas is a necessary element of effective leadership and one of the reasons that ASGW has declared one of the core group work competencies to be "knowledge of ethical considerations unique to group work" (see the ASGW brochure, "What Every Counselor Should Know About Groups"; available at http:// www.asgw.org).

Group Leader Orientation:
Individual, Group, or Theory

Group leaders are often faced with decisions about whether they should act in the interests of an individual, in support of the group, or in accord with a theoretical framework. Sometimes counselors feel caught between the "devil and the deep blue sea" when individuals lock horns with the group or when the group makes demands that are out of step with the counselor's theoretical rationale. Although no easy solution exists to this issue, Dinkmeyer and Muro (1971) cast some light on the subject: "No individual is sacrificed to a theory, no participant is required to respond to a given group technique, and no group member is in any way made to respond to queries that the counselor himself (herself) would not care to have asked of him (her)" (p. 95). The implication seems to be that the interests of the individual come first, the group next, and the theory last. And the key criterion should be whether counselors are willing to put themselves in a similar spot.

These ideas help, but they also are a bit naive in light of pressures placed on leaders in training and the leader's more extensive personal experience and maturity. Leaders may be willing to do some things that are beyond the capability of the members. Training programs consciously and unconsciously mold leaders according to certain theoretical and philosophical biases that are difficult to lay aside in the interests of groups or individuals. Similarly, certain individuals in the group who disrupt, resist, and abuse the group process may be difficult to support even when support is professionally appropriate. The solution to this situation therefore requires that leaders develop their own leadership protocol combining their theoretical perspective with their knowledge of the group process, their understanding of individuals who compose the group and the objectives of the group, all under the auspices of acceptable professional practice standards and ethical guidelines and then face individual instances of conflict with openness and flexibility to be sure the best possible route is followed. This is also a particularly important place to involve supervision and peer consultation.

As indicated at the beginning of this section, the manner in which group leaders resolve these issues determines leadership style and effectiveness. Leadership style is influenced by leader personality and training, the needs of group members, the nature of their problems, and the goals of the group. An effective leadership approach accounts for all these factors in resolving the issues and facing the challenges of group leadership. In addition, it operates within the context of group development. Effective leaders are able to guide their individual behavior so that what they say and do and how they handle the various issues of leadership are not antithetical to therapeutic and constructive group functioning.

Special Considerations

What might be termed special considerations for the group leader may have many dimensions. Every group member potentially qualifies as a special consideration on the basis of his or her individual uniqueness. The different purposes associated with different types of groups call upon leaders to make special efforts. But the intent of this discussion is to denote several areas that subsume individual cases and diverse groups and that when realized give the leader a sense of appreciation for the struggle, turmoil, and pressure group members experience in garnering benefit from the group process.

The first area is the realization that *personal growth and change is a difficult and often painful process*, especially when associated with the psychological and personal-social components of one's life. Maslow (Katz, 1973) perhaps stated it best:

> We must appreciate that many people choose the worse rather than the better, that growth is often a painful process and may for this reason be shunned, that we are afraid of our own best possibilities in addition to loving them, and that we are all of us profoundly ambivalent about truth, beauty, virtue, loving them and fearing them too. (p. 80)

When we group leaders begin to feel frustrated with members' inabilities to act in ways to improve their lives or contribute constructively to the group task, we must try to stop and sense the real effort, almost superhuman at times, required to do so. What may seem to all outward appearances the best and most sure fire solution to a client's problems may for that person be a nemesis. What to the leader and the group is an obviously good, appropriate, and possible action may be totally threatening to the person who must carry it out. Thus, when encountering resistance we must bear in mind the possibility that the inner fear of change is a stifling factor in members' desires for and thrusts toward growth. Seigelman (1983) noted that, "Major life change is not made easily. It usually takes some external deadline . . . some outrage, or burnout . . . or some outside pressure . . . to get us moving. We don't divert the course of our lives lightly or easily—at least not if we are prudent" (p. 77).

Resistance to change by members in the group *may be the result of an internal conflict* associated with the needs to be adequate in coping with life. Combs and

Snygg (1959) have proposed that two major forces that motivate us to be more adequate in our lives also are the cause of resistance. Every person experiences a desire to maintain the self as it is known (self-preservation) and a desire to improve the self (self-enhancement). These desires create a major conflict because in order for the latter to succeed some part of that which is dear to the former must be given up. This struggle is one of the major barriers facing group members in their effort to change. The risk of giving up that which is known about oneself, even though it causes problems, in exchange for something promising but unknown and untested is not easy. The group leader's ability to acknowledge and relate to this perpetual human dilemma in members can do much to turn a confounding barrier into a facilitating resource.

While these first two areas deal with the special consideration of common psychological factors within individual members, the third area concerns the relationship of individual members in the group. The reaction of individual members in the group generally epitomizes humanity's lifelong struggle to "differentiate (a self) while retaining a feeling of unity with others" (Mahler, 1969, p. 33). The whole developmental process in life is a journey from dependence to independence to interdependence, and now with the extension of life expectancy and the added developmental stages of aging and dying, possibly back to dependence (DeSpelder & Strickland, 2005). Every human being wishes to be his or her own person while at the same time feeling part of a group. Finding the right balance is an extremely difficult task and maintaining it in all situations once found is nearly impossible. In interpersonal relationships the quest for autonomy and for intimacy and connection often creates our greatest frustrations. No wonder then that group members at times flounder desperately in striking a suitable equilibrium between independence and conformity in the group process. Not surprisingly this equilibrium is easily upset, throwing both the individual and the group into a dither of defensive maneuvers and assertive challenges. Rybak and Brown (1997) frame the struggle as follows:

> Once members have developed some cohesion and a beginning level of integration, the next developmental task is for members to differentiate enough from each other so that each finds a unique place and role in the group. (p. 40)

These dynamics pose a critical question for group leaders at any given moment in the group. Is integration that draws members together or differentiation that individuates members most important? Leaders "must decide whether to pull members together as a group or let them differentiate as individuals. The orchestration of such decisions is the way they guide the group through its developmental stages" (Matthews, 1992, p. 163). The group leader who is sensitive to the existence of these connecting-differentiating dynamics and cognizant of the fragile nature of individual-group relationships negotiated in the group will be able to act more constructively, less critically, and more patiently in helping the group prosper.

The importance of these *special considerations* has primary relevance to the leader and subsequent relevance to group members. Leaders who understand the pain of growing, sense the fear of change, feel the inner conflict in the struggle to improve one's self, and appreciate the battle waged between individual dynamics and group pressures will have a more caring attitude in working with the group. This attitude will relieve many of the pressures and anxieties leaders experience, especially when groups do not go well. They will spend less time worrying, expend less energy in group- or self-flagellation, and concentrate more intensely on helping the members and promoting a therapeutic atmosphere in the group. It will also help the leader create a "loving therapeutic atmosphere" and be a "loving figure" thereby defusing the transferential issues that can emerge if members become defensive, frustrated, or disappointed (Bemak & Epp, 1996, pp. 122–123). This attitude of patience, encouragement, understanding, peace, and confidence will be transferred to group members, and give them reassurance that their struggles are worthwhile and that they are understood and appreciated.

Learning Activities

The activities described in the following section fall into two categories. The first is methods or strategies for obtaining leadership experience that are grounded on a solid base of professional training and supervision principles. The first eight learning activities are within this category. The second category contains exercises designed to assess leader characteristics or abilities and develop leader competencies. The last eight activities are in this second category.

Leadership Training and Supervision Experiences

Leading Groups in Undergraduate Classes

Many undergraduate classes in education, psychology, social work, communication, human relations, and other disciplines incorporate small group experiences into their requirements. These groups tend to have specific course related goals and are required so that attendance is mandatory. Even when provided as an adjunct option for extra credit or broadening the learning endeavor, the groups are well received. Instructors are often amenable to graduate students in group classes leading these groups. The workload for professors is reduced, the learning potential for their students is extended, and graduate students receive an excellent opportunity to acquire valuable group leadership experience. A formal program of cooperation between the graduate and undergraduate instructors is preferable. However, if such an agreement does not exist, personally contacting undergraduate instructors and working out an individual independent study or field work experience is suitable. An advisable procedure is to be under some type of formal supervision (for credit) for liability purposes rather than volunteering your services.

Rotating Group Leadership

One method of obtaining an initial exposure to group leadership is to rotate leadership responsibility among members of groups formed as part of a group dynamics course. A schedule can be organized beforehand designating the sequence of leaders and subgroup membership. This type of experience serves the purpose of introducing prospective leaders to the role and function of group leadership and exposes them to a number of leadership styles, since each member's approach will reflect his or her own personality. A more important purpose is to give members an opportunity to assess the skills and characteristics of effective leadership. These sessions can be video taped for purposes of feedback and discussion of the individual's approach and issues of group leadership. The psychological pressure of this experience should be low key because members will not get an in-depth leadership experience, probably leading the group only once or twice during the course of a quarter or semester. The focus on general group leadership dynamics should be retained as the main emphasis, and the evaluation of individual performance should be secondary.

Rotating Coleadership

A variation of the method just mentioned, which gives added depth to the leadership experience, is to rotate coleadership responsibility in the group. In this way two members can be in charge for longer time periods—say three to five sessions—and get a more definitive picture of the leader's role. Sessions can be video taped and feedback from the instructor and the group can be given to the coleaders after each session. An overall evaluation can be conducted at the conclusion of their sessions. This strategy also lends itself to variations such as alternating partners, matching coleaders on the basis of personality similarities or differences, and having coleaders model specific philosophies or theories of group leadership to expose members to a broader range of leadership possibilities. It also places members who assume the leadership roles under less pressure since they have a mutually available source of help and reinforcement in the form of the coleader.

Coleadership with an Experienced Leader

One of the very best ways to develop group leadership skills is the mentoring or apprenticeship process where a prospective leader co-leads with an experienced professional. According to McCue-Herlihy (1996), "mentoring is an intentional, insightful, supportive process in which a more skilled or experienced person serving as a role model, nurtures, befriends, teaches, sponsors, encourages and counsels a less skilled or less-experienced person for the purpose of promoting the latter's professional and/or personal development" (p. 171). The advantages of this approach are numerous. The experience is an intense and complete immersion in the leader's role. It supplies the prospective leader with a role model to follow and a source of support in crisis situations. It helps the new leader understand the responsibility involved by placing that responsibility directly on his or her shoulders, and it provides a safe place to experiment with the development of a personal style and approach. The difficulty in implementing this approach is finding enough experienced leaders to serve as mentors. Even then problems may occur in arranging schedules and getting the necessary approval to participate. However, these problems should not deter the counselor trainee or counselor educator from trying to develop such a program. If conscientious efforts are made to locate groups and experienced leaders, professional leaders are usually more than willing to take on novices as coleaders and teach them the ropes.

Coleadership with Supervision

Another good way to develop valuable leadership experience is to have two potential leaders co-lead groups under the supervision of an experienced group leader. When experienced leaders can't be found to take on a coleader, this alternative serves equally as well. It has many of the same mentoring advantages as the previous strategy and may be less threatening to the potential leaders. Sometimes new leaders tend to be withdrawn and passive in the presence of an experienced leader. In this case, both leaders are on an equal footing, feel more responsibility, and have less opportunity to be passive. This type of experience tends to be more action oriented and less observation oriented. An added dimension that serves as a control factor and a learning impetus is the inclusion of a supervisor. This method requires less time on the counselor educator's part than co-leading but still gives new leaders the benefit of experience and knowledge through feedback and evaluation sessions. Supervision of this nature introduces additional variables into the group process like video taping or observation, but these tend to be accommodated easily by both the leaders and the group. DeLucia-Waack (2002) has formulated a written guide to assist leaders in preparation for supervision that can be adapted to any of the formats here the involve supervision.

One problem with coleadership (this pertains to all the strategies that involve co-leading) is that success depends on the ability of the coleaders to work out an effective team approach to the group. Sometimes personality conflicts and differences of group leadership style become obstacles that interfere with the development of a therapeutic group atmosphere. Coleadership thus adds an important variable to the process. Coleadership is recommended generally as a viable leadership form by many group experts (Corey, 1995; Donigian & Malnati, 1997; Gladding, 1991) and advocated for certain types of groups (e.g., groups that focus on gender issues, relational problems, or intimacy difficulties). Carroll and Wiggins (1997) discuss in detail the advantages and disadvantages of coleadership (pp. 83–85) and note that in practice coleadership is for "experienced counselors, not for two neophytes who feel insecure in their role and lack confidence in their leadership" (p. 83). In addition, Riva, Wachtel, and Lasky (2004) reviewed the research literature on coleadership and found that coleadership though common was not necessarily validated as more effective. They noted the importance of coleaders working out their relationship as a critical component of the experience, but found little evidence that the model actually had a positive effect on the group process. As a training format, however, prospective leaders can examine the utility and relevance of coleadership as an appropriate learning device based on the intuitive sense that if coleaders develop a positive relationship in their group approach, they have a greater capacity for helping individuals and the group than a single leader.

Supervised Leadership in Practicum, Internship, or Field Work

As has already been indicated, group leadership experience should be the focus of a separate fieldwork experience. Once the counselor has developed a solid cognitive and experiential background in group work, the only way left to develop group leadership ability is by leading groups. The advantages of a practicum/internship setting should be utilized to facilitate that process. The supervision provided by the trainee's field supervisor and the practicum/internship director is an invaluable source of learning. In addition, the sharing of experiences with other practicum students or interns adds significantly to the learning and experience of the group leader. More effort is required, however, in establishing specific group counseling field placements to complement the general fieldwork requirements. In this way counselors in training will have access to a more formal means of developing their group abilities on an experiential level.

Groups for Group Leaders

One specific type of leadership training format is the group for group leaders. The general nature of this procedure is to draw together a small group (six to eight members) of counselors who are interested in further developing their expertise in groups. Under the direction of one or more qualified group experts, the group functions as both an intensive group experience and a leadership training process. In other words, the group leaders themselves form the group in which they gain their leadership experience. There are three basic components to this approach. The first, of course, is the personal experience of each person as a member of the group. The second is related to those activities in the group that are designed to give the members experience in the leadership role, and the third is a cognitive component involving feedback and discussion of various leadership skills, functions, and issues.

This format allows much room for flexibility. One variation is for the group to be handled by two experienced group experts using a format of one experiential session and one cognitive session each week. One expert serves as the facilitator of the experiential session, while the other observes the experiential session, using observations as the basis for discussion and feedback in the cognitive session. During the experiential session members can rotate leadership responsibility or simply work with leaders as they emerge. The facilitator is there not to lead the group but to lend expertise, become personally involved, and assume ultimate responsibility in case negative circumstances arise in the group. The follow-up session is an analysis of the experiential session concentrating on group dynamics, group theory and essentials of group leadership.

Peer Consultation

One of the often untapped resources among professional counselors is the knowledge and experience of colleagues. The unfounded myth that seeking assistance from fellow professionals is tantamount to an admission of incompetence has long been an inhibitor to sharing expertise. The group work field has been no exception. However, due to the increased concern for promoting and assuring ethical practice and with a substantial push from credentialing and licensing/certification requirements where peer consultation is more typically being mandated, this resource can and should be used to acquire group leadership expertise.

Several suggestions for making effective use of peer consultation as a professional resource in regard to developing group counseling expertise follow:

1. Obtain a total department/agency commitment to the use of group methods in counseling and therapy so that all members have a vested interest.
2. Develop a group program so that the need for expertise becomes apparent to all concerned.
3. Set aside specific time slots for consultation to occur rather than depending on catch-as-catch-can meeting arrangements.

4. Arrange schedules that allow for observation and don't create added pressures on either the group leader or peer consultant.

5. Develop settings where observation can take place without causing discomfort to the group, the leader, or the observer and without interfering in the group process.

6. Exchange roles so that equal opportunity is afforded to be the consultant and the consultee. Nothing is more irksome than to always be asking for consultation and never being asked for feedback in return.

7. Develop guidelines for consultation that specify criteria for evaluation and establish a format for giving feedback. These guidelines should be the product of discussion and input involving all parties in the consulting relationship and should be agreed upon prior to any consultation occurring.

If these general guidelines are used, the threat involved in exposing one's methods and approach to one's colleagues is alleviated. As such, peer consultation is a professionally enhancing method of improving one's group skills while insuring ethical and competent practice. It can also be a morale building experience for the total department, agency, or group practice.

Leadership Training Activities

Group Leaders in My Life

Divide an 8½ × 11 sheet of paper into three columns both lengthwise and widthwise (nine sections total). In each section of column 1 identify one group in which you have been a member and from which you have personally benefited. In each section of column 2 identify the names of the leader(s) of each of those groups. In each section of column 3 describe the characteristics or traits of each group leader. Circle or underline the traits you believe you have. In small groups (three to four persons) share the characteristics identified in the third column, including your own. Use data from the activity to discuss traits of effective group leaders.

Classified Ad

Write a classified ad for a group leader. Include information such as personality traits, training, qualifications and credentials, expectations of the leadership role, setting, and clientele of the group. This activity may be used to initiate a discussion of the essential nature and qualifications of a group leader. Instructions may be varied so that members write classified ads for themselves as group leaders. Have group members read their classified ads to the group and facilitate a discussion around content. An effective follow-up activity is to have the group write a composite classified ad using the data and discussion from the individual ads.

Consensus Leadership Traits

Have each person in the group write down two or three traits that represent effective group leadership. Form dyads and have the two members develop a composite list. Continue to merge subgroups (dyads to foursomes and foursomes to groups of eight, etc.) until a total group consensus or composite is attained. Use the consensus traits to initiate a discussion of effective group leaders.

Dimensions of Group Leadership

Using the Dimensions of Group Leadership scale in Figure 6.1, have each group member place an asterisk at the point on each continuum that reflects his or her self-perception on that polarity. When completed, have members connect the marks to create a profile. Have each person present his or her profile to the group. Discuss results in terms of similarities and differences. Use the continuum constructs to derive goals for individuals to work on as group leaders. Continuum items may be added or deleted to create a scale that is appropriate to the group.

A modification of this activity is to use the line-up format and have group members physically place themselves on each continuum so that both self-assessment and comparative personality data are available for discussion. This version allows access to feedback from others in the process as group members jostle to find their place and space in relation to others on each of the variables.

As a group leader I am:		
Talkative	_/_/_/_/_/_/_/_/_/	Quiet
Directive	_/_/_/_/_/_/_/_/_/	Nondirective
Humorous	_/_/_/_/_/_/_/_/_/	Serious
Confident	_/_/_/_/_/_/_/_/_/	Hesitant
Prepared	_/_/_/_/_/_/_/_/_/	Unprepared
Structured	_/_/_/_/_/_/_/_/_/	Nonstructured
Confrontive	_/_/_/_/_/_/_/_/_/	Supportive
Comfortable	_/_/_/_/_/_/_/_/_/	Ill at Ease
Personable	_/_/_/_/_/_/_/_/_/	Aloof
Authoritative	_/_/_/_/_/_/_/_/_/	Facilitative

Figure 6.1 Dimensions of group leadership.

1. Put a check mark in column one after the three characteristics you feel describe the general type of personality you portray most of the time as a group leader.
2. After doing the above place the first name of each of the other members of your group in one of the other columns. Then check the three characteristics you think best describe each of them as group leaders.

	ONE (Self)	(Other Member Names)			
gentle					
gracious					
agreeable					
understanding					
considerate					
calm					
soft spoken					
reserved					
quiet					
sincere					
warm					
sweet					
cheerful					
carefree					
confident					
witty					
decisive					
dominant					
intellectual					
serious					
dignified					
mature					
animated					
enthusiastic					
outgoing					
radiant					
vivacious					

3. Share perceptions in the group giving an explanation for each rating.

Figure 6.2 Personality inventory analysis.

Personality Inventory Analysis

Since personality is a crucial factor in group leadership, the personality characteristics in Figure 6.2 enable prospective leaders to assess for themselves—and obtain feedback as to—their primary personality traits. Using the Personality Inventory Analysis or a modification thereof, have each member place a check mark in column one (self) identifying three characteristics that describe the general type of personality they portray to others most of the time. Then have members write in the names of the other group members (one in each column) and place check marks by three traits that they believe best describe each person's personality. Share these data by having each person first share his or her own perception and then get feedback as to what other members perceive. Process the information in light of similarities and differences in perceptions. Seek to build self-knowledge, self-awareness, and self-esteem since each of the descriptions can be construed as constructive. Also, help members create composite personality sketches by combining traits and integrating self and other perceptions.

Nature of Leadership

The nature of group leadership (Adapted from Johnson and Johnson, 1982, pp. 36-39) can be summarized in two key polarity perspectives. The first is *leaders make the group versus the group makes the leader*. In this perspective the leader is either the one who controls the fortunes of the group or is a pawn in the hands of the group that controls its own fortune. The second is *leaders are born, not made versus leaders are made, not born*. This perspective contrasts innate ability of the leader with learned ability as the key to effective leadership.

Divide the group in half; assign one group, "the leader makes the group" perspective and the other group, "the group makes the leader" perspective. Have each group discuss its position and make a case for its accuracy (10–15 minutes). Then create dyads by pairing partners from each group and giving them 10 minutes to convince each other of the correctness of their position. Repeat the same process, using the "leaders-are-born" and "leaders-are-made" perspectives. First, have the group discuss their position and then form dyads. After each polarity has been addressed, conduct a brief follow-up discussion to cull the group's reaction and position on each perspective. A final activity is to have each person present their personal position on the two polarities. When all individuals have presented, facilitate a group discussion on the merits of the various perspectives and come up with a general group view. This activity tends to elicit many tangential issues relative to group leadership, which may be valuable to pursue.

Analysis of Group Skills

The form in Figure 6.3 is useful in helping prospective group leaders assess their attitudes and behaviors in the group and determine goals for themselves with respect to improving skills. Items may be added or changed to depict any of the skill areas described earlier in the chapter.

This form is to help you think about your leadership attitudes and behavior in groups.

Directions:

1. For each item, circle a number along the 5-point scale that fits you best.
2. When you have completed all the items, go back and star three or four scales you would like most to change.
3. Draw an arrow (← or →) to show in which direction you want to change.
4. Select one group skill (from the three or four starred scales) that you would be most willing to work on during this class or supervision period.
5. Write a contract with yourself to improve this behavior or skill. In the contract, identify specific behaviors that you would like to develop. This contract will be renegotiated periodically.

    a. Ability to listen to others in an alert and understanding way
       Very poor 1 2 3 4 5 Very high

    b. Ability to express ideas and thoughts clearly
       Very poor 1 2 3 4 5 Very high

    c. Willingness to tell others what I feel
       Conceal everything 1 2 3 4 5 Reveal everything

    d. Willingness to accept direction from others
       Usually unwilling 1 2 3 4 5 Very willing

    e. Tendency to take over and dominate a group
       Don't ever try 1 2 3 4 5 Try very hard

    f. Reactions to comments about my behavior
       Ignore them 1 2 3 4 5 Incorporate them

    g. Understanding why I do what I do in groups (insight)
       Don't usually know 1 2 3 4 5 Understand very well

    h. Reaction to conflict and expressions of anger in a group
       Become   Become
       immobilized and ineffective 1 2 3 4 5 stimulated and more effective

    i. Reaction to expressions of affection and warmth in a group
       Become   Become
       immobilized and ineffective 1 2 3 4 5 stimulated and more effective

    j. Tolerance for opinions and viewpoints different from my own.
       Very low 1 2 3 4 5 Very high

    k. Ability to lead in a group
       Very low 1 2 3 4 5 Very high

Figure 6.3 Analysis of group skills.

Problems Leading Groups

This activity is useful in eliciting discussion of leadership problems in supervision. Pass out 3 × 5 cards and have each member describe a problem he or she is having as a group leader. The cards are placed in the center of the table and each person draws a problem making sure it is not his or her own. Each person reads the problem to the group, discusses it, and makes suggestions as to how he or she might deal with it. The group then discusses the problem sharing ideas and perceptions. Repeat the process until all problems have been addressed.

7
Group Member

The evidence of effective leadership shows up in the lives of the persons being led. Consequently, leadership is the catalyst for constructive action and therapeutic process within and between group members. The key question for leaders who want to assess how they are doing is "How are you (members) doing?" not "How am I (leader) doing?" In the final analysis, group work is all about members, and leadership is merely the bridge between who they are when the arrive and who they are when they leave with productivity being the residual effect in either their individual lives as persons or their collective life as group members or both.

Nature, Roles, and Behaviors

The most valuable resources a group has at its disposal are its members. The members are crucial to the success of the group and it is imperative that group leaders understand them and their behaviors. Of primary importance is the relationship of each member to the group. The individual decisions of members regarding their own involvement determine the impact of the group as a thera-peutic tool for solving problems or a dynamic process for addressing its agenda. Each member has to decide whether he or she is in the group to relate to others with mutual respect and personal self-reference or for exploitation. "The group is completely dependent upon the decision and capacity of each person to share his (her) self-perceptions and to encourage others to do the same" (Dinkmeyer & Muro, 1971, p. 74). Even when a positive commitment is made to become involved, however, problems created by group membership are many.

The fact that counselors must work with a group of clients at one time creates a number of problems for both the leader and members. Lakin (n.d.) enumer-ates several of these problems: (1) A basic problem of control occurs because the leader is not always able to stay on top of the process, and members are not always sure of the authority structure. (2) The issue of responsibility is clouded. Throughout the group process members and the leader engage in a jousting contest over the nature and allocation of responsibility. (3) Although closeness and cohesiveness are continually developing as a group matures, the extent of that closeness is difficult to define for group members. Intimacy is still primarily a dyadic quality, and therefore group relationships have more social attributes than affectional qualities. The problem, however, is knowing how to differentiate and where to draw the line relative to relational closeness. (4) Even though direct communication typical of small groups perpetuates the group process, that communication is sometimes difficult to follow. The multiplicity of member actions and reactions gives members and the leader a vast amount of input to comprehend. (5) The numerical superiority of members creates a competitive possibility that challenges the expertise and leadership of the counselor directly and indirectly.

The leader must be able to cope with each of these situations and adequately deal with them for the good of the group and its members. Understanding the dynamics of member behavior can provide a solid foundation for doing so. The purpose of this chapter is to consider the various aspects of group membership of which a group leader needs to be aware. Topics covered will include the nature, roles, and behaviors of group members.

Nature of the Group Member

The group member is really a unique form of client. This is because each one brings to counseling all the individuality that personality differences allow for (Krause & Hulse-Killacky, 1996), and each one must learn to cope with and make use of both the counselor and the group process. In therapeutic groups this combination of personal diversity and the task of functioning adequately as a client in a group gives the group member a quality that is not characteristic of clients in individual counseling, consulting relationships, or even in marital/family counseling where each client's place is circumscribed by a preexisting relational unit.

Just as in leadership, the key factor in membership is personality. Groups are composed of individuals who "overtly and covertly present their unique needs, likes and dislikes, strengths and weaknesses" in the group (Krause & Hulse-Killacky, 1996, p. 91). Those various and sundry characteristics clients manifest in their personal lives are part and parcel of the group process, weaving an intricate pattern in each group that can never be replicated or even simulated in another group. This attribute makes group work the dynamic process it is and makes every group a new and challenging experience to the sensitive and aware group leader.

To enumerate all the personality traits that are conducive to good group membership would be an impossible task. However, one general characteristic appears to be mandatory. *The effective group member must be able to relate fairly well in a small group situation.* This rather simple social criterion is essential for both the person to benefit and the process to work. Clients who are antisocial, severely shy, or withdrawn do not have the social ability to function in groups. Other extremes in personality dynamics such as hostility, narcissism, depression, psychosis, total noncompliance, conduct disorders, oppositional defiance, and borderline features may also mitigate against group participation (Jacobs, Harvill, & Masson, 1994; Ohlsen, Horne, & Lawe, 1988; Yalom, 1995). Such clients are best worked with individually or referred to professional resources for intensive treatment including therapy groups designed specifically for such dysfunctional clients. However, if the client can function at a minimal level of effectiveness in a small group, all other personality traits that may disrupt or impede the group process and the individual's growth can be worked with to some degree, as the remainder of this chapter will attest.

The basic criteria for determining minimal group effectiveness is the client's responsiveness to the leader and other members as noted in the screening interview and the first few group sessions. If evidence exists of interactive qualities in the person that (1) enable a process of give and take to occur, (2) demonstrate a degree of interpersonal initiative, and (3) indicate awareness of the interpersonal influence of others, the probability of adjusting to the group is increased.

Beyond the individual differences and the group adaptability requirement, group members have several other factors in common. These factors define the general nature of the group member. As we've already discussed, all human beings have the same essential needs that motivate their behaviors and direct their courses of action. In most cases, typical group members are experiencing deprivation in meeting some of these needs. Therefore, they tend to be wary of any procedure that purports to meet their needs when they have not been able to do so themselves. Although naturally wary of the group, most members also experience a hope (usually unexpressed and secret in the initial stages of the group) that the group will be a place where they can find fulfillment and learn the means of satisfying their needs.

Since most of our human needs are met through the process of social interaction and relationship formation, the typical group member is usually experiencing difficulties in relating to others. This difficulty may be with one or two specific relationships or relationships in general, encompassing peer, family, work, community, and school associations. Due to the existence of these inherent relational difficulties in the individual member's lives, each person tends to be hesitant to interact unreservedly in initial group sessions for fear that relational difficulties will also emerge there. Most group members would like to interact amiably, freely, and personally in the group, but this desire is normally camouflaged by caution. Pistole (1997) notes that "as the group develops into a social microcosm, members begin to exhibit their typical patterns of relating and thereby present their interpersonal problems in group interaction" (p. 13).

Interpersonal Relationship Factor

The character of group members' relational problems is described categorically by the Interpersonal Problem Matrix depicted in Figure 7.1. While this schemata is useful in delineating the nature of the group relative to focus, content, membership, and level of therapeutic intervention, it is included here to explicate the interpersonal difficulties group members bring into the group. Levels I and II are most relevant for our purposes in discussing member behaviors and Level III indicates the prospective interventive mode that relates to the type of group process that is most relevant (Trotzer, 1985).

The matrix is generated by intersecting three dynamic dimensions of interpersonal problems. Level I (horizontal axis), Nature of Interpersonal Problems, depicts four categories of interpersonal problems emphasizing the dynamics involved.

These problems are:

1. Forming Relationships
2. Maintaining Relationships
3. Changing Relationships
4. Conflict in Relationships

Level II (diagonal axis), Interpersonal Problem Focus, is divided into four broadly construed categories representing the basic relational domains in which we experience interpersonal problems. These categories are:

1. Interpersonal Skills
2. Family Relationships
3. Peer Relationships
4. Hierarchical Relationships

Level III (vertical axis), Intervention Level, depicts the purpose of the group relative to the degree of difficulty or seriousness of the interpersonal problems and the intensity and timing of the intervention itself. The three categories are:

1. Reconstructive, referring to a focus that is personality-specific and designed to help clients make extensive personal changes in order to improve their interpersonal effectiveness (e.g., psychotherapy groups).
2. Remedial, referring to an interventive focus that is problem-specific and

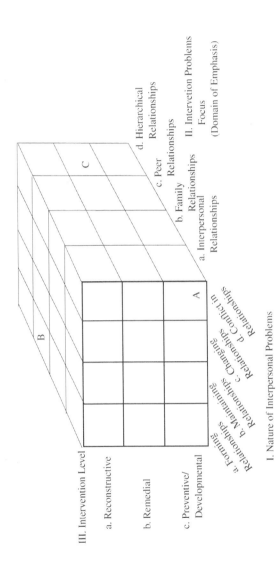

Figure 7.1 Trotzer's interpersonal problem matrix.

designed to resolve interpersonal concerns that are impeding growth and development of the individual (e.g., counseling groups).

3. Preventive/Developmental, referring to the process of providing personally relevant information and skills in order to help clients prepare for, work through, and/or circumvent typical interpersonal problems (e.g., psychoeducational groups).

Each of these levels translates into a type or form of group work delineated in chapters 2 and 10 of this text.

The interaction of these three vectors generates descriptive cubicles that suggest the general nature of relational problems, the domain in which problems occur, and the basic character of the group process needed to rectify them. For example, the cube labeled A in Figure 7.1 represents a *conflict/interpersonal skills/preventive* interaction. Since we know that conflict in relationships is inevitable and actually a means by which relationships grow and develop (Rybak & Brown, 1997), we can propose a counseling group that teaches conflict resolution skills as a preventive measure. Such a group would be relevant to any number of target populations. Cube B (Figure 7.1) is *forming relationships/peers/reconstructive*. An example of this cube would be a therapy group for individuals who are social isolates that is designed to help them form friendships. The group process would be extensive and intensive to enable the group members to make personal changes and acquire the interpersonal skills necessary to form friendships in their social network (peers). Cube C (Figure 7.1) is *changing relationships/hierarchical/remedial*. An example is a training group for supervisors who had been promoted to positions of authority over former peers and who are subsequently confronted with the task of developing this new relational pattern.

While the matrix does not produce mutually exclusive categories, or cover all possible permutations of interpersonal problems, it is very useful in conceptualizing and planning group work with respect to relationship issues. Combined with a particular group model for structuring group counseling (e.g., Trotzer, 1979, 1980), it has considerable utility for addressing members' interpersonal concerns.

Application to Task Groups

The interpersonal relationship factor discussed above manifests itself in the course of interactions in task groups as well. Members bring their interpersonal abilities, skills, experience, styles, and issues with them into the group, and these factors become part and parcel of group life dynamics. As members engage in interpersonal communication relative to the purpose of the group all the elements of interpersonal relationship issues and resources surface that contribute to the nature of the group milieu (Beebe, Beebe, & Redmond, 2005). Effective task group leaders learn how to mobilize these factors when constructive and address these factors when they disrupt or distract in order to help the group be effective and efficient in the course of addressing its agenda.

Motivational Factor in Clinical Groups

In the clinical domain, specific problems or personality issues prompt individuals to join counseling or therapy groups. This fact then is another common characteristic of group members. All are in clinical groups because they are experiencing a problem or problems that they have not been able to resolve satisfactorily on their own. The fact that they have problems and have indicated an inability to solve them is a duality that generates frustration and creates a natural defensiveness in a social milieu like the group. A basic assumption and expectation from both the clients and others' perspectives is that one should be able to handle one's own problems and that failure to do so suggests inadequacy, weakness, and lack of determination or drive. In addition cultural, ethnic, or family values and mores that mitigate against displaying vulnerability may be at work. As a result, members generally experience a great deal of ambivalence when they enter therapeutic groups. No matter how well screened, oriented or prepared they are, when the group begins to interact most members experience an internal conflict between sharing themselves and their problems and retaining an aura of privacy and self-concealment. Matthews (1992) reframed this typical member experience as follows: "One motive (of member behavior) is the desire to escape from group experience with their old way intact. Another is the contradictory desire to use the experience to actualize new potential. Maslow (1967) calls these two motives the omnipresent defensive and growth impulses" (p. 165).

Members experience this approach-avoidance conflict in groups for a variety of reasons. They are not sure what others in the group will think if they reveal their problems. They are not sure of the nature of the group process itself, and they are not sure of themselves and their own role in the group. This being the case, the group is doomed to fail unless a trump card can be played that will tip the balance in favor of proceeding. That something extra can either be the personality of the leader, the internal emotional pressure created by the members' personal concerns, the attraction of the group, or the generic value of the therapeutic group process.

The counselor who can obtain member confidence and is viewed as a caring, supportive, friendly, and helpful person is a vital force in securing commitment to the group process on the part of members. On the basis of leader explanations beforehand and conduct during initial sessions, many members decide whether they will risk involvement.

Psychological turmoil is another factor that often influences members to commit themselves to therapeutic groups. When the pain, frustration, or anxiety caused by personal problems becomes great, the risk involved in sharing one's issues in the group becomes a lesser and often secondary consideration. The need to ventilate issues and obtain the group's help overcomes the fear of self-disclosure and the need to protect oneself. This motivation, however, often places individual members at risk because they sacrifice their defenses for the sake of psychological relief thus becoming vulnerable. Therefore, the group atmosphere in general—and actions of the group leader in particular—must be such that the relief of pain incentive does not devastate the individual or undermine the group's development as an effective therapeutic process.

The attraction of the group is probably the most influential in convincing members to involve themselves in the group as a means of working on their problems. Cartwright (1951) stated that "the more attractive the group is to its members, the greater is the influence the group can exert on its members" (p. 388). Ohlsen (1970) affirmed this notion, calling the attraction of the group one of the key dynamic forces in its effectiveness. When the member is attracted to the group, the group becomes a setting where individual behavior can be affected (Fullmer, 1971). The group's attractiveness derives from many sources: the social nature of the process, the promise of personal need fulfillment, and the anticipation of help for one's problems (Caple & Cox, 1989). Whatever the reason, members react to the group's appeal by immersing themselves in the process.

Finally, Corey, Corey, and Callahan (1990) have noted that the therapeutic process in groups purports to offer and invoke certain values and incentives. These include: "Self disclosure, risk taking behavior, learning to be direct, questioning of one's life, choosing for oneself, increasing awareness, and autonomy" (p. 69). These factors separately or combined may be the impetus for member involvement.

The final common factor among most group members is a deep and sincere desire for success. This desire also tends to be covered by the defensive mechanisms of members as they enter into the nebulous domain of the group, but it is usually clearly revealed when an atmosphere of trust and safety is created. Even when obstacles to change seem insurmountable, members tend to retain a glimmer of hope that things will work out. Usually when this flickering flame of optimism is extinguished, the group process loses its impact and more intensive psychotherapeutic treatment is required. At times, however, the group process itself may have to rekindle that flame in some clients, which accounts for the overlap between counseling and psychotherapy mentioned in chapter 2.

Application to Task Groups

Membership in task groups is more likely prompted by the nature of a job description or organizational structure, personal, avocational, or vocational interests and voluntary choices that relate to the nature of the group. Members may bring personal issues with them into the group that affect the dynamics and process of the group, but they are not the direct prompts that motivate them to become group members. Consequently, the emergence of personal issues or problems becomes a process factor that may need to be addressed in order for the content or agenda dimension to proceed in a functional and effective manner. Task group leaders must develop the ability to note, assess, and address personal issues in task groups as a means of removing process obstacles and incorporating the personal dimension of group members' lives into the productivity dimension.

Roles of the Group Member

The role of the group member is crucial to the nature and effectiveness of the group. Systemically, roles in groups always imply relationships and interpersonal functions (Rugel, 1991). That fact is certainly relevant in clinical groups. The role of each group member is a composite of subroles and role functions. MacKenzie (Rugel, 1991) has delineated four functional roles that emerge in the course of counseling and psychotherapy groups. They are the "structural, social, divergent and cautionary roles" (Rugel, 1991, p. 75). For purposes of our discussion these functional dynamics will be addressed in the context of four subroles: the client, the helper, the model, and the reality check.

The *client role* is self-explanatory. It is that aspect of a member's involvement when the group is focusing on that individual's concerns. All members of counseling groups have problems. At some point they must assume the position of being helped in order to make effective use of the counseling process. When the client role is mobilized the member is functionally task or goal oriented and as such lends a structural impetus to the group in line with the group's purpose (Rugel, 1991). Members who continually refuse to explore their concerns in the group deny the most vital component of their group membership and thus obstruct any efforts made to help them. Ohlsen, Horne, and Lawe (1988) referred to these members as *non-clients* and Corey and Corey (1977) cited eight reasons that may explain such *nonparticipating behavior*. They are:

1. The feeling that one doesn't have anything worthwhile to say.
2. The feeling that one shouldn't talk about oneself or that one should be seen and not heard.
3. Fear of looking foolish; not knowing the appropriate thing to say or do.
4. Fear of certain members in the group or of the authority of the group leader.
5. Resistance, particularly if the person doesn't really want to be a member of the group.
6. Uncertainty about how the group process works.

7. Fear of being rejected or of being accepted.
8. Lack of trust in the group; fear of leaks of confidentiality (p. 40).

These reasons should be explored in the group. Functionally, members who avoid the client role may be manifesting what MacKenzie (Rugel, 1991) called the *cautionary role* where their wariness of overdependence on the group motivates them to maintain a psychological distance. Members who relentlessly function in this manner may not be appropriate for group counseling and should be offered individual counseling where the role of being a client is clearly defined.

The *helper role* has already been alluded to. One of the advantages of group counseling is that the member has the opportunity to be both the helper and the helped. In the helper role members seek to give assistance in whatever way possible to the member who happens to be working on a problem or in need of support, understanding, encouragement, or even confrontation. The functional dynamic involved in the helper role is focused on the needs of other group members for emotional support and acceptance (Rugel, 1991). This *sociable role* assistance may take the form of listening, sharing, giving feedback, suggesting alternatives, confronting, or participating in group activities such as role playing. The helper role has a real therapeutic impact on the client being helped and on the helper. The client values the help received because it originates from peers. For helpers the opportunity to be of assistance builds self-confidence, self-efficacy and self-esteem. It provides them with another perspective that takes their minds off their own concerns temporarily and restores a psychological balance. Each helper adds a dimension to the counselor and the group and increases the group's resources in a geometric progression because of the subsequent interaction between unique member personalities. The more willing, creative, and effective the helper is, the more efficient the group process will be. Members who refuse to show concern for others in the group and fail to function in a helping capacity risk not getting the group's help when they need it. In addition, some members resist giving up the client role, continually demanding the group's help and attention in a self-centered manner. They are inconsiderate of other members' needs in this regard and must be helped to realize that their function as helpers in the group is equally important as their client role.

The group member is in a *model role* as well as observing others. Dustin and George (1973) pointed out that group members offer a great number of models and sources of reinforcement. This social learning dynamic functions in the group to help members learn socially adaptive behaviors and skills by emulating fellow members who already exhibit them (Miller, 2002). The variety of personal attributes among group members accounts for many modeling opportunities during counseling. Some members may be models because of their verbal skills, others because of their personal attractiveness, social skills, emotional sensitivity, common sense, or intellectual abilities. Sometimes leaders include members in the group to serve as models. For example, sociometric stars and isolates are placed together in the same group with the intent being that the isolates will identify with and pattern their behavior after the socially effective stars. It is a good idea is to know the particular area in which each group member can serve as a model so that modeling may be utilized appropriately. Being a model also gives members feelings of worth, prompts accountability and helps them learn responsibility.

Besides demonstrating relevant adaptive behavior as models, group members also represent the society outside the group. As such they function as a *reality check*, helping other members assess their concerns in light of realistic criteria and select alternatives that have a reasonable chance of working. This role is part of the group's society in microcosm characteristic and functions effectively only when members do not deny reality, distort their perceptions, or hesitate to express honest opinions out of fear of or sympathy for the member whose problem is being discussed. This aspect of the member role has tremendous vitality because no matter what the circumstances or setting the group is in, members usually know what is necessary to adapt themselves constructively. The problem is that they are not always willing to admit it. Thus, the leader must see that members handle this role responsibly and to the benefit of the group and its members.

The model role and reality check role provide the context in which the divergent nature of member functionality emerges (Rugel, 1991). Models can be detrimental or negative and reality can be denied or distorted. Consequently, oppositional dynamics can emerge in the group and generate conflict and problems. The path toward constructive, realistic solutions and resolutions is often strewn with obstacles emanating from perspectives of difference. This process, however, is helpful to the group because it helps the group face challenges and develop norms for dealing with conflict (Rybak & Brown, 1997; Kraus, DeEsch, & Geroski, 2001).

All the members will demonstrate strengths in certain of these aforementioned roles and weaknesses in others. But at some time during the group process all members must portray each of these four roles to some degree if the group is to maintain mutual responsibility, commitment, and therapeutic influence.

Application to Task Groups

All of the above-described roles have their direct counterparts in task groups. The *client role* becomes the *contributing role* where each member takes responsibility to do their share of the work regarding the purpose or task of the group; the *helper role* becomes the *resource role* where each member contributes their own unique and special talent or ability to the accomplishment of the task; the *model role* and the *reality check* are essentially the same as described above, but are carried out in the context of the group's purpose. As members perform these roles in task groups they contribute to and experience what Hulse-Kilacky, Killacky, and Donigian (2001) identify as characteristics of successful groups where members:

- Feel listened to.
- Are accepted for their individuality.
- Have a voice.
- Are part of a climate in which leaders and members acknowledge and appreciate varied perspectives, needs and concerns.
- Understand and support the purpose of the group.
- Have the opportunity to contribute to the accomplishment of particular tasks (p. 6).

Task group members therefore wear many of the same hats, but do so in the context of the group's purpose rather than their own personal agendas.

Behaviors of the Group Member

Group members exhibit many kinds of behavior in the group. These behaviors are the material the group and the leader must work with to accomplishing the purposes of the group and help individual members resolve their problems. Five generic categories of member behavior will be discussed here: resisting behaviors, manipulating behaviors, helping behaviors, emotional behaviors, and subgrouping behaviors. Effectively understanding these behaviors will make dealing with them an easier task.

Resisting Behaviors

Resistance is perhaps the biggest nemesis the group counselor faces in the effort to develop a therapeutic milieu. The source of this resistance is within members themselves. Resistance is usually more blatant during early stages of the group and tends to become more subtle and potentially destructive during the later stages. Ohlsen, Horne, and Lawe (1988) describe resistance as the failure to cooperate in the therapeutic process or the blocking of another client's treatment in the group. Members resist the group process for many reasons (Corey & Corey, 2006). They fear that other members will not accept them if they disclose their problems. They worry that if they share one problem it will lead to others, creating a snowballing effect that they cannot control. Some members resist because they are not willing to suffer the pain involved in solving their problems, and others resist simply because they feel incapable of making changes or achieving their goals. For these reasons Rybak and Brown (1997) refer to resistance in group members as *avoidance behaviors* because they are characterized by actions that inhibit the flow of information and disclosure from within and between members. In contrast, Kraus, DeEsch and Geroski (2001) reframe these tendencies into "challenges" that the leader can view "as a source of therapeutic energy" (p. 31).

Dinkmeyer and Muro (1971) pointed out that resistance to personal explorations is particularly evident during early sessions when trust and cohesiveness are minimal. This social resistance is common in most new social environments. Social resistance is the most easily overcome because once common ground is established, rapport develops quickly and the foundational elements of a sharing relationship are formed. Resistance later on in the group when members are confronting their problems becomes a more individualized form of resistance related to taking the steps necessary to resolve problems. This type of resistance is sometimes very difficult to detect and must be watched for closely by both members and the leader.

Ohlsen (1970) gave four potential liabilities of resistance in its various forms: (1) Resistance increases the possibility that confidentiality will be broken. Members who do not commit themselves personally to the group are much more apt to divulge proceedings to outsiders. (2) Resistance increases the amount of acting out behavior. Members who have no ties to the group have less to risk and therefore are more willing to engage in overt disruptive behavior in order to escape from group pressure or protect themselves against involvement. (3) Resistance encourages members to be dependent on each other for meaningful relationships rather than working on improving their lives. Members may resist making changes in order to turn the group into a permanent social gang rather than the temporary therapeutic milieu it is supposed to be. (4) Resistance helps members escape responsibility for coping with their unwillingness to cooperate in the group process. If members never have to face up to their resistant behavior, they will not have to confront the painful areas of their lives or have to expend the energy necessary to change.

Overcoming resistance is a ticklish issue but one that must be faced. Social resistance during the early stages of the group is best handled with methods characterized by warmth and acceptance. Establishing a common ground of experience through group activities or sharing here and now feelings about the group tend to be very effective. For the more complex and serious forms of individual resistance, the possibilities are not so well defined nor is effectiveness assured. Ohlsen (1970) noted that two common techniques used to cope with resistance are interpretation and confrontation. He added, however, that both are questionable because "interpretation tends to encourage intellectualization and to make clients dependent" and confrontation places members on the hot seat where "the full therapeutic impact of the group is no longer felt continuously by the client" (p. 138). Both of these techniques, however, do have utility once a solid relationship of trust and acceptance is established between members. If interpretation is used prior to a good relationship being formed, members may resent the intrusion into their privacy and become even more resistant. However, interpretation at the proper time and stated in a tentative manner can be very helpful. The same is true of confrontation. Often at the point where individual members are resisting, a well timed confrontation can have a meaningful result. This is especially true if the confrontation is generated by group members who have already clearly demonstrated their acceptance and caring for the individual being confronted.

Ohlsen (1970) pointed out another appropriate method of coping with resistance. He suggests utilizing the screening interview as a means of preventing resistance by turning responsibility for convincing the counselor of readiness for group counseling over to the prospective client. Giving clients responsibility for convincing the counselor that they are ready for group counseling, committed to its purposes, prepared to work toward achieving their own individual goals, and willing to develop and maintain a therapeutic climate enables them to accept considerable responsibility for their own growth. Within such a climate, clients tend to perceive resistance as deviant behavior (p. 120).

Kraus et al. (2001) outline a menu of six helpful questions that can help a leader respond to the challenges that emanate from resistance and may provide the cues necessary for responding. With respect to specific incidents of resistance the questions are:

1. Were group members appropriately selected?
2. Is the challenging incident related to the group system?
3. Is the incident a function of the stage or the dynamics of the group?
4. Is this incident a symptom of an individual member's style of functioning?
5. Is this incident related to issues raised in the group?
6. Is this incident an artifact of my own responses to the group or to individual members? (p. 33)

Processing resistant incidents or member behaviors using these questions can provide creative insights and possible means for responding in a manner that energizes the group and helps it move along in a constructive manner.

Resistance is portrayed in many different ways, but whatever its behavioral manifestation, the objectives of protecting oneself and preventing interpersonal connection remains the same. Some of the more common resisting behaviors are discussed in the paragraphs that follow.

Monopolizing

There are many descriptions of monopolizing group members (Corey & Corey, 2006; Carroll & Wiggins, 1997; Donigian & Malnati, 1997; Higgs, 1992). Dinkmeyer and Muro (1971) described them as persons who must hold the group's attention and who become anxious when the focal point shifts to another member. This type of behavior may be a defensive overreaction to fear of attack or isolation from the group. Ohlsen (1970) said, the monopolist "does seem to be a self-centered recognition-seeker who tries to maintain a place for himself (herself) in the center of the stage" (p. 188). Kranzow (1973) stated simply that a monopolist dominates group discussion. A monopolizing member stymies group interaction because other members do not get the opportunity to react or to present their own concerns and points of view. This form of resistance also can create many negative, unexpressed feelings in group members. They dislike having one person monopolize the discussion but do not have the courage or opportunity to take the floor themselves. They therefore internalize their feelings and express them through nonverbal reactions, may become passive-aggressive or make debilitating, behind-the-back comments outside the group. The leader should tune in to these reactions drawing the members out and helping them express their feelings. This will curtail out of group comments and also may help monopolists see that they are generating negative attitudes toward themselves.

The group members may unwittingly reinforce monopolizing behavior by expecting the monopolist to take over in periods of ambiguity and tension. Members can develop a subconscious dependence on this type of group member to take over, so even though they do not particularly relish the idea of a one-person show, they do nothing to prevent it. Monopolists also provide a handy excuse for other group members not to reveal themselves. Thus even when a monopolizing person desires to change, expectations are such that he or she will receive little support for not monopolizing. This situation may have to be pointed out to the group from time to time in order to help the group understand and cope with all the dynamics of monopolizing.

Monopolists are often not aware of their behavior and may actually feel that they are behaving correctly. Dinkmeyer and Muro (1971) stated:

> Even when an individual is revealing what appears to be significant aspects of self, he (she) may be either consciously or unconsciously trying to control the group's potential impact on him (her). As long as an individual is speaking he (she) holds the group's attention, prevents interaction, and minimizes the probability of being confronted by another group member. (p. 20)

Monopolists tend to be very verbal and therefore initially can put everyone at ease, including the leader. Once monopolists are established the only way to unseat them is through some form of confrontation, which may result in negative repercussions throughout the group process. Therefore it is necessary to identify this behavior early and to act to create a more balanced pattern of communication characterized by total member participation. Yalom (1985) noted that the key to dealing with monopolizing members is not to silence them. "You do not want to hear less from (them); instead, you want to hear more" (p. 378). The message to be conveyed to monopolizers is that you want to hear more meaningful disclosures. In some cases if monopolists persist, they may need to be offered individual counseling as a substitute until they can function more effectively in the group. However, once the problem has been identified, members who are authentically engaged in the group process can be helped to overcome their penchant for monopolizing by setting simple behavioral criteria for participation such as only speaking after six other comments have been made by others, asking for permission before commenting and/or setting a time limit (e.g., 1 minute) for verbal input.

Excessive Talking

A mild form of resistance that is often mistaken for monopolizing is excessive talking (Higgs, 1992). This phenomenon is typically evident in early stages of the group process and during periods of heightened anxiety. Verbal members of the group may respond to anxiety or tension by increasing their verbal output as a protective or stress reduction mechanism. The characteristic that distinguishes excessive talking from monopolizing is that it tends to be "catching" (i.e., other members' verbalizations are elicited and the group begins to babble). In these situations interventions to slow down the pace and giving process feedback to the group noting the phenomena help the group and individual members reduce or restrain their talking. In addition, as anxiety in the group is alleviated by rapport and acceptance and the contingent issue generating the tension is addressed, the pace of verbalizing also recedes to a more serious and constructive level.

Hostility

Hostile members exhibit a form of resistance that is difficult to work with because very few avenues of approach are open to the group for making personal contact and gaining trust and confidence. Hostility is usually the result of being hurt, let down, or abandoned by someone whose love and acceptance were needed. On the basis of this experience, the hostile person no longer expects to be accepted or loved and therefore tends to be demanding, brutal, sullen, and defiant. Detection of hostility is as much an emotional process as it is a behavioral one. Hostile clients tend to generate visceral reactions of fear, edginess, tension, and even anxiety in those around them. Thus, other members attempt to either avoid or placate them, both reactions that interfere with constructive group interaction.

Hostile clients require infinite patience tempered with firmness and caring. They must be given an open invitation to let down defenses and join the group on a personal level and must be made aware that the group understands how difficult that may be. On the other hand, hostile members must not be allowed to control the group by attitudes and behavior. In fact, if the group can become involved in personal, warm, trusting, accepting interaction in spite of the hostility, it may convince hostile members of the group's sincerity. Reflection and empathic understanding are useful methods of approach (Ohlsen, Horne, & Lawe, 1988). Confrontation is the most risky because it gives the hostile member a good reason to lash out under the pretense of being attacked. If members can convince hostile clients that they really care and make good on their commitments, these clients can be worked with.

Kraus et al. (2001) describe a version of hostile members as *counterdependents*, "members who balk at authoritative structures such as conforming to the norms of a group even though established by the group" (p. 41). Rather than viewing these members as aberrant or threatening to the group, they frame the counterdependence as typical in groups just like dependence or independence thus making it a continuum issue instead of a polarizing issue. A counterdependent member can be viewed as helping the group raise and address underlying issues that might otherwise be neglected or avoided.

Silence

Silent periods and silent members usually cause feelings of uneasiness, tension, or consternation in the group (Corey & Corey, 2006; Carroll & Wiggins, 1997; Donigian & Malnati, 1997; Higgs, 1992). But a distinction must be made between silence that is constructive and silence that is resistant and destructive. A warm and accepting silence that gives individuals time to think and reflect is useful in the group in spite of its dis-ease. This type of silence can be a motivating factor when the ambiguity it creates results in tension that influences members to share themselves or their feelings in a personally relevant way. Similarly, some group members can become deeply involved in the group interaction even though they do a minimum of talking. These members may, in fact, use silence as a means of removing defenses and with time the effect becomes evident. Other members usually are quite adept at recognizing this type of silent member.

A destructive silence generally results in tension and anxiety in the group that interferes with effective action. It is motivated by fear of self-disclosure and elements of confusion and insecurity. It is an effective resisting behavior because it places the responsibility and pressure on other members or the leader to carry on the group process while at the same time protecting the individual from self-revelation. Hinckley and Herman (1951) indicated that silence may mean (1) members are holding back as a punitive measure against the leader or certain members, (2) members are avoiding reality and/or escaping conflict, (3) a particular client is hiding, or (4) certain members have difficulty in communicating with others. In some cases individual members are silent because they do not get the opportunity to talk, are not assertive in speaking out, or simply do not want to interrupt. In other cases, cultural factors may account for silence (Ho, 1984; Ipaye, 1982; Kaneshige, 1973; Merta, 1995). For example, Native American and Asian clients may view silence as a mark of respect rather than as resistance. Lifton (1966) added that silence may be a reaction of shock or support. Personality traits that tend toward quietness in social situations and verbal patterns that are deliberate and slow paced also contribute to silence in individual members.

In dealing with group silence, the leader must develop an ability to determine the tolerance level of members and the point at which the ambiguity is no longer producing constructive or therapeutic results. Intervention is appropriate at that point—either in the form of initiating a group activity, reflecting the leader's own feelings, reflecting the leader's perception of the group atmosphere, asking a leading question or introducing a round that surveys the group in a brief and succinct manner (i.e., "Let's do a quick round where each person gives a one word or brief phrase descriptor of where you are at this time."). Often this type of intervention is greeted with spontaneous relief by the members who then assert themselves verbally in an effort to purge their anxious feelings and prevent the recurrence of that type of silence. In addition, responses made during the round may serve to focus the group or give it a direction.

Individual silent members must be encouraged to talk but not necessarily put on the spot to do so. Opportunities can be provided to them in the form of go-rounds or questions directed to the group so that the silent member's participation is in the context of just another perspective. Responding to nonverbal cues that indicate the silent member is thinking, feeling, reacting, or about to say something also can facilitate participation. Use simple statements like "Cheryl, you seemed to be thinking about something just now, and I wonder if you would share it with us?" or "Daniel, you seemed to react to what Jack just said; would you explain what you felt?" Note the tentative nature of these statements. Too forceful or too direct statements may increase resistance. Always give the silent client an option rather than forcing the issue. Response to nonverbal cues is an important skill to develop in working with silences or silent members. This skill is not only important for the leader to develop but for members to master as well.

Withdrawal

Withdrawal and silence tend to go hand in hand, but silence is not necessarily indicative of withdrawal. Withdrawal is usually associated with a negative self-concept in members and may be reflected in the positional dynamics that emerge between members and the leader. Referred to as *proxemics* by Donigian and Malnati (1997), withdrawal is the emotional and physical distance that emerges between a member and the group or between the group and the leader.

Group members may resist involvement by maintaining or encouraging social distance between themselves and the group. This may be communicated by a member actually placing his or her chair apart from the group or sitting in a manner that creates physical barriers or distance between themselves and the group. The member may take on the role of an isolate in the group, maintain an observer posture, or resist involvement by criticizing what is going on, either verbally or nonverbally (Kranzow, 1973). Withdrawal tends to be an obvious challenge to group members to demonstrate their care and concern by making a supreme effort to bring the person into the group, or it enables members to resist having to reveal and work on their problems in the group. The withdrawn member, however, usually does not cut off all communication with the group. In fact, often while seeming withdrawn, the person is actually listening intensely. I recall an incident in my therapy group at the Minnesota State Prison where an inmate refused to participate in the group and would go into his cell when the group convened. His cell was just off the area where the group met. During one of the sessions he yelled out a comment as the group was interacting, indicating that despite his withdrawal he was avidly aware of what was going on. To work effectively with withdrawal, an avenue must be located and used to expand the withdrawn member's participation in the group. Many of the same techniques used in silence are relevant for withdrawal, especially those related to the leader "drawing out" the member. In certain cases confrontation coupled with support is also useful, especially if the member does not know how to ask for the group's help.

Leaders may inadvertently reinforce withdrawal dynamics in the group by not recognizing it as a group phenomenon where the group maintains a distance from the leader as a protective device. This makes it easier for individual members to further withdraw without notice because it occurs in the context of a group norm or tendency. "The greater the distance between group members, the less likely they are to reveal their personal thoughts and feelings and the more likely they are to engage in restrictive solutions such as denial and intellectualization" (Donigian & Malnati, 1997, p. 19). Thus, leaders need to maintain active involvement with both members and the group in order to circumvent such systemic dynamics.

Absences

One of the easiest ways to avoid involvement in the group and resist its therapeutic impact is to simply not show up for the group meeting. Absences early in the group process may indicate members' lack of interest, lack of commitment, or fear of the unknown. If the group process is not clearly explained, and if a commitment to participate is not obtained beforehand or at initial contact, absences can be expected. Later in the process absences take on a different meaning. Hinckley and Herman (1951) stated that members may use absence as a means of testing the limits of acceptance in the group and to determine their status. Johnson (1963) added that as a group develops and members sense that subsequent interaction may penetrate into areas that are frightening, potentially harmful, or embarrassing, they may use absence as a means of resistance and escape.

The peculiar aspect about absence is that being out of sight does not mean being out of mind as far as other group members are concerned. A natural tendency is for the group to discuss absent members, especially if other members have feelings they will not express when the absent person is there. This may itself be a form of resistance, and the leader must see to it that the group does not use it to avoid confronting their own concerns. On the other hand, this can be an opportunity for members to work with their feelings in preparation for constructively dealing with the absentee. Often when members find out about the tendency to discuss the absentee, they will make more concerted efforts to attend the group sessions rather than risk being talked about.

Absence can be handled by simply contacting the absentee in a nonconfrontative manner to demonstrate concern. At the same time, the responsibility issue can be stressed. Once clients have indicated they will be in the group, they have an obligation to themselves and other members to be there. Of course, a positive group relationship and climate reduces absences. In cases where absence is obviously an effort to avoid responsibility for one's problems, confrontation addressing accountability may be called for.

Cross Talking

A group form of resistance behavior is cross talking where group members engage in parallel conversations simultaneously disrupting both the flow and the focus of the group. Cross talking is a natural phenomenon in most groups but usually dissipates as the group gets down to business either on its own or at the behest of the leader. However, it becomes problematic when a pattern emerges where it erupts spontaneously and continues in spite of or in direct disregard to leader intervention or member discomfort. This behavior must be dealt with directly on a here and now process level because of its disruptive influence and propensity to undermine cohesiveness and generate chaos in the group.

This phenomenon occurs frequently in groups that lack clear purpose and commitment, where members are required to participate, or where the general purpose of the group is growth or learning rather than therapy or counseling. A specific example of this latter case is required group experience in graduate level group classes. Cross talking as a pattern is also a signal that the group may be of excessive size for the purposes involved to the point where effective group cohesiveness and atmosphere is delimited. If that is the case, the appropriate intervention is to subdivide the group into smaller units and/or design smaller groups in future planning.

Intellectualizing

Probably the most uncomplimentary label that has developed in the annals of group work is *intellectualizing*; in some ways no more negative charge can be leveled at a group member. Intellectualizing as such basically implies that members are not personally involved and are using the cognitive domain as a shield (Higgs, 1992). Because of the exaggerated overtones of this term, its real meaning has been distorted. Its connotations are more feared though much less distinct and less understood than the denotative qualities of the term. As a result, members and leaders hesitate to point it out when it occurs because of the strong reaction that might be stimulated.

Intellectualizing is nevertheless a very common resistance mechanism in groups. Most members realize that discussing a topic is easier than talking about themselves. They also know that interacting in discussions is easier when devoid of emotional qualities and personal implications. They prefer to discuss how they got to be like they are (there and then), or what they would like to be (if and when), rather than become involved in a discussion of their present thoughts, feelings, behaviors, and problems (here and now). Whenever verbalizations take on qualities that move the focus away from the person to a topic, event, situation, or issue that has little relevance to the group or its members' problems, intellectualizing is occurring. This does not mean these discussions are uninteresting or unemotional. In fact, the contrary is quite often the case. But the point is that the work of the group is not being attended to.

The best safeguard against intellectualizing is to encourage members to relate their discussions directly to themselves and to keep the focus within the group rather than outside the group. Intellectualizing is often a means of keeping the group going to avoid silence or keeping the leader happy, especially when members are not sure of the group's purposes. Clear and specific goals can help circumvent this problem so that members can address themselves to communication that is personally meaningful and facilitative of group progress. In addition, helping members personalize their comments through reflection, restatement, clarification, modeling, tone setting, and probing can prevent intellectualizing from impeding group progress. Poppen and Thompson (1974) described the nature of nonintellectualizing communication: "Talking about something one of the group members likes becomes more meaningful when he (she) describes his (her) complete feelings about it, indicates how important its value is to him (her), or states how he (she) acts in accordance with this value" (p. 96). The purpose of working with intellectualizing is not to eliminate thinking from the group process. It is to make the cognitive process a resource to the person in working out problems rather than a wall to hide behind. The therapeutic counterpart of intellectualizing is cognitive restructuring which is a legitimate group focus and process.

The Old Pro

As more and more individuals have experienced involvement in small group interaction of a therapeutic nature, another resistance phenomenon has emerged—the old pro syndrome.

The likelihood that any particular group will include one or several members who have had previous small group experience is high. Accordingly, an experiential differential exists such that the less experienced–more experienced continuum can be used by more experienced members to avoid personal involvement. The old pros manifest themselves in a variety of ways. They may exude a sophistication that is read as "I know what this is all about, and it doesn't threaten me a bit." They may make numerous references to their previous group experience to solidify their position, impress other members or the leader, justify their actions in the group, or indicate they have less need for help than the others. A common reaction of the old pro is to become "Mr. or Ms. Co-counselor," to minimize personal involvement by assuming a quasi-leadership role (Dinkmeyer & Muro, 1971). This type of member also may begin to share seemingly personal information early in the group, which turns out to be a rehash of what they have already said or dealt with in previous group experiences.

Old pros have the potential of being helpful or detrimental influences in the group. If the leader can help them model effective membership behaviors to help other members overcome fear and distrust of the group, they can be tremendous assets. In fact, this type of person may be able to accommodate very well to functioning as a leader in the peer facilitated groups described in chapter 10. However, remember that this member's first purpose is to work on personal concerns. If past experience is being used to avoid that purpose, it must be dealt with immediately.

Experienced members can generate negative feelings in other members who resent their superiority. Old pros also may engage in advice giving, which can be disturbing to other members and is in itself a form of resistance. Powder-maker and Frank (1953) explained that giving advice diverts attention away from one's own problems, exhibits superiority to others in the group, and may conceal contempt and hostility for the one seeking assistance. Finally, the old pro may attempt to become the group's superego, the one who keeps telling the group what it should or should not do (Kranzow, 1973). This type of member may represent a direct challenge to the leader or become a divisive threat to the group process. For all these reasons old pros must be dealt with as quickly as possible to prevent problems.

But oddly enough the group leader often fails to spot the old pro before some damage has already occurred. Leaders wanting to facilitate a positive group experience may be extremely appreciative and condoning of the behavior of the old pro initially. As a result, this person becomes firmly entrenched in that role before the group leader realizes it. Several precautions should be taken. Placing experienced members together in a group counters using their experience as a resistant tool because they can keep a check on each other. An individual interview with the experienced member before or during the group to point out the member's position, enlist cooperation, and reaffirm the basic purpose for being in the group may be all that is needed. During group sessions, probing and questioning the old pro may be effective and drawing out other members' feelings in the form of feedback to the experienced member is invaluable. Remember though that the old pro image may be no more than a facade with very little solid basis. If confronted too strongly such a person may become confused, hurt, and even devastated. Feedback therefore should help them realize what they are doing and amply encourage them to continue to function in a helping capacity with other members. The difference between advice and support or assistance can be pointed out, and reinforcement given for suggesting alternatives as options to members rather than telling members which choice to make.

The Joker

Humor is probably the least offensive form of resistance in the group. The member who can get the group laughing helps relieve strain and tension and removes some of the pain and discomfort of addressing problems. Humor also calls attention to the person, but often at the cost of serious consideration of certain necessary and personal factors. The joker has a lot of group support because group members tend to associate laughter with happiness, and certainly no one should be criticized for making others happy. Therefore, the joker has a natural defense alliance that is difficult to penetrate, especially early in the group. Unfortunately, the joker's problems are usually so well camouflaged in joviality that other members seldom take them seriously. The group may depend on the joker to lighten things up when interaction gets too heavy making it difficult for that member to give serious input or get help from the group when needed. This locks the joker into a circumscribed role that conveys an expectation obligating the member to serve as the group's court jester.

The most effective way of coping with humorists is through reflection of the underlying serious aspects of their communication. To be able to laugh with them and yet respond to them seriously and personally will not only help them overcome the use of humor as resistance but also will help other members see them in a more serious perspective.

The Housekeeper

Dinkmeyer and Muro (1971) described this resistant member as the person who is doing everything for the group except participating in it. Housekeepers set up the room, get extra chairs, pass out materials, and generally take care of any possible technical details of the group. They are especially adept at running errands. They associate with the group but don't involve themselves in the interaction. Reinforcement of their participation and control of the amount of chores they do will help this type of member make therapeutic use of the group more likely. Encourage housekeepers to engage in self-disclosure and giving feedback. In this way housekeepers feel useful to the group and become more involved in it as they engage in give and take discussion with the members on a personal level.

The Help-Rejecting Complainer

Yalom (1985) has identified the help-rejecting complainer (HRC) as one of the most frustrating resistive group members. A subcategory of the monopolizer, the HRC is a discloser, but not a closer. This type of member holds the focus of the group with an unending litany of complaints or problems that by definition are insolvable. No matter how understanding the group is, catharsis does not generate a shift in emphasis and no matter what the group suggests, an obstacle always is present. HRC's are master "yes-butters" and their standard response is often "I tried that and it didn't work."

The HRC is almost completely self-centered and has difficulty tolerating anyone else being in the limelight. They solidify their position in the group early because of their seeming willingness to discuss their problems, but that's as far as they go. As the group continues, they generate an underlying tension in the group that manifests itself as irritability, frustration, and anger either stifled or expressed impulsively as group members struggle with the discomfort of dealing with the HRC.

One of the more common interactions that emerge in the group is when an HRC and an advice giver lock horns. Since both members are engaging in nonproductive group behavior, the tension level in the group escalates. This tension can be used constructively if the leader or other group members can shift the focus from content (the topic of the interaction) to process (what's happening in the group). This detaches the group from the grip of the HRC and gives an opportunity to look directly at the behavior and impact of the person in the group.

The key to coping with an HRC is not buying in emotionally to the plight of that member's life. Instead, focus on process, zero in on how the person is coming across, and solicit feedback about the behavior manifested in the group rather than trying to solve the problems being described in the HRC's discourse. Additional measures are *limit setting* where specific boundaries are established around how much group time the HRC can use for themselves and *paradox* where the leader goes with the flow overstating the insolubility of the HRC's problems. Both of these methods make use of boundaries to generate change in behavior. In the first case, boundaries are set and adhered to placing the responsibility for staying within them on the HRC, while in the second case the HRC'S own boundaries are breached creating the reactive initiative to change behavior to regain a sense of being in control.

Since a common dynamic of HRC behavior is "to frustrate and defeat the group and the therapist" (Yalom, 1985, p. 391), mobilizing group resources to address the problem is vitally important. If the group is not stimulated to respond constructively, neither the group nor the individual will realize the therapeutic potential of the group process.

The Self-Righteous Moralist

Another resistant group behavior pattern identified by Yalom (1985) is the self-righteous moralist (SRM). "The most outstanding characteristic of the self-righteous moralist is the need to be right and to demonstrate that the other person is wrong" (Yalom, 1985, pp. 392–393). The critical distinction here is not that the member is secure in his or her own values and lives up to them irrespective of circumstances or negative repercussions—a quality that generally garners respect even from those whose values differ. Rather, the SRM's mission is to be right and superior to others to the point where what others think or feel about him or her is unimportant and/or disparaged. A SRM's security is based totally on personal ascendance that has the tendency to generate intense resentment in other group members. This reaction develops quickly and locks the SRM into a role that is difficult to escape. Members no longer see the SRM as a person because every comment he or she makes generates a negative emotional reaction even among members who may generally espouse the same values.

Yalom (1985) identified the dynamic of shame as the force that undergirds the SRM's behavior. Due to feelings of inferiority stemming from lack of success or recognition, the SRM seeks superiority on the basis of "immobility of character rather than achievements" (Yalom, 1985, p. 393). Another dynamic of the SRM's behavior is projection. Often the SRM takes an uncompromising stand on things that internally stem from a distinct sense of vulnerability. SRMs believe and feel that if they do not take an absolute position and hold it, the next step is to be totally consumed by the very thing they are so against. This facet becomes especially evident when issues related to sex, drug and alcohol use/abuse, authority, beliefs and values, or character traits such as honesty, trustworthiness, and fidelity arise in group discussions.

Given the fragility of their shame based defensive mechanisms, their intrinsic fear of vulnerability, and the group's emotional reactivity, dealing with the SRM is an extremely delicate and often unsuccessful process. Once again, separating content from process is recommended because it takes the focus off of the topic upon which the SRM solidifies his or her position and places it on the person. However, because the importance of others is often disregarded by the SRM, very little leverage can be generated from group dynamics. Confrontation places the SRM at risk due to the brittle nature of their defenses. More often than not, the SRM is ostracized rather than worked with. However, if group members' feelings can be processed sufficiently to the point where the group can endure or even benevolently tolerate the SRM's participation, over time he or she may be able to risk (experiment with) softening his or her stance and learn a more flexible mode of interpersonal relating that begins to reconstruct the basis of achieving a sense of self-esteem.

The Rescuer

One of the more subtle resisting behavior patterns is the rescuer (Jacobs, Harvill, & Masson, 1994). The rescuer is mobilized into action whenever negative intensity arises in the group. Rather than face and work through negative affect, the rescuer rushes to the aid of the upset member via smoothing, reassurance, and sympathy. They engage in what Corey and Corey (1977) call "band-aiding" behavior by which they try to turn the focus from pain to feeling better without addressing the basis or cause of the distress. They patronize rather than support and try to change the level of interaction from personal to social and the emphasis from personal pain to pain avoidance.

Rescuers can be helped to understand and change their behavior by processing their actions after an incident of rescuing occurs. They also can be tutored via modeling and direct instruction to respond empathetically rather than sympathetically. At critical times their rescuing attempts can be blocked or diverted so that therapeutic business can be attended to. Most important is to work on facilitating self-disclosure by rescuers so that they can experience first hand the helping process and then translate it into use with others. In most cases, a rescuer can be transformed into a vital helping resource in the group.

Difficult Members

Kottler (1992) has identified 14 characteristics of difficult clients (see box next page) that in turn have been translated into four categories of difficult group members (Kottler, 1994b). These categories effectively summarize the nature of resisting behaviors.

1. The "characterologically difficult" or members "who exhibit rigid personality traits such as character disordered clients (who) may not do well in group settings" (p. 4);
2. Acting out group members who behave "provocatively, seductively or aggressively" (p. 5);
3. The entitled member who seeks control by dominance in time and focus (p. 5); and
4. The manipulative member (pp. 6-7 and discussed in detail later in this chapter).

Kottler (1994b) noted that difficult members (and resistant behaviors) "are as much a matter of the leader's perception as are their actual behavior" (p. 7). Leaders must have the ability to deal with difficult members while protecting the rights and well being of other members in the process. Kraus et al. (2001) add that the leader's own expectations may be at the core of the problem in that as members fail to live up to the leader's expectations they are perceived by the leader as being counterproductive. This personalizes the challenge and may be fueled either by the leader's insecurity or possibly countertransference issues. It is important for the leader to process their own feelings and perceptions intrapersonally and in reflective sessions with colleagues or supervisors as a basis for response. In most cases, the results will point the leader back to trusting the group process rather than prompting an intervention that is not based on leader issues but on what is best for the group.

✳ Kottler's Characteristics of Difficult Clients

1. Have uncontrollable diseases that impair interpersonal functioning.
2. Have hidden agendas that they are unwilling to reveal.
3. Ignore appropriate boundaries.
4. Refuse to accept responsibility for their plight and tend to blame others.
5. Are argumentative.
6. Fear intimacy.
7. Are impatient and unrealistic about what group work can do for them.
8. Are inarticulate or lack verbal skills.
9. Are unduly literal or concrete, or have an intolerance for ambiguity.
10. Are significantly divorced from reality.
11. Are "empty" inside and unable to access internal states.
12. Are despondent and express abject hopelessness.
13. Have little impulse control and are prone to explosive tantrums or outbursts.
14. Feel entitled to special privileges. (Kottler, 1994b, p. 4)

Responding to Resisting Behaviors

Several basic strategies that pertain specifically to resisting behaviors are presented in the following discussion. They are identified in a general hierarchical order of preference from the perspective of (1) relevance and potential for effectiveness, (2) degree of seriousness with respect to the behavior, and (3) appropriateness with respect to timing (earlier vs. later in the group process). The general guideline for responding to any potentially detrimental group member behavior is based on a "for the good of the group" criteria. When any behavior persists to the extent that the therapeutic effectiveness or the functional productivity of the group is jeopardized, action to deal with the behavior first as an ingroup task and second via referral or removal of the member from the group must be initiated. In most cases, except where delimited by traits already specified, member resistance is best viewed as an opportunity for growth and the group process should be trusted to address it and work it though (Kraus, et al. 2001). It is in that context that the following recommendations are presented.

Empathy

First and foremost is the use of empathy as a means of dealing with resisting behaviors. Since most resistances are essentially defense strategies, the impact of an empathic ear goes a long way in establishing a trust base that enables the group member to risk vulnerability. In fact, the more aggressive the resistance, the more potent accurate empathy becomes.

Limit Setting

This tool is especially appropriate for resisting behaviors that manifest themselves via garnering an inordinate amount of the group's time and attention (Kottler, 1994b). Placing limits on the amount of time a person can retain the group's attention and holding vigorously to those limits places the initiative for responsible group participation on the shoulders of the resistant member.

Using Paradox

Based on the premise that resistance is a matter of gaining control, going with rather than blocking resisting behaviors creates a paradox where the group member gets more control, attention, and affirmation than he or she is comfortable with. This produces a reactive change in the direction of more appropriate boundaries both as a person and as a group participant.

Contingency Contracting

This strategy is particularly relevant to resisters who are big on problem sharing but come up short on problem solving. Contract with the group member for time in the group based on action outside the group or behaviors/conditions inside the group. Such contracts may be in the simple form of a ratio of responding to others statements versus self statements. For example, five responsive statements must be made before one self statement can occur. Contingency contracting raises the issue of accountability both in and out of the group.

Giving Responsibility

In some cases resisting behaviors can be translated into effective group behaviors by assigning a resister responsibility to assist another person in the group. This technique is useful for resisters whose patterns of behavior are based on inferiority, low self-esteem, or lack of self-confidence. It is also helpful with members who have difficulty when the focus is not on themselves. It is guardedly appropriate for persons who resist involvement via patterns such as the old pro.

Confrontation

Confrontation whereby the behavior of the group member is addressed on a here and now process level is the ultimate ingroup format for dealing with resistant behaviors. Confrontation is often necessary when the other methods have not worked and the resisting behavior is jeopardizing the group process. However, several basic guidelines are necessary for effective confrontation to occur. Johnson and Johnson (1982) note that confrontation is not hit and run. Make sure time is sufficient to work through the confrontation. Take time to hear and understand all points of view (both the group members' and the resister's) and define the problem as a mutual problem (a problem for the group) and not just the confronted member's problem. Keep feedback directed at the behavior rather than the person and make sure each person owns rather than projects their feelings. Encourage the confrontee to sift through and cull out relevant data and express positive potential for redirection rather than pose threats when possible.

Removal From the Group

Ultimately, some group members will not be able to accommodate to the group and will place the whole group at risk if they maintain their involvement. In such cases removal from the group is appropriate. If at all possible, this process should be implemented with options for continued therapeutic help such as individual counseling or referral to another more appropriate group. The task of ending should be addressed with the leaving member if possible, but whether or not the departing group member participates, those that remain should be given an opportunity to process their thoughts and feelings.

Manipulating Behaviors

The primary difference between resisting behaviors and manipulating behaviors is that the former are used as a direct protection of self, and the latter are used to control others. In either case the resulting interference with therapeutic growth is the same. Manipulating behavior is directed at getting others to act in a way that is not threatening to self and enables the person to feel in control. It is steering the group and its members to meet one's own needs without their knowledge. Shostrom (1967) pointed out that manipulation is actually one end of a continuum; the other end is actualization. All manipulating behaviors have counterparts that are potentially beneficial to the effector and the recipient of the action. This is also true within the group process. The idea is not to eliminate these behaviors but rather to transform them into their actualizing forms so that the group and its members can benefit and progress.

Manipulation is another of those terms that raise the hackles of purported targets. It can be used to mount an attack against those who are seemingly restricting one's psychological, physical, social, or intellectual freedom. Manipulation—or the suspicion of it—motivates members to watch out for their own hides in order to prevent becoming helpless pawns in the hands of a ruthless controller. It generates distance, blocks communication, prevents cohesion, and generally creates a group atmosphere characterized by restraint and distrust.

Interestingly enough, the group leader is typically the first to be suspected of manipulating and only later does the suspicion transfer to members. On one hand, leaders may be suspected of manipulation when members are not clear about the leader's role or intentions. On the other hand, group members are likely to be manipulative in their actions toward the leader and fellow members as an inevitable and natural consequence of the interaction between multiple personality variables and the ambiguous nature of the group situation. In other words, manipulation is often a first response, interpersonal, coping mechanism when confronted with uncomfortable circumstances or dynamics. The purpose of this section is to point out some of the more common types of manipulating behaviors and to discuss their relevance to group work. As Shostrom (1967) so aptly observed, manipulation need not be directed from a position of strength and power but can also be done effectively from a position of weakness. Figure 7.2 clearly demonstrates this possibility and shows the positive quality of each type of manipulating behavior. Note the counterparts of each behavior and that each can exert a great amount of influence on others regardless of position.

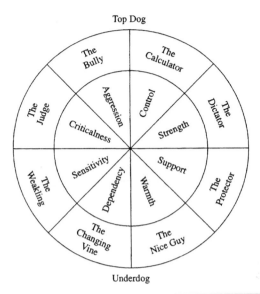

Figure 7.2 The manipulative types. Adapted from *Interpersonal Diagnosis of Personality: A Functional Theory and Methodology for Personality Evaluation,* Timothy Leary (1967) and *Man, the Manipulator,* E. L. Shostrom (1967). Reprinted by permission.

Socializing

Socializers interact extremely well in the group, but their purpose is to extend the group relationship into a social relationship rather than to work toward the goals of the group. Ohlsen (1970) described a socializer as "a person who so thoroughly enjoys the quality of his (her) relationships with the members of his (her) counseling group that he (she) may wish to substitute these relationships for those with his (her) important others" (p. 180). Socializers correspond to Shostrom's (1967) nice guys, who can control the actions of others because they are pleasant, friendly, and well liked. They are people no one wants to harm. Nice guys, also can influence members to not upset things by getting into nitty gritty problems. They may misuse the capacity for exuding warmth to reinforce nontherapeutic behaviors in the group members and even promote distortion of reality by the default mechanism of using their niceness to discourage addressing issues that might generate conflict or discomfort. In its actualizing form the warmth of the nice guy approach is particularly relevant to developing cohesiveness in the group and to stimulating the synergy that can emerge from authentic relational dynamics that enable members to address and overcome challenges and thereby feel more connected as a team.

Socializers need to be reminded of the purposes and intent of the group. Sometimes it is necessary to block suggestions and input of this type of member so that the group does not become distracted and lose sight of its goals. Socializers can be helped to use their abilities as models, especially for those members who lack social skills. However, they also must be encouraged to utilize their social competence outside the group as appropriate. Once they realize they can function authentically in their relations with significant others, they will have no more need to manipulate group members into social alliances and will be able to approach them openly in the context of doing therapeutic group work and accomplishing the goals for which the group was formed.

Scapegoating

This behavior directs attention toward another individual or group of individuals in order to divert attention from oneself and avert responsibility, fault, or blame. An individual member is consciously or unconsciously identified as the personification of all that is wrong in and/or out of the group. Through the use of projection or displacement, members can attribute their own problems to others and thus avoid any personal responsibility. The subject, willingly at times and unwillingly at others, is made to feel responsible and required to do penance for the entire group.

Scapegoating is obvious when the entire group gangs up on one particular individual in a barrage of negative feedback. It also can be subtle, as when the group consistently turns its attention to a key person only when the interaction gets to be particularly disturbing or threatening. In either case, the skills usually needed to deal with it are blocking, protecting, and confronting. Leaders must intervene to protect the well being of the persecuted member and to get members to face up to their actions and take responsibility for themselves. Of special importance for the leader is to see that the group does not use scapegoats that are outside the group so all can concur and thus avoid responsible action.

Clark (1997) identified the dynamic of scapegoating as projective identification. When a member who experiences marked self-contempt or low self esteem projects those feelings on to another member in the group, and that person absorbs, internalizes, and enacts the projection, the dynamic of scapegoating is generated. When this occurs other group members are enticed to join in the projection or an antithetical response in the form of subgroup counter attacks is produced. Both responses are harmful to the group process and require leader intervention. The intervention must have a dual focus that acts to protect the target member and at the same time acknowledges the instigator's underlying feelings. Consequently, combining skills like blocking, reframing, empathy, cognitive restructuring, and confrontation may be required.

Dependency

Dependent clients operate from a position of weakness. They need someone else to show them the what, how, and why of everything they need to do in order to solve their problems or to be contributing members. They treat others as experts and as the only means of help available. In this way they force others to take control and thus do not have to face the anxiety of being independent or autonomous. Ohlsen (1970) stated that "dependent clients have had their dependent behaviors reinforced by persons who needed to have someone dependent upon them or by important others such as parents and teachers who did not bother to teach them, during the normal process of growing up, how to behave independently" (p. 167). Shostrom's (1967) representation of this type of person is the clinging vine. These people completely entwine themselves around others, allowing the others to guide, direct, and shield them from autonomy or independence. The actualizing dimension of dependency relates to the fact that the person is on a dynamic continuum or pathway that leads from dependence to independence to interdependence, and the group's task is to encourage and prompt the person to embark on the journey. When the member does so and experiences the merits of their effort, they become a model that testifies positively to others who may be stuck in the clinging vine position both in and outside the group.

Leaders and members both fall subject to manipulation by the dependent client because of the appeal to one's pride, sympathy, and expertise. The lesson, of course, that dependent clients must learn is responsibility for self. They must learn to engage in independent behavior, make their own decisions, and avoid dependency reinforcing relationships. Leaders and members alike must refuse to make decisions for the dependent client and must firmly resist taking control. Reinforcement of independent actions within the group is a good place to start and placing the member in choice making situations is very helpful. Affirmation, empowerment, encouragement, and accountability are all critical elements in addressing dependency.

Submissiveness

Submission differs from dependence in that not only do the clients want someone else to tell them what to do but they also want someone else to do it for them. Submissive clients are completely other-controlled persons who will do almost anything to get the approval of people that they treasure (Ohlsen, Horne, & Lawe, 1988). They correspond in some ways to Shostrom's (1967) weaklings because they have no authority or will power to act on their own and they lack even a minimum of courage to assert themselves in any way. They present such a needy countenance that others automatically come to their aid. In group situations they are difficult to deal with because any direct contact with them must be made through a wall of defenders who completely blunt any hurtful intrusions. The weakling also tends to be the dominant focal point because no one else seems to need as much help. Such a person may control the group action and emphasis and effectively disable the helping process from having an impact on anyone else. In contrast, the actualizing dimension of being a weakling is sensitivity, a trait that is vital to empathy, awareness of diversity factors especially related to discrimination, oppression and bias and support. The submissive member can play a crucial role as an "encourager" to other members as they make the effort to overcome obstacles and barriers in their lives.

The all or nothing feature of the submissive client is its source of power. I recall an inmate in my Intensive Treatment Unit therapy group at the Minnesota State Prison who was so thoroughly submissive that fellow inmates, guards, and even administrative officials took over responsibility for his well being and care. So "weak" was this person that normal responsibilities such as obtaining meals, exchanging linens, and performing required routines were carried out for him by others in a joint care taking effort by inmates and prison officials.

The things that help submissive clients change are learning to be assertive, taking interpersonal risks, and expressing a positive social interest in the welfare of other group members. The use of modeling and role playing can be very helpful in accomplishing the first and second tasks and structuring interaction through the use of interpersonal activities will facilitate the third. In addition, empathy expressed through reflection can be beneficial. However, if a tendency toward sympathy and overprotectiveness on the part of members does occur, the leader should step in to redirect and limit the interaction.

Aggression

The aggressive group member has been labeled variously as a pusher (Kranzow, 1973) and a bully (Shostrom, 1967). Both labels represent key identifying traits since the first emphasizes a desire to move ahead as quickly as possible and the second refers to methods used. Aggressive members are very active, influencing the pace and direction of the group by sheer willfulness and a desire to have others see and do things their way. They instill fear and timidity in other members and can single handedly create a stalemate in the group progress. Aggression is often combined with hostility, which results in a formidable challenge for even the most experienced and competent group leader. The Achilles' heel of aggressive clients, however, is that they are usually overreacting to a basic feeling of insecurity that they feel will make them susceptible to being hurt, embarrassed, or disliked. Their aggression, therefore, is an attempt to act first in what they are sure is a situation designed to reveal their weaknesses and make them vulnerable to attack.

Aggressive members must learn that the group is a safe place to let down defenses and that other people are not out to harm them. They need to experience support and acceptance from the leader, who as an expert represents a special threat, and the members. The leader can encourage other members to stand their ground to the threatening forays of the aggressive member and at the same time help the aggressive member realize that other members' independence does not constitute a personal attack or diminish their own importance in the group. The actualizing dimension of aggression is assertiveness with regard to one's own issues and initiative with regard to group business. Both contribute constructively to the work and process of the group enabling energy to be directed toward problem-solving, strategic planning and implementation of action plans. As bullying is transformed into assertiveness, insecurity is replaced with confidence and the potential of the person as a leader emerges.

Criticism

Being critical is an effective way to put people on the defensive and control their actions. The key features of this manipulative behavior are evaluation and judgment. Evaluation is based on one's own frame of reference and criteria, while judgment attributes a negative or positive quality to the results of that evaluation. Critical group members may operate under the guise of objectivity so that their assessments seem to be nonpersonal observations of behavior. In reality, however, they may simply be using the role of judge to invoke their own rules and thereby direct the interaction of the group. Criticism also tends to make others avoid contact with the critic and hide true feelings. It communicates the opposite of acceptance, which is disruptive to the group. For these reasons Shostrum (1967) uses the term calculator to refer to this type of member behavior because they activate their comments at times and in ways that place the person or group on the defensive and divert energy away from constructive process. The actualizing dimension of this trait is objectivity that provides a counter-balance to emotionality enabling the person and the group to assess all aspects of a situation or perspective.

Constructive feedback is definitely a valuable part of the group process when it is given in the interests of the receiver and out of a sincere concern for his or her welfare. When used as a tool of control, however, it is unwarranted. The leader must be careful not to model critical behaviors that can be misconstrued by members and emulated to accomplish their own selfish motives. Ground rules are helpful in keeping critical feedback in check; asking members to speak only for themselves and their own perceptions is also important. Poppen and Thompson (1974) stated that criticism should be directed only at those things a person can change and should be concerned with the here and now and questions of "what" and "how" not "why." Since much criticizing is done to avoid being criticized, members must learn both how to receive and how to give feedback. Especially important is for critical members to experience being constructively criticized. In this way they realize the impact of their behavior and can make alterations accordingly.

Domination

Domination is distinct from aggression and monopolizing because it pertains to every aspect of group life, from members to goals to topics of discussion. Dominators through force of strength control the action of the group. They may do it verbally and actively or passively and nonverbally. Shostrom (1967) referred to this type of person as the dictator or someone whose will must be done. Dominating group members can determine the entire character and personality of the group if allowed to act unopposed and unquestioned in the group. Thus, channels of interaction and diversity of communication patterns are restricted, and in turn the flexibility and freedom of the group are limited in meeting individual needs. Dominating members usually pose the most serious threat to the leader because they like to call the shots. The most difficult form of dominating member is the one who acknowledges the group leader on the surface but works behind the scenes to subvert the leadership role.

Dominators must learn to use personal power constructively to facilitate rather than restrict freedom and openness. Their strength should be mobilized, and they should be given ample opportunity to lead but must not be given any more authority or control in the group than other members. Leaders should welcome the challenge to their leadership role as an opportunity to find out more about their own attitudes toward domination and authority. By supporting the independent actions of other members and respecting the input of the dominating member, without giving it more credence than that of other members, the leader can effect a constructive balance of power that will help the dominator learn interdependence in relationships inside and outside the group.

Mothering

The mothering group member creates dependency by being the shield and buttress for other members in the face of adversity, attack, or crisis. By supplying this support the "mother" garners a position of power in the group, which can be wielded to stifle interaction or direct it in a more personally desirable vein. This control can be maintained simply by threatening to remove the support and thus is a potent force in the group's development. Shostrom (1967) referred to this type of person as the protector, who becomes the chief defender of the rights and welfare of others. This type of person is usually above reproach in the eyes of the group members and successfully avoids dealing with any personal problems by continually supporting others as they work on their own.

The mother role (Kranzow, 1973) is a positive addition to the group in that it provides interpersonal nurturing and sees that needs of members are met. However, this type of member must learn to expose personal needs so that others can respond in kind, thereby creating a symbiotic relationship that leads to mutual growth. As in real life, where mothers must learn to give up their nurturing role as their offspring mature, so the mothering group member must realize members must be granted independence, autonomy, responsibility for their own lives, and freedom from emotional badgering.

Calculating

As noted previously, the calculator (Shostrom, 1967) is a very special type of group member who can steer the group by gauging input for effect and then interjecting it at the precise moment when it will have the most impact. Calculating members are hard to pin down because they are usually very intelligent in the use of their involvement and have the patience to withstand attacks while waiting for the proper moment to counterattack. The calculator often makes highly sensitive and penetrating remarks that contain an element of surprise. Calculators are capable of submarining unsuspecting group members and devastating them at will. As a result, other group members keep a wary eye on them.

Calculators must be handled carefully in the group and, in fact, may not be good group member material. The reason is the difficulty encountered in engaging them in the continuous interaction of the group since they have enough self-control to decide when and if they will participate. They must learn to be sensitive to the feelings of others since their remarks smack of intellect rather than emotion. They may have to be taught through modeling how to both self-disclose and give constructive feedback. If they are willing or can become willing to receive the group's help, they can be valuable assets because they can estimate accurately the impact of certain behaviors. But if they cannot be brought around to full time, personal participation, probably the better procedure is to work with them on an individual basis.

In responding to manipulating behaviors leaders must walk a careful path between compassion and confrontation. They must avoid the "compassion trap" of reacting "too sympathetically or treating group members as more fragile than they really are" (McBride & Emerson, 1989, p. 28). And they must act firmly and directly to intercept detrimental actions. "Because manipulative clients thrive in an atmosphere of tension, conflict, hostility and chaos where they feel more powerful, it is especially important to rely on confrontation rather than interpretation as the preferred intervention" (Kottler, 1994b, p. 7). Combining caring, directness, and firmness in responding to manipulative behavior produces best results.

Helping Behaviors

Helping behaviors are those behaviors members engage in that stimulate and promote the therapeutic group process to the mutual benefit of members. They constitute what Rybaek and Brown (1997) call approach behaviors and incorporate many skills and functions described in chapter 6. The leader therefore has a responsibility to model and teach them to members so they can help one another thereby generating a process ripple effect that benefits the group and its members. In addition, many members have a lot of natural ability in helping others that combined with altruistic motives contribute meaningfully to the helping process. The major helping behaviors are discussed in the following paragraphs. A direct correlation exists between the presence of these behaviors and the effectiveness of the group.

Listening

Active, nonjudgmental listening is a necessity in effective groups. Members who conscientiously listen to one another communicate the essential ingredients of therapeutic, helping relationships. This type of listening conveys empathy, acceptance, caring, and respect to the speaker. It is a means of valuing the other person and indicates openness. One of the basic ground rules in any group should be that members are to listen to everyone for the purpose of understanding who they really are and what they really think and feel. Reaction skills described in chapter 6 are the core of effective listening. Group members can learn them through the use of such exercises as Active Listening, described at the end of this chapter. Listening facilitates the group process by establishing the kind of communication base upon which trust and helping relationships can be constructed.

Facilitating

This behavior is important because its purpose is to engage all group members in the interaction of the group. Kranzow (1973) described the facilitator as a person who sees that everyone's needs are met and that all cards are out on the table. Facilitators make efforts to draw group members together, help them talk about themselves, and share their concerns. They tune in to nonverbal cues to draw out less verbal members, ask leading questions, and solicit feedback. Facilitating behaviors assist the problem solving process because they bring out material for consideration that is crucial to constructive action. They are other-directed and therefore are an integral part of the helper role. As more facilitating is done by members, less responsibility for doing so is needed by the group leader, and the members grow in self-confidence, self-esteem, and responsibility in the group.

Leading

At different times during the group process different members may emerge in a leadership capacity. This fluctuation is a common feature of all groups, and group counseling is no exception. Leadership may be assumed or given for a specific purpose or period of time or may be a more permanent role function throughout the group process.

Leading in the therapeutic sense means that the member functions to help group members resolve their problems and accomplish group purposes or tasks. Leading behaviors are important because they serve to disperse responsibility among group members, lifting the burden of responsibility from the leader and giving members the opportunity to take responsibility for the direction of their own lives and the group. They provide an important learning experience that helps members be more assertive and responsible in their lives outside the group. Leading may manifest itself in relation to content or process and incorporates a variety of methods ranging from reflecting feelings, making suggestions, and directing organized activities to leading by example. Leading helps provide structure to the group interaction, decreasing ambiguity and making the group a comfortable and predictable social environment in which to discuss problems or address the agenda for the group.

Self-Disclosing

Johnson (1972) defined self-disclosure as revealing how a person is responding to a present situation, "giving any information about the past that is relevant to understanding how he (she) is reacting to the present" (p. 10). It is the ability to share oneself with others on a personal level. Pierce and Baldwin (1990) describe appropriate self-disclosure as

> sharing ones persistent reactions to what is happening in the group, and it is revealing current struggles, unresolved personal issues, goals and aspirations; pain, joy; strengths and weaknesses; and the meaning of certain personal experiences. Appropriate self-disclosure is *not* revealing one's innermost secrets or digging into one's past; it is not expressing every fleeting reaction to others; it is not telling stories about oneself, and it is not letting the group pressure dictate the limits of one's privacy. (p. 152)

Self-disclosing is at the center of the client role. If clients cannot learn to reveal themselves, especially in regard to their problems, they have little chance of benefiting from the group. Self-disclosure depends on an atmosphere of trust, warmth, and acceptance but is a very specific behavior that can only be performed by the particular individual. To self-disclose for someone else is impossible because the material shared is from the hidden or private sector of one's own life. Self-disclosure initiates the problem solving process in the group and paves the way to understanding, on which action and change are based. In task groups, by comparison, self-disclosing pertains to sharing perceptions, abilities and resources related to the group agenda and extends to personal material and issues when related to the process component of group interaction as a means of facilitating the effectiveness or relevance of group content (Hulse-Killacky, Killacky, & Donigian, 2001).

Giving Feedback

Johnson (1972) referred to feedback as self-disclosing how one person is reacting to the way in which another person is behaving. Feedback is the mechanism through which the group can give assistance to individual members, assess the group process, inform the leader or direct the course of group action. It is the means by which reality testing is incorporated into the group and is the means of helping members arrive at specific decision points regarding change. Feedback is basically the ability to share one's perceptions without stating that they are absolutely correct and without forcing the recipient to accept them. As part of the helper role it is designed to provide as accurate and as comprehensive a picture as possible to the recipient but always allows him or her to make the final decision about what to accept or reject. In giving feedback, maintaining a tentative posture and expressing it in a personalized manner is of particular importance. Feedback is only one person's perception of reality and must be expressed as such.

Leveling

This helping behavior is really the combined action of self-disclosing and giving feedback. Leveling is the open expression of members as they really are and really feel (Satir, 1972). It involves awareness of one's bodily reactions, thoughts, and feelings and utilizing this knowledge in one's communication with others. Perhaps Rogers' (1962) description of congruence—where internal awareness and external expression are one—is an appropriate definition of leveling. Leveling is the basis of open and honest communication and is the principal means of assuring authenticity and genuineness in interpersonal relationships. This behavior is especially important when feelings, reactions, and perceptions are being withheld from the group for some reason, causing a stoppage of therapeutic action and communication in the group. Many times the group needs to engage in leveling so as to clear the air of old feelings that are interfering with an individual's freedom to interact or curtailing free expression in the group. Leveling is both a remedial group behavior and a developmental one.

Keeping Confidence

Confidentiality in the group is the responsibility of all group members and emanates from the value of respect for privacy. Keeping confidence is the specific behavior that carries out that responsibility. Poppen and Thompson (1974) contrasted keeping confidence with gossiping, pointing out that the latter is destructive to the group process, implies lack of commitment to the group, and is a violation of group trust. The trust issue is certainly at the root of this behavior. If members do not feel their disclosures will remain only within the group, they will not risk exposure. Keeping confidence is therefore one important means of establishing trust. It is also a very individual behavior. Vorrath and Brendtro (1985) pointed out that each member must realize that the development of trust in all its dimensions is completely dependent on him or her. If members cannot keep each other's disclosures and the group's interactions confidential, the meaning and importance of both will either deteriorate or never materialize. A basic ground rule therefore must be the establishment of confidentiality, and group members must be made aware of their obligation to respect the confidence of each other and the group. From an ethical perspective, confidentiality is a group responsibility that cannot be guaranteed by the leader since it resides outside the purview of his or her personal action. However, the leader must do everything possible to model, nurture and establish confidentiality and then hold members accountable for maintaining it.

Personalizing Communication

This behavior basically refers to communication within the group that utilizes first and second person pronouns (I and you) rather than third person (he/she, him/her, and they/them). Poppen and Thompson (1974) referred to this as the use of I-language. Third person references are an attempt to dissociate oneself from one's own behavior or from direct contact and communication with others. A simple comparison of the difficulty in using the various personal pronouns in conversation makes this fact clear. The third person is the easiest form of pronoun to use because it implies objectivity and personal distance in one's communication. Thus, referring to a member in the group as "he" or "she" avoids making the comment directly to the person and means you are talking *about* the person rather than *to* or *with* the person. The second person pronoun is more difficult to use because it makes the communication relate directly and specifically to another person. Feedback should always be stated in terms of "you" rather than "he" or "she" so that the message is personal rather than impersonal. The only exception to this guideline is the use of a particular communication exercise that incorporates a third person approach into its format. Examples of this would be the behind the back technique or describing yourself as your own best friend.

The first person pronoun is the most difficult to use because it places the speaker on the firing line. It is the principal means of exposing one's perceptions, feelings, and opinions. This being the case, members often resort to third person references to avoid personal involvement or to defuse emotional communications. However, the group leader should model personalized communication and request members to use it as well. In this way they learn to take responsibility for their own actions in the group. They also become more careful about what they say and how they speak to each other, which effectively improves the nature and usefulness of communication in the group. Group members can learn to use this type of communication very quickly if the leader simply asks them to repeat their third person statements using appropriate first or second person pronouns. In this way group communication becomes either a personal expression of one's own frame of reference or a personal message to another member.

Emotional Behaviors

The next category of member behaviors is composed of actions characterized by emotional qualities that are difficult for the members, leader, and the group to cope with effectively. These behaviors are generally associated with the extremes of normal emotions and involve overt physical or verbal expressions that tend to stymie even the most experienced and sophisticated leaders and members. Emotions, especially in extreme form, are a challenge to process and tend to either stimulate a defensive reaction of avoidance or withdrawal or generate escalation as members catch the emotions and spread them throughout the group. Ambivalence is the order of the day whenever someone begins to express strong feelings negatively or positively. Yet, a well known fact is that group dynamics often generate strong feelings. If these reactions are not handled appropriately and responsibly, they can be detrimental to individuals or the group itself. Rather than approaching these behaviors in the blind hope that all will turn out well in the end, a better procedure is for the leader to be prepared in the advent of their occurrence and have some strategies and ideas as to how to respond in a therapeutic manner (Kraus, DeEsch, & Geroski, 2001). This section will only discuss a few of the most common emotional behaviors that occur in the group, but the concepts and principles noted can form a basis for dealing with many group behaviors related to the affective domain.

Venting Negative Feelings

In an atmosphere of safety members frequently verbalize strong negative feelings such as anger, hatred, hostility, and frustration toward people and situations both in and out of the group. This type of ventilation can scare members but is cathartic and may be therapeutic if members do not overreact by withdrawing from or attacking the member and if follow-up action is taken to help the person work through the feelings. Because social mores generally restrain the expression of strong negative feelings, these feelings sometimes have a tendency to accumulate within the individual rather than dissipate. This is especially true if the individual is continually exposed to the situation or the person that stimulates those feelings. The group's first task is to hear the person out and in the process try to determine if the feelings are temporary or the result of a chronic situation or relationship. If the former, simple catharsis may be sufficient with follow-up to develop preventative measures that will reduce the possibility of recurrence. In the latter case, a more problem-oriented approach must be taken in which plenty of opportunity is provided to express feelings but with an emphasis on understanding the problem, developing alternatives, forming a plausible plan, and acting to implement it.

When members are experiencing strong negative feelings, they are more likely to take risks that they would not normally take. Thus, after feelings are expressed and equilibrium restored, the member may feel sheepish and embarrassed especially if the atmosphere in the group is ominously neutral or quiet. This may cause the person to draw back and develop hostile feelings toward the group. Therefore, processing is necessary to get the feelings and reactions of group members out in the open as quickly as possible after ventilation has occurred. In this way the focus is directed to others and the member is assisted in moving beyond the incident.

Members who ventilate cannot always remember what they said afterwards. Therefore an important procedure is to get back to that member after a short respite to work through the feelings and situation again. The member can determine the role emotion played in the situation by obtaining feedback from other members and can be helped to think more rationally about alternatives and options available.

When negative feelings are directed toward another member in the group the handling of the interaction is a much more serious matter because the welfare of the group is at stake. This type of behavior is often a derivative of confrontations that take place in the group. Also, strong feelings built up over time in the group make the ground fertile for a verbal attack in which these feelings come pouring out in rapid order. A preventative measure is to encourage members to express their feelings as they occur, emphasizing immediacy rather than holding them back in hopes they will disappear. During the exchange keep in touch with reactions of the one being attacked/addressed and restrict ventilation to one person at a time so that a ganging up effect does not materialize. At this point deal with the feelings of the expressor/attacker rather than allowing the focus to turn to the receiver. The initiator must first come to grips with personal awareness before relating to anything the recipient of the barrage might say in response. The follow-up then can then shift to the receiving member and the group's reactions. Other members' perceptions can be used as a means of dealing with allegations made. The total group should be involved so that a precedent of one member attacking and another defending is not set. Maintaining the perspective that venting negative feelings is primarily therapeutic to the person doing it is a necessity. Otherwise possible damage may result if too much stock is placed in the emotional charges leveled at another member. Once emotional equilibrium has been restored, the charges can be reevaluated but without the contingent threat introduced by the emotional component of the communication.

Physical Aggression

Physical aggression directed toward persons has no place in groups of any kind. To assuage that possibility, a very clear and firm ground rule against it must be laid down, with violation resulting in immediate consequences including expulsion from the group. However, the possibility is real that some members may attempt to vent their feelings through physical means because they are not capable of verbal expression or because verbalization alone is not a sufficient outlet. In these cases introducing physically expressive activities to release the feelings without a personal attack is appropriate. For example, arm wrestling or attempting to push one another to the floor by pressing on shoulders are useful exercises. Punching bags, batakas (foam bats), cushions, and pillows also can be used. Alternatively, have a physically aggressive person lie on the floor and have all other members take a firm hold on the person's arms and legs. The person then tries to get up while the members do all they can to restrain him or her. The strenuous nature of this exercise tires the member quickly and by doing so greatly lessens tension and the emotional impulse to be physically aggressive. Verbal follow-up after this activity helps the member deal constructively with the situation that caused the feelings. Note that these physical activities are relevant in very limited situations where clear boundaries and expectations exist and appropriateness is predetermined.

With members who have a tendency toward being violent, a prearranged agreement can be worked out so that the member is isolated when aggressive feelings begin to emerge. The use of timeout partners, described at the end of this chapter, is also effective in dealing with this type of member behavior. Purposes are to calm the person down, temporarily interrupt the situation that is generating the feelings, and allow time to think or process.

The physically aggressive or violent member must be helped to find better ways of reacting and behaving. This may involve several steps such as: (1) physical expression in a nonthreatening and nonharmful manner, (2) substitution of verbal expression for physical expression, and (3) development of self-monitoring cues that can help prevent impulsive physical outbursts. The member can then become a more productive and adjusted individual who can seek self-expression and fulfillment in socially appropriate ways. In fact, groups are one of the most effective arenas for helping undersocialized members develop social skills pertaining to strong emotions.

Crying

Probably the most uncomfortable emotional behavior experienced in the group is crying. Even though crying is a natural reaction to sharing a very painful experience or situation, the psychological pressure involved in shedding tears is significant. Social attitudes about crying, especially for male members, include connotations of weakness and lack of self-control. Fear of others' reactions is a major constraint to emotional expression through crying. As one young woman blurted in reaction to breaking down during her discussion of a particularly hurtful relationship, "I'm afraid you all think I'm just a slobbering idiot." The fear of embarrassment and being seen as a fragile person forces many members to contain their tears. This frequently results in mounting pressure, especially if the member continues to work with the painful material. The end product of this buildup then is, in the mind of the crier, far worse because no control over feelings exists. For this reason members often withdraw from the arena of action when they suspect tears are imminent in an effort to avoid a gusher.

Seeing a person cry also has significant impact on other members. They want to help the person but may not really know how. They also may develop the attitude of "boy, that's not going to happen to me," and then withdraw or pursue an entirely cognitive course in the discussion of their problems. This hesitance and inaction often makes a person who cried feel isolated. If the group does not react spontaneously to support and affirm the member, the leader must take steps to do so. Verbalization on the part of others especially in the form of reflection is necessary. And some form of physical gesture such as touching the person's arm or putting an arm around his or her shoulder may be appropriate depending on the person, cultural mores, and situation. Supportive touch when initiated by group members is usually quite affirming, but may need to be modeled by the leader to assure appropriateness. More than anything, the group must communicate that they are aware of the various implications that make crying difficult and at the same time convey the message that crying is a normal expression of one's feelings in many situations.

The characteristics of trust and acceptance—if intricate parts of the group atmosphere—alleviate much of the resistance to crying. However, the group must take care not to seduce a member into crying just to demonstrate its ability to handle it or to prove vulnerability. Some leaders function under the misguided notion that crying is synonymous with deeply meaningful group interaction or personal disclosure and direct their efforts to see that members reach that point. Group members need to view crying as a natural part of certain self-disclosures requiring the support and attention of the group. However, it is not necessarily a symbol of group progress. Nor should efforts be made to belabor distraught members. They should be helped to regain their composure after a reasonable period of time. This is particularly important if the member must leave the group to attend classes, go home, go to work, or relate in other social situations. Few things are more uncomfortable than facing persons outside the group knowing your eyes are red and swollen from crying. If composure has not been restored by the end of the group session, the member can be retained or worked with until he or she is able to function in their typical demeanor outside the group.

Crying is another form of ventilation that can be therapeutic. In some cases really no other way exists to express one's pain so effectively. Once these feelings are out the task of working on problems that generate them is easier. Group members understand the seriousness and have a deeper sense of the person. The overreaction that must be guarded against is when the member begins to wallow in self-pity or to use crying to demand the group's attention. When this happens the leader should intervene to bring the member up to a more cognitive level, with emotions placed in proper perspective, and turn attention to coping, managing, or making necessary changes.

Affection

Extremes in negative or painful emotions are not the only emotional behaviors difficult to cope with in groups. Extremes in positive feelings, especially related to affection, also cause problems. Normally, much more social restraint is related to the expression of affection than to the expression of negative feelings. The reasons for this are that erotic or sexual implications may be associated with showing warm feelings (Bemak & Epp, 1996), and that rejection is much more threatening than punishment. If someone expresses warmth, caring, affection, or love in an overt manner, it may raise questions about the real motivation behind the actions. Similarly, if a person reveals a positive feeling to another person, who rejects it, little recourse is available for the rejected person other than to withdraw with hurt feelings. If someone addresses us negatively, however, the possibility is always open to respond in kind. Strong positive feelings therefore remain quite disguised in many social situations.

In a cohesive and close group the possibilities of overt physical and verbal expression of affection increase. As Bach (1954) stated:

> in giving of love and sympathy the group as a rule naturally goes much further in overt expressions than any other professional therapist (or counselor) would, could, or should ever do. At such moments the group demonstrates a truly remarkable intensity in its expression of support. (p. 96)

In most cases, the physical expression of affection is what causes the most concern. Authorities, family members, and other significant persons with a vested interest in the group members or the group process may perceive any expression of physical affection with suspicion. They may even exert pressures on the leader and/or group members that produce inhibitions, create feelings of guilt, and cast a negative reflection on the entire group process. Ethical practice guidelines restrict the extent of physical touch to appropriate supportive contact and touch. Thus, the spontaneous expression of physical affection is judiciously limited. In addition, structured activities that involve physical touch should have clear guidelines and precise purposes. Generally speaking, members should be encouraged to utilize verbal means of expression of affection.

However, expressions of warmth should be tempered by an awareness of how the receiver may respond. They should never be used to embarrass or make another person feel uncomfortable for the sake of gratifying one's own ego. Neither should verbal expressions incorporate a demand to which the other person must respond. They must simply be a reflection of one's own feelings. Following these guidelines can alleviate much of the discomfort and difficulty associated with affectionate behaviors and can make them a viable therapeutic influence in the group process. Once again, as with all of the critical incidents that are associated with the member behaviors already discussed, processing is critical in order to both recognize the nature and impact of the behavior in the group and attribute meaning to its occurrence.

Acting Out

Acting out behaviors may incorporate any number of previously mentioned resistant, manipulative, or emotional behaviors but constitute a very special category (Kottler, 1994b) because of their intent to flaunt the authority of the group leader or the freedom and acceptance of the group. Johnson (1963) felt that a frequent cause of acting out behavior is the negative feelings individuals have toward the group leader that cannot be expressed. As a result the member engages in overt arts which are designed to threaten, frustrate, irritate, and intimidate the leader. Ohlsen, Horne, and Lawe, (1988) presented a varying perspective indicating that acting out may simply be a matter of members using treatment as an excuse to do things they ordinarily would not do. Acting out behavior may take the form of tardiness, absences, use of drugs or alcohol, or overt, ingroup, aggressive actions. In all cases, these actions immediately bring attention to the member and usually are disruptive to the group process.

Acting out also may be a group test administered by the member to determine boundaries of group interaction and to find out exactly where he or she stands with the leader and members. Kraus et al. (2001) reframe acting out as challenging behavior that is associated with an individual member's unique psychology and personality. Horne and Campbell (1997) use the metaphor of "round pegs in square holes" to describe such behaviors. For example, they indicate that acting out may be the result of an individual member's perception that they are not being heard, understood, and do not have a place or space in the group. They act out as a means of being recognized. Whatever the motive, efforts should be made to involve all members in the discussion rather than letting the acting out behavior degenerate group interaction into a one-to-one confrontation. This is difficult to do especially if the overt behavior is directed at the leader. Other members are naturally curious about how the leader will handle it. Nevertheless, the leader should attempt to get members to express their feelings and perceptions so that the instigator is given feedback from a variety of viewpoints. In this way the entire group takes responsibility for coping with the acting out member. Another effective approach is to use Glasser's (1965) question "What are you doing?" (avoid asking "why," which would lead to rationalizations). This request makes the member assess his or her own behavior rather than forcing others to react. If these ingroup strategies do not work, then an alternative is to ask the acting out person to take a break (time out) and return to the group when functioning in an acceptable manner. If acting out continues unabated in a disruptive fashion, individual counseling may be more appropriate because the member will not have an audience. In more extreme cases the need may be to make a referral to inpatient psychotherapy.

Subgrouping Behaviors

The generic definition of a group is *three or more persons* because with the introduction of the third and succeeding members the phenomenon of group dynamics emerges. Part of those dynamics is the potential for coalitions to form. Consequently, the formation of subgroups is a naturally occurring phenomenon in all forms of group work. As a group develops, coalitions become an integral part of group life. As such, subgrouping is one of the major group member behaviors of which leaders must be aware and must learn to utilize effectively.

In one sense subgrouping behavior serves as a barometer of group health. If subgroups emerge, dissolve, and reemerge in the course of group interaction, and the membership of coalitions varies from topic to topic and issue to issue, the group has fluidity that enables it to maintain resiliency and flexibility. On the other hand, if subgroups solidify with the same members coalescing all the time regardless of the topic or issue, the group develops a rigidity that interferes with and undermines the dynamic nature of the group. Therefore, as long as subgroups retain variable membership, reorganize in response to different focal points, and function generally within the overall norm structure of the group, no particular concern need be raised. However, if persistent patterns of polarization combined with consistent subgroup membership continually emerge across all group interactions, action to dissolve or derigidify the subgrouping process is necessary.

Yalom (1985) noted that subgrouping, or fractionalization, is an inevitable part of the group process and if not attended to can be a destructive force. Subgrouping may occur in one of two general ways: (1) within the context of the group itself, and (2) as a result of external group contact and interaction. Within the group, subgrouping is by far the easiest to deal with because the dynamics are present in a first hand, here and now form that can be processed as they are occurring. In heterogeneous groups, coalitions between members with more similar concerns, problems, values, or perspectives tend to occur. Such coalitions provide excellent material and opportunities for learning acceptance, generating dialogue, and appreciating diversity. These are commodities that have unlimited value in relating to and coping with the world outside the group. The primary facilitative factor in dealing with ingroup subgrouping is raising what is happening to the awareness of the group members rather than letting such dynamics hover beneath the surface where assumptions and suppressed emotions can begin to ferment into misunderstandings that will jeopardize healthy group functioning.

Out of group subgrouping dynamics are much more complicated to cope with. Subgroups with an out of group derivation may arise in several different ways: (1) members may seek out contact with other members based on what they have observed or heard in group, (2) social contact outside the group such as getting together for a beer or cup of coffee may serve as impetus for a subgroup emerging, and (3) on occasion, intimacy between two group members may generate a dyadic coalition. Note that while social incentives motivate members to connect outside the group, equally strong privacy incentives inhibit group members from becoming intimately involved with each other so as not to become the focus of group discussions. Members often view socializing as nonproblematic but tend to draw the line on close relationships at least until the group is over.

Yalom (1985) depicted the problem of subgrouping as stemming "from the belief of two or more members that they can derive more gratification from a relationship with each other than one from the entire group" (p. 334). With respect to dyadic intimacy he stated, "members who become involved in a love-sexual relationship will almost inevitably award their dyadic relationship higher priority than their relationship to (the) group" (p. 335). He added that members who "violate group norms by secret liaisons are opting for need gratification rather than pursuit of personal change" (p. 337). Thus, the evidence is that subgrouping in any of its derivatives is potentially destructive to the group.

Out of group connections that lead to subgrouping are not all negative. In fact, outside contact negotiated in the group for purposes of accountability and support may be an effective means of extending the group's therapeutic influence. Women's groups at times use the *in-relation* propensities of women to therapeutic advantage by incorporating out of group contact. (Juntunen, Cohen, & Wolszon, 1997; McManus, Redford, & Hughes, 1997). If such contacts occur in the context of overall group goals and norms and do not lead to collusion and the emergence of a no talk subterfuge, they can be very helpful and therapeutic. The obvious key is that any significant out of group contacts or experiences are open and above board and that material from such contacts is accessible to the group. Yalom (1985) observed that "it is not the sub-grouping per se that is destructive, but the conspiracy of silence that surrounds it" (p. 339). His research has indicated that such suppression of expression not only leads to a deterioration in therapeutic group process, but also is a contributing factor to attrition and drop outs as individuals fail to cope with being included or excluded in a subgroup.

The general guidelines for dealing with subgrouping behavior are as follows:

1. Make expectations relative to subgrouping behavior clear both in screening interviews and in the context of group interaction. Some group leaders make specific groundrules that delimit or specify out of group contact. While subgrouping cannot likely be absolutely forbidden, actions that would encourage or exploit it are to be avoided.
2. Bring all coalescing, colluding, and subgrouping behavior that occurs in the group to the group's attention for purposes of processing.
3. Establish a guideline and expectation that the group be informed about extra group activity among members.
4. As a group leader, do not collude with subgroups overtly or covertly by not disclosing what you perceive and/or know about the subgroup.

Application to Task Groups

All of the group member behaviors described above are relevant to task groups in the sense that they will affect the process and flow of the group in respect to the group agenda and the work that the group is designed to perform. Resisting, manipulating, helping, emotional and subgrouping behaviors are part and parcel of work groups, and leaders will have to recognize and respond to them in order to achieve maximum efficiency and effectiveness in attaining the objectives of the group. Resisting and manipulating behaviors may manifest themselves in relationship to the group purpose, the leader, members or the group as a whole. Helping behaviors are resources in the group, and emotional behaviors can generate disruptions and distractions. Subgrouping is also common especially in regard to power issues, strategic planning and leadership style. In each case the leader and the group must address the challenge of behaviors that are counterproductive and mobilize those behaviors that are productive.

Concluding Remarks

Most group member behaviors, as diverse as they are, can be predicted according to the climate of the group, the leader's knowledge of human reactions, and the dynamics involved in forming a number of individuals into a group. Most of the detrimental effects of the negative behaviors described in this chapter can be prevented or curtailed if precautionary measures are taken to ensure a healthy group atmosphere and transformed into constructive dynamics if the leader is willing to act to address and work with them. The positive behaviors, whether actualized counterparts of negative behaviors or helping behaviors, can also be incorporated into the group process by laying clear ground rules and by modeling, teaching, and intervening when necessary. The most important step is to recognize the behaviors in the group and use that awareness to inform and direct the process of the group.

Learning Activities

The following activities can be used to teach members effective group behaviors and skills, help them understand their own and other members' actions in the group, and help them cope with the more difficult emotional behaviors that may occur. Generally, the activities included in this section pertain to enhancing appropriate and therapeutic member behaviors and to understanding the nature of member actions and experiences in the group.

Active Listening

This activity can be used to teach members the helping behavior of active listening by developing the specific skills of restatement, reflection, summary, and clarification. The exercise has four parts and requires at least an hour to do. Even more time is preferable, and the exercise can be done in two sessions, concentrating on Parts 1 and 2 in the first session and 3 and 4 in the second.

1. **Making Contact**
    Have members pair up with another group member, usually a person they know least well. This can be done nonverbally through the use of milling, or it can be accomplished simply by numbering off. Once partners are together have them disperse around the room so that there will be as little noise interference or distraction as possible during the exercise.
2. **Hearing and Being Heard: The Skill of Restatement**
    a. *Verbal Communication*. Have one partner make a personal statement about himself or herself. The other partner must repeat that statement word for word exactly as it was said. If the statement is repeated with even the slightest variation, the first partner must reply with an emphatic "No, you're not listening," and then reiterate the statement until it is repeated exactly right. Each partner does this with three different statements. When repeated accurately, confirm the listener with positive feedback: "That's right, good listening!"

b. *Inflection or Tone of Voice.* Repeat the procedure as described in 2.a. except this time incorporate an emotional quality in the statement expressed through fluctuation in the speaker's tone of voice. This time the partner must repeat the statement exactly, word for word and in the same tone of voice. Do this three times each.

c. *Nonverbal Communication or Body Language.* Repeat the procedure as described, but this time include gestures for emphasis in the statement. The partner must repeat the statement exactly, word for word, in the same tone of voice, and using the same gestures.

This part of the activity teaches the skill of *restatement* and focuses on the various levels of communication: the verbal level (word for word), the inflection level (same tone of voice), and the nonverbal level (same gestures).

3. **Transition: Restating in Your Own Words**

Have the partners carry on a conversation on any topic they choose for a period of 10 minutes. However, before adding to the conversation each person must summarize in their own words what their partner just said. The following ground rule must be followed:

Once the first statement has been made, the other person can make a statement only after summarizing the ideas and feelings of the first speaker accurately and to that speaker's satisfaction. All individual comments must be restated satisfactorily before continuing. See to it that this rule is followed for the entire 10 minutes.

The purpose of this segment of the exercise is to help members realize how often their own thoughts interfere with hearing other people out. By repeating their partner's statement before making one's own comment, chances are greater that complete communication will take place. The object is to concentrate on what the other person is saying rather than on organizing what is about to be said. The skill of *summarization* is also learned.

4. **Understanding and Being Understood**

a. *Declarative Statements.* Have one partner make a personal declarative statement about himself or herself, or his or her life, thoughts, or feelings. The other partner then responds by saying "Are you saying. . . ?" and adding what she or he perceives the meaning of the statement to be. If the statement is accurate, the first partner says "yes" and if inaccurate "no." The responding partner must get three "yes" answers to the same statement (i.e., three different meanings) before she or he proceeds to make her or his own statement. Repeat this process three times for each partner using a different statement each time. This part of the activity teaches the skill of *reflection.*

b. *Personal Questions.* Have one partner ask the other partner a personal question. Instruct them to make the questions as personal and honest as possible because the questions will not have to be answered. The questioned partner responds by saying, "Are you asking...?" and then adds what is perceived to be the meaning and intent of the questioner. She or he must get three "yes" answers from the questioner (i.e., three different meanings) before asking his or her own personal question. Repeat this process three times for each partner using a different question each time. The basic premise behind this exercise is that most questions are essentially camouflaged declarative statements representing a directive or reflecting the questioner's point of view or expected answer. The skill taught in this part of the exercise is *clarification.*

The complex nature of communication is pointed out using the two basic forms of expression: the declarative statement and the question. The activity reveals how one person really has difficulty in understanding another's personal communication and stresses the fact that one statement or question can have a multitude of meanings.

Nonverbal Communication Exercise

The purpose of this exercise is to help members develop their skills in nonverbal communication of feelings and utilizing them to improve the communication process in the group. It is also an effective device for leading members in a step by step manner in addressing feelings that are a part of their personal lives.

1. *Recognizing Feelings*
   Divide the group into dyads and have them sit facing each other with one partner facing the board and the other facing away from it. The leader writes a feelings word from the following list on the board and the person facing the board tries to communicate that feeling nonverbally and as naturally as possible to the partner. After five seconds, call time and have the observer try to identify the feeling using reflective leads like "You seem to be feeling...." or "I get the sense you are feeling...." Repeat this activity about four times and then reverse positions and do it again with different words. Then ask partners to think of a feeling they have experienced often or recently and try to communicate it nonverbally to each other. Discuss the difficulties involved in communicating and identifying feelings using only nonverbal cues. Also discuss the differences in communicating positive and negative feelings noting similarities and contrasts. Here are some feelings words that can be used.

Hostility	Anger	Love
Joy	Happiness	Anxiety
Frustration	Confusion	Suspicion
Satisfaction	Pride	Fear

2. *Feelings and Situations*

    Since most feelings are hard to separate from the situations they are associated with, it is often easier to communicate the feelings given a context in which they occurred. Divide the group into subgroups of four. Ask one member of each group to come to you and give that member a description of one of the following situations. The member then returns to the group and attempts to naturally and nonverbally communicate the emotions associated with the situation. Other situations can be substituted or added at the leader's discretion. The other group members try to determine the feelings and make educated guesses about what the situation might be. Repeat this procedure until all four members have had the opportunity to communicate a situational feeling.

    a. You are bored and tired during a class discussion. How do you portray that feeling nonverbally?

    b. Another person does something or says something that hurts your feelings deeply. How do you portray those feelings nonverbally?

    c. You feel affection for another person but at the same time you are not sure the other person feels the same way you do. How do you show your feelings nonverbally?

    d. Your closest friend is leaving town for long time and you will have no chance to see her/him while she/he is gone. How do you show your feelings nonverbally?

3. *Personal Situations*

    Reconvene the entire group if it is a counseling size group or stay with groups of four if larger. Have the members think of a recent past experience that was quite emotional for them. Have individual members in turn demonstrate those feelings nonverbally while the group observes. Observers then discuss what they perceived without comment from the person who expressed the feelings. After the discussion is concluded, the presenter indicates how accurate the group's perceptions were and shares feelings with them including the situation or circumstances if they so choose. Repeat this process until all have participated in conveying a personal feeling. (This particular segment of the exercise was suggested by Dr. Wayne J. Kassera, College of Education, University of Wisconsin-River Falls.)

Barriers to Communication

Sometimes members can understand communication barriers more clearly if they are depicted in a physical manner. The purpose of this exercise is to help group members realize the importance of communication in the group and think about strategies for overcoming obstacles.

Form dyads and have members begin a personal sharing type of discussion. Instruct them to sit *back to back* as they talk and not to turn around. After several minutes, have them change their position to *side by side* but without looking at each other. Next, have members *face each other but avoid eye contact*. During these changes they should continue to share. Finally, have them carry on a *normal face-to-face conversation*. Stop the conversation after a few minutes and ask for reactions and feedback. Point out the importance of eye contact and careful listening in communication.

Then, have the partners reengage in their discussion. Number off members in each dyad as a one or a two. Start with both partners *sitting*. After a few minutes ask the number 1s to *stand up* while continuing the conversation. A few minutes later ask the number 1s to *stand on their chairs* while talking. Again, after a few minutes instruct the 1s to *sit down*. Repeat the entire procedure giving the same instructions to the number 2s. When both are at an equal level sitting again, ask for feedback and reactions, paying special attention to the impact of position and role on the communication process.

Cartoon of Member Reactions

The caricatures depicted in the cartoon in Figure 7.3 can be duplicated and passed out to members to help them discuss and understand the various defensive reactions or postures members display in groups. The handout can be used in several ways:

1. It can be used simply as an open-ended stimulus for discussion.
2. Members can write and discuss captions for each figure, attempting to identify the message that is being conveyed.
3. Members can label each figure with an appropriate name that represents the behavior displayed (e.g., Hostile Harry); or
4. Members can use the cartoon as a means of identifying their own and others' reactions, placing names of the members beneath the caricatures and then getting feedback from others as to what they think.

Since the caricatures are exaggerations they should be used in a lighthearted vein and not as a means of castigating any one member for their behavior or for giving

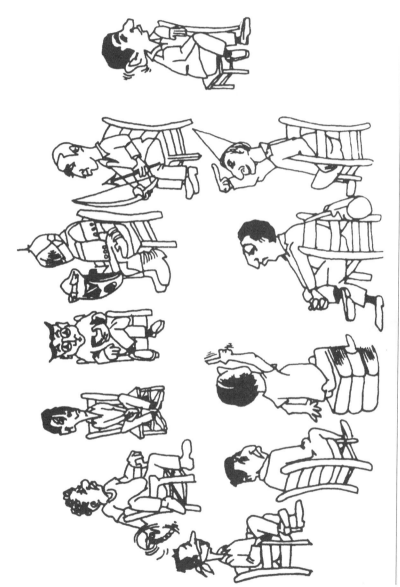

Figure 7.3 Caricatures of group member reactions.

negative feedback. Follow-up discussion might center on how to help each of these types of persons be more comfortable, involved, and open in the group.

Time Out Partners

The time out partner activity (Poppen & Thompson, 1974) lends itself well to working with the more negative or counter productive member behaviors. At any point in the action the leader can call "time out" and have members pair off for a short time to counsel or coach each other. Partners can be selected at random, the same partners can meet together for a period of time, or some criterion (such as using stars with isolates) can be used to match partners. The idea is to stop the group interaction temporarily to give individuals a respite from the pressures of group interaction and to provide them with time to relax, reassess and process their involvement and behaviors. Members usually respond well to this activity and occasionally initiate the request for a time out period themselves. The time out concept can also be applied on an individual basis where certain members or the entire group go off by themselves for a short time and then return to the group. This technique can easily be adapted to a variety of different group settings, such as the task, classroom, psychoeducation or guidance groups, and psychotherapy groups.

Dollar Game

An excellent activity for helping group members understand manipulative behavior is to have each member bring a dollar to the group meeting (fifty cents or a quarter can be used for children). Instruct the members to place their dollars in the center of the group. Then tell them that their task is to decide as a group which individual is to receive all the money. No deals to share the money can be made and the individual chosen will in fact get all the money for personal use. Tell them they must come up with a rationale for disbursing the money to the one person and that no lottery or luck of the draw process can be used.

Allow the group to interact until they reach consensus on the group member who is to receive the money. Give the money to that individual. Conduct a follow-up discussion directed at describing the rationale developed, and sharing feelings and reactions to the task particularly emphasizing values and strategies used in the negotiation process. After some discussion pass out a copy of Shostrom's (1967) Top Dog/Underdog diagram (Figure 7.3) and have members assess the types of manipulative strategies that were used in the group interaction. Have members identify their own strategies and also give their perceptions of other members' strategies.

A variation of this activity for children is to use a free trip to a special place like Disney World as the thing group members must decide to give to one member.

Also, the Closed Fist exercise described at the end of chapter 4 can be used for the same purpose as this activity.

Sharing Fears Activity

As a stimulus to introduce the helping behavior of self-disclosure, Childers and Couch (1989) suggest an anonymous fear sharing activity. Members are asked to write their fears, anxieties, or concerns about the group on 3×5 cards, which are then passed to the leader. The leader randomly selects and reads the cards anonymously, solicits group discussion, and processes member's responses. As the cards are read and processed, self-disclosing by members begins to occur.

Name and Sign Activity

The following activity is designed to dissolve the barriers to connecting and communicating that exist in first or early group sessions. It helps members feel at ease, participate effectively in the group, and as a group and helps members get to know one another in a nonthreatening manner.

1. Members stand in a circle with the leader(s).
2. The leader begins the activity by giving his/her name and making a physical sign: "My name is Jim and my sign is (enacts a gesture, e.g., wave, hand signal, dance).
3. The group responds in unison by saying: "You are Jim and your sign is (the group makes the gesture).
4. The process then moves clockwise or counter clockwise with each member giving his/her name and sign. After each new person's disclosure, the group responds in unison starting with that person and then repeating the name and sign of each previous person.
5. Continue until the entire circle of members has been introduced and the group has responded in unison to the entire circle.
6. Once successfully completed individual members can be invited to do the whole circle.
7. The activity can be replicated as an interpersonal warm-up activity at the beginning of succeeding group sessions as a means of helping members remember names and connect socially with each other.

8

Best Practices in Group Work

Lynn S. Rapin
Robert K. Conyne

"Best Practices" in group work are the vital link between ethical integrity, effective process and efficient productivity in all types of groups.

Introduction

by James P. Trotzer

Professional ethics and standards of professional practice have catapulted to the forefront as predominant concerns in the helping professions. Encompassed in the tumultuous maze of legal, ethical, and professional dynamics are the providers, consumers, and overseers (professional organizations and governmental agencies) of mental health services. Codes of ethics and statutory parameters to govern and guide professional practice have been established and are in a perpetual state of being devised and defined, revised and refined, tested and applied. The field of group work is no exception to this emphasis and process. Consequently, the inclusion of a specific chapter on best practices in group work is designed to provide you with the most current perspectives on professional and ethical practice in group work.

Pedersen (1998) has noted that "ethical guidelines are a necessary but not sufficient condition for promoting ethical behavior" (p. 23). Herlihy and Corey (1996) have explicated the functions of ethical codes as educational tools relative to professional conduct, sources of accountability relative to professional responsibility, and catalysts relative to improvement of the profession. The purpose of this chapter by Lynn Rapin and Bob Conyne is to incorporate those elements into the training dimension of this text with regard to group work.

The emphasis of the chapter is to develop a pragmatic connection between codes of ethics, standards of practice, and literal performance. The relationship of the chapter to professional ethics is to provide concrete group work guidelines and practices that will implement the moral principles that undergird codes of ethics (Kitchener, 1984; Welfel & Kitchener, 1992). These principles include:

1. *Autonomy*: Preserving the free agency and self-determination of the client.
2. *Beneficence*: Promoting that which is good (therapeutic) for the client and facilitating the client's growth and development.
3. *Nonmalfeasance*: Applying the first directive of the Hippocratic Oath that stipulates "above all else—do not harm." Refraining from engaging in any actions that are hurtful to the client.
4. *Justice and fairness*: Treating all clients equally and with equity.
5. *Fidelity*: Being honest, reliable, faithful in conduct and not engaging in deceptive manipulative or exploitative behaviors.

Referring to the Best Practices Guidelines as explicated, and learning and engaging in best practices behaviors will assist you in understanding and implementing both the spirit and the letter of ethical codes of professional conduct.

In relationship to a specific code of ethics (American Counseling Association [ACA] Code of Ethics and Standards of Practice, 2005), the following statement will suffice:

Best Practices in Group Work Guidelines are intended to clarify the application of the ACA Code of Ethics and Standards of Practice to the field of group work by defining a group worker's responsibility and scope of practice involving those activities, strategies and interventions that are consistent and current with effective and appropriate professional, ethical and community standards. (p. 1; excerpted from ASGW Best Practices Guidelines by Lynn Rapin and Linda Keel, adopted by ASGW Executive Board March 29, 1998)

In relationship to the helping modalities, this chapter delineates group work as an entity that presents certain unique issues compared to the other helping modalities (e.g., individual counseling, couple, or family counseling). Group counseling—while in some respects ameliorating some of the ethical dilemmas attendant to individual counseling and family counseling—raises its own challenges to ethical practice due to the nature of the process and its reliance on group dynamics and peer pressure. Consequently, the best practices as elucidated will be of utmost utility.

Finally, this chapter in some respects is the core of the text as all the other chapters are reflected in it and reflect on it. You will note as you read, the direct relationship the guidelines have to the other sections of the text. Therefore, it is with a great deal of enthusiasm, appreciation, and confidence that I present Lynn Rapin and Bob Conynes' chapter. I believe that its merit will be self-evident and that you will benefit conceptually and practically from its content and activities.

Overview

Group work practice can be enhanced and barriers to its implementation can be reduced or eliminated through the proper application of best practices. Our purpose in writing this chapter is to provide a basic primer on best practices in group work, with application to four widely accepted types of group work identified by the Association for Specialists in Group Work (ASGW) including task groups, psychoeducation groups, counseling groups, and psychotherapy groups (ASGW, 1990; ASGW, 2000). In addition, chapter contents, although generically reflective of ASGW's perspective, represent our own thinking and should not be construed as being in any way an official statement of ASGW.

Definition of Best Practices in Group Work

Best practices in group work refer to those activities, strategies, and interventions that are consistent and current with effective and appropriate professional, ethical, and community standards. These practices should address not only what occurs within group sessions but, also, necessary activities and involvement occurring before and after group sessions. That is, best practice guidelines for group work need to be comprehensive in scope.

ASGW Best Practice Guidelines

Since its inception in 1973, the Association for Specialists in Group Work has produced a series of organization documents to support group work training and practice (see http://www.asgw.org for ASGW documents). In 1998, ASGW published the *ASGW Best Practice Guidelines* to replace earlier versions which were written as independent ethical guidelines for group counselors. The Best Practice Guidelines were developed with the input from counselors and group work specialists (Keel & Rapin, 1997; Rapin & Keel, 1996a, 1996b, 1997), and are being used as a basis for training protocols (Thomas, Pender, Brock, Gambino, Morrow, & Neill, 2005).

Upon publication of the Best Practice Guidelines, formal consideration of ethical issues reverted to the American Counseling Association and its adjudication of the Code of Ethics and Standards of Practice (2005). This step was taken at the request of the American Counseling Association (ACA) to reduce the legal liability of any ACA division, including ASGW, that had developed a set of ethical standards, and to promote the unification of the counseling profession.

Planning, Performing, and Processing

We organize the best practice guidelines into the "3 P's" of group work leadership practice: Planning, Performing, and Processing (Conyne, 1997, as reported in Conyne, Smith, & Wathen, 1997).

Planning In Planning, group leaders must be concerned with all steps that are preliminary to conducting the first group session, including but not limited to designing the group, choosing appropriate meeting space, and recruiting and selecting group members.

Performing In Performing, group leaders apply the group work plan effectively and appropriately to positively affect group members and achieve its purpose. Some important components of Performing include the delivery of core competencies in group work, attending to confidentiality throughout the sessions, and developing therapeutic conditions.

Processing In Processing, leaders meet between sessions as they evaluate what occurred in the preceding session, derive meaning from events and experiences, and consider any impact on the next and upcoming sessions. In addition, in the case of coleaders, processing involves examining the quality of their interaction during group sessions.

Ethical choice points and dilemmas can occur at every planning, performing and processing step. As this text is organized, you will find that many of the guidelines in the current chapter match content headings of other chapters. This is understandable because the group leader has ethical responsibilities in every aspect and stage of group work, from participation as a student leader-in-training through direct experience with group members to professional instruction, evaluation and consultation about groups.

We propose that orienting yourself to the best practice elements of planning, performing, and processing will assist you in identifying and limiting potential ethical dilemmas. At the same time, we appreciate that guidelines can only serve as a road map to decision making. The unique personal attributes of the group leader, leader skills, member needs, group goals, leader and member roles and behaviors in interaction with the particular group and theoretical orientation combine for a wide range of decision points.

As you read through the guidelines, consider potential choice points and options you have for responding. The reader can also increase understanding of ethical issues by consulting other ethics sources including two special issues of the *Journal for Specialists in Group Work* (1982, 1990), texts devoted entirely to ethical practice (Burke & Miranti, 1992; Corey, Corey, & Callanan, 1993; Herlihy & Corey, 1996) and texts which apply the guidelines, for example, to failures in group work (Conyne, 1999).

Section A: Best Practices in Planning Group Work

Best Practice Planning Guideline A1:
Be Aware of Professional Context Codes of Ethics

Counselors have both professional and regulatory obligations that guide their practice. Codes of ethics define the ethical responsibilities required of members of professions toward the persons whom they serve. Further, accompanying standards of practice provide minimum expected behaviors required of practicing professionals. Specific procedures must be followed when there is a complaint about the ethical practice of a professional association member. There are a number of ethical decision-making models (Forester-Miller & Davis, 1995; Forester-Miller & Rubenstein, 1992; Kitchener, 1984) available to assist you at ethical decision points, and issues surrounding ethical and legal practice in groups require close monitoring (Rapin, 2004).

These published codes of ethics, standards of practice, and complaint procedures are available to the current and future members of professional organizations, and to their clients. Ethical codes are not static but are revised periodically to reflect current practice. Changes in professional training, delivery and reimbursement systems, for example, may influence specific ethical principles or standards of practice.

Counselors look to their primary national organization, The American Counseling Association (ACA), and its divisions to guide their group practice. The ACA Code of Ethics and Standards of Practice (ACA, 2005), generally addresses group work. The Association for Specialists in Group Work (ASGW) Best Practice Guidelines expressly focuses on group work ethical and practice issues. Because ASGW is a division of ACA, its Best Practice Guidelines operate in addition to the general ACA ethical code.

Counselors or their colleagues may have membership in other professional associations which also have codes of ethics and practice standards germane to general practice and, in some instances, to group work. Some of these other codes include those of the American Psychological Association (2003), the National Association of Social Workers (1999), the National Board for Certified Counselors (2002), and the American Group Psychotherapy Association/National Registry of Certified Group Psychotherapists (2002).

Licensure, Certification, and Accreditation Counselors are regulated by state licensing bodies, and they also can be certified as being properly trained and educated. As of this writing, licensure for counselors has been enacted in 48 of

50 states. Certification is available through different bodies, including the National Board for Certified Counselors (2002), and the American Association of Group Psychotherapy's National Registry of Certified Group Psychotherapists (http://www.groupsinc.org/stdnt/certreq.html). The Council for the Accreditation of Counseling and Related Educational Programs (CACREP; http://www.cacrep.org) has accredited 459 counselor education training programs within 188 institutions. These accredited programs are evaluated as meeting at least the minimal standards for counselor training, including the area of group work.

It may seem overwhelming to the counselor in training or new graduate to absorb all the professional practice context components we have briefly summarized above. However, the professional context that emerges strongly influences group work training and practice, requiring practitioners to be cognizant and responsive as they engage in best practice.

Group Work Best Practice Planning Guideline A2: Develop Conceptual Underpinnings

Value of Group Work

Some counselors and their supervisors do not believe that group work is effective. Evidence to the contrary is building. For example, group counseling has been found to be equally as effective as individual counseling, and sometimes more so (DeLucia-Waack & Bridford, 2004; Horne & Rosenthal, 1997; Seligman, 1995; Sleek, 1995). Group psychotherapy has been demonstrated through a series of studies to be strongly effective (Burlingame, Fuhriman, & Johnson, 2004; Burlingame, MacKenzie, & Stauss, 2003; Fuhriman & Burlingame, 2001; Taylor, Burlingame, Fuhriman, Kristensen, Johansen, & Dahl, 2001). Psychoeducation groups with a preventive focus have been evaluated as showing promising to good evidence for effectiveness (Burlingame, Fuhriman, & Johnson, 2004; Kalodner & Coughlin, 2004), and in the context of larger prevention programs, have contributed to strongly positive effects (Conyne, 2004a,b).

Task groups (Conyne, 1989; Hulse-Killacky, Killacky, & Donigian, 2001) deserve more attention in this discussion, as they are the newest form of group work for counselors to be considering. Task groups occurring in the workplace (Wheelan, 2004) are ubiquitous, for example, with problem-solving task groups being used by 92% of Fortune 1000 companies (Lawler, Mohrman, & Ledford, 1995, cited in Wheelan, 2004). Over half of the workers in organizations employing 100 or more people were members of group-based teams, and psychoeducational skill training in groups occurs frequently within these task group settings. Contrasted with wide adoption of a variety of task groups within work settings, effectiveness research remains a kind of new frontier to be explored and consolidated. Consistent positive findings have been reported by Sundstrom,

DeMeuse, and Futrell (1990) about work teams, the value of focusing on goal setting and performance feedback (Guzzo, Jett, & Katzell, 1985) and attending to group development in a task group's performance (Buzaglo & Wheelan, 1999).

In sum, group work across its wide spectrum is used heavily. Its effectiveness needs no longer to be assumed or left to anecdote. Research in group work is accumulating to demonstrate its effectiveness, allowing Corey and Corey (1997) to assert with regard to counseling groups, "… groups are the treatment of choice, not a second-rate approach to helping people change" (p. 5). At the same time, additional work to demonstrate value is needed. Clearer linkages need to be demonstrated between process and outcome, training and practice, and between research and application in the field (Burlingame, Fuhriman, & Johnson, 2004).

Scope of Practice

It is important that all group workers define their scope of practice (Conyne, Wilson, & Ward, 1977). The ASGW Training Standards (2000) require group workers to be able to define group work in general, the core competencies that all counselors should be able to deliver, and each of the four group work specializations (task, psychoeducation, counseling, and psychotherapy groups). Group work itself is defined in the training standards as:

> A broad professional practice involving the application of knowledge and skill in group facilitation to assist an interdependent collection of people to reach their mutual goals, which may be intrapersonal, interpersonal or work related. The goals of the group may include the accomplishment of tasks related to work, education, personal and interpersonal problem solving, or remediation of mental and emotional disorders. (ASGW, 2000)

As mentioned above, group work is divided into four group work types (ASGW, 2000). Task groups are intended to enhance or correct performance and production goals in work groups, such as committees, classes, or planning sessions. Psychoeducation groups are intended to transmit needed psychological information and to develop member skills. Counseling groups are intended to help members to cope more effectively with common but difficult problems in living. Psychotherapy groups are intended to reduce psychological and/or emotional dysfunction in members who usually are diagnosed or diagnosable. All group types hinge on utilizing interpersonal and group processes in the educational or the healing process (Conyne, 1999).

Advantages and disadvantages of each group work specialization and the conditions under which each can properly be used also need to be understood. Group workers need to be aware of their strengths and limitations in relation to performing group work leadership. Awareness and knowledge of all these areas allow counselors to select a scope of group work practice that suits their assets and which fits presenting situations.

Conceptual Framework

Group workers cannot be effective if their leadership is driven by techniques, directed by presenting issues, or prompted by reliance on intuition alone (Corey, Corey, Callanan, & Russell (1992). It is necessary for them to develop a general conceptual framework that can be referred to for practical guidance, prediction, and to test reality (Conyne, Goodman, & Newmeyer, in press). For some group workers, development of a conceptual framework may involve drawing from counseling and personality-based theories, such as those belonging to the psychodynamic, behavioral, cognitive-behavioral, humanistic, or transpersonal orientations (Corey, 1995; Peterson & Nisenholz, 1995), and applying them to group counseling. Corey and Corey (1997), for instance, prefer a combination model drawn from selected theories, which they describe as "thinking, feeling, and behaving." For others, it may involve focusing on interpersonal, interactional, social psychological, ecological, or systemic models of change (e.g., see Bemak & Conyne, 2004; Forsyth, 1990; Napier & Gershenfeld, 1993; Shaw, 1981), and applying them to group work. In all cases, conceptual underpinnings need to be incorporated with personal values, strengths and limitations, and represent an appropriate fit with cultural and situational demands. These considerations are further reflected in Planning Guidelines sections on Professional Disclosure Statements and Professional Development.

Best Practice Planning Guideline A3: Conduct an Ecological Assessment

In ecological assessment (Conyne & Clack, 1981; Conyne & Cook, 2004) the group worker is interested in understanding the cultural, demographic, economic, political, social, health, and psychological needs of community members. In addition, community members' attitudes about group work are influenced by factors of culture and diversity, and both need to be accorded high importance in any ecological assessment.

Multiple Assessment Issues

The group worker must become focused on understanding the local community. Some of the issues that need to be assessed include: What needs exist in this community that group work might be able to address? What resources could be harnessed in order to provide groups? How would group work fit within the organizational mission? What type of group work might be developed and delivered using strategies that are culturally appropriate and which include adequate opportunities for community participation?

Likewise, the group worker needs to research the professional literature to discover what approaches have worked elsewhere. In doing so, leads can be found to suggest how successful group work might be adapted to local use.

It is usually wise to decide not to conduct an ecological assessment alone for two reasons: (a) it is too complex for one person to accomplish well; and (b) involvement of others at this stage can facilitate their later approval. Formation of a small representative planning group can be helpful.

Match Group Work Type

As we have discussed earlier, group workers can choose from a variety of group work types (task, psychoeducation, counseling, and psychotherapy groups) to serve the needs of their clients and to match the presenting situation. More than one type of group could be used with clients. For example, at-risk populations could be served by both psychoeducational and counseling groups, and task groups within an organization might be linked with psychoeducational skill training.

Best Practice Planning Guideline A4:
Implement Program Development and Evaluation Principles

Group Goals, Themes, and Activities

Once ecological assessment has produced information allowing for identification of the type of group(s) to be offered for specified client populations, the group leader needs to define the purpose of the group(s) and set specific group goals for both leader and members. The leader should further use program development skills to formulate the activities or themes of the group and to identify potential techniques which might be most appropriate for the group type, theoretical orientation and population (Conyne, Goodman, & Newmeyer, in press; McKay & Paleg, 1992).

Evaluation Plan

An evaluation plan should be developed to look at both process (formative evaluation) and outcome (summative evaluation) dimensions (Fitz-Gibbon & Morris, 1987; Patton, 1997). Evaluation questions, measures and tools should be identified prior to the start of the group so that planned evaluation can be conducted (Craig, 1978; Hadley & Mitchell, 1995).

Best Practice Planning Guideline A5:
Identify Resources for Managing the Group Program

Several practical considerations related to resources should be considered prior to implementation. These resources are the nitty-gritty necessities used to make a plan work.

Fees and Insurance

Fees and group member payment obligations often need to be clearly identified across each of the group work types. Group charges should be established consistent with agency or organization guidelines and in consideration of the financial status of prospective group members. Many organizations have sliding fee scales to respond to the varying income levels of potential group counseling or group psychotherapy clients. When counselors are providing fee-based task or psychoeducation group training or consultation within organizations or communities, contracts need to be developed to clearly define responsibilities in relation to cost and payment.

One of the current challenges in counseling is that of providing services which might be covered in whole or part by insurance. Fees consistent with professional and community standards may vary greatly from reimbursement limits set by insurance plans. Further, membership on insurance panels greatly affects reimbursement levels, with a late 1990's common effect of reducing fees (*Psychotherapy Finances*, 1997). A group could thus have some members whose fees are fully paid by insurance, some who have insurance covered by a managed care contract at a discounted fee, members who have no insurance coverage and pay full fee, and members with reduced fee due to income variability.

Funding

Adequate funding must be available to support group offerings. Costs might include "hard moneys" to support preparation of materials and supplies necessary and, also, such "soft" needs as supporting professional development of staff who may need additional training and/or supervision including continuing education requirements that must be met for licensure.

Leaders/Coleaders

A determination of whether it is appropriate for the group to be led by one leader or coleaders should be made. If coleaders are appropriate, the model of leadership they would employ (apprentice model, rotating model, supervision model) needs to be identified. It also is important that leadership styles of coleaders be discussed and integrated so that group members are not confused or harmed by different orientations or approaches. Research and analysis suggests that coleaders need to progress through their own development as a team prior to beginning work with a group (DeLucia-Waack, & Fauth, 2004; Dugo & Beck, 1997; Riva, 2004; Wheelan, 1997).

Meeting Space

Identifying available group meeting space and any necessary privacy requirements (especially with counseling or psychotherapy groups) ensure that groups can actually take place in the desired setting. It is not unusual for there to be no dedicated space for groups, whether the organization is an agency, business, school or private practice. Flexible negotiating with administrative authorities may be necessary to convert space for appropriate group work.

Marketing and Recruiting

Any recruitment or marketing must be accomplished considering the setting for the group. Professional development presentations to staff about the group offering(s), staff discussion with clients about group benefits, community education presentations, consultation with referral agencies and individuals, community service announcements, media presentations, and Internet announcements are among appropriate options. Reliance upon just one approach is not recommended, however. The best strategy is to use multiple approaches, being sure to integrate nonpersonal ones, such as stand-alone fliers, with a personal contact, and also providing opportunities for those interested to immediately and concretely take action (Wilson, Conyne, Bargett, & Smith-Hartle, 1987).

Other organization settings require alternate strategies. School settings have unique resources, including the classroom teacher, administrators who work with at-risk students, parents, and students themselves. Business organizations have Employee Assistance Programs, managers and supervisors, in-house publications, and employees themselves as potential referral sources.

Best Practice Planning Guideline A6:
Develop a Professional Disclosure Statement

An essential step in the planning process, applicable to group counseling and to group psychotherapy, is the preparation of a professional disclosure statement. These printed statements are often required by law and serve to inform potential group members of the group leader(s)' scope of practice, licenses and certifications, specific qualifications in conducting the group or groups being offered, and fees for service (see Table 8.1 for a basic format example).

Table 8.1 Professional Disclosure Statement Format Example.

Identification:
> Pat Jones, Adolescent Group Coordinator
> Community Mental Health Center
> 110 Main Street
> Central City, Your State
> Phone: (123) 456-7890
> Email: pj@ccc.com

Education:
> Master's Degree (M.A.) in Community Counseling from State University (CACREP Approved Program) and specialist in advanced counseling from State University

Licensure and Certification:
> Licensed Professional Clinical Counselor
> Your State License No. 12345
> Certified, National Board for Certified Counselors

Professional Associations:
> American Counseling Association
> Association for Specialists in Group Work
> Your State Counseling Association

Scope of Practice:
> Provision of community counseling services within the mental health setting

Specialization:
> Group work with adolescent clients in the Mental Health Center who experience behavior, drug, and alcohol issues

Purpose and Goals of Group Counseling:
> Assist adolescents in resolving conflicts and increasing problem solving skills as they face risk situations

Group Structure:
> Time limited, closed groups; ongoing open groups; groups are frequently co-led

Previous Experience Leading Groups:
> Two years as a junior group co-leader and four years as senior group co-leader

Fee Schedule:
> Groups follow the agency fee schedule provided to all clients

Credentialing Agency Address:
> Counselor Licensing Board
> 123 Central Avenue
> Capital, Your State

Best Practice Planning Guideline A7: Prepare the Group and its Members

Once the counselor has selected the type of group(s) to be conducted, it can be determined whether it is appropriate or not to screen members prior to admission to the experience. Counseling and psychotherapy groups generally require pre-screening to ensure a good match between member and group. When counselors are using psychoeducational or task groups, they may be working with intact groups in which individual member screening is not always possible.

Informed consent

A group plan cannot succeed without integration with the real people who will become its members. Information prepared during preceding planning activities is provided during screening to ensure that prospective clients of counseling or psychotherapy groups are fully informed, willing, and appropriate to participate in the group. Clearly delivered information about goals of the group, ground rules for participation, possible activities, leader qualifications, and leader and member responsibilities fosters member involvement and ownership of the group experience.

Confidentiality and its limits

A delicate balance is required to both educate potential counseling and psychotherapy group members to the importance of confidentiality within and outside the group experience and to provide information on the limits of confidentiality (e.g., legal privilege does not apply to group discussions and that the group leader(s) cannot guarantee confidentiality of information shared among group members). Members need to understand that documentation for treatment plans, insurance approval, and claim filing requires that the group leader(s) provide confidential information in writing that may not be protected beyond the sponsoring organization.

Best Practice Planning Guideline A8: Pursue Professional Development

Group workers have both opportunity and obligation for continuous learning. In addition to the learning opportunities present in every group session, more formal opportunities for professional enhancement are plentiful. Continuing education through professional meetings, professional development workshops, academic experiences, professional supervision in groups, coleading experiences, professional presentations and personal development all enhance counselors' abilities to serve group members. Responsible group workers integrate research and practice literature into group design and evaluation.

Best Practice Planning Guideline A9: Be Aware of Trends and Technological Changes

Counselors should be aware of and appropriately respond to technological changes and trends as they affect society and the profession.

Managed Care

Mental health delivery systems, including group counseling and group psychotherapy, have been significantly affected by legislative health care reform and changes in the insurance industry. Managed care has and will continue to influence group counseling and group psychotherapy, including access to services, delivery of group and other treatment modalities, documentation, confidentiality, reimbursement, and outcome evaluation. On the positive side of managed care, there is some indication that group counseling and group psychotherapy services may become a preferred delivery format in the future for reasons of both economy and effectiveness (Spitz, 1996). Group workers must be active participants in understanding managed care issues and in developing appropriate responses to them.

Demographics

Group workers must respond in their training and practice to changing population demographics and client needs. These include, for example, increased sensitivity to multicultural and diversity issues as the population becomes more diverse, responding to AIDS and other serious health trends, working with an aging population, and adapting to the impact of anticipated and unanticipated societal and world conditions—such as the heightened concern and security surrounding personal and national safety in this post-September 11 age.

Technology

Counselors must keep abreast of technological advances that affect their work. Access to the Internet presents both opportunity and challenge in many areas (e.g., in research, information exchange, advertising, and service provision). Online groups are now a reality (Page, 2004) and online technologies, such as Blackboard and distance learning, provide options for group workers to adopt and adapt. Locally, we have been exploring the use of hand-held personal responders, in conjunction with small group work, in large classrooms as an instructional technology (Goodman & Huether, 2004), and of how group work can be effectively integrated within Problem-Based Learning as an important instructional strategy (Conyne, Goodman, Newmeyer, & Rosen, 2004). Counselors must adhere to ethical guidelines related to use of developing technologies (Bloom, 1997; NBCC, 1997a). Preparation and flexibility are essential for future professional success.

Section B: Best Practices in Performing

The performance of group counseling involves effectively adapting the group work plan to fit situational demands. It is seldom that a preconceived plan, no matter how well developed, can be implemented without undergoing substantial modification. The group worker then must use effective and appropriate competencies and strategies to affect the revised plan, with the goal of meeting group and individual member goals. In the case of task groups, organizational/community goals also need to be closely considered because task groups typically are formed within organizations or communities.

Although Performance is a portion of group leadership (surrounded by Planning and Processing), it often is considered to be the "first among equals." Performance is what most often is thought of as comprising group leadership. It is what the leader(s) actually do during the course of group counseling sessions. What best practices are associated with performance?

Best Practice Performance Guideline B1: Know Thyself

As many experts have observed (e.g., Corey & Corey, 2002; Gladding, 2003), it is fundamentally important that group counselors (and all group workers) be aware of their strengths and weaknesses and of their stimulus value to others. One of the best ways that future group workers can become aware of themselves as interpersonal beings is to become a member of one or more therapeutic group experiences and avail themselves of the opportunities to self-disclose and to give and receive feedback in the group setting.

Best Practice Performance Guideline B2: Effectively Deliver Group Competencies

Core Group Competencies

As described in the ASGW Professional Training Standards, all counselors should be able to perform the foundation skills of group work and understand basic knowledge of groups. For example, they should be able to open and close group sessions, encourage the participation of group members, and to engage in appropriate self-disclosure in groups. As well, all counselors must possess a working knowledge of groups, including being able to identify the principles of group dynamics, to describe specific ethical issues that are unique to group work, and to deliver a clear definition of group work.

Unique Competencies within Each Group Work Type

Additional to the core competencies, that form a foundation for all group work, more specialized competencies accompany each of the four group work types. General competencies thought to be necessary within each type of group work (ASGW, 2000) are summarized next.

Task Group Competencies Application of principles of normal human development and functioning through knowledge and skills based on educational, developmental, and systemic strategies to promote task and goal accomplishment.

Psychoeducation Group Competencies Application of principles of normal human development and functioning through knowledge and skills based on educational and developmental strategies to promote personal and interpersonal growth and the prevention of future difficulties with people who may be at risk.

Counseling Group Competencies Application of principles of normal human development and functioning through knowledge and skills based on cognitive, affective, behavioral, or systemic strategies to resolve problems of living with people experiencing transitory maladjustment or desiring enhancement.

Psychotherapy Group Competencies Application of principles of normal and abnormal human development and functioning through knowledge and skills based on cognitive, affective, behavioral, or systemic strategies to remediate dysfunctional behavior and promote growth with people who may be experiencing severe and/or chronic maladjustment.

Best Practice Performance Guideline B3:
Adapt Group Plan

As stated above, group workers need to learn the conditions under which their plan is to be used as is, to be modified, or to be abandoned. They need to develop adequate and reliable professional judgment, such that they can determine when and how to proceed with their groups (Conyne, Wilson, & Ward, 1997; Kottler, 1994). While this capacity emerges through experience and training, it can be advanced through appropriate supervision and by working in coleadership arrangements where processing of group events and experiences can occur openly and genuinely between sessions.

Best Practice Performance Guideline B4:
Master Therapeutic Conditions and Dynamics

Effective group workers understand what we call the "Holy Trinity" of therapeutic conditions and dynamics: (a) group development, (b) process observation, and (c) therapeutic conditions. We believe these conditions and dynamics apply across the group work spectrum.

Group Development

Many sequential and cyclical models of group development exist (MacKenzie, 1997). The sequential model described in this text is as useful as any, maybe more so because it also ties group developmental tasks to each stage. But whichever model is chosen, it can provide the group worker with a powerful schematic for generally predicting future events and for interpreting occurring ones. Possessing such knowledge allows the group leader to bring perspective to practice, and it contributes to leader competence and confidence.

Process Observation

Group workers must be able to assess and diagnose what is occurring in their groups, not only in terms of what is being said (content) but, also, how content is being presented and received (process). Examples of important group process observations include being able to notice levels of participation, influence, styles of decision making, group tone, task and maintenance behaviors, how affect is dealt with, and the operating norms of the group (Hanson, 1972). Noting such processes within sessions and across them helps to determine how the group is working and how members are progressing.

Therapeutic Conditions

Yalom's (1995) therapeutic conditions or factors are accepted by most experts as axiomatic to effective group counseling and psychotherapy (Crouch, Block, & Wanless, 1994). The capacity to generate these 11 conditions, such as universality, instillation of hope, and altruism, needs to be well within the repertoire of all group counselors, regardless of theoretical orientation. We believe these therapeutic conditions also can be generalized as educational conditions, as well, and are applicable to all group work types. In addition, with Task groups, it is important to give particular attention to goal clarity, decision-making procedures, and the relationship between the group itself and its "sponsor," that is, the larger organization of which it is a part and by whom the group may have been initiated.

Best Practice Performance Guideline B5: Choose Appropriate Interventions

Group workers need to be able to select interventions from a range of possibilities that fit the presenting situation. Considerations such as intervention level (individual, interpersonal, group), type (conceptual, experiential, structural), and intended intensity (high, medium, or low) are important to understand and utilize (Cohen & Smith, 1976; Conyne, Goodman, & Newmeyer, in press).

Best Practice Performance Guideline B6:
Attend to Here-and-Now and to Meaning Attribution

Group workers generally can help members find increased therapeutic value in interactions that are focused on present experience and events. Competencies demanded by each group work type, for instance, demand attention to here-and-now dynamics. But attention to here-and-now experience is not enough. As Lieberman, Yalom, and Miles (1973) showed with regard to encounter groups, members need to learn how to attribute meaning (make sense) to their experience (Hill, 1969; Yalom, 1995). And, what is done and understood needs to be applied and/or adapted appropriately and effectively in the extra-group (some would say, "real world") environment.

Best Practice Performance Guideline B7: Collaborate with Members

Help Members Develop Goals

Groups tend to flounder when members do not understand the general group purpose or if they do not receive help in translating their sometimes vague intentions into more concrete goal statements (Johnson & Johnson, 1997). Working with group members to define feasible and meaningful goals for the group experience is an excellent motivational tool that can accelerate positive outcomes.

Coequal Partners

Leaders and members are co-equal partners in all types of group work. Wheelan (2004) points out with regard to task groups, for example, that a key to successful intervention allows group members to decide what and how to change in targeted areas. Thus, leaders are experts in the theory and process of group work; members are experts in their own experience and life situation. Working with members, seeking to empower them through harnessing their own resources, represents an important way for group workers to approach leadership.

Best Practice Performance Guideline B8: Include Evaluation

If evaluation occurs in group work at all, it is most likely to be at a group's conclusion, to be formal in nature, and too often (although this is rapidly improving), to be cursory. Outcome evaluation needs to be supplemented by process evaluation. So, it is important for leader(s) to collect information along the way. One way for this to occur is for leaders to evaluate each session informally with their group members. Doing so reinforces an ethic of collaborative learning and will help to keep the group on a proper course. This kind of evaluation need not be complex, sophisticated, or lengthy. In fact, we recommend it be simple, friendly, and short, and be integrated with discussion. A very usable format is that developed by Hill (1969), called the Post Meeting Reaction Sheet (PMRS), where leaders and members discuss at the end of each session such issues as personal learning, participation levels, and overall satisfaction.

Best Practice Performance Guideline B9: Value Diversity

Group workers need to establish a group value that fully incorporates diversity (Conyne, Tang, & Watson, 2001). An interesting way to think broadly about diversity can be found through considering the term "respectful," used as an acronym by D'Andrea and Daniels (1997b). The authors argue that counselors should integrate within their work attention to a broad range of client differences, including: Religious/spiritual identity; Ethnic identity; Sexual identity; Psychological maturity; Economic class standing; Chronological challenges; Threats to one's well-being; Family history; Unique physical characteristics; and Location of residence.

RESPECTFUL

Best Practice Performance Guideline B10: Maintain a Constant Ethical Surveillance

Group work is an intricate, complex intervention that demands great attention, focus, and skill of its practitioners. Ethical challenges can be found in every session, and these are especially sensitive for group counselors and group psychotherapists. Examples include: How to safeguard and protect the rights of each member while, at the same time, encouraging risk taking; How to develop a common agreement about the sacred trust of confidentiality while explaining to members that it is not possible to guarantee it; How to help members understand the leader's position on a topic while not imposing his or her own values on the member. Group counselors need to develop a solid understanding of the ACA Code of Ethics and Standards of Practice (ACA, 2005), to employ a process of ethical decision making to help them determine appropriate courses of action in morally or procedurally uncertain instances (Forester-Miller & Davis, 1995), and to be able to consult with trusted colleagues when murkiness is the state of affairs. Group psychotherapists need to be aware of the American Psychological Association ethical code (APA, 2003). Licensing ethics and applicable law are equally as important.

Section C: Best Practices in Processing

Life is fast-paced. Events and experiences occur as if in a blur. Speed characterizes life in group work, as well. So much happens, from so many directions, that group members and group leaders alike often are unable to keep up let alone make sense of what is occurring (Conyne, Wilson, & Ward, 1997). That is why the processing element is so crucial.

Best Practice Processing Guideline C1: Consistently Schedule Processing Time

Purpose for Processing

Processing is often overlooked in group work, taking a back seat to Performing and to Planning. As it is linked to Planning and Performing, we refer to Processing as between-session analysis, evaluation, and reflection engaged in by group leaders in order to guide the group forward productively. Processing by group leaders is necessary in order for them to better understand what occurred, draw meaning from events and experiences, and to make appropriate or necessary adjustments to the plan for next sessions (DeLucia-Waack, 2002; Ward & Litchy, 2004).

Before- and After-Session Processing

Before- and after-session processing is similar to processing that may occur within sessions, which is conducted to help members integrate experiential with cognitive learning. However, before- and after-session processing is distinguishable as a leadership step which is conducted to help the group stay on course and to be effective. Never forget, ignore, or avoid making time to process before and after sessions, no matter how difficult it is to schedule or how threatening it may seem to do (Conyne, 1989, 1999). Doing so makes a commitment to your learning and to the group and its members.

 Before a session, leaders are concerned with adequate preparation and making sure goals and strategies are linked, the session plan matches the developmental progress of the group, and leader roles are clear. After a session, leaders are focused on understanding what occurred, examining member and leader behavior, assessing the relative effectiveness of the session, and seeking to draw deeper meaning from events and experiences.

Best Practice Processing Guideline C2: Engage in Reflective Practice

Learn from Experience

As Yalom (1995) has pointed out with regard to within-session performance of group leadership, the here-and-now experience of the group needs to be informed by reflectively arcing to illuminate the process. He means that here-and-now experience needs to be considered and understood, resulting in the attribution of meaning (Lieberman, Yalom, & Miles, 1973). This is accomplished by reflecting back (arcing) on concrete group experiences, resulting in an integration of experiential and cognitive learning. Likewise, Argyris, Putnam, and Smith (1985) discussed the action scientist role, Lewin (1951) posited the value of action research, and Conyne, et al. (1997) described the group worker as a reflective practitioner.

These perspectives all share placing the value of synthesizing with doing, of action with reflection, of theory with practice. Group counselors must actively and systematically allocate time, energy, and focus to learning from their experience as leaders and to appropriately incorporate learning outcomes into their ongoing groups. For between-session Processing, assiduously keeping session by session journals, processing before and after sessions with a coleader or with a supervisor, applying concepts to practice, reviewing session evaluation results, and critiquing video tapes made of sessions represent some of the strategies to use in nurturing the reflective practitioner role.

Pragmatic and Deep Processing

Two types of processing between or after sessions are possible: (a) pragmatic processing, and (b) deep processing (Conyne, 1999; Conyne, Smith, & Wathen, 1997). In pragmatic processing, the focus is placed on noting and describing the dynamics of members and their interactions, including such matters as who talks to whom and identifying decision-making procedures that have been used. In deep processing, leader(s) probe more intensely the relationship between what has occurred and their values, cognition, and affect. Here, leaders risk confronting themselves and each other, intending to move to a deeper level of personal meaning that could have both immediate and lasting impact on their professional practice.

Best Practice Processing Guideline C3: Use Evaluation Data

Evaluation is a central part of Processing. "Utilization-focused evaluation" as conceptualized by Patton (1997) makes evaluation data central to group work practice. Unless one is conducting basic experimental research, it is of little value to ask questions about a group that do not have pragmatic importance. Conversely, it is of high value to ask questions and to produce data that are directly relevant to ongoing group issues.

Evaluation can be focused on monitoring the ongoing processes and performance of a group. Questions of effort, efficiency, appropriateness, satisfaction, group process, and congruence with the group plan are often important for monitoring (Craig, 1978). In Performing Guideline B8 we discussed collaborating with group members to include evaluation within each session. In Processing, the focus of evaluation is on studying evaluation data between sessions, designing methods for gathering evaluative data in future sessions, and using data produced for making any necessary adjustments in the group plan.

Evaluation also can be focused on determining group outcomes. Outcomes address such summative matters as overall satisfaction, involvement, effectiveness, and goal accomplishment. For example, an outcome evaluation can be designed to test if the general purposes of the group and the individual goals of members were met. Quasi- or experimental designs (Campbell & Stanley, 1963) are suited to these kinds of bottom-line questions, the answers to which have assumed considerably more significance with the advent of managed care and its emphasis on what works.

Conclusion

Group work is rapidly developing as an essential helping methodology. According to some experts, it and other forms of group work may become the preferred forms of help-giving in twenty-first century America. Given the importance of group work, it is necessary that best practices be developed to help guide training, delivery, and research across its wide spectrum. This chapter represents an effort in presenting these best practices. Its contents emerge from ethical guidelines previously adopted by the Association for Specialists in Group Work, and it is compatible with both the Code of Ethics and Standards of Practice of the American Counseling Association (2005), and the ongoing work of ASGW's Ethics, Professional Standards and Diversity Committees.

The set of best practices presented in the chapter are organized within three major sections: (a) Planning, (b) Performing, and (c) Processing, as are the learning activities that follow. Implementation of these best practices will assist practitioners in their provision of effective, appropriate, and useful counseling groups.

Learning Activities

Planning Activities

1. Imagine you are a staff member in a mental health center that has no group services. Generate for your real or imagined setting at least six points you would need to consider in developing a psychoeducation group program. Share and discuss contributions in a small learning group of three to five members (60 minutes).

2. Design a Professional Disclosure Statement containing appropriate information for a group counselor and present it to a partner; then reverse. Now do the same for group psychotherapy. Discuss your similarities and differences (45–60 minutes).

3. You recently were appointed the "Group Work Coordinator" in your agency. No systematically-organized group work presently is being done, except for an occasional psychotherapy group. Your charge is "to get approval of a comprehensive plan for a 'full-blown' group work program in the next 90 days." Write notes detailing how you might proceed with this complex task and be prepared to share your thoughts in a total class discussion (45 minutes).

Performing Activities

1. Self-assess your strengths and areas for improvement as a group counseling leader. List strengths and improvement areas in two columns. Select one strength and one improvement area and indicate how you might utilize the strength in a group of your choice and enhance the area of improvement. Discuss these with a partner, and then reverse roles (60 minutes).
2. Organize into a group of six people and select a leader. Conduct a 20-minute group discussion addressing the topic, "How I think psychoeducation groups can be helpful to people." After 20 minutes, stop the group and engage in an evaluative discussion, asking (a) What was the accuracy of understanding among the group members about what a psychoeducation group is? (b) How did the meeting go? (c) How satisfied were you with your participation? (d) How might you be able to improve your working together, using this information?
3. Focus statement: "Psychotherapy and task groups are polar endpoints on the group work continuum." Discuss the accuracy of this statement and analyze it in terms of group leader behavior, considering roles, competencies required, and training needed. Meet with a partner to discuss the statement comparing and contrasting your perspectives (30 minutes).
4. Your class might be considered a task group. Why? What is transpiring that fits the definition of a task group? What could be added to more closely approximate it? Discuss this matter as a whole class, with a student volunteering to lead that discussion (30 minutes).

Processing Activities

1. Break into pairs to complete the following exercise. Suppose you have just joined with a co-leader to offer a psychotherapy group. Individually identify what characteristics would be important for you to discuss with your co-leader to ensure a successful group. Discuss your ideas with a partner. Summarize ideas from your dyad and share with the whole group (60 minutes).

2. What specific steps would you take to assure adequate processing of your group experience? Prepare your answer, and then discuss your steps with others in a small discussion group of three to five participants (45 minutes).

3. As part of your new role as "Group Work Coordinator," you need to develop procedures to help determine if group work services are effective, efficient, appropriate, and adequate. Develop ideas to address this task and discuss your ideas with a partner and report your results to the larger group. (30 minutes).

4. Identify a specific group experience or event you have encountered as a member or leader. Describe its dynamics (pragmatic processing). Go beyond this to identify your thoughts and feelings and, also, what this experience meant to you (deep processing). Share the results of your work with a partner; reverse roles and reciprocate (60 minutes).

5. Use the check list in Figure 8.2 as a guide for planning a group. Have you done everything you need to do to plan for, perform and process your group experience? For *no* responses, return to this chapter and identify what additional actions you need to take.

Best Practice Guidelines Training Activity

The format for this activity was created by R. V. Thomas (Rollins College) and D. A. Pender (Southern Illinois University) (cochairs of the Ethics Committee for the Association for Specialists in Group Work (2004–2005). This activity has been modified from the ACA (2005) presentation to focus on use in the classroom. Content is based on Association for Specialists in Group Work (1998). ASGW Best Practice Guidelines, *Journal for Specialists in Group Work, 23*, 237–244. This activity introduces students to ASGW Best Practice Guidelines in group work and helps them clarify their responsibilities to ethical clinical practice. Students will engage in an experiential learning activity that helps bring to life the three sections of the Best Practice guidelines. Practice tips from seasoned practitioners are offered as pearls of wisdom based on years of successful clinical experience. Please note, prior to this activity you must secure seasoned practitioners, counselor educators, or counselors who would be willing to participate in the activity and are willing to be in the inner circle of the practice pearls portion of the activity.

The training activity will require students to:

- Define the Best Practices in Group Work.
- Become familiar with the three sections of the Best Practices in Group Work.
- Receive tips for ethical practice from seasoned practitioners.
- Construct a plan to implement a best practice idea in their current setting (for students this might include practicum or internship sites.

Table 8.2 Best Practices in Group Work Checklist.

Check List Items	Yes	No	NA
Section A: Best Practices in Planning Group Work			
A1: Be Aware of Professional Context.			
Have awareness of professional context			
Have reviewed Codes of Ethics			
Have complied with licensure, certification, and accreditation requirements			
A2: Develop Conceptual Underpinnings.			
Have developed conceptual underpinnings			
Have understanding of the value of group counseling			
Have defined my scope of practice			
Have developed a conceptual framework			
A3: Conduct an Ecological Assessment.			
Have completed an ecological assessment			
Have identified and answered key assessment questions			
Have matched group work type to population			
A4: Implement Program Development and Evaluation Principles.			
Have implemented program development and evaluation			
Have defined group purpose			
Have defined group goals			
Have identified group themes			
Have selected appropriate activities			
A5: Identify Resources for Managing the Group Program.			
Have identified resources for managing the group program			
Have complied with fee and insurance policies			
Have secured necessary funding			
Have made leadership\co-leadership decision			
Have secured meeting space			
Have completed marketing and recruiting			
A6: Develop a Professional Disclosure Statement.			
Have developed a professional disclosure statement			
A7: Prepare the Group and its Members.			
Have prepared the group and its members			
Have completed any required screening			
Have provided informed consent			
Have described confidentiality and its limits			
A8: Pursue Professional Development.			
Have identified relevant professional development activities			
A9: Be Aware of Trends and Technological Changes.			
Have awareness of relevant trends and technology			
Have understanding of managed care impacts			
Have understanding of client demographics			
Have understanding of technology impacts			

(Continued)

Table 8.2 (Continued)

Check List Items	Yes	No	NA
Section B: Best Practices in Performing Group Work			
B1: Know Thyself.			
Have understanding of personal limits (self-knowledge)			
B2: Effectively Deliver Group Competencies.			
Have understanding and skill in group competencies			
Have knowledge and skill in core competencies			
Have group counseling (or other type of group) competencies			
B3: Adapt Group Plan.			
Have group plan			
Have considered adaptation contingencies			
B4: Master Therapeutic Conditions and Dynamics.			
Have skill in therapeutic conditions and dynamics			
Have understanding of group development			
Have skill in process observation			
Have knowledge of therapeutic conditions			
B5: Choose Appropriate Interventions			
Have chosen appropriate interventions			
B6: Attend to Here-and-Now and to Meaning Attribution.			
Have prepared to attend to here and now and meaning attribution			
B7: Collaborate with Members.			
Have plan to collaborate with group members			
Have plan for member goal development			
Have respect for member contributions			
Have developed Co-Equal Partnership.			
B8: Include Evaluation.			
Have plan to include evaluation			
B9: Value Diversity.			
Have value for diversity			
B10: Maintain a Constant Ethical Surveillance.			
Have plan to maintain a constant ethical surveillance			
Section C: Best Practices in Processing Group Work			
C1: Consistently Schedule Processing Time.			
Have schedule for processing			
Have purpose for processing			
Have plan for before and after session processing			
C2: Engage in Reflective Practice.			
Have activities to engage in reflective practice			
Have focus on learning from experience			
Have plan for pragmatic processing			
Have plan for deep processing			
C3: Use Evaluation Data.			
Have plan to use and integrate evaluation data			
Have made consultation and training contacts			

Introduction (10 minutes)

Overview Refer to chapter 8 material and briefly discuss the history of Best Practices. How did these guidelines evolve? Provide short overview of each section (planning, performing and processing) and discuss the purposes/rationale for Best Practices and why we need these guidelines?

Learning Activity (20 minutes) Divide students into three microlab groups. Each group is asked to focus on one of the three sections of Best Practice Guidelines. Assign a group facilitator (a graduate student or member selected by the group) to facilitate the group. Thus, there are three group activities occurring simultaneously each focusing on a different Best Practices section. Examples of selected activities for each section are provided below. However, any of the Best Practices guidelines can be used and the format can be repeated with different guidelines until the whole set of Best Practices is addressed.

Section A Learning Activity:
Planning Section—Professional Disclosure Statement

The instructor informs the first work group that their task is to collectively generate the items that a group worker should include in a professional disclosure statement. After students have discussed their spontaneous response, the instructor will offer the best practice guideline for comparison.

Section B Learning Activity: Performing Section—Group Plan Adaptation

The instructor informs the second work group that their task is to brainstorm ideas for an activity to prompt member self-disclosure. After each participant offers an idea, ask the group to decide what type of group and stage of group development the suggested activity would be appropriate for. Then discuss the skill it would take to manage the activity. Finally, ask if the activity would need to be adapted if the group included members from diverse ethnic or racial groups, were all of one gender, or of different chronological ages.

Section C Learning Activity: Processing Section—Reflective Practice

The instructor informs the third work group that their task is to create a post group process note format for a group of their choice. Students identify a group type (i.e., task group, counseling group, psychoeducational group) to use as an example. They then brainstorm several kinds of reflective questions that might be important to address after conducting a session. For example, after conducting a psychoeducational parenting group, what questions might group leaders process in order to make sense out of the group experience. Processing questions should include focusing on:

1. understanding what occurred in the session,
2. examining member's and leader's behaviors,
3. assessing the effectiveness of the session, and
4. seeking to draw deeper meaning from events and experiences.

After-session processing helps the group stay on course and be effective. Then, alter the type of group (e.g., counseling group to a psychotherapy group) and see what changes students feel should be made to the original list of processing questions.

Practice Pearls (20 minutes) Arrange an inner and outer circle for discussion. The inner circle should be composed of seasoned participants (at least three or more years of experience). The outer circle is composed of those who are new to group work or less experienced (students, etc.). The following three questions are posed:

1. What are the most important lessons you have learned about planning a group?
2. How have you used your personal strengths or become self-reliant on your strengths in group work and how has that affected your groups?
3. What do you think the challenges are in doing deep group processing?

The inner circle discusses and shares their answers to the questions offering tips or advice and ideas for successful practice. The outer circle listens and then contributes any ideas they have about the section topics discussed. Reactions to the information are then exchanged between the inner and outer circle.

Ideas to Action: (10 minutes) What is your plan? Students are asked to reflect and share in dyads what they will take from this activity and how they will implement their new learning into their practice of group work. In other words, "How will you make a best practice idea come alive when you leave here?" For example, they might decide to implement a new learning idea that supports Best Practices in a current group they are running or planning; discuss a new idea with fellow group workers at their professional (practicum or internship) site; or decide to implement a training program in their professional organization or work site.

Activity Modifications This activity can be modified to include more time in each component. This allows for more processing and exchange of information between participants. In addition, (depending on class size) you may want to keep students in one group and focus on one Best Practices section rather than dividing them into three sections and then repeat the format focusing on the second and third sections.

9

Multicultural and Diversity-Competent Group Work

Niloufer Merchant

Style of leadership and the tools that are prevalent in group work . . . reflect the prevailing politics and values of the time. W. Lifton (Christensen, 1990, p. 136)

Introduction

by James P. Trotzer

So stated Walt Lifton, group work pioneer, in an interview conducted by the *Journal for Specialists in Group Work* for a series on the History of Group Work. In his observation Lifton captured both a reflective reality and a projective direction that is crucial to group work and particularly relevant to the focus of this chapter.

As a reflective reality, the current sociopolitical climate and emerging cultural pluralism in the United States and the technologically prompted reality of the world as a global community all converge to bring a multiplicity of cultures and diversities into our lives and profession. As a projective direction, the fact that multicultural and diversity factors must be accounted for is no longer a matter for debate. From former President Clinton's Initiative on Race, to the board room of every international corporation, to the state and federal agencies that must provide health and human services, whether in the public or private sector, the mandate is the same: culture and diversity must be acknowledged, understood, accounted for, incorporated, and valued.

As the face and fabric of our society and culture change during this century, counseling as a profession and group work as a particular dimension of that profession must, and will respond to the challenges put forth so eloquently by Dean Mahesh Sharma of Cambridge College (May 8, 1998). Speaking as an outsider to the profession at a conference on Multicultural and Spiritual Dimensions of Counselor Supervision, he put forth four challenges or questions. I paraphrase these challenges as follows:

> *The Browning of America*: How will counseling cope with, account for, and incorporate multicultural factors as the fabric of society changes to a pluralistic configuration of cultural, racial, and ethnic diversity and complexity?
>
> *The East versus West*: How will counseling acknowledge, account for, cope with, and resolve the philosophy of life differences manifested in an Eastern philosophy that values community and emphasizes ego submersion and a Western philosophy that values individuality and stresses ego emersion? Put in more colloquial terms, how does Western psychology that values a culture emphasizing individuality where "the squeaky wheel gets the proverbial oil" mesh with Eastern psychology that promotes the value of community as the context for culture and warns that "the nail that stands out gets pounded?" (Markus & Kitiyama, 1991).
>
> *Emergence or Reemergence of Spirituality*: How will counseling acknowledge, account for, incorporate, and value spirituality with its many faces and facets in the lives of clients?
>
> *The Downside of Technology*: How will counseling respond to the problems created by the ever increasing impact of technology that (a) produces an ever widening gap between the rich and the poor, the "haves and have nots," and (b) generates an insidious separation of the humane from the human as technical contact replaces personal touch in the relational realm?

These challenges and issues provide a suitable umbrella for our consideration of multicultural group work because what better place is there to confront and work through the inherent tension between the dynamics of individual personality and the interpersonal dynamics of peer influence than in the context of the small group process as explicated in this book?

The challenge of diversity has been taken up with great enthusiasm in the field of group work. The Preamble of the Association for Specialists in Group Work's Principles for Diversity Competent Group Workers (ASGW, 1999) avers a commitment to "understanding how issues of diversity affect all aspects of group work" (p. 1). Andy Horne and Janice DeLucia-Waack as editors of the *Journal for Specialists in Group Work* have made poignant efforts to spur recognition and utilization of the multicultural perspective in group work. Horne (1994) challenged authors to emphasize multicultural implications in their writings and work and DeLucia-Waack (1996) declared unequivocally that "multiculuralism is inherent in all group work" (p. 218).

I concur with Arredondo (1994) who concluded that all counseling, including group counseling, must be reframed as multicultural counseling. To do so with regard to group work, however, requires that group leaders develop competencies that include cultural awareness and sensitivity relative to their own and other's characteristics of culture and diversity and proficiency in using that competence in forming, leading, and utilizing groups. Failure to do so will produce detrimental effects either out of ignorance or because cultural differences when magnified or denied will undermine therapeutic dynamics (Vacc, 1989). Rather, diversity competent group leaders will have the attitudes and beliefs, knowledge and skills to facilitate a group process where diversity and culture are not only acknowledged, understood, and valued but also mobilized for the collaborative productivity of the group and the therapeutic benefit of its members. Hence, the crucial importance of this chapter.

Niloufer Merchant has been and is in the vanguard of multicultural group work as a professor, a practitioner and a consultant to ASGW in the development of the Principles for Diversity Competent Group Workers. Her chapter provides an eminently erudite and practical perspective while contributing a cutting edge authenticity that gives the contemporary group worker a reflective reality for the present and a projective direction for the exciting challenges of doing group work in the twenty-first century. Special acknowledgement is made of Rod Merta who contributed this chapter to the third edition of this text and graciously granted permission to use the material in the construction of the current chapter.

The Case for Diversity-Competent Group Work

Interest in diversity-competent group work has surged in the past few years (Conyne, 1998; Corey, 1995; D'Andrea & Daniels, 1997a,b; DeLucia, Coleman, & Jensen-Scott, 1992; DeLucia-Waack & Donigian, 2004; Granrose & Oskamp, 1997; Greeley, Garcia, Kessler, & Gilchrest, 1992; Merta, 1995; Pack-Brown, Whittington-Clark, & Parker, 1998). A major catalyst for this surge in interest has been the development of the Multicultural Counseling Competencies (Association for Multicultural Counseling and Development, 1996) and the operationalization of these goal-like competencies into objective-like explanatory statements, strategies, and recommended activities (Arredondo, et al., 1996; Sue, Arredondo, & McDavis, 1992). The Association for Specialists in Group Work has since adopted the competencies and has adapted them to group work, entitling them the Principles for Diversity Competent Group Workers (ASGW, 1999).

The focus on multicultural counseling in the United States has evolved from the study of just ethnic minority groups, to the broader context of understanding multiculturalism that includes all people, both minority and majority populations, and the intersection of multiple sociocultural factors in addition to the personal and other psychological, familial and historical variables of the individual in counseling (Arredondo, Rosen, Rice, Perez, & Tovar-Gamero,

2005; Haley-Banez, & Walden, 1999). A review of the literature in group work reveals that race, ethnicity, and other cultural variables such as ability (mental/physical), age, gender, region of the country, religion, sexual orientation, and socioeconomic status have largely been overlooked as constituting group dynamics that can impact the group process (see Merta, 1995). In this respect, it would be appropriate to say that all counseling (including group counseling) is "multicultural counseling" (Arredondo, 1994). The inherent complexity in understanding human behavior from a multicultural context, however, creates a dynamic tension between understanding all the dimensions in all their complexities, thereby creating too broad a focus, and giving salience to any one dimension, thereby generating too narrow a focus. Counseling from a multicultural context therefore cannot be seen from an either/or perspective, but must encompass a both/and point of view. In other words, the broad and the narrow focus are alternatively the foreground or background and have to be considered as a gestalt of the whole.

This chapter will address diversity-competent group work from a broad view of multiculturalism with examples of how it will impact specific sociocultural dimensions, and/or the intersection of those dimensions. This perspective is consistent with the definition of diversity as outlined in The ASGW Best Practices in Group Work guidelines (1998), which defines best practice related to diversity as "group workers practice with broad sensitivity to client differences including but not limited to ethnic, gender, religious, sexual, psychological maturity, economic class, family history, physical characteristics or limitations, and geographic location" (p. 19). In other words, cultural identity is viewed in all its dimensions, *apparent* and *unapparent*, including the intersection of the various sociocultural factors. This perspective will be discussed in more detail later in the chapter.

Definitions

In an attempt to reduce ambiguity for the reader, various terms relevant to multicultural group work will be defined, while other terms will be defined as they occur within the text of this chapter. *Culture* has been defined broadly as "any group of people who identify or associate with one another on the basis of some common purpose, need, or similarity of background" (Axelson, 1993, p. 3). The term *value*, "the principles or standards that individuals or groups of people use in determining their behavior" (Axelson, 1993, p. 33), is perceived by the author as constituting the basic element of a culture. *Stereotype* can be defined as "the application to others of personality theories that we all have about people whom we have met or have experienced in some way at some time" (Axelson, 1993, p. 35). Typically, African Americans, American Indians, Asian Americans, Arab Americans, and Hispanic and Latino Americans along with European Americans are referred to as *racial/ethnic* groups. Groups such as the elderly, feminists, people from Appalachia, gays and lesbians, people who are deaf, are referred to as *cultural groups*. The terms *multicultural, cross-cultural and diversity* are often used interchangeably to refer to racial/ethnic minority groups and all other cultural groups (Sue, Arredondo, & McDavis, 1992). Much of the literature in the multicultural counseling field has heavily focused on racial/ethnic minority groups, with only recent inclusion of all sociocultural dimensions (Haley-Banez & Walden, 1999; Myers et al., 1991). As a way to be inclusive of the multiple identities of the various sociocultural dimensions, and to remind ourselves of the constant inter-play of these dimensions, the terms *diversity or culture* will be used for the purposes of this chapter to refer to all cultural groups, racial/ethnic and nonracial/nonethnic cultural groups.

Group Work Practice in Traditional Societies

The fact that group work existed in numerous cultures long before its appearance in the Western psychological practice must be recognized. Group work and healing in groups in a variety of forms has been practiced by Native peoples across the world for eons and represents a natural form of healing (Garrett & Osborne, 1995; Pack-Brown, Whittington-Clark, & Parker, 1998). These practices and beliefs continue on in many of the cultural practices of Asia, Africa, and indigenous peoples of the Americas and Australia today. According to Garrett and Osborne (1995), the "Circle of Life" pervades all practices in Native American traditions. They state that "Native Americans have always believed that healing and transformation should take place in the presence of the group" (p. 34). The importance of social networks, such as tribe, group, family and community are also evident in Asian (Chen, 1995; Yu & Gregg, 1993; Chung, 2003), African (Loewy, Williams, & Keleta, 2002; Pack-Brown, Whittington-Clark & Parker, 1998), and Latin American (Sue & Sue, 1999) cultures that emphasize the power of group work in healing. As such it is important to first honor and acknowledge the long and rich history and numerous contributions to group work practice that have not been recorded in written form.

Value Orientation in Group Work

The current practice of group work in the counseling and psychology field has typically been based on Eurocentric, Western values, with the assumption that these values are universal in nature. In order to practice diversity-competent group work it is important to deconstruct the implicit and explicit value assumptions that guide group work, particularly in the United States. Underlying assumptions in Western group counseling have been identified as follows (Delucia-Waack & Donigian, 2004; Leong, 1992; Leong, Wagner, & Kim, 1995):

The underlying Western Assumptions

Assumption 1: *Western psychology asserts that creating an environment that encourages open and free exchange of feelings and thoughts about any topic is a primary goal in group work.*

Therefore, self-disclosure, verbal and emotional expressiveness, and direct communication are valued over self-reticence, quiet or silent behavior and indirect forms of communication. Additionally, identification of strengths and weaknesses is important to the therapeutic process. Direct confrontation of weaknesses and public validation of individual strengths is encouraged and essential to the change process, rather than, modesty, humility, and subtle, indirect ways of acknowledging strengths and weaknesses (Leong, 1992; Yu & Gregg, 1993). Many cultural differences are evident in the amount of value placed on verbalization and direct communication and some cultures endorse the notion of verbal and direct communication while other cultures are in direct conflict with this value orientation. Expressing feelings in an open and direct manner and bringing attention to oneself may be culturally inconsistent in Asian communities (Chen, 1995; Leong, Wagner, & Kim, 1995). On the other hand, African Americans value engaging in emotional dialogue and may tend to distrust those members that do not verbalize their thoughts as a result of the historical experience of racism (Greeley, Garcia, Kessler, & Gilchrest, 1992; Merchant, 1991). Eurocentric values of asserting oneself in relationships, using "I" statements, making eye contact and talking directly to individuals may be consistent with some cultural values such as the Latino (in communicating with peers and those who are younger) and Israeli cultures. However, such values may be in direct opposition to the values of other cultures such as the Native American communication style that emphasizes avoidance of eye contact as a sign of deference and respect to elders and authority figures (DeLucia-Waack & Donigian, 2004; Garrett & Garrett, 1994).

Assumption 2: *In Western psychology maturity is judged by the level of autonomy and self-sufficiency, while interdependence and group loyalty is perceived as a lack of self-actualization or differentiation and a sign of dependency.*

Self–related phenomena such as self-esteem, self-concept, self-respect, self-efficacy, are more prevalent in the English language than other-related phenomena (Leong, 1992). Indigenous and eastern cultures on the other hand tend to heavily rely on community, family and group networks and employ group problem-solving methods (Lee, Oh, & Mountcastle, 1992).

Assumption 3: *Western psychology values and utilizes an individualistic orientation rather than a collectivistic orientation as a guide to appropriate behavior in group work.*

The collectivistic orientation is clearly evident in various cultures. In the Afrocentric perspective, the concept of self is embedded in the value orientation that "I am because we are" versus the Eurocentric perspective that "I think therefore I am" (Pack-Brown, Whittington-Clark, & Parker, 1998). Similarly, the collectivistic framework in the Asian perspective emphasizes achievement of goals of harmony and unity in family and community versus the focus on accomplishment of personal goals of independence and achievement separate from one's family and social networks (Chen, 1995). For example, discussion of wrong doing from an individualistic perspective may generate feelings of individual "guilt", in contrast to a collectivistic perspective that produces a sense of "shame" or "loss of face" to family and community. The collectivistic orientation is also evident in the concept of *familismo* in the Latino culture where family interests come before individual interests.

Assumption 4: *The notion of healing from a Eurocentric perspective is based on separation of mind, body and spirit and focuses on self-control, choice, and improvement of relationships in the physical world.*

On the other hand, non-Western perspectives are typically based on the interconnectedness of mind, body and spirit, the belief in *fate* and *karma* in Asian cultures, (Sheikh & Sheikh, 1989) and/or relationships with ancestors in the spirit world in the African or Native American traditions (Garrett, Garrett, & Brotherton, 2001; Myers, et al., 1991). The metaphysical and more holistic perspectives of well being and healing at times directly contradict the linear, concrete methods of Western counseling and therapy approaches and therefore may be more responsive to indigenous or nonlinear approaches to healing (Lee & Armstrong, 1995; Yeh, Hunter, Madan-Bahel, Chiang, & Arora, 2004).

Assumption 5: *The Western framework of group counseling values unstructured and spontaneous interactions between members (Delucia-Waack & Donigian, 2004) where the group leader plays the role of an "interaction catalyst", a "modeler" or "communication facilitator" that guides the process without controlling the session and member behavior (Gladding, 1999).*

Many other cultural norms call for more structured, hierarchical and sometimes restricted interactions (e.g., male-female interactions in Muslim cultures). Relationship with the group leader is also seen differently in non-Western cultures, where the helper is seen more as an "expert" or "authority" figure (Conyne, Wilson, & Tang, 2000; Lee & Armstrong, 1995).

These inherent value orientations and what is considered good practice in group work may not always be a good fit for those group members whose cultural perspectives don't match those values. What is even more treacherous is the underlying assumption that the Eurocentric framework is *universal* leading to much of the cultural insensitivity towards culturally diverse clients. The Principles for Diversity Competent Group Workers (ASGW, 1999) provides a framework by which group workers can understand their own worldviews, the worldviews of group members and accordingly provide culturally relevant group interventions.

Principles for Diversity Competent Group Workers

The Association for Specialists in Group Work (ASGW) endorsed the Principles for Diversity Competent Group Workers in 1998. This document, based on the seminal work of Sue, Arredondo and McDavis in 1992 and the subsequent development and operationalizing of the Multicultural Competencies by the Association for Multicultural Counseling and Development (AMCD), provides cultural competency guidelines geared specifically for group workers (ASGW, 1999). In contrast to the AMCD multicultural competencies, the ASGW competencies take a broader focus on diversity and include effectiveness in working with gays, lesbians, bisexuals or transgendered persons, and persons with physical, mental/emotional, and/or learning disabilities in addition to racial and ethnic minorities. The competencies are discussed in relationship to three characteristics: (1) Awareness of Self, (2) Group Worker's Awareness of Group Member's Worldview, and (3) Diversity-Appropriate Intervention Strategies. Based on these characteristics, a culturally competent counselor is one who is

actively in the process of becoming aware of her or his own assumptions about human behavior, values, biases, preconceived notions, and personal limitations; who actively seeks to understand the world view of his or her culturally different client without negative judgments; and who is in the process of actively developing and practicing appropriate, relevant, and sensitive intervention strategies and skills in working with his or her culturally different clients. (Sue, Arredondo, & McDavis, 1992, p. 482)

The competencies also focus on three *domains* that interface with each characteristic: (1) attitudes and beliefs, (2) knowledge, and (3) skills. *Attitudes and beliefs* refer to a group worker's awareness of his or her stereotypes, biases, and values toward culturally different group members and how these attitudes might affect cross-cultural group work. *Knowledge* pertains to the group worker's understanding of his or her own world view, the world views of his or her group members, and of relevant sociopolitical influences (i.e., immigration, prejudice, discrimination, oppression, and powerlessness). *Skills* refer to the specific interventions and strategies, individual and institutional, to be employed with culturally different group members.

As mentioned earlier, the group work competencies are inclusive of all *apparent* and *unapparent* differences. The emphasis on *unapparent* differences is especially important, as issues related to disability, sexual orientation, class, etc. may not be readily evident or observable. However, they play a crucial role in the cultural identity of the individual (Haley-Banez & Walden, 1999).

Group Worker's Awareness of Self

The emphasis in the first domain (*attitudes and beliefs*) is on increasing awareness of one's own cultural identity with respect to culture, race, ethnicity, nationality, gender, sexual orientation, class, religion, spirituality, mental and physical abilities, and other sociocultural factors. These, of course, are in addition to the personal, psychological, familial, and other historical factors that contribute to who we are as individuals. How a person identifies oneself "culturally" is usually a conglomerate of many factors, with some factors having more salience at any given time than others. So for instance, as an Asian Indian American, educated, able-bodied, straight female who was raised Muslim, and an immigrant of 20 plus years in the United States, all of these identities have been critical in my identity formation, particularly those identities where I have experienced minority status. Those identities where I am more part of the majority are not always as visible to me, and therefore need intentional exploration to better understand myself as a group leader and my impact on group members.

Examination of diverse cultural identities necessitates the parallel examination and *knowledge* of oppression in society. As a diversity-competent group worker it is vital to understand our values, biases and stereotypes and acknowledge and accept issues of racism, sexism, heterosexism, classism, abelism, and other forms of oppression (ASGW, 1998). This means that we must also examine our privileges with respect to each of these identities. Understanding White privilege for instance, is critical in understanding the issues related to how oppression is perpetuated in society related to race. If we accept the notion that each one of us has both *privileged* and *oppressed* status (Croteau, Talbot, Lance, & Evans, 2002), and therefore struggle with internalized cultural superiority and oppression, then we can more fully (and humbly) explore our own cultural identity and its impact on others.

In addition to defining oneself on the basis of cultural variables, values, and stereotypes, several identity development models have been proposed in understanding the process of cultural identity formation. Identity development models related to race and ethnicity (Cross, 1978; Helms 1990; Jackson & Hardiman, 1983; Merchant, 1991, Sodowsky, Kwan, & Pannu, 1995; Sue & Sue, 1999), gender (Downing & Rousch, 1984), and sexual orientation (Cass, 1979) suggest a developmental process by which a person evolves in their level of consciousness about those identities. Helms' (1995) statuses and their corresponding information processing strategies for White identity development are as follows: *contact* (denial, obliviousness, or avoidance of anxiety evoking racial information), *disintegration* (disorientation, confusion, and suppression of information that would force one to choose between own group loyalty and humanism), *reintegration* (distortion of information in an own group enhancing manner), *pseudo-independence* (reshaping racial/ethnic or cultural stimuli to fit one's own liberal societal framework; *immersion/emersion* (reeducating and searching for internally defined racial and cultural standards), and *autonomy* (flexible analyses and responses to racial material). Similarly, Black racial identity development proposed by Cross (1978) and Helms (1990) and later generalized to all people of color, (Helms, 1995) include: *Pre-Encounter* (denigrate one's own racial identity and idolize the Euro American frame of reference), *Encounter* (confusion about Black identity, and realization that he/she had been "brainwashed"), *Immersion-Emersion* (pro-Black/anti-White sentiments), *Internalization* (identification with Blackness, feelings of inner security, and tolerance and acknowledgement of Whites and White culture), *Internalization-Commitment* (actively involved in responding to all forms of oppression). Cultural identity developmental models proposed by Sue and Sue (1999) and Merchant (1991) describe a similar process.

Slightly different models have been proposed for more specific ethnic groups such as Asian American (Kim, 1981), Latino (Ruiz, 1990), feminist (Downing & Roush, 1984), and sexual orientation identity development (Cass, 1979). However, they all suggest movement from naivete to greater levels of awareness leading to pride in one's identity and activism related to all forms of oppression.

The group leader's level of identity development with respect to the various sociocultural dimensions can impact relationships with group members. Based on studying individual counseling relationships between counselor and client, Helms (1990) suggested four relationship types, viz., *parallel* (group leader and coalition of the group share the same racial identity stages), *crossed* (group leaders' racial identity development are opposite to that of the coalition of the group), *progressive* (group leader is at a more advanced racial identity stage than characterized by a coalition of the group) and *regressive*, (group leader is in a less mature racial identity stage than the group coalition). Parallel relationships are suggested to result in inertia as the group is not likely to challenge each other in moving to more advanced stages. In crossed relationships the group leader and coalition of the group are at cross-purposes and relationships are likely to be contentious, whereas, in regressive relationships the group leader may tend to see the issue of race as the clients' problems. Therapeutic work is least conflicted when the group leader is in a progressive relationship as the leader is likely to move the coalition to more advanced stages of racial identity development. As a general rule, the more the group leaders have explored for themselves the various identities related to race, gender, class, sexual orientation and so forth, the more effective they will be in understanding and encouraging movement in the cultural identity development of group members.

Equally important in understanding ethnic and cultural identity is the process of *acculturation*. Berry (1990) differentiates between acculturation at the population level (ecological, social, cultural and institutional changes) and the individual level. He referred to the latter as psychological acculturation, a process by which individuals modify their behavior, identity, values and attitudes as a result of coming in contact with another culture. Berry and Kim (1988) proposed four attitudes related to acculturation: *assimilation* (individual maintains daily interactions with host culture, but minimal interaction with culture of origin), *separation* (individual maintains interaction with culture of origin, but avoids interaction with host culture), *marginalization* (does not feel she/he belongs or is interested in either host or native culture), and *integration*, also referred to as *bi-cultural* (individual maintains active interest and daily interactions with host and native culture). The integration attitude is considered to be the most beneficial, while marginalization is considered to be most problematic. The process of acculturation is an elusive and complex construct, and hence more multilinear models for assessing acculturation have been developed (see Kim & Abreu, 2001, for a detailed discussion). Nevertheless, the complex interaction of acculturation and cultural identity needs to be considered in understanding oneself and the group process. The acculturation attitudes impact the cultural identity development process and vice versa (Sodowsky, Kwan, & Pannu, 1995). Additionally, internal conflicts experienced by individuals caught between cultures can significantly impact their adjustment and mental health. Receptivity to Western style group counseling may also vary with level of acculturation. Leong, Wagner and Kim (1995) suggest that individuals who are bicultural or assimilated may be more responsive to group work based on a Western value systems.

As a diversity competent group worker one needs to develop the *skills* in seeking out educational and training experiences to enhance self-awareness with relation to values, biases, and cultural identity and strive to unlearn behaviors that perpetuate oppression. This could take the form of seeking out training and educational opportunities, consulting regularly with other professionals on cultural issues, and providing referrals to other qualified individuals as necessary (Arredondo, et al., 1996).

Group Worker's Awareness of Group Member's Worldview

In addition to knowing one's self in a cultural context, group workers need to examine their *attitudes and beliefs* about other cultural groups. For instance, what are our stereotypes, biases and prejudices towards other racial and ethnic groups, sexual minorities, the disabled, the poor, the elderly, or other forms of religions/spiritualities? What *knowledge* and information do we have about the cultural heritage, history, traditions, and sociopolitical forces (i.e., immigration, prejudice, discrimination, and oppression) of people who belong to these groups? How informed are we about the family structures, hierarchies, values, and beliefs of diverse cultural groups? What is our knowledge base about the multiple intersections of various identities as well as racial/gender/sexual orientation identity development and acculturation issues, and how they may impact an individual? The models of cultural identity development and acculturation process apply to understanding group members' worldview. The more informed we are about the cultural context that impacts individuals, the more effective we will be in understanding the impact of that context on group process and dynamics (Delucia-Waack and Donigian, 2004; Sue & Sue, 1999).

The *skills* related to increasing awareness of group members' worldview involves group workers familiarizing themselves with relevant research, educational experiences, and actively involving themselves with various cultural groups and individuals of diverse backgrounds outside of the group setting. The group leader can research a given cultural group by means of literature and media, consult with professionals who have had experience with that cultural group, and make direct contact with people of that cultural group. Arredondo et al., (1996) offer specific activities for accessing such resources and obtaining such awareness. Although not a substitute for pregroup research, consultation, and direct contact with the member's culture, contact with a member before and during the group, provides the group leader with an opportunity to identify members with respect to their diversity.

Diversity-Appropriate Intervention Strategies

The group workers *attitudes and beliefs* about the religious/spiritual beliefs, indigenous helping practices and other intrinsic help-giving networks, as well as the value placed on providing alternative forms of assistance to clients that don't speak the language, and/or meeting other needs, are critical in the type of interventions made. Appreciation and valuing of different beliefs and practices will allow the group leader to be more accommodating of group members needs. It is important therefore, that group leaders examine their attitudes about the practices of culturally diverse groups and increase their *knowledge* base about culturally responsive intervention strategies. Group workers need to be knowledgeable about institutional barriers that may prevent group members from participating in the groups or the settings in which they are offered. Further, they need to be knowledgeable about potential bias in assessment instruments, and group evaluation procedures and be cognizant of the specific linguistic, and other cultural factors that may negatively impact the results (ASGW, 1999). In a recent grant project on groups for girls of color in local junior high and high schools, we, the project coordinators, implemented an extensive qualitative evaluation process that involved focus groups, interviews and written documentation of progress on self-identified goals. We found that the data received from written documentation was very minimal, which may have been in part due to lack of comfort with expressing themselves both in English, and in written form.

So what would it look like for a group leader to be operating from a diversity-competent stance? What *skills* would a group leader need to effectively lead a diverse group? The remainder of the chapter will focus specifically on diversity-competent intervention strategies and will be organized according to the ASGW Best Practice Guidelines (ASGW 1998). The guidelines suggest that group workers' responsibilities involve three broad functions, i.e., Planning, Performing and Processing. Diversity competent group leadership will be further discussed within the ecological framework offered by Conyne & Bemak (2004). Group work discussed in the ecological context provides a broader, more holistic and collectivistic worldview, and takes into consideration the multiple levels and systems that are so essential in addressing the complexities of diversity and multiculturalism.

Diversity-Competent Group Leadership Skills

Planning for Diversity-Competent Group Work

Partner with Target Population Group purpose, goals, and outcomes should be clearly defined in planning for the group as it will determine the type of group that will be offered. According to Conyne and Bemak (2004), the planning for groups should be ecologically centered, where the leader can be viewed as an "architect who partners with others to create a design that fits needs and terrain" (p.10). Thus in order for the group to be contextually valid, i.e., accurately reflect "the needs, culture, and values of prospective members and be located in a place and at a time that are appropriate" (Conyne & Bemak, p. 11), the group leader needs to partner with representatives of the target population whenever possible in the planning step. I have frequently encountered that lack of deliberate planning with respect to the unique needs of the target population will invariably lead to problems later. For example, my experience in offering groups to culturally diverse and/or low income participants has been that lack of transportation and child care are the most frequently cited reasons for inability to attend groups. In order to recruit and retain diverse group membership considerations have to be given in the planning process to provide for basic needs to be met in order for members to be present. Provision of food, where possible, is also another consideration, as it eases the stress on group members of feeding themselves and/or their children prior to coming to groups, especially in the evenings. Attending to the location of the group is equally important. Holding the group in environments that are comfortable to the clients is critical, and this can often be determined in consultation with potential group members. In providing outreach for women of color through a sexual assault center, I quickly found that holding the group at the sexual assault center itself would inhibit some members from participating due to the taboo related to direct reference to sexual matters in many cultures. Instead, conducting the group at a local American Indian center drew more participants since it was considered a culturally "safe" and neutral place to meet regarding sexual violence issues.

Determine Type of Diversity-Related Group to be Offered In addition to determining whether the group is a task, psychoeducational, growth, counseling or therapy group, it is important to determine the type of group based on the diversity goals identified for the group. Is the group specifically focused on diversity issues (e.g., support group for lesbian mothers, race relations group for students on campus), or is the primary focus on other specific or general goals (e.g., eating disorder group in a hospital or group for nontraditional students on campus) where diversity considerations are part of the group process? Curiously, the discussion of multicultural and diversity-competent group work in counseling and related fields has not given much attention to the differences in these types of groups and instead has tended to discuss diversity related issues in groups as being universal to all types of groups regardless of the focus. Planning for diversity-focused groups requires specific attention to the content and process of group that may be different from other groups. Based on the types of diversity-related group work discussed in the literature, it appears that there are three types of groups: (1) Culture-specific groups that focus specifically on the needs of a particular cultural group; (2) Intercultural learning groups that promote better relations and reduce oppression and bias between diverse groups; and (3) Groups that have other content focus but consider diversity issues as an important consideration in the group.

Culture-Specific Groups Culture-specific groups are geared towards a certain cultural population or a group of people that share common experiences as a result of their diversity. The goals of the group are to provide support, education, spiritual guidance/healing, counseling/therapy and/or other services within their shared cultural context. In addition to some of the groups mentioned above, groups under this category could include such groups as acculturation groups for new immigrants, support groups for parents of children with special needs, and groups to enhance cultural identity for ethnic minority adolescents. In the multicultural group counseling literature considerable attention has been given to the application of culturally relevant theoretical models and techniques in working with culturally-specific groups. For example, the use of Afrocentric principles that emphasize interdependence, collective survival, emotional vitality, harmony, and the respect for wisdom of elders and the oral tradition have been extensively discussed in working with Africans and African Americans (Lee, 1987; Lowey, Williams, & Kaleta, 2002; Pack-Brown, Whittington-Clark, & Parker,1998; Rollock, Westman, & Johnson, 1992). Similarly, the use of Native American healing traditions such as the Talking Circle, the Sweat Lodge, and other practices have been applied to group work with Native Americans (Colemant & Merta, 1999; Garrett, 2004). Group work more akin to Asian values of collectivistic social orientation, harmony and subtlety in communication (Chen, 1995; Chen & Han, 2001; Leong, 1992; Pope, 1999; Yu & Gregg, 1993;) and culturally responsive models for Latino clients (Baca & Koss-Chiono, 1997; Guanipa, Talley & Rapagna, 1997; Villalba, 2003) also emphasize the need for working with culturally homogenous groups.

Some themes that emerge in culture-specific groups relate to the experience of oppression (from external sources and internalized oppression), identity development based on their diversity, self-empowerment, learning survival and coping mechanisms, healing past trauma, advocating for one's rights, and challenging the status quo of the systems within which they exist (Baca & Koss-Chiano,1997; Dufrene & Coleman, 1992; Pack-Brown, Whittington-Clark, & Parker,1998; Lowey, Williams, & Kaleta, 2002; Merchant, 2002). By virtue of sharing a cultural context, members often feel freer to engage in self-exploration as they don't have the added pressure of having to explain themselves or teach others about their culture (Merchant, 2002). As a leader of culturally-specific groups, one has to be well conversant with the cultural history, and sociopolitical forces that impact the cultural group, and the various support systems and resources within the community. Strategies and techniques used by the group leader should be in sync with cultural values, beliefs and practices. Furthermore, the group leader should be familiar with the nuances of within-group differences and be able to effectively address tensions and conflicts that may exist between members, historically or interpersonally. For example, both as a member and a facilitator of a faculty of color group that advocated for the rights of people of color on a university campus, I have consistently witnessed the tension between those who were critical of the predominantly White administration, and those who were more conciliatory towards the same administration. Each group viewed the other with suspicion, as one coalition was labeled "radical" or "militant," while the other was viewed as "assimilated" or having "sold out" to the administration. As a facilitator of the group I had to be well aware of the "bigger picture" that led to this tension, and constantly negotiate between members so that the tasks and goals that we had set out for ourselves could be accomplished.

There are differing opinions about whether the group leader needs to be from the same cultural group as the participants, or if that is irrelevant as long as the leader is culturally competent. Those that advocate for the group leader as being of the same cultural group and/or gender (for gender-specific groups) feel that the group leader serves as a role model, and has a connection to the lived experience of group members that a group leader outside that cultural group would not be able to provide (Bailey, 2005; Holcomb-McCoy, 2005). On the other hand, there are others that argue that if the group leader has a deep knowledge and understanding of the cultural group, they can be equally effective in making that connection. Further, due to the dearth of group counselors belonging to minority groups, there is often not the luxury to wait for cultural matches (Bemak, 2005; Merchant, 2002; Muller, 2000, 2002).

Intercultural Learning Groups Intercultural learning groups are those that strive to promote knowledge and understanding and improve relationships among diverse groups with the ultimate goal of addressing systemic change.

Examples of such groups are diversity training and sensitivity groups, race-relations groups, safe-zone training, and other types of groups that promote greater understanding about cultural and diversity issues (Gardenswartz & Rowe, 1993; Landis, Bennett, & Bennett, 2004). The membership in the group typically involves people of both minority and majority status. Since the civil rights movement and the subsequent women's, disability, and gay rights movements, a considerable amount of time and energy has been devoted to helping minority and majority populations better understand and relate to each other. Such groups are provided in a variety of settings: schools, private and public industry, churches, nonprofit organizations, human services, etc. Planning for groups that promote understanding about diversity requires particular attention to the context in which it is provided. Some groups are offered in reaction to an incident in a particular setting, whereas others are part of ongoing educational efforts in that setting. Some groups are voluntary, while others are mandatory. In the planning stage it is necessary to determine who the participants will be, their particular experiences with diversity and their identity development with respect to their diversity.

The themes within groups enhancing relations between diverse cultural groups typically involve cultural sharing, understanding historical and current contexts, examining differences in communication styles, personal biases, various forms of oppression, and internalized cultural superiority and oppression, and exploring strategies for advocating institutional change (Finkel, Ragnar, Bandele, & Schaefer, 2003; Gardenswartz & Rowe, 1993; Landis, Bennett, & Bennett, 2004). The last few decades have shown increased diversity training efforts in the workplace. Most often these trainings are offered as one-time workshops and typically involve large and small group interaction among members. In some instances more long term training is provided, leading to in-depth exploration of issues. Facilitators of such trainings are usually well versed in addressing diversity issues, but not always trained in group work. Many times I have observed intense interactions between workshop participants that lead to negative outcomes due to the limited knowledge of group process and dynamics on the part of the facilitators. It is important that group work competencies are incorporated in diversity training and race-relations efforts to be effective.

Other-Content Focused Groups Groups that have a focus on other-content related issues but consider diversity dynamics as an important part of the group process call for slightly different group leadership skills. Take for instance a support group for survivors of domestic abuse, or group for children of divorced parents. In groups such as these, the leader, while addressing the many issues related to the focus of the group always needs to be aware of the overt and covert cultural manifestations in the group. In a group for children of divorced parents, one or two participants may be from a different cultural background.

As a group leader, one needs to address the personal and family struggles of the group members, but understand those issues in the context of the culture they are part of. Additionally, the intergroup interactions between members may be impacted by the level of acculturation, racial identity development, and the differences in communication styles. The leader may also need to respond to coalitions formed within the group either by identity attitudes related to various sociocultural factors and/or by cultural/racial backgrounds.

The issues therefore that surface in groups that have other content goals may be different from culture-specific groups which may in turn be different from groups that promote understanding about diversity. The group leader needs to understand the uniqueness and the complexities of each type of group. The literature on group diversity competencies therefore requires a more extensive discussion of the various nuances of group work with diverse populations.

Group Composition A review of literature regarding selection of group members to a diverse group depicts mixed opinions regarding the diversity composition of the group. For instance, some studies suggest that the quality of interaction worsens when the percentage of one racial group increases relative to the other (Giles, 1977). Other studies suggest that clients are reluctant to join groups in which they are a racial minority and that people are increasingly comfortable in joining groups where there are people more like them (Davis, Cheng, & Strube, 1996; Tatum, 1997). J and U models have also been proposed in relationship to describing interracial group dynamics. In the J model behavior and attitudes of White people are not affected by Black participants, until the percentage of Black people increases beyond a certain tipping point, typically 30%. The U model contends that an equal number of Black and White group members is the least harmonious. It is important to note, however, that all of these earlier studies were based on the perspectives of White and male members (see Davis, Cheng, & Strube, 1996 for a more detailed discussion). More recently, McRae (1994) suggests that it is not simply the racial groupings that impact group dynamics, but racial identity attitudes. According to McRae, subgroup coalitions can form within and across racial groups based on similar racial identity attitudes and not just by skin color.

What all of this discussion on racial composition and racial identity attitudes suggests is that group leaders need to be cognizant of the impact of cultural differences and identity with respect to the effect of various forms of diversity on group process, and consider that in the selection of members to groups. If the goal of the group is to provide a safe and supportive environment for members to discuss their cultural issues, it may be desirable to select members that are more similar in their identity development, whereas if the goal is to promote greater cultural understanding and movement in identity development, then it may be more effective to incorporate members that are at varying levels of identity development.

Pregroup Screening The pregroup screening process is an important step in beginning to identify and. address issues related to culture/race/ethnicity/nationality/visible and invisible disability/religion/spirituality/language needs/and sexual orientation. This is an opportunity for the group worker to discuss the group member's specific needs related to diversity issues and brainstorm ways in which barriers can be minimized and how best to address those issues in the group. For instance, a gay member may be very reluctant to come out to other group members due to the lack of safety, and the fear of encountering homophobic attitudes. If the group member discloses this information to the group leader in the prescreening process, then facilitator and member can collaboratively identify what conditions can be created in the group to develop the safety, and if appropriate, how the group leader can facilitate the coming out process without psychological harm to the group member or detriment to the group process.

The prescreening inquiry can take the form of dialogue alone or the dialogue can be facilitated by having the prospective member first complete a simple form in which he or she voluntarily identifies himself or herself by relevant cultural variables (e.g., race/ethnicity, religion, region of the country, and sexual orientation), values (e.g., pro-life position on abortion, sexual equality, and youth orientation), and offensive stereotypes (e.g., Latinas being dependent, religious fundamentalists as being rigid in their thinking, lesbians as being masculine in grooming and dress, New Yorkers as being fast paced and rather abrupt). At first glance, some cultural variables will be more readily apparent than others: race/ethnicity or gender in contrast to religion or sexual orientation

When making such inquiries the group leader needs to avoid being insensitive and unnecessarily intrusive. By introducing the terms cultural variable, values, and stereotypes by means of providing definitions and examples, the group leader can then inquire as to whether any of the variables are personally relevant. Pressure to have members identify themselves on all eight variables (race/ethnicity, ability, age, gender, geographical region, religion, sexual orientation, socio-economic status (SES) or any identified values or stereotypes by the leader is neither sensitive nor necessary. In the dialogue or on the aforementioned form, allow the prospective member to select or identify the variables, values, or stereotypes relevant to him or her while ignoring or omitting those that are not.

Performing Diversity-Competent Group Work

According to Conyne and Bemak (2004), *performing* is "where the rubber meets the road" and involves the adaptive implementation of the plan and group interventions by the leader. Ecologically-centered performance requires attention to the big picture (i.e., the ever changing systemic, cultural, political, and historical context, as well as to group process and individual needs). As a diversity-competent group worker one needs to draw on the various cultural competencies discussed earlier in implementing interventions in the group setting. The leadership skills described under *performing* help operationalize and expand the diversity competencies articulated by ASGW (1999)

Prepare Group Members for Multicultural Group Work As noted in the multicultural counseling competencies (Sue, Arredondo, & McDavis, 1992), the culturally skilled counselor must assess the appropriateness of a particular counseling approach for a culturally different client. Group work theories and techniques are not culture free, but like counseling theories and techniques, in general, reflect the values of the dominant or majority culture. The majority culture in the United States is usually best epitomized by the middle-aged, middle-class, European American male. For counseling, however, the majority culture might be more accurately identified as middle-aged, middle-class, European American, androgynous male or female. Counseling values or human relations norms (i.e., attention to feelings, willingness to show vulnerability, personal and direct expression), as articulated by Kanter (1977), appear to be more representative of females and androgynous males than traditional males. Anecdotal reports of male aversion to counseling and evidence of underutilization of services by men (Feldman, 1990; Pasick, Gordon, & Feldman, 1990) appear to support such a conclusion. The more at variance a prospective group member (e.g., a lower SES, inner city, African American, or Hispanic male adolescent) appears to be from the majority culture, the more important it is for the group leader to identify group members related to their diversity, to facilitate informed consent, and to begin structuring the group experience.

Consistent with ASGW (1998) Best Practice Guidelines for group work, group leaders need to provide prospective members with informed consent. *Informed consent* entails providing a prospective group member information on all aspects of a particular group: the nature or theoretical basis of the group, the various techniques that will be used, and the values or norms, expectations, and characteristics of the group (e.g., nondirective group leadership, non structured interactions, self-disclosures of a personal nature with a focus on feelings, and member to member feedback of a candid and possibly negative nature). With such information the prospective member can decide on participating in the group or not. Again, with a more culturally diverse individual, the group worker needs to emphasize existing cultural differences between the group and the prospective member. Although the group worker can and may need to facilitate informed consent during the first group session, with the individual, the group worker should attempt to do it during a pregroup screening interview to allow for more individual attention and sensitivity. The member needs to be made aware of the group, initially given the choice of participation, and the opportunity to exit the group at any time. Although involuntary or mandatory group member's choices are reduced, informed consent is even more of a necessity (see Corey, 1995). With court or agency mandated group members, the group worker must not only inform the individual of eliciting cultural differences in regards to the group but often in regards to the agency, legal system, and society as well. For example, in leading a substance abuse group with recent immigrant Latino clients who are unfamiliar with laws, and treatment modalities in the United States, it may be necessary to spend considerable time attempting to explain culturally different and changing mores and laws regarding alcohol and drug use (e.g., stiffer DWI or DUI sentencing, illegalization of marijuana, and differing penalties for cocaine and crack abuse). To be more effective in facilitating informed consent, the group worker should provide a written description of the group (see Corey, 1995), possibly in the form of a contract and preferably in Spanish or any other language of relevance to prospective members.

Structuring Structuring is defined by Cormier and Cormier (1991) as "an interactional process between counselors and clients in which they arrive at similar perceptions of the role of counselor, an understanding of what occurs in the counseling process, and an agreement on which outcome goals will be achieved" (p. 51). Merta (1995) inferred from the literature in multicultural counseling that structuring group work may actually take two forms: (1) informing members prior to and during the group process of what to expect from a particular group, and (2) modifying the group to be more accommodating to culturally different group members. As already noted, the first form of structuring began with the group worker providing the culturally diverse individual with information about the group to facilitate informed consent. Even after the group has begun, the structuring continues as the group worker must be prepared to interrupt a group session to clarify for a culturally diverse member any aspect of the group process that appears to be confusing or frustrating. The group worker may wish to use before or after group session contacts with a group member for such efforts at clarification. It may not always be clear to the group worker whether a reticent or apparently contrary group member is sincerely confused as to group expectations or is intentionally resisting them.

Norming In leading any group the leader needs to intentionally create a norm that discussion of cultural differences is valued, acceptable and important. Members should be encouraged to share how their diversity impacts their participation, and how they are impacted by the diversity of others in the group. The group leader can create an environment where learning about each other's culture, and being genuinely but respectfully curious about each other's cultural norms, practices, and preferences are desirable interactions.

The use of inclusive language is another way to create a welcoming environment. Using the term partner instead of husband or wife demonstrates an openness to all forms of relationships. In using ethnic labels, to the extent possible, listen for how members want to be referred to themselves—Latino versus Hispanic, Korean American versus Asian American, and the like. The group leader should also be comfortable addressing issues such as communication style differences, oppression related to their diversity and minority status or power and privilege as a result of majority status in society.

The group-work diversity competencies assist in creating norms in groups that allow for some measure of safety in expressing personal values, and beliefs without fear of being labeled racist, sexist, homophobic, and the like. However, it is also important to understand that such safety is relative, as most people who have been oppressed have never felt safe. Regardless, group facilitators need to ensure that an environment is created where group members can both express themselves and engage in deep listening in order to move to greater understanding of themselves and each other. If you want to have members be aware of the cultural identities of other members, the group facilitator can use a *round*, a technique in which every member takes a turn responding to a question or topic initiated by the group leader (Gladding, 1991; Jacobs, Harvill, & Mason, 1994). The opening round should ideally be initiated during the first session. The leader should preface the round by stating the importance of being culturally aware of each other and respecting and being sensitive to cultural differences as a norming initiative. As was recommended for the prescreening interview, the leader may wish to introduce the terms cultural variables, values, and stereotypes. Use of the aforementioned form for cultural identification might be used to facilitate the round. Again, members should be encouraged to identify themselves only by those variables, values, and stereotypes that they deem relevant and safe. Since personal disclosures can sometimes take on a self-perpetuating nature, the leader needs to preface the round by cautioning members to disclose only that information they feel comfortable in sharing; and second, the leader needs to be prepared to halt a member's disclosure and check out with the member whether further disclosure is warranted. Such a round may appear rather time consuming, but it certainly could be used in lieu of such traditional ice breakers as having members compare themselves to some animal. If normed and facilitated sensitively, I have found that opening rounds provide validation for group members regardless of cultural identity. With younger or more reticent members, the group leader may wish to first use *dyad* work in preparation for the round. The dyad work could consist of pairing members, having them take turns completing the cultural identification exercise, and then having the dyad partners take turns introducing each other to the group by his or her cultural identity.

With or without cultural identification of group members by means of pregroup screening or completion of a round, the group leader must engage in *ongoing cultural identification* by being alert to member's disclosures and non-verbal behaviors and by being willing to follow-up with inquiries into the nature of a member's cultural identity. Let's assume that an Asian American woman was receiving feedback from other members on her hesitancy to speak in the group. The group leader needs to be alert to the realization that her cultural identity might be a factor in her hesitancy and may intervene by inquiring as to how such feedback coincided with her own cultural upbringing.

Model Cultural Respect and Sensitivity Regardless of the cultures represented in one's group, the group leader must strive to model respect by communicating and demonstrating that all cultures are valued and all members are treated equally. Similarly, the group leader must strive to model cultural sensitivity by being aware of, showing respect for, and protecting the values and personal boundaries of one's members. It is not uncommon that people, including counselors, are often selective as to whom they bestow cultural respect and sensitivity. Whereas a counselor may be theoretically committed to respecting Latino Americans, he or she may be openly contemptuous of traditional gender roles in the Latino community. Whereas that same counselor may model respect and sensitivity toward a Navajo disclosing traditional religious beliefs, he or she may communicate contempt for an African American disclosing religious fundamentalist beliefs. Although voicing support for gays and lesbians, a group worker may prompt a gay member relating a romantic encounter to hurry up by unintentionally revealing his or her discomfort. In modeling cultural respect and sensitivity, I do not believe that a group worker can show preferential treatment for one cultural group at the expense of another without alienating other group members. As noted in the first and second competency characteristics, modeling cultural respect and sensitivity is dependent on our cultural awareness of others and ourselves. Cultural disrespect often takes the form of discounting another's values, often out of ignorance of those values, and by proselytizing one's own. Respect comes from increased familiarity with culturally different groups obtained through research, consultation, and especially personal contact. Sensitivity begins with respect and is dependent on one's proficiency at using skills often practiced in individual counseling: core conditions, listening skills, open ended probes, and confrontations (Cormier & Cormier, 1991; Young, 1994).

According to Yalom (1985), *culture building* refers to a collaborative process between leader and members in which the group culture—"an unwritten code of behavioral rules, or norms—must be established that will guide the interaction of the group" (p. 108). Although structuring and culture building are similar concepts, structuring primarily occurs between the leader and an individual member during the prescreening interview and contacts before and after sessions, while culture building involves the leader and all the members and occurs within the session. Yalom contends that the group leader serves as technical expert and a role model in the building of the group culture, for example, modeling norms that emphasize a here and now focus, member to member feedback, and working through conflict. As for a multicultural group, the leader must serve as a technical expert by being knowledgeable of the value differences, stereotypes, majority and minority stage identities, and sociopolitical forces operating within a multicultural group, so as to intervene to work through conflict and avoid cultural group think.

The group leader needs to transcend political correctness by making inquiries into a member's cultural identity, but it is important that the member has at least implicitly approved such inquiries by having them take the initiative in culturally identifying themselves. Although culture building is a group consensual process, the group leader must model cultural respect and sensitivity and must be vigilant and willing to intervene to maintain a culturally respectful and sensitive group culture.

Although interacting with group members in a genuine manner, making inquiries into the nature of a member's cultural identity, and testing out our own stereotypes are necessary interventions in a diverse group, they can be overdone. Use of these interventions does not give a group leader or another group member license to bombard a culturally diverse member with a whole series of personally, intrusive questions. The group leader must balance genuineness with cultural sensitivity.

Demonstrate Neutral but Active Leadership

Similar to the need for balancing genuineness and sensitivity, the group leader must strive to balance genuineness and respect in the form of equal treatment of group members. Regardless of modality—individual, family, or group—I have found that by occasionally disclosing some of my own values, I increase my cultural similarity with my members but only to the extent that those members share my values. In racially/ethnically and culturally heterogeneous groups, I believe that by disclosing my own values, biases, stereotypes, and personal limitations, my group members perceive my behavior as genuine and often a stimulus for engaging in similar risk taking. Despite the potential gains, I may make such disclosures at the risk of being perceived by some members as being biased. To avoid perceptions of bias and partiality, I believe the group leader must limit his or his disclosures to reinforcing group norms (i.e., cultural identification, cultural respect and sensitivity, genuineness) and stating universals (i.e., failure to test stereotypes, tendency to be ethnocentric regarding our values, etc.). By intentionally communicating personal values, failing to model cultural respect and sensitivity to all members and cultures represented in a group, permitting stereotypes to be stated but go untested, and extending preferential treatment to any member regardless of cultural identity, the leader is likely to sacrifice the members' perception of him or her as a neutral and objective leader who will facilitate the group impartially.

Such neutrality should not be mistaken for a laissez faire style of group leader-ship. Lewin identified three styles of group leadership: authoritarian (directive and structured, leader centered), democratic (nondirective but active, group centered), and laissez faire (no structure or direction, group led) (Gladding, 1991). Although the leader should avoid being directive, he or she cannot afford to be laissez faire. By being overly directive, group members are limited in their interaction and hence their cultural exploration. By being too laissez faire, nega-tive norms are as apt to develop as positive ones, conflict will likely be avoided or left to become abusive, and the group is likely to experience cultural group think as the values and stereotypes of the majority will dominate and eventually be imposed on minority members.

Be Alert to and Work Through Cultural Group Conflict "Most white people do this patronizing number: They never disagree with you, even when you are talking the worst sort of garbage. It is near impossible to have a decent, human conversa-tion with them. They are so busy trying not to say anything offensive—so busy trying to prove they aren't prejudiced—that they freeze up, get all constricted, formal. They never just talk." (Attributed to the African American narrator in *Primary Colors: A Novel of Politics*; Anonymous, 1996, pp. 35–36).

Just as political correctness can cause a group leader to interact with culturally diverse members in a less than genuine manner by failing to explore cultural differences and by opting not to disclose personal biases and limitations or test out stereotypes, it can cause that same group leader to avoid cultural group conflict as illustrated in the quote above. As noted by Yalom (1995), "conflict can be harnessed in the service of the group, if the intensity does not exceed the members' tolerance and the proper group norms have been established" (p. 344). Conflict resolution of cultural conflict is properly performed when the group leader does not prematurely rescue members from receiving negative feedback while still insuring that the feedback does not become abusive.

As noted by Greeley, Garcia, Kessler, and Gilchrest (1992), group workers may hesitate to acknowledge the existence of cultural differences and avoid working through conflict for fear of offending members or making them feel uncomfortable. Such avoidance is unfortunate because acknowledgment of cultural differences and working through cultural conflict can result in greater group cohesiveness as well as greater multicultural awareness.

Attend to Interplay of Multiple Cultural Identities and Differences in Commu-nication Styles As discussed earlier in the chapter, the different levels of cultural identity development stages are likely to impact member to member interaction and leader to member interaction. This interaction is further affected by the differences in communication style between cultural groups. While much has been written in the literature advocating the position that we understand people along multiple dimensions, Croteau, Talbot, Lance, and Evans, (2002) contend that in fact there is insufficient conceptualization regarding the interplay of the multiple dimensions both at the individual level and the group level. In a year-long study of the process and outcome of a racial awareness group with equal numbers of Black and White, and male and female students, I observed several interesting interactions across racial groups and across racial identity stages (Merchant, 1991). Several White members entered the group at the pre-encounter or denial stages, whereas the Black members were in varying stages of racial identity development. Trust-building was difficult as White members were afraid to express how they felt for fear of being labeled as racist, while Black members at more advanced racial identity development stages were frustrated at the level of naivete and ignorance about racial issues among White members. The Black members were more vocal in expressing their thoughts and feelings and often took on the "teaching" role, while White members were quieter and took on the "listening" role. This led to even more distrust of White members by some Black members, who saw the White members as not being open or willing to engage with them interpersonally. It took a considerable amount of processing by the leaders to facilitate understanding between members. Dividing members into same race groups for short periods of time before bringing them back as a larger group allowed for freer expression and processing of issues. It was also interesting to note that many of the White members focused on personal feelings and tended to see themselves as *individuals* in sorting through what it meant to be White, whereas Black members tended to process feelings and issues in relation to their role in their cultural *group* and the larger community.

The complexity of interactions is likely to increase when we consider the interplay between issues of race/culture/ethnicity with other statuses such as gender, age, sexual orientation, or class. Take for instance the interaction between a middle-class, young, gay man who is Jewish, a heterosexual, working class, older woman who is of German American heritage, and a heterosexual, middle-aged man who is middle class and African American. In addition, let's assume that the Jewish gay man has done much work in understanding his identity as a gay man, but not what it means to be Jewish, or a White male in this society; that the German American heterosexual woman has worked on developing a feminist identity and is well aware of the impact of class on her life, but has not explored issues related to sexual orientation or race; and that the African American, heterosexual man fully understands what it means to be a Black male in this society, understands the impact of class, but has not really examined his identity as a heterosexual male. Let's assume even further that the group leader is an Asian Indian, heterosexual, middle-class, middle-aged female who is an immigrant, but has not really explored any of the issues related to race, class, gender, or sexual orientation, but understands her experience as an immigrant to this country. Now add to this layer the complexity of differences in communication styles that may be individually or culturally related. The implicit assumption in the example above is that all the individuals are able-bodied. Apparent and unapparent disabilities will contribute to yet another layer of diversity.

What you have in the above example is a complex set of dynamics that can go awry in a group setting if not appropriately addressed. It behooves us therefore to not only understand ourselves as group leaders along the multiple dimensions, but to comprehend the multiple dimensions of group members as well as the interplay of those dimensions in a group setting. If this group was a counseling group for people struggling with depression, the theme of depression would be a common theme, but the experience of the depression, and how members relate to each other in the group setting will be impacted by the various levels of identity development. Diversity issues may be more readily addressed in culture-specific and intercultural learning groups, but may go unaddressed in groups focusing on other content unless cultural issues are validated and considered in the group process.

Be Sensitive to Language Needs The group leader needs to be sensitive to specific language needs, and accommodate member needs in a way that best meets the needs of that group member and the rest of the group. If language (including sign language) interpreters are used, the group leader will discuss with the specific member as well as the rest of the group, ways in which barriers can be minimized and accommodations that need to be made by the group leader and group members. Loewy, Williams, and Keleta (2002) describe an intervention with female East African refugees where an interpreter was utilized so members could communicate in their native languages. The authors suggest that if an interpreter is used, she/he should be seated on the left or the right of the group leader so that the leader can maintain eye contact with the group member and stay focused on the group instead of the interpreter. Language interpretation for just one member of the group presents unique challenges as simultaneous conversations in the group may create noise interference. The group leader needs to appropriately address this with the language interpreter prior to group so as to identify ways that they can be most effective.

Guidelines for the use of interpreters for deaf members in a group have been suggested by Card and Schmider (1995). The authors recommend that the group leader meet with the interpreter prior to the group to explain the purpose of the group, rules related to confidentiality, and other logistics. Having the same interpreter paired with the same client for the duration of the group is desirable for the sake of continuity and consistency.

Be an Advocate and Exercise Institutional Intervention Skills The group leader may find it necessary to make interventions on behalf of group members at the institutional level. This may take several forms and can be carried out at various stages of the group process. A group worker who sees the necessity to alter ways in which groups are typically implemented in their work setting, may need to lay the ground work with administrators and other colleagues in offering services that are more culturally responsive. Recruiting a diverse membership to the group may call for intentional solicitation of referrals from people or institutions that serve a diverse population. In order to provide support for group members unable to afford transportation, additional funding may need to be sought to assist them to get to and from the group. Providing interpreter services, and other amenities, such as food and child care, etc., may involve additional costs. Ideally, agencies that have made the effort to provide culturally responsive services have already considered these needs requiring less effort on the part of the group worker.

Institutional interventions can also be made when the group worker recognizes that a "problem" arises from racism, sexism, homophobia or other forms of bias. In conducting a group for adolescents of color in a residential treatment setting an incident arose that required institutional intervention on my part (Merchant, 2002). An African American group member described an incident at a local mall where he was treated in a prejudicial manner by a server at a fast food restaurant. The group member was angry but did not react as the staff person accompanying him advised him to walk away. The member was validated for not responding aggressively (something he would have been previously inclined to do), and also for his feelings of anger for being wrongfully treated. On behalf of the client, conversations were held with the staff member who, along with the group member, followed up with the fast food restaurant to hold the server accountable for his behavior. This empowered the group member, and also gave him strategies to appropriately address issues of racism. Such interventions, although outside of the group context, provided for meaningful discussions within the group and with key individuals in the institutional setting.

Incorporate Traditional and Spiritual Healing or Seek Consultation when appropriate Application of traditional healing techniques and concepts in group counseling has been provided by several authors (Colemant & Merta, 1999; Garrett & Osborne, 1995; Garrett, 2004; Lowey, Williams, & Keleta, 2002; Wilbur, Wilbur, Garrett, & Yuhas, 2001). The use of the sweat lodge (a cleansing ceremony that heals body, mind, and spirit, and at the same time brings people together) has been advocated in working with Native Americans as a way to combine traditional healing ceremonies with other treatment approaches (Colemant & Merta, 1999; Garrett & Osborne, 1995, Garrett, 2004). Lowey, Williams, and Keleta (2002) describe the use of the Kaffa Intervention, a traditional coffee ceremony, in a counseling group with East African women refugees. Caution should be exercised in the use of such techniques, as group leaders need to be immersed in the cultural context and be very familiar with the healing techniques before implementing them in the group. If traditional healing is seen as the best fit for group members, then the group worker could consult with or invite traditional healers into the group.

Processing Group Work

The evaluation of group work according to Conyne and Bemak (2004) involves processing group events and experiences (formative evaluation) and determining whether the overall goals of the group have been met (summative evaluation). Conyne (1999) proposed a five-step model for *deep processing* that facilitates formative evaluation and the derivation of meaning both within the session and between sessions, viz., *transposing* (leader describes observations without interpretation; *reflecting* (leader connects subjective awareness, feelings, thoughts, and sensations to observations); *discovery* (leader links observations and reflections to external sources, theory, and life experiences; *application* (leader converts deepened understanding to action steps); and *evolving* (leaders are actively involved over time in creating sustaining principles that guide their group work). This deep processing needs to be ecologically and contextually grounded in that consideration is given to the type of the group, individual and group goals, context in which it is offered, and the culture and abilities of the members. Summative evaluation on the other hand is at the end point of the group and can take the form of processing the group experience with members and determining whether individual and group goals were met within the context of the group and a better fit was achieved for the individual in their everyday life outside the group (Conyne & Bemak, 2004).

Diversity-competent group work embraces the concept of deep processing within an ecological context. Understanding and processing each members experience with a holistic framework that takes into consideration individual, family, community, and societal influences is the very essence of diversity-competent group work. Given that the group is a microcosm of society (Yalom, 1985), group work presents a rich opportunity to process the multiple social realities of members within the context of the group.

Summative evaluation of group work in a cultural context is imperative in determining whether individual and group goals were met. Assessment tools used should be culturally relevant and used with sensitivity. Asking for written responses in English from individuals who do not speak the language fluently (as mentioned in an example earlier), will negatively impact data collection. Qualitative data collection methods such as interviews, focus groups, and participant observation may be most suited in working with culturally diverse populations (see Merchant & Dupuy, 1996).

Conclusion

Becoming a diversity-competent group worker is critical in effective group work practice. It involves a thorough examination and understanding of one's own world view, that of others' worldview, and using culturally relevant skills and interventions. Admittedly, the issues related to diversity may at times seem overwhelming, and difficult to attend to at all times. This overwhelming feeling can lead to psychological paralysis or a sense of failure. A frequent argument I have heard is that "attending to diversity is divisive" and that instead one should focus on the "similarities and what unites us." It is important to note that consideration of diversity does not preclude addressing similarities and unity. As mentioned earlier in the chapter, it is not an either/or perspective but a question of foreground versus background and addressing issues that seem to be the most salient at a given time. Addressing the inherent complexities related to diversity does not imply that we get bogged down in the complexities. It simply means that being aware of the complexities and addressing them when necessary will facilitate rather than impede group process.

Learning Activities

Engaging in self-examination particularly with respect to cultural understanding requires involving cognitive, behavioral, and affective dimensions (Delucia-Waack, & Donigian, 2004). In contrast to more traditional didactic approaches (e.g., lecture, class discussion), calls for increased experiential training in multicultural counseling have multiplied resulting in a varied assortment of experiential activities (McRae & Johnson, 1991; Merta, Stringham, & Ponterotto, 1988; Pedersen, 1988, Pope-Davis, Breaux, & Liu, 1994). The following activities can be used in any group setting to better understand the diversity represented in the group: Name Activity, Neighborhood Blue Print Activity, and Relationship Comfort Activity.

Name Activity An activity that I have used frequently in classroom settings, intercultural learning groups, and most any group is the activity related to names. Participants are asked to reflect on what their name means to them (either first, last, or both) within a personal, family or cultural context. Participants often have rich stories to tell about their family background and cultural heritage. One caution to remember is that family history, names, and cultural heritage also carry a lot of pain for some. For example, African American participants may have difficulty in sharing the history behind their last names due to loss of familial and cultural connections as a result of slavery. Similarly, new immigrants to this country sometimes change difficult sounding names to names that are more anglicized for ease of pronunciation. People who are adopted, and/or do not feel a strong family or cultural connection may also struggle with sharing the history behind their name. Therefore, in presenting this activity, it is important to acknowledge upfront that this activity can generate many different types of emotions, but can lead to a deeper understanding of familial, historical, and political contexts from which we come. This introductory activity can quickly bring to light the diversity reflected in the group, and the personal and cultural histories of group members. The group leader can identify themes related to family and cultural background, link members with respect to their similarities, and generate excitement in learning about members who are different from them. It also provides the opportunity to link individuals to an ecological context and to provide an understanding of the sociocultural context we live in. Depending on the context in which it is used, the activity can be conducted in dyads, with large group sharing at the end, or as a round with the whole group.

Neighborhood Blue Print Participants are asked to draw a blue print of the neighborhood they grew up in or the neighborhood that has the most significance to them. They may also draw characters, homes, or other icons that hold meaning to them in their neighborhood. I have used this activity several times as an introductory or ice-breaker exercise, again either in dyads or the whole group, and have been impressed by the level of interest it generates among participants. This activity provides an opportunity to discuss issues related to class, cultural history, and personal stories about growing up or living in a certain neighborhood. Again, caution should be used as this exercise may not always be easy for participants who have experienced trauma related to living in a certain neighborhood, frequent relocations, or feel shame regarding their living conditions. If one's own neighborhood is difficult to draw, group members could be given the option to draw the type of neighborhood they would like to live in, and/or any type of neighborhood that holds interest to them. This activity can provide another way to address the diversity and the ecological context of group participants, such as socioeconomic issues, geographic location, urban versus rural experiences, and the type of diversity they have been exposed to in their living environments.

Relationship Comfort Activity Introduce this activity by indicating the purpose is to explore and examine one's racial/ethnic and cultural values, personal preferences and perceptions via a consideration of close or intimate relationships. Have group members consider and reflect on the following four relationships with regard to personal comfort/discomfort and the degree of personal interest/disinterest. Ask members to rank order the four privately and think about what generates their feelings and thoughts regarding each relationship. Indicate that actual rankings will not be shared, but that a discussion of what emerged from the individual assessment process will follow. State specifically that any sharing will be based on personal choice and that no one will be asked to share anything that they are not comfortable with sharing, and that the right to defer or pass will be honored.

Think about the following relationship possibilities (other relationship statements can be created to reflect other cultural or racial/ethnic factors), and privately rank order them on the basis of your personal comfort.

1. A romantic relationship with someone of a different race.
2. A romantic relationship with someone of a different religion.
3. A romantic relationship with someone significantly older than you are.
4. A close friendship with someone of a different sexual orientation.

Upon completion of the individual assessment process, conduct a round to obtain initial thoughts and feelings that the activity generated in the group. Use the responses as a means of guiding the direction of the discussion. Generally consider the relationship of race, religion, age, and sexual orientation in relationships and especially in regard to dyadic attraction and intimacy. In addition, explore the reactions and perspectives of group members when exposed to these relationships in the community (i.e., What do you think and feel when you become aware of such a couple?). This activity is particularly useful in intercultural learning groups that have developed to the work stage of the group process. (This activity is adapted from Beebe, Beebe, & Redmond, 2005, p. 346).

10
Differentiating Groups

The vibrant tapestry of group work is woven from the unlimited capacity of small groups to be molded and melded to meet the needs and purposes of the members who comprise them, the goals and objectives of systems and organizations in which they are formed and the unique traits, perspectives, abilities and protocols of group workers who lead them.

Up to this point we have concentrated on the nature of the group process and the integral components that interact to create that process—namely the leader and the members. However, groups have many different facets that come into play in the context of translating group process into practice. The purpose of the next three chapters is to focus on the technical dimensions of group work as a means of providing hands on tools for implementing group programs.

As the field of group work has grown, acquiring merit as a human service modality, it has developed a technology of its own that has both affirmed its validity and enhanced its reliability across client populations and settings. The fact that groups are here to stay is well established. Conyne (1985) observed that "groups are a dominant, omnipresent force in our lives, and they most likely will continue to be so well into the future" (p. 61). This is because research and clinical practice have demonstrated that group work is an entity with specific knowledge, procedures, processes, and mechanics that can be beneficially learned, applied, and adapted in most human contexts. The challenge is no longer one of proving the potential and relevance of group work in facilitating growth, enhancing productivity, and resolving problems. The challenge now is how to most effectively and efficiently utilize group process. This is where the elements of differentiation, organization, and evaluation of groups become important. Unless group leaders can effectively do all three, the prospects of establishing effective groups and developing functional group programs are curtailed.

This chapter will focus on the first of these three components of group work. Differentiation will be addressed from the standpoint of process and focus perspectives and via group typology based on the nature of groups and client populations served. In chapter 11, organization will be discussed in a general to specific manner. Starting with the perspective of outreach and guidelines for planning group programs, we will then delineate group composition factors and technical considerations for forming groups and conclude with an example of a group counseling format. Evaluation will be discussed in chapter 12 from a practitioner's perspective that differentiates research from evaluation and provides specific tools and suggestions for evaluating process and outcome.

Differentiating Between Groups

The term group usually conjures up the image of a particular type of group or group approach, most likely one the counselor has been exposed to, trained in, experienced, or led. This often creates a limited purview from which it is difficult to build a flexible and varied group program that will serve a variety of purposes and meet a wide range of client needs. The ability to differentiate between groups based on process characteristics and qualities unique to certain group formats and purposes will provide a solid basis for organizing and implementing appropriate and comprehensive group programs (Trotzer, 1975). Consideration will be given first to process perspectives that attribute contextual diversity to groups and then group typology will be described from a context, process, and client perspective.

Socio-Process and Psyche-Process Groups

Coffey (1952) initially proposed the idea that groups could be categorized as socio-process groups (task oriented in nature) or psyche-process groups (person oriented in nature). Kemp (1970) expanded on this idea, relating it particularly to group guidance and counseling. A socio-process group is one in which goals are external to the group and involves tasks for which the group is given or assumes responsibility. "The intent of the (socio-process) group and its specific reason for being is not primarily the self-improvement of members" (Dinkmeyer & Muro, 1971, p. 126) but rather it is to accomplish a set task. The socio-process group is thus task oriented and attempts to utilize the resources (members) of the group in the most efficient and effective manner to accomplish its mission. The group is problem oriented only to the point of resolving difficulties that are directly associated with the task or are interfering with the group's progress in working on the task. Members receive gratification and fulfillment as a result of their contribution to the task, their cooperation with other members, and ultimately from the accomplishment of the task itself. The leader is primarily responsible for getting the job done by keeping the group goal oriented, assessing the group's resources, and mobilizing them to achieve its task goal. Examples of socio-process groups are committees, athletic teams, work groups in business and industry—such as quality circles or think tanks—task force groups, and other such groups that interact to attain an end result in the form of a program, policy, product, victory, and so forth. The emergence of the task group as an entity in the group work rainbow is testimony to the reality of the socio-process group (Hulse-Killacky, Killacky, & Donigian, 2001).

A psyche-process group is one in which goals come from within the group, particularly from the internal frame of reference of individual group members themselves. The process is person oriented as opposed to task oriented, and individual growth, personal learning, and personal problem solving are the focuses. Group interaction itself is of primary importance. Member satisfaction results from involvement and interaction with group members, increased knowledge about self and others, and from personal problem solving, change, and growth. The leader is responsible to the members, not to a task, and functions to create a therapeutic climate in the group, facilitate interaction, and protect group members if that becomes necessary. Examples of psyche-process groups are counseling and therapy groups, marital enrichment, encounter, sensitivity, and personal growth groups.

Schmuck and Schmuck (1971) noted that both socio- and psyche-process groups can be either individual oriented or group oriented in purpose. That is, the interaction of any group benefits either individuals separately or the group as a unit. For example, classrooms are individual socio-process groups, whereas industrial work groups tend to be group socio-process groups. Therapy groups are examples of individual psyche-process groups while T-groups are group psyche-process groups. The individual focus therefore means that results are gauged in terms of what each individual member achieves as a function of group interaction. The group focus, by contrast, results in increased group efficiency and increased knowledge and awareness of the group process itself.

In most guidance, psychoeducational, counseling, and psychotherapy groups the primary goal is to use the group process for the benefit of individual members. This goal is basic to the nature of therapeutic groups. Therefore, if groups do not promote the best interests of the individuals involved, they are not effectively serving the cause of human growth and development. On the other hand, the group emphasis in certain groups like class meetings, guidance classes, T-groups, consciousness raising groups, and human relations groups may serve an extremely important function in helping members learn cooperation, collaboration and respect for one another and appreciation of those who have ethnic, racial, or cultural characteristics different from their own.

Although all counseling and psychotherapy groups are basically psyche-process in concept, the socio-process concept is often used, particularly as a basis for leadership strategies. Some leaders prefer to start their groups on a structured task or activity oriented basis. They use tasks to develop a group atmosphere in which members get to know each other, gain trust for one another, and develop cohesiveness through working together on the activities. Gradually then, the leader turns the responsibility and focus over to members and facilitates the evolution of the psyche-process so members can get down to the business of working on their own problems and concerns. Conversely, groups such as committees and work teams that are socio-process in concept may utilize psyche-process strategies to get started. Before receiving a specific task to work on, members of the group spend time and effort, often via T-group, encounter group, or human relations methods, getting to know each other and building a group relationship. Emphasis is on acceptance of self and others and interpersonal communication. Once the members have begun to develop a relationship where personal needs are met, they are then assigned a task to accomplish, switching the emphasis of the group from psyche-process to socio-process.

In either of these strategies the leader can move back and forth between the two processes as the group needs dictate. At times, the psyche-group may benefit from the structure and responsibility of a task and the socio-group may need to reestablish the person to person quality of their group interaction. The tenor of the group can change depending on its overall purpose and the needs of the members.

Wilbur and Roberts-Wilbur (1994) further refined the dynamics of socio-process and psych-process into three categories of group processes: task-process groups, psycho-process groups, and socio-process groups. The task-process form is characterized by a predetermined task or project to which the group is assigned. The group interacts in a manner that Waldo (1985) typifies as *extra-personal* where gathering information and completing tasks are pre-dominant activities. The psycho-process form is designed to change behavior of the group participants, and meets Waldo's (1985) criteria for being *intrapersonal* in nature because the impact of group interaction is realized in the individual lives of the members. In contrast, the socio-process form is a more cognitive, interactive process where attitudes, values, beliefs, ideas, and opinions are surfaced and examined in a format that qualifies as *interpersonal* (Waldo, 1985) because emphasis is on sharing information, orientation, and discussion (Polcin, 1991). All three forms relate directly to the ASGW group work typologies delineated in chapter 2.

Finally, a recent group work development has further exemplified the importance of the process delineations just described. The emergence of the Process Observer as an official entity in groups of all forms has made it possible to directly identify and utilize process components and dynamics to enhance group effectiveness. A process person is incorporated in the group for purposes of tracking process dynamics and bringing observations of such to the attention of the leader and group members. Consequently, process becomes a recognized and considered dimension of the group activity regardless of its purpose and nature (Trotzer, 1997a, 1997b, 1997c, & 1998b). Task groups, class groups, work groups, committees, and leadership teams such as the ASGW Executive Board have all utilized and benefited from inclusion of a Process Observer into their deliberations thereby creating a vital link between process and content (Krause & Hulse-Kilacky, 1996).

Different Focuses in Groups

Groups also can be distinguished on the basis of the focus of the interaction in the group. Patterns of communication in a group define its nature and solidify characteristics that can be used to describe it. Several basic focuses tend to occur in groups. Each has advantages and disadvantages. Each can promote the effectiveness of the group or disrupt it. The leader has to be aware of the type of focus that will best serve the interests of members and achieve the group's goals and act to see that that focus is developed and maintained. Each focus is briefly discussed in the following pages.

Here and Now Perspective

This focus is on what is happening to and in the individual and the group at the moment. The concentration is on the action and interaction as it develops in the group. This orientation brings out members' feelings and thoughts that are part of their present awareness and deals with current behavior. It maintains that what individuals are like in the group is representative of their personalities and actions outside the group. The basic assumption is that personality is consistent in human beings, and that the group can use what occurs in the group as material for helping members resolve problems outside the group. As Sklare, Keener, and Mas (1990) note: "The group is a microcosm of society, behaviors similar to that which members exhibit outside the group will come to life in the group" (p. 144). The here and now focus is an integral part of growth groups, is highly significant in counseling and psychotherapy groups (Carroll, 1986; Yalom, 1995) and has procedural importance in other groups. The here and now is a firm foundation for beginning communication and relationships because all parties have equal access to the stimuli of interaction. It provides a common starting point and is a necessary component of any effort to increase self-knowledge and improve social adequacy. It is also the perspective that gives feedback its most meaningful impact. However, the here and now also can be a means of avoiding problem issues that involve the outside world. Too much emphasis on the present (in the group) interaction can lead groups away from reality instead of closer to it.

One of the charges leveled against marathon groups and encounter groups is that they become so enmeshed in the here and now interaction of the sessions that little if any transfer of learning occurs. Participants have to wait until another opportunity arises to engage in a similar process to use their newfound insights and skills. This focus also can stymie group members in their development of plans for action that have a future, outside the group application. The group leader therefore must be able to assess when the group needs to get to the here and now but also must sense when that focus is running counter to the process of therapeutic change.

There and Then Perspective

This focus deals with events, behaviors, or feelings that occurred in the past but are still interfering with the adjustment of the individual or the group in the present. This perspective may draw on either conscious or subconscious material in its effort to identify causes and to clarify and resolve problems (Donigian & Malnati, 1997). This perspective should not be misconstrued as displaying dirty laundry or looking for skeletons in someone's closet. The past is a natural element in any person's life and in the group's life and can contribute meaningfully to the helping process if utilized in the proper manner. The individual's past is an extremely important theme in group therapy and has importance, but to a lesser degree, in group counseling. The group's past, typified in comments like "remember last time," is important in growth groups, counseling groups, and therapy groups but has less value except for transition purposes in other groups. The there and then is particularly useful if members have unresolved feelings about past events that are currently stifling growth or functionality. Conflicts unsuccessfully dealt with, feelings of guilt, actions that are regretted, and traumatic experiences stemming from rape, physical abuse, incest, substance abuse or trauma are examples of past material that can be brought out and worked through beneficially in the group.

The important thing to remember about this focus is that efforts should always be made to bring the person up to date so that the disclosure does not become just another unsatisfactory means of handling the situation. The past is of value when it can perpetuate adjustment to the present and stimulate growth in the future. Frequently, members use the there and then to avoid getting into the here and now problems of their lives. A common ploy in groups is to play the "remember when" nostalgia game as a means of procuring a reprieve from working on problems. The group leader must sense when the there and then is losing its impact in the helping process and help the group move on to a more valuable focus. Similarly, the leader must help the group avoid rehashing its past to such an extent that it never catches up to itself. Some groups continually dwell on clarifying past behaviors, perceptions, and intentions. They get to the end of their sessions feeling that they have analyzed their group history without ever having experienced it as a present phenomenon.

Tichy (1997) asserts that the there and then focus is of particular importance to leadership. In his book *The Leadership Engine,* he points out that the leader's past is a prologue to his or her current leadership approach in that it provides the basis for what he calls a "teachable point of view." A leader's past experience is a basis for stories that have merit with regard to style and character of leadership, modeling, teaching, and motivating members. Stories from the leader's formative years related to values and beliefs and their professional experience especially related to successful leadership efforts all combine to demonstrate that leaders have a usable past that serves them well when utilized appropriately.

Social Value Perspective

This focus basically asks the question "What does society expect and how does that affect me?" It attempts to assess a person's thoughts, feelings, and behaviors in light of their usefulness in daily life. This perspective makes full use of the group as a mini-society reflecting the standards, norms, and expectations of the outside world. The social value focus is the key to reality testing that needs to be done in the group to make the process meaningful for transfer of learning. The basic idea is that if members can provide realistic feedback and evaluations, individuals can make better decisions and develop plans for change that have a higher probability of success. The necessity of this perspective in most groups is obvious, especially when problems are involved or strategic planning is needed. As Glasser (1965) noted, most problems initially reflect a denial or distortion of reality, and if the group does not attempt to reestablish the member's or the group's contact with reality, the process has little positive effect. In guidance groups, counseling groups, and therapy groups this perspective is mandatory. In all other groups it is important from the standpoint of credibility and productivity. Individual members may resist this perspective because it demands that they face problems in light of others' perceptions and not simply their own. In an effort to protect their members, groups sometimes deny reality and on occasion actually distort it. When this situation occurs, the relevance and usefulness of the group process in solving problems is negated. Whenever leaders become part and parcel of a group's refusal to be a reality check and do not act responsibly to include that focus, they are acting unethically. There are times when the leader may have to stand alone and confront members with reality in order to force them to deal realistically with each other's problems.

Skills and Tools Perspective

This focus, as the rubric implies, is concerned with providing group members with the technical means of resolving their problems, living more effective lives, and making growth facilitating decisions. This perspective provides a focus around which entire groups can be built since it concentrates on providing members with certain basic skills that will enhance their personal welfare or group skills that relate to team building and group efficiency. A group can be organized to help members learn a variety of skills ranging from decision making to social interaction skills and conflict resolution to team work (Gazda & Brooks, 1985; Johnson & Johnson, 1997). This perspective can perpetuate both preventative and remedial helping group methods. Gazda has promoted this perspective stating "I think we need to employ a model in which, after clients' deficits are identified in the interview format, they are put through a systematic, structured, intensive skills training program" (Ritter, West, & Trotzer, 1987, p. 296). The skills and tools perspective is an essential part of guidance and psychoeducational groups and can be one of the means of implementing action during the work stage of counseling groups. This focus has relevance in therapy groups, incidental impact in growth groups, and training value in task groups.

The expertise of the leader is especially important to this focus for two reasons. First, he or she must recognize when the lack of certain skills is a major part of a member's or group's problems and be able to act to fill that void in the group. Second, he or she must have the wherewithal to teach the needed skills. The only draw back to this perspective is that it can become a rigid and inflexible means of running groups if the leader begins focusing only on teaching the skills and not on the persons in the group. In other words, the group can develop into a classroom type group with a leader centered structure and academic content but little personal relevance to group members.

Agent of Change Perspective

The philosophical basis for this focus is that each person is responsible for learning about himself or herself, and the group is an arena in which that learning can take place. Reddy (1985) believes this perspective will become increasingly important as group work reaches for its zenith in society's effort to meet personal, social, and business needs. She stated, "with the breakdown of the family unit and a continuing depersonalized society, individuals will be in, if not seek out, small groups of people to fulfill their affiliations, tasks, and personal, interpersonal and organizational needs" (p. 106). The main objective is to change oneself in a desired direction and to help others do the same. Self-acceptance, self-knowledge, and self-responsibility are associated with this perspective. It also contributes to members' understanding and acceptance of others.

The material for group discussion is personal functioning and involves self-disclosure and direct feedback as the principal means of acquiring self-understanding. This focus tends to be the primary emphasis in growth groups because of the basic assumption that participants in these groups are healthy, functional individuals who willingly involve themselves and who are capable of governing their own lives. The advantage of this perspective is that, ideally, each member chooses the amount of involvement, disclosure, feedback, or change desired. However, in reality, sometimes one has difficulty assessing whether the person, the group, or the leader is the motivating force in the interaction. All helping groups should advocate self-responsibility, but especially in counseling groups members need to *learn* how to be responsible for themselves before they can *practice* it. Therefore the group leader may need to help the group develop this perspective over time rather than use it as the primary means of promoting change throughout the entire group process.

Summary

The perspectives described tend to complement each other in effective groups. Certain focuses may be primary in certain types of groups but the others serve a countering and balancing function in keeping group interaction relevant, productive, and therapeutic. Most groups with which the counselor works will utilize all of these focuses to some extent. The typical counseling group may run the full gamut of perspectives during its course. Guidance and psycho-educational groups, though mainly concerned with the skills and social value perspectives, will incorporate other focuses as well. Once again, the needs of the members and the purposes of the group will determine the validity of the focus that the leader promotes in the group. The leader should not hesitate to redirect or reframe the focus when necessary to help groups engage in constructive interaction.

Typology of Group Work

Group workers should have a specific awareness of the many different types of groups relevant to their particular settings. Effective groups in helping settings have in common process characteristics that we've discussed in previous chapters. But they also have unique attributes that differentiate them from each other and broaden the impact of the group process as a means of increasing the counselor's effectiveness. Generally, helping groups can be broken down into six major categories:

1. Guidance and life skills groups (psychoeducation),
2. Counseling groups,
3. Psychotherapy groups,
4. Support and self-help groups,
5. Consultation groups, and
6. Growth groups.

Each category has characteristics relative to focus, leadership, size, and purpose that distinguish it. General traits and characteristics of the broad categories in which each of these groups fit are delineated in chapter 2. Each of these six major categories and representative types of groups are presented on the following pages.

Guidance and Life Skills Groups

Under the general rubric of psychoeducation, guidance groups are primarily school oriented both conceptually and practically, whereas life skills groups have broader applicability to any mental health private practice or agency. Both use a similar format adapting content to the setting and clientele served. The process involved is that of

> providing personally relevant information and skills and encouraging interpersonal interaction, discussion, and sharing in order to help group members understand themselves, their development, and their world, thereby facilitating effective decision-making, appropriate adjustment, and satisfactory personal growth. (Trotzer, 1980, p. 342)

The types of guidance groups a counselor should be familiar with are large and small group guidance, classroom meetings, guidance classes, human relations groups, and life skills groups. However, research by Dansby (1996) has found that "types of groups vary greatly by school level with apparently more counseling groups being conducted with younger students and more guidance groups with older students" (p. 238).

Large Group Guidance

Large group guidance is primarily concerned with dispensing information to help in personal planning and decision making. Emphasis is on presenting educational and vocational information of a personally relevant nature in an interesting manner to large numbers of clients who need the same information. Large group guidance is used when information can be presented in a straightforward manner with little risk of misunderstanding. Methods usually involve a presentation in the form of films or lectures followed by an opportunity for discussion and questions. The process is content oriented and cognitive in nature and stresses environmental factors as well as generic personal attributes. The leader generally presents the information and directs and controls discussion.

Large group guidance can be effectively used in orientation and articulation situations to help clients understand a system and how to move through it. Although called large group guidance, it is still advantageous to limit groups to a size where the counselor can keep tabs on how information is being received. A general guideline is to work with groups no larger than the usual class size. Using groups larger than this may get the information to more people at one time but also may inhibit discussion to the extent that the process could become self-defeating. The length of time involved in these groups can vary from 15 minutes to an hour. Longer presentations result in diminishing returns due to the loss of client attention and interest. Large group guidance also helps counselors give out general information in a relatively small amount of time, thus freeing the counselor to concentrate on other aspects of the group program.

Small Group Guidance

Very often small group guidance is an outgrowth of a large group presentation. In a school situation, for instance, scheduling procedures may be explained in a large group, but the actual working out of an individual's schedule can be done in a small group. In fact, it is indeed strange that school counselors who are often saddled with scheduling responsibilities do not opt more frequently for handling this task in small groups rather than on a one on one basis. Time is saved and monotony is lessened for everyone. Small group guidance allows clients to discuss their own situations and allows for asking specific questions. Clients who refuse to ask questions in a large group are much more willing to do so in a small group.

Emphasis in small group guidance is on providing educational, vocational, and personal information. Methods, however, concentrate on the discussion aspect rather than on presentation, and efforts are made to involve all members in the interaction. The process is cognitive stressing both content and skills. Focus is on relating environmental and informational factors to personal goals, values, attitudes, and responsibilities. The leader alternately facilitates group discussion and presents information.

Small group guidance is particularly useful in helping clients develop social skills and decision-making skills to help them be more successful in their lives. In addition, vocational and educational planning in small groups for members who have common interests and goals is an efficient use of counselor time. For example, clients desiring to explore common career areas can benefit from small group guidance sessions, sharing their interests, concerns, and knowledge with other clients headed in the same direction. Generally, small group guidance is appropriate when clients are beginning to make specific use of information or need to develop some skill to enhance personal effectiveness. Group size should be restricted to 8 to 12 members, because larger groups decrease the probability of interaction by the total group membership. Sessions of 30 to 60 minutes tend to be sufficient, and the frequency of meetings should depend on the topic discussed and the needs of group members.

The content and focus of most guidance groups in schools tend to be catego-rized in one of the following areas (Thompson & Poppen, 1979):

1. *Self-concept development.* Group sessions address the question of "Who am I?" They are designed to help participants deal with identity crises as-sociated with growing up, develop positive self-concepts, and engage in self-exploration and values clarification.
2. *Student self-discipline.* The focus is on learning to be responsible for self and acting in a responsible manner toward others. Decision-making and coping skills are often intrinsically involved.
3. *Effective peer relations.* The emphasis is on understanding and effectively coping with peer pressure and utilizing peer dynamics constructively. Exploration of the impact of peers on individuals is stressed and human relations skills are taught.
4. *Effective interpersonal relationships with non-peers.* The focus is primar-ily on developing effective adult-child relationships and communication encompassing teacher-student, parent-child, and other such relationships that involve a transgenerational or hierarchical authority type of interac-tion.
5. *Academic progress of all learners.* The emphasis is on educational progress in orientation, articulation, and study skills. General educational information and requirements, or teaching specific learning skills, may be involved.
6. *Career development.* Educational-occupational information, career deci-sion-making, and vocational development are addressed for the purpose of helping participants make effective career choices.
7. *Effective classroom or work environment.* The focus is on developing a cooperative (cohesive) learning environment and a positive learning atmosphere characterized by effective communication.

Within these broad categories specific group guidance programs are developed and tailored to the specific needs of participants and conditions of the environ-ment (Trotzer, 1980).

Classroom Meetings

Classroom meetings utilize a ready-made group situation, although, of course, the situation is limited to schools. School counselors who conduct classroom meetings enhance their own roles in three ways:

1. By direct contact with the counselor, the students become more cognizant of who the counselor is and more familiar with the counselor role.
2. By becoming involved in the classroom milieu, counselors are kept aware

of the kinds of experiences and pressures both students and teachers face, which makes them more sensitive to both groups.

3. By developing a working relationship with teachers, school counselors will perpetuate their impact as consultants and referral sources.

The general format and implementation of class meetings is described by Glasser (1969). He discussed three main types of classroom meetings: (1) the social, problem solving meeting where the goal is to change behavior, (2) the open ended meeting where the goal is to change thinking, and (3) the educational-diagnostic meeting where the goal is to determine what students have learned and where weaknesses still exist.

Class meetings can facilitate the development of productive and positive classroom relationships and therefore should involve the entire class. By structuring the meetings into the regular routine, students learn that they have a specific time when what they have to say takes precedence over what the teacher or counselor has to say.

Thompson and Poppen (1979) described seven types of classroom meetings based on their focus:

1. *Involvement meetings*: to promote student involvement and sense of belonging.
2. *Rules and responsibilities meetings*: to deal with class operational procedures and expectations.
3. *Thinking meetings*: to increase students' thinking and verbal abilities.
4. *Values clarification meetings*: to clarify personal values and develop tolerance of differences.
5. *Hypothetical dilemmas*: to pose hypothetical problem situations and develop action plans.
6. *Actual problem solving*: to deal with real problems in the classroom.
7. *Class council*: to provide a vehicle for class governance (pp. 157–159).

Whatever the focus, the process is discussion oriented with the goal of maximizing total student participation. Although the process is mainly cognitive, efforts are directed at finding out what the students think. The counselor serves as a facilitator of the discussion and as a model to the teacher who should be present in the class. In this way counselors help teachers develop their own skills so that eventually the counselor can bow out. The meetings should be at least 30 minutes in length but can vary depending on class involvement, topic of discussion, and leader time commitment. Frequency is a key factor. Glasser (1969) maintained that elementary school classes should have a class meeting every day. In secondary schools, one or two meetings a week is a realistic goal for counselors to seek. Thus, the counselor's time must be carefully planned. To be effective he or she must develop a programmed sequence of conducting class meetings and training teachers so that as responsibility for one class meeting is turned over to its teacher another class can be added.

Guidance/Psychoeducational Classes

The oldest of any guidance technique was first proposed in the form of vocational guidance classes as part of the school curriculum. Through the years, however, the guidance class gradually became so routine, monotonous, and irrelevant that both counselors and students perceived it as no more than a necessary evil at best. However, with the recent emphasis on career, mental health, and psychological education, the guidance class is once again assuming its meaningful place in school curricula. Guidance classes (using many different names and rubrics) are courses taught by the counselor whose content and structure are based on developmental psychology and guidance and counseling principles. They may be elective or required and usually last for one quarter or semester, during which time students consider personally relevant topics and information in both an experiential and academic manner. They also make use of what Schmuck and Schmuck (1971) called the "splendid myriad of different individual styles and emotional experiences" (p. 4) that make up a classroom group. For best results class size should be limited to approximately 20 people. The format of guidance classes is highly variable, depending on needs of students and the personality of the counselor. However, several forms enjoy fairly consistent emphasis and acceptance among counselors.

Career Guidance Classes The career guidance class (Hoppock, 1976) helps students explore vocations and make vocational choices based on self-knowledge and knowledge about the world of work. Students do various career projects, research numerous vocations, and assess their own vocational interests and abilities. Offshoots of this type of group are appearing in greater quantity throughout the educational process. The main purpose of these classes is to prepare students for a vocational choice that is personally satisfying and contributes meaningfully to society.

Feelings Classes The feelings class as described by Faust (1968) has a guidance class format that concerns itself with the affective domain of students' lives. The purpose of the class is to give attention to the emotional development of the student. Five main ideas are stressed:

1. Many kinds of feelings exist.
2. Nearly everyone experiences all the different feelings.
3. To have these feelings is all right.

4. Having a feeling is different from expressing a feeling.
5. Feelings can be expressed in ways that are not harmful to yourself or others, and in many cases these methods of expression are helpful.

Feelings classes should not be confused with sensitivity training or encounter groups. Rather, they are to teach people that recognizing and knowing how to express a feeling is as important as having the feeling in the first place. The leader must be able to work with clients' feelings in a constructive manner. The critical importance of human emotions which supports such group efforts has been elucidated by Goleman's (1995) national best seller *Emotional Intelligence*.

"Knowing Me" Classes In these classes students have an opportunity to learn how wonderfully complex and interesting they are as persons. Under the direction of the counselor, they engage in a variety of self-assessment and interpersonal learning activities. They discuss results among themselves and hear presentations on various aspects of human development. These classes can be held for any age group, but they are particularly interesting to middle school and junior high students because they are in that ambiguous stage of preadolescence where change and the imminence of change are major factors in their experience. The leader must be adept in the psychology of the particular age group with whom he or she is working and have the ability to organize class sessions around the individual differences of class members.

Human Relations Groups

Human awareness and human relations are becoming an increasingly important aspect of the group process. Within the context of education, Birnbaum (1969) stated that human relations training

> holds tremendous potential for improving education by dealing with affective components, reducing unnecessary friction between generations and creating a revolution in instruction by helping teachers to learn how to use the classroom group for learning purposes. (p. 82)

Gazda (1971b) added that we have a responsibility to educate children in human relations to prepare them to cope adequately with their ever expanding worlds. Not to do so would be a tragic and inexcusable mistake. In general, human relations groups are a means of contributing to the psychological education of both children and adults. The counselor trained in group process has the resources to be in the forefront of this movement.

Human relations groups can vary in size from six members to six dozen members; the larger groups are broken down into smaller subgroups all under the direction of one leader. Focus is on development of competencies in communication and relationship formation, and the process entails demonstration, experiential involvement in activities, and group discussion. Understanding and appreciating individual differences and similarities especially in terms of racial, cultural, and other diversity factors are stressed. The leader structures and guides interaction and facilitates discussion. Sessions are usually organized in a planned sequence and meet for a specified number of meetings. Each meeting usually lasts one to three hours or is arranged in a workshop format of longer time periods. Members benefit from involvement in the sessions because the social skills and knowledge of self and others are immediately relevant to their lives.

Life Skills Groups

Life skills groups have many labels but one basic commonality: they use a structured, experiential, group training format to teach participants specific skills that enable them to improve their life adjustment. Gazda has identified four generic life skills areas that delineate the content of these groups. They are:

1. Interpersonal communication or relationships,
2. Fitness and health maintenance,
3. Problem solving and decision making, and
4. Establishing one's personal identity and life's purpose (Ritter, West, & Trotzer, 1987, p. 296).

Training programs in each of these skill areas can be developed that are applicable to four specific settings: community, home, school, and work. Numerous resources have been developed in the life skills area by leaders in the field such as George Gazda (Gazda, 1984b; Gazda & Brooks, 1985) and David Johnson (Johnson, 1972; Johnson & Johnson, 1979; 1997). You also are referred to Drum and Knott's (1977) book *Structured Groups for Facilitating Development* as a prototype work in the life skills area.

Planning Guidance and Life Skills Groups

The group process model described in chapters 4 and 5 is a useful resource in organizing and planning groups of a guidance, psychoeducation or life skills nature. Figure 10.1 presents the basic content and process components that provide a planning framework for these groups.

Content considerations include selection and development of a general theme based on the needs of the population to be served. Specifications of overall goals emanate from the theme. The nature of the goals brings the sequential order of the program into perspective, with each session addressing relevant topics.

CONTENT									
THEME									
OVERALL GOALS									
SESSIONS	1	2	3	4	5	6	7	8	X
TOPICS									
OBJECTIVES									
ACTIVITIES									
MATERIALS									

SECURITY	Getting Acquinted	⟶
	Setting Boundaries	⟶
	Interpersonal Warm-Up	⟶
	Establishing Trust (Basic Rapport)	⟶
ACCEPTANCE	Personal Sharing	⟶
	Giving Feedback	⟶
	Group Cohesiveness	⟶
	Accepting Self	⟶
	Accepting Others	⟶
WORK	Self Assessment	⟶
	Recognizing Ownership	⟶
	Learning and Applying Information	⟶
	and Skills to Personal Life	⟶
	Mobilizing Group Resources	⟶
	Realtity Testing	⟶
CLOSING	Unfinished Business	⟶
	Giving Support	⟶
	Confirming and Affirming Growth	⟶
	Saying Goodbyey	⟶
		Follow-Up

Figure 10.1 Group guidance: Program development format.

Specific objectives for each session are planned and topic related information, activities, and materials are selected for presentation and discussion. Thus, as participants move through the sequence of sessions they engage in experiences that culminate in achievement of goals of the program, which, in turn, meet the objectives for which the group was organized. However, structuring content is only part of the organizational task; it is the horizontal dimension of the model. The group process also must be accounted for in the planning of topics, selection of activities, and organization of sessions. Group process is the vertical dimension of the model. The sequential interaction between process and content form the basis for an effective group guidance program.

Developmental tasks provide a basis for selecting activities appropriate to the stage of development in which the group is. Accounting for process tasks increases the relevance of activities and facilitates movement to the next stage of the group process. The choice of activities, then, should be based on both process and content considerations. In other words, any activities chosen should facilitate the realization of both process and content objectives. For example, an initial session of a career guidance group might use a get acquainted activity that includes sharing vocational goals along with other "who are you?" tasks. Process and content thus are integrated, providing experiences and an atmosphere conducive to personalized learning relative to the focus of the group guidance program. Individual group sessions can be further organized and planned using phases of a group session described in chapter 5.

Counseling Groups

Counseling groups are distinguished from guidance groups in that they are problem oriented and remedial in nature. Group counseling focuses on helping people explore and confront specific dissatisfactions in their lives with the express purpose of understanding their concerns and discovering and implementing ways of resolving their problems (Trotzer, 1972). The group leader attempts to develop an atmosphere in which members can talk openly about their problems without fear of rejection or reprisal. He or she encourages members to help each other, facilitates communication, protects individuals if that becomes necessary, and functions, in many other ways that have already been described. Since members feel safe and have the opportunity to both help and be helped, the process becomes one of conscientious concern for each other. This group also serves as a reality testing ground, where members can try out alternatives and obtain feedback about their probable success prior to attempting to make changes in the real world.

Since group counseling is a primary focus of this book, little additional information about it is necessary at this point. Group size should be limited to 4 to 10 members to preserve the personal focus in the group. Verbal techniques and conscious awareness are emphasized, and groups meet as often and only for as long as is necessary to resolve problems. Session length ranges from 45 to 90 minutes with the ideal length of time being one and one-half to two hours. The focus of the group varies with the nature of the members' problems, and therefore group counseling is a quite flexible tool. The following descriptions of some types of counseling groups attest to this quality of flexibility.

Common Problems Groups

The common problems group (Blocher, 1966) uses the most typical of all group strategies. Most practitioners agree that homogeneous groups have many advantages. Members share concerns and therefore do not feel isolated from the experiences of others. Comments such as "I feel that too," "That's the same problem I have," "We're all in the same boat," and "I'm glad I'm not the only one who has that problem" abound in these groups. Members benefit by observing others working out problems similar to their own. This strategy is highly relevant because it can be adapted to any type of problem that a number of clients have in common. Examples include problems with drugs/alcohol, dating, parents, losses (death or divorce), and so forth. Certain variations can improve the effect of the group, such as using role models or opening the group to new members as individuals resolve their problems and leave.

Case Centered Groups

An alternative to the common problems group is the case centered group (Poppen & Thompson, 1974), which uses a problem solving approach with a heterogeneous group. Whenever the focus is on a problem different from their own, other members are cast in the role of helpers, providing valuable feedback, information, and support based on their own experiences in overcoming that problem or simply offering assistance as interested, concerned, and objective helping persons. Diverse group membership is valuable for motivating interaction and maintaining group interest. Only in extreme circumstances where members' problems are so different that little basis exists for understanding one another is heterogeneity seriously disruptive to the group process. The only disadvantage is that some people may feel the other members cannot help them with their problems because of lack of experience or understanding. Heterogeneous groups are often much more interesting to leaders, making the task of leadership more stimulating.

Human Potential Groups

Human potential counseling groups (Otto, 1967) focus on personal strengths and positive resources of the person as a means of overcoming obstacles that are preventing him or her from realizing his or her potential. This type of group is unique due to the process involved. It can be utilized in homogeneous or heterogeneous groups and attempts to resolve problems by concentrating on what individuals can do rather than what they can't do. Members are asked to examine their resources and then apply those resources to their concerns. The key quality of this approach is that it counters effectively the negative connotations and feelings of inferiority usually associated with having problems. Even when group leaders do not adhere completely to this format they incorporate sessions that stress the positives for balance and perspective. By operating from a strength base members grow in self-esteem and self-confidence, improve their self-concepts, and have more positive attitudes toward changing their behaviors, feelings, or cognitions.

Problem Solving Groups

Current dynamics and developments in the mental health field coupled with the economic expediency introduced by managed care have prompted the emergence of counseling groups that are characterized as short term, pragmatic, and solution focused. Problem solving groups are formed of individuals who specify before meeting the problem(s) in concrete terms that each is going to address in the group. The format is then structured and directed by the leader who provides the guidelines, parameters, techniques, and activities for the group to perpetuate the problem solving process. These groups may meet for extended, workshop type time frames (two to three hours) for four sessions over a one month period with a follow-up session, or may be conducted in a day long format with a follow-up session. In any event, the methods utilized reflect the influence of brief family therapy and solution focused therapy along with techniques adapted specifically to problem solving (Trotzer, 1998c; Trotzer, 2001).

Psychotherapy Groups

Therapy groups differ from counseling groups more on the basis of who is in them, who leads them, and where they take place than on the basis of process variations or therapeutic dynamics. Clients tend to be more disturbed and often carry a *DSM-IV* diagnosis. Leaders tend to have had their clinical training in settings that treat mental health disorders (e.g., hospitals, mental health centers, or other outpatient treatment programs). Leaders also tend to have more academic training, clinical experience, and credentials and are usually certified or licensed as psychiatrists, psychologists, clinical social workers, pastoral counselors, or clinical mental health counselors. The majority of therapy groups convene in agency, private practice, or hospital settings (inpatient or outpatient). The factors that delineate counseling from therapy are described in chapter 2. Yalom (1983) distinguished inpatient from outpatient group therapy by differentiating process based on the level of functionality of the patients. Higher level inpatient groups meet for one hour and fifteen minutes during which time they work through a four phase process of (1) orientation/preparation, (2) agenda formation, (3) agenda filling, and (4) review of the meeting. Lower level inpatient groups meet for only 45 minutes in somewhat smaller groups and work through the same phases but in a much more structured, leader activated manner.

Therapy groups also tend to be open ended and long term. In hospital settings they may meet daily and in outpatient situations they may meet more than once a week as well. For additional information on therapy groups you are referred to Yalom (1983, 1995).

Support and Self-Help Groups

Groups in this category are differentiated by the following traits:

1. Group membership is homogeneous with each member experiencing or having experienced the particular problem that called the group into being,
2. Peer support and assistance takes precedence over expert (professional) resources and assistance.
3. If a leader is present, he or she is primarily a facilitator and/or also may be in need of the same support as the group members.

Pearson (1986) differentiated between mutual help/self-help groups and support groups on the basis of professional group leadership. He pointed out that any group that "truly functions as a group involves mutual help" (p. 66). Therefore, a distinction must be made between professionally organized and led groups which he calls support groups and groups which are couched in the context of "fellow sufferers giving aid to and receiving assistance from each other" (p. 66) which he calls mutual help or self-help groups. Surgeon General C. Everett Koop supports this distinction in his *Workshop on Self-Help and Public Health* (1990) in which he defined self help groups as "self governing groups whose members share a common health concern and give each other support and material aid, charge either no or only a very small fee for membership and place high value on experiential knowledge in the belief that it provides special understanding of a situation. In addition, such groups may also be involved in information, education, material aid, and social advocacy in their communities" (Klaw & Humphreys, 2004, p. 630–631).

The rise of self-help and mutual aid groups in contemporary society has been identified by Katz (1981) as an emerging social movement. At the time, he estimated that 500,000 self-help groups existed in the United States with a membership of 23 million people. That number has since grown extensively. A more recent survey conducted by Kessler, Mickelson and Zhao (1997) found that 7% or about 11 million Americans participated in self-help groups in the year prior to the survey, and 18% of adults have done so at some point in their lifetime. There are currently more than 800 self-help organizations in the United States that address a plethora of health and social problems and most sponsor self-help groups (Klaw & Humphreys, 2004). Such figures make group workers take note. What is the appeal of these groups, and in what capacity do professional group workers relate?

Silverman's (1985) definition of mutual help groups gives us some clues to answer the first question.

A mutual help group is an aggregate of people sharing a common problem or predicament who come together for mutual support and constructive action to solve their shared problem. The help offered is based on the participants' experience in coping with their problems and is not the result of any professional training or education group members possess. (p. 237)

The appeal, merit, and practicality of these groups are based on members "having been there." Examples of such groups abound starting with Alcoholics Anonymous and all the other anonymouses (narcotics, gamblers, overeaters, etc.). Physical ailments (kidney transplants, cancer, spinal bifida, HIV positive/AIDS), physical disabilities (paraplegics, amputees), and losses of various types (death, divorce) generate many mutual help groups. Other self-help groups have emerged for those who have lived or do live with and/or care for people with illnesses or difficult circumstances or conditions. Examples include Adult Children of Alcoholics (ACOA), parents of HIV positive/AIDS patients or other ailments and caretakers of aging parents.

While many such groups abound and are appealing, the role of the professional group leader is not all that clear. In fact, Shapiro and Shapiro (1985) warned that the trend toward population specific specialization in group work has produced "an increased reliance on self-help and ingroup chauvinism" based on "an underlying notion that only someone who shares an affliction can successfully treat it" (p. 85)—a trend that is counter to the values and power of professional group work. Traditionally, competition, skepticism, and distrust existed between lay experts and professionals who have vied for the same client turf. However, some positive shifts are occurring. Some of the reasons for the shift are the efforts to delineate between professionally led and nonprofessionally led groups, the sharing of expertise both ways, and the concern for valid research to document therapeutic impact.

For more in depth discussion of this group category you are referred to the May, 1986 (Volume 11, Number 2) special issue of the *Journal for Specialists in Group Work* edited by Richard Pearson and to Silverman's (1985); chapter 12 on mutual help groups in *The Group Worker's Handbook: Varieties of Group Experience* edited by Robert Conyne, and Klaw and Humphreys' chapter on The Role of Peer-Led Mutual Help Groups in Promoting Health and Well-Being in DeLucia-Waack et al. (2004).

Peer Facilitated Counseling Groups

A small but established development in group counseling that has gained acceptance and support in a variety of environments from schools to prisons to community settings is the use of peer counselors as group leaders or coleaders. These groups are distinctive from self-help groups because the designated leader, though a peer, is trained by a professional group worker and supervised. Kranzow (1973) noted that in peer facilitated groups members frequently are responsive to peer pressures and controls. Peer leaders tend to speak the same language literally and figuratively and members find it easier to identify with and trust the peer leader. Blaker and Samo (1973) pointed out that information gained from peers is usually more impressive than the same information provided by experts. Peer led groups also are applicable to all age levels (Brown, 1965; Gumaer, 1973; Hamburg & Varenhorst, 1972; Vriend, 1969).

Counselors who utilize the peer facilitator approach are themselves extremely important to its success. They must be involved in the selection and training of peer counselors and must be responsible for their supervision once the groups are under way (Tindall, 1989; Tindall & Gray, 1985, 1989). They serve as a referral source and as a resource in crisis situations. Counselors who pursue this course of action therefore are not only going to make their own jobs easier, but will be able to expand the helping function in their settings.

Consultation Groups

The counselor's consultant role can be immensely expanded through effective use of the group process. As a group specialist the counselor's expertise can be utilized by larger numbers of people across varied settings. In fact, Reddy (1985) emphasized the utility of group expertise in the form of a rhetorical question: "Does 'group specialist' signify a profession or does it represent a set of skills to be used by a broad range of professionals in many different fields?" (p. 105). For our purposes the answer is yes to both questions, and the counselor's consultant function is his or her primary means of demonstrating proof. In the schools, for example, parents, teachers, administrators, and other professionals can all be conveniently gathered under the umbrella of consultation in the interest of improving their own effectiveness and promoting the welfare of clients. In business and industry consulting groups can be an integral part of employee assistance programs and personnel work (Kirby, 1985).

The leader in these groups performs most leadership functions with specific emphasis on moderating and facilitating the process. The purpose and composition of the group varies and session length depends on the nature of the focus. Membership and group size are determined on the basis of relationship to the focus for which the group is organized. The two basic types of consulting groups are the case centered consulting group and the C-group (Dinkmeyer & Muro, 1971).

Case Centered Consultation Groups The counselor organizes case centered consultation groups when specific problem situations or cases arise that need the immediate attention of outside resources to facilitate resolution. Persons involved in these groups include significant others who have some direct relationship to the problem situation or person being discussed. Additional members should be drawn from resource personnel who have expertise that relates to the problem. The exact membership of the group, however, is dependent on the nature of the initiating problem.

The main focus in these groups is on clarifying the problem and the relationship of each member to it and then, through environmental or systemic intervention involving a plan devised by members, acting to deal with that problem. The counselor's role is to facilitate discussion, contribute to it, and serve as a catalyst in getting the group to deal directly with the problem. The leader should first attempt to orient the group toward expressing their perceptions about the problem. Once understanding and consensus has been largely achieved, the leader then can turn the group to consideration of alternative solutions leading to a specific plan of action (Kirby, 1985). If effectively conducted, these groups can have a definite impact on improving communication and developing respect between the various participants.

C-Groups

The C-group, developed by Dinkmeyer and Muro (1971), combines didactic and experiential procedures to provide group members with practical, relevant training that generalizes to their professional lives. This approach is labeled C-group because many of the factors that account for its success begin with C. These components are described as follows:

1. The group *collaborates*, works together on mutual concerns.
2. The group *consults*. The interaction within the group helps members develop new approaches to issues or problems.
3. The group *clarifies* for each member what it is he or she really believes and how congruent or incongruent his or her behavior is with what he or she believes.
4. The group *confronts*. The group expects each individual to see their own self, purposes, attitudes and to be willing to confront other members of the group.
5. The group is *concerned* and *cares*. It shows that it is involved.
6. The group is *confidential* insofar as personal material discussed in the group is not carried out of the group.
7. The group develops a *commitment to change*.

Participants in the group are concerned with recognizing what they can really only change themselves. They are expected to develop a specific commitment involving an action they will take before the next C-group meeting to change their approach to a problem (Dinkmeyer & Muro, 1971, pp. 272–273).

This type of consulting group is useful for all professionals in the helping fields. Participants can develop their helping skills and work out solutions to common problems. Within the school, it's particularly useful for teachers. The emphasis on the teacher-advisor system in schools for example, stresses the need for teachers to develop their helping and group leadership skills.

The C-group can be an effective method of working with families. It can help parents develop the ability to relate to their children and find creative solutions to their problems. The counselor can use these groups to help these people realize they have much in common with other parents and also have the ability to help each other overcome their problems in raising children. The C-group model is also adaptable to business/industry and professional agencies where supervisors, coworkers, and colleagues can be assembled for purposes of addressing common problems and issues.

Growth Groups

Growth groups are organized for the purpose of helping psychologically healthy people become more sensitive, aware, fully functioning, and self-actualized through the use of the group process. Members are assumed to be responsible for themselves and capable of handling ambiguous situations and intense personal interaction. They grow by expanding their levels of personal effectiveness.

A great deal of controversy exists over what constitutes a growth group. Certainly titles are no indication of what is involved in the process. The most common types of growth groups, however, are the sensitivity group or T-group and the encounter group. Although commentaries on each of these groups abound, the terminology tends to be so similar that it is often difficult to ferret out distinctions.

One distinction is that the T-group has a distinct point of origin emanating from the work of Kurt Lewin and developed by the National Training laboratory (NTL) in Bethel, Maine (Ward & Litchy, 2004). Therefore it has an eminently traceable history, whereas the encounter group has grown out of a broad range of social and psychological endeavors. Significant contributions have certainly been made by Gestalt psychology, by Carl Rogers, and by Institutes such as Esalen in Big Sur, California, but the encounter movement is still a melting pot in which influences are quickly subsumed. Beyond that distinction, however, the encounter group places its primary emphasis on the individual's growth in the group, while sensitivity groups stress individual learning and learning about the group process as well. From this point on, differences become more a matter of degrees than contrasts. Encounter groups use more confrontation, while T-groups emphasize awareness, sensitivity, and learning about self and others. Birnbaum (1969) affirmed that in encounter groups "emphasis is on direct exposure of beliefs and feelings that usually are not put on public display by individuals. The objective is to stimulate an exchange that is inhibited by a minimum of reserve and defensiveness in order to achieve a maximum of openness and honesty" (p. 83). Encounter groups, on the whole, tend to be more intense and emotional than sensitivity groups. Encounter groups lean toward a problem oriented focus while T-groups tend to be more process oriented. This focus on process is implied in the definition of a T-group by Bradford, Gibb, and Benne (1964):

> A T-group is a relatively unstructured group in which individuals partici-
> pate as learners. The data for learning are not outside these individuals
> or remote from their immediate experience with the T-group. The data
> are transactions among members, their own behavior in the group, as
> they struggle to create a productive and viable organization, a miniature
> society. (p. 1)

Similarities associated with all growth groups are numerous. They are characterized by open, close, direct psychological contact that stresses spontaneity, freedom of expression, and intense interaction. The focus is on the here and now action of the group and ambiguity is commonly used to generate interaction. Methods utilize verbal and nonverbal techniques aimed at expanding the members' conscious awareness and zeroing in on their feelings and perceptions. One of the major issues in growth groups is the development of trust so that members can be as truly themselves in the group as possible. The time span of growth groups is usually brief but intense, ranging from one to two week workshops or weekends during which members spend many hours together to ongoing sessions over a specific period of time. Spending hours together without interruption often heightens the intensity of interaction. Finally, growth groups are face to face groups with no organizational structure and no imposed tasks and rely heavily on feedback and reinforcement as the tools for self-learning.

Growth groups peaked in popularity during the mid-1960s and early 1970s and in retrospect created two major issues for the field of group work (Dies, 1985). The distinction between growth and remediation was blurred and many of the leaders particularly of the more intensive group experiences had dubious credentials. Thus, the issue of quality control always must be raised with growth groups relative to both the nature of the experience and the leadership.

Vriend (1985) noted the critical importance of this issue by delineating between the encounter group model (model B) and the counseling group model (model A). Encounter groups develop their own norms and content, evolve through inevitable stages, function with a facilitator who guides the process but does not determine its nature, and cause (allow) change in members. Counseling groups presuppose a trained group leader who takes responsibility for and determines the structure of the experience, teaches group members therapeutic group behavior, and bases interventions on a rationale emanating from counseling theory (p. 66). Vriend contended that the training of group leaders must be based on the counseling group model for the profession to survive.

Growth Groups in Schools

The encounter group per se has no relevance to the vast majority of counseling programs in schools because of its intense confrontative nature, its assumption of adult maturity, and the time arrangements required to use it. And the impact of encounter groups is hard to determine. Birnbaum (1969) points out this basic weakness, "Because of the failure to follow through with concrete plans for specific action, it (the encounter group) too often remains a memorable experience, but not one that produces change" (p. 96). Some of the encounter methods, however, are useful to the group counselor and can be integrated into group counseling to the mutual benefit of the members and the group process.

Sensitivity groups also have little general relevance to the school. This is mainly because of the misconceptions people have about T-groups as well as for some of the same reasons noted above. However, in specific situations and in certain clearly defined areas a case can be made for using them. Because T-groups stress both self-learning and understanding of the group process they can help well adjusted students become more cognizant of their own self-characteristics and improve their human relations skills. As a social laboratory, it allows group members to gain insight into their own behaviors, develop better understanding of others, and increase their awareness of processes that help and hinder group action. Schmidt (n.d.) described two basic T-group concepts that give the method advantages:

1. People can learn best about themselves by producing behavior, becoming aware of that behavior, analyzing the behavior and its consequences, and then drawing generalizations.
2. People can learn about their own assumptions and values by being placed in a setting where there is considerable ambiguity. The ambiguity permits them to project their own meanings into the situation and to compare their projections with those of their colleagues.

If counselors do decide to use sensitivity type groups, the best procedure is to label them with a less auspicious title and clarify precisely the nature of the process and its objectives before starting the groups.

Conyne's Typology of Group Work Grid

Conyne (1985) has made an admirable effort to categorize the variety in group work by creating the Group Work Grid presented in Figure 10.2. Responding to the observation that "generally missing from our major texts (on group work) is attention to the range of group experiences available today" (p. x), he created this matrix to conceptualize group work as a means of expanding the horizon of group work and consolidating practical understanding about group work. The Group Work Grid is comprised of two major interactive dimensions: (1) the purpose of the group work intervention and (2) the level of the group work intervention. *Purpose* is further delineated into correction and enhancement and *level* is divided into individual, interpersonal, organizational, and community subcategories. Within the purpose dimension is embedded the process factor of whether the group is personal (psyche-process) or task (socio-process) in orientation. The result is a working model of group typology that has breadth and depth. Each section of the grid represents a type of group that is explicated in the book Conyne edited and entitled, *The Group Worker's Handbook: Varieties*

		Intervention Level Emphasis				
		Correction		Enhancement	
		Personal	Task	Personal	Task
Individual	Type	Personality Change	Rehabilitation	Personal Growth	Skill Development
	Eg.	*Psychotherapy*	*Remedial Social Skills*	*Personal Development*	*Human Relations Skills Training*
Interpersonal	Type	Interpersonal Problem Solving	Resocialization	Interpersonal Growth	Learning
	Eg.	*Counseling*	*Social Control*	*T-Groups*	*Systematic Group Discussion*
Organization	Type	Employee Change	Organizational Change	Management Development	Organization Development
	Eg.	*Employee Assistance*	*Social Climate*	*Team Development*	*Quality Circles*
Community-Population	Type	Secondary/ Tertiary Prevention	Community Change	Health Promotion/ Primary Prevention	Community Development
	Eg.	*Manual Help*	*Action*	*Life Transition*	*Futuring*

Figure 10.2 Conyne's group work grid.

of Group Experience (1985) to which you are referred for further understanding of both the variety of groups and their specific nature.

Client Populations and Group Work

The interaction between specific client populations and settings is another basis for delineating groups. Each client group and setting flavors the group process with unique dynamics and characteristics that leaders must take into account and work with to generate effective therapeutic impact. The parameters of this book do not allow for explication of the almost endless variety of group possibilities based on population and setting, but Seligman (1982) has made an estimable attempt to present a representative sample. You are referred to his book *Group Psychotherapy and Counseling With Specific Populations* as an adjunctive resource in differentiating group work (Trotzer, 1984). In addition, the *Journal for Specialists in Group Work* has made a conscientious effort to publish articles about group work practice that represent the full gamut of settings, group types, and populations. Finally, DeLucia-Waack, Gerrity, Kalodner, and Riva (2004) give extensive consideration to examples of counseling and psychotherapy groups across settings, age groups, populations and topics including multicultural groups in Parts III-VI of their book *Handbook of Group Counseling and Psychotherapy.*

Learning Activities

The following activities can be used to compare and contrast the basic characteristics of socio- and psyche-process groups. First, divide the class into small groups of four to eight members. Depending on the number of groups you have, give half the groups a socio-process activity such as the NASA space project and the other groups a psyche-process activity like the here and now face. Next, repeat the process, reversing the activities. Follow-up discussion should focus on distinctions between and similarities of the two processes. In additional discussion, the class can compare the effects of having one process precede the other. In this way, elements of leadership strategy in using these processes can be identified.

NASA Space Project

First, administer the NASA Decision Form individually to each group member. After each person has completed an evaluation of the items, give the group another Decision Form and read the instructions for Decision by Consensus. Instruct the group to fill out the group decision form based on the discussion in the group.

You are a member of a space crew scheduled to rendezvous with a mother ship on the lighted surface of the moon. Due to mechanical difficulties, however, your ship was forced to land at a spot some 200 miles from the rendezvous point. During re-entry and landing, much of the equipment aboard was damaged and, since survival depends on reaching the mother ship, the most critical items available must be chosen for the 200-mile trip. Below are the 15 items left intact and undamaged after landing. Your task is to rank order them in terms of their importance in allowing your crew to reach the rendezvous point. Place the number 1 by the most important item, number 2 by the second most important, and so on through number 15, the least important.

_____ Box of matches
_____ Food concentrate
_____ 50 feet of nylon rope
_____ Parachute silk
_____ Portable heating unit
_____ Two .45 caliber pistols
_____ One case dehydrated milk
_____ Two 100 pound tanks of oxygen
_____ Stellar map (of the moon's constellation)
_____ Life raft
_____ Magnetic compass
_____ 5 gallons of water
_____ Signal flares
_____ First aid kit containing injection needles
_____ Solar powered FM receiver-transmitter

From "Lost on the Moon: A Decision Making Problem," *Today's Education* (1969). Reprinted by permission.

NASA Decision Form

Research in group dynamics has revealed that the manner in which groups utilize their member resources is a critical determinant of how they perform. In this exercise you are asked to use the technique of group consensus. This means that the ranking for each of the 15 survival items must be agreed upon by each member before it becomes a part of the group decision. Consensus is difficult to reach. Therefore, not every ranking will meet with everyone's complete approval. Unanimity, however, is not a goal (although it may be achieved unintentionally), and it is not necessary, for example, that every person be as satisfied as he or she might be if he or she had complete control over what the group decides.

What should be stressed is the individual's ability to accept a given ranking on the basis of logic, whatever his or her level of satisfaction—and his or her willingness to entertain such a judgment as feasible. When the point is reached at which all group members feel this way as a minimal criterion, you may assume that you have reached a consensus as it is defined here and the judgment may be entered as a group decision. This means, in effect, that a single person can block the group, if he or she thinks it necessary.; At the same time, it is assumed that this option will be employed in the best sense of reciprocity. Here are some guidelines to use in achieving consensus:

1. Avoid arguing for your own ranking. Present your position as lucidly and logically as possible, but consider seriously the reactions of the group in any subsequent presentations of the same point.
2. Avoid win-lose stalemates in the discussion of rankings. Discard the notion that someone must win and someone must lose in the discussion; when impasses occur, look for the next most acceptable alternative for both parties.
3. Avoid changing your mind only in order to avoid conflict and to reach agreement and harmony. Withstand pressures to yield that have no objective or logically sound foundation. Strive for enlightened flexibility; avoid outright capitulation.
4. Avoid conflict-reducing techniques such as the majority vote, averaging, bargaining, coin flipping, and the like. Treat differences of opinion as indicative of an incomplete sharing of relevant information on someone's part and press for additional sharing—either about task or emotional data—where it seems in order.
5. View differences of opinion as both natural and helpful rather than as a hindrance in decision-making. Generally, the more ideas expressed, the greater the likelihood of conflict will be; but the richer the array of resources will be as well.
6. View initial agreement as suspect. Explore the reasons underlying apparent agreements; make sure that people have arrived at similar solutions for either the same basic reasons or for complementary reasons before incorporating such solutions in the group decision.
7. Avoid subtle forms of influence and decision modification; for example, when a dissenting member finally agrees, do not feel that he or she must be rewarded by having his or her own way on some later point.
8. Be willing to entertain the possibility that your group can excel at its decision task; avoid doom saying and negative thinking.

From "Decision by Consensus," Jay Hall (1969). Reprinted by permission.

NASA Key
Decision by Consensus

Little or no use on moon	15	Box of matches
Supply of daily food required	4	Food concentrate
Useful in tying injured together, help in climbing	6	50 feet of nylon rope
Shelter against sun's rays	8	Parachute silk
Useful only if party landed on dark side	13	Portable heating unit
Self-propulsion devices could be made from them	11	Two .45 caliber pistols
Food, mixed with water for drinking	12	One case dehydrated milk
Fill respiration requirement	1	Two 100-pound tanks of oxygen
One of the principal means of finding directions	3	Stellar map (of the moon's constellation)
CO_2 bottles for self-propulsion across chasms, etc.	9	Life raft
Probably no magnetized poles; thus, useless	14	Magnetic compass
Replenishes loss from sweating, etc.	2	5 gallons of water
Distress call when line of sight possible	10	Signal flares
Oral pills and injection medicine	7	First aid kit containing injection needles
Distress signal transmitter; possible communication with mother ship	5	Solar-powered FM receiver-transmitter

From "Lost on the Moon: A Decision-Making Problem," *Today's Education* (1969). Reprinted by permission.

Under no circumstances should individuals change their own answers. After the group has completed the task, give them the key and have them calculate their individual scores by totaling the absolute value of the difference between their ranking and the key's ranking on each item. The instructor can calculate the group score to demonstrate the scoring process. The lower the scores, the more accurate the ranking of the items in terms of their practical relevance on the moon. Have the group answer questions such as the following:

1. Was the group or the individual more effective in performing the task?
2. Who emerged as the leader in the group?
3. Who seemed to be the expert in the group?
4. Who talked most and least in the group discussion?

5. Who seemed to get the group to accept his or her opinion most often? How did he or she do it?

You may wish to have members discuss these questions prior to determining their scores and then use the scores as a means of assessing the accuracy of the group's perception.

Here and Now Face

The here and now face (Kranzow, 1973) is a psyche-process activity designed to help members disclose and discuss their feelings and emotions. Instruct the members to draw a face that represents the feelings they are experiencing at the present time. Below the face, have them write a verbal description of those feelings and the reasons for them. The discussion should include both what the feelings are and why they exist in the person at the present time. Some leaders use a format statement like "I am feeling (member fills in what) because (member fills in why)." This activity is a means of generating a discussion of the importance of feelings in our lives and brings the group into personal contact with one another.

Cooperation Squares

Cooperation is one of the key components of any task oriented group, and this activity focuses specifically on the factors involved in working together. Make puzzle squares out of cardboard, following the patterns illustrated in Figure 10.3. Six-inch squares are a satisfactory size. Divide the class into groups of five and give each group a package containing five envelopes with equal numbers of pieces but from different puzzles, (five different puzzles to a group). Then read the following instructions and rules:

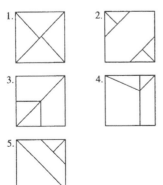

Figure 10.3 Puzzle design

In this package are five envelopes, each of which contains pieces of cardboard for forming squares. When the leader gives the signal to begin, it is the task of your group to form five squares of equal size. The task will not be completed until each member has a perfect square of the same size as that held by the other members. The following rules must be followed in working on the problem:

1. No member may speak. The task is to be completed entirely without words.
2. No member may ask another member for a puzzle piece or in any way signal that another person is to give her or him a piece.
3. Members may, however, give pieces to other members.

The instructor's task is to see that the rules are adhered to. Follow-up discussion generated by this activity usually centers around the importance of cooperation and communication in effective group functioning. Conversation may also turn to a consideration of good and bad rules.

Life Picture Map

This psyche-process activity (Kranzow, 1973) is oriented toward helping members develop the time competence perspective so important in self-actualization (Johnson, 1972). Ask group members to draw an illustrated road map that represents their past, present, and future. The map should pictorially depict experiences the members have had, obstacles they have overcome, what their present lives are like, what their goals are for the future, and what barriers stand in the way of accomplishing those goals. Upon completion of the drawings, have the members share their maps with the group, explaining the various illustrations. Follow-up discussion should just be allowed to evolve from a consideration of the pictures.

Paint a Group Picture

This activity essentially combines many of the elements of both psyche-process and socio-process groups. It focuses on the nature of the group itself, its personality and atmosphere, but uses a task approach to do so. Divide the total group into groups of four to eight and supply the subgroups with paper and paints (crayons also will suffice). Ask them to paint a picture as a team that reflects the personality of their subgroup. The picture should be creative and integrate individual efforts. Some leaders require the groups to decide on a group name and sign the picture with it. Materials need not be limited to paints. The group can use a variety of media to make a group sculpture or group collage. Discussion should revolve around the experiences of group members in this activity. Feelings of shyness, embarrassment, and artistic inferiority are common. Information about who got the choice spot on the painting, the role of wit, and who emerged as leader also are germane to the discussion. If several groups have participated, each group can present and explain their picture to the rest and describe the interaction that took place.

Eight Topics for Group Discussion

The following eight topics are useful in generating personal discussion in groups and also can be used effectively in determining the locale of problems. The topics can be handled one at a time or in combination. Members can use them in interviewing each other, or they can be incorporated into a general group exercise to stimulate discussion.

1. List three people who have influenced you greatly in your life.
2. Briefly describe three experiences you have had that you feel you will remember the rest of your life.
3. List three things at which you are particularly good.
4. List three things that really interest you.
5. List three things that you would like to accomplish in the future.
6. List three decisions you have made that have changed your life in some way.
7. List three values or beliefs that are important to you and that you live by.
8. List three problems that you have right now that you have not been able to resolve.

The number of things required in each instruction can vary, and directions can be added or substituted depending on the leader's interests and the nature of the group. How each topic is handled is also the prerogative of the leader.

11
Organizing Group Work

Any amount of group knowledge, training, and experience is useless if counselors cannot implement the group process into the framework of their work environments. Even the most conscientious and enthusiastic attempts to use groups will fail if appropriate methods of organizing a group program are not utilized.

Put Ecology First in Planning

Conyne and Bemak (2004c) make a solid case for group work as an independent entity in human systems and particularly in mental health practice. For that reason they espouse an ecological perspective as the foundation of planning, performing, and processing group work and as the basis for organizing group programs.

> A group is a contextualized, living, social system through which information is produced and processed, always established within a multitude of changing forces. A group never stands alone, but rather, is always influenced by and influencing its context. (p. 9)

This viewpoint promotes the ASGW (2000) definition of group work expounded by Conyne, Wilson, and Ward (1997):

> Group work is a broad professional practice that refers to the giving of help or the accomplishment of tasks in a group setting. It involves the application of group theory and process by a capable professional practitioner to assist an interdependent collection of people to reach their mutual goals which may be personal, interpersonal, or task-related in nature. (p.14)

Therefore, whether organizing a group program or setting up a particular group, the objective of the group worker is generate an entity that is ecologically effective in creating "a dynamic, contextualized social system that is productive (task groups), educational and skill-building (psychoeducation groups), adept at interpersonal problem solving (counseling groups), or psychological reconstruction (psychotherapy groups)" (Conyne & Bemak, 2004c, p. 12). To do so, the group worker must espouse an ecological perspective and conduct an ecological assessment, the purposes of which are to become informed of the needs of perspective members, assess the appropriateness of the group process to meet those needs as well as determine the relevance of the proposed group in the systemic context where it will be conducted. In doing so, the reciprocal effect of informing the members and the system of the availability and relevance of the proposed group or groups will also be realized. Consequently, when the motives, message, and mission of the group worker are ecologically sound, the planning and implementation of groups and group programs will flow smoothly.

Perspective of the Group Worker: Outreach

To effectively organize a group, counselors need to develop a dynamic perspective of their role and function. That perspective can be summarized as *outreach*. "Too often, we (counselors) have donned our clinical robes within the safe confines of a remote office and waited for the world to beat a path to our door. The counselor who would work with groups cannot afford the luxury of solitude—it is he/she who must make contact with...possible clientele" (Dinkmeyer & Muro, 1971, p. 140).

The counselor must take the responsibility for building a group program based on the knowledge and confidence that the group approach has a great deal to offer. In all probability, most administrators, staff members, and clients will be cognizant of neither the potential of the group process nor the counselor's own expertise in that area.

Another reason for the outreach perspective is to assure the counselor of a solid foundation on which to build a group program. Too often counselors filled with professional zeal have ventured forth on group missions without a clear conception of objectives in mind and have found themselves in the deep water of professional criticism without a lifeboat of accountability to rescue them. To establish groups simply on the merit of the group process itself is not sufficient. As Mahler (1969) pointed out, the fundamental question that must be asked is "for what purpose is this group being organized?" The outreach perspective provides necessary information about the needs of clients in the systems in which they interact so that accurate and clearly defined goals can be established to answer that question. Outreach is the key because it enables the counselor to enter the domain of clients, to penetrate their life spaces, and make contact directly with people and factors relating to their problems. In this manner counselors can not only clarify their own roles and the nature of the group process but also make both of them relevant to their clientele and their environments.

The purpose of this chapter is to provide the counselor with practical methods for setting up a group program. The full gamut of administrative procedures related to group organization and composition are considered. Material for this chapter emanates from a clinical and experiential base bolstered by the ever increasing empirical foundation provided by group research. In many cases definitive guidelines for use in organizing group programs remain in a formative state. However, the wealth of clinical knowledge derived from practice provides an invaluable resource in lieu of and in conjunction with research findings (Corey 1995, Corey & Corey, 2006; Dinkmeyer & Muro, 1979; Gazda, 1984a; Gladding, 2003; Jacobs, Harvill, & Masson, 2002; Mahler, 1969; Ohlsen, Horne, & Lawe, 1988; Yalom, 1995). (For an excellent, in depth account of organizing an effective and comprehensive group program in an elementary school read Litrell and Peterson's (2002) article detailing the efforts of Claudia Vangstad in an Oregon Elementary school.)

Organizational development of group programs is discussed from the perspective of schools or institutional settings and embellished with considerations from agency/practice settings.

Determining the Need

The best way to get a group program off on the right foot is to determine where a need for one exists. Counselors should not organize groups simply because it is part of their professional role or because counselor educators have told them to do so. Groups should only be proposed after the counselor has done some background investigation to determine what the problems are and whether they can be effectively worked with using a group approach. Counselors have many sources of information in this regard, and they should make use of all of them to obtain as comprehensive a picture of needs and problems as possible. In school situations the major sources are students (potential clients), teachers, learning specialists, school psychologists and social workers, administrators, families, student records, and data bases. In agency/practice settings clients and referral sources such as physicians, pastors, attorneys, and professional colleagues both in and out of your own setting are useful resources. The counselor must keep two guidelines in mind to successfully conduct this needs assessment (1) the nature of the approach must be outreach, going out to make contact with the various populations and talking with them on their home ground; and (2) the purpose of this contact is to listen and understand not to suggest. After the counselor has accumulated input and evaluated it carefully, then the time is right for proposals and suggestions.

Potential Group Members

Potential members are the most obvious sources of information and in many respects the most accurate. In schools, of course, these potential members are students. School counselors can use their normal role contacts with students in guidance and counseling situations to develop a conception of the general concerns and problems of the population they work with. This in itself is not enough, however, since many students will never darken the door of a counselor's office for any reason. The counselor must get out and mingle with students, holding informal conversations with them in the areas where students congregate, such as the student commons, the gym, or hallways. Setting up rap sessions in some classes simply to get student opinions is effective, and even establishing a rap corner or rap room near student gathering places so they can drop by and chat is helpful. Some counselors have created Web sites to conduct surveys and set up chat rooms that students can log in to and talk about issues, concerns, or questions.

More formal procedures might involve the use of survey instruments. Open ended questionnaires that stimulate reactions (including statements like "the thing I worry most about is…") can be used anonymously to tap client opinions of needs. Problem checklists, your own or standardized ones like the Mooney Problem Checklist, can be administered to determine what areas give clients the most concern. In many cases, designing the survey instrument yourself is preferable because you can include items that are appropriate to the unique environment in which you work. Another effective method is to use the "agree-disagree" format (see Figure 2.5) and design statements dealing with specific problem areas (like problems with parents) and then let the clients come up with their own conception of the most accurate statements. These methods help the counselor determine whether the group approach is appropriate or not and for what reasons.

In agency/practice settings one's own caseload is the most viable source of potential group members especially as individual cases emerge that have commonality or needs that are conducive to a group approach. Web sites are particularly effective in soliciting input and information that is directly related to the formation of groups.

The importance of understanding the needs of clients before starting groups cannot be overstated. Ponzo (1991) has aptly warned of the dangers of group work that does not address client needs: "Just as nutritious food has no value if it is hostile to the consumer's palate, so too are curative factors or critical factors rendered impotent if they do not match the discriminating wants, needs and desires of our clients" (p. 22).

Faculty/Staff Referral Sources

Another school source of valuable information that often goes untapped is teachers. Teachers represent an aggregate of individuals whose cumulative experience in relating to students far surpasses that of any other group. The counselor who cultivates a positive working relationship with them, meets them on their own ground (classroom, faculty lounge, *their* offices, and hallways), and approaches them with a sincere interest in learning from their experience will find the results beneficial. Counselors can use many approaches to obtain vital information from teachers. They can ask permission to attend various department meetings and listen as they discuss students and problems related to their particular areas of interest and expertise. Organizing voluntary rap sessions during coffee breaks and free periods also can be effective. Socializing is still the most accepted and best informal way of making contact. Some counselors have developed suggestion boxes so students and teachers can express their concerns and ideas to the counselor. Developing this relationship with teachers helps them feel more a part of the process of organizing the group program rather than feeling it is imposed on them. They begin to be supportive of it rather than threatened by it.

In agency/practice settings directly contacting referral sources to solicit their input as to the types of problems or issues that need attention can be very productive. Once referral sources realize your interest and emphasis is emanating from their input, both your relationships and your client referrals will improve.

Education Specialists

Other resource groups of vital importance in the school are the education and learning specialists. Specialists in learning disabilities and giftedness, school psychologists, social workers, and other adjunct educational staff can be polled for input relative to the clientele they serve and problems they address. Attending Individual Education Planning (IEP) meetings, parent conferences, community agency consultations, and other such interactive meetings can provide critical information about special problems and special populations.

Administrators

Sitting down with school administrators for a few minutes of straight talk will usually produce positive results. Administrators inevitably have a focus group of students they are particularly concerned about (usually because they are a pain in the neck, represent the educational system's failure to work, or are a threat to it). If the counselor approaches the administration indicating an interest in helping and a concern for the students, administrators will usually respond, even if they have reservations about counseling or the group process. The counselor must be careful not to make any promises at this point, however, since that might create expectations that are unrealistic. The information received should be contemplated for a time before the counselor returns with positive suggestions and alternatives. Counselors who approach administrators this way often realize greater respect and support from the administration. Administrators soon realize the counselor is making efforts to help students and also to improve the efficiency and effectiveness of the school. Colleagues, administrators, and board members in community agency or private practice environments can provide the same type of input as school officials.

◊ *Families*

Families represent another source of information for counselors. Counselors in schools find students' parents especially helpful, but more difficult to contact than other sources. The counselor can make use of incidental contacts with parents to garner their opinions and can use the consultation function with parents to do so as well. Questionnaires and surveys, preferably brief, can be sent to parents and usually result in an adequate percentage of returns. Such efforts have been greatly expanded with the advent of email as long as such contact has been cleared and approved on all levels including administration and the parents. The counselor's participation in parent programs, parent nights, and parent school organizations (e.g., parent/teacher associations) is a valid use of counselor time. Counselors can organize sharing/discussion sessions around topics related to student problems, use the "agree-disagree" strategy, and conduct surveys as part of the regular agenda. In any case, families should always be considered as a crucial source of information, since their perspectives are definitely a factor in many of the concerns clients will express in counseling groups.

◊ *Student Records and Data Bases*

Within schools, counselors can find information in student records and data bases that is valuable to needs assessment with respect to groups. Access to such information must be attained with permission and with a clearance with regard to privacy and confidentiality. The best approach is to do such processing in an organized manner, using a specific set of criteria for determining problems. If the counselor can organize guidelines for the kind of data being looked for, an aide can do the work of tabulating. Given the efficiency of computer technology information processing that used to be tedious and minimally productive has now become relatively efficient and effective. The best method is to define specific problem behaviors or student characteristics and then accumulate frequencies based on comments and demographic data. However, whenever a data base or personal information resource is used be sure to do so with the latest version of public records laws and privacy regulations in mind.

Examples of data that provide cues to needs that groups may address are demographics on single parent and remarried families where adjustment factors related to death or divorce and blended family living are prominent. Children who are coded as exceptional (learning disabled or gifted) often manifest adjustment issues, absences, or other characteristics that may signal problems.

Once the counselor has accumulated information from all these sources and evaluated it, a decision can be made, based on needs, as to how groups can be used and what specific problems will be addressed. At this point, the counselor is ready to take the next step of setting goals and recontacting the various groups to inform them of program proposals.

Establishing Goals

Goals are extremely important to group counseling because they provide a direction for both the leader and members and supply an appropriate yardstick for assessing the value of the group experience. Goals fall into two major categories—general group goals and specific individual goals. *General goals* refer to the overall objectives of the group and are the basic reasons for which it is formed. *Specific goals* are those directly related to individual members and their personal lives. The relationship between the two has been expressed by Dinkmeyer and Muro (1971): "The group counselor and the group must be flexible enough to allow individuals to work on personal concerns, and broad general goals of the group must not be so rigid that the individual is sacrificed to some theoretical construct" (p. 139).

The most important consideration is to determine if group work and a particular type of group is the most appropriate means of dealing with problems or issues revealed by the needs assessment. The counselor must then make sure that goals are in accord with and matched to the needs of prospective members. The counselor's professional judgment must be utilized in this process. In regard to counseling issues, Mahler (1969) pinpointed a number of situations that lend themselves to individual counseling, group counseling, or both; they provide useful guidelines in making the decision to use group counseling. These situations are detailed in Figure 11.1. Counselors are not to view group counseling as a cure all; however, they are to make specific professional decisions for or against its use. In this way the possibility of success is enhanced and the usefulness of the group approach assured.

Some of the general goals that have relevance to group counseling are as follows:

1. To develop relationships that will help individual members meet their developmental and psychological needs;
2. To help members in their identity seeking process (Mahler, 1969);
3. To help members change undesirable behaviors (Dustin & George, 1973);
4. To help members develop social skills and resolve problems in social relationships;

❝ Individual Counseling Tends To Be More Appropriate:

1. When the client has a crisis problem that is very complicated, both as to causes and possible solutions.
2. When confidentiality is highly essential to protect the client and others.
3. When working through the meaning of test results in terms of one's self-concept.
4. When fear of talking in a group is so extreme that the person does not seem to be able to get started in the group.
5. When an individual is grossly ineffective in relating to his peers and sets off such a strong immediate reaction that the group is more likely to be rejective than acceptant.
6. When a person's awareness and understanding of his or her own feelings, motivations, and patterns of behavior are very limited or so complicated that he or she feels lost and unable to share in a group.
7. When sexual behavior, particularly of a deviant nature, is involved.
8. When one's need for attention and recognition is too extreme to be managed in the group situation.

◦ Group Counseling Tends To Be More Valuable in the Following Areas:

1. Learning to better understand a variety of other people and finding out how others perceive things.
2. Learning a deeper respect for other people, particularly those who are different in many ways from oneself.
3. Gaining greater social skills in talking and relating to others.
4. Learning to share with other people, especially gaining a deeper sense of belonging from participation in a group in which one is a respected and accepted member.
5. Being free to talk about concerns, problems, values, and ideas with others who are facing similar situations.
6. Getting several persons' reactions to one's problems and concerns.
7. Finding support from a group of peers, which is often of greater value to a student than support from an interested adult.
8. Giving each person an opportunity to spend more time with a counselor.
9. Being able to involve oneself rather slowly in the counseling process and to withdraw partially if a discussion becomes too threatening.
10. Giving the counselor a chance to see clients in a broader and more active social setting than individual sessions provide.

❧ Both Group and Individual Counseling Tend To Be Equally Valuable in the Following Areas:

1. Being accepted as a worthwhile individual.
2. Being responsible for one's own behavior.
3. Deepening the understanding one has of human behavior.
4. Being able to explore wider variations in one's emotional life and gaining greater confidence in the control of one's emotions.
5. Increasing one's self-confidence and trust in one's own perceptions.
6. Gaining strength to be an individual in one's own right.
7. Examining one's interests and values and moving toward integrating them into a life plan.

From *Group Counseling in the Schools.* C. A. Mahler (1969). Reprinted by permission.

Figure 11.1 Situational guidelines for use of individual counseling, group counseling, or both.

5. To help members increase their acceptance and understanding of self and others;
6. To help members deal with an identified and specified problem area they have in common;
7. To help members develop self-confidence and self-responsibility in directing their own lives;
8. To help members deal with concerns and problems related to the educational and vocational decision making process;
9. To help members examine feelings, attitudes, values, and ideas about themselves and their world; and
10. To help members learn new and desirable adaptive behaviors (Dustin & George, 1973).

Certainly many more general goals could be identified, but these are sufficient as examples. Individual goal definition comes later in the process, when group members actually begin to prepare for and interact together in the group. Once these general goals are defined, the counselor must orient all concerned people to the nature of specific and general goals and the group process in order to enlist their support and cooperation.

Orienting Significant Others

The principal purposes of orienting significant others are to help them understand the nature and intent of the group process, clarify misconceptions, answer questions, and generally obtain their support and cooperation. Orientation should certainly include all parties who were contacted during the needs assessment period of the organizational plan. They deserve to know what use you have made of the information they shared and in most cases are seriously interested in the suggestions you have developed. Orientation regarding the group process, its nature, and its goals should encompass the vast majority of staff members, referral sources, and, if applicable, the families of those selected for participation.

Counselors have a variety of options available to orient staff members in a school situation. They can organize inservice programs, make presentations at staff meetings, or contact members individually or in small groups (at department meetings). Methods should involve presentation, explanation, and preferably demonstration with a follow-up period allowed for questions. Important topics for orientation might include advantages of the group process (chapter 2), rationale for group counseling (chapter 3), the nature of the group process (chapters 4 and 5), the role of the leader (chapter 6), ethics and best practices in group work (chapter 8), and distinctions between types of groups (chapter 10).

Demonstration is a particularly useful mechanism because staff members have an opportunity to observe the group process firsthand. Organization of a live demonstration group composed of former group members is a useful method for orienting significant others (staff, administrators, parents) to group process and dynamics. This type of procedure may be a bit threatening because the counselor is automatically subjected to evaluation by colleagues. Also, if the group members are from the same school as the staff being oriented, members may feel some anxiety because they are under the scrutiny of past, present, or future teachers. On the other hand, former group members are typically the best advocates for group work which tends to counter the anxiety factor. One way around this is to use a video tape that has been properly edited. In any case, the consent of participants must be obtained before proceeding. If the group members are minors, the written permission of their parents is obligatory. With regard to questions of permission, confidentiality, and privacy involving minors in groups, Ritchie and Huss (2000) provide a useful and practical guideline stating that they "operate under the belief that ethically the child is the client but legally the parent is the client" (p. 154).

Another option is to use staff members to role-play a typical group counseling session. Staff members thus can experience directly the dynamics involved. A mini-demonstration involving the use of a specific group exercise also may suffice. Finally use of commercial video tapes can also be incorporated into staff orientation (Carroll, 1985; Stockton, 1992).

Whatever approach to orientation is chosen, specific things need to be communicated. Dinkmeyer and Muro (1971) enumerate them:

1. Teachers should be aware of the nature of groups—of how and why students are selected and what their goals are.
2. Faculty members should be aware of the necessity of confidentiality (and also be clear about the difference between confidentiality and privileged communication).
3. Teachers should understand that the primary purpose of the group is not to promote a systematic attack on the school, the staff, or society at large.
4. The organizational and mechanical steps of group organization should be explained to the faculty.
5. The counselor should make his or her point of view known to the staff, especially in terms of group composition.
6. The faculty should know that wherever possible the counselor will report back to them on the group's progress (pp. 141–142).

Generally speaking, the same ideas apply to orienting families with the one difference being that they may be more wary and concerned than staff members. Parents can be invited to the school for presentations and demonstrations, met with individually, or talked with over the phone. Sometimes information sent home in the mail is sufficient. But when group members are minors, precautions always should be taken to obtain written, informed consent from parents.

Orienting Potential Clientele

The purposes of orienting potential clients are to help them understand the nature and goals of group counseling, to answer questions, and to elicit and nurture an interest in participation. Zimpfer (1991) in a review of literature pertaining to pretraining and orientation of group members identified three general objectives: (1) clarification of expectations, (2) presentation of guidelines for group participation, and (3) provision of models for effective behavior in groups (p. 264). Bowman and DeLucia (1993) explicated these objectives stipulating the purposes of preparation as: (1) to establish rapport, allay "excessive" anxiety and orient clients to the group, (2) to assess the client's psychological dynamics and interpersonal skills, and 3) to establish therapeutic goals, expectations and a problem focus (p. 68).

Basic forms of orientation are cognitive: provision of information; vicarious: observation of role models or examples; experiential: involvement in a structured experimental activity, and a combination of all three (cognitive-vicarious-experiential). These forms can be incorporated into both dyadic and group orientation formats (Bowman & DeLucia, 1993).

Based on the premise that member preparation is an essential task of the group leader, Bowman and DeLucia (1993) conducted a study to determine the impact of preparation relative to enhancing group effectiveness and preventing drop outs. Results of the study: (1) supported the positive impact of preparation on client attitudes, beliefs and expectations about group therapy; and (2) confirmed the combination of information, vicarious exposure, and opportunity to practice (cognitive-vicarious-experiential) as the most effective form of preparation. These findings support Korda and Pancrazio's (1989) contention that competent and adequate preparation is one of the key factors that limits negative outcomes in group work. DeRoma, Root, and Battle (2003) using a format that incorporated pretraining as an introductory feature of each group session with combat veterans grappling with anger and anxiety also found positive effects when results were compared with a control group that did not receive such training.

In a practical sense one of the most effective ways of reaching students in schools is to give presentations in classes that all students must attend. For example, in the high school the counselor can make a presentation in each grade level's English classes. In this way two purposes are served: (1) students are familiarized with the group process and its probable benefit to them, and (2) students increase their general knowledge of the counselor's role and function. This type of systematic approach ensures consistency in presenting group information because counselors can prepare materials to complement the presentation and utilize all the formats described above. Typical topics that could be covered in these presentations are the nature and process of group counseling (chapters 2, 4, and 5), the role of the group leader (chapter 6), the role of the group member (chapter 7) and ethics in group work (chapter 8). Questions also should be dealt with as they arise. A key part of these sessions should be a mini-demonstration, in which class members participate in a brief but effective small group activity. Many of the activities listed at the end of most chapters of this book lend themselves well to demonstration. In this way students are given not only a cognitive introduction to the group process but an experiential one as well. Another element of a class presentation should be a sign up sheet that members can fill out to indicate their interest in participating in a counseling group. A similar sheet also should be available in the counselor's office for those students who decide to volunteer at a later date. Nelson (1971) warned that volunteers should not be obtained by a show of hands in these presentations because of the possible reactions to popular or unpopular students' actions in responding and the importance of protecting privacy of prospective participants.

The counselor can use regular guidance and counseling contacts to spread the word about group counseling, but, as has already been stressed, this alone is insufficient. Effective orientation of staff, administration, and parents yields positive results because they inform potential clients of the group possibility and often refer them. Another vehicle is to use the announcement approach, where concise, clearly worded blurbs are passed out in classes, posted on bulletin boards, placed on the Web site or run in the school newspaper stating that a certain type of group is being organized and that interested students should check with the counselor. Although this sounds a lot like a Madison Avenue approach, catchy phrases, creative designs, and art forms will attract attention and produce results. One counselor got together with the art department and produced some very effective posters that attracted a substantial number of inquiries and an eventual commitment to group counseling by one-half of those who inquired. Finally, as already noted, some counselors have mobilized computer resources to set up a Web page where announcements of groups can be posted and a chat room where questions about group counseling can be addressed.

When orienting potential clients in schools, Muro and Freeman (1968) highlighted some points that may be particularly helpful:

1. Students should be told in simple terms about the nature of group counseling. It may be helpful to inform prospective members that they will be given an opportunity to learn more about themselves, their plans, and the ways other students see them.
2. Prospective group members should know that group meetings are confidential and the topics discussed in groups are not for general discussion outside the group meetings.

3. Students should be informed that they are not joining a therapy group. Students frequently associate any type of counseling activity with those who are in some way unhealthy.
4. The counselor should prepare a schedule of the times she or he has available for working with groups. Within this limitation, the number of meetings a week and the duration of counseling should be a topic to be decided after the groups have been formed.
5. Students should know whether or not volunteering to participate would mean they would be selected as group members. It is best to inform teachers and students of the number of students the counselor wishes to have in a group and how the final selection will be made if the number of volunteers is too large.
6. It is beneficial to inform the students that those who wish to participate may be interviewed individually. This will give the counselor an additional opportunity to make decisions about placing the student in a group. In addition, students may wish to ask the counselor personal questions about group participation that may be embarrassing to ask in a class size group (pp. 314–331).

If the counselor has adequately performed the needs assessment and orientation steps, then the time is appropriate to proceed to the actual organization of specific groups. Note that although my primary emphasis is on group counseling, other types of groups described in chapters 2 and 10 also may be called for at this point. If so, the counselor must make the proper administrative arrangements and proceed in the manner prescribed by the nature of the group. For group counseling, however, further organizational steps are usually required before the groups actually convenes.

Selection and Preparation of Group Members

Selection and preparation of group members go hand in hand in the minds of most writers and practitioners (Corey & Corey, 2006; DeLucia-Waack, 1997b; Dinkmeyer & Muro, 1979; Gazda, 1984a; Gladding, 2003; Mahler, 1969; Ohlsen, Horne, & Lawe, 1988) because they are both associated with a pre-group individual interview with prospective group members. Riva, Lippert, and Tackett (2000) in a survey of randomly selected ASGW members found that the individual intake interview was the most frequently endorsed method of preparing group members with a minority (11%) of responders using a group intake process. They note that critics of the individual interview point out that interpersonal behavior, a key variable in effective group participation, is not readily assessed in an individual interview. However, the individual interview still remains the predominant method.

Once clients have indicated an interest in participating in a counseling group, a good idea is to schedule them, for an interview on either an individual or group basis. Important areas of emphasis during individual interviews should be: (1) client expectations, (2) counselor assessment, and (3) client commitment. Corey and Corey (1987) state that the key screening question for the group leader in the pregroup interview is: "Should this particular *person* be included in this particular *group* at this *time* with this *leader*?" (p. 81). These same factors can be addressed in a group intake with the additional benefit of the leader observing and assessing each member's interpersonal capabilities as they participate in the group. Ritchie and Huss (2000) recommend the group intake interview because it "requires less time and allows group leaders to observe communication and interaction skills of members in a group setting" (p. 150).

Member Expectations

Purposes of the interview from the client's perspective are to ask questions and develop realistic expectations about the group process. Ohlsen (1970) stated that "clients profit most from a counseling group when they understand what is expected of them before they decide whether to join" (p. 82). They should be informed that responsibility to change and help others change is part of their commitment and that they will be expected to work toward the "mutually aligned goal of personal\social growth" (Dinkmeyer & Muro, 1971, p. 38). Clients should be given an opportunity to describe problems with which they hope the group can help. They should be told that the group will engage in free and honest expressions of feeling and that members will have the opportunity to discuss their own and others' problems constructively. In addition, every effort should be made to dispel any myths the member may have regarding group counseling (Childers & Couch, 1989). If group leaders are interested in eliciting change in group members, clients must be truly ready for constructive group participation.

Counselor Assessment

From the counselor's perspective, purposes of the screening interview are to evaluate the client's readiness for group counseling, develop that readiness if it's not present, gather information that will facilitate selection and placement, and generally get to know the client. The counselor's role is not to counsel the client at this point but rather to clarify the nature of the group process and to obtain data that will facilitate decisions in regard to the client's group participation. The counselor's professional judgment is involved here. The impact of each client on other individuals as well as on the total group must be considered. Counselors must keep in mind various factors discussed later in this chapter to facilitate placement of selected members in the most beneficial groups. Generally, the counselor must try to determine how each client will best fit into group counseling and organize various groups around that knowledge. The ethical principle that guides this clinical decision is found in the *Code of Ethics and Standards of Practice* (American Counseling Association, 1997) and states:

> To the extent possible, counselors select group members whose needs and goals are compatible with the goals of the group, who will not impede the group process, and whose well-being will not be jeopardized by the group experience. (p.2.)

Member Commitment

Nelson (1971) indicated that three steps exist in securing commitment from potential group counseling members. The first is the indication of interest in participating. The second is the individual interview. And the third is arrival at the group session. Of the three he felt that the individual interview may be the most vital. Ohlsen (1970) emphasized the importance of commitment, stating that "those who profit most from group counseling recognize and accept the need for assistance and are committed to talk about their problems, to solve them, and to change their behavior when they are accepted for group counseling" (p. 80). The screening interview should facilitate the securing of this type of commitment.

The pregroup, group meeting is another commonly used screening device. Potential group members are brought together as a group to orient them to the purpose and process, assess their readiness for group counseling, and elicit their commitment. The advantage of this procedure is that the group leader gets a first hand opportunity to assess the interpersonal competence of each member with respect to their ability to function effectively in a group.

Sometimes individual or pregroup group interviews are not convenient or time does not permit them. In that event a wise procedure is to use the initial group session for group screening during which the same objectives and information just discussed are considered. In fact, some group leaders prefer not to have pregroup interviews so as to avoid preconceived attitudes that have a tendency to form as a result of them. These counselors prefer to handle problems of readiness and commitment as they emerge in the group and to use the group as an arena and resource for dealing with them. In most cases however, the counselor will be wise to make some type of pre-group contact, if only to waylay some of the grossly destructive factors and misconceptions that will undoubtedly hamper group progress.

Group Composition Factors

The group counselor is like a baker who must put together all the right ingredients in the proper proportions in order to come up with a satisfactory product. There are certain factors that must be weighed in the organization of any group. Too much of one thing or too little of another can cause problems. No magic formula exists for putting together all the right ingredients in their proper amounts. Research has not fully delineated specific guidelines either. But practical experience, combined with investigative efforts of researchers has revealed some tendencies the professional counselor as developmental scientist and clinical artist can use to organize groups that are catalytic to therapeutic change (Riva & Huss, 2000; Roark & Roark, 1979).

Homogeneity Versus Heterogeneity

The issue of homogeneous and heterogeneous groups was already posed in chapter 10 in discussing common problems groups and case centered groups. Both types have advantages and disadvantages, but the counselor who is working with a typical range of clients does not have to take a stand at any one particular place on this issue. A more appropriate procedure is to maintain a flexible attitude, making decisions based on the nature of the problems and clients being worked with. Commonality certainly enhances identification and facilitates the cohesive development of the group. But too much similarity can spoil the process and lead to boredom, stagnation, and disinterest. Bach (1954) noted that heterogeneity gives members the experience of learning to relate to different kinds of people. Unger (1989) affirmed this notion stating, "If group therapy is to help one prepare for everyday realities of life, it seems ultimately desirable to emphasize its heterogeneous aspects" (p. 156). However, Mahler (1969) warned that too wide a variation may create problems in communication and relationship formation. Nelson (1971) and Dustin and George (1973) took a more middle of the road perspective and advocated that groups should include some members who have different concerns. All things considered, balance seems to be the key. Groups should have enough diversity to generate interest but also enough commonality to help members feel comfortable and identify with one another. Certain groups that deal with specific concerns like disruptive behavior may tend toward homogeneity, whereas other groups that deal with a broader category of concerns like social competency may be more heterogeneous in nature. As noted in chapter 9, multicultural factors directly or indirectly related to the group purpose will raise diversity as a component in groups subsequently emphasizing the importance of the homogeneity-heterogeneity factor.

Where clients are in their efforts to deal with an issue also may affect whether homogeneous or heterogeneous groups are more appropriate. For example, McBride and Emerson (1989) noted that for adults molested as children (AMACs), homogeneous groups are more appropriate during the initial phase of treatment because discomfort is eased. However, if clients are further along in their progress, say at the point of dealing with the fact of having been abused (past the denial and denial break through phases) then a more heterogeneous group may be more appropriate.

Counselors must find their own solutions to this issue relying on research, clinical experience, and client input to develop the type of experience that will be most beneficial to the group members and the group's purposes and that will accommodate the counselor's personality and leadership style.

Age and Maturity

For most groups in schools, a generally advisable procedure is to put members together who are roughly the same age. This is less important for adult groups, but still a consideration. Most practitioners agree that maturity more than age is the key. However, leaders hesitate to group on this basis because the specifications of maturity levels have not been clearly delineated. Dinkmeyer and Muro (1971) felt that for organizing groups of children more attention should be given to developmental factors than to chronological ones. Ohlsen (1970) made a far more comprehensive assertion that social maturity is simply more important than age. Until clearer guidelines are established by research, the counselor is generally warranted in using age guidelines in the placement of group members but should temper them by restructuring groups that have obvious inequities in social maturity. Members tend to be more comfortable in their own age groups because of the importance of peer relationships. Any variation of this type of grouping should be done with specific purposes in mind (e.g., putting teenagers and parents together to increase communication, connectedness, and understanding) or to effect certain special treatment procedures in the group (e.g., using socially competent seniors as models for sophomores who lack certain social skills). On the other hand, some of the most effective, fascinating, and dynamic groups I have led have involved working with adults in adult education settings, graduate schools and private practice where a broad range of ages were represented, contributing diversity that made these groups complex, interesting and resourceful.

Gender

The literature contains general consensus that same gender groups are preferable for preadolescents and mixed gender groups are more appropriate for adolescent and adult groups subject, of course, to the theme or focus of the group. Ginott (1968) felt that mixed gender groups were appropriate for preschool children since no compelling reasons exist to separate them. But for school age children he firmly adhered to same gender groups because boys and girls are in the process of developing their masculine and feminine identity. The mixed gender group has merit because it is a more natural environment with immediate relevance to the outside world and is a safe but effective way for males and females to deal with their problems and further their normal social-emotional development (Ohlsen, 1970).

Mahler (1969) supported the ideas expressed here but did note particular situations that call for one or the other of the gender groupings. Groups organized to work with discipline problem clients are more effective if they include only same gender members, whereas, social problems groups should definitely be mixed. He also pointed out that when counselors are in doubt regarding the gender grouping of clients they should consult the clients. In most cases, especially from adolescence on up, the inclusion of both sexes stimulates interest even though it may also be a bit threatening to members. The relational developments that result from group interaction between the sexes are valuable regardless of the specific goal for which the group was formed.

Social and Psychological Factors

Riva et al. (2000) noted a host of factors that pertain to selection criteria including factors that are both for and against inclusion. Inclusion criteria variables such as moderate social ability, ability to tolerate frustration, commitment to changing interpersonal behavior, willingness to see other group members as helpful, and willingness to help others all portend a positive acclimation to the group. On the other hand, factors such as difficulty trusting and relating to others, introversion, difficulties with shyness, friends, socializing, and loneliness all tend to preclude effective participation. Member expectations are also crucial. The more a member expects the experience to be beneficial the more beneficial it will likely be. The reverse is also applicable. In addition, psychological mindedness is noted as a positive predictor of effective membership. Described variously as the inclination to be attracted to and the tendency to resonate with the interpersonal nature of the group process and the introspective nature of the content, psychological mindedness is considered a promising criteria for inclusion.

Additional factors to consider in the selection and placement of group members are: (1) verbal ability, (2) diversity characteristics and personality, and (3) prior acquaintance and friendship. Verbal ability, especially its potential, must be assessed so that extreme differences do not interfere with the communication process in the group. If ability is comparable, the more expressive members can model verbal behaviors for less expressive members; drawing out a quiet person can be an appropriate goal for a group. But if members who lack verbal abilities and skills are placed with those who verbalize with ease, it can be a very frustrating experience. In fact, if members with low verbal ability are put on the spot by the leader or other members, they can suffer extreme embarrassment which can lead to withdrawal or aggression and cause damage to their self-concepts. The best procedure is to work with these members in groups of their own and occasionally admit carefully selected models until they have upgraded their skills and self-confidence.

To consider *diversity characteristics* and *personality* requires a tremendous amount of counselor time and sensitivity but is important as a basic criterion for selection and placement. Understanding the nuances of various cultural, environmental, family, ethnic, racial, and personality factors and their impact on group interaction is a difficult but important task. Diversity is a topic that is addressed in detail in chapter 9 by Niloufer Merchant. Benefit will result from giving serious attention to these factors prior to the commencement of the group in an effort to address factors that might generate difficulties in the group. Differences, especially those related to culture, ethnicity, and race, should not be a reason for excluding members but should be noted as factors that affect group interaction and have beneficial potential to group members. DeLucia-Waack (1996) stated that "multiculturalism is inherent in all group work and in fact enhances the effectiveness of all group work" (p. 222). Since understanding self and others is an important goal for any group, cultural background, diversity, and personality differences definitely contribute to the broadening of that understanding. In individual cases, however, decisions may have to be made to redirect or omit a person from participation in a specific group based on characteristics that preclude effective adjustment and involvement in that group.

Prior acquaintance and friendship can be touchy subjects in member selection. In some instances, including friends in the same group has adverse results because they tend to support one another in a cliquish manner, which deters the group process. Prior friendships also make contact outside the group a more critical and influential factor that can be disruptive and undermining. In addition, including friends in the same group also may have detrimental effects on their friendship. On the other hand, the group can benefit from members whose friendships are the support needed to help them reveal and work on their problems. The group also can improve friendships by helping members learn behaviors that are conducive to deeper understanding and better communication. The best way to decide on this factor is to obtain additional information on the individuals and their friendships and develop clear ground rules relative to outside the group contact and discussions. For example, Rittenhouse (1997), citing the importance of relationships as a critical factor in the development of self-esteem and healing in feminine psychology, emphasizes contact between members outside the group for purposes of support and accountability. To frame such contact therapeutically, however, three parameters must be implemented: (1) contact is voluntary; (2) contact is reported to the group, and (3) contact is not destructive/harmful to the person or disruptive/harmful to the group process.

In some respect, to expect that groups be composed of persons who do not know each other is unrealistic because in many situations groups are composed of persons who already relate to each other in some other arena. and therefore do not qualify as being strangers. The group counselor needs to be concerned with relationships that may interfere with the group process or be detrimental to the individuals involved, and in many circumstances even these can be worked with in the group.

The counselor's main concern regarding these factors is to develop a reasonable balance in the group's composition to facilitate the helping process rather than detract from it. If members are included who function reasonably well in small group situations and if extreme variations are avoided, the resulting effect will most likely be positive.

Technical Considerations

In addition to the various selection and placement factors, the group worker also must be concerned about several technical factors that can enhance the group's effectiveness. Decisions and strategies in these areas affect the nature of the group. These factors also affect the group's initial reaction to the leader, influence effectiveness, and establish the boundaries within which the leader will operate. The major technical factors of group organization are discussed in the following subtopics.

Voluntary Versus Forced Participation

Counselors must make a basic decision about the kind of group member they wish to work with in each group that is organized. The three basic types are volunteers, forced volunteers, and forced participants (non-volunteers). Volunteers decide to participate of their own volition or on the basis of group counseling information they have received from presentations, friends who have participated, or other sources. The volunteer is most likely to benefit from group counseling. Johnson (1963) indicated that clients who are experiencing pain and seek help on their own are easier to work with than those who have been coerced by family or friends. Ohlsen (1970) also affirmed that the volunteer is more apt to profit than the nonvolunteer, and Mahler (1969) maintained that for this reason the decision to participate should be left up to the individual. The counselor who works with volunteers is much more likely to experience success. The underlying factor in the volunteer member is motivation. The old saw, "How many counselors does it take to change a light bulb? Only one, but the light bulb has to really want to change!" applies here. The member who chooses to become a member is likely to get the most out of the group experience. Volunteering is also an effective means of ensuring commitment since these members take responsibility for thrusting themselves into the interaction of the group. Thus, the success of the group process is more assured with volunteers, but the extent of its impact in terms of numbers is limited. Many clients who could benefit from the group process will not freely volunteer, and if counselors restrict themselves to volunteers they will be limiting their effectiveness.

Forced volunteers are like "Mr. or Ms. In Between." They have professed their interest in participating but only because they were cajoled, bugged, or directed to do so. They enter the group under the guise of volunteering but experience great ambivalence because of the pressure that was used to help them decide to participate. Forced or prompted volunteers may represent an obstacle in the group because they are hiding behind the facade of willing participation which translates into resistance or because they adopt a passive aggressive posture relative to group pressure. Thus, they must resolve their dissonance in regard to being in the group in addition to trying to resolve their problems. More time must be spent with forced volunteers in the initial stages to create trust and acceptance. If addressed effectively, these members can convince themselves that the decision was in their own best interests no matter what its genesis was, and then they will commit themselves to the process. But if pushed too fast and too hard, they may regret the decision and negate all efforts of the group to help them.

Mahler (1969) advocated required participation for certain clients (for example, acting out boys). He felt that involuntary attendance should be required whenever "group counseling is being used to help people who are causing trouble or having difficulty adjusting to a situation in which they find themselves" (p. 60). The counselor must decide whether the effort of working with *forced participants* will result in positive change or have diminishing returns. Realizing that the returns may be less than hoped for and tend to be in contrast to those of volunteer groups, the counselor may still be able to work effectively with groups composed of forced participants. Gazda (1968) summarized the issue of voluntariness:

> An individual must either have or be capable of developing a desire to change at the time he/she enters a group. Involuntary clients can be assisted, however, if they remain in counseling long enough to experience the beneficial effects of the process. (pp. 268–269)

Basically, the decision about which kind of group members counselors will work with is between two main types: (1) members who volunteer, and (2) members the counselor feels the group process can help. On the basis of these two criteria, counselors can organize all their groups. The only precautions are that selectivity is still important among volunteers and that the counselor must be willing to admit that group counseling cannot help everyone (Childers & Couch, 1989).

Open Versus Closed Groups

Another decision the counselor must make is whether the group will be open or closed. In open groups, old members leave and new members rotate in as the group per se continues. In closed groups, the same members stay together from the beginning to the end. Both types have advantages, but counseling groups in schools have the tendency to be closed groups. Dinkmeyer and Muro (1971) gave one good reason for this: "A group must develop, it must move through or pass through certain phases for optimal effectiveness. Such movement requires time and a sense of cohesiveness" (p. 148).

The introduction of new members can impede this process of development because it automatically places members at different developmental levels process wise. If the decision is made to open a group to a new member, the leader should discuss it first with the group and make the integration of the new member the responsibility of the group. In most groups, introductions of new members should be done one or two at a time so that the group can more easily absorb the new person without experiencing a great deal of pressure or causing undue regression in the group's development. Certainly, adding new members will cause some growing pains, but if it is done on an individual basis and if a good therapeutic rapport exists among members, the impact will be slight. In fact, the new member's development will probably be accelerated, and initiating a new member can be a positive experience for the group as well.

In contrast, in agency/practice settings, open ended groups are more typical and practical due to the ebb and flow of case loads and client turnover. More than one member may be added at a time but two or three should be the maximum as three already represents a significant minority with sub-grouping propensities that could undermine the group process. Additionally, in inpatient settings where groups meet more frequently or even daily, open ended groups are more common.

In most cases, however, staying with a set group membership is preferable because it facilitates the sense of cohesiveness, which enhances identification and belongingness and helps the group move in a more consistent developmental manner to its culmination point. Within a closed group the possibility is higher that all the business of the group will be finished—new, unfinished, or old—while in an open group, new members always introduce new business and their entrance into the group may effect changes that prevent old business from being fully completed. (Frederick S. Perls, Gestalt psychologist and well-known group therapist, used the terms new business, unfinished business, and old business in reference to the material considered in group therapy and encounter group sessions.)

Group Size

No magic number determines the absolute effectiveness of the group counseling process, but reasonable considerations necessitate limiting group size. Roark and Roark (1979) recommend a size range of 5 to 12 members. For practical and therapeutic reasons, however, counseling groups should be limited to 10 or fewer members. Mahler (1969) stated:

> The main dangers of groups with more than ten members are that some members may not get adequate attention or be able to participate fully,

that others can avoid involvement, that the counselor may have difficulty giving adequate attention to each member, and that the group may tend to become more of a class than a counseling session. (p. 55)

For adolescents and adults, groups of 6 to 10 can be handled effectively by a leader. That size of a group is large enough to maintain interest due to the diversity in the group, gives members an adequate opportunity to participate, and yet is large enough for members to feel safety in numbers. For children, groups of four to six are more appropriate. Mayer and Baker (1967) indicated that the size of groups for children should vary with the age and maturity level of the counselees. Although some group experts stress a specific number, generally the group leader must decide what a workable group size is. This decision should be based on the counselor's own effectiveness and comfort in various sized groups and on knowledge of group members. In most cases the 10-member limit should be adhered to, and therefore the decision applies mainly to establishing what the minimum size will be. My own clinical experience has indicated that the most intense, effective, satisfying, and interesting interaction has occurred in groups of five to eight members.

Time and Frequency of Meetings

Roark and Roark (1979) delineated time into calendar time and clock time. Calendar time refers to the schedule of group meetings, and clock time refers to the length of individual sessions. The optimal frequency of sessions and length of individual meetings have not been definitely established. Both tend to conform to the administrative structure within which the group is formed. In schools individual sessions mirror the length of class periods, and frequency tends to be established on the basis of student and counselor availability. Mahler (1969) stated that groups should meet at least once a week for a minimum of 10 sessions, although urgency may require more frequent meetings. Dinkmeyer and Muro (1971) suggested twice weekly meetings, reducing or increasing frequency with the development of the group. Based on a review of research, Roark and Roark (1979) recommend that closed groups meet twice weekly over a 10 week span. The more often the group meets the greater the tendency to be cohesive; however, members should have time between group sessions to reconsider group interaction, prepare themselves for the next session, and simply relax and unwind. Relative to frequency, weekly sessions are still the most common.

As far as length of each session is concerned the class period approach is practical for schools but isn't necessarily ideal for the group process. Class periods tend to be too short because groups need the first 10 to 15 minutes to warm up and settle down to the work of the group. This time is important and should not be eliminated. Although members can be made aware of it and can work to reduce the amount of time needed for warm-up, work time in the group often gets limited to 20 to 30 minutes depending on the length of the class period.

The preferable time period for group counseling is one and one-half to two hours. With more flexible scheduling procedures in some schools, the possibility increases to set this amount of time aside for group counseling without raising havoc with the student's schedule. However, the class period is still the primary unit at this point, so the leader should see that groups begin and end promptly. This facilitates maximum use of time and good public relations with other staff members since students don't show up late for their classes. For children, shorter time periods are appropriate, ranging from 20 minutes to an hour depending on the attention span of members and the practical learning and administrative requirements of members' classroom environments.

In agency/practice settings scheduling relative to clock time is not a problem. However, when in the day group sessions are scheduled is crucial. Prime group time is one and one-half to two hours in the late afternoon or evening which is the most convenient time slot for children, adolescents, and adults who must coordinate school, work, and family schedules.

The number of sessions again depends on the goals of the group and the nature of the members. Quarters, semesters, and school years do provide some natural time periods for groups to meet, but they should not be rigidly subscribed to. Interestingly enough, however, even in agency/practice settings clients tend to think and behave on the basis of school year time frames. At least 10 to 12 sessions are necessary for groups to develop a substantial therapeutic group process, and more are preferable. Members need to be informed of the termination date of sessions so they can pace their work accordingly and do not get left in midstream. Even when groups continue on an open ended basis, the advisable procedure is to give members a couple of weeks notice before disbanding, and to have a guideline for departing members to notify the group two to four weeks prior to termination.

Scheduling

In school situations, scheduling is consistently one of the group counselor's biggest challenges, especially if group counseling does not enjoy the support and cooperation of administration and staff. Dansby (1996) simply states that "lack of time and lack of access to the students remain the primary obstacles to conducting groups in schools" (p. 238). For this reason the counselor must do a good job of orienting significant others and networking and developing a positive working relationship with teachers as a preventative and facilitative measure. Whenever possible, group meetings should be scheduled during students' free periods or in conjunction with a relevant curriculum offering, such as a "knowing me" class.

A second strategy is to rotate meeting times so that students don't miss the same classes all the time. Mahler (1969) suggested an additional strategy for groups organized to help troublemakers. He suggested that groups should meet during the period when the trouble normally occurs. In any event, arranging schedules should take into account both the members' and the counselor's obligations and responsibilities and should show a concern for the perspective of significant others. Clearly relate the schedule to members, stressing the necessity of staying with the schedule but allowing enough flexibility to make justified exceptions.

In agency/practice settings clients' schedules rather than agency or practitioner schedules create the scheduling obstacles. Most of the resistance relative to engaging in and committing to the group is worked through by addressing the scheduling issue. (Scheduling and payment issues are on par with each other for raising and working through resistances.)

Physical Arrangements

To say that the room makes the group would be an exaggeration, but it does help. The physical setting is a significant factor and especially influences the nature of group interaction during the early stages when the development of rapport and establishing member comfort are important. Mahler (1969) stated that the group room should be small but large enough to accommodate everyone without crowding. It should have sufficient privacy so that the group neither distracts others nor is distracted by others. Nothing is more disruptive than to have to compete with noises outside the group and nothing is more embarrassing than having an outsider, especially someone members know, enter the room in the middle of a personal discussion. Muro and Freeman (1968) recommended that the same room should be used for each meeting since roaming seems to hinder group progress. The decision to meet around a table or without one, to use chairs or sit on the floor (with pillows, cushions, or bean bags) is up to the leader and the group. Having a suitable facility is a big help in this regard.

Roark and Roark (1979) extended physical arrangements to include the way in which the room is set up and people are seated advocating a circle format as most conducive to effective group interaction. Donigian and Malnati (1997) also place much emphasis on physical arrangements dynamically in their discussion of proxemics (the physical and emotional distance between members and leader; pp. 17–19). The decor of the room can contribute to members' comfort, but the leader always must be on the lookout for group members using the setting as a resistance ploy or an excuse not to become involved. No matter how poor the facility, my experience has been that the group interaction can overcome any physical-setting barrier if members develop a supportive milieu and concentrate on each other and the purposes for which they are meeting.

Relevance to Task and Other Groups

Discussion of organizational factors in this chapter focused on application to counseling and therapy groups because of their circumscribed status in the mental health field. Psychoeducation groups are also affected by these considerations, but to a lesser degree because their focus and format is derived from content, and process variables are integrated into the formats utilized rather than used to create those formats. Task groups also are affected by the variables that were discussed, but the impact is less critical because the purpose of the group (agenda or job) takes precedence, and many of the factors are determined by the organizational or work setting in which they operate. Consequently, certain group decisions as to when, where, how long, and even decisions as to who may come either from the nature of the task, the milieu of the organization or the administrative structure of the workplace. As leaders of task groups, the more critical factors are process related addressing such things as making sure group meetings have warm up and closing phases and using leadership skills and process observation to keep content and process in touch with one another as the group proceeds about its business.

However, most if not all of the topics discussed in this chapter have relevance to task groups. Task group leaders will benefit from maintaining an ecological orientation and perspective and would do well to conduct ecological assessments in framing and forming their task groups. Considerations relative to group composition, selection and orientation of group members apply as do the comments regarding the importance of member expectations, leader assessment of members and member commitment. All the technical factors discussed relate to task groups in some manner and especially apply when teamwork and team building are the focal point of a system or organizational plan. Certainly task groups will vary depending on the setting and the purpose for which they are convened, but the process will be a critical part of the experience, and the competent group worker will integrate many of the factors discussed in this chapter into that process.

Summary

The basic steps in establishing a group program are as follows:

1. Determine the needs of the clients, utilizing as broad a range of resources as possible, and do an ecological assessment to determine the influence of the environment on those clients and the relevance of group work to that environment.
2. On the basis of the needs assessment determine the relevance of group counseling (or other types of groups) and establish general goals for which groups are to be organized.

3. Orient significant others in order to help them understand the group process and enlist their support and cooperation in organizing the group program.
4. Orient potential clientele to clarify the nature of the group process and its benefits to them and solicit their interest in participating.
5. Select and prepare group members, preferably on the basis of a screening interview (individual or group) in which questions are answered, assessments are made, expectations are developed, and commitment is obtained.
6. Develop specific groups, taking into account the group composition factors that will result in the most tenable helping relationships. Organize groups in accordance with the specific technical qualities that facilitate positive interaction.
7. Hold the first group meeting.

Learning Activities: De-Mythologizing Group Work Activities

The ideas and contents for the following activities were derived from the Childers and Couch (1989) article entitled "Myths about Group Counseling: Identifying and Challenging Misconceptions."

The scales and activities described below can be used in training group leaders by making use of both scales or in prescreening procedures with prospective group members as a means of generating questions and discussion about prospective group participation. The members' scale has also been useful in initial group sessions to stimulate discussion of member expectations.

Group Member Perception Scale

Provide prospective group members with the scale below and have them rate their perception of each item according to the directions.

Individual Members (PreGroup Screening Interview) Review each item with the prospective group member discussing his or her rating and the meaning of it relative to his or her expectations and perceptions of group counseling. Use the statements to explore the member's expectations and as a means of orienting him or her to the nature of the group process.

Group Process Activity Have group members share their ratings item by item and facilitate a discussion of expectations, perceptions, and concerns leading to a discussion of group ground rules. A follow-up task is to have the group develop a list of their own reflecting realistic perceptions and characteristics of group counseling.

Group Leader Perception Scale

Provide prospective group leaders or leaders in training with a copy of the next scale and ask them to rate the items according to their perception of group counseling and group work. When all participants have completed the rating, have them share their ratings with each other and facilitate a discussion processing the information for the purpose of developing statements that reflect a realistic perspective of groups and group process. The final objective is to have the group compile a list of statements agreed to by the group that reflects the reality of group dynamics, process, and theory.

Direct Group Members as Follows:

Please read the following statements that represent typical thoughts or feelings people may have about counseling groups. Examine each statement carefully and circle the rating that most accurately represents your thoughts and feelings as you anticipate becoming or being a group member.

My view of this statement is that it is:

Very Inaccurate	Somewhat Inaccurate	Not Sure	Somewhat Accurate	Very Accurate
VI	SI	NS	SA	VA

Stimulus Statement	**Personal Rating**
1. Counseling groups are for sick people.	VI SI NS SA VA
2. Counseling groups force people to lose their identity.	VI SI NS SA VA
3. In counseling groups you "gotta spill your guts."	VI SI NS SA VA
4. Group counseling is a second class treatment process.	VI SI NS SA VA
5. Counseling groups tear down psychological defenses.	VI SI NS SA VA
6. Counseling groups are confrontative, hostile, and attacking.	VI SI NS SA VA
7. All counseling groups are "touchy-feely."	VI SI NS SA VA
8. Counseling groups are artificial and unreal.	VI SI NS SA VA
9. Counseling groups are environments for brainwashing.	VI SI NS SA VA

Note: Items adapted from "Myths about Group Counseling: Identifying and Challenging Misconceptions," J. H. Childers & R. D. Couch, Journal for Specialists in Group Work (1989).

Present the Group Leader Perception Scale as Follows:

Please rate the following statements about group counseling. Examine each statement carefully and circle the rating that most accurately represents your thoughts and feelings as you anticipate becoming or being a group leader.

My view of this statement is that it is:

Very Inaccurate	Somewhat Inaccurate	Not Sure	Somewhat Accurate	Very Accurate
VI	SI	NS	SA	VA

Stimulus Statement	**Personal Rating**
1. Everyone benefits from a group experience.	VI SI NS SA VA
2. Leaders can compose groups to assure effective outcomes.	VI SI NS SA VA
3. The group revolves around the "sun" of the leader.	VI SI NS SA VA
4. Leaders can direct change through the use of structured exercises.	VI SI NS SA VA
5. The medium of change in groups is an emotional here and now experience.	VI SI NS SA VA
6. The majority of learning in groups comes from self-disclosure and feedback.	VI SI NS SA VA
7. One can work effectively with groups without understanding group process and dynamics.	VI SI NS SA VA
8. Changes in intensive small group experiences are not maintained over time.	VI SI NS SA VA
9. Discussion of racial-cultural differences will offend group members.	VI SI NS SA VA
10. Groups can be truly homogeneous.	VI SI NS SA VA
11. Group member differences do not affect process and outcome of task groups.	VI SI NS SA VA
12. Group work theory is appropriate for all clients.	VI SI NS SA VA

Note: Items 1–8 are adapted from Myths about Group Counseling: Identifying and Challenging Misconceptions, J. H. Childers & R. D. Couch, Journal for Specialists in Group Work (1989). Items 9–12 are adapted from Multiculturalism is Inherent in all Group Work, J. L. Delucia-Waack, Journal for Specialists in Group Work (1996).

12
Evaluating Group Work

Evaluation produces the data that becomes the group practitioners' main contribution to the viability and growth of the group work profession. Evaluation results serve as evidence of the efficacy of group work and spark a heuristic flame that researchers can pick up and turn into a veritable conflagration. Consequently, evaluation is a central factor in processing the impact and effectiveness of any of the group work modalities.

Research or Evaluation: No Longer A Practitioner's Dilemma

In the past, conscientious group workers were typically confronted with a conflict between a professional obligation to do all they could to expand and clarify the knowledge and understanding of group work and a role responsibility to extend and apply group work to the greatest number of clientele as was meaningfully possible. The professional obligation prompted counselors to become responsible contributors to the broad professional community of group workers thereby emphasizing a research perspective, and the role responsibility specifically defined the service function of counselors in the particular settings in which they work thereby stressing the practice perspective. As such, the research perspective emphasized by counselor educators as part of the research orientation of higher education, and by the professional literature and professional associations seemed incompatible with the role perspective nurtured by the work setting, where the interest was on the pragmatic impact of the group worker rather than his or her knowledge of the field, theoretical prowess or reputation in professional circles. Consequently, meeting the research expectations of the profession and the accountability emphasis of the job required a superhuman effort that often resulted in a choice to focus on practice only at the expense of research. Fortunately that dilemma is no longer relevant. Group workers in their roles as researchers, practitioners, counselor educators and trainers have forged a viable means of resolving the dilemma and transforming the component parts into a collaborative initiative that enhances the group work profession practically and conceptually as is eloquently pointed out and demonstrated by Stockton, Toth, and Morran in chapter 16 of this text.

A Realistic Perspective

Group workers can best carry out their responsibilities relative to the research-practice conundrum by cultivating certain perspectives described below that ameliorate conflict and forge a working relationship between practitioners and researchers. The recommendations are as follows:

Leave the Major Burden of Group Research to Group Researchers and Become a Collaborator with Group Researchers

Since most studies are generated by researchers at universities, graduate students and other professionals whose requirements and job descriptions primarily entail research, the group practitioner need not assume further responsibilities in this area. Ohlsen (1970) stated, "Considering (their) commitment to service, the time required to obtain adequate financial support for research, the difficulties involved in appraising outcomes of counseling and (their) own feelings about (their) research skills, one would not expect the practitioner to do much research" (pp. 284–285). Therefore, a more appropriate role is for the practitioner is to become a collaborator with group researchers (Dies, 1985; McCoy, 1997; Riva & Kalodner, 1997), participate in well designed and carefully conceived research projects, and offer his or her groups to researchers for studies and data collection.

Become a Consumer of Group Research

The procedures and findings of research projects reported in various professional journals and at professional meetings and conventions are invaluable sources of help to the group worker. As a consumer, the group practitioner can integrate this information into practice to make the group process even more effective. Dinkmeyer and Muro (1971) confirmed this point of view stating that the "practicing counselor is more a research consumer than he (she) is a producer" (p. 303).

Being a consumer is made convenient by professional journals such as those listed below and the vast resources available through the Internet and group related Web sites. For example, critical reviews of group research on selected topics frequently published in the *Journal for Specialists in Group Work* are reflective of efforts made by journals to produce user friendly research data. A fine example of such a comprehensive review of group research is Horne and Rosenthal (1997).

The following professional journals provide extensive information in group research:

1. *Group Dynamics: Theory, Research and Practice*
2. *International Journal of Group Psychotherapy*
3. *Journal for Specialists in Group Work*
4. *Journal of Child and Adolescent Group Therapy*
5. *Journal of Group Psychotherapy, Psychodrama, and Sociometry*
6. *Small Group Behavior*
7. *Small Group Research*
8. *Social Work With Groups*
9. *Group Psychology and Psychotherapy*

Concentrate on Developing Experience and Expertise as a Group Leader

One of the major weaknesses of many group counseling research projects traditionally has been that they do not utilize leaders who have extensive group counseling experience and competence (Cohn, 1967; Mahler, 1969). This particular factor has been greatly ameliorated over the past two decades (Barlow, Fuhriman, & Burlingame, 2004; Burlingame, Fuhriman, & Johnson, 2004), but the need for diligence in this arena persists. Thus, when the research fails to demonstrate significant results, it may be due to lack of leader expertise rather than lack of power in the group process. By building one's expertise in practice, the counselor will contribute to a more extensive population of competent group leaders who can be called upon for help in research projects (Dies, 1983).

Become an Evaluator of Group Work in Your Own Setting

Even though counselors may not be in the position to do research, that does not negate their responsibility for evaluation of the effectiveness of group work in their own environments. Early in the development of the group work field, Cohn (1967) emphasized that the group practitioner needs "to be persuaded that evaluation is necessary to determine actual outcomes rather than depending solely upon his (her) own individual perception of outcomes" (p. 28). Counselors must be interested in assessing the results of their group programs. They need to be accountable to their clients, themselves, their environments, and their profession, and an evaluation emphasis can meet that need. In addition, evaluation results are grist for the research mill and often provide the seeds from which research projects grow. To that end resources to assist in evaluation are being developed. DeLucia-Waack and Bridbord (2004) have identified and described a host of evaluation instruments that can be used by practitioners in addition to the ones developed particularly for a specific group project or program.

Research Versus Evaluation

The basic difference between evaluation and research is that *evaluation* is concerned with what is happening or what has happened in order to determine the value and worth of the assessed occurrence in that situation, while *research* is designed to assess the nature and impact of a particular treatment for purposes of testing theoretical hypotheses, expanding knowledge or predicting and generalizing results to other situations. Research also entails a formal design for comparison and replication purposes and incorporates the use of descriptive and inferential statistical methods. Research makes use of accumulated knowledge and procedures that compose a professional discipline in its own right. Evaluation is less formal and is not restricted by rigorous statistical and procedural limits. Its procedures are associated with the specific area being evaluated rather than with an outside body of professional knowledge. An analogy might be that evaluation is to the group worker as teacher-made tests are to the classroom instructor. In both cases the practitioner utilizes information from formal testing or research methods but adapts it to fit particular content, methods, clientele, and environments. Evaluation uses discovered results as a means of developing, revising, or consolidating a very specific treatment (i.e., group work). Research is more oriented toward defining overall group work characteristics in order to standardize the process as a formal and specified procedure of the counseling profession.

The Place for Evaluation

Evaluating group counseling is pivotal to both the individual group experience and the ongoing group program. Rapin and Conyne (chapter 8) and ASGW's Best Practices Guidelines (ASGW, 1998) emphasize the critical importance of evaluation by making a specific place for it in planning, performing, and processing group work. Evaluation is particularly important to group practitioners who wish to determine whether group work is effective or not and who may need such information not only to enhance the quality of the group experience but to justify the viability of groups in the context of their work environments.

The purpose of this chapter is to examine evaluation from a practical perspective and provide the rationale and resources to assist group workers in effectively evaluating their efforts. Both process and outcome evaluation will be considered and specific techniques and tools will be described. The chapter will culminate with an illustrative group counseling example reflecting in an integrative manner the material presented in chapters 10–12. Learning activities will conclude the chapter.

Basic Assumptions

In presenting evaluation as the focus of this chapter, the following basic assumptions were made to insure that a practitioner oriented perspective was maintained.

1. Professional counselors are primarily interested in the impact group in its various forms has in their own settings, and global answers to group questions though relevant are of secondary importance.
2. The typical counselor in most settings does not have the wherewithal in terms of time, interest, skill, and access to financial resources or multidisciplinary professional expertise needed to conduct significant group research.
3. Group work (particularly counseling and psychotherapy groups) has been demonstrated to be effective in the literature (Ward, 2004; Burlingame, Fuhriman & Johnson, 2002; Burlingame, Fuhriman, & Mosier, 2003), but evaluation is necessary to denote its specific impact.
4. Effective evaluation practices in individual settings will create fertile ground and a solid data base for formalized, extensive, and specific research projects in group work.
5. Effective evaluation procedures will—in and of themselves—contribute significantly to the expanding experiential base necessary for conducting successful group work and solidifying the professional field.

Methods of Evaluation

Group workers must develop evaluation procedures that are relevant to the types of groups they lead and describe the inherent group processes. Just as classroom teachers develop evaluative practices in accordance with subject matter and teaching methods and businesses develop marketing analysis procedures commensurate with their products, so counselors must construct evaluation procedures appropriate to their area of expertise. The counselor can learn much from the experiences and findings of researchers since many of the factors which undermine research also undermine evaluation. By eliminating or at least decreasing error factors and paying particular attention to specificity, effective evaluation can be implemented. The following discussion describes various procedures to help the counselor assess both the process and the outcomes of group counseling.

Process Evaluation

Process refers to what goes on in the group and has three components: the leader, the members, and the group interaction (Donigian & Malnati, 1997).

Efforts to evaluate group process are designed to increase understanding of group dynamics and to help counselors improve effectiveness in utilizing the group as a helping vehicle. Evaluation of process is generally associated with observation, analysis, and feedback. Specific goals include: (1) determining leader methods, attitudes, and characteristics to assess the effectiveness of approach; (2) determining member attitudes, reactions, and characteristics to better understand the effect of the group on the individual; and (3) identifying the focus and themes of group interaction to establish their relevance to the goals of the group and its members. Various methods discussed in the following paragraphs lend themselves well to process evaluation.

Expert Evaluation

One method of process evaluation is to ask colleagues or other professionals who have expertise in group work to observe your group sessions and give you feedback. This can be done either on a consistent basis as in a supervision relationship or on a selective basis where the expert is asked to observe when the group is at an impasse or not going well. The leader then uses the observer as a resource in finding ways of improving the group interaction. If colleagues are used, follow the procedures detailed in chapter 6 (Learning Activities: Peer Consultation). To prevent distractibility, have the observer watch the group by an indirect means such as a one way mirror or by closed circuit TV. Some counselors have found that observation by a group of experts followed by a roundtable discussion with the leader is professionally growth producing.

Member Process Observer Evaluation

Appointing a group member to be the process observer and rotating the responsibility through the group membership as the group progresses is another method that is gaining wide acceptance. Brief training in process observation is usually necessary but once in motion this approach adds immensely to the group experience. Input from the process observer during the group, at the end of group, and on an impromptu basis stimulates the group and gives each member an additional learning experience as well (see chapter 6: Process Observation: Group Leaders Resource and Reference).

Member Evaluation

Another source of process evaluation is the group participants themselves. Who is really better qualified to evaluate process than those who are affected by it? Some counselors use what might be called 3 × 5 evaluation methods. This format involves giving members 3 × 5 cards at the end of each session and asking them to write down their honest impressions or appraisal of the session. They also may include suggestions for improvement. An alternative is to have cards or sheets printed with a number of descriptive continuums to which members can respond by circling the rating that best represents their reaction to the group (e.g., a seven-point scale of boring to extremely interesting). The cards (filled out anonymously) are collected by the leader and used to help assess the group's development in an ongoing manner.

Some leaders ask members to keep journals or logs of their reactions to each group meeting, turning them in at the succeeding session (Yalom, 1995). This procedure tends to give a more comprehensive picture of the group process but creates a disadvantage because the counselor is always a week behind. This can be rectified if members are willing to turn in their logs at a time prior to the next meeting. Then leaders can make use of the material and adjust their approaches accordingly. Another option is to simply collect the journals at the end of the entire group process as a learning device for future reference.

Yalom (1995) suggested the use of leader process summaries dictated immediately after each session, typed, and distributed to members between sessions as a means of evaluating group process, facilitating flow from session to session, and extending the depth of group interaction. Group members also can take on this task as a means of presenting their view of the group process.

Evaluation of Audio and Video Replays

The most extensive method of process evaluation uses either recorded or videotaped replays of group sessions. Certainly no better way exists for analyzing one's actions and the interaction of the group than to review and re-experience the action to get a clearer understanding of the process. The major disadvantage of this approach is time. Busy counselors seldom have the opportunity to go over sessions without sacrificing some other aspect of their jobs or personal lives. For this reason tapes tend to be used extensively in training but seldom on the job. One means of circumventing the time problem is to listen to excerpts that the leader feels left something to be desired, involved a crisis, was particularly therapeutic, contained vital information, portrayed a critical incident or represented a significant disclosure. It is a good idea to get members used to being recorded so that it does not become a disruptive element. Some counselors make the mistake of introducing the tape recorder or videotape at crucial points in the process that they want to look at more closely. They bring the recorder or video camera to the session for the first time and then are surprised when the interaction is completely different. Whether you listen to the sessions or not, get the group accustomed to being taped so you can use the recordings if the need arises. These recorded sessions also can be used to stimulate professional discussion and obtain constructive feedback at staff meetings if permission has been obtained from group members for supervision purposes.

Interaction Evaluation

A more formal method of evaluating the group process is for counselors to familiarize themselves with a group interaction scale such as Bales (1950) Interaction Analysis Scale, the Hill Interaction Matrix (Hill, 1966) or Simon and Agazarians's (1974) Sequential Analysis of Verbal Interaction (SAVI). For extensive discussion of these and other formal instruments of evaluation the reader is referred to De-Lucia-Waack (1997b) and DeLucia-Waack and Bridbord (2004).

Scales can be used by counselors to analyze taped sessions on their own or counselors can train observers to use them. In either case the scales can be used to quantify interaction patterns and evaluate them qualitatively. The conscientious use of these sophisticated methods can yield valuable results for the counselor's own understanding of the group process and as a guide to productive group interaction (Zimpfer, 1986).

Group Themes

The group process can be assessed effectively on the basis of themes or topics the group considers. Bates (1966) and Muro and Denton (1968) first introduced this evaluation procedure with adolescent and college student populations. A theme is a "point of focus in the group's interaction with a clear beginning and stopping point" (Dinkmeyer & Muro, 1971, p. 111). Identification of these themes gives the group leader a solid basis for determining whether the group is engaging in meaningful goal oriented interaction or not. If not, the leader can exert influence to get the members to do so.

Process Evaluation Scales

Two process scales have been developed from material in this text. The Leadership Process Evaluation Scale (Figure 12.1) is constructed from information pertaining to leadership skills found in chapter 6. The Member Process Evaluation Scale (Figure 12.2) is constructed from descriptions of members' behaviors in chapter 7.

The Leadership Process Evaluation Scale is helpful in assessing the nature and effectiveness of the counselor as a group leader. Each leader response is observed and identified on the basis of the various skill categories. The impact of that response is then evaluated on a five point scale of Very Effective (5) to Very Ineffective (1). By accumulating frequencies of each skill, leaders can determine the characteristics of their leadership roles, functions, and styles. By calculating

Instructions: Observe the group leader, noting each response he or she makes. Identify that response as representative of one of the skill categories listed on the scale. Place an X in the Incidence (7) column each time you observe an identifiable skill. Then note the impact of that response by rating the response in the Effectiveness (*E*) column on a 1 to 5 scale:

    5 Very Effective: Helpful to the group process and person(s) involved
    4 Effective: Helpful to either the group process or person(s) involved
    3 Appropriate but neutral in impact
    2 Ineffective: Inappropriate or distracts group process or person(s) involved
    1 Very Ineffective: Distracts group process and impedes person(s) involved

Be sure to identify each response and evaluate its impact. Frequencies of each skill can be calculated by tabulating the marks in the *I* column. Leader effectiveness means can be determined for each skill as well as on an overall basis by adding the ratings in the *E* column for each skill and across all skills and dividing by the appropriate frequency.

Note: Counselors who use this scale should attach an addendum describing each skill for reference purposes. This information can be obtained from Chapter 6.

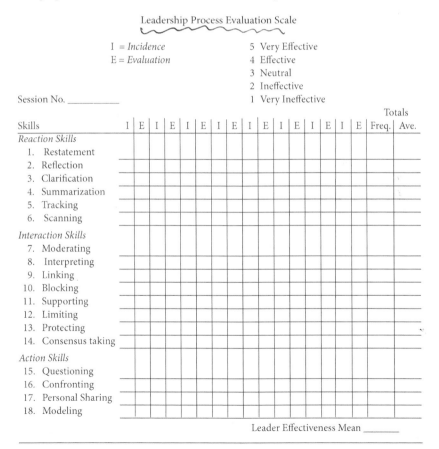

Leadership Process Evaluation Scale

I = *Incidence*	5 Very Effective
E = *Evaluation*	4 Effective
	3 Neutral
	2 Ineffective
Session No. _____	1 Very Ineffective

Skills	I	E	I	E	I	E	I	E	I	E	I	E	I	E	I	E	Freq.	Ave.
Reaction Skills																		
1. Restatement																		
2. Reflection																		
3. Clarification																		
4. Summarization																		
5. Tracking																		
6. Scanning																		
Interaction Skills																		
7. Moderating																		
8. Interpreting																		
9. Linking																		
10. Blocking																		
11. Supporting																		
12. Limiting																		
13. Protecting																		
14. Consensus taking																		
Action Skills																		
15. Questioning																		
16. Confronting																		
17. Personal Sharing																		
18. Modeling																		

Totals

Leader Effectiveness Mean _____

Figure 12.1 Leadership process evaluation scale.

Instructions: Provide each group member with an ID number to assist the rating process e.g., numbers 1–8 or letters A–H for an eight member group). Observe the group interaction, identifying member behaviors according to the categories listed on the scale. Note the incidence of the behavior by placing the member's ID number in the Incidence column each time the behavior occurs. Except for those exceptions noted on the scale, there must be a member ID number recorded for each behavior that can be identified. When the group is completed, total the incidence numbers for each behavior category by counting the number of ID entries in that category. This gives you the frequency of the behavior in the group session. A behavior profile can be developed for each group member by plotting the number of times a member's ID number appeared in each behavior category.

Note: Counselors who use this scale should attach an addendum describing the characteristics of each behavior for reference purposes. This information can be obtained from Chapter 7.

Member Process Evaluation Scale

Session no. _____ Number of Members in Group: _____

Member Behaviors	Incidence	Total
Resisting Behaviors		
1. Monopolizing		
2. Excessive Talking		
3. Hostility		
4. Silence*		
5. Withdrawal		
6. Absence*		
7. Cross Talking		
8. Intellectualizing		
9. Old Pro		
10. Joker		
11. Housekeeper		
12. Help Rejecting Complaining		
13. Self-Righteous Moralizing		
14. Rescuing		
Manipulating Behaviors		
15. Socializing		
16. Scapegoating		
17. Dependency		
18. Submissiveness		
19. Aggression		
20. Criticism		
21. Domination		
22. Mothering		
23 Calculating		

FIGURE 12.2 Member process evaluation scale

Member Behaviors	Incidence	Total
Helping Behaviors		
24. Listening#		
25. Facilitating		
26. Leading		
27. Self-Disclosure		
28. Giving Feedback		
29. Leveling		
30. Keeping Confidence#		
31. Personalizing Communication		
Emotional Behaviors		
32. Venting Negative Feelings		
33. Physical Aggression		
34. Acting Out		
35. Crying		
36. Affection		

\# Behaviors labeled with this sign may be recorded as a group behavior as well as an individual member behavior by simply recording the sign each time the group engages in the behavior.

* Absence need only be recorded once per session designating those members not present by ID number.

FIGURE 12.2 Member process evaluation scale. Continued.

means based on the evaluation ratings, leaders can determine their effectiveness in using each skill and on an overall basis. Group leaders can use this information to improve their skills and cultivate the use of skills they deem more helpful. They can clearly determine whether they are making appropriate progress in the use of their skills.

The Member Process Evaluation Scale is useful in helping the group leader evaluate the behavior of individual members. It also depicts characteristics of the group interaction at any one point that can be related to the process of group development. Each member should be given an ID number to facilitate the evaluation process. Then members' behaviors are observed and identified according to the categories listed on the scale by placing the member's ID number in the appropriate column. Other than exceptions noted on the scale each member behavior is recorded in the incidence column. Accumulation of behavior frequencies depicts the interaction in the group and tabulation of each member's behaviors results in a profile of that person's participation. Information from this scale helps counselors understand the members and the group process better and gives them definite areas that need to be worked on in the group. It also indicates when the group atmosphere is becoming more therapeutic and less resistant and manipulative.

Process evaluation is perhaps the easiest type of evaluation to do. It concerns itself only with what is happening within the confines of the group interaction and does not concern itself with external matters. The process, however, is only important as it relates to the impact witnessed outside the group. As Dies (1985) indicated, one of the bridges that must be built in group research and practice is the bridge between process and outcome. Our attention therefore must turn to the outcomes of group work because only in the context of external results is the value of the group process validated.

Outcome Evaluation

Outcome is what happens in a group member's life as a result of experience in the group. Outcome shows how goals, purposes, and objectives for which the group is organized are manifested in terms of change or impact in group members' feelings, thoughts, and behaviors. The degree to which that change occurs determines the relative success or failure of the group process. Evaluation of outcomes is a difficult task because neither the treatment nor the subjects can be adequately controlled, and the evaluation criteria are often difficult to define.

If change is observed, the question of whether it was caused by the group is moot, and if no change occurs, one wonders if the criteria were valid or if the method of evaluating was appropriate.

Despite the difficulty, group workers can do much to make evaluations of outcomes meaningful and concise in their own settings. It can be done by heeding the various warnings researchers have proffered, by making evaluations an inherent aspect of the group program, and by designing evaluation procedures specifically related to clients, the setting, and the type or focus of the group. Some of the basic considerations for effective outcome evaluation are discussed in the following subtopics.

Importance of Goals

Although we have discussed goals in regard to organizing group programs, I must emphasize them further here because goals are the roots of effective outcome evaluation. This topic is introduced with an appropriate quotation and warning from Ohlsen (1970):

> A counselor may be tempted to use vague general goals, to select for groups only clients with some common goals, and to ignore individuals' unique goals when appraising clients' growth. . . . Such errors often account for a counselor's failure to obtain significant results when he (or she) tries to assess outcomes of group counseling. Carefully defined, precise goals stated in terms of measurable or observable outcomes are necessary if the counselor is adequately to assess changes in clients. (p. 43)

He continued by advising that group counselors should learn from the behavioral counselors:

They have not attempted to improve the global adjustment of clients. They have merely focused their attentions on one or two precise behaviors, for which they usually have adequate measuring devices to assess predicted changes. (p. 255)

Group counselors should address themselves to measuring change in individual members rather than on a total group basis. In this way individual assessment will add up to a composite of group change. Cohn (1967) advocated this approach, considering it the easiest way to demonstrate change as a result of group counseling. Specific goals for individuals in groups must be developed so that evaluation is on an individual basis leading to a cumulative group effect. In other words *general group goals are important in organizing a group program, but specific individual goals are necessary to determine outcomes.* This perspective is intrinsic to counseling since "counseling's worth rests on the notion of furthering individual development and helping individuals face and learn to deal with painful and distressing problems. Therefore, appraisal must focus on individual change" (Ohlsen, 1970, p. 256). Dinkmeyer and Muro (1979) add that each group member should be afforded the opportunity to define and clarify goals that are unique to them within the context of the group.

So the message is clear: to evaluate outcomes of group work accurately we must develop individual goals within the group process. With this in mind let's turn our attention to implementation. Some counselors use the screening interview to help clients identify individual goals they wish to work toward in group counseling. Members then come to the first session with certain goals already specified. If this method is used, a natural initiating activity during the first session is to have members share their goals as a means of getting acquainted and establishing a work oriented attitude among members.

Another approach used in brief, solution oriented group counseling is to have members come to group with a detailed description of a problem they wish to solve or issue they wish to resolve. Solutions are then generated in group which upon implementation solve the problem or resolve the issue (based on member reporting data) (Trotzer, 1998c; 2000; 2001).

Other counselors structure goal setting sessions into the group counseling process, during which each member discusses and selects specific goals on which to work. In this case not only are the counselor and the client aware of the person's goals, but the rest of the group is cognizant of them as well.

Once individual goals are clarified and established, an excellent evaluative device is the behavioral contract (Dustin and George, 1973). Members are asked to specify in writing the actions they will take in an effort to achieve their goals. This contract negotiated in the group is then signed by the client and counselor

Scale Value	Scale Level Descriptor	Specific Problem Solving Behavior
+2	Much better than expected outcome	
+1	Better than expected outcome	
0	Expected outcome	
-1	Worse than expected outcome	
-2	Much worse than expected outcome	

Name: _____

Goal Statement: (expected outcome) _____

Figure 12.3 Goal attainment scaling.

and witnessed by the group. Each can receive a copy of the others' contracts so that the group can monitor progress and determine if a client successfully fulfilled the contract obligation. It also has built in evaluative criteria and implies or even denotes evaluation procedures. As such its use is recommended as a procedure for outcome evaluation.

Another evaluation method that has great utility for assessing individual change in counseling and therapy groups is called Goal Attainment Scaling (GAS) (see Figure 12.3). Developed by Kiresuk and Sherman (1968) and adapted to group counseling by Paritzky and Magoon (1982), GAS is a standard score device which translates any group member's goal into a measurable form using a 5-point scale from minus 2 (much worse than expected) to plus 2 (much better than expected). This procedure requires each group member to identify specific, concrete, measurable, problem solving goals they want to attain. The individual's goal is then represented as 0 (expected outcome) and serves as the target for which the member is to strive. A reasonable unit of variation from the target is determined to complete the scale in increments of 1 unit per integer above and below the target. Progress is then periodically assessed by the members and leader. The overall objective is to demonstrate progress and ultimately to be on target. This procedure allows for individualized group member goals and provides a means of clearly identifying progress. Combining GAS scores across all group members demonstrates the overall effectiveness of the group counseling process.

Self and Other Reports

Two important sources of outcome data are the clients themselves and those important others who have extensive contacts with them. If change occurs, it must be recognized by the party who changes and by those with whom that party interacts and relates. Cohn (1967) identified the distinguishing quality between self-reports and other reports of client changes when he wrote, "In both cases subjectivity operates, but in one case it is subjectivity of the (clients) involved, and in the other the subjectivity of a not-so-interested observer" (p. 31). In other words, self- and other reports tend to have inherent bias due to their subjective nature, but this in no way precludes their importance to the evaluation of outcomes. In fact, these reports are really front line evaluation procedures because of their kinship to the group process itself. Since group work is a people oriented process, its effects have people oriented meanings. Thus, the counselor should be immensely interested in whether clients themselves think they have changed and whether others around them concur. Ample evidence is available to indicate that what one thinks and perceives affects what one does. These thoughts need to be gotten out in the open as a means of gauging the influence of the group process on members and to assess the reception of significant others to member changes. Once reports have been obtained their validity or invalidity can always be tested.

The self-report can take many forms ranging from feedback given directly to the counselor or group to the use of instruments like Q-sorts, rating scales, semantic differentials, or personality inventories. The general purpose is to provide a self-based evaluation of the client's experience or change. In many cases researchers have found that no changes were noted on formal criteria (such as standardized instruments) but that group members reported positive reactions to their experience (Trotzer, 1971; Trotzer & Sease, 1971). Thus, the self-report can serve an especially important function if discrepancies are found or if no changes are evident on selected formal criteria. If discrepancies occur, the counselor must investigate the possible causes, which often leads to productive changes in the group process, individual members, or both. If no changes are noted on other criteria, counselors are compelled to reassess their criteria in light of positive self-reports of group members.

As far as other reports are concerned, Ohlsen (1970) pointed out that "when counseling is effective, important others should notice some of the changes in behavior and attitudes" (p. 258). If those around the client perceive changes, most likely the change has been extensive enough to overcome the normal expectations that tend to resist acknowledgement of change. If others notice it, most likely it exists. But this prompts an additional motive for using self- and other reports.

Sometimes changes clients make have an adverse effect on their relationships with important others. Cohn (1967) stated that counselors must find out whether "changes in growth in a given member act as a freeing device for other persons to whom he (or she) significantly related or whether individual growth will cause a disruptive pattern in his (or her) group relationship outside of counseling" (p. 19). In the latter case, the group member may need assistance in coping with problems generated as a result of efforts to change. Such input addresses the systemic nature of the change process reflecting the resistance to change or the acknowledgement of change in the client's world outside the group, both of which are critical to an individual member's success in implementing changes in their life.

Those persons involved in these evaluative reports are generally the clients themselves, parents, and other family members, teachers, coworkers, colleagues, supervisors, and selected peers both in and out of group. The counselor can use formal or informal methods in obtaining their reports. An informal method might entail devising a brief rating sheet that concentrates on the specific problem area the client is addressing and administering it periodically to the client and selected significant others. A comparison of the raters' perceptions of changes can then be made. This procedure is advantageous because it alerts those around the client to the client's efforts and generates more positive expectations. The balancing effect of both the client's and others' perspectives counters bias. When using significant others or any outside referent, be sure to build in appropriate release of information mechanisms.

Other useful methods of acquiring significant other reports are Q-sorts, semantic differentials, rating scales, open ended questionnaires, and structured face to face interviews. These procedures enable respondents to express their personal perspectives relative to the change process and provide a basis for determining whether change has occurred in the interpersonal realm of the member's experience. In most cases, it is preferable to use methods involving both self- and other perceptions in order to obtain a more comprehensive, balanced, and accurate evaluation of change.

Outcome Criteria

The selection of criteria for the evaluation of outcomes must be done in accordance with the points already considered. The criteria must be adaptable to the individual goals of the client, not the client to the criteria. Criteria must be specific and observable or measurable so that it can be validated. For groups conducted in schools, Cohn (1967) added another guideline that criteria "should probably be limited to variables that can be demonstrated to have some rather direct bearing on the child's school performance" (p. 32). A more general application of this idea is that criteria chosen should have a direct impact on the client's performance in the setting in which the group is organized and in the client's living environment. However, tangential criteria should not be excluded if they pertain to the individual goals of the client.

Cohn (1967) delineated two kinds of criteria, behavioral and affective (including attitudes, feelings, and values), both of which have relevance to group counseling. In schools the most readily available criteria are the educational variables of grades (in specific classes), grade point average (GPA), and a host of standardized tests (especially achievement and aptitude). Numerous other tests and inventories also can be called on to measure a variety of other variables. Examples include acceptance of self and others (Berger, 1952), self-concept (Tennessee Self Concept Scale-Counseling Form, Fitts, 1965), dogmatism (Rokeach, 1960), and many other personality type measures (see also DeLucia-Waack, 1997b). See Burlingame, Fuhriman, and Johnson (2004) for a comprehensive review of studies using outcome and process scales and DeLucia-Waack and Bridbord (2004) for a review of instruments related to measuring group process, dynamics, climate, leadership behaviors and therapeutic factors.

Before counselors choose to use any of these or other criteria they must ask the following questions:

1. Is this criteria merely convenient or does it actually measure a relevant variable?
2. Can this criteria be related to the individual goals of the clients?
3. Is change in a positive direction on these criteria indicative of change that results in problem resolution?
4. Can results be described simply and clearly to the client and significant others?
5. Will results reflect the influence of the group process?

If criteria are selected in this manner, the counselor will have a creditable basis on which to support claims regarding the efficacy of the group process.

Follow-up Procedures

Probably the most serious concern in the helping professions is whether positive change that is realized at the end of treatment is maintained over time. A related question is whether a latent effect occurs that generates positive change sometime after the treatment is completed. These same questions plague the group worker. Mahler, (1969) felt that "if we use immediate criteria measures the outcomes of a short group counseling program might be somewhat superficial" (p. 210). He stressed therefore that follow-up is more important than immediate results. Cohn's (1967) guidelines also emphasize that delayed evaluation is preferable.

The follow-up idea is extremely important in evaluation of group work outcomes. Counselors should make every effort to maintain contact with their former group members over an extended period of time to keep tabs on whether changes (actual or professed at the close of group sessions) have been integrated into the client's life style. This need not take an inordinate amount of time. But contact either personally or by questionnaire should be made, and data should be tabulated for reference purposes. Some counselors follow a general routine of contacting ex-group members after three months and again after six months. Others operate on a more casual basis with no specific schedule. They simply keep in touch with group clients over a period of time. Another method is to reconvene the entire group periodically for follow-up sessions to find out how members have progressed. These sessions often turn into extremely interesting and revealing interactions. In any event, the extent to which changes are retained is a good indicator of the potency of the group process in helping individuals resolve their problems, attain their goals or accomplish their tasks.

Summary

The key to effective group work evaluation is the relationship between process and outcome. An overemphasis of one or the other therefore will be detrimental to both (Krause & Hulse-Killacky, 1996; Hulse-Killacky, Killacky, & Donigian, 2001). A philosophy of using multiple assessment tools will greatly increase the reliability and importance of evaluation procedures. Obtaining data and feedback from a variety of relevant sources serves to clarify the nature of the group process and delineate its effect on the group members. The three principal concepts to keep in mind are: (1) make evaluation an inherent and established part of a group program; (2) develop relevant general goals based on assessed needs for organizing groups, but concentrate on specific individual goals to assess outcomes; and (3) utilize evaluation results to improve the group process, increase the expertise of the group leader, and establish group work in its various forms as accountable in helping people solve their problems, attain goals, complete tasks and become productive.

Illustrative Group Counseling Example:
An Interpersonal Problem Solving Group in a Mental Health Center

The counseling group described below took place in a mental health center (Trotzer, 1985). The group consisted of eight adult members, five female and three male, and was facilitated by a male-female coleadership team. All group members were referred to group counseling by their individual therapists at the center. Group members had become involved in individual therapy for a variety of reasons but were referred to the group to work specifically on the interpersonal dimensions of their lives. The group met for a total of 30 hours including an intake/orientation interview, an exit interview, and 14 two-hour group sessions over a four month period.

Overview of the Group Process

Orientation/Intake Interview The coleaders conducted an intake interview with each of the prospective group members for purposes of screening, orientation, and goal setting. The individual's therapist also was contacted with the client's permission to obtain relevant information. During this one hour interview each client was helped to identify interpersonal problem areas in his or her life and asked to specify particular problems or issues he or she wanted to work on in the group. Group ground rules were reviewed and questions were answered. The client was introduced to the Goal Attainment Scaling process (Figure 12.3) described earlier in the chapter, and a commitment to group participation was obtained.

Based on the content of the intake interviews, the leaders determined to utilize a semi-structured approach to the group introducing specific activities related to relevant topics as well as providing for open ended, problem focused interaction. The nature of the clients' interpersonal problems indicated that attention to four specific interpersonal skill areas would be a helpful adjunct to the group counseling process. These areas were communication skills, social skills, assertiveness skills, and conflict resolution skills. Consequently, two sessions were devoted to each of these areas. (Refer to chapter 11 for a specific format for organizing a group counseling program.)

Sessions 1 and 2 These sessions were primarily devoted to the forming and security aspects of the group. Members became acquainted with one another through structured activities and began engaging in self-disclosure and giving feedback. Group rules were reiterated and clarified and time was devoted to making contact on a person to person basis. Each person also shared why they were in the group, what issues they wanted to work on, and something about their current status.

Sessions 3 and 4 The focus of these sessions was on communication in a context of building cohesiveness and acceptance in the group. Members engaged in lab activities related to active listening and practiced various forms of interpersonal communication (Miller, Nunnally, & Wackman, 1975; Beebe, Beebe, & Redmond, 2005). Time also was spent identifying the specific interpersonal problem areas in clients' lives that served as content for the process of learning effective communication skills.

Sessions 5 and 6 Social skills were emphasized in these sessions combining the use of role playing and behavior rehearsal with out of group tasks and assignments to facilitate the application of social skills. The principle of in group and out of group connectedness thus was established prior to any intensive consideration of interpersonal problems. In addition, the perspective of responsibility for self and individuation/differentiation in the context of the group was explored.

Sessions 7 and 8 Assertiveness principles and techniques were integrated into these sessions thereby extending the responsibility dynamics introduced previously. Members practiced assertiveness skills in the group and targeted situations where they could use them outside the group.

Sessions 9 and 10 Lab activities teaching the various strategies of conflict resolution and helping group members identify their own tendencies in conflict situations were used. Conflict situations in each client's life were identified and analyzed from the viewpoint of effective conflict resolution thus introducing the dynamics of the work stage of the group process. Conflict resolution contracts were drawn up for each member with respect to a relationship outside the group.

The approximate ratio of structured activity to spontaneous interaction for these first 10 sessions was 1 to 1 1/2 hours structure to 1/2 to 1 hour open ended. The last four sessions, however, were mostly oriented toward the open ended form of interaction following the lead of members as they zeroed in on the specific problems in their lives.

Sessions 11–14 The focus of these sessions was directed by the content of problems on which group members were working. A check in system was used where each group member updated the group as to his or her progress and indicated whether or not specific attention (time) was needed during the session. A goal board was constructed so that members could be quickly apprised of each other's goals and progress. Sessions were primarily work oriented and devoted to making plans, testing them in the social laboratory of the group, and reporting on their efforts outside the group. The final session involved reviewing individual and group progress, making commitments to continue working individually, and saying goodbye.

Exit Interview An exit interview centered around the Goal Attainment Scale procedure that had been introduced in the orientation session and developed during the group meetings was conducted by the coleaders with each group member. Emphasis was on helping the individual assess and take credit for his or her own efforts and change and determining the overall effectiveness of the group counseling process.

Follow-up A three month follow-up questionnaire and survey consisting of two parts was sent to group members by the leaders. Part 1 consisted of questions related to the client's individual goals/progress and current status. Part 2 consisted of questions designed to solicit feedback relative to the group process experience and merits of group counseling for interpersonal problem solving.

Learning Activities

The learning activities described in this section are primarily designed to prepare the group counselor for the orientation aspects of organizing a group program. A secondary gain, however, is the development of leadership skills and expansion of the counselor's repertoire of group activities and experiences. Use these activities in conjunction with the material covered in chapters 10–12.

Class Presentation

Using material from the various chapters of this book, prepare and deliver a 15–20 minute talk on group counseling designed to clarify potential clients' understanding of the group process and inspire their interest in participating. After the talk, conduct a question and answer discussion in which class members, posing as potential clients ask questions that typically might emerge in such meetings. Upon completion of this discussion, ask the class to critique the presentation noting strengths, weaknesses, and possible omissions and revisions.

Staff Orientation

Have class members pose as teachers, referral sources, administrators, or parents and present a brief description (15–20 minutes) of the distinctions between different types of groups. Follow up the presentation with a demonstration that involves all or some of the members so that they will be able to experience the nature of one of the types of groups firsthand. Conduct a follow-up discussion to answer questions. Class members should try to anticipate typical questions teachers, administrators, referral sources, or parents might ask. Finally, critique the presentation.

Demonstration Videotape

Develop a video tape using class members or other persons to demonstrate the group counseling process. Making it could be a class project with one member designated as the leader and other members playing various member roles. This tape can serve as a means of stimulating class discussion about the group process and the leadership role. It can be shown to counselors in the field, referral sources, teachers, administrators, and families to get their reactions and feedback. The tape may be a useful resource to the student going into his/her internship or the counselor going into the field. It could also be duplicated for use on the job.

Demonstration Activities Project

Instruct each class member to compile a list of three to five group activities that could be used in a classroom situation, with prospective clients, or in a staff orientation session to experientially present the group process. These activities must be obtained from sources other than this book and must be written up in detail covering goals, materials needed, procedures, instructions, and the population for whom each activity is best suited.

Each class member then can be asked to demonstrate one of the activities in class. Duplicating these papers so that each class member can have a copy is a good way of supplying valuable material for future reference. These activities will also serve as a resource in leading groups since counselors will be able to adapt them readily to group sessions. See ASGW's *Group Work Experts Share Their Favorite Activities: A Guide to Choosing, Planning, Conducting and Processing* edited by DeLucia-Waack, Bridbord, and Kliener (2002) for examples.

13
Communication Activities in Groups

If group leaders were carpenters, they would have tool chests that would accompany them to every site where they applied their leadership talents, skills, and functions. In that tool chest would be a host of activities that could be pulled out and used in different types of groups, . . . in diverse settings, with a wide variety of clients for a multitude of purposes. Every skilled carpenter knows the tools that are needed for the job, why and how they work, and when to use them. In addition, dedicated carpenters keep the tools of their trade sharp, in good condition and up to date so that the final result does not display poor craftsmanship or shoddy labor. In other words, the tools are used to make their mark, but not leave their mark on the finished product. The same is true of activities that leaders use in groups. Activities are tool of a group leader's trade, but they are only tools and must be used in a manner that produces a group experience and result that is not flawed by the evidence a particular activity leaves in the aftermath of its use (Trotzer, 2004, p. 76). ❧

Structured activities in groups have emerged as a viable and integral component of group work and as a vital element in facilitating the group process (Bates, Johnson, & Blaker, 1982; Corey, Corey, Callahan, & Russell, 1982; Gladding, 1994, 2000; Jacobs, Harvill, & Masson, 2006; Johnson & Johnson, 1997; Ohlsen, Horne, & Lawe, 1988). Labeled variously as group procedures or techniques, structured exercises, catalytic activities, or human relations activities, they all can be subsumed under the general rubric of communication activities, the term we will use to identify them in this chapter. Although the genesis of communication activities is difficult to determine, the activities themselves have emanated from a wide range of psychological, sociological, communicational, and educational endeavors. Because of the growing reliance on and use of communication activities in all types of groups (group models and protocols: Furr, 2000; Jones & Robison, 2000; Kulic, Dagley, & Horne, 2001; counseling and therapy groups: Gore-Felton & Speigel, 1999; Loewy, Williams, & Keleta, 2002; Portman & Portman, 2002; Samide & Stockton, 2002; Stanko & Taub, 2002; Williams, Frame, & Green, 1999; psychoeducation groups: Akos, 2000; Asner-Self, & Feyissa, 2002; Daignault, 2000; Hage & Nosanow, 2000; Martin & Thomas, 2000; Sommers-Flanagan, Barrett-Hakanson, Clarke, & Sommers-Flanagan 2000; Vacha-Haase, Ness, Dannison, & Smith, 2000; training/teaching groups: Brenner, 1999; Cummings, 2001; Kees & Leech, 2002; Marotta, Peters, & Paliokas, 2000; Smaby, Maddux, Torres-Rivera, & Zimmick, 1999), and the increased awareness of their existence and utility in both professional circles and the public sector, a special need is for the group leader to have an understanding of their nature and use. Perhaps Bates, Johnson, and Blaker (1982), who call communication activities "catalytic activities," have stated the perspective toward communication activities best: "Catalysts are not the most important part of a leader's arsenal, but they do provide added potential for leading creatively" (p. 162).

The proliferation of information regarding communication activities in the literature is almost at a saturation point. With the general emphasis on human relations training, diversity, and multicultural awareness, the expansion and adaptation of the growth group on college campuses and in society at large, the appeal of encounter groups as a form of white collar hippie movement and the use of sensitivity training, T-Groups, and quality circles in business and industry, the amount of professional material is almost overwhelming. However, the low key hysteria (both for and against) communication activities fanned in the sixties and seventies by the popular media (Howard, 1968; Human Potential, 1970) has evolved into a solidly professional perspective that emphasizes pragmatism, ethics, and conceptual validity. The initial confusion in the public sector—and to some extent in professional circles—as to the use of communication activities in groups has largely been clarified and focused. The mention of communication activities is less likely to conjure up comments about touchy-feely experiences, brain washing, seduction, or unethical practice, but such issues are still cause for concern because they represent a potential threat to group work and can curtail the effective use of communication activities in the group process. This concern has long been recognized by many professionals in counseling and psychotherapy who strongly voiced the need to develop ethical standards and guidelines to regulate the use of these activities and to ensure leader competence (Lakin, 1969, 1970; The Personnel and Guidance Journal, Vol. 50, No. 4, 1972; Verplanck, 1970; Whiteley, 1970). These expressions have produced the ethical and training standards that now epitomize both the training and the practice of professional group leaders with respect to communication activities (Association for Specialists in Group Work, 1998; American Counseling Association, 2005; see also chapter 8 of this volume and Trotzer, 2004)

The purpose of this chapter is to address the nature and use of communication activities as a means of assisting group leaders in resolving the normal dilemmas that arise when consideration is given to using them in groups. The chapter will: (1) present a model for categorizing communication activities, (2) discuss a rationale for their use, (3) identify guidelines for selection, (4) describe psychodrama as a particular form of communication activity, and (5) conclude with sample communication activities that reflect the chapter's contents.

Categorizing Communication Activities

Despite the plethora of terms and the variation in definitions, certain characteristics generally distinguish communication activities from other group procedures and methods used by group leaders. First, communication activities call for specific directions and parameters that give group members a format and/or a focus for their interaction. Whenever the leader makes an explicit and directive request of a member for the purposes of focusing on material, augmenting or exaggerating affect, practicing behavior or solidifying insight" he or she is using a form of communication activity (Corey, Corey, & Callanan, 1982, p. 1). Second, communication activities often entail the use of materials or props for carrying out the activity (e.g., pencils, paper, paint, material objects, and so forth) (Gladding, 1998). Finally, communication activities can be standardized to a large degree, enabling leaders to use them in identical or adapted form in a variety of group settings and with diverse clientele.

Leader Attitude Toward Communication Activities

The group leader's attitude toward communication activities should reflect a professional commitment to ethical standards and his or her personal responsibility to group members. Communication activities are only tools that must be used judiciously to enhance the group process for the benefit of group members. These activities are not mechanisms that should be exploited, used to generate emotional highs, or entertain group participants. Any experimentation should be done for specific purposes, such as determining the impact of a technique to ensure its most effective use in a particular group setting or familiarizing group leaders with an activity so that they have greater awareness of its impact and more confidence in using it. Communication activities should not become ends in themselves and should always relate directly to the group process, the purposes of the group and the needs of group members. They must be consistent with the rationale and philosophy of the group leader and have a specified purpose from a pragmatic (group related) and conceptual (theory related) perspective.

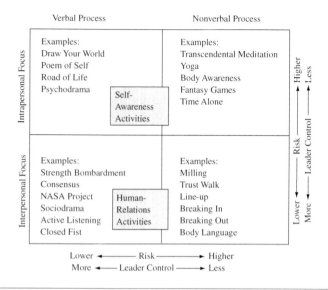

Figure 13.1 Categorizing communication activities. (Adapted from a model presented by Roy Evans, Clinical Psychologist, Minnesota State Prison, during a group counseling workshop at the University of Wisconsin-River Falls, Summer, 1972. Reprinted by permission.)

Identifying Traits of Communication Activities

Figure 13.1 presents a model comprised of two dimensions that is helpful in differentiating the nature of communication activities. The first relates to the *focus* of the activity and is divided into two parts, intrapersonal and interpersonal. *Intrapersonal activities* are designed to help people engage in the introspective process that leads to greater self-knowledge. They emphasize a greater understanding of one's inner self as the basis for making constructive decisions, personality dynamics, living a more effective life, changing one's feelings, thoughts, or behaviors, and actualizing one's potential. They stress personal learning about the subject of self. *Interpersonal activities* are designed to help people explore, understand, and improve their relationships with others. Their focuses are on the social self, group and system dynamics and human relationships. Activities revolve around interpersonal interaction, and emphasis is on relational qualities and characteristics that enhance effective communication, promote meaningful human encounters, and facilitate meeting social-psychological needs.

The second dimension of the model involves the *process of communication* used in the activity and is divided into verbal and nonverbal categories. *Verbal activities* concentrate on the use of words as the primary means of communication. The form of verbal exchange may make use of either the speaking or writing capacities of the participants. *Nonverbal activities* encompass a broad range of media from art forms to body language to internal communication processes. The nonverbal dimension of communication activities is identified by the fact that the primary action takes place without the use of or dependence on words.

The combination of these two dimensions provides us with a perspective for assessing the nature of communication activities. *Verbal intrapersonal activities* help individuals engage in introspective self-examination and then verbally share their perceptions in the form of self-disclosure. Examples include such activities as Draw Your World, Poem of Self, Road of Life, and Life Story. Psychodrama is a very sophisticated form of this type of activity. *Nonverbal intrapersonal activities* provide a format for introspection but the experience takes place totally within the confines of the individual and is not accessible to others except through that person's verbal interpretation of what was experienced. Examples of ingroup activities include meditation, yoga, body awareness exercises, fantasy games (Schutz, 1967), and Time Alone (Katz, 1973). Out of group activities may involve a variety of creative writing activities or tasks. (See Wenz & McWhirter (1990) and Gladding (1992a; 1992b; 1998) for specific writing activities that can be incorporated into group work.) Most of these activities include some type of sharing, but their main thrust is on providing each person with an internal experience for personal enrichment, problem solving and learning.

One prominent example of an intrapersonal activity that has a long history of effectiveness in therapeutic groups is journaling (Riordan, 1996; Riordan & Matheny, 1972). Referred to variously as diary writing, journaling, or keeping a log, Riordan (1996) has dubbed the use of writing as an adjunctive dimension of counseling as *scriptotherapy*. Group members are asked to or recommended to keep a journal of their thoughts, feelings and experiences over the course of the group. This serves the purpose of intrapersonal processing and effectively develops a conceptual bridge for members between group sessions. As a communication exercise specific instructions can be given as follows:

"When you have finished the session, take 15 minutes to record your observations and feelings" (Riordan & White, 1996, p. 97). These entries can be collected and reviewed by the group leader or simply left to be a personal summary and a possible stimulus for members to voluntarily relate or share in the course of group interaction.

Verbal interpersonal activities are designed to engage people in interaction with others and are characterized by dependence on verbal feedback and sharing. Examples include Strength Bombardment, Consensus, Active Listening, and The Closed Fist. Sociodrama is a form of this type of exercise because it focuses on common problems in social relationships that all group members can benefit from working on and uses mainly verbal role-playing techniques to do so. *Nonverbal interpersonal activities* are designed to provide members with experiences in interpersonal relationships without using the normal communication channel of words. Although these activities usually entail a verbal follow-up, the main action takes place during the activity. Any clarification, interpretation, sharing, or feedback takes place after the experience and is subject to modification when translated into the verbal domain. Activities such as Trust Walk, Milling, Line up, Breaking In, and body language activities are examples.

Generally speaking we can classify all verbal and nonverbal intrapersonal activities as _self-awareness activities._ Similarly, verbal and nonverbal interpersonal activities can be labeled _human-relations activities._ No absolute rigidity exists in this model because many activities include both verbal and nonverbal components and some may incorporate all four quadrants of the diagram. Also, many exercises can be altered to fit the various categories with just a little creativity on the part of the group leader. In effect then, this model is a reference for determining the characteristics of communication activities. As such it is a useful resource in training group leaders to select and use communication exercises in groups.

Some specific considerations of this model have direct relevance to group counseling and psychotherapy. The therapeutic group process is primarily a verbal process whose effectiveness depends on communication among group members. Therefore the leader must always incorporate a verbal sharing component into any activity that is used.

Activities should always end up in the verbal interpersonal realm. In point of fact, the processing phase when using communication exercises is the most important dimension (DeLucia-Waack, 1997a; Ward & Litchy, 2004). Kees and Jacobs (1990) emphasize that

> without adequate processing the leader cannot be sure of what learning has taken place. If done correctly, processing can provide members with additional learning about themselves and other members of the group. Through processing, members may also develop a plan of action for transferring this learning to their lives outside the group (p. 23).

Processing in the verbal interpersonal domain facilitates greater group cohesiveness and communication and alleviates problems of member dissociation that sometimes occur, especially with nonverbal and intrapersonal activities. It also enables members to benefit from each other's experiences and encourages modeling and identification. DeLucia-Waack (1997a) notes that processing by both individuals and the group is critical. "The effectiveness of group work interventions and strategies is greatly increased when the intervention (_communication activity_) is processed (_verbally_) at the individual (_intrapersonal_) and group (_interpersonal_) level" (p. 3).

Two underlying continuums also are part of this model and warrant careful attention by the group leader. The first is the element of risk involved in using these activities. At the beginning of the chapter I mentioned some general concerns with communication activities, but here I will be more specific. Verbal activities are less risky than nonverbal in the perception of both group members and significant others outside the group. This is especially true in school situations and with adolescent groups. Nonverbal activities should be carefully selected and used judiciously. Extensive physical contact and physically dangerous activities *Risk* should be avoided. Risk also is somewhat higher in intrapersonal activities than in interpersonal ones. The risk here is psychological in nature because of the focus on self-disclosure. Usually a person can give feedback more easily than be self-disclosing and can talk more easily about what is happening between people than engage in introspection. In other words, low impact self-assessment activities and interpersonal activities should take precedence over exercises requiring in depth self-disclosure until the group is ready for them. In this way an atmosphere of trust and acceptance can be established that reduces the risk of sharing more private thoughts about one's self and one's problems.

Bates, Johnson, and Blaker (1982) in adapting this model noted that a within quadrant intensity factor mirrors the overall risk dimension. Within each section activities can be refined more definitively on the basis of being low, medium, or high in intensity. Group leaders can thus select activities that are appropriate to the level of group interaction and commensurate with the nature of group dynamics. (2) The second continuum is leader control. The amount of control the leader has in guiding, facilitating, and limiting the interaction in using communication activities is directly related to their nature. Verbal activities lend themselves to much greater control than do nonverbal. At least when members are talking the leader can tune in to consistencies and discrepancies between members' words and their experiences. In nonverbal activities much of this awareness can be lost or hidden. And nonverbal communication by its very nature is much more difficult to follow anyway. Because the experience takes place without the usual verbal cues of the expressive domain, the leader has less contact with it. Similarly, interpersonal activities are more conducive than intrapersonal to leader direction, especially in the nonverbal intrapersonal area. Maintaining a common level of involvement in these activities is difficult because some members may go very deep and others may do nothing. The result thus can be detrimental to group cohesiveness and development.

These considerations should not deter group leaders from using communication activities in their groups, but they should be aware of these issues and take them into account in choosing and implementing activities (DeLucia-Waack, Bridbord, & Kleiner, 2002; Trotzer, 2004). Risk will always be involved because change and growth do not occur without it. Control problems will always exist because of individual uniqueness, the diversity of member commitment and involvement, and the nature of the group process. Leaders must act to reduce these problems by carefully utilizing techniques that are consistent with their philosophies and rationales of group counseling and that are best suited to the needs of the group members.

Rationale and Use of Communication Activities

By viewing any small group experience as an on going developmental process and each group session as a mini-reflection or prototype of that process, we can build a generic rationale for using communication activities in different types of groups. This rationale provides a framework that encompasses individual differences in group leadership styles and helps leaders explain and justify activities to group members and other interested parties. To relate communication activities to the group process, I will discuss their purposes and how they are introduced into the group. The three basic ways of using communication activities are to: initiate, facilitate, and terminate (conclude or close). Each will be described separately (Trotzer, 1973).

 Initiation

Communication activities can be used in group work to initiate the group process. This includes beginning the overall group process, starting individual sessions within that process, and interjecting a new or different focus during the group session. For example, at the first session of a 10 session counseling group of graduate students, the leader asked members to describe themselves in the third person as if they were their own best friend. The members described themselves using their first names and "he" or "she" rather than "I" or "me." The leader initiated this activity to set the tone for both that particular session and the overall group process. Members began the process of getting to know one another and sharing themselves with others. The self-consciousness created by the newness of the group and having to talk about themselves was lessened because members could step outside themselves and speak more objectively. This example points out one of the purposes in initiating activities: giving members a structured format in which they can have a common experience. Some of the discomfort of beginning the group was lessened, and the common focus established a basis on which the group process could build (Furr, 2000; Jones & Robison, 2000; Kulic, Dagley, & Horne, 2001).

Hetzel, Barton, and Davenport (1994) reported that the use of structured activities was particularly useful in beginning their men's groups. They observed that "a few exercises were helpful during the initial sessions of the group in developing a sense of trust among members, but no more than one activity should be included during each session" (p. 59). Their use of communication activities in an initiating manner thus helped the individual members and the group process get off to a constructive start.

Stockton, Rohde, and Haughey (1994) found that structured group exercises at the beginning of each session resulted in participants being significantly more satisfied with their group experiences. In addition, they discovered that groups where structured activities were used did significantly less recycling to earlier developmental group tasks and stages.

A second purpose for using communication activities to initiate is to orient the group toward a topic that will be useful to effective group functioning in accord with the purpose of the group. The focus is not on content of the topic but on aiding the group members to function as a group. For example, a group of male high school juniors was formed because of their disruptive classroom behaviors. They exhibited a great deal of discomfort, resistance, and distrust during their first two sessions. The counselor suggested the trust walk as an initiating activity for the third session. The trust walk made the issue of trust concrete since each individual experienced being dependent on another person and being responsible for another person. When the activity was over, the leader helped group members express their feelings about the experience and make the transition from being trusting and trustworthy in the activity to being so in the group and in their own lives.

Using communication activities to start group interaction lessens the discomfort created by the ambiguity of an unstructured situation. Members are able to relax and lower interpersonal barriers, thus opening channels of communication that can subsequently be used to confront and resolve problems in the group. Also, the simulation experience and modeling effect of the activities help group members learn important aspects of effective interpersonal communication and group dynamics.

Counselors who use communication activities to initiate group interaction gain the benefit of group control. They become the experts who direct the group interaction, lifting this responsibility from the members' shoulders. The counselor becomes the guide, and members become the guided. Structuring group interaction by using an activity gives the counselor a better sense of what is going on and what to expect. This provides the leader with, a kind of security that is not as readily accessible to the leader who does not initiate. Leaders who are more comfortable and effective in structured settings or who want to make things happen (Poppen & Thompson, 1974) tend to use more initiating activities. In fact, some leaders resemble orchestra conductors or movie directors, putting activities together in sequence and molding and directing the group process from start to finish.

One drawback to using communication activities for initiating purposes is that the counselor may create a dependency propensity in which members expect the counselor to provide the direction all the time. To circumvent this possibility, the leader must be able to integrate the initiating activity into the group process and facilitate the shift of responsibility back to the members. The communication activity should not be an isolated experience but an integral part of the life cycle of the group process.

Another difficulty is in choosing appropriate initiating activities. The counselor's choice of an activity should be based on his or her knowledge of the group process, the purpose of the group and the unique qualities of the group members. For best results, leaders should choose activities with which they are familiar. Even then, at times an activity will not be effective. This situation may be avoided if the leader maintains a tentative attitude when suggesting activities and remains sensitive to the group's reaction as the activities are being described. Leader willingness to alter or change the activity based on members' reactions usually enhances success. Having more than one activity in mind also gives the leader flexibility in dealing with situations created by member resistance or by the failure of a particular activity to work.

Finally, when leaders use initiating activities they provide members with targets toward which to direct their resistance. Members can grasp the opportunity to be uncooperative in a very specific way. However, resistance is normal and if the leader is prepared for it the activity also can serve as a means of dealing with it in a constructive manner. Since members know clearly what is expected of them, they can direct their resistance at a nonpersonal target but also are likely to experience group pressure to participate. The end result is that through the activity members often find that their reasons for resistance are unwarranted and can comfortably make the transition from resistance to cooperation and involvement.

Facilitation

The primary purpose of using communication activities to facilitate is to help the group use its resources to the fullest extent (Poppen & Thompson, 1974). For example, a group of sixth-grade girls who were central figures in cliques found it difficult to talk to one another without getting into heated arguments. The group leader used active listening as an activity to help them learn listening skills and thereby improve their communications with one another. The girls not only began to relate to each other in the group but used their listening skills with noticeable effect in the classroom.

The main point to keep in mind when using communication activities to facilitate the group process is that the activities should be derived from or suggested in response to a situation or dynamic that has emerged in the group. A typical facilitating activity is role playing. Role playing is a procedure in which a problem is dealt with by having the principals involved act it out in the safety of the group with other members participating as actors or observers. For example, a ninth-grade girl was discussing her problem of communication with her parents about dating and curfews. The counselor asked the girl to role play a typical conversation with her parents on this topic, using other members as auxiliaries. The counselor directed the role playing by keeping the actors in character and guiding them through the use of role reversals, alter egos, and role substitutions. When the role playing was over, the leader facilitated a follow-up discussion to consolidate what had transpired regarding the problem. In this particular case, role playing also was used to help the girl try out some alternative approaches to the problem as well.

⊘Facilitating activities help to clarify problem situations, present alternatives, alleviate anxiety producing circumstances, and break through impasses that occur in groups. They can be used to perk up the group interaction when normal communication channels stagnate or break down. They can help a group consider an issue that they feel is relevant but do not know how to approach. Facilitation procedures should be catalytic, stimulating, and enhancing to group interaction without creating a noticeable structure that will distract members from their stated purposes.

Facilitating activities usually enjoy ready acceptance by group members. Because they are based directly on the interaction of the group, their probability of success is increased. Since facilitating activities are designed to provide avenues for reaching goals set by the group and do not suggest content, the group experiences an autonomy and responsibility with respect to the nature and focus of the material discussed. Facilitating techniques thus help members learn their responsibility in the group and at the same time help the leader establish guidelines and boundaries within which the group interaction occurs.

The facilitative use of communication activities is difficult to master. Its relevance and effectiveness is dependent on the leader's creativity, spontaneity, and sensitivity in here and now situations. The leader must exhibit a willingness to follow and respond rather than lead and direct. A facilitative leader must have a capacity to tolerate ambiguity, allowing the group to take responsibility for its own direction. Responding effectively requires a knowledge and awareness of numerous activities that are usable in groups (DeLucia-Waack, Bridbord, & Kleiner, 2002). This knowledge should include details of procedure, applicability, and probable effects of each activity. The ability to respond with the right activity at the right time has to be developed through experience in the leadership role.

Termination

Communication activities are useful at the end of individual group sessions, when individual members terminate, and when the total group is being disbanded. Their major purposes are to consolidate and integrate what has been learned in the group and generate closure. More specifically, they help members clarify and review what has transpired, provide reinforcement for changes that have been made, and encourage members to implement these changes in their daily lives.

Terminating activities that bring closure to a group provide a jumping off place for members. For example, a go-round at the end of a session asking members for their reactions to the session or to the problems or topic under consideration creates a format in which members can express their feelings before the group disperses. An activity such as this aids both the leader and members in understanding where the group is and provides a natural ending point.

The impact of termination activities removes some of the awkwardness associated with closure. It helps individual members say goodbye and gives the group an opportunity to send them off on a positive note. For example, a member of a therapy group for prison inmates obtained a parole. At the member's last session, the leader suggested an adaptation of the Hope Chest activity in which group members presented the departing member with symbolic gifts they felt would enhance his success in readjusting to society. The gifts served to pinpoint the gains he had made and warned of vulnerabilities that still needed attention. In addition, the positive feelings generated had a remarkable effect on the group itself that was evident in their efforts to work on their own problems during the following weeks.

When a group is being disbanded, members usually recognize that termination is called for but experience some ambivalence about it, especially if a sense of belongingness and cohesiveness have developed in the group. This desire to "end but not yet" triggers the enthusiastic involvement typifying the ending phase of a group and may even result in members suggesting their own closing activities. For example, during the final session of a group of college freshmen who initially were having a difficult time adjusting to a large university, one member suggested that each member show how he or she felt about every other member. Members individually went around the group expressing their feelings toward each other, first nonverbally and then verbally. This activity clarified the relationships between individual members and also focused on their learning in the area of developing relationships.

Ambivalent feelings about terminating also may affect group leaders. They may feel reluctant to disband a group because of the effort expended in getting it to function effectively. Or they may feel that something the group— or an individual in the group—needs for a more complete or well-rounded experience has been overlooked or neglected. In either case, a closing activity may be useful. For example, during the course of a human relations group composed of high school seniors, the group members had looked critically at themselves and each other offering constructive criticism to each other but focusing primarily on their weaknesses in relating to others. The leader felt a balance was needed, and he also felt a great deal of personal involvement in the group. Therefore, he suggested a segment of the technique called Strength Bombardment in which every member including the leader gave every other member only positive feedback. This activity helped to remove some doubts that members had about relating to others and served to strike a balance between critical and positive feedback. It brought the group together and helped them realize how much they had learned about themselves and each other. It also showed emphatically that, regardless of difficulties a person may have to resolve, strengths and other good qualities can aid and sustain them in that process.

Termination activities involve very little risk. The group is generally cohesive and cooperative at this point, ensuring the effectiveness of most activities suggested. And since members recognize that the group is ending, the chances of opening new problems or going overboard emotionally are small. One drawback is that the high degree of closeness and satisfaction the group may experience may not be present in the daily lives of individual members. This could create distortion in their perceptions of the group process and temporarily block out the effort that was involved in getting to the ending point. It may even give rise to wishes to prolong the group, which the leader must handle warmly but firmly. This reaction is a normal phenomenon associated with the completion of difficult but successful projects and is soon replaced with a more realistic perspective.

Flexibility of Communication Activities

Many communication activities can be used in all of the ways previously described. They can be revised and adapted to fit into the group process as initiating, facilitating, or terminating activities. Most also can be redesigned to conform to a leader's particular style or to meet the unique needs of a particular group. The main point is that all communication activities are intended to provide a means by which group members can interact with each other (Blaker & Samo, 1973). They can and do add flexibility and breadth to the group process. But it must be remembered that the focus of the group is on persons and purposes—in that order—and that communication activities are only important and useful to the extent they contribute to the therapeutic growth of individuals in the group and resolution of problems for which the group was formed or address the tasks for which the group was organized.

Guidelines for Selecting Communication Activities

The group process can be greatly enhanced by the proper selection and judicious use of communication activities. For example, McMillon (1994) found that intentionally structured groups had a positive impact on problem solving and interpersonal communication among a population of underprepared, first-year minority college students. However, naive and careless use of structured activities casts a bad reflection on the counselor and the group counseling process and may endanger group members in a psychological, moral, or physical sense.

Blaker and Samo (1973) warned that communication games can become ends in themselves in the hands of incompetent leaders who discover their potential for reducing inhibitions. However, communication activities do aid the group process if selected for a specific purpose and introduced in the right way (DeLucia-Waack, Bridbord, & Kleiner, 2002; Trotzer, 1973, 2004). The following guidelines are designed to help the group leader make wise choices in selecting communication activities for use in the group process (Trotzer, 2004; Trotzer & Kassera, 1973).

1. *Select activities on the basis of their purpose, relevance, and desired outcomes.* This is the most important rule and supersedes all other considerations. Communication activities should not be implemented because they produce

Intentional activities

emotional highs. All too frequently popularity and familiarity are the only bases for selecting an exercise rather than the why and wherefore of its use. The impact of an activity should be considered above all else, and if that impact is not in accord with the needs of the members and the purposes of the group, the activity should not be used.

Jacobs, Harvill, and Masson (1988) suggest seven generic reasons or purposes for using communication exercises:

1. To generate discussion and participation.
2. To get the group focused on a common topic or issue.
3. To shift or deepen the focus.
4. To provide an opportunity for experiential learning.
5. To increase the comfort level.
6. To provide the leader with useful information.
7. To provide fun and relaxation.

These process parameters provide a general framework within which specific activities can be selected.

2. *Select activities that have a solid conceptual framework and rationale relative to human growth and development and interpersonal communication.* Activities should not be selected on the basis of pragmatism alone. Each activity also should have a psychological, conceptual basis that validates its use from a theoretical perspective. This guideline serves as a check and balance to the often intuitive use of structured activities that can initiate interactions that are not consistent with principles of human growth and development, the group leader's philosophy, and/or the psychological rationale of the group.

3. *Select activities that are familiar and comfortable for you to use.* The enthusiasm and confidence of the leader in presenting an activity are often the cues that mark its reception by the members. The leader's discomfort with a technique will be picked up by the group and could cause resistance to and even the failure of the activity. Activities that have been experienced should take precedence over those that have been observed or read about. Do not use techniques you have heard about just to see what will happen. To increase your repertoire of activities, first attempt new techniques under controlled conditions so that the process can be carefully observed and the impact or outcome evaluated.

4. *Select activities that are primarily verbal rather than physical.* Physical contact is often the first issue raised against the use of communication activities in group work and should be included only after careful consideration. Members' cultural, religious, and personal values and beliefs may mitigate against activities that involve physical contact. Consequently, activities need to be selected and adapted to facilitate inclusion and participation

rather than resistance, intrusion, or exclusion. From a leader's perspective, Birnbaum (1969) noted that nonverbal techniques require a minimum of experience and knowledge to stimulate an initial response but demand a maximum of expert knowledge and sophistication to extract a positive educational outcome. Most desired outcomes in groups can be attained either by verbal or nonverbal activities that involve a minimum of physical contact. For example, hand or arm holding in a trust walk is acceptable, but the extended physical contact of an activity such as body sculpturing (Schutz, 1967) is better avoided. Remember that any nonverbal activity should always involve a verbal sharing component. This enables the leader to assess more accurately the effect of the activity and to make the necessary adjustments to handle problems.

In addition, modifications that accommodate individual belief systems and religious or cultural mores can be made to generate inclusion rather than to delimit the group from access to a particular experiential learning activity that involves touch. For example, in a mixed gender training group that included a male whose religious practice forbade physical contact with females, the leader enlisted his assistance as a verbal consultant to the group as they addressed the task of getting the group physically into a two foot square area. He participated verbally by contributing suggestions as to strategy and was thus included in the activity and could participate directly in the processing portion of the activity. In this particular case, it also enabled the group to expand its diversity awareness and sensitivity and enabled the individual to share his beliefs without threat of rejection or judgment.

5. *Select activities that do not rely on jargon or labels and that can be presented in terms that do not stereotype, invoke negative connotations or produce overtones that stigmatize.* Many times people react to the connotations of names without knowing the real nature of the process to which the name is given. In selecting and discussing activities, group leaders should take that tendency into account. Often the same activity can have many different labels. "Let's see if you can show us how you reacted in that situation" could be termed psychodrama, sociodrama, or role playing. However, there is a considerable difference in connotation between labeling it psychodrama as opposed to role playing. Activities selected should be explained in everyday language or in neutral terms.

6. *Select activities that are commensurate with the maturity level of group members.* The members' abilities to immerse themselves in an activity without undue difficulty, tension, or embarrassment is extremely important to the effective use of any technique. Similarly, the activity should have characteristics that appeal to members' interests. If members feel they are being manipulated, talked down to, or treated without respect, they will resist and shun involvement. If the activity itself is unattractive or unstimulating,

they will lose interest or be easily distracted. For example, the use of puppets to aid third graders in exploring their feelings may be more effective than role playing. Eighth graders, however, would probably prefer role playing, and adults may benefit from a full blown psychodrama integrated into the session. If a leader feels a particular activity has merit and accomplishes a desired purpose, it can most likely be modified to fit the age level and maturity of the group. In fact, this type of leader action is constructive because it indicates the leader is person oriented rather than technique oriented and is willing to alter activities to meet the needs of the group.

7. *Select activities that are compatible with and adaptable to the physical setting in which the group is meeting.* If the physical setting does not allow for an activity to be fully experienced or interferes with it being carried out, the activity should be avoided. For a large group that meets in a small room, using dyads for a verbal activity requiring high concentration may create confusion and interfere with accomplishing the purpose intended. Similarly, techniques that require members to leave the room should be carefully screened and explained and are best avoided if any indications are present that clients may not be able to handle the activity responsibly. The loss of leader control in these activities could result in misunderstanding from outside observers who witness the actions of group members as well as from the members themselves.

8. *Select activities that allow for maximum member participation.* Some activities require physical skills or emotional endurance that may be frightening, distasteful, or overtaxing to some group members. Physical activities always should be prefaced with a caution to members and an option to observe rather than participate. Strenuous activities are best avoided. Activities that require members to move in a way that might cause embarrassment should be used only when members have been advised in advance of this factor. For example, for some activities members might prefer to wear jeans rather than dresses or skirts. Selection should take into account the psychological, intellectual, and experiential levels of group members. Techniques requiring extensive self-disclosure and feedback may not allow for maximum participation if members are at different levels with respect to trust and acceptance or if they have varied skill capacities or experiential contact with communication activities. In addition, consideration of cultural and diversity factors is necessary to facilitate maximum relevance and participation (see chapter 9).

9. *Select activities that allow group members to control their own levels of involvement and disclosure.* Guideline 8 is directed at external factors that must be considered to promote maximum member participation in an activity. Guideline 9 focuses on internal factors that allow for maximum involvement by each individual member. Communication activities should promote personal

freedom and empowerment, not simply reduce inhibitions. Techniques that force members to do something they are not ready for or find too threatening should be avoided. Birnbaum (1969) pointed out that confrontation techniques, for example, are easy to implement but very difficult to handle constructively because of the psychological pressure placed on individuals being confronted. Members should be allowed to decide how they will involve themselves and to what depth they will go. Activities that interfere with an individual's right to personal privacy or undermine his or her free agency should not be used in groups. A general guideline that states "participation is expected but the depth of involvement and sharing is up to each individual" included in the instructions or ground rules often alleviates the undue pressure dimension of communication exercises.

10. *Select activities that will result in outcomes you are confident that the group and you as a leader can handle.* Activities that precipitate the expression of strong feelings are always risky and should be used with caution. If the possibility of loss of control is apparent in the use of any technique, it is best avoided. Leaders must always consider their own capabilities and the composition of the group in selecting activities. As member involvement increases and leader experience expands, the range and depth of activities that can be effectively utilized increases. However, experience is not a license to experiment freely; it is rather a safeguard against the inappropriate handling of member reactions. A conscientious concern for the hidden psychological triggers embedded in activities is a necessary component for effective leadership when using communication activities.

11. *Select activities that can be culminated in the time frame available for the group meeting.* Leaders should have a good idea about how much time is necessary to fully implement an activity. Nothing is more frustrating to a leader or to group members than to run out of time in the middle of an activity in which everyone is involved and interested. Select activities that can be presented, experienced, and processed during the time limits of the group. Do not begin an activity that cannot be worked through before the session ends. And hurrying to get through an activity usually defeats its whole purpose by forcing members to concentrate on the activity rather than on themselves or each other. If an activity has not been satisfactorily concluded at the end of the time period, sometimes the better procedure is to hold the group over rather than to have members leave with unexpressed or unresolved feelings that could produce misunderstandings or disgruntlement detrimental to the group.

12. *Select activities that are easy to process and integrate effectively into the flow of group interaction.* In order to counter the myopic tendencies produced by structured activities, select communication activities on the basis of their processability. Key processability features are: (1) the interaction generated

is reflective of the group process, and (2) the content is relevant to group member problems or purposes for which the group was formed. Activities that produce experiences that the leader and members can effectively integrate into the flow of the group interaction are preferable to those that are self-contained or require extensive translation to make them fit. A distinctive trait of a processable activity is that the group moves directly back into their interactive pattern without spending excessive time and energy finishing or closing the activity.

Creative Arts Communication Activities

Gladding (1997, 1998) makes a strong case for using communication activities derived from the creative arts (e.g., painting, music, dance, drama, poetry, and writing). These particular techniques inspire members and groups and provide mechanisms of sharing that tap otherwise inaccessible resources. In addition, they may provide channels of expression to members who may struggle with the straightforward verbal processes relied on in groups. Gladding (2000) notes that creativity oriented communication activities are advantageous because they are multicultural, energize, promote insight and self-awareness, communicate messages on multiple levels, are playful, nonthreatening, and open up new options (p. 8). He also notes the following reservations or precautions relative to using creativity based activities:

- They may be inappropriate in some situations.
- They may become gimmicky.
- They are not effective when applied with most artists.
- They may not be useful for group members who are emotionally labile.
- They may take up too much time that could be more productively used in other ways.
- They may lead group members to be too self-occupied and introspective (p. 9).

(For resources related to creative arts-based activities and creativity see Galdding (1998) *Counseling as an art: The creative arts in counseling* and Jacobs (1992) *Creative counseling techniques: An illustrated guide.*)

Psychodrama: A Special Form of Communication Activity

Psychodrama is both a group process in and of itself and a tool to be used in the context of group counseling and therapy. As such, it is a sophisticated and elegant form of communication activity and therefore merits separate consideration in the context of this chapter.

Psychodrama was conceived and nurtured into being by Viennese psychiatrist, J. L. Moreno (1964) who brought it with him to New York City in 1925. Using the tools of the stage and the conceptual framework of psychology, he and his colleagues developed psychodrama into an entity in and of itself with wide ranging application to therapy across many populations and settings. Psychodrama is now an approach to therapy with training programs and skilled practitioners who practice it exclusively. However, it is also a viable tool for group leaders to learn and use in the context of other group process applications.

The calling card or seminal identifying trait of psychodrama is _action_. It is a form of therapy or training in which participants enact or reenact situations in their lives that are of emotional significance to them. The process is active, not passive and relies on behavioral expression rather than verbal description. The environment (where the action takes place) provides free space that can be used expressively whether it occurs in an office, in a classroom, or on a stage. The main actor essentially performs therapy on him or herself.

The key conceptual dynamic of psychodrama is known as _surplus reality._ This term refers to the perspective that whatever is occurring in the action whether it is drawn from the past, present, or future, and whether it represents reality or fantasy, it is all happening in the here and now. As such, the present is expanded experientially to encompass the whole of life experience.

Psychodrama has a distinct quality that enables greater honesty to occur with less effort. It requires more energy and purposeful honesty to disclose what cannot be seen by others (that which occurs outside the group or is hidden inside the person) than to acknowledge what is occurring before the group in the here and now. Thus, psychodrama is useful in helping people deal with issues in their lives that are often harder to talk about than to act out.

Techniques

Psychodrama can be credited with the development and adaptation of numerous techniques that have utility to the group practitioner, whether the form of psychodrama is applied or not. Several examples are briefly described in the following subtopics.

The Soliloquy. Taken from drama where an actor steps out of the context of the play to express a supplementary perspective to the audience, this technique is essentially designed to help a client think out loud.

The Double Another person assumes the place of the main actor to assist him or her in expressing his or her experiences. The double plays a key role in helping that which cannot be expressed to emerge and bringing out distortions in that which is expressed. The double can take many forms such as the following:

1. Colorless double: relies primarily on restatement
2. Satirical double: uses humor and paradox in responding
3. Passionate double: expresses the emotions of the main character
4. Oppositional double: takes an opposing side in order to create a dialogue between sides
5. Physical double: mirrors gestures, behavior, and body language
6. Multiple double: represents different aspects of the person such as their past, present, and future or his or her thoughts, feelings, and actions.

The double is also referred to as the alter ego to emphasize the role as an extension of the person who is the central focus.

Magic Shop This technique casts the therapist or other group member in the role of a Shopkeeper who barters with clients for qualities, values, and experiences they want based on the principle that they must give something valuable (pay a price) to get something valuable. (Additional techniques are described in the learning activities section of this chapter).

The psychodrama process is composed of five elements and three phases which combine to create the therapeutic context.

Five Elements

The Stage The stage is the arena of action. Everything that happens on it occurs in the here and now. It is a space limited only by the imagination and creativity of participants and the director. It is the area where the drama occurs and is differentiated from the area that contains the observers or audience.

The Protagonist

The protagonist is the main actor, the star of the psychodrama. He or she is the one who is working through a problem or issue in action. He or she is performing therapy on him or herself, but is also the one who defines the limits of the drama (is in charge of how far the action will go). The protagonist acts out his or her problem from a subjective point of view.

The Auxiliaries The auxiliaries are the extensions of the world of the protagonist. They are the supporting cast who assist the protagonist in carrying out the drama. Operating from an objective point of view, the auxiliaries perform three important supplementary functions besides assisting the protagonist. They provide support for the protagonist, they give input to the director, and they are therapeutic agents to the main actor helping him or her clarify, understand,

and modify his or her life experience. More skill is required of auxiliaries than of protagonists, which is one reason that trained auxiliaries are often included in groups that utilize psychodrama.

The Director The director is the one in charge of producing the drama. He or she has the technical skills and tools necessary to help the protagonist act out his or her story and mobilize auxiliaries to that end. The director is in charge of the entire process of the psychodrama not just the action. He or she plays three key roles in the process. Besides being producer, he or she is also analyst and therapist merging, combining, and separating these roles in the best interests of the main actor. The director must not only be skilled in psychodrama, but also must be able to trust it as the final arbiter and guide in the therapeutic process (Moreno, n.d.).

The Audience The audience represents the world and is the source for both protagonists and auxiliaries. Audience members are all participants even if their role is that of spectator. They are particularly essential with respect to the sharing phase of psychodrama where the audience gives back to the protagonist in exchange for that which was given them.

Three Phases

The Warm-up Purposes of the warm-up phase are to assist participants in connecting with each other, develop an atmosphere of rapport and safety, and generate content out of which can emerge the selection of a protagonist. As such, the security stage tasks of getting acquainted, interpersonal warm-up, and trust building are addressed along with the acceptance stage tasks of personal sharing and building cohesiveness and closeness.

The warm-up is the precursor to the action and sets the atmosphere in which the drama can unfold. It usually involves a structured activity that will generate personal content in the form of issues or problems that will lend themselves to being acted out in a psychodrama. Many of the activities at the end of chapters in this book are effective tools for the warm-up phase of psychodrama. The purpose of the warm-up is to generate interaction between participants that enables them to open up and share experiences thereby assisting the director in identifying a potential protagonist.

The Drama The drama phase is the action or core of the psychodrama. Once the protagonist has been elicited he or she works with the director to act out the story. The arena is divided into stage and audience and the drama is carried out to a suitable end point using auxiliaries as appropriate.

The Sharing Once the protagonist has reached the climax and ends his or her story, the final phase of the psychodrama is invoked by the director. This is the follow-up to the drama where the audience shares with the protagonist what his or her story has meant to them. This is not a time for analysis, advice giving, or therapy. It is a time when members of the audience give a piece of themselves to the main actor. This is crucial for closure for both the protagonist and the audience and is the phase in which the impact of the drama is generalized beyond the designated client-protagonist.

Phases of psychodrama are recycled each time a drama is enacted much like groups recycle stages as they evolve to deeper or different levels of interaction. Each of these phases and each of these elements are central to the psychodrama's effective use. Training in psychodrama is eminently available and a recommended adjunct to group leadership training. Much of the psychodrama literature (especially that of J. L. Moreno and Zerka Moreno) is published by and available from Beacon House, Inc.(P.O. Box 311, Beacon, NY 12508). Additional resources are Greenberg (1974) and Leveton (1977).

Concluding Comments

Resources for finding communication activities to utilize in group work abound. Some of them are Johnson (1981); Johnson and Johnson (1997); Pfeiffer and Jones (1969–85); Bates, Johnson, and Blaker (1982); Jacobs, Harvill, and Masson (1988); Stevens (1972); Simon, Howe, and Kirchenbaum (1972); Thompson and Poppen (1979), Rosenthal (1998), Morganette (1990, 1994), and DeLucia-Waack, Bridbord, and Kleiner, (2002). However, selection and implementation are the bailiwick of the professional leader.

Communication activities are valuable tools in guiding and facilitating the group process and improving individual self-understanding. They contribute to the helping process and give leaders and members a means of coping with problems that are a part of therapeutic group interaction. They are useful in task groups for addressing process dynamics, training, team building and addressing group tasks. There are, however, precautions that must be considered. These activities should not be viewed as an end in themselves but rather as means to an end. They should be used with considerable discretion and only in the context of ethical practice.

Learning Activities

Communication activities described in the following pages are organized around their primary use in initiating, facilitating, or terminating the group process. Remember, however, that these activities are flexible and can be used in ways other than described here.

Initiation

Describe Yourself as Your Own Best Friend The purpose of this activity is to help members get to know one another through the process of self-disclosure. The anxiety of talking about oneself is reduced by the objective third person approach, which helps members cope with the discomfort of the group environment and feelings of self-consciousness.

Have group members individually describe themselves as their own best friend using their name ("This is my best friend John . . .") and the appropriate third person pronoun referent (he or she). Each member can be his or her own best friend or describe their self as they think an actual best friend would. After each person has completed his or her description, other members can ask questions to obtain or clarify information. These questions are also framed in the third person. (e.g., "What does John like about himself?") The person responds to the questions in the third person. The leader's role is to help members maintain the third person approach and to ask leading questions as a guide or model for other members. Also an effective approach is to have the leader be the first person to do the activity. In this way he or she can set the tone for the group, model self-disclosure, and demonstrate how the activity should be done.

Name Tags, "able" and "ing" This is a good beginning activity, especially in groups where members are not familiar with each other (Kranzow, 1973). Have members make tags that state their name and include three words ending in "ing," and three words ending in "able" that describe what they are like. The six words should describe their personality traits (e.g., interesting, loving, irritable, likable). Encourage members to be creative and invent words that best fit their personality (e.g., funning, angerable). After name tags are completed have members introduce themselves to one another. ("My name is Toni, and I am fascinating. . . " or "I see your name is John, and you are memorable."). After the participants have had the opportunity to meet each other, convene the total group and have the members explain why they chose the words they did. Other group members also can respond by adding "ing" or "able" words they think are appropriate to individual members.

Building Blocks Go-Round This is another good initiating activity that breaks the ice of a new group and helps members get to know each other—at least by name—very quickly. Sit in a circle and have one member start by stating his or her name. The person next to him or her must repeat the first member's name and then give her or his own. This continues with each person repeating the names of every preceding person until each member can flawlessly state every other person's name in the group. Then add a piece of information, such as how each is feeling at the moment, and repeat the entire process using names and feelings. You can continue to build in this way, adding categories such as major interest, goal in life, main concern, marital status, job, and so forth. Choose items of information that will be most conducive to group growth and sharing. You may want to intersperse position changes in the group during this activity to help members remember persons rather than positions and sequences. This activity, especially the name part, can be repeated at the beginning of the first few sessions until people are completely sure of one another's names. This takes very little time and removes some of the natural embarrassment and frustration members experience when they think they should remember a person's name but don't and are afraid to ask.

Draw Your World

This activity initiates the process of self-disclosure in the group and incorporates a visual dimension into the process of sharing. Provide group members with an 8½ × 11 sheet of paper with a large circle on it and ask them to create a picture that represents their world. They may use symbols, pictures, words, phrases, or a combination. The purpose is to portray their personal world as they see it and as they fit into it. When the picture is completed have members embellish their pictures with the following information: At each of the four corners of your world (N, S, E, W) write two words or brief phrases that describe: (1) how your family sees you; (2) how your friends see you; (3) how your colleagues or coworkers see you; and (4) how you see yourself. Have each member show their picture to the group and describe his or her world and answer questions about it. When all have shown their pictures, have them share the descriptions. Additional perceptions that may be solicited are those of employer, teachers, students, neighbors, etc.

Appleton and Dykeman (1996) have suggested a modification of this activity that has worked effectively with Native American groups. They call it Make a Picture of Your World. They distribute magazines to the group and ask members to do a rapid perusal of them and tear or cut out pictures that reflect who they are and their world. Members then form these pictures into a collage depicting their life that is then shared with the group. Processing is integrated into the sharing to generate group interaction.

Lifeline Activity   Miller (1993) describes this activity as "a near surefire, bona fide strategy in fostering self-disclosure, group cohesion and group feedback" (p. 51). Use the following instructions to introduce the activity:

Draw a horizontal line across your card (usually a 5 × 7 index card). Put a dot at each end of the line. Over the left dot, place a zero. This dot represents your birthday. Write your birth date under this dot. The dot on the right represents your death. This next part is optional. Over the right dot, put a number that indicates your best guess as to how many years you will live. Now place a dot that indicates where you are right now on the line between birth and death. Above the line, experiences that were positive, happy, or rewarding should be plotted chronologically. Below are plotted experiences that were negative, unhappy, or painful. The distance above or below the line indicates the degree of positive or negative impact or feeling. Try to portray at least two or three positive and negative events or experiences in such a way that you will be able to identify them. Take your time and when you are finished put down your pencil so I will know you are finished. (p. 52)

Processing will require consideration of time limitations and be adapted to the nature and purposes of the group. Modifications for children, adolescents, and adults will also be necessary as developmental dynamics impact both the product developed and the resulting process.

Facilitation

Role Playing Role playing is one of the most flexible facilitation techniques in groups and every counselor should develop expertise in its use. Role playing in its simplest form means reenacting or acting out a situation in the group as if it were occurring in actuality. Role playing makes use of simulation and modeling to help group members look more intensely at problem areas, both for deeper understanding of their concerns and for alternative solutions. It provides members with a highly realistic basis for transfer of learning to the real environment making the prospect of change less threatening and the implementation of change less difficult.

Role playing can be appropriate any time a member gets into a descriptive discourse of a problem situation that involves other people. It is especially helpful when a person is having difficulty expressing a situation clearly or if a story seems to have discrepancies. Ask whether the member is willing to role play the situation and, if so, ask for a brief description of the people and setting. Select other group members to play the roles of the people involved, and have the member give the participants a brief description of the personalities of the people they are playing. Then begin the role play, making sure that participants stay in their roles until the role play is concluded or is concluded by the leader or member. Some leaders prefer to run through the whole situation whereas others approach it in small vignettes, stopping along the way to assess what is happening, to ask for feedback, or to point out something relevant to the problem. Make sure sufficient time is available when a role play is completed for discussion in which participants and observers can reflect on what happened.

Many role-playing techniques can be used by a counselor. A few examples are briefly described below:

Open Chair Technique. In this particular technique only one role player is involved. It is useful when the problem under consideration involves only the member and one other person. Two chairs are placed facing each other and the member sits in one and the counselor in the other. A conversation is started, and as soon as it gets going the counselor leaves the chair. The client continues the conversation playing both roles, moving to the appropriate chair to speak for each party.

The open chair technique is also effective when an individual is struggling with inner conflicts that can be polarized into a dialogue depicting the two sides of the struggle.

Role Reversal. This technique is similar to the Open Chair except that two persons (or more) are involved throughout the role play. The member and the other person begin a conversation and at an appropriate point the leader intervenes to make them switch chairs and roles. The leader helps the conversation continue smoothly through the switch by repeating the last line that was stated before the reversal. In this way the continuity of the role play is maintained, and participants get to look at things from each other's point of view.

Role Substitution. In many role-playing situations, a useful technique is to have the main participant stand back and watch him or herself in action. Once a role-playing situation is in full swing the counselor can ask another member to play the part of the main actor. The role play continues with the main person watching his or her double in operation, trying to gain insight or glean a greater awareness of the situation.

Alter Ego. To facilitate clearer and deeper understanding in a role play, the leader may ask a group member to become an alter ego to one or several of the participants. This person is a helper to the person in the role, representing some aspect of that person. The alter ego can operate independently or can be given specific instructions such as "interject now, and express the feelings of the person in the role." This technique is very useful but requires some training and practice before a member can function effectively in the role of alter ego.

By combining any number of these techniques and extending the time and scope of the role play, the group leader can create a full scale sociodrama or psychodrama if that is beneficial to the member or the group. In school settings, sociodramas are quite appropriate whereas psychodrama is relevant in treatment programs for chemically dependent clients and in a wide variety of out patient therapy groups.

The Line Up Many times groups get into discussions that involve being more than or less than something. Some members may see themselves as more quiet or more shy than other people in social situations. Or some members may feel they are more trusting or committed in the group. The lineup is a useful facilitating technique in such situations. Clearly define the issue in terms of a continuum (most talkative to least talkative in social situations), and establish two points in the room to represent the two ends of the continuum. Then have members place themselves on the continuum where they feel most comfortable or that most accurately describes them. The first time through each member chooses a spot on the line but no ties are permitted (two or more people at the same point). When the line has been established repeat the activity, but this time each person's position is determined by the other members. Follow-up discussion can focus on the discrepancies and consistencies between the two lineups and the natural tendency for clustering in the middle on most issues. An additional procedure is to do a follow-up line up where each person places themselves where they would like to be. This helps members set goals to work toward in the group.

Katz (1973) has suggested another version of the line up. Place the group members in a straight line in the middle of the room (order is not important). Then designate the wall in front of the members as one endpoint of the continuum and the wall behind them as the other endpoint. Ask members to close their eyes and on a signal move to the spot where they feel they belong on the continuum. In this way the intragroup comparative nature of the exercise is minimized and each member reacts more independently and personally to the continuum issue itself.

Relationship Analysis Many group members have relationship problems. Poppen and Thompson (1974) suggested a format to help members assess what is happening in their relationships and with the group's help identify whether they are balanced (mutually respectful). This procedure involves five basic steps:

1. Describe the relationship.
2. Specify the limits (specific boundaries) in the relationship.
3. State the responsibilities each person has in the relationship.
4. Note the degree of freedom within the relationship.
5. Designate the amount of personal recreation (time alone) for each person in the relationship.

Discuss each step in the group and determine if the relationship is unbalanced and what can be done to achieve mutual respect in the relationship. The basic ideas behind this facilitative technique are: (1) all relationships have some limits and some specific areas of freedom, (2) every person should have designated responsibilities (even a child), and (3) personal recreation time (time alone) is important. If members can learn these principles, they can act constructively in resolving many of their relationship problems.

Three Things I'd Like To Change This activity can be used to facilitate a work oriented focus on specific problems of group members. Many times group members have difficulty resolving their problems because they do not know exactly what they want to change. This activity helps them identify clearly the areas that need changing. Have members write down three things about themselves that they would like to change. Have each member share their list with the group, giving brief explanations of each item. Then have each member select one area from the list and describe it in more detail following these four basic behavioral steps:

1. Describe what you do not like about the way you are (*problem*).
2. Describe how you would like to change (*goal*).
3. Discuss with the group how you might be able to change and form a strategy for doing so (*plan*).
4. Try out the plan, and report back to the group on your progress (*follow-up*).

For the last two steps some counselors like to use the contract system (Dustin & George, 1973), whereby the group member writes up a plan as if it were a contract and signs it in the group's presence. This increases the specificity of the plan, promotes the individual's commitment to it, and gives the group a solid basis for holding the member accountable and reinforcing, encouraging, and evaluating the member's progress. This same procedure can be used for each of the desired changes noted on the initial lists.

Button and Flower Technique Thomas, Nelson, and Sumners (1994) recommend an activity the helps members "recognize the connection between current situations that automatically elicit strong negative feelings" and abusive experiences from their past (p. 108). Paper, pen, and a box of buttons are needed for this activity. Each member is asked to draw a flower composed of petals, each of which describes a repetitive situation where he or she experiences strong negative reactions. When completed, a button is placed on a flower petal of one member (representing a situation that pushes his or her button), and the situation is processed in the group to assist the person in identifying, understanding, and dealing with the situation and the real origin of his or her feelings. This technique is used facilitatively over time and is particularly helpful in groups where members are dealing with and working through repercussions of traumatizing experiences.

Write Your Play Thomas, Nelson, and Sumners (1994) use this activity to help members "realize the complex nature of breaking the abuse cycle and the tendency to continually replay the victim, caretaker or abuser role with their partners, families and peers" (p. 108). Each group member is helped to describe in detail recurring situations in their lives where interactions are characterized by the same negative, destructive, and self-defeating dynamics, and behaviors. Relative to that scenario, each member is then asked to: (1) name the play, (2) identify the roles played by the member and others involved, (3) describe the plot (pattern), and (4) recognize the familiar ending. Once the play has been fully developed, the member is asked to rewrite the play giving it: (1) a new name, (2) new roles, (3) a new plot with different behaviors leading to (4) a new ending. Processing has deep impact on the life of the member whose play it is and on the members who enact similar scenarios in their lives leading to empowerment and breaking the abuse cycle.

Termination

Crystal Ball This terminating activity requires the use of some object that resembles a crystal ball. Members are asked to think about the future and consider what and where they would like to be five years hence. (The timeframe is arbitrary and can be varied according to the age level and particular setting of the group.) The crystal ball is then passed from person to person and members describe as imaginatively and creatively as possible what they see for themselves in the future. Another way of proceeding is to have members project what they see in the future for their fellow members. This activity tends to give members a future orientation but is based in large measure on the learning and experience that have taken place in the group.

3 × 5 Evaluation Some leaders like to get feedback regarding the group process at the end of each session. A kind of ongoing evaluation takes place that serves the leader's purposes for planning and revision and also helps members assess their experiences during that particular session. One means of doing this is to distribute 3 × 5 cards on which members express their reactions, opinions, or suggestions about the group session. This evaluation can be done during the last five-ten minutes of each session and cards can be deposited in a box as members leave or shared as a round before the members leave. This activity also provides a cue to members that time is up and yet allows an opportunity for the expression of any feelings that members were not able to state during the meeting. Over time these cards can supply counselors with valuable feedback about their effectiveness and the progress of the group.

Hope Chest This activity is helpful for closing a group on a positive note accentuating the qualities of interpersonal support that have developed. Ask the group members to silently consider their hopes and wishes for every other member in the group. Pass out blank sheets of paper to members and have them write at the top "Hope Chest for (their own names)." Then have the members pass their sheet to the person on their right. When the exchange is made, ask each member to draw a symbol or picture, designate a gift, or write a statement that reflects specific hopes for the person whose name appears at the top. Continue this process until each person in the group has made an entry on each sheet. When the sheets return to their owners, each member reviews the information and in turn holds up his or her Hope Chest for the group to see. The members then explain their contributions as feedback and acknowledgement. A variation of this technique is to have members exchange symbolic gifts that represent wishes for one another.

Harman and Withers (1992) use a modification of the Hope Chest: A blank sheet of paper is taped to each member's back. Members are given magic markers and 30 minutes to write comments reflecting their hopes for each other. Colors are alternated to camouflage the source of feedback. Upon completion of the time period, sheets are removed and each member reads and reflects on the comments. The feedback and experience are processed in the group as a closing activity.

14
Family Theory as a Group Resource

We become who we are in our families of origin. (Teyber, 1997, p. 10)

Without exception patients enter group therapy with a history of a highly unsatisfactory experience in their first and most important group—their primary family. (Yalom, 1985, p. 15)

The family is the first group in which individuals learn to interact. (Donigian & Hulse-Killacky, 1999, p. 124)

Troubled families make troubled people. (Satir, 1972, p. 18)

The impact of family dynamics is manifested in the predispositions members bring with them in the form of group expectations and their views of themselves as persons and participants. (Trotzer in Donigian and Hulse-Killacky, 1999, p. 124)

The family group is a system that sends its members out into the world to become members of other groups that exist in systems or become systems. Group work is the process of creating groups of individuals whose experience in other groups implicitly and explicitly impacts their participation in the group being formed. Therefore, group leaders who are informed by systems theory generally and family theory specifically will be drawing upon a vital resource as they help their groups create a history that will impact the individual members in the context in which the group is formed and the systems in which they live.

The Relevance of Family Theory

The impetus for including a chapter relating family theory and systems thinking to group process emanated from a variety of sources not the least of which was my own evolutionary development as a professional. Trained initially in an individually oriented, client-centered, Rogerian model that emphasized necessary and sufficient therapeutic conditions in the counselor-client relationship and the mobilization of the inner resources of the client to resolve his or her problems, I quickly realized that a major discrepancy existed between what happened in the counselor's office and what happened in the client's life. The helping process that relied on the therapeutic relationship to mobilize intrapsychic forces for the purpose of implementing change often was insufficient to overcome the seemingly insurmountable obstacles presented by the client's social system.

Introduction: The Case for Integration

In an effort to improve the transferability of the therapeutic process to the ongoing life experiences of clients, I became interested in the group process, which because of its nature as a social milieu, offered advantages (as noted in chapter 2) that greatly enhanced the probability of constructive change. However, even the group process was limited in that it could only represent reality. As a social laboratory group members could approximate the real world, but a gap still existed between their experiences in the group and their experiences outside the group.

The desire to work directly with a piece of client reality instead of a second hand account or an approximation, coupled with the observation that in both individual and group counseling problems typically had a family connection, resulted in my becoming involved in family counseling. However, my evolution was far from complete. The old expression *what goes around comes around* typifies what happened next. I moved from a position at a university where I was training counselors in all three modalities to a position as a practicing clinician where I was immersed in using all three modalities. This shift produced a basic dilemma because unilateral decisions as to appropriate modality and approach were not always easy to make. Consequently, questions of whether these three modalities were mutually exclusive, sequential, or tangential with areas of commonality as well as uniqueness were raised. Whether I wanted to or not, I had to grapple with the challenge of integration. This chapter is part of my response to that issue—particularly from the perspective of relating group process and family theory.

Integrating Group and Family Counseling

Efforts to develop a conceptual and pragmatic interface between group counseling and family counseling as differentiated but related therapeutic modalities have been emerging in the literature, in training, and in clinical practice for at least four decades. From the group perspective, Ohlsen (1979) noted the high incidence of counselors doing marital work and compiled a set of articles that applied group methodology to couples. West and Kirby (1981) followed suit demonstrating the relevance of group methods in dealing with family issues and problems. Becvar (1982) reviewed literature comparing the family and other small groups and concluded that small group theory is a valid and useful resource in understanding and working with families. In 1982, the Association for Specialists in Group Work created a Commission on Family Counseling specifically to address the relationship between family counseling and group counseling. That commission presented an initial program at the 1984 American Association for Counseling and Development Convention in Houston, Texas comparing and contrasting group and family counseling (Ritter, West, & Trotzer, 1987). The Commission also presented a subsequent program in New York in 1985 on integrating and differentiating group and family counseling in theory, training, and practice (Trotzer, West, Ritter, & Malnati, 1985), and a program in Chicago, Illinois entitled, Group and Family Perspectives on a Simulated Family Session (Trotzer, West, Ritter, Malnati, & Hovestadt, 1987). The work of that commission culminated in a special issue of *The Journal for Specialists in Group Work* entitled "The Interface of Group and Family Therapy" (1988) edited by Hines (1988a) in which the similarities and differences between group and family therapy were explored (Hines 1988b), and initial efforts toward an integrated perspective were launched (Trotzer, 1988b). Connors and Caple (2005) traced the development of this integration with a review of group systems theory updating its status to include the work of Agazarian (1997), Donigian and Malnati (1997), and McClure (1998) in which they assert that "systems thinking is an important way to expand and strengthen the supra-individual theory base of group practitioners beyond interpersonal theories" (pp. 93–94).

The fact that family counseling has emerged as a therapeutic modality in its own right is reflected in the growth of marriage and family training programs and the incorporation of such training into counselor education programs (Hovestadt, Fennell, & Piercy, 1983). The growth of professional organizations promoting marriage and family counseling such as the American Association for Marriage and Family Therapy (AAMFT), the International Association for Marriage and Family Counseling (IAMFC), and Division 43 (Family Psychology) of the American Psychological Association (APA) also attest to the emergence and relevance of family theory and family therapy. While the popularity of marriage and family counseling has prompted some counseling practitioners to make exclusionary commitments to family therapy as the modality of choice across the board, a strong case exists for family theory and family therapy to be a resource to the other counseling modalities as well as being a preferred interventive entity in its own right. In fact, Horne (Campbell, 1992) has framed family counseling as one of the developmental phases the counseling profession has gone through in its maturing process. He noted that the sequence of individual counseling, group counseling, marriage and family counseling, and currently multicultural counseling (since broadened to diversity-competent counseling; see chapter 9) are substantiated as critical stages of development in the counseling profession with a cumulative effect on training and practice.

Research and clinical practice supports the idea that a group and family integration is not only viable, but a recommended core competency and emphasis in professional training programs (Shapiro & Shapiro, 1985). Ruevini (1985) addressed the critical issues facing group work in the future:

> Group workers ... should realize that they need to involve themselves not only with the important issues of group methodology, research and the effectiveness of various available theoretical frameworks, but also with issues of the viability, importance and central position of the family group as a critical factor in people's lives. (p. 88).

He goes on to promote training in family therapy as an essential component of group leadership training. Matthews (1992) proceeds a step further by examining and explicating the link between general systems theory (GST) and group process. Connor and Caple (2005) validate this connection by pointing out the interdependent nature of systems thinking and its direct relationship to group work. They point to: (1) "a solid body of research (that) establishes the critical connection between the personality and functioning of individuals and their past and present relationships;" (2) "50 years of group research which have established the effectiveness of interpersonal group therapy in helping individuals with mental health issues," and (3) "decades of social and psychological research (that) establish the importance of family, group and community membership to the well being of individual members" as evidence of the merit of systems thinking relative to group work (p. 100).

The purpose of this chapter is to present the utility of family theory as a resource in group work. The basic premise is that just as group theory and techniques can be useful in understanding and helping families (Becvar, 1982) so family theory and techniques can be useful in understanding and helping individuals in groups (see Trotzer "Family-Centered Therapy" responses to "Critical Incidents in Group Therapy" in Donigian & Hulse-Killacky, 1999, pp. 124–126, 157–160, 191–193, 221–223, 259–261, 304–306). This chapter will first differentiate between group and family dynamics and then discuss family theory as a group resource. Family theory in relationship to group process and content and as a basis for developing group techniques and activities will also be presented. Guidelines and precautions for using family-based group techniques will be discussed, and the chapter will conclude with group learning activities derived from a family theory base.

Differentiating the Family Group from the Counseling Group

A family is a group with a history, structure, and organizational hierarchy that the counselor must join while a counseling (or other type of group: therapy, psychoeducation, or task) consists of individuals brought together by a counselor to create its own history and structure. The family group will continue regardless of interventive efforts while a counseling or other type of group will eventually dissolve (Trotzer, 1988). Consequently, the family is a unit of relational reality that has continuity over time while the counseling group is artificially created to approximate relational reality which is time limited. Note, for purposes of convenience and efficiency, the discussion that follows will focus on counseling groups as our primary type of group. However, material covered has relevance for other types of groups as well.

Tavantzis and Tavantzis (1985) noted additional differences between the family group and the counseling group. The purpose of counseling groups is to enable members to interact as equals in a safe environment where mutual help is a derived norm. The thrust is to create the possibility for members to share their vulnerabilities and experiment with new attitudes and behaviors. The leader takes a responsible role in creating a safe atmosphere, but greatly relinquishes that role to the group as the group evolves. As Pistole (1997) notes, "In a family, the parents remain the authority and source of security and protection. In groups, the counselor's goal is to relinquish this position and manage the multiple relationships more as a partner" (p. 12).

In family groups, hierarchies take precedence over equality relative to membership, and the security of the group is more than an artifact of the group process. Vulnerability and freedom are greatly curtailed by the family members' "shared history and interlocking roles and patterned behavior" (Tavantzis & Tavantzis, 1985, p. 4). The therapist must be continuously cognizant of the safety factor in the family as it extends beyond the therapy room. Hansen (Ritter, West, & Trotzer, 1986) observed that if people get nicked up in individual counseling or chewed up in group, they can still turn to others for support and sustenance. But, if they get nicked up in family counseling, the most meaningful people in their lives are doing the attacking (p. 297). Thus, family members both bring their stressful environments with them and take them home while group members can get respite from their stressors in either environment (the group or their life) by moving from one to the other. However, one advantage of group work is that generic similarities between the counseling group and the family group can bring family issues to life in the group while providing a space where those issues can be examined without the contingent threat of family retaliation (Pistole, 1997). Yalom (1995) refers to this phenomenon as a recapitulization of one's family of origin or a family reenactment where members learn from and experience the group as if it were one's family.

In counseling groups (with some exceptions) membership is primarily voluntary whereas in family counseling members often attend involuntarily (parents bring children; wives coerce husbands).The advantage of working with a family is that you get to work with a piece of reality without having to rely on second hand accounts (individual counseling) or approximations of social reality (group counseling). However, the disadvantage is that the resistance factors are accentuated. As Yalom (Forester-Miller, 1989) observes in groups and families "some of the basic processes are the same in that you are using interpersonal analysis" (p. 198). The difference is that "there are ongoing relationships in the family that you want to alter, where the group is much more a kind of dress rehearsal for life" (p. 198).

While family theory and group theory both address the process involved in their respective units, the focus of change differs. In family counseling, the unit of change is either the family with subsequent impact on the individual or change in the individuals with subsequent impact on the family system. In groups, however, the unit of change is the individual.

Hovestadt (Ritter, West, & Trotzer, 1987) stated that the purpose of change in family counseling is to generate a higher level of functioning and satisfaction in the family system which is in contrast to group counseling where the goal is to improve the functioning of the individual (p. 296). In addition, the epistemology of the change process differs. Most individual and group approaches tend to be based on linear thought process models of causation whereas family counseling is based on systemic thinking which posits circularity with patterns and sequences as the causal framework (Couch & Childers, 1989). Change then only occurs when the pattern or sequence of interaction—rather than the individual per se—is modified. However, both modalities are interventive in nature attempting to utilize and/or create interpersonal dynamics that will result in therapeutic change. This particular factor paves the way for integration between the two modalities as will be explicated in the remainder of this chapter.

Family Theory as a Resource

The significance and centrality of family data and experience are not new ideas in a therapeutic sense. Freud relied on family data particularly from a person's infancy to explain psychodynamically the characteristics of personality development. (Miller, 2002) Adler emphasized the impact of a person's childhood family recollections in regard to the development of social interest and the emergence of his or her private logic and basic mistakes (Dreikurs, 1964). However, family dynamics remained only a factor in the conceptualization of human problems. The family was treated vicariously within the individual and the subsequent resolution of family dynamics was left unaddressed until the family theorists and their systemic orientation emerged in the 1950s and 1960s (Zuk, 1971). Since then, the field of family theory and therapy has blossomed into a fully developed conceptual and clinical entity as a bonafide approach to resolving human problems (Mikesell, Lusterman, & McDaniel, 1995).

Family theory provides conceptual models that relate directly to group counseling in terms of process, content, and techniques. For group leaders who wish to utilize family theory as a resource, understanding the following conceptual components is recommended as a minimum basis for incorporating family concepts into group work:

1. Overview of the growth and development of family theory and family therapy (Barnard & Corrales, 1979; Goldenberg & Goldenberg, 1996; Nichols, 1984);
2. The family as a system, i.e., systemic thinking from both a structural and strategic perspective (Madanes, 1981; Minuchin, 1974);
3. Intergenerational family dynamics (Boszormenyi-Nagy & Krasner, 1986; Boszormenyi-Nagy & Spark, 1973; Bowen, 1966);
4. The developmental life cycle of the family (Carter & McGoldrick, 1988; Walsh, 1982);
5. The impact of divorce and the dynamics of single parent and remarried (blended) families (Cantor & Drake, 1983; Sager, Brown, Crohn, Engel, Rodstein, & Walker, 1983; Visher & Visher, 1979, 1988);
6. The importance, impact, and relevance of ethnicity, diversity, and culture in family systems (McGoldrick, Giordano, & Pearce, 1996).

An introductory course in marriage and family counseling or family dynamics will address most of the above noted material and a follow-up course in marriage and family theories and techniques will provide the conceptual depth necessary to use family theory as a resource in leading groups. *The Family Crucible,* a classic text by Napier and Whitaker (1978), the highly acclaimed contemporary book on American families, *All Our Families* (2nd Edition) edited by Mason, Skolnick, and Sugarman (2003) and *Marriage and Family: Better Ready Than Not* (Trotzer & Trotzer, 1986) are recommended as required reading.

Family Theory and Group Process

The family is a social unit that teaches its members about social interaction and supplies them with skills, perceptions, and rules relative to how one is affected by and acts in social (interpersonal) situations. In group counseling, each individual member reflects his or her family heritage—a factor that significantly affects the process of group development. For example, "attachment theory describes individual and dyadic aspects of significant relationships that develop within the family and so it can be an aid in exploring and interpreting behavior in adult relationships" (Pistole, 1997, p. 10). Such family theory constructs that explain the dynamics of family influence can be useful in helping group leaders address the tasks involved in starting a group and building a cohesive group structure while accounting for individual differences. For example, a person raised in an enmeshed family (Minuchin, 1974) may experience great difficulty connecting in the group during its initial stages due to loyalty or guilt issues, while a person raised in a disengaged family (Minuchin, 1974) may rapidly identify with the group but have difficulty or actually resist forming a committed attachment. Such reactions emanate from family-based social expectations and rules that influence members' behaviors and experiences in the group. As such, family theory provides a useful perspective as group members negotiate ground rules and establish group norms.

Family theory also provides process tools for the group leader. For example, Zuk (1981) has identified three key roles that the therapist plays in negotiating the therapeutic process. These roles are that of *celebrant, go-between*, and *side taker*.

The *celebrant* is the role of official who presides over significant events such as a minister presides over a marriage or a judge over a trial. This role is crucial in establishing that an interaction or a problem is real and definitive so that it can be treated as a fact of life. This is the means by which problems are acknowledged and established as the focus of attention.

The *go-between* is the mediator role. This role is facilitative in nature enabling people with different perspectives to connect with and understand each other. The go-between sees that communication occurs, makes sure everyone is heard, and serves as the channel for translating differences into understandings.

The *side taker* is the influence dimension of the counselor role where he or she judiciously chooses to take sides in the best interests of generating constructive change and problem resolution.

Based on the premise that a family therapist cannot help but be drawn into emotional intensity among clients, these roles enable him or her to act constructively in spite of becoming emotionally inducted into the family system. The same dynamics affect the group leader when group members become engaged in intense interpersonal interactions. As such, being cognizant of and able to utilize these roles are valuable process assets to group leadership.

Another systemic construct that relates directly to the group process is the separateness-belongingness dimension of human experience. "The oscillation between individualizing and grouping or differentiation and integration according to GST (general systems theory) is the basic dialectic of all human systems" (Matthews, 1992, p. 162). In groups, this dynamic is manifested in the members' "conflict between responsibility to self and responsibility to the group" (Matthews, 1992, p. 163) and in the vacillating balance between the individual influencing the group and the group influencing the individual. "Therapy conducted in groups has the advantage of treating the members in the context of this fundamental dance of life" (Matthews, 1992, p. 163).

Applying this construct to process, Matthews (1992) summarizes the essence of leadership as delineating "whether differentiation or integration is needed" (p. 163) and deciding "whether to pull members together as a group or let them differentiate as individuals" (p. 163). The "orchestration of such decisions is the way (leaders) guide a group through its developmental stages" (p. 163).

The process applications of family theory to group counseling are innumerable. As groups develop cohesiveness, they take on more characteristics and traits that make them just like a family in many respects. As Saygar (1996) observed, "healthy functioning families, as any well functioning groups, respect diverse perspectives and individual differences, embrace an overall mood of warmth and caring and operate via clear yet flexible structures" (p. 81). The reverse of these characteristics can also be true generating dysfunction in both a family and a group. However, as noted by Gazda (Ritter, West, & Trotzer, 1987), groups can generate feelings that are similar to families but certain dimensions are always missing. Therefore, family theory is useful in understanding and guiding the group process, but should not be used as a means of recreating group experiences that are meant to be family experiences. Rather groups are arenas for recapitulating family dynamics for the purpose of reconstructing emotional experiences for corrective therapeutic reasons (Yalom, 1995).

Family Theory and Group Content

In terms of content, a significant portion of problems and issues raised in group counseling are directly or indirectly related to family. Trotzer's (1985) Interpersonal Problem Matrix designates marital and family problems as a major subgroup of the category "Conflicts in Relationships" (p. 101). Yalom (1985) stated that "without exception patients enter group therapy with a history of a highly unsatisfactory experience in their first and most important group—their primary family" (p. 15). Although somewhat overstated for counseling groups, family experience does provide developmental and residual problems that are often addressed in groups. Satir (1972) stated simply that "troubled families make troubled people" (p. 18), and their troubles (or problems) tend to emerge in counseling groups.

Ruevini (1985) acknowledged the family as the source of pain in a past, present, and future sense, but also credits it as a major source of productive and positive support—especially in periods of crisis. Family theory, therefore, is a vital resource relative to the content of problems addressed in groups both from the standpoint of clearly delineating their nature and developing practical and realistic interventive strategies the individual member can use in dealing with them. For example, adolescent counseling groups typically address problems related to the existence and nature of boundaries established by significant adults in their lives, the resulting dynamics of differentiation, and the emerging generation gap. Subsequently, constructs drawn from the adolescent stage of the family life cycle are particularly applicable (Carter & McGoldrick, 1988; Walsh, 1982). In groups for young adults, understanding and utilizing individuation and differentiation concepts and helping group members establish and communicate *I positions* where they are separate from but connected to parents, siblings, and family are helpful group resources (Bowen, 1966).

Content applications of family theory are even more germane to group counseling than the process dimensions. Increased familiarity with the dynamics and perspectives of family life in relationship to individual development will enhance understanding of group member problems and improve the probability of constructive resolution strategies and potential change. Therefore, family theory has a direct relationship to the therapeutic impact of group counseling and therapy.

Family Theory and Group Techniques

The primary means of integrating family theory constructs into group counseling are structured group techniques called communication activities in this text. As noted in chapter 13, structured activities have utility as initiating, facilitating, and terminating tools in groups (Bates, Johnson, & Blaker, 1982; Trotzer, 1973). Coupled with family theory as an idea generation base (Trotzer, 1985), the group counselor can develop a myriad of activities that enhance group process and surface relevant material for group interaction.

Family-based group techniques are advantageous for both intrapersonal and interpersonal reasons. Intrapersonally, such techniques are engaging because they tap a common experience (i.e., everyone has a family background). In addition, one's own family background is an arena where each person is more expert than anyone else. Thus, a common focus is generated where everyone has something meaningful to contribute. Interpersonally, a family focus stimulates generic curiosity. Since everyone is a member of a family, each person tends to reflect on how his or her family is different from or similar to other families. Family-based group techniques provide a natural bridge between members facilitating cohesiveness and creating a context where similarities and differences can be acknowledged. Thus commonality and connectedness is enhanced *and* diversity and uniqueness is promoted. Effectively used, family-based group techniques will facilitate the group process and generate foci in accordance with the problem solving purpose or psychoeducational emphasis of the group's existence (see Mathis & Tanner, 2000). Several examples of such techniques follow.

Family-Based Group Techniques

Family Rules and Group Rules

One of the fundamental constructs of family theory is based on the premise that the family is a system. A system is a number of parts related in such a way that a change in one part affects all other parts (Barnard & Corrales, 1979). Systems operate on the basis of rules that are communicated to its members in either spoken form (verbalized edicts that specify expectations and consequences) or unspoken form (nonverbalized operational rules that only family members know). These rules create the basis of group members' social expectations referred to previously. One activity, Rules I Grew Up With, that surfaces these expectations is particularly useful as an initiating activity in the early stages (e.g., security stage) of group counseling. The activity instructions are:

Rules I Grew Up With
1. Explain the difference between spoken and unspoken rules (Barnard & Corrales, 1979).
2. On a blank sheet of paper create two columns, one labeled Spoken and the other Unspoken.
3. Have group members list examples of rules they grew up with in the appropriate columns.
4. Have group members share their lists and explain their entries.
5. Process the activity in relation to member expectations about the group and relate the material to ground rules for group interaction.

The Rules I Grew Up With activity facilitates the expression of group members' expectations and begins the process of forming group norms. Group ground rules whether established by leader directive or group consensus are reflective of spoken rules and norms which evolve in groups are reflective of the unspoken variety. Just as families need effective boundaries, so do groups. In group counseling, therapeutic ground rules and norms can be forged out of the composite of group members' experiences with family rules. This activity also lays the ground work for helping members adjust to environments with differing boundaries (e.g., school or work setting) and modifying expectations that have been molded in family environments that are contributing to adjustment problems. Therefore, the material generated by this activity has both process and content relevance.

Sibling Position and Group Relationships The family theory contention that significant aspects of a person's personality are forged in the family is useful in facilitating the development of relationships in the group. Constructs such as Toman's (1976) family constellation and ordinal position in the sibling hierarchy lend themselves well to an activity that effectively assists group members in connecting relationally. The Sibling Position Personality activity helps group members get acquainted and form relational bonds.

1. Have group members identify themselves according to their birth order (oldest, second, middle, youngest, only, or an appropriate modification of such, e.g., oldest of the second set of three) and include details such as gender of siblings and spacing chronologically. Instruct the person to refrain from giving details as to their experience in that position.

2. Ask the group to discuss what they know about each person based on their birth order identification only (e.g., "What do you know about John who is the oldest of three with two younger sisters?"). The focus person only listens during this discussion.

3. After the focus person's traits are proscribed by the group, ask that person to respond with their perspective of themselves (verification, clarification, refinement, modification, or disconfirmation). Repeat this process (i.e. steps 1-3) for each group member.

4. After each member has been processed individually, discuss how different combinations of sibling position personalities might be expected to relate (e.g., "How would a youngest and an oldest relate?" or "What might be happening between an oldest and a second child?").

Process the activity in light of possible group dynamics and interaction patterns in the group. Discussion usually brings the group's attention to itself and the relationships forming as a result of group interaction. This activity is particularly useful in the cohesiveness (acceptance) stage of the group and helps members get to know each other quickly and effectively without excessive emphasis on self-disclosure.

Family Legacy as a Group Resource Intergenerational family constructs are particularly useful in the work or problem solving stage of the group. Decision making in personal, interpersonal, vocational, recreational, and spiritual spheres of life are often influenced by the legacies a person inherits from his or her family of origin. The Houses in Your Life activity is useful in exploring the psychodynamic forces operating in group members' lives.

1. Have group members draw caricatures or bring photographs of the following family homes:
   a. Maternal grandparents
   b. Paternal grandparents
   c. Parents (step-parents if applicable)
   d. Current home (if different from parents)

Note: Extended family generational homes such as great grandparents' homesteads or immigrant families' original homeland domiciles can also be included.

2. Have members identify and share the following information relative to each home:
   a. A significant memory
   b Traits, attitudes, or values associated with that home or generation.
3. Process the shared information in light of each member's current life style, decisions and problems.

Family of origin dynamics tend to be intricately involved in most problems group members discuss. In fact, Mathis and Tanner (2000) have organized an entire group process around family of origin themes using structured activities. These activities facilitate the emergence of legacy material that tends to remain beneath the surface when considering here and now problems and future oriented decisions. Consequently, a broader base of information becomes available to the individual and the group that can be mobilized as part of the problem solving process.

These examples illustrate how family theory can be integrated into the group process through the vehicle of a structured group technique. (Additional activities are described at the end of the chapter.) However, the material from family theory also can be integrated without reliance on structured techniques. Using the leadership tools described in chapter 6, group leaders can introduce family dynamics in the context of using their reactive, active, and interactive skills to carry out their leadership functions.

Guidelines and Precautions

Although family-based group techniques are relatively easy to develop and utilize, there are several important guidelines and precautions that must be observed.

1. *Remember the loyalty factor.* Whenever individuals are invited or induced to discuss their family, an automatic loyalty conflict is created—particularly if negative information is involved. Consequently, group leaders must learn the skill of multi-directed partiality (Boszormenyi-Nagy & Krasner, 1986). This skill enables the counselor to be partial to both the discloser's side and the family's side without taking sides, thus enabling a constructive dialogue to ensue between the sides in the safety of the group context. Raising the family's side of a group member's perspective enables the group member to disclose without feeling like a traitor because the group leader demonstrates fairness and caring not only for the member but for his or her family as well.

2. *Seek resources not skeletons.* The purpose of family-based group techniques

is to generate material that will enhance the understanding of the individual member and provide assistance in helping that member deal with his or her problems or concerns. While family material can be extremely enticing from an interest perspective, leaders must avoid getting distracted by family story telling. If the material emerging cannot be directly related to the group process or the concerns of the individuals, measures should be taken to redirect the discussion.

3. *Avoid meddling in families.* A basic premise of group counseling is that the group can only directly affect persons who are in the group. This fact must be recognized and continually reaffirmed when using family-based group techniques. Leaders must avoid doing long distance family therapy or turning group members into therapists for their own families. The tendency to meddle in families must be watched for and curtailed. Keeping the focus on the person rather than the family during sharing and discussion will circumvent the tendency to dabble in family dynamics without a clear purpose with respect to the individual member.

4. *Build family-based group techniques from concepts rather than content.* Most people are private where information related to their families is concerned. This is particularly true in certain cultures and ethnic groups. Group techniques should be created out of a sound conceptual framework and not merely for the purpose of eliciting particular information. The structure of the technique should be such that members do not feel threatened by either the process or the content of the desired disclosure. Apprise group members of the construct under girding the activity which relates to all group members so that they will feel comfortable in supplying the subsequent information.

5. *Use care in selecting family-based techniques that elicit emotional or traumatic disclosures.* Family encounters often produce the most painful emotional reactions. Psychological wounds garnered in the context of family relationships tend to produce emotional responses whether they represent recent or old wounds. Leaders must be sensitive to the traumatizing potential in family-based activities, discard high risk activities, and modify instructions to temper the level of emotional impact.

Note: In therapy groups with members who have experienced intrusive acts in a family context (e.g., incest, sexual, physical, emotional abuse, or other trauma) this guideline does not constitute avoidance, but rather a monitoring of disclosures to maintain a pace and focus that facilitates working through of such experiences in a therapeutic manner (Courtois & Leehan, 1982).

Concluding Comment

Family theory provides a vast resource base for the group counselor. Whether used from a dynamic perspective as a means of understanding and assisting group members, as a catalyst relative to group process and content, or translated into group techniques, it is a valuable entity for extending the group practitioner's expertise. When used ethically and wisely, the impact and utility of group work as a therapeutic modality will be enhanced.

Learning Activities

The learning activities that follow are divided into five loosely defined categories based on the nature of their conceptual origins, the content produced, or the general focus of the activity:

1. Impact of the family,
2. Exploring family dynamics,
3. Individual development in a family context,
4. Exploring legacy dynamics, and
5. Couple's group activities.

Impact of the Family

Introduction Dyads: The Family Perspective

This activity is an excellent initiating activity for groups. Using a format of revolving dyads, have group members introduce themselves from the following perspectives:

1. *Grandparent (legacy) Perspective*: Introduce yourself as if your grandparents were introducing you: "This is my grandson/daughter (name). He/she..."
2. *Family of Origin Perspective*: Introduce yourself as your parents would introduce you: "This is my son/daughter (name). He/she... "
3. *Sibling Perspective*: Introduce yourself as your siblings (brother/sister) would introduce you: "This is my brother/sister (name). He/she...."
4. *Intimate Partner Perspective*: Introduce yourself as your intimate partner (spouse, lover, financé, etc.) would introduce you: "This is my (husband/wife/partner, etc.) (name). He/she...."
5. *Family of Creation Perspective*: Introduce yourself as your children would introduce you: "This is my mother/father (name). He/she...."
6. *Self Perspective*: Introduce yourself as you would introduce you: "My name is ____. I am... "

Step family perspectives can be added or substituted depending on the group. For any perspective that does not currently exist or apply (e.g., member does not have children or was an only child), the member should make up an introduction as they would like it to be if it did exist. Each member can also be given a 3×5 card to record significant traits that emerge from each introduction. These data can be self-recorded or the result of feedback from the partner who picks out one or two traits that stood out in the introduction.

A God, Higher Power, or Supreme Being perspective reflecting the spiritual dimension of human experience can also be incorporated into the dyadic rounds (e.g., "Introduce yourself as God or a Higher Power would introduce you).

When all perspectives have been shared convene the total group and process the activity from the perspective of how it helped group members get to know one another and how family relationships affect personality development and identity.

Exploring Family Dynamics

Family Tree One of the places where love and belonging is crucial to the growth and development of a person is in the family. This activity is designed to help each person consider how family background has contributed to who he or she is today. Furnish each person with paper and crayons for drawing. Instruct group members to draw a symbolic tree. The type of tree should represent each person's family; its color should symbolize feelings about childhood, the ground should represent the nature of growth and development, and the background should indicate dominant childhood memories.

After members complete the drawings (10 minutes), pair members off and have them explain their drawings to each other. Have them discuss how they fit into their respective families at the present time (15 minutes). Form groups of four (two pairs) and have each person discuss their partner's tree and family relationship, pointing out things that seem interesting and significant (25 minutes).

Family Sculpture Another activity that demonstrates the relational connection or pattern of family relationships is the family sculpture. Select a volunteer to create a family sculpture using other group members. Have him or her design a sculpture of his or her family that represents the relationships as he or she sees them. The sculptor should include him- or herself in the sculpture. When completed have the sculptor assume the position of him- or herself in the finished product. Then have the sculptor describe why he or she placed each person in the position he or she did and what his or her own relationship is to that person and the family. After that discussion have the same volunteer form another family sculpture using different members of the group (the first sculpture should remain intact except for the sculptor). The second sculpture should be a desired picture of the family (how the person would like it to be). If the same people are used, remind each person to remember their original position so the first sculpture can be reformed for comparison and contrast. Follow-up discussion should deal with similarities and differences between the two sculptures. You can repeat this several times but usually once or twice is sufficient to generate meaningful discussion. This technique is very useful as a tool in helping clients who are experiencing problems in their families.

Draw Your Childhood Table

1. On a large sheet of paper draw the shape of the table your family ate at when you were growing up (as a child between ages 7 and 12 if you want to raise school age family dynamics or as a teenager between ages 13 and 17 if you want to raise adolescent family dynamics).

2. Place members of your family around the table in their usual places using rectangles around names of males and circles around females. Identify parents and include yourself. An example is provided in Figure 14.1.

3. On the surface of the table write descriptors (words and phrases) which describe the family atmosphere and what it was like for you to live in this family.

4. Near each member at the table write at least two phrases or comments that describe his or her personality.

5. Have each member share their family table with the group.

If used as a homework task, have members write a one page description of their family of origin.

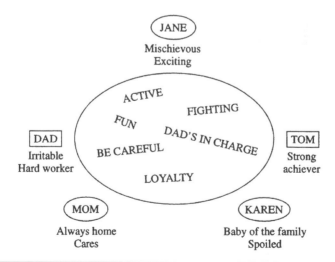

Figure 14.1 Example of table with family members seated in regular positions for meals plus words to describe personalities and feelings.

This activity can be modified to the present family table and used to explore current family dynamics. Another version is to have members do both their childhood and current family tables. Processing then involves comparing and contrasting one's experience in their family of origin and family of creation.

Another effective method of processing the material from this activity is to use the *family-o-gram technique*. Each person at the table is assigned a typical statement or comment that typifies their personality and role in the family. These statements are assigned to group members who represent the family members. The focus group member then stands in the center of a circle organized in the seating arrangement depicted in the family table. Starting with a parent figure the member rotates around the table receiving the phrase consecutively in a rapid fire manner. Each family member attempts to capture both the content and affect of the message. Have the focus member rotate around the table at least three times without interruption or discussion. The family-o-gram is concluded by having each family member repeat their phrase or statement at the same time in an attempt to solicit the focus member's attention while he or she stands still with his or her eyes closed. The activity is then processed in light of the messages and perceptions the group member carries with him or her from his or her family experience (see Trotzer, 1998a for additional features of this activity).

Belongingness-Separateness Activity All families provide their members with two basic experiences growing up: experiences of belongingness and experiences of separateness. The experiences combine to create a dynamic force in identity development (Trotzer & Trotzer, 1986). Belongingness experiences are of two types: those that are engaged in freely and with enthusiasm and those that are forced upon children and participated in with some resistance. Separateness similarly is divided into activities that were encouraged and discouraged (Figure 14.2).

Belongingness		Separateness	
Free Choice	Forced	Encouraged	Discouraged

Figure 14.2 Sample sheet of belongingness-separateness activity.

Pass out a sheet with columns as identified in Figure 14.2 and have group members identify belongingness and separateness experiences they had in their families growing up.

Have group members share their experiences either column by column or overall. Process the information in terms of the impact of these experiences on the respective identity, personality, and values of each person in the group. This activity is effective in helping members get to know each other on a deeper level and begins to surface the unmet needs and strengths in group member's lives. It also raises the topic of individuation and differentiation, a vital dynamic that is often associated with well being.

Individual Development in a Family Context

Individuals In the Family Life Cycle Pass out the diagram shown in Figure 14.3. Have group members plot the following information about themselves and their family.

1. Place a dot and the initials of each family member (parents, spouse, siblings, children, grandparents, self) on the birth to death Individual Development (ID) line.
2. If married, draw a line from the age at which marriage occurred (ID line) to the marriage dot on the Family Life Cycle (FLC) line. (If divorce and/or remarriage has occurred, add that information by identifying age at divorce on the ID line and draw a line from age at remarriage to the marriage dot on the FLC line.)
3. Life expectancy date: Have males draw a line from their current age on the ID line to the dot representing 72 (male life expectancy) on the FLC line. Have females draw a line from their current age to the dot representing 78 (female life expectancy) on the FLC line.
4. Family life cycle data: Draw a line straight up from the age of your oldest child on the ID line to the FLC line. (This approximates the family life cycle stage the family is in.) If a step-family is involved, draw a line straight up from the age of the oldest child in each biological family unit (Yours, Mine, and Ours).

The information charted can be processed as a means of getting acquainted and understanding the context in which each member is living. Data such as individual development via decade of life, stage of the family life cycle, years left to live and/or years of married life left, and complexity of living in single or remarried families all tend to emerge in the sharing and provide valuable material for developing closeness, acceptance, and understanding in the group and pinpointing problem areas for discussion.

FAMILY LIFE CYCLE (FLC) LINE

| Establishment | New Parent | Pre-school | School Age | Adolescent | Young Adult | Launching | Parental Middle Years | Aging Family (72) (78) | Spouse's Death |

INDIVIDUAL DEVELOPMENT (ID) LINE
Marriage

| Birth | 2 | 6 | 12 | 18 | (22-24) | | 30 | 40 | 50 | 60 | 70 | Death |

Developmental Tasks

| Trust | Autonomy | Initiative | Identity (Who am I?) | Differentiation —Seeker Self —Merger Self | Generativity | Integrity |

Figure 14.3 Individual and family development.

Family Life Cycle Analysis This activity is designed to help members look specifically at their experiences in their family from a developmental perspective.

Answer the following questions or respond to the directives relative to your family's current position in the family life cycle. Briefly review the typical stages of family life (Trotzer & Trotzer, 1986, pp. 225–234).

1. In what stage of development is your family at this time? Explain why you made that assessment. (Remember, some families may be in more than one stage at any one time.)
2. Write one sentence describing how each person in your family is currently experiencing the family (include yourself), e.g., if you have five people in your family write five sentences.
3. What issues or problems is your family currently dealing with that are typical of the family's stage of development.
4. What is your family doing to deal with the issues or problems listed above?
5. Describe the nature or condition of the marital relationship in your family. Indicate how it contributes and/or hinders the family's ability to deal with the tasks and problems of its developmental stage.

Have each group member share their analysis with the group for the purpose of pinpointing common issues and problems emanating from the stages of family development represented.

This activity is useful in agenda setting as group members identify issues they are grappling with that can be worked on in the group.

Five Roles Activity Everyone plays many different roles as a normal part of daily life. Some of these roles are more important than others, and some roles cause conflicts with others. This activity is designed to help members clarify their values with regard to several of the most important roles they play. Have each group member write five commonly played roles on five different 3×5 cards. Seat the group in a circle with their roles on their laps. Citing a crisis mandate (e.g., "Something happens in your life and because of that circumstance you must give up one role."), ask them to decide individually which role they would be most willing to give up. Have them crumple up that card and throw it into the middle of the circle. Continue the same process without discussion until each member has one role left. Then have the members discuss why they kept that particular role, how they decided to eliminate the other roles, and what their feelings were as they proceeded to discard roles.

An alternative procedure is to have a discussion after each decision and an extensive discussion relative to priorities and values at the end.

Another modification is to make certain roles mandatory as part of the five, such as job, parent, spouse. This creates a set of dynamics (sometimes referred to as systems clash) that typifies the stressors in each person's life when demands of job, personal interests, and family compete for time and energy. Process the activity in terms of daily decisions made to allocate time, energy, and resources to these roles and relative to priorities and values that often conflict with behavior and create stress and tension in daily living.

Expectations and How We Live Describe the chart in Figure 14.4. (*Note*: Categories on this chart are generic and can be modified, deleted, or expanded to be more relevant to the members of your group.) The instructions are as follows:

1. Fold the sheet so that only the Importance column is showing and rank the categories 1 through 9 based on their importance to you where 1 represents the most important. (This is the *cognitive* dimension and typifies ideal or value based priorities.)
2. Fold the sheet so that only the Time column is showing and rank the categories 1 through 9 on the basis of actual time spent in doing the activities of that category where 1 represents the most time spent. (This is the *behavioral* dimension and represents how time is allocated.)
3. Fold the sheet so that only the Satisfaction column is showing and rank the categories 1 through 9 on the basis of personal satisfaction experienced in each category where 1 represents the most satisfaction. (This represents the *affective* dimension and reflects the nature of inner emotions related to experience.)
4. Unfold the sheet so all rankings can be compared. Have each member analyze their rankings for congruence (importance, time, and satisfaction are directly related) or incongruence (discrepancies exist between the importance, time, and satisfaction columns).
5. Have group members share their rankings and analysis in the group.

This activity is particularly useful in groups where stress and stress management are topics of importance.

Exploring Legacy Dynamics

Family Genogram Activity Genograms are useful tools in helping group members explore their personhood and legacy. The instructions that follow are for a limited or working genogram that can be constructed quickly. For more extensive information about genograms refer to McGoldrick and Gerson (1985).

Categories	Importance	Time	Satisfaction
1. **Work:** This category includes all jobs or tasks you perform for which you are paid. (Include full time and part time) (School, full time or part time fits here)			
2. **Family:** This category includes activities and time spent with all or some (at least one) members of your nuclear family, meaning parent(s) and children.			
3. **Extended Family:** (Family of origin) This category includes time and activities with members of your extended family (parents, siblings, grandparents, aunts, uncles, etc.)			
4. **Marriage:** This category includes time spent specifically with your spouse exclusive of other family members. (Includes social activities together)			
5. **Personal:** This category includes individual activities and interests you pursue apart from your family/ marriage/work. (Hobbies, recreation, time alone, etc.)			
6. **Organizations:** This category includes time and activities in groups you belong to such as civic or professional groups, community organizations, clubs, etc.			
7. **Domestic:** This category includes activities or tasks you are responsible for to run and maintain your household e.g., chores, cleaning, cooking, house maintenance, etc.			
8. **Church:** This category includes church related and other activities that have a spiritual dimension and require time and commitment to pursue.			
9. **Step Family:** This category includes all activities with step-children if you differentiate them from the family category above.			
10. **Write your own:** _____ _____ _____			

Figure 14.4 Expectations and how we live.

1.   Construct a genogram of your family consisting of at least three genera-
     tions of persons that you have known personally or know about through
     other family members.
2.   Be sure to include both sides of your parents' families and in cases of
     step-families include significant generational relationships such as step-
     grandparents.
3.   Most genograms will include:
     a. your generation (spouse and/or siblings)
     b. your children (if applicable)
     c. your children's children (if applicable)
     d. your parents
     e. your grandparents
     f. your great-grandparents
4.   Indicate birth order via gender, sequence, and age (e.g., see Figure 14.5).
5.   Use circles to designate females and squares to designate males.
6.   Indicate deaths by placing an X over the person indicating their age at time
     of death, date of death, and cause.
7.   Indicate divorces with slashes through the line connecting the two persons
     and separations with dashes.
8.   Use dash lines to indicate adoption.
9.   Place a star by those family members you resemble the most.
10. Place a check mark by those family members you resemble the least.
11. Optional: Identify facts, traits or tendencies in your family such as
     alcohol/substance abuse, diseases (cancer, heart attacks, etc.) by appropriate
     designations (e.g., circle alcohol/substance abuser in red).

Creating a genogram is a good homework assignment and can be used for both
getting to know one another and exploring a person's background in greater
depth in relation to a particular problem such as substance abuse. Have group
members present their completed genograms to the group and then brainstorm
possible dynamics that may be operating in the person's life. Some groups continue
to develop genograms over the course of the group process so the technique has
both short term and long range utility.

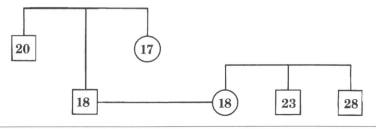

Figure 14.5 Example of sibling level.

Marriage and Family: The Impact of Legacy The following activity may be used in total or in part to help group members explore the impact of their family of origin and family legacy on their lives particularly in the context of current family relationships. The activity can be administered as a homework task or used as a guide to structuring discussion around each of the topics built into the activity.

The Revolving Slate

Growing up in our family of origin often produces resolutions about marriage and family that we find are tested once we become married and have a family. We are often surprised, shocked, or even disappointed that patterns or traits are repeated even when we had determined they would not be.

1. Make a list of statements you recall making as you grew up in your family that reflect how you wanted your marriage and family life to be. Most of these statements will take the form of resolutions or vows starting with stems such as:
   - When I'm married...
   - The person I marry will (will not)...
   - I will never...
   - My children will (will not)...
2. Indicate which of the preceding statements are the most important to you and why.
3. Have you altered any of the preceding statements or found any to be inaccurate. If so, how does that make you feel and how did the change occur?

Adopting-Adapting

Growing up in our family of origin produces certain experiences and values that we wish to emulate in our own marriage and family. Complete the following tasks to help you discover how the positives in your family legacy have influenced you.

1. Make a list of experiences in your family of origin that have resulted in treasured memories.
2. Complete the following statement: The traits and values I admire most about my family are..."
3. Identify one of your treasured memories that you would like to *adopt* or have *adopted* in your marriage or family of creation in the same way you experienced it. Explain why and indicate problems you have had or may have in doing so.
4. Identify one of your treasured memories you would like to *adapt* or have *adapted* in your marriage or family of creation. Explain how you would like to modify (or have modified) it and why.

Opposing-Rejecting

Growing up in our family of origin produces certain experiences and impressions we want to negate or avoid reconstructing in our own marriage and family. Complete the following tasks to help you discover how the negatives in your family legacy have influenced you.

1. Make a list of experiences in your family of origin that have resulted in negative memories.
2. Complete the following statement: The traits I consider undesirable and the values I disagree with in my family of origin are...
3. Identify one thing you will do or have done in your family of creation that makes sure the negative experience you had will not be repeated. Explain how that change will affect your children's experience.
4. Identify how one of the above listed experiences could be (or has been) handled differently in your marriage or family of creation. Indicate how you discovered the means of changing it.

Decisions Across the Generations

Every generation is faced with choices and decisions that must be made in the course of forming its identity in and impact on the flow of life. These decisions may be repetitive emerging in every generation or may be unique to the historical time frame or context in which the person and family lives. This activity is designed to explore the generational relatedness or nonrelatedness of personal decisions. It is best conducted as an out of group process where group members actually discuss with grandparents and parents what they consider their most important decisions were and are. In the absence of the opportunity to obtain the data first hand, the group member can project the data from memory or conjecture. Have group members identify the most important decisions (specific choices) that their: (1) grandparents made, are making, and must make; (2) parents made, are making, and must make; and (3) they have made, are making, and must make. Upon completion, have group members share the data comparing and contrasting their contemporary generational decisions (problems and issues) with those of the previous two generations. Process the activity in light of common and different problems and in terms of assets and resources that are available from past generations that can be mobilized in resolving current problems.

Couples Groups

The activities that follow are particularly appropriate to couples groups where intimate partners can benefit from sharing with each other as well as in the group. The resource for these and other couples activities is *Marriage and Family: Better Ready Than Not* (Trotzer & Trotzer, 1986).

Expecting To Be Loved One of the most significant aspects of an intimate relationship is the love dimension. However, the definition of love and, more particularly, how it is expressed is the root of many relational issues. The following activity is useful in helping couples assess and express their similarities and differences relative to the behavior of demonstrating love. Have each group member rank the five categories described in Figure 14.6 on the basis of their own preference for giving and receiving love. Then have them rank their perception of their intimate partner's preferences for giving and receiving love. Use 1 to represent the top preference.

When the individual rankings are completed have each couple share their rankings with each other using them as a basis for discussion. When the couple dyads are finished, reconvene the group and process the activity in light of gender preferences and characteristics and personality traits of the couples and individuals in the group. When working with mixed gender couples discuss rankings

Five Categories Relative to Expressing Love	Me	Spouse
1. **WORDS**: One way to express love is simply by saying "I love you," or "You look nice in that dress," or "I like the way you did that." Verbal statements affirming love bring a great deal of emotional security to some of us.	—	—
2. **GIFTS**: A second love language is gifts. They need not be expensive to be valuable. A gift says, "He or she was thinking of me when we were apart." You cannot select a gift without thinking about the person to whom you will give it. It is a deliberate act of love.	—	—
3. **ACTION**: Doing things for your spouse can be a powerful communication of love. Cooking a meal, washing dishes, dusting, vacuuming the floor, taking out the garbage, putting gas in the car, etc., are all ways of expressing love.	—	—
4. **TIME**: Spending quality time with your spouse is also a means of expressing love. Quality time is giving your spouse your undivided attention. Whether you are sitting on the couch, taking a walk, or sharing a meal at a quiet restaurant, when you focus on listening and sharing with your spouse, you are communicating love.	—	—
5. **TOUCH**: Physical touch is recognized as an important way to express love. Kissing, embracing, holding hands, sexual intercourse, or other affectionate physical contacts are a means of communicating love.	—	—

FIGURE 14.6 Expecting to be loved.

and choices in gender determined inner-outer circle formats where men discuss their choices in the inner circle while women listen, and then women discuss their choices in the inner circle while men listen. Process the results with regard to insights and observations relative to the impact of gender, culture, ethnicity, and values regarding the expression of love.

Attraction Dimension in Couples The following is a good get acquainted activity because it focuses couples on a typically positive time in their lives and provides a comfortable channel for couples to share themselves with each other.

1. Complete the following statements with respect to your partner. Share your responses with your partner.
    a. When I first met you I was attracted to you because . . .
    b. When I got to know you I was attracted to you because . . .
    c. Now I am attracted to you because . . .
2. Tell the story of your courtship and marriage. (Use this task as a means for couples to introduce themselves to the group.)
    a. 1st Partner: Share with the group how you met and became involved with each other.
    b. 2nd Partner: Describe how you decided to get married or become a committed couple.
3. In the columns in Figure 14.7 indicate specific examples of things that attract you to your partner. Fit them into the category you believe is most appropriate.
    a. Share the column information in same gender subgroups. Each partner shares his or her perception of the attraction dimension in his or her intimate relationship.
    b. Reconvene the group and discuss the importance of attraction as a relationship characteristic in intimate relating.

Similarities (Howe we are alike)	Differences (How we are different)	Exchanges (How we contribute to each other)

Figure 14.7 Sample sheet for categorizing specific things that attracted one to his or her partner.

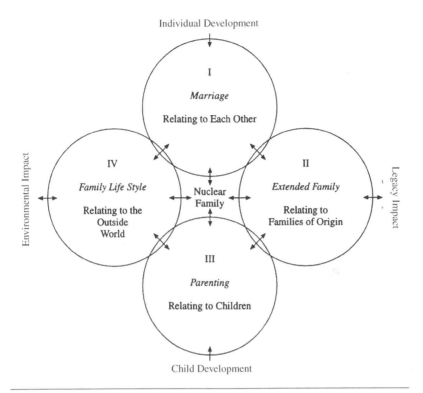

Figure 14.8 Basic arenas of marital conflict.

Basic Arenas of Marital Conflict Distribute and briefly explain the diagram located in Figure 14.8 (Trotzer & Trotzer, 1986, pp. 185–187). Have each couple identify a list of specific issues from their own relationship that relate to the four arenas of marital conflict. Have them identify three issues they would be willing to discuss in the group. Convene the group and have each couple share the issues they would like to discuss and give a brief description of them to the group. When all couples have shared their issues, form an agenda for group work either by selecting a problem/issue of common concern to the couples in the group or by having each couple identify a priority issue. Organize the work of the group around the agenda making sure each couple's issue or version of the issue is addressed.

Relationship Analysis Inventory Give a brief introduction to the activity by describing the four component parts of an intimate relationship (Trotzer & Trotzer, 1986, pp. 162–170). Have partners complete the Relationship Analysis Inventory (Figure 14.9) individually and then share their results with each other. Have them identify the area(s) they want to work on in the group. Have each couple share what they learned about their relationship with the group and use the information to solidify the group and create a work focus.

The Relationship Analysis Inventory also can be used as a homework task for the couple to work on together. Each couple then presents their analysis to the group. The results are processed as a means of identifying work areas and setting agendas for the group and the individual couples.

Select an intimate relationship you are currently involved in (boy/girl friend, fiancé, spouse, intimate partner) and fill in the columns below as follows:

1. Togetherness: indicate those activities the two of you participate in together.
2. Apartness: Indicate those activities you engage in separate from your partner.
3. Pushing-Resisting:
   a. Identify the things about you your partner does not like or wishes you would change.
   b. Identify the things about your partner that you do not like and wish he/she would change.
4. Leading-Supporting:
   a. Identify the things you take the initiative in while your partner gives you his/her support and encouragement.
   b. Identify the things your partner takes the initiative in where you give him/her your support and encouragement.

Marital Vows Activity Marriage vows raise the issue of commitment and their content elicits the definitions and values that under gird that commitment. The following activity is appropriate for both premarital and postmarital couples groups and can be utilized as either a group activity or a combined couple and group activity. If a combined approach is used, the sequence can be either couple-group or group-couple. Results will vary based on sequence, but the end result will be a deeper understanding, appreciation, and meaning for couples relative to their own commitment to each other and for the group relative to the importance of commitment in marriage. The instructions are as follows:

Group-Couple Sequence: Read the example of typical marriage vows below and then as a group create a generic version emphasizing the elements the group feels are most important. You may wish to use either traditional or contemporary language.

✸ Marriage Vows

(name), will you have (name) as your (husband/wife)? Will you live with (him/her) according to God's will? Will you love and comfort (him/her),

INSTRUCTIONS: Select an intimate relationship you are currently involved in (boy/girl friend, fiancé, spouse, intimate partner) and fill in the columns below as follows:

1. Togetherness: Indicate those activities the two of you participate in together.
2. Apartness: Indicate those activities you engage in separate from your partner.
3. Pushing-Resisting: a) Identify the things about you your partner does not like or wishes you would change.
   b) Identify the things about your partner that you do not like and wish he/she would change.
4. Leading-Supporting: a) Identify the things you take the initiative in while your partner gives you his/her support and encouragement. b) Identify the things your partner takes the initiative in where you give him/her your support and encouragement

1. Togetherness	2. Apartness	3. Pushing-Resisting	4. Leading-Supporting
		a) b)	a) b)

Figure 14.9 Relationship analysis inventory.

honor and support (him/her), in times of joy and trial, as long as you both shall live?

I, (name, take you, (name), to be my (wife/husband) from this day forward, as long as I live; to be with you in times of joy and suffering and wealth and poverty; to love and honor you, according to God's will; I therefore pledge you my faithfulness.

Each couple then uses the generic form as a stimulus to develop their own personalized version that is then shared with the group. (For the *Couple-group Sequence* simply modify the steps as follows: Typical marriage vows, personalized marriage vows (couple), and generic marriage vows (group).

As a group, discuss and respond to the marriage vows shared and then have couples review and, if desired, refine or revise their vows based on input from the discussion. Using the group leader as presider, each couple may wish to recite their vows to each other in the presence of the group as a commitment/recommitment experience.

Marriage: The Sexual Dimension Sex in marriage or a committed relationship serves four basic functions. Sex is the means of expressing and experiencing intimacy. Sex is the means of meeting each person's need for sexual gratification and physical release. Sex is the means by which partners reproduce themselves (biological procreation). Sex is the means by which physical pleasure and enjoyment is experienced. All are important facets of the sexual dimension of the marriage relationship (Trotzer & Trotzer, 1986, pp. 181–185). The instructions for this activity are as follows:

1. Personally rank *intimacy, need, pleasure,* and *reproduction* in order of priority for you as a person.
   ___ Intimacy   ___ Need
   ___ Pleasure   ___ Reproduction
2. Share your ranking and your explanation with your partner.
3. Suggested Personal Sharing Tasks (Between Partners)
   a. Share a special memory of your sexual life together.
   b. Share the most enjoyable aspect of sex for you.
   c. Share one thing you would like to change or add to your sex life.
   d. Identify differences between you and your partner with respect to sexual relating.
   e. Discuss how you think you obtained your perspective and values relative to sex (What influences you to see sex as you do?)
   f. Share your perception of the current state of your sexual relating.

g. What sexual experience (s) do you anticipate with each other? (Share your sexual fantasies).

4. Have a group discussion of the four dimensions of sexuality reviewed in the opening paragraphs of this activity. Discuss similarities and differences relative to:

a. Values and religious perspectives,

b. Influence of legacy and family of origin,

c. Gender perspectives, and

d. Developmental dynamics (age, family status, etc.).

15
Crisis Response
A Group Work Priority

Given the escalating amount and ever increasing impact of natural, human-made, and accidental disasters in our local, national, and global communities, the application of group work is vital to the physical, psychological, mental, and emotional well being of victims, responders, witnesses, and bystanders. Group work may well become the predominant human response vehicle of our generation, thus making group leadership skills and group process expertise in the various forms of group work a basic necessity for meeting the needs of people affected by disasters across the entire continuum of crisis response from rescue and recovery to community action planning and preparation.

Context

Monday, September 10 (2001)

- On Monday, a hose in my sink broke just when I needed to rush out the door, and I thought life was being unfair.
- On Monday, when you asked people how they were doing, without much thought, or much contemplation, they replied "fine" or "good."
- On Monday, the papers and the news magazines were filled with stories about the new fall TV schedule.
- On Monday, there were not many people in the religious section at the bookstore.
- On Monday, the American flag hung, for the most part, unnoticed at government buildings and at schools.
- On Monday, I passed strangers without much regard.

Tuesday, September 11 (2001)

- On Tuesday, September 11, all that changed.
- On Tuesday, September 11, different things seemed important.
- On Tuesday, September 11, blissful naiveté was lost. Sanctity was mercilessly shaken.
- On Tuesday, September 11, somebody tried to take America apart.
- On Tuesday September 11, America came together.
- On Tuesday, September 11, there were no Republicans, Democrats, yuppies, blue collars, or any other labels. There were only Americans.
- On Tuesday, September 11, the best of the human spirit spit back into the eye of the worst.
- On Tuesday, September 11, America was knocked to its knees.
- On Tuesday, September 11, America got back up again.

USA Today, Friday, September 21, 2001, p. 21A

The Eminence of Disasters

We live in a world where disasters of every kind and variety are increasing on a monumental scale. Trauma producing events whether natural, human-made, or accidental in origin are accumulating at an ever-increasing rate, and their impact is projected far and wide through the media producing hosts of impacted bystanders and witnesses in addition to the victims, first responders, and persons directly affected by the cause. For example, statistics tell us that there were three times as many natural disasters in the 1990s than there were in the 1960s, and that the cost of damages caused by these disasters was nine times greater (Annan, 1999). In other words, there are more natural disasters in our world today, and they are more destructive than at any time in our previous recorded history.

The year 2000 set a record for the number of natural disasters worldwide killing 10,000 people and causing $30 billion dollars in losses. That year there were 850 natural disasters counting wildfires, volcanic eruptions, earthquakes, landslides, floods, hurricanes, tornados, typhoons, lahars (volcanic mud flows), and droughts. A record for economic losses incurred by natural disasters, $89 billion dollars, was set in 1998. During that year 32,000 people were killed and more than 300 million were driven from their homes. In 1999, that record was broken when natural disasters killed 75,000 people and caused $100 billion dollars in economic losses. Thus, in the three year period from 1998 to 2000, 117,000 people lost their lives and $219 billion dollars in economic losses were caused by natural disasters (Ward, 2001). In addition, countless millions of people were displaced and injured. Therefore, besides being unpreventable, the two additional things that natural disasters have in common is that they cause devastating destruction to property and traumatizing damage to people in the form of death, injury, and loss.

Recent events such as the tsunami of December 26, 2004, in which more than 250,000 people were killed and untold billions of dollars of damage incurred, and hurricane Katrina assaulting the Gulf Coast of the United States killing more than a thousand people and nearly devastating the entire City of New Orleans, are evidence that no part of our world is immune to cataclysmic catastrophes, and although many of the natural disasters are predictable, *none* are preventable. The Red Cross enumerates hurricanes, flash floods, earthquakes, tornados, fires, and hazardous waste spills among the traumatic events that prompt their response and mobilize their services. Add to these figures those of terrorist attacks such as occurred on September 11 in which 2,819 people lost their lives in the New York City Twin Towers attack and over 4,167 deaths occurred all toll, and the insidious nature of trauma is no longer an aberration or exception, but becomes part and parcel of everyday life (www.newyorkmetro.com/news/articles. wtc.1year.numbers.htm: retrieved June 2, 2004).

A Personal Anecdote: The Preparation and The Prompt for this Chapter

In May of 1999, I had the privilege of going to Taiwan to deliver a speech and conduct a group counseling workshop at a Counseling Conference at National Changhwa University of Education. Following the conference, my gracious host, Dr. Sophie Woo, arranged for a few of us to spend a brief holiday up at Sun Moon Lake in the high mountains of Taiwan. During our stay there, we took a wonderful boat ride on the lake and we stopped to visit the island shrine in the middle of the lake. While I greatly appreciated the beauty of the lake and its surrounding mountains, I was especially touched by the peaceful charm of that little island in the center of that magnificent lake. I was so impressed that I shot a whole roll of film trying to capture the essence of that special place to keep it in my memory and share it with my family back home. Little did I know that those pictures were going to document a place that would be devastated by a natural disaster.

On September 21, 1999 Taiwan experienced an earthquake that measured 7.6 on the Richter Scale, the impact of which left 2,105 dead, 8,713 injured, 100,000 homeless, 12,000 buildings destroyed and caused $3.1 billion dollars in damages (Trotzer, 2001b). When I heard the news of the earthquake, I immediately began calling and e-mailing my friends and colleagues to find out if they were safe. To my great relief, I found that none had been seriously affected by the tremor. However, in one of my contacts with Dr. Woo, she informed me that the epicenter of the quake was 7.75 miles from Sun Moon Lake and that whole area, including that beautiful little island, was severely devastated. It was a very eerie and scary feeling to know that I had been walking around on that very place just a few months before. It took me some time to come to grips with that fact, and there is still a residue of unreality associated with the facts especially when I look at the pictures.

Subsequently, on August 1, 2001 I received another invitation to go to Taiwan to deliver a keynote address on the theme of "Responding to Crises Caused by Natural Disasters." I chose as my specific topic, "Helping Children Cope and Recover from Natural Disasters" and developed a rationale and format for training counselors in conducting crisis intervention groups. The model was designed as both a practice framework and a training vehicle so that crisis intervention services could be rendered directly to children, and service providers could be trained in its use. My research and preparation for the address involved soliciting information from many of my colleagues who had been directly involved in many of the disasters that had occurred in the United States including the earthquakes in California, the hurricanes in Florida, the shootings at Columbine High School in Colorado, the Oklahoma City Bombing, the tornados in the Midwest, and the floods in New England. Little did I know that six weeks of preparation for the Taiwan presentation was preparing me for a traumatic event much closer to home.

As part of the invitation, I had been given a due date for a typed copy of my paper (Trotzer, 2001b) to be delivered to Taiwan for translation—that date was September 10, 2001. I dutifully sent out my paper on that date, and the next day found out I had been preparing material that would be put to use immediately. On September 11, 2001 the United States experienced our generation's Day of Infamy, and I was immediately called upon to utilize the training material, rationale, model, and format to train local counselors and community leaders in conducting crisis response discussion groups in their schools and organizations. Within two weeks I had trained over 100 community leaders in the model that is the core of this chapter under the auspices of the University of New Hampshire System College for Lifelong Learning (now Granite State College). This chapter is the result of the preparation elicited by the Taiwan earthquake and the prompt triggered by the September 11 attacks.

As a side note, in my research preparing for the Taiwan address, I came across a report prepared by Dr. David Petley, a geologist whose particular expertise is the seismological region that encompasses Taiwan. He noted that Taiwan sits on a location where two of the earth's tectonic plates, the large Eurasian Plate and the smaller Philippine Plate, converge. He made the observation that Taiwan's aggressive tropical climate and significant seismic activity cause major landslides, rock falls, and other hazards throughout the island. He also noted that seismologically speaking, Taiwan experiences as many as 1,000 earthquakes per year (Trotzer, 2001). Fortunately, most of those tremors are only measured by a seismograph and not ever felt by the people who live there. However, the meaning of that information is blatantly clear: If you live in Taiwan you can expect to experience more earthquakes, and since earthquakes cannot be prevented, it is essential to prepare for them and have plans in place to respond when they occur. However, as I reviewed that material again in writing this chapter, I could not help but think,

"Wouldn't it be great if we had a seismograph that detected terrorism?" If we did, we certainly would do all we could to prevent events like those of September 11. Such an instrument will not likely be developed, but the importance of preparation and response is critical, and therefore I offer this chapter.

Overview

The purpose of this chapter is to present a perspective of crisis response that emphasizes and integrates the relevance of group work and group process. A general overview of the components of disaster response and the general nature of a disaster plan will be reviewed followed by specific suggestions and considerations for implementing such a plan in community agencies and schools. The role of the counselor as a group work expert will be specifically emphasized leading to the description of several models for using groups in response to crises. Finally, the rationale and format for training crisis intervention discussion group leaders will be presented. This model is applicable to local, national, or global crises involving human-made, natural, or accidental disasters. It can be used in the immediate aftermath of the event and as an ongoing follow up to the event. It is a form of psychological first aid, an initial step toward recovery, an interventive means of engaging in the recovery process and a process for revisiting and reviewing one's progress over time relative to the initiating event.

Generic Objectives of Disaster Response: P&P and R&R

The Broad Strokes of a Disaster Response Plan

In the game of baseball the expression "hitting for the cycle" is used to describe a batter who hits a single, double, triple, and homerun in one game I want to use that phrase as a metaphor for effective disaster response. Every disaster response program must "hit for the cycle" and encompass what I call the P&P and R&R of disaster response. The four generic objectives or "the cycle" of a disaster response plan are *Preparation* and *Protection*, *Relief* and *Recovery*. Together they create a context for the group work blueprint that I will present in the rest of the chapter.

Preparation Preparation involves the development of plans, procedures, and policies for responding to disasters. Resources are identified and responsibilities are assigned in the event of a disaster. This information is recorded in a manual or guidebook, and training is dispensed to those who provide services related to disaster and those affected by the disaster so that all are familiar with the disaster response program. A major portion of the preparation phase is helping people anticipate disasters and disaster-proof their communities, businesses, schools, homes, and families to the greatest extent possible. In addition, information relative to safety and relief is communicated to the constituents of the area the disaster response plan covers. Kofi Annan, (1999) Secretary General of the United Nations, has emphasized the importance of preparation especially in regard to natural disasters because we have satellite surveillance that is revolutionizing disaster early warning, and the Internet can provide instant dissemination of that warning data. He pointed out, however, that without a clear plan for disaster response that information has little effect. On the other hand, in places where extensive plans are in place death tolls have been reduced dramatically.

Protection Protection refers to the concrete resources available to people in time of crisis. The location of "safe haven" places prior to, during, and after a disaster are identified and provided in the event of a disaster. Protection has both a community dimension and a personal or private dimension. In other words, it involves stipulating "safe havens" in the community, the school, the work place, and in the home.

Relief Relief is the crisis intervention aspect of the disaster response plan. It encompasses the immediate help and assistance that is mobilized before, during, and immediately after the disaster in the form of rescue, food, water, shelter, medical care, clothing, and all other essentials to the saving, preservation, and maintenance of life. Relief also encompasses mobilizing identified resources and allocating trained personnel to address the mental, emotional, and psychological impact of a disaster in people's lives in the form of crisis intervention (Kulic, 2003; Jordan, 2001, 2002)

Recovery Recovery refers to the long-term response plan that is designed to help the victims regain stability and rebuild their lives following the disaster. It includes both economic and psychological programs that can be used to help people respond to, work through and move beyond the crisis, and it brings the disaster plan full circle to preparation because those who survive go on to use their knowledge and experience to construct prevention and preparation programs for future disasters. While victims may be the primary focus of recovery in disaster plans, contemporary reality expands this focus to persons identified as "first responders" (those who become directly involved in providing rescue and relief), those who are connected to the victims, whether closely or distantly related, and the large pool of witnesses and bystanders who are brought into contact with the trauma through the news media particularly through visual exposure via TV and the Internet. These people also must be accounted for in the relief and recovery process (Boss, 2002; Figley & Barnes, 2005; McKenry & Price, 2005).

A Blueprint for Disaster Response

An ancient African proverb espouses the wisdom that "It takes a village to raise a child." With regard to disasters that proverb is best adapted to, "It takes a village to protect a child," or even "It takes a village to protect its inhabitants—adults and children alike." While the main focus of this chapter will pinpoint schools and mental health agencies, the community is the umbrella under which the school operates and the context in which the agency functions. Consequently, I will note three levels (community, school or agency, and specific counseling or mental health program) of a comprehensive disaster response plan, commenting briefly on the community level and more extensively and specifically on the school/agency and counseling/mental health program levels.

Cultural Context Comment

The United States, like many other countries, has experienced a wide range of natural disasters—hurricanes in the East and South, tornados and floods in the Midwest, earthquakes in the West, Nor'easters and ice storms in the North. These natural disasters coupled with human-made disasters stemming from violence and accidents have prompted communities and schools to develop disaster relief plans and programs. Much of the information that follows is drawn from sources related to those programs. Consequently, it is offered with the knowledge and expectation that cultural differences must and will be considered in the use and adaptation of the suggestions whether in the sense of cultural diversity in the United States or cultural/political differences in the other countries. It is also recognized that direct application of some of the material may not be appropriate or relevant in other countries or cultures. Therefore, I offer these ideas and suggestions with the hope that they will be processed from a cultural perspective and adapted and applied in a cultural context that will make them useful to the communities, schools, families and students for whom they are intended.

The Community

Every community, however it is defined, should have a *Community Action Plan* for purposes of responding to natural, human-made or accidental disasters. This plan is created by, involves, and is carried out by community leaders, professionals, experts, social servants, and volunteers drawn from the broad spectrum of community resources. All sectors of society are tapped to contribute to the action plan including government, law enforcement, medical, health care, social services, religion, education, and any other group that has resources to give and services to provide.

Time and the focus of this chapter does not allow for an in depth review of a comprehensive community action plan. But I will emphasize one critical element that must be part of every action plan because it relates directly to the school and the students and families in the school system. Every community action plan should include a *Community Crisis Intervention Team* (CCIT) of trained professionals and resource personnel who can be mobilized immediately in time of crisis. This team (a crisis intervention cohort group) can provide relief services to the school or other community setting immediately following a disaster and can provide preventive services to the school in preparation for disasters.

The personnel on the CCIT should be trained in "critical incident stress management" (Everly & Mitchell, 1997) or a similar form of response framework (e.g., American Red Cross Disaster Mental Health Services Training). They must be capable of providing psychological first aid directly to those affected by the disaster *and* be able to train others to provide that first aid as well. Recent literature has supported the qualification that these team members be skilled group workers because the impact of the group process is both quantitatively and qualitatively advantageous (Everly, Lating, & Mitchell, 2000). The group approach is particularly relevant because of its capability to decrease vulnerability and increase resiliency in the same process (Shakor & Fister, 2000) while extending its influence to greater numbers. Mental health professionals, including school and mental health counselors, are often primary members of such teams. However, other school, health, medical, social services, and law enforcement experts are also part of the team. As such, the team is a resource that can be activated immediately after a disaster occurs to provide services in the school and classroom to students, parents, teachers, and others affected within the school environment. A specific group model for the delivery of these services will be reviewed later in this chapter. If any community does not have a community action plan, I strongly advocate that immediate attention be given to developing one.

For those communities that do not have a plan, I suggest the use of a community dialogue and action planning process such as Weisbord's (Weisbord & Janoff, 1995) large group problem solving and visioning process called Future Search, which is adaptable across cultures and provides a means of mobilizing the best and brightest resources in a community to address a critical issue or problem (in this case disasters). Resource personnel in the community referred to as "stakeholders" are brought together for the purpose of devising a community action plan. Bertram (2000) described this process as "a large group, facilitated experience involving stakeholders, all of whom are concerned about and vested in addressing and resolving to their satisfaction, a complex, controversial, and entangled issue" which is certainly an apt description of the problems created by natural, human-made or accidental disasters (personal communication).

The School

Every school system and school should have a *Strategic Action Plan* (SAP) developed and in place in the event of a disaster. This strategic plan should incorporate a training dimension for all school personnel, a crisis response dimension and a recovery program dimension. The plan should address the needs of students and their parents in *preparing for, responding to,* and *recovering from* disasters. The plan should consider school personnel as both victims affected by the disaster and resources to victims of the disaster. This distinction is crucial because school personnel in the helping role are not exempt from the impact of the disaster if they live in the community affected by it (Young, 1997). Consequently, their relief and recovery needs must also be addressed as part of the training program, and through debriefing sessions following the delivery of relief and recovery services. In that way the best possible assistance to students and their parents can be assured, and the potential ramifications of what has been identified as "vicarious trauma" (impact of victim's trauma on the helping professional) can be addressed (Trippany, White, & Wilcoxen, 2004).

Every school should have a *Crisis Management Team* (CMT) composed of school personnel (administrators, counselors, teachers, school nurses, school psychologists) who are specifically designated to develop a crisis response plan for the school and deliver training, relief and recovery services in regard to disasters or traumas that may affect the school and its students. In many cases the school counselor because of specialized training in trauma response and group work will serve on or lead the team. The primary preparation task of this team is to provide training to teachers in crisis intervention. Given the extensive nature and amount of crises that impact students and the status of teachers as being on the front line for addressing such events, crisis intervention training is now considered a necessity for all teachers. In addition to training, every school should have a *safety plan for protection* that can be followed in the event of a disaster, a *crisis intervention plan* that can be mobilized in the school immediately after a disaster and a *disaster recovery program* including services to students and their families over the extended period of time it takes for students, their families, the school and the community to rebuild their lives following the disaster.

Counseling and Mental Health Programs

The counseling program of a school and the mental health program of agencies should provide and perform the primary services associated with preparation, relief and recovery with regard to disasters and other traumas that will affect community members, students, and their families. Operating under the rubric of a *Crisis Response Program,* counselors are the frontline resources in the school with regard to both training and the delivery of relief and recovery programs and services. Counselors play many roles in the conduct of their profession with regard to crisis. They are consultants to teachers, administrators and parents relative to student needs. They are primary providers of relief in the form of individual and group services immediately following a disaster, and they are the principle providers of recovery programs and services relative to psychoeducation, counseling, referral, and therapy. *Consequently, counselors need to be specialists in disaster response so that they can be a resource to the school in preparing for, during and after the occurrence of a disaster.*

Two Key Principles of Disaster Response

Last and Least Principle

In responding to disasters, children tend to be last and least on the priority list of communities, adults, and parents.

Natural disasters, for example, are different from other traumas and crises because of the immense damage to property and the environment that they leave in their wake. Consequently, much of the community energy is diverted to the task of cleaning up and rebuilding after the destruction. Adults get caught up in their own recovery and involved in getting their lives and property back in order, and children are left in the background and may even become viewed as nuisances. Parents are often overwhelmed by the simple fact that they have to clean up their property and reconstruct their homes. In addition, the financial losses and cost of recovery place extreme burdens on adults to put all their energy and resources into re-establishing and reordering their physical lives and reasserting their economic stability. Coupled with their own personal, emotional, and psychological responses to the disaster, these factors tend to push the needs of children down on the adult priority list once the immediate impact of the crisis is over, and the children are determined to be physically safe. For that reason, it is imperative that the school, the common gathering place for children, have a disaster response program that meets the needs of children and extends that program to parents as well.

This same type of last and least response occurs with regard to human-made and accidental disasters. Adults in their own emotional enmeshment with the event (e.g., September 11) may become so immersed in the event that they do not realize the impact on their children. They may, in fact, simply attempt to protect their children from exposure as the primary means of response and then neglect to notice the emotional effect on the child. Here again, the school is often the place where symptoms show up and where opportunities abound to talk about and process the crisis event with peers and teachers. Consequently, the importance of group expertise and group programs relative to crises become critical in transforming children from a "last and least" category to a "first and foremost" domain.

Crisis and Trauma Versus Loss and Grief Principle

Trauma and Crisis are to Relief as Loss and Grief are to Recovery

Any disaster response program must clearly distinguish between the crisis and trauma relief phase and the loss and grief recovery phase that follow in the aftermath of a disaster. Crisis and trauma create reactions that must be expressed, shared, recognized, validated, and affirmed as a major feature of any crisis intervention process, program or response. The characteristics of victims, first responders, related significant others, and bystanders or witnesses immediately following a disaster are cause and effect traits that are common to the general population of persons who experience or are exposed to a disaster. While degrees of effect will vary and responses of individuals will reflect their uniqueness and individuality, the general guidelines that direct crisis intervention are different from those that guide loss and grief work even though they may have parallel and common elements (Hacker, 2001). In contrast, responding to loss and grief requires a long-term developmental perspective and process. Consequently, intervention relative to trauma and crisis is related to relief while intervention related to loss and grief is related to recovery. In an effective disaster response program, anxiety over trauma (fear, panic, loss of control) takes psychological priority over mourning (pain and grief from loss) though both are sequentially essential. The relief process of crisis intervention sets the stage for, opens the door to and gives a running start in the loss and grief work of the recovery process for disaster victims in all their various forms.

With these perspectives in mind I will turn my attention to the specific model for training leaders and conducting crisis intervention discussion groups.

Crisis Intervention Discussion Groups

Rationale and Development

The following model and format for crisis intervention discussion groups is informed and influenced by a number of models for group crisis intervention and is not either a reinvention of the wheel or presented as an original framework. Rather, it is a modification of several models that is expanded and refined to meet crisis needs in a wider context with a more diverse population of participants across a broad spectrum of traumatic events and a time continuum that encompasses immediate response, follow-up and long term processing and recovery. It is applicable to natural, accidental, and human-made disasters of a local, national, or global origin, but it is also uniquely applicable to community-specific events such as the death of a student by suicide or a teacher in an accident or from an illness such as cancer. It is also specifically informed by the dynamics, principles, practices, and processes inherent in effective group work that have been elaborated in the previous chapters of this text.

The basic framework of the model is derived from Brock's (1998; Brock, Sandoval, & Lewis, 1996) Classroom Crisis Intervention approach which in turn has been impacted by Mitchell's (Mitchell & Everly, 1996) Critical Incident Stress Management format. It is designed to be primarily relevant to community or collective disasters as opposed to personal disasters. Some general considerations are discussed first, and then the model itself is described.

Personal Disasters Versus Community (Collective) Disasters

The distinction between these two types of trauma is that collective disasters affect people in a wider circle beyond the immediate victims or those directly affected. For example, personal disasters affect you, your family, close friends or colleagues, but do not encompass the larger community beyond the possible extension of sympathy, condolences or support. Events such as death of a spouse or child, loss of a job, divorce, and such may qualify as traumatic or disasters, and may elicit sympathy and empathy from outsiders but do not meet the criteria of a collective disaster. Collective disasters generate witnesses and bystanders who are emotionally affected by the event in ways that affect their lives even though they may not be closely related to the person or persons who are directly affected. This occurs because of the ripple effect of community connections and the exposure to the event though the media and through the permission such events give to community members to talk about it in their private and public conversations. For example, September 11 created a nation of eyewitnesses through the media that produced a new category of potential post-traumatic stress victims—people who witnessed the events on TV. *Newsweek* (Gossard, 2002), in reporting a study published in the *Journal of the American Medical Association* in the aftermath of the attacks, identified three key traits that distinguish collective disasters: (1) they give people permission to open up and talk about the event; (2) there is a direct link between posttraumatic stress disorder (PTSD) symptoms and the number of hours people watch the event and its coverage on TV, and (3) the closer people are geographically/physically to the event, the greater the amount of PTSD symptoms. This proximity factor is relevant to all forms of traumatic impact especially in regard to more personal and local events such as murders or suicides (Miranda, Molina, & McVane, 2003). These factors are applicable to local as well as national or global events and serve as the impetus for providing a setting where people can constructively process their experiences.

Dynamics of Processing Traumatic Events—The ABC'S(s)

The nature of human experience is essentially a combination of factors that encompass our emotions (affect), actions (behavior), and thinking (cognition) combined with a perspective or attitude derived from a sense of something greater than ourselves (Spirituality) and a sense of our inner nature (human spirit). Consequently, the acronym of the ABC'S(s) can be used to depict the nature

A = Affect (feelings and emotions): What did you feel?

B = Behavior (actions, behaviors): What did you do?

C = Cognition (thoughts, ideas, perceptions): What did you think?

S = *The big S* (Spiritual or Faith Dimension: God or Higher Power):

Did you turn to the spiritual as a resource in the crisis or Blame or castigate God for the cause?

Did your faith grow or decrease?

s = *The small s* (The Human Spirit: The nature and resiliency of our humanity):

Did the experience bring out the best or the worst in your and other's human nature?

Figure 15.1 The ABC'S (s) of Sharing and Processing Experiences.

of human response to trauma or disaster (see Figure 15.1). In other words, the nature of our response to a traumatic event will include an affective dimension (emotions or what we feel), a behavioral dimension (actions or what we do) and a cognitive dimension (thoughts or what we think). In addition, the impact of a trauma typically prompts a Spiritual response in some way that moves us toward or away from faith as a resource in responding to or explaining the event and typically raises the question of our mortality in light of the trauma especially if loss of life is involved. This is referred to as the big "S" (capital letter). Then there is the small "s" that relates to the human spirit that also surfaces on our radar screen in the context of the disaster usually in the form of whether the trauma brings out the best or the worst of our human nature and whether there is resiliency or despair involved (Boss, 2002). In any event, these ABC'S(s) factors serve as the basic rubric for processing disasters that is built into the format of crisis intervention discussion groups. This rubric is vital to both immediate response processing and after the fact, long term processing when the dimension of time is introduced into the discussion. (e.g., What did you feel then? and What do you feel now?)

Figures 15.2 and 15.3 illustrate the impact of disasters relative to emotions and behavior producing what I have labeled as Escalation Debility with regard to affect or emotions and De-Escalation Debility with regard to behavior or actions. Emotionally disasters prompt multiple emotions that either overwhelm and immobilize or produce panic reactions, disorganization and chaotic behavior. Emotions may be either repressed or suppressed to assist in the coping process or they may become the prompt for behavior that is destructive at worst and non-productive at the least. The key to effective emotional responding is *expression*, and therefore one of the first objectives of a crisis intervention process is

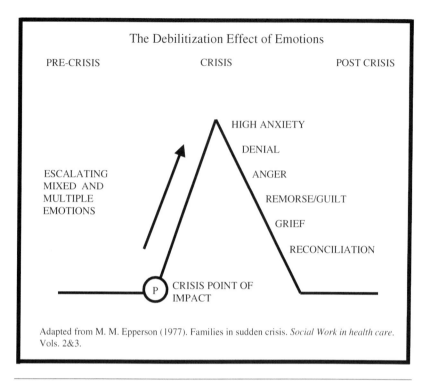

The Debilitization Effect of Emotions

PRE-CRISIS   CRISIS   POST CRISIS

HIGH ANXIETY

DENIAL

ESCALATING
MIXED AND   ANGER
MULTIPLE
EMOTIONS   REMORSE/GUILT

GRIEF

RECONCILIATION

P   CRISIS POINT OF
IMPACT

Adapted from M. M. Epperson (1977). Families in sudden crisis. *Social Work in health care.* Vols. 2&3.

Figure 15.2 Emergency response to crisis escalation debility.

to provide opportunity, assistance, support and guidance for that expression. Behaviorally, the impact of crisis has the tendency to produce disorganization and chaos, immobility and confusion, helplessness and panic. In other words, escalation of emotions produces debility because it prompts reactive behavior and restricts or interferes with cognitive functioning, rational thinking and thought directed choice-making. On the other hand, de-escalation behaviorally results when emotions prompted by the crisis prevail, displacing rational thought and thereby producing disorganization (i.e., nonproductive action or inaction) and chaos in the immediate aftermath of the crisis. Crisis intervention generally and crisis intervention groups specifically act to intervene in both of these debilitating processes truncating both the escalation of emotions and the de-escalation of behavior thereby prompting the reassertion of cognition as the basis for decision-making and action. That is why most crisis response experts recommend that psychological first aid in the form of activities such as crisis intervention groups be introduced within 24 to 72 hours or as soon as possible after the crisis. It is preferable to address the crisis in the first few days after its occurrence because people are talking about it anyway and the intervention

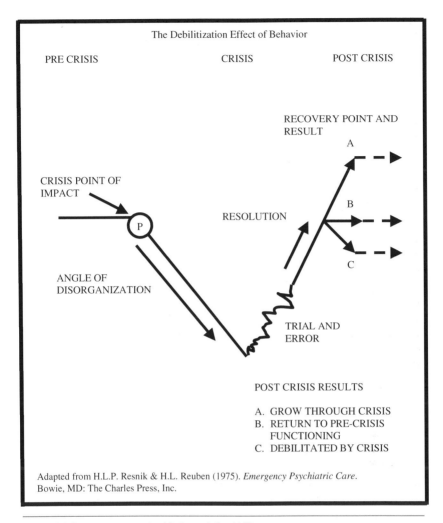

The Debilitization Effect of Behavior

PRE CRISIS   CRISIS   POST CRISIS

RECOVERY POINT AND
RESULT

A

CRISIS POINT OF
IMPACT

B

RESOLUTION

P

ANGLE OF
DISORGANIZATION

C

TRIAL AND
ERROR

POST CRISIS RESULTS

A. GROW THROUGH CRISIS
B. RETURN TO PRE-CRISIS
    FUNCTIONING
C. DEBILITATED BY CRISIS

Adapted from H.L.P. Resnik & H.L. Reuben (1975). *Emergency Psychiatric Care.*
Bowie, MD: The Charles Press, Inc.

Figure 15.3 Emergency response to crisis de-escalation debility.

gives them a forum or format to do so constructively. In other words, thinking is resurrected as the mediator of action. As a side note, foreknowledge of an action plan in regard to a crisis such as a natural disaster also truncates these escalation dynamics because people have a concrete resource base for action that can be resorted to in the face of crisis.

Carmichael (2000) has utilized *The Wizard of Oz* (Baum, 1985) as a metaphor in developing a psychoeducational group program for helping children understand, work through, and learn about the impact of tornados, a natural disaster that is common in the Midwest. The familiar story is directly related to the event, and the characters effectively epitomize the various aspects of the ABC'S(s) model noted above. For example, the Tin Man relates to affect and emotions, the Cowardly Lion corresponds to behavior or actions, and the Scarecrow represents cognition or thinking. Other symbols in the story are also related to the model such the Red Slippers that represent human resiliency or the human spirit in the face of crisis and the Wizard representing a spiritual resource in the form of a higher power. The story is thus an excellent resource for teaching, stimulating interaction and prompting sharing in groups.

The Crisis Intervention Gap

Most schools and community organizations now have crisis intervention plans that mobilize community resources in the immediate aftermath of the crisis. This form of psychological first aid is not only typical but crucial to an effective response. However, once these intervention team members leave the premises, there is often a gap that must be filled in by those who work in the setting. In schools this task falls to teachers and counselors who work with the students on a daily basis. The model that you will learn in this chapter is especially relevant to filling in that gap. The more teachers, administrators, and counselors who are trained in such a model, the easier it is to work it into the ongoing life of the school or community organization over time, thus accelerating the recovery process rather than letting it stall for want of effective leadership and a relevant forum.

Crisis Intervention Group Model:
A Six-Step Process for Psychological First Aid and More

The format for conducting crisis intervention discussion and support groups outlined in Figure 15.4 and described below derives from a model developed by Brock (1998) for the Lodi, California School System and is adapted and expanded for processing all forms of disasters and trauma. The process involves six steps for the group and a debriefing session for the leaders and facilitators of the process. Groups range in size from small groups (4–12 members) to classroom size groups and in many cases groups may be intact groups such as an actual classroom group or a work group. This last type of group provides an atmosphere of familiarity to the members as they become involved in the process. If groups are being organized for purposes of crisis intervention, the composition should be homogeneous and size restricted to 10 to 20 students to facilitate maximum involvement. The six steps of the process are as follows, and the recommendation is that all six phases be experienced in each session. Specific activities will be included at the end of the chapter to use in training leaders in this model and in carrying out some of the tasks in the group.

OVERVIEW OF THE MODEL

1. Step One: Organizing and Starting the Group
   a. Introductions: If you are new to the group, introduce yourself and tell a little about your background and expertise.
   b. Getting Acquainted: If the group is an intact group you can forego this task. Otherwise, do a brief get acquainted activity. (Basic information like names, affiliation, work role etc.)
   c. State the Purpose of the session: "Our purpose today is to talk about the terrorist attacks on September 11, 2001 and to share our experiences relative to that event."
   d. Set the Boundaries and Expectations:
      1) Everyone is encouraged to participate.
      2) Everyone's viewpoint will be heard and respected.
      3) State timeframe for the meeting
      4) Outline the sequence of the session (the six steps)

2. Step Two: Start with the Facts (Establish the Facts and Dispel the Rumors) Address:
   a. Disinformation: Withholding information as a means of misinforming (Provide up to date, accurate information).
   b. Misinformation: Wrong information that members may have (Correct inaccurate information).
   c. Myth-information: Rumors and fabrications that have been disseminated or created by members to fill in the gaps. (Dispel rumors, myths and fabrications).

   Suggestion: A well-written news article or Internet information piece or official statement from your organization can be distributed and reviewed.

3. Step Three: Sharing Stories (Everyone has a story, everyone is a story-teller and every story is valid.)
   a. There are no right or wrong reactions to disasters: Everyone's experience is valid. With the exception of self and other destructive reactions, all reactions are normal.
   b. Depending on time, everyone gets a chance to tell his or her story.

4. Step Four: Sharing Reactions and Processing the stories.
   a. Discuss the common themes and feelings
   b. Normalize and affirm each person's feelings and experience
   c. Introduce the time dimension using the ABC'S(s) model
      1) Affect: Key questions
         • What did you feel then?
         • How do you feel now?
      2) Behavior: Key questions
         • What did you do?
         • What are you doing now?
         • What do you intend to do?
      3) Cognition: Key questions
         • What did you think before it happened?
         • What do you think now?
         • What did you think when it happened?

Figure 15.4 The crisis intervention group model: a six-step process for psychological first aid.

5. Step Five: Empowerment
   a. Brainstorm what can be done
      1) What are some good things you can do to respond?
   b. Note Resources:
      1) Family, friends, fellow survivors or witnesses
      2) Support groups in the community
      3) Professional Services: Counseling/therapy

6. Step Six: Closure
   a. Summarize the session
   b. Ask for feedback from the group
   c. Offer assistance
   d. Follow up with those who need more help
   e. End in a positive manner: Emphasize hope and encourage recovery.

7. De-Briefing (If multiple leaders conduct Crisis Intervention Groups in one setting, gather them together for a follow-up session.)
   a. De-Briefing Tasks
      1) Help leaders Share and Process their experiences.
      2) Evaluate process and impact of groups.
      3) Follow-up with those who need more help and make referrals.
      4) Solicit Suggestions and Feedback for "What's next?"

Figure 15.4 The crisis intervention group model: a six-step process for psychological first aid. Continued.

Step I: Organizing and Starting the Group (Framing, Forming, and Focusing the Group) The group leader has four tasks to address in this first phase of the group. All or some may apply depending on the composition of the group and the leader's relationship to the group.

1. Introductions: If you as a leader are new to the group, introduce yourself and tell a little about your background and expertise. You are the outsider to the group and both your resume and your discussion of your expertise give the group a point of contact with you.
2. Getting Acquainted: If the group is an intact group you can forego this task. Otherwise, do a brief get acquainted activity. Basic information such as names, affiliation, work role, or other pertinent data is appropriate as this provides the group with a point of contact with each other and you a point of contact with them.
3. Stating the Purpose: This is a very important task because it establishes both the focus of the group and sets a boundary relative to the content of the sharing. It helps the group focus and lends a sense of security to the process as each member knows what is going to be talked about. For example, a statement such as, "Our purpose today is to talk about the terrorist

attacks on September 11, 2001 and to share our experiences relative to that event" is appropriate. Always stipulate the specific event that prompted the meeting upfront so everyone is on the same page.

4. Set the Boundaries and Expectations: Minimal but clear boundaries regarding participation should be stated. Encourage everyone to participate, but also acknowledge the right to pass or defer. Emphasis is on the opportunity to talk not pressure to talk (Shaffer, Brown, & McWhirter, 1998). State the timeframe of the meeting so that participants know whether all will get a chance to share their stories or not. In response to disasters this is very important. If enough time (i.e., group is open-ended) will be given for all to share let that be known. If there is a time constraint, let that be known also. Finally, outline the sequence of steps so that the group is aware of the road map for the session. Sometimes a brief handout stating this information is useful so that members can refer to it as the session proceeds.

One basic premise for leaders relative to structure and boundaries is, "the closer the event—the more directive the leadership" (e.g., state or inform groups of the specific boundaries); "The farther you are from the event—the more facilitative the leadership" (e.g., ask for input and suggestions as to important boundaries as well as stipulate them).

Step II: Start With the Facts (Establish the Facts and Dispel the Rumors) The purpose of this phase is to provide accurate information about the disaster and give as much factual detail as is possible about the event. Efforts should be made to identify and defuse rumors and correct misinformation. This step is particularly critical for laying the groundwork for later personal sharing and discussion because it creates a sense of security and trust based on fact rather than myth and fear. Three factors typically related to disasters must be addressed. Each represents an obstacle that can interfere with effective group processing of the event:

1. Disinformation: Information about disasters in often withheld either purposefully or inadvertently. When that occurs, the group members may turn to rumors or create their own versions of the facts.
2. Misinformation: Many times members come into the group with wrong information and this must be corrected in the course of the process by providing accurate, up to date information.
3. Myth-information: The human mind and the social interaction process tend to fill in the gaps in information formulating creative bridges between the informational pillars relative to the event. Consequently, when either disinformation or misinformation is disseminated, members generate their own explanations or myths that are then passed on as if they were facts.

The most effective practice for starting with the facts is to have a brief but accurate account of the event that can be read and handed out to the group. This dispels the rumors and informs the group giving a basis for trust and security. A well written news article or Internet piece or a formal organizational statement can be distributed and reviewed. This should be brief and factual only, and not a commentary.

Step III: Sharing Stories (Everyone Has a Story, Everyone Is a Storyteller and Every Story Is Valid) In this step, members are invited to share their experiences relative to the disaster in the form of story telling where each person in the group is given opportunity to share as much or as little of their experience as they choose. Most stories follow a format of where the storyteller was, what happened, how he survived, and what she did during and after the disaster. The key to this phase is validating all stories and affirming the experiences of each storyteller. This phase extends as long as there are stories to be told and storytellers to tell them. Emphasize that there are no right or wrong reactions to disasters. Everyone's experience is valid and will be respected with the exception of self and other reactions that may be destructive.

Step IV: Sharing Reactions and Processing the Stories (The Key to This Phase Is Reflecting) The sharing reactions phase is devoted to the emotional reactions and feelings associated with the disaster. Special efforts are made to identify reactions and normalize them in the context of the event (i.e., "This is what people who have experienced earthquakes feel like afterward."). Themes and traits endemic to typical emotional reactions and mental perceptions are drawn out in the discussion, affirmed, explained, and corrected if necessary. Guidelines for processing include the following suggestions:

1. Discuss the common themes and feelings.
2. Note unique and unusual reactions.
3. Normalize and affirm each person's feelings and experience.
4. Introduce the time dimension using the ABC'S(s) model. The longer the time between the event and the group discussion, the more critical the time dimension becomes. Examples of time dimension questions are:
   a. Affect: Key questions
     • What did you feel then?
     • What do you feel now?
   b. Behavior: Key questions
     • What did you do?
     • What are you doing?
     • What do you intend to do?

   c. Cognition: Key questions
- What did you think before it happened?
- What did you think when it happened?
- What do you think now?

During this phase, you may also want to prompt the Spiritual dimension (big S) and the human spirit dimension (small s) by raising awareness that disasters often prompt responses in these two domains (such as the event causing movement toward or away from faith and precipitating the emergence of either the best or the worst expression of our humanity).

Step V: Empowerment The focus of empowerment is identifying coping strategies and resources that students can use to recover from the trauma and impact of the disaster. The tone is action oriented (i.e., What you can do!) and concrete (i.e., Where you can get or give help or assistance!). Members are encouraged and supported in the process of coping with the disaster and moving on with the grief, loss, and rebuilding aspects of their lives. Describe resources and opportunities for further processing and ways to reach out in assistance or help to those directly affected. Brainstorm ideas for helping the victims or those in need. Develop a "Good Things To Do" (GTTD) list. Identify resources such as family, friends, fellow survivors, or witnesses/bystanders. Describe the availability of support groups and professional services. Have specific referral information available.

Step VI: Closure This phase is designed to bring closure to the group in a number of different ways. It is an ending celebration of the crisis intervention phase, although more such work may continue. It brings to a close a common experience in which members have shared and processed their experiences as a means of coping and growing beyond them. It gives each person an opportunity to say goodbye, affirming them and sending them out with things to do, people to see, projects to complete, and plans to follow. As a leader, make sure you summarize the session, ask for feedback from the group, offer assistance, and follow-up to those who want or need more assistance and end on a positive note stressing hope, and encouraging recovery.

Debriefing Phase

The final phase of this process, especially if conducted in a school using teachers, counselors, and school personnel, is to hold a debriefing session with the leaders to process the experience, work though and share feelings as leaders, get a sense of the impact of the process and identify a direction for the disaster response program to go as a result. Individual members who may be in need of additional assistance can be noted as well. Debriefing is also critical for crisis intervention team members who go into schools or community settings to conduct crisis intervention group sessions. It is necessary for the psychological well being of the leaders, aids in the formulation of follow up and helps make improvements in the delivery of the services. It is also the time to make appropriate referrals. Most important, as noted earlier, debriefing serves as an antidote to vicarious trauma effects that leaders may experience in working with their groups (Trippany, White, & Wilcoxen, 2004).

Identifying Group Members in Need of Additional Assistance

One of the responsibilities of a crisis intervention group leader is to assess the membership population for signals that additional assistance or help might be warranted. Although ground rules and the structure of the format do a great deal to help members feel secure and work through their experiences relative to the trauma, there are often occasions where members signal a need for more intensive psychological assistance. Here are a number of cues and clues to look for in regard to offering additional assistance and making a referral. These factors have both a product and a process dimension in that a member may be psychologically fragile and thus need more direct individual care or potentially disruptive to the group requiring intervention for the sake of the group process (Shaffer, Brown, & McWhirter, 1998).

When in the context of a provided opportunity to assist in processing and coping with the crisis (e.g., the Crisis Intervention Group), a person manifests the following symptoms, immediate intervention, follow up, and referral may be needed. The member:

1. Underreacts: Member manifests withdrawal, isolation, flat affect, and inattentiveness in the face of invited/supported expression and a norm of sharing.
2. Overreacts: Member is unable to contain emotions or behavior in the context of the group ground rules, expectations and parameters.
3. Displays or implies suicidal or homicidal behavior or threats.
4. Distracts: Talks at length about other topics: Member is unable or unwilling to stay with the topic and focus despite repeated requests to do so.
5. Specific request for help: Member states a need for or desire to have more help.
6. Manifests dissociative, disoriented, or disturbing (paranoid, psychotic, etc.) behavior: Member acts strangely, incoherently, or oddly in the social context of the group.

In these cases, referral for therapeutic or protective intervention is appropriate.

Learning Activities

The activities presented below are intended for use in training group leaders in the crisis intervention discussion group model outlined in Figure 15.4. They are organized in sequence to relate to each of the steps in the format.

Icebreaker and Orientation Activity

Pass out 3 × 5 cards and divide the training group in half. Identify one half as Feelers and one half as Thinkers.

1. Leader states: "When I present you with the following stimulus, your task is to jot down your feelings if you are a feeler and your thoughts if you are a thinker.
2. Show a photo, slide, transparency, or newspaper page depicting the disaster that is most common to the experience of the trainees (e.g., the September 11, 2001 terrorist attack).
3. Instruct trainees to be spontaneous (i.e., do not edit or contemplate; write what comes to your mind or your heart).
4. In a large group processing format, ask trainees to share their entries one at a time, alternating between the feelers and thinkers. Process by noting how feelings and thoughts get interchanged and by noting the nature of the expressions.

Get Acquainted Dyads: Sharing your Disaster Experiences

The purpose of this activity is to engage trainees in a process of sharing their personal experiences with community disasters to get acquainted and to form training work groups.

1. Pass out 3 × 5 cards to each person.
2. Explain the difference between Community and Personal Disasters.
3. On your 3 × 5 card jot down three Community Disasters that you have experienced in your lifetime excluding September 11, 2001. (Note: For training purposes have trainees exclude the event that you intend to use to demonstrate the group process model. For example, in the United States September 11 is a common denominator for most participants (i.e., almost everyone had a response they remember and can talk about). Therefore, it serves as an effective training focus. Another example would be November 22, 1963 (the assassination of President John F. Kennedy); in Asia, the Tsunami of December 26, 2004 might be appropriate.

Get Acquainted Dyads (Option I)

4. Chose a partner and share your name, affiliation, and your community disaster experience and one of the dimensions of the ABC'S(s) model. Rotate through three dyads at the directive of the leader.

   a. 1st Dyad: Share your affect (What did you feel?)

   b. 2nd Dyad: Describe your behavior (What did you do?)

   c. 3rd Dyad: Share your cognition (What did you think?)

   d. Join with another dyad and form a group of four: Share your lists (three disasters) briefly to get a sense of the nature of the disasters reflected in the experience of the group. Discuss the impact of the disasters on the S's (Spiritual and human spirit).

   e. Process the activity getting feedback on the experience regarding the ABC'S(s) and list the types/nature of disasters reflected in the trainees' experience.

Get Acquainted Dyads (Option II)

1. Chose a partner and share your name, position, and, *one* of your Community Disaster Experiences using the entire ABC'S(s) model and then join with another dyad to form a work group.

2. Process as described above.

Step-Related Training Activities

Step I: Organizing and Getting Started

State the Purpose of the Group For example: "Our purpose to learn and experience the crisis intervention group discussion process by focusing on the events of September 11, 2001 and to address, share, and discuss your experience of the disaster from that time to the present." (The content of this statement would be determined by the disaster event you choose to use for the training session.)

State the Workshop Training Ground Rules

1. Everyone is a participant. There are no spectators in this workshop. However, the level or depth of your participation is your choice.

2. Principle of Assumed Ego Strength: Because this is a training workshop and we are time-limited, you will at times be interrupted before you are finished with an activity. I expect you will be able to handle those interruptions in a cooperative manner without frustration or resistance.

Work Group Task: Boundaries

Step One Make a list of ground rules that you as a group believe are necessary for effective group discussion and sharing of disaster experiences. (5 minutes)

Process: Ask for one ground rule from each group and note the therapeutic trait inherent in each one.

Step Two: First the Facts Your task: Make a list of the facts as you know them to be regarding the September 11, 2001 terrorist attacks (or other event that is the focus of the training). Criteria for a fact: All group members must know and agree to it being a fact. If someone does not think it is a fact, do not place it on your list. (5 minutes)

Process: Ask for one fact at a time from each work group until a list is created on the board. Note the difficulty in establishing the facts. In a group situation this activity can be used as a lead-in to the sharing of the formal statement regarding the event.

Step Three: Telling Your Stories Your Task: Give every member an opportunity to tell his/her story of when he/she first heard of or experienced the event. Instruct other members to practice active listening skills and demonstrate support and empathy while each person shares their story. (20 minutes)

Note: As the leader, you may want to model the story telling by telling your own story to emphasize your connection to the event and to provide an example relative to content and time limit.

Step Four: Sharing Your Reactions and Processing Your Stories Your Task: Identify and discuss the following: (20 minutes)

1. What were the common themes in your stories?
2. What unique reactions were noted?
3. Introduce the Time dimension.
   a. How are your feelings different or the same now?
   b. How has your thinking changed? What did you think then? What do you think now?
   c. How has your behavior changed? (Then and now)
4. What is your primary concern now?
5. What about the big S and the little s?

Process: Open discussion to the large group with regard to the above themes.

Step Six: Closure Your Task: Share your ABC's regarding today's workshop (Debriefing)

Affect: What are your feelings? How did you resonate to the training session?

Behavior: What do you plan to do with what you learned?

Cognition: Share one thing you learned.

Acknowledgments

I would like to thank the following experts in crisis intervention and counseling in the schools, universities, and communities in the United States who willingly shared their knowledge, expertise, and resources with me in preparation for the presentation that formed the foundation for this chapter. Dr. Carol Hacker (deceased), Counselor, Columbine High School, Certified Trauma Specialist, Jefferson County Schools, Golden, CO; Dr. Burt Bertram, Inner Change Facilitators and Rollins College, Orlando FL; Dr. Anne Geroski, University of Vermont, Burlington, VT; Dr. Becky Schumacher, University of North Florida, Jacksonville, FL; Dr. Rose Raska, Director of Guidance, Seminole County Schools, Sanford, FL; and Dr. Robert Dingman, Marshall University and Consultant to the American Red Cross, Virginia Beach, VA. I am much in their debt for the concepts, information, and resource materials they shared with me. I would also like to thank Dr. Judy Zubrow, Associate Dean of Faculty at Granite State College in New Hampshire who organized and promoted the training program that used this material the week following September 11.

16

The Case for Group Research

Rex Stockton
Paul L. Toth
D. Keith Morran

Theory, practice, and research are the triadic pillars that give stability, vitality and viability to the field of group work. Theory informs practice. Practice prompts and refines theory. Research validates practice and tests conceptual hypotheses for pragmatic relevance and accuracy.

Group Research: A Practitioner-Friendly Proposition

The fact that many practitioners shy away from clinical research is no surprise. From their first statistics and research courses people begin to avoid that which they have difficulty with or are not introduced to in a way that makes practical sense. Group workers may feel they have not been adequately trained in research methodology, that the research concepts and skills they learned were not adequately reinforced through applied practice, or that those who do research carry out their studies in a world removed from day to day practice. So, we hope that this chapter will give the reader an appreciation as to what research can do in terms of influencing practice. The authors are researchers *and* practitioners who value research and enjoy pursuits of acquiring new knowledge. Whether research is analyzing basic information that might influence group practice in general or evaluating factors that have an impact on a particular group program, applying scientific reasoning to group work enhances practice, teaching, and future inquiry efforts. We will begin by talking about basic scientific inquiry and some of the effects of research on applied practice.

Until the 1960s, polio infantile paralysis was a scourge. During the summer months, when it frequently raged, many localities had to close swimming pools, theaters, and other places where children liked to congregate. A multitude of resources went into developing iron lungs and other methods to treat the consequences of the disease. One of the authors vividly recalls stories in his local newspaper of improved treatments of those who were affected by the disease. However, it wasn't until the development of vaccines that prevented polio that the epidemic was stopped. Prior to this, energy and resources that were poured into developing ways to treat the illness were well spent. However, in this case, the best payoff went into the basic research that developed the vaccine. Having effective treatment procedures and instruments is important, not having to use these procedures and instruments is even better. In many cases basic scientific research provides us with the methodology to investigate better treatment and prevention. Practice can be enhanced by the application of knowledge that was uncovered through scientific research.

To put scientific research in the mental health field into perspective let us consider the case of depression. Depression is a mood disorder that affects an estimated 18.8 million American adults in a given year (National Institute of Health, 2001). Counselors who have practiced any length of time inevitably have worked with depressed clients. Seasoned counselors will be old enough to remember when mood disorders, especially major depressive disorder, were treated much less effectively than they are today. Two areas of inquiry have helped us understand and treat depression more effectively: (1) the advent of medication that affects certain synaptic responses in the brain, and (2) the development of treatment that enhances a person's self-perceptions. Basic scientific research has provided the field with a better understanding of the brain's biochemical functions and the importance of cognitive and behavioral interventions for the treatment of depression.

An organized program of biological research into chemical processes that occur in the brain has resulted in the development of drugs that regulate those processes and help control depression. Initially, it was unclear to researchers which neurotransmitters were involved with depression, so the earlier drugs were developed to target a wide area of the brain. Further research helped pin-point specific neurotransmitters (serotonin, norepinephrine, and dopamine) as being involved in depression. This enabled a new group of drugs (e.g., selective serotonin reuptake inhibitors (SSRIs)) to be developed, which have been quite successful in the treatment of depression (Goldenberg, 1990; Price, 2004).

A similar programmatic research approach focused on the cognitive aspects of depression. In 1967 Seligman and Maier began a cognitive revolution in psychotherapy treatment not by initially working with human clients, but by painstakingly investigating responses of animals to inescapable situations. The laboratory work of Seligman and Maier (1967), Overmeier and Seligman (1967), Maier and

Seligman (1976), and Maier, Seligman, and Solomon (1969) found that if animals were presented with a mild electric shock when they had no opportunity to escape, they would continue to take shocks even when escape was made available (Rosenhan & Seligman, 1989). If escape was hopeless, the animals became helpless and passive and did not engage in behavior (escape) that would ultimately benefit them. This exploration with animals led Seligman and others to investigate this phenomenon further. They discovered that learned helplessness also occurs in humans. With this information in mind, they hypothesized that persons with depression could be helped by changing their cognitions from thinking they are ineffective in controlling life events to believing they can have an impact on their future (Rosenhan & Seligman, 1989). Helpful therapeutic treatment for depression has come from researching learned helplessness in people.

The research of Seligman and others is an illustration of how inquiry works in the sciences. In order for a problem to be understood and appropriate solutions to the problem developed, it is important to understand its basic components. Breaking down a problem and researching its component parts offers glimpses of insight into the workings of the entire piece.

In all types of research it is critical that the researcher have a sound and systematic strategy as a guide in seeking valid answers to the research questions posed. The following section of this chapter briefly presents some of the most commonly used research strategies within the individual and group counseling fields.

Research Methods

Within the social sciences in general, and group counseling in particular, a wide variety of research methods are employed. The selection of a certain methodology depends on the purpose of a given study and the realities of the research setting. Two of the most basic categories of inquiry are quantitative research and qualitative research. Quantitative research involves the collection and analysis of numerical data while qualitative research involves primarily (though not exclusively) non-numerical data such as written descriptions (Hittleman & Simon, 1997).

Quantitative descriptive research is a type of inquiry where the researcher wishes to describe a given phenomena as it currently exists (e.g., what is the average number of self-disclosures made by members of a counseling group in each session?) (Sprinthall, Schumutte & Sirois, 1991). Such studies, for example, often collect data on various relevant variables across multiple participants and report these data in the form of such aggregate statistics as frequencies, means, standard deviations, or percentages.

Also included under the quantitative research category are a variety of experimental approaches including true experimental designs, quasi-experimental designs, and single subject research designs. Experimental designs involve the active manipulation of one or more independent variables (e.g., treatment versus no treatment) to determine if the different treatment conditions result in differences on the dependent (outcome) measures. True experimental designs are characterized by their purpose of establishing firm cause-and-effect relationships among variables and by their use of direct manipulation of independent variables and the control of extraneous variables through the use of random selection (Ingersoll, 1998). Quasi-experimental designs represent an alternative, or compromise, to the true experiment. Such designs may be employed, for example, when random assignment to experimental conditions is not possible (or practical), thus, the effects of extraneous variables cannot be tightly controlled (Hittleman & Simon, 1997). Although researchers using quasi-experimental designs can reach tentative decisions concerning cause-and-effect relationships, such relationships can be established with much greater confidence when true experimental designs are used. Within the social sciences, however, it is often not possible to meet the rigid requirements of the true experiment; thus, quasi-experimental designs are among the most frequently used.

Single subject designs are another type of experimental methodology that can address cause-and-effect relationships (Odom, Brantlinger, Gersten, Horner, Thompson, & Harris, 2004; Shavelson & Towne, 2002). Somewhat contrary to the name, single subject designs often involve more than one participant in the study (e.g., the members of a counseling group may be treated as a single entity and several groups may be studied). When using single subject designs, the researcher will typically begin by establishing a baseline measure for the dependent (outcome) variable. The researcher will then take repeated measures of the dependent variable across time while systematically implementing and withdrawing the independent (treatment) condition. By comparing the participant's performance during and in the absence of the treatment, causal inferences can be made. This type of research design has the advantage of requiring a limited number of participants; however, the establishment of external validity requires replication across multiple participants, settings, etc.

Another category of quantitative research methodology, though not experimental in nature, is the ex post facto design. This design is used when the researcher cannot actively manipulate the independent variables of the study but can only assign participants to conditions based on a pre-existing characteristic (e.g., gender or ethnicity) (Sprinthall, Schumutte, & Sirois, 1991). Such studies do not allow for cause-and-effect inferences but do help to establish associations between variables that can lead to predictions. Correlational studies are one example of this type of research.

Qualitative research designs have become increasingly prominent in recent years and are likely to remain so. Brantlinger, Jimenez, Klingner, Pugach, & Richardson (2005) define qualitative research as "a systematic approach to understanding qualities, or the essential nature, of a phenomenon within a particular setting" (p. 195). As noted above, qualitative studies are characterized by the use of text, rather than numerical values, to document and analyze variables (Hittleman & Simon, 1997). Qualitative researchers use a variety of data collection techniques such as interviews, document analysis, and observation. Some of the typical methodologies of qualitative research include case studies, historical research, ethnography, and naturalistic inquiry.

It should be noted that the descriptions of research strategies presented above represent only a few of the many possible research approaches. Additionally, many of these same strategies, or combinations of strategies, are often used in evaluation studies where the purpose is to investigate the processes and/or outcomes of specific programs or interventions rather than for purposes of generalizing findings to other populations or settings.

Dealing with Extraneous Variables and other Problems

In the true experimental method, a researcher attempts to test a hypothesis by experimentally manipulating one variable (the independent variable) to measure its effects on another variable (the dependent variable). In order to show that there is a causal relationship between these two variables, the researcher must carefully rule out other possible, or extraneous, hypotheses (Ingersoll, 1998). One way this is done is to control, to the extent possible, outside factors that are irrelevant to the purpose of the study, but that nevertheless may have an effect on the outcome. These factors are known as extraneous variables. Many steps are typically taken by investigators in order to control or eliminate the impact of extraneous variables. The most powerful method of doing so is randomization. If participants are randomly assigned to treatment or control conditions, it can be assumed that extraneous variables are relatively equal across groups; such variables are thus not likely to significantly impact results (Ingersoll, 1998). When randomization is not possible, other methods of controlling for extraneous variables can be used. One such method is to carefully match (matching) the participants in experimental groups on these variables. For example, if researchers were concerned about gender as an extraneous variable, they could ensure that there were equal numbers of males and females in each group. Another method is to hold the extraneous variable constant for all participants (e.g, selecting only female subjects for the study).

The problem of extraneous variables becomes even more challenging in group research. This is because of the complexity of the group experience. Interactions among group members and leaders create many extraneous variables not present in other types of research (e.g., members' reactions to a given intervention may not be independent since one member's reaction may influence other members' reactions). The work of Stockton and Morran (1981) is an example of using an experimental design to control for extraneous variables. In this study group members were instructed to give feedback to each other and then to rate the credibility, desirability, impact, and helpfulness of the feedback they received. Group researchers know that extraneous variables such as social influence and other effects resulting from interpersonal communication may influence the type of feedback members give to each other. So, in order to control for these effects in this study, members were instructed to write down their feedback before being asked to orally communicate it. Additionally, members rated feedback from others anonymously. Using these methods allowed the researchers to state with more confidence that experimental results were due to the effects of the feedback and not other interactional factors.

In addition to the problem of extraneous variables, Fuhriman and Burlingame (1994) mention several types of methodological problems in the group research to date. They conclude that the most serious threats to the soundness of the research base involve construct validity issues. Specifically, although many studies report positive client outcomes as a result of group therapy, few studies actually describe in detail the characteristics of the therapy or the therapist. Thus, it is very difficult to determine what it was that actually occurred to produce the positive outcomes. Despite these technical problems, researchers in group counseling have done solid work and continue to do so. As Burlingame, Fuhriman, and Johnson (2004) have noted, research today "presents the field with not only a clearer understanding of the effectiveness of group treatment and the processes involved but also more refined questions regarding the relationship of group processes to successful client change" (p. 50).

Expanding the Use of the Scientific Method

The scientific method, the standard approach to scientific inquiry, is able to provide answers to many significant questions. However, this type of tightly controlled research can not answer all the complex questions within the human domain. Research into problems of human interaction are too complex to be answered with absolute clarity. Depending on the methods employed, certain facets of the truth are revealed. Since it is tremendously difficult to control for all extraneous variables in the life of the group, it becomes much harder to make group research fit into a nicely designed package that is free from error and clean of confounding elements. Therefore, it is typical for a study to answer only a part of the question being explored by the investigation. A study that investigated the effects of structured group exercises on group counseling is a good illustration of both the limitations and usefulness of this type of research. Stockton, Rohde, and Haughey (1994) had participants in an experimental condition begin their group sessions with a 20 minute structured exercise. The researchers assumed that this structure would affect the following developmental variables: cohesion, engagement, avoidance, and conflict. The researchers also thought that satisfaction with the experience would be higher for those involved in the exercises than those who were not. The results of this study suggest support for the effectiveness (with some important cautions) of structured group exercises early in group development. Though this was a relatively sophisticated study, there were limitations. In this case, groups focused on personal growth instead of pathology and participants were quite similar as to socioeconomic and academic variables. Even with these qualifications, the study provided some support for the use of low risk structured exercises. It remains to be seen whether or not these findings are valid for different types of groups with different types of participants. This was one study that answered only a portion of the overall question being posed by the investigators, but still added to the overall knowledge of group work and offered suggestions for future studies. This is how research works—the researcher discovers a bit of new information as he or she moves along *and* poses new or additional questions to examine via continued research.

Given the complexity of interpersonal interactions that are magnified in group therapy, it is especially important for group researchers to expand our use of the scientific method. Polkinghorne (1988) wrote, "knowledge is understood to be the best understanding that we have been able to produce thus far, not a statement of what is ultimately real" (p. 2). Polkinghorne went on to say that science should not be an endeavor that, like cooking, follows certain procedures so as to produce certain results. Instead, science should become "the creative search to understand better, and it uses whatever approaches are responsive to the particular questions and subject matters addressed" (p. 3). Likewise, Wampold (1986) wrote that research should consider "using any methodology, provided the methodology is appropriate to answer the research question and provided the methodology is applied correctly" (p. 38). Additionally, using one type of research method often provides insights that can be explored using another approach. For example, by using qualitative research methods and procedures (interviews) McDonnell (1996) elaborated in rich detail the experiences of beginning group leaders as they started and worked their way through their first group leadership experience. Using this information, it is possible to devise experimental studies that will address the same issues. An area young in its theoretical development, group work has much to gain from such a cooperative and interactional system. The vital importance of practitioners in the early and continued development of other applied fields such as medicine and engineering attests to the possibilities for group counselors to make the same kind of contributions to group work.

Group Research that Works

The field of group counseling has significant information about applied practice. A variety of studies and synthesizing reviews have impacted current practice. Research has helped mold ideas of what is best practice. For example, the impact of research on group practice can be found in a series of studies related to group structure. Riva, Wachtel, and Lasky (2004) define structure as a "broad term that encompasses many different techniques and interventions that have as their primary goal the development and maintenance of a healthy therapeutic group" (p. 40). Until the work of Bednar, Melnick, and Kaul, (1974), the conventional wisdom in group work called for a very low level of structure within the group. For example, Whitaker and Lieberman (1964) believed that groups should evolve with minimal input from the leader. However, Bednar, Melnick, and Kaul's (1974) review of small group research led them to believe that a lack of structure in the early stages of a group may actually impede the development of group process. Groups with low structure often suffered from high dropout rates, high levels of distress, and avoidance of interpersonal communication.

Bednar, Melnick, and Kaul (1974) argued that the implementation of a certain degree of structure in early group sessions would facilitate and enhance the development of group process. More specifically, they argued for the use of pre-therapy training to help clarify role expectations for clients. This training included modeling, practicing of good group behaviors, and helping clients develop an understanding of group development.

Like a good scientist practitioner, Bednar implemented a systematic research program to investigate his theoretical formulations. Through a series of studies he and his colleagues (Evensen & Bednar, 1978; Lee & Bednar, 1977) examined different aspects of the theory. These studies were designed to examine the effects of group structure, in the form of pre-therapy training, on people with varying levels of risk taking dispositions (i.e., high risk takers versus low risk takers). Consistent with Bednar's theory, results of the studies indicated that high risk takers exposed to a high level of structure in pre-therapy training were more involved than others in self-disclosure and exchanging interpersonal feedback. These subjects also reported higher levels of group cohesion and depth of communication. High levels of structure were also shown to be particularly influential in increasing the amount of self-disclosure and interpersonal feedback in those with low risk taking dispositions (Evensen & Bednar, 1978; Lee & Bednar, 1977).

Through these research studies, Bednar was able to gain empirical support for his ideas. The classic work of Bednar and his colleagues has had a major impact on the way the majority of group workers think about and plan for the initial stages of group counseling. Although there is still much to be learned about this topic, it does demonstrate that a well developed and implemented program of research, that looks at a topic in a variety of ways, can have a beneficial effect on or provide insights into good practice.

Another example of programmatic work that changed the way group leaders think about how to conduct their practice can be seen in the efforts of the Indiana University research group. Conventional wisdom in the 1960s and 1970s had assumed that powerful negative feedback was appropriate in early therapeutic group development. This view held sway until the research of Jacobs and Spradlin (1974), in a series of analogue studies, demonstrated that in a laboratory setting much better results were produced by beginning with positive feedback. This was followed by research on actual counseling groups done at Indiana University which has supported the notion that feedback can have a positive impact on group members and be seen as helpful if the feedback meets some of the following qualifications: (1) corrective feedback is given after the group moves along in the developmental process (Morran, Stockton, & Harris, 1991; Morran, Stockton, & Robison, 1985; Stockton & Morran, 1981); (2) positive feedback is given prior to corrective feedback (Davies & Jacobs, 1985; Morran, Stockton, & Harris, 1991; Stockton & Morran, 1981); and (3) corrective feedback focuses on specific behaviors (Morran, Stockton, & Harris, 1991).

Understanding and Engaging in the Research Process

This section will discuss ways to sharpen research and evaluation skills for those either in graduate school or those who have completed graduate work and wish to increase their knowledge and ability in this area. It is our hope that training programs will provide more focus on group research since graduate schools are one of the major arenas where people develop research skills. Gelso (1993) tells us that graduate school training has a great impact on the student's attitude toward research and his or her commitment toward continued research after graduation. The result of a positive research training experience may be the development of practitioners who are excited about inquiry and able to become good consumers, perhaps even taking part in research themselves. Medicine and other fields are filled with examples of practitioners who have applied their research skills, curiosity and creativity to solving major medical and social problems. The same may also be true of group counseling, but practitioners need to first apply research skills to the work they do.

Although dated, Wampold's (1986) suggestion, that research training employ a model similar to clinical instruction, is still relevant. This is a sound idea not only for graduate instruction but also for developing research and evaluation in the practice setting. Just as students in counseling begin their clinical training by developing beginning skills, beginning researchers (practitioners or students) should start by developing basic research skills. For example, in order to insure that the first counseling experience is a positive one, the student's first client is often a classmate from whom the student can receive encouragement and non-threatening direction (after all, the peer playing the client will have to be the counselor as well). Likewise, in order to make a counselor's first evaluation or research project a positive experience it should be non-threatening, fairly simple in design and analysis, and of interest to the counselor.

Taking Wampold's (1986) suggestion to train counselors to do research by using a model similar to clinical training has implications for the practice setting as well. Just as students who graduate with a masters or doctoral degree in counseling continue to benefit from ongoing supervision, consultation, mentoring, and peer discussion, so also persons in the field benefit from these ongoing experiences in their clinical work (Stockton & Toth, 1997). Likewise, one will become a more astute researcher from supervised practice, inter- and intra-agency consultation, and peer group discussions focused on research. A supportive research environment in which to proceed with research efforts is essential to successful outcomes. Gelso (1993) and Gelso, Mallinckrodt, and Judge (1996) have stressed that a research environment can be created in any setting whenever there is a critical mass of individuals and resources available. Since early efforts so heavily influence later paths, it is essential to gain support from peers and a working alliance with supervisors in order to maximize chances for early success. Moreover, research training at the postgraduate level is available. The American Educational Research Association (AERA) offers professional workshops in research methods at their annual conventions. Divisions of the American Counseling Association (ACA) like the Association for Specialists in Group Work (ASGW) sponsor informal discussions at their annual conventions, also. The ASGW gatherings provide opportunities for persons less experienced in group research to ask questions and engage in dialogue with those who are more experienced. It is an opportunity to discuss research ideas and problems with peers experienced in a variety of group research methods. It can be a golden opportunity for those beginning research projects to employ the collective wisdom of seasoned professionals before they get their programs off the ground. Moreover, ASGW sponsors group research papers at their annual conferences and the annual convention of the ACA. These are additional opportunities to hear what types of research are being done in the field.

While at the University of Iowa, Toth followed a developmental model of research training in an advanced group counseling course he taught. In this course, group research was introduced in a non-threatening way. Students began a project by reviewing journal articles. Next, they conducted a literature review that was informed by their perusal of journal articles. This research project required students to design a study that could be conducted at the local community counseling center where they had participated in field observations throughout the semester. So, the students' inquiries were informed both by literature in the field and by what they observed in the practice setting. The instructor focused on positively reinforcing students' research activities and maximizing success through early introduction to a minimally intimidating research involvement (Gelso, 1993).

Another example of the importance of graduate student research in group counseling is found in the work of the group research team developed by Stockton at Indiana University. The research team has been engaged in a long term program of inquiry. The team has been composed of faculty members and students in training (who, in some cases, continue working with the team following their graduation). Beginning with an earlier focus on such factors as cohesion, goal setting, self-disclosure, and feedback, in the past few years the team has also been concerned with group leader instruction. Two primary questions have guided the work: What is it that group leaders need to know? And, what teaching methods are best suited to the instruction of group leaders? Thus, the goal of the team is to be able to richly describe a group experience from the perspective of members as they are trying to make changes in their lives and also from the perspective of leaders as they attempt to apply skills they have learned. Students are involved in this apprenticeship type program at the level they are prepared and feel comfortable. Typically, they begin with necessary activities that do not require high technical sophistication, e.g., library literature reviews, assisting in preparing information, administering and collecting forms for research projects, and coding data. At the same time these activities are taking place, team members are involved in weekly seminars. At these meetings current projects are discussed or future projects contemplated. These projects range from dissertations to pilot studies to long term continuing projects. The discussions range from practical support for data gathering to brainstorming about beginning projects to research design or statistical analysis.

Through our own research experience and our ongoing involvement with training and mentoring novice researchers, we have found that there are some key stumbling blocks that often hinder research endeavors. Here are some of the research tips that we frequently find helpful for our students:

1. When planning a research or evaluation project, join or form a group of others interested in research and meet with them on a regular basis. Two (or more) heads are better than one when discussing and planning a research study.
2. Do a careful literature review to find out what is already known within the area of your intended research.
3. Formulate specific research questions and/or hypotheses and state them clearly.
4. Choose or create measures that are directly related to the questions of the study.
5. Choose a research design that can validly address your particular question(s); consult with others as needed.
6. Evaluate your resources for conducting the study: Can you recruit enough participants? Are the experienced judges or raters you need available? Can you get the help you need for coding data and doing the statistical analyses?
7. Be realistic in terms of how much to take on in any one study. For example, it may be quite feasible to administer questionnaires to 200 participants but unrealistic to attempt to interview 200 participants unless you have

access to a large staff of assistants. Some studies look great on paper and have the potential to address numerous important research questions; however, they may require more time, knowledge, or resources than the researcher has available. A simple study that can be completed is much more valuable than a complex study that is never finished.

Program Evaluation

The purpose of this section is to discuss the importance of evaluation research in the field of social sciences. More specifically, information regarding how to carry on program evaluation is given, and questions one might ask in this endeavor are addressed.

Counselors are increasingly being called upon to be accountable for the work that they do. As funding becomes less available, it is being left up to human service professionals to document the effectiveness of their programs. This is particularly true in the world of managed care, but is also increasingly true in all other areas of counseling. Private practitioners, counseling centers, and other provider programs that do not begin to inform consumers' representatives of their worth are likely to be undercut by other competition, or simply cut out of the mental health provider system. Correspondingly, school counselors are also increasingly called upon to provide evidence of the efficacy of their services. Evaluating group counseling and psychoeducational programs in the school setting is advised in order to justify to the principal, superintendent, or board of education the necessity of spending valuable resources on such programs. Thus, more and more often counselors are expected, even required, to be involved in program evaluation. Often they may be put in charge of organizing and implementing such an evaluation. Therefore, it is increasingly important that counselors be knowledgeable about and skilled in program evaluation.

Evaluating your group counseling programs for any setting provides data to support the work that you are doing as well as giving you information about the quality of the work you are doing. By evaluating your group counseling programs you can begin to create a reciprocal relationship between program quality and evidence of efficacy. Thus, you are not only informing yourself but you have evidence for those who might want to know if what you are doing works well. Now it is not only those in the middle (i.e., managed care corporations) that are looking for evidence of therapeutic results but the whole fabric of the counseling endeavor including consumers, advocates, overseers, providers and sources of funding.

Evaluation Questions

Process evaluation addresses questions geared to finding out if a program is being implemented and done so in ways that were intended. Hubbard and Miller

(2004) discuss both process and outcome evaluation questions. They propose the following key process questions: (1) To what extent has an intervention been implemented as planned?; (2) What factors are causing an intervention to be implemented differently than planned (or not to be implemented at all? How might those factors be addressed?; (3) To what extent is an intervention reaching the intended (target) population; and (4) Who within the target population is not being reached by the intervention, and what are the obstacles to participation for these individuals (families, groups, communities)?

Outcome research questions are geared to finding out whether or not the program is accomplishing its purposes. Hubbard and Miller (2004) suggest the following types of questions: (1) How well did the program achieve its goals and objectives?; (2) Who benefited most from the intervention or what components of the program had the greatest impact?; (3) Did the program have unintended consequences (positive or negative)?; and (4) What was learned that would inform future interventions or other similar programs?

Evaluation Procedures

Before proceeding with any evaluation of a program, it is important to determine specifically what information is being sought. In other words, why is the evaluation being done. For example, sometimes program evaluation is necessary to provide accountability for government sponsored programs or for other funding agencies, such as managed care providers or foundations. Program evaluations are also used for purposes of policy making. Often, decisions such as whether or not to continue a program or how much financial and political support it will receive are based on evaluation data (Hubbard & Miller, 2004). Other times, program evaluations are conducted by conscientious counselors who simply want to get an idea of the effectiveness of their programs and make improvements where needed. It is important to keep the purpose of your evaluation in mind while planning. Some issues to consider when planning the evaluation include what services will be evaluated, how the data will be collected, who will be involved in and/or affected by the evaluation, and how the information will be used. It is important to make explicit the information you are looking for by developing a specific list of questions to be answered in the evaluation.

Some types of evaluation will involve the use of written evaluation instruments. Published instruments may be acquired from several sources. There are many self-report type instruments published in journal articles that may be reproduced and used at no cost. Other standardized instruments may be purchased from publishing companies. Other resources include compendiums of reviews and test descriptions; the best known of these is the *Mental Measurements Yearbook* series published by the Buros Institute of Mental Measurement (Impara & Plake, 1998). Often journal articles will describe instruments. An excellent example of such an article is by DeLucia-Waack (1997b), which describes a number of instruments designed specifically to measure the efficacy of groups. Readers interested in group assessment will find this resource particularly helpful.

You may want to develop your own instrument: It may be helpful or even necessary to develop a questionnaire to answer questions that are unique to your own work. Developing your own instruments will help to ensure that data collected corresponds specifically to the information you are seeking (Fairchild & Seeley, 1996). If you are going to develop your own instrument you should consider consulting with a specialist since the application of psychometric procedures takes particular training. Below we discuss some self-developed evaluation instruments. It should be noted that many of the following examples of program evaluation are rather simple in their executions. Nevertheless, they are still important in that they answer specific questions raised by specific counseling situations in the field. They help to discern the program's strengths and weaknesses and offer bits and pieces of important information to the broader field of group counseling.

Post-group evaluations can be accomplished in a number of ways. Group members can be asked open-ended questions at the conclusion of the group that will serve to elicit evaluative responses. For example, members can be asked: "Were you able to discuss your problems in the group?" A Likert type scale, where students are asked to respond to a series of questions on a 5-point continuum, could be used at the group's conclusion to determine group effectiveness.

A good example of an outcome evaluation of a group counseling program was done by the bereavement directors of two hospice programs (Housley, 1996). The directors wanted to investigate the effectiveness of the children's grief groups they conducted. This evaluation involved administering pre- and posttest measures to the participant children and their parents, as well as to a control group of children and families that the directors recruited from local public schools. The evaluators of the hospice groups designed their study to answer specific questions:

1. Do the children feel differently about themselves after participating in the grief support group?
2. What are the children's perceptions of the effectiveness of grief support groups following their participation?
3. What are strengths and weaknesses of the group experience as perceived by the children?
4. What were the undesirable outcomes of participation in the group?
5. What was the effectiveness of the group as reported by the parents?

To answer these questions, the children in both groups were given the Death Concept Scale and the Piers Harris Self-Concept Scale. The parents in both groups were administered the Child Behavior Checklist and an Information Questionnaire. In addition, semi-structured interviews were designed and administered to the children and parents in the treatment group. In general, the investigators found that participation in the groups was effective and beneficial. This study is a good example of an evaluation designed to meet the needs of the program itself. By planning out the questions to be answered, the investigators were able to design an effective combination of quantitative and qualitative measures to assess the effectiveness of their program. While the evaluation was effective and helpful, it was also simple enough to be performed by practitioners without an extensive research background.

Another example of the effectiveness of field evaluation for therapy groups can be seen in a study by Toth (1997) and a colleague at a large university counseling center. In order to determine the effectiveness of their grief therapy group for college students who had suffered the death of a significant other, Toth and his colleague conducted an evaluation of their grief group. Five students who had experienced loss by death within the last two years participated in a short term grief therapy group. They agreed to fill out measures to determine the severity of their bereavement and their experiences in the group at four times during the eight treatment sessions.

In this study, the group leaders used the Brief Grief Experience Inventory (Lee, Munro, & McCorkle, 1993) to measure the extent of each client's bereavement and progress in symptom reduction, and had members write a journal entry four times during the course of the therapy expressing their perceptions of significant events that took place in the group. Journal entries included responses to the following questions:

1. Describe a personally significant experience from today's group session. Please be as specific as you can about the event. What made this particular experience meaningful? Was the event helpful? If so, how was it helpful?
   a. List two thoughts about the experience.
   b. List two feelings regarding the experience.
   c. List two physical reactions to the experience.
2. Are there any other thoughts or feelings you wish to discuss about today's group session? Do you have any other comments you would like to share?

This study is an example of how evaluation procedures can be utilized and helpful information can be gathered even with a small number of participants and lack of experimental control. Even though statistically significant results would not be expected from a sample size as small as this, significant policy information regarding the members' group experiences was gathered. When examining the group members' responses to questions posed to them it was clear that the members experienced a good deal of therapeutic gain. Nearly all the members appreciated the feeling of universality they shared with others. Sharing their grief with others interrupted the members' feelings of isolation and despair. They began to talk about feeling normal in spite of their grief. The members were also grateful to have a forum to deal with their feelings of loss. The group provided a safe place to explore thoughts and feelings they were not able to share with peers.

Even a study with a small number of participants, though not experimentally significant, can provide useful information. The next time a group like this was convened, the leaders were more informed about how to meet members' needs. Recommendations that were made after reviewing the data included: (1) taking more group time to involve members in interpersonal interaction as well as honoring the time members need to tell their grief stories, (2) a longer period for treatment could prove helpful since eight one and one half hour sessions did not seem long enough to members or leaders, and (3) consider group as a mode for treating distress due to losses other than death (Toth, 1997).

Curriculum evaluation in classroom settings can help improve the quality of teaching and may result in more highly trained counselors. For example, Toth taught the here-and-now intervention to masters level group counseling students (Toth & Stockton, 1996), and wanted to add another intervention to this skill based curriculum. With help from an advanced doctoral student at the University of Iowa, he developed a training program to teach group leaders to give and facilitate feedback in interpersonal therapy groups (Toth & Erwin, 1998). In order to help determine the efficacy of this technique, they utilized many of the above mentioned evaluation techniques with his introduction to group counseling course. Toth and Erwin wanted to know whether or not students' self-confidence about giving and facilitating feedback improved through the training interval. They wanted to know the students' experiences in the training program, i.e., did students find this training helpful, enjoyable, and/or stimulating? In order to discover this information they constructed evaluation measures specifically for these purposes. Students responded to a survey measuring their confidence in making feedback interventions prior to and after being trained in the intervention. Students also responded to a series of questions and were asked to comment on various aspects of the training program so that the researchers could determine the most interesting, helpful, and useful portions of the training. The evaluation helped clarify the researchers' perceptions of the program and supplied valuable data regarding the students' perceptions of the program and development of self-confidence. This evaluation enabled the researchers to make decisions about how to best meet students' training needs in the face of classroom and curricular limitations.

How to Access Information

When doing research the first step that one has to take is to get informed. The researcher has to find information in the field that already exists about the topic. Alternatively, before you thoroughly study a topic you may have a question that you are interested in pursuing and your curiosity about this question may be what inspires you to pursue further understanding. However, it is the review of literature that provides grounding for your further pursuits of the problem in question. A good review allows the investigator to establish what is already known about a topic. There should be a logical progression of knowledge, or at least some understanding of gaps in the knowledge base. When completed, the review should be able to demonstrate the need for the next logical study in the area being examined.

Current group textbooks play an important role in dissemination of research knowledge as it applies to group practice. However, there is always a lag time between the knowledge base available and the publication of any text. Another source of research information is reviews done by writers who compile, analyze, and make sense of what we know about an area in a research review. There are a number of good reviews regarding group research; including the well known publication (released every five years) *The Handbook of Psychotherapy and Behavior Change,* by Bednar and Kaul (1994), *The Handbook of Group Psychotherapy,* by Fuhriman and Burlingame (1994), and the *Handbook of Group Counseling and Psychotherapy,* by DeLucia-Waack, Gerrity, Kalodner, and Riva (2004). Other reviews of literature can be found in a variety of counseling journals. Reading these reviews can help one gain perspective on what groups are, why they work the way they do, and how to be most effective as a group leader.

A good first step in undertaking any research or evaluation project is to find out what work has already been done in that area, as well as what other professionals are currently doing. Methods for investigation have changed quite dramatically in recent years with advances that have been made in technology. In the not so distant past, reviewing the literature on a topic involved proceeding manually through card catalogs with note cards in hand to take notes. Collecting information today is a much different process. With use of a computer it is possible to gain access to a vast amount of information electronically. This information comes in a variety of forms, including electronic data bases and Internet sites. It is also possible to communicate with other professionals through list serves and mailing lists. While the use of such resources may initially seem intimidating, becoming familiar with them can make the task of collecting information a much easier and faster process.

Databases of research formerly available only as print indexes, such as Educational Research and Information Clearinghouse (ERIC) and PsychLit, are now published on CD-ROM and are available at many libraries. These databases allow the user to quickly generate lists of publications on topics of interest. They also offer the advantages of "being able to experiment with various keywords, follow interesting leads (e.g., the works of a particular author), and limit the final output to only those references that are right on target . . ." (Sexton, Whiston, Bleuer, & Walz, 1997, p. 132).

Even newer and more easily accessible resources are available over the Internet today, and it is possible to access an incredible amount of information from professional organizations, online journals, and even from live communication with other professionals. A big advantage to using the Internet is that most sites are frequently updated, so that the user often has access to the most current information available. Such a vast amount of information is now available that it can be difficult to know where to begin. Efficiently searching the Internet for information has become a skill in and of itself. However, there are several key sites that can provide good starting points for the professional interested in gathering information about group counseling.

Professional organizations such as the American Counseling Association (ACA), the American Educational Research Association (AERA) and the American Psychological Association (APA) also have Web sites that are full of helpful information. For example, at the ACA Web site counselors can chat with colleagues on the World Counseling Network, which holds regularly scheduled discussions on specified topics. The AERA Web site contains online journals and publications; this site allows you to search abstracts of AERA journals since 1966. It also provides access to list serves such as the Education Research List, which is a forum for general discussion of education research. Similar resources are available at the APA Web site; you can browse APA journals by topic, for example, as well as get access to the PsychInfo database online. A number of other Internet sites of interest to group counselors are listed below.

1. American Counseling Association: http://www.counseling.org/
2. American Educational Research Association: http://www.aera.net
3. American Psychological Association: http://www.apa.org/
4. Association for Specialists in Group Work: http://www.asgw.org/

Of particular interest to group counselors may be the Association for Specialists in Group Work (ASGW) Web site. At this site a counselor can gain access to information on all aspects of group work by selecting the Resources for Group Workers icon, which provides links to many excellent resources on all aspects of group work. The research area of this site may be particularly useful to counselors embarking on a research or evaluation project. The electronic listserv Groupstuff, operated by Stockton, can also be accessed from the resources icon of the ASGW site. Through this listserv, counselors can exchange information, questions, ideas, and feedback related to group topics.

There are numerous other sites with a seemingly infinite amount of information available. Perhaps the best way to learn about what is available is to just explore; the possibilities are almost endless. The sites mentioned here and listed above are good starting points.

Summary

As we have pointed out, research plays a very important role in the way we think about and conduct group practice. In this chapter we have identified some of the problems and challenges inherent in doing research in general and in group work specifically. We have tried to present to the reader the trade offs that are inevitably necessary in conducting this type of research. In doing this, we have used actual studies to illustrate how the knowledge base in group work has developed through a combination of research and evaluation approaches. We have noted that research knowledge develops incrementally and stressed the importance of programmatic efforts to this end. Finally, we have emphasized the value of becoming familiar with the literature and have encouraged our readers to develop and carry out their own studies.

Final Note

While the finishing touches were being applied to this fourth edition of *The Counselor and the Group: Integrating Theory, Training and Practice*, the *Journal for Specialists in Group Work* published a special issue recognizing the contributions of Rex Stockton to the field of group work (Association for Specialists in Group Work, 2005). The guest editor of and a contributing co-author to that special edition was Paul Toth (2005), and Keith Morran (2005) contributed an article featuring a follow up interview to his 1992 interview in which many of the themes reflected in this current text are featured. The special issue details the influential work of Dr. Stockton over more than 30 years of an on-going career that is validated not only by his research, publications, professional leadership and honors recognizing such but also by the professional contributions of those he has taught and mentored and who have become leaders in the group work field in their own right. This living legacy was acknowledged by Ward (2005) who attributed Dr. Stockton's contributions to "an uncanny ability to stimulate others to work together to accomplish a great deal" thereby justifying the accolade defining him as "the quintessential group worker" (p. 198).

Therefore, it is with added pleasure that this final chapter is not only included but acknowledged for its erudite explication of the integral role that group counselor educators, group practitioners, and group researchers play in the foundation, formation and advancement of the field of group work. You are encouraged to read that special issue cover to cover because it is not only a testimony to a professional group work legend in his own time, but a demonstration of just what can be done when the group process is effectively utilized and applied across all levels of the group work profession from higher education to research to clinical practice.

References

Agazarian, Y. (1997). *Systems centered therapy for groups.* New York: Guilford Press.

Akos, P. (2000). Building empathic skills in elementary school children through group work. *Journal for Specialists in Group Work, 25,* 214–223.

Akos, P. (2004). Investing in experiential training appropriate for pre-service school counselors. *Journal for Specialists in Group Work, 29,* 327–342.

Akos, P., Goodnough, G. E., & Milsom, M. S. (2004). Preparing school counselors for group work. *Journal for Specialists in Group Work, 29,*127–136.

Alberti, R. E. (Ed.). (1977). *Assertiveness: Innovations, applications, issues.* San Luis Obispo, CA: Impact Publishers.

Alberti, R. E., & Emmons, M. L. (1995a). *Your perfect right: A guide to assertive behavior* (6th ed.). San Luis Obispo, CA: Impact Publishers.

Alberti, R. E., & Emmons, M. (1995b). *Your perfect right: A manual for assertiveness trainers.* San Luis Obispo, CA: Impact Publishers.

Allport, G. W. (1960). *Becoming.* New Haven, CT: Yale University Press.

American Counseling Association. (2005). *Code of ethics and standards of practice.* Alexandria, VA: Author.

American Group Psychotherapy Association/National Registry of Certified Group Psychotherapists. (2002). *Guidelines for ethics,* Retrieved February 9, 2006 http://www.groupsinc.org/group/ethicalguide.html.

American Psychological Association. (2002). Ethical principles of psychologists and code of conduct. *American Psychologist, 57*(12), 1060–1073.

American Psychological Association. (2003). *Ethical principles of psychologists and code of conduct* Retrieved February 9, 2006 from http://www.apa.org/ethics/code2002.html.

Anderson, A. R. (1969). Group counseling. *Review of Educational Research, 39,* 209–226.

Anderson, J. (1984). *Counseling through group process.* New York: Springer

Annan, K. A (10 September, 1999). An increasing vulnerability to natural disasters. *The International herald tribune.* Retrieved August 8, 2001 from http://www.unorg/Overview/SG/annan_press.htm.

Anonymous. (1996). *Primary colors: A novel of politics.* New York: Warner Books

Appleton, V. E., & Dykeman, C. (1996). Using art in group counseling with Native American youth. *Journal for Specialists in Group Work, 21*(4), 224–242.

Argras, W. S. (Ed.). (1978). *Behavior modification: Principles and clinical applications* (2nd ed.). Boston: Little Brown.

Argyris, C., Putnam, R., & Smith, D. M. (1985). *Action science.* San Francisco, CA: Jossey-Bass.

Arredondo, P. (1994). Multicultural training: A response. *The Counseling Psychologist, 22,* 308–314.

Arredondo, P., Rosen, D. C., Rice, T., Perez, P., & Tovar-Gamero, Z. G. (2005). Multicultural counseling: A 10 year analysis of the *Journal of Counseling & Development. Journal of Counseling & Development, 83,* 155–161.

Arredondo, P., Toporek, R., Brown, S. P., Jones, J., Locke, D. C., Sanchez, J., & Stadler, H. (1996). Operationalization of the multicultural counseling competencies. *Journal of Multicultural Counseling and Development, 24,* 42–78.

Asner-Self, K. K., & Feyissa, A (2002). The use of poetry in psychoeducational groups with multi-cultural-multilingual clients. *Journal for Specialists in Group Work, 27,* 136–160.

Association for Multicultural Counseling and Development. (1996). *Multicultural competencies.* Alexandria, VA: Author.

Association for Specialists in Group Work. (1989). *Ethical guidelines for group counselors.* Alexandria, VA: Author.

Association for Specialists in Group Work. (1982). Group work and organizational development. *Journal for Specialists in Group Work, 7*(1).

Association for Specialists in Group Work. (1982). Special issue: Ethical issues in group work. *Journal for Specialists in Group Work, 7*(3), 138–214.

Association for Specialists in Group Work. (1990). Special issue: Ethical and legal issues in group work. *Journal for Specialists in Group Work, 15*(2), 66–127.

Association For specialist in Group Work (2005). Special issue: The contributions of Rex Stockton. *Journal for Specialists in Group Work, 30*(3), 197–298.

Association for Specialists in Group Work (ASGW). (1983). *ASGW professional standards for the training of group workers.* Alexandria, VA: Author.

Association for Specialists in Group Work (ASGW). (1990). *ASGW professional standards for group counseling.* Alexandria, VA: Author.

Association for Specialists in Group Work. (1991). ASGW *Professional training standards for the training of group workers.* Alexandria, VA: Author.

Association for Specialists in Group Work. (1992). ASGW: Professional training standards for group workers. *Journal for Specialists in Group Work, 17*(1), 12–19.

Association for Specialists in Group Work (ASGW). (2000). ASGW professional standards for the training of group workers. *Journal for Specialists in Group Work. 25,* 327–342.

Association for Specialists in Group Work (ASGW). (March, 2000). Psychoeducational group work. *Journal for Specialists in Group Work, 25,* 29–121.

Association for Specialists in Group Work (ASGW). (September, 2001). Special issue: The use of groups for prevention. *Journal for Specialists in Group Work, 26,* 205–292.

Association for Specialists in Group Work (ASGW). (March, 2004). Special issue on teaching group work. *Journal for Specialists in Group Work, 29,* 1–148.

Association for Specialists in Group Work. (1988). The interface of group and family therapy: Implications. *Journal for Specialists in Group Work, 13*(2).

Association for Specialists in Group Work. (1998). ASGW best practice guidelines. *Journal for Specialists in Group Work, 23,* 237–244.

Association for Specialists in Group Work. (1998). ASGW *principles for diversity competent group workers.* Alexandria, VA: Author.

Atkinson, D. R., Morton, G., & Sue, D. W. (1993). *Counseling American minorities* (4th ed.). Dubuque, IA: Brown & Benchmark.

Aubrey, R. F. (1973). Organizational victimization of school counselors. *The School Counselor, 20,* 346–353.

Axelson, J. A. (1993). *Counseling and development in a multicultural society.* (Rev. ed.). Monterey, CA: Brooks/Cole.

Baca, L. M., & Koss-Chioino, J. D. (1997). Development of a culturally responsive group counseling model for Mexican American adolescents. *Journal of Multicultural Counseling and Development, 25,* 130–141.

Bach, G. R. (1954). *Intensive group psychotherapy.* New York: Ronald Press.

Bach, R. (1970). *Jonathan Livingston Seagull: A story.* New York: Macmillan.

Bailey, D. F. (2005). Response to the EGAS approach. *Professional School Counseling, 8*(5), 398.

Bales, R. F. (1950). *Interaction process analysis.* Cambridge, MA: Addison-Wesley.

Bandura, A. (1969). *Principles of behavior modification.* New York: Holt, Rinehart, and Winston.

Bandura, A. (1997). *Self-efficacy: The exercise of control.* New York: Freeman

Barlow, S. H. (2004). A strategic three-year plan to teach beginning, intermediate, and advanced group skills. *Journal for Specialists in Group Work, 29,* 113–126.

Barlow, S. H., Fuhriman, A. J., & Burlingame, G. M. (2004). The history of group counseling and psychotherapy. In J. L. DeLucia-Waack, D. A. Gerrity, C. R. Kalodnar, & M. T. Riva (Eds.), *Handbook of group counseling and psychotherapy* (pp. 3–22). Thousand Oaks, CA: Sage.

Barnard, C. P., & Corrales, R. G. (1979). *The theory and technique of family therapy.* Springfield, IL: Charles C. Thomas.

Bates, M. (1966). Themes in group counseling with adolescents. *Personnel and Guidance Journal, 44,* 568–575.

Bates, M., Johnson, C. D., & Blaker, K. E. (1982). *Group leadership: A manual for group counseling leaders* (2nd ed.). Denver: Love.

Baum, L. F. (1985) *The wizard of Oz.* Morris Plains, NJ: The Unicorn Publishing House.

Beck, A. T., & Weishaar, M. E. (1995). Cognitive therapy in R. J. Corsini & D. Wedding (Eds.), *Current psychotherapies* (4th ed., pp. 285–320). Itasca, IL: F.E. Peacock.

Becvar, D. (1982). The family is not a group—or is it? *Journal for Specialists in Group Work, 7*(2), 88–95.

Bednar, R., & Kaul, T. (1994). Experiential group research: Can the canon fire? In A. E. Bergin & S. I. Garfield (Eds.), *Handbook of psychotherapy and behavior change* (4th ed., pp. 631–663). New York: Wiley.

Bednar, R. L., & Langenbahn, D. M. (1979). Structure and ambiguity: Conceptual and applied misconceptions. *Journal for Specialists in Group Work, 4,* 170–175.

Bednar, R., Melnick, J., & Kaul, T. (1974). Risk, responsibility and structure. *Journal of Counseling Psychology, 21*(1), 31–37.

Beebe, S. A., Beebe, S. J., & Redmond, M. V. (2005) *Interpersonal communication: Relating to others* (4th ed.). Boston: Pearson: Allyn & Bacon.

Bemak, F., (2005). Reflections on multiculturalism, social justice, and empowerment groups for academic success: A critical discourse for contemporary schools. *Professional School Counseling, 8*(5), 401–406.

Bemak, F., & Chung, R. C. (2004). Teaching multicultural group counseling: Perspectives for a new era. *The Journal for Specialist in Group Work, 29,* 31–41.

Bemak, F., & Conyne, R. (2004). Ecological group work. In R. Conyne & E. Cook (Eds.), *Ecological counseling: An innovative approach to conceptualizing person-environment interaction* (pp. 195–218). Alexandria, VA: American Counseling Association.

Bemak, F., & Epp, L. R. (1996). The 12th curative factor: Love as an agent of healing in group psychotherapy. *Journal for Specialists in Group Work, 21*(2), 118–127.

Benjamin, A. B. (1987). *The helping interview with case illustrations.* Boston: Houghton Mifflin.

Berger, E. M. (1952). The relationship between expressed acceptance of self and expressed acceptance of others. *Journal of Abnormal and Social Psychology, 47,* 778–782.

Berry, J. W., & Kim, U. (1988). Acculturation and mental health. In P. Dasen, J. W. Berry, & N. Sartorius (Eds.), *Health and cross-cultural psychology* (pp. 207–236). Newbury Park, CA: Sage.

Berry, J. W. (1990). Psychology of acculturation: Understanding individuals moving between cultures. In R. W. Brislin (Ed.), *Applied cross-cultural psychology* (pp. 232–253). Newbury Park, CA: Sage.

Berry, J. W. (1994). Acculturation and psychological adaptation: An overview. In A. Bouvy, F. J. R. van de Vijver, P. Boski, & P. Schmitz (Eds.), *Journeys into cross-cultural psychology* (pp. 129–141). Amsterdam: Swets & Zeitlinger.

Bertram, B. (Jan. 21, 2000). Large group problem solving and visioning process. Association for Specialists in Group Work National Conference. Deerfield Beach, FL.

Bieschke, K. J., Matthews, C., & Wade, J. (1996). Training group counselors: The Process observer method. *Journal for Specialists in Group Work, 21*(3), 181–186.

Bieschke, K. J., Matthews, C, Wade, J., & Pricken, P. A. (1998). Evaluation of the process observer method: Group leader, member and observer perspectives. *Journal for Specialists in Group Work, 23,* 50–65.

Birnbaum, M. (1969). Sense about sensitivity training. *Saturday Review,* November 15, 82–89.

Blaker, K. E., & Samo, J. (1973). Communications games: A group counseling technique. *The School Counselor, 21,* 46–51.

Blocher, D. (1966). *Developmental counseling.* New York: Ronald Press.

Bloom, J. W. (1997). Guidelines for the new world of webcounseling. *NBCC NewsNotes, 14*(2), 1–2.

Bonney, W. C. (1969). Group counseling and development processes. In G. M.Gazda (Ed.), *Theories and methods of group counseling in the schools.* Springfield, IL: Charles C. Thomas.

Boss, P. (2002). *Family stress management: A contextual approach* (2nd ed.). Thousand Oaks, CA: Sage.

Boszormenyi-Nagy, I., & Krasner, B. R. (1986). *Between give and take: A clinical guide to contextual therapy.* New York: Brunner/Mazel.

Boszormenyi-Nagy, I., & Spark, G. M. (1973). *Invisible loyalties: Reciprocity in family therapy.* Hagerstown, MD: Harper & Row.

Bowen, M. (1966). The use of family theory in clinical practice. *Comprehensive Psychiatry, 7,* 345–374.

Bowman, V. E., & DeLucia, J. L. (1993). Preparation for group therapy: The effects of preparer and modality on group process and individual functioning. *Journal for Specialists in Group Work, 18*(2), 67–79.

Bradford, L. P., Gibb, J., & Benne, K. (1964). *T-group theory and laboratory methods.* New York: Wiley.

Brammer, L. M., & Shostrum, E. L. (1976). *Therapeutic psychology: Fundamentals of counseling and psychotherapy* (3rd ed.). Englewood Cliffs, NJ: Prentice-Hall.

Brantlinger, E., Jimenez, R., Klinger, J., Pugach, M., & Richardson, V. (2004). Qualitative studies in special education. *Exceptional Children, 71,* 195–207

Breier, C. A. (1997). Group counseling is like.... *Together, 25*(2), 12.

Brenner, V. (1999). Process-play: A simulation procedure for group work training. *Journal for Specialists in Group Work, 24,* 145–151.

Brock, S.E. (1998). Helping Classrooms Cope with Traumatic Events. ASCA, *Professional School Counseling, 2*(2), 110–116.

Brock, S. E., Sandoval, J., & Lewis,S. (1996). *Preparing for crises in the schools: A manual for building crisis response teams.* New York. Wiley.

Brown, N. W. (2004). *Psychoeducational groups: Process and practice* (2nd ed.). New York: Brunner Routledge.

Brown, S. L. (1991). *Counseling victims of violence.* Alexandria, VA: American Counseling Association.

Brown, W. F. (1965). Student to student counseling for academic adjustment. *Personnel and Guidance Journal, 43,* 811–816.

Burke, M. T., & Miranti, J. G. (Eds.). (1992). *Ethical and spiritual values in counseling.* Alexandria, VA: American Counseling Association.

Burlingame, G. M., Fuhriman, A., & Johnson, J. E. (2002). Cohesion in group psychotherapy. In J. C. Norcross (Ed.), *Psychotherapy relationships that work* (pp. 71–87). New York: Oxford University Press.

Burlingame, G. M., Fuhriman, A. J., & Johnson, J. (2004). Process and outcome in group counseling and psychotherapy. In J. L. DeLucia-Waack, D. A. Gerrity, C. R. Kalodner, & M. T. Riva (Eds.), *Handbook of group counseling and psychotherapy* (pp. 49–61). Thousand Oaks, CA: Sage.

Burlingame, G. M., Fuhriman, A. J., & Mosier, J. (2003). Differential effectiveness of group psychotherapy: A meta-analytical perspective. *Group Dynamics, Theory, and Research, 7,* 3–12.

Burlingame, G., MacKenzie, K., & Strauss, B. (2003). Evidence-based small group treatments. In M. Lambert, A. Bergin, & S. Garfield (Eds.), *Handbook of psychotherapy and behavior change* (5th ed., pp. 647–696). New York: Wiley.

Burke, M. T., & Miranti, J. G. (Eds.). (1992). *Ethical and spiritual values in counseling.* Alexandria, VA: American Counseling Association.

Buzaglo, G., & Wheelan, S. (1999). Facilitating work team effectiveness: Case studies from Central America. *Small Group Research, 30,* 108–129.

CACREP. (1994, January) *CACREP accreditation standards and procedures manual.* Alexandria, VA: Council for Accreditation of Counseling and Related Educational Programs.

Campbell, D., & Stanley, J. (1963). *Experimental and quasi-experimental designs for research.* Chicago: Rand McNally.

Campbell, L. (1992). An interview with Arthur M. Horne. *Journal for Specialists in Group Work, 17*(3), 131–143.

Campbell, L. (1996). Samuel T. Gladding: A sense of self in group. *Journal for Specialists in Group Work, 21*(2), 69–80.

Cantor, D. W., & Drake, E. A. (1983). *Divorced parents and their children.* New York: Springer.

Caple, M. C., & Cox, P. L. (1989). Relationships among group structure, member expectations, attraction to group and satisfaction with the group experience. *Journal for Specialists in Group Work, 14*(1), 16–24.

Card, K. J. & Schmider, L. (1995). Group work with members who have hearing impairments. *Journal for Specialists in Group Work, 20,* 2, 83–90.

Carmichael, K.D. (2000). Using a metaphor in working with disaster survivors. *Journal for Specialists in Group Work, 25,* 7–15.

Carroll, H. A. (1969). *Mental hygiene: The dynamics of adjustment* (5th ed.). Englewood Cliffs, NJ: Prentice-Hall.

Carroll, M. R. (1973). The regeneration of guidance. *The School Counselor, 20,* 355–360.

Carroll, M. R. (1985). Critical issues in group work in education: Now and 2001. *Journal for Specialists in Group Work, 10*(2), 98–102.

Carroll, M. R. (1986). *Group work: Leading in the here and now.* Alexandria, VA: American Counseling Association.

Carroll, M. R., & Wiggins, J. D. (1997). *Elements of group counseling: Back to the basics* (2nd ed.). Denver, CO: Love.

Carter, E. A., & McGoldrick, M. (Eds.). (1988). *The family life cycle: A framework for family therapy* (2nd ed.). New York: Gardner Press.

Cartwright, D. (1951). Achieving change in people: Some applications of group dynamic theory. *Human Relations, 4,* 381–392.

Cass, V. C. (1979). Homosexual identity formation: A theoretical model. *Journal of Homosexuality, 4,* 219–235.

Chen, C. P. (1995). Group counseling in a different cultural context: Several primary issues in dealing with Chinese clients. *Group, 19,* 45–55.

Chen, M., & Han, Y. S. (2001). Cross-cultural group counseling with Asians: A stage-specific interactive approach. *Journal for Specialists in Group Work, 26,* 111–128.

Childers, Jr., J. H., & Couch, R. D. (1989). Myths about group counseling: Identifying and challenging misconceptions. *Journal for Specialists in Group Work, 14*(2), 105–111.

Christensen, E. W. (1990). Walter Lifton's Pioneering contributions to group work. *Journal for Specialists in Group Work, 15*(3), 132–140.

Chung, R. Y. (2003). Group counseling with Asians. In J. L. DeLucia-Waack, D. Gerrity, C. R. Kalodner, C. R., & M. T. Riva (Eds.), *Handbook of group counseling and psychotherapy* (pp. 200–212). Thousand Oaks, CA: Sage.

Clark, A. J. (1989). Questions in group counseling. *Journal for Specialists in Group Work, 14*(2). 121–124.

Clark, A. J. (1992). Defense mechanisms in group counseling. *Journal for Specialists in Group Work, 17*(3), 151–160.

Clark, A. J. (1993). Interpretation in group counseling: Theoretical and operational issues. *Journal for Specialists in Group Work, 18*(4), 174–181.

Clark, A. J. (1997). Protective identification as a defense mechanism in group counseling. *Journal for Specialists in Group Work, 22*(2), 85–96.

Clark, A. J. (1998). Reframing: A therapeutic technique in group counseling. *Journal for Specialists in Group Work, 23,* 66–73.

Coe, D. M., & Zimpfer, D. G. (1996). Infusing solution-oriented theory and techniques into group work. *Journal for Specialists in Group Work, 21,* 49–57.

Coffey, R. S. (1952). Socio and psyche group process: Integrated concepts. *Journal of Social Issues, 8,* 65–74.

Cohen, A. M., & Smith, R. D. (1976). *The critical incident in growth groups: Theory and technique.* La Jolla, CA: University Associates, Inc.

Cohn, B. (1964). Group counseling with adolescents. In B. Cohn (Ed.), *Collected articles: The adolescent and group counseling* (unpublished). Board of Cooperative Educational Services. Yorktown Heights, NY, 10598.

Cohn, B. (Ed.). (1967). *Guidelines for future research on group counseling in the public school setting.* Washington, DC: American Personnel and Guidance Association.

Cohn, B. (1973). Group counseling presentation. Spring Group Guidance Conference, University of Wisconsin-Oshkosh.

Colemant, S. A., & Merta, R. J. (1999). Using the sweat lodge ceremony as group therapy for Navajo youth. *Journal for Specialists in Group Work, 24,* 55–73.

Combs, A. W., & Snygg, D. (1959). *Individual behavior* (Rev. ed.). New York: Harper & Row.

Connors, J.V. & Caple, R.B. (2005). A review of group systems theory. *Journal for Specialists in Group Work, 30,* 93–110.

Conyne, R. K. (Ed.). (1985). *The group worker's handbook: Varieties of group experience.* Springfield, IL: Charles C. Thomas.

Conyne, R. K. (1989). *How personal growth and task groups work.* Newbury Park, CA: Sage.

Conyne, R. K. (1996). The Association for Specialists in Group Work training standards: Some considerations and suggestions for training. *Journal for Specialists in Group Work, 21*(3), 155–162.

Conyne, R. K. (1998). What to look for in groups: Helping trainees become more sensitive to multicultural issues. *Journal for Specialists in Group Work, 23*(1), 22–32.

Conyne, R. (1999). *Failures in group work: How we can learn from our mistakes.* Thousand Oaks, CA: Sage.

Conyne, R. (2004a). Preventive counseling: Helping people to become empowered in systems and settings (2nd Ed.). New York: Brunner-Routledge.

Conyne, R. (2004b). Prevention groups. In J. DeLucia-Waack, D. Gerrity, C. Kalodner, & M. Riva (Eds.), *Handbook of group counseling and psychotherapy* (pp. 621–629). Thousand Oaks, CA: Sage.

Conyne, R. K., & Bemak, F. (Guest Editors) (2004a). Teaching Group Work. *Journal for Specialists in Group Work, 29*(1).

Conyne, R. K., & Bemak, F. (2004b). Preface. *Journal for Specialists in Group Work, 29,* 3–5.

Conyne, R. K. , & Bemak, F. (2004c). Teaching group work from an ecological perspective. *Journal for Specialists in Group Work, 29,* 7–18.

Conyne, R., & Clack, J. (1981). *Environmental assessment and design: A new tool for the applied behavioral scientist.* New York: Praeger.

Conyne, R., & Cook, E. (Eds.). (2004). *Ecological counseling: An innovative approach to conceptualizing person-environment interaction.* Alexandria, VA: American Counseling Association.

Conyne, R. K., Dye, A., Gill, S. J., Leddick, G. R., Morran, D. K., & Ward, D. E. (1985). A retrospective of "critical issues." *Journal for Specialists in Group Work, 10*(2), 112–115.

Conyne, R. K., Dye, H. A., Kline, W. B., Morran, D. K., Ward, D. E., & Wilson, F. R. (1992). Context for revising the Association for Specialists in Group Work training standards. *Journal for Specialists in Group Work, 17*(1), 12–19.

Conyne, R., Goodman, J., & Newmeyer, M. (In press). *Group techniques: How to use them purposefully.* Upper Saddle River, NJ: Merrill-Prentice-Hall.

Conyne, R., Goodman, J., Newmeyer, M., & Rosen, C. (2004, January). Working with group processes in Problem-Based Learning. Presentation at the National Conference of the Association for Specialists in Group Work, New York City.

Conyne, R. K., Harvill, R. L., Morganette, R. S., Morran, D. K., & Hulse-Killacky, D. (1990). Effective group leadership: Continuing the search for greater clarity and understanding. *Journal for Specialists in Group Work, 15*(1), 30–36.

Conyne, R. K., & Horne, A. M. (2001). Special Issue: The use of groups for prevention. *Journal for Specialists in Group Work, 26*(3).

Conyne, R. K., Smith, J., & Wathen, S. (1997, October). *Co-leader and supervisor processing of group phenomena.* Paper presented at the annual meeting of the North Central Association for Counselor Education & Supervision, St. Louis, MO.

Conyne, R., Tang, M., & Watson, A. (2001). Exploring diversity in therapeutic groups. In E. Welfel & R. E. Ingersoll (Eds.), *The mental health desk reference* (pp. 358–364). New York: Wiley.

Conyne, R. K., Wilson, F. R., & Tang, M. (2000). Evolving lessons from group work involvement in China. *Journal for Specialists in Group Work, 25,* 252–268.

Conyne, R. K., Wilson, F. R., & Ward, D. (1997). *Comprehensive group work: What it means & how to teach it.* Alexandria, VA: American Counseling Association.

Conyne, R., Wilson, F. R., Kline, W., Morran, D. K., & Ward, D. (1993). Training Group Workers: Implications of the new ASGW training standards for training and practice. *Journal for Specialists in Group Work, 18*(1), 11–23.

Corey, G. (1995). *Theory and practice of group counseling* (4th ed.). Monterey, CA: Brooks/Cole.

Corey, G., & Corey, M. S. (1977). *Groups: Process and practice.* Monterey, CA: Brooks/Cole.

Corey, G., & Corey, M. S. (1987). *Groups: Process and practice* (3rd ed.). Monterey, CA: Brooks/Cole.

Corey, M. S., & Corey, G. (1992). *Groups: Process and practice* (4th ed.). Pacific Grove, CA: Brooks/Cole.

Corey, G., & Corey, M. S. (1997). *Groups: Process and practice* (5th ed.). Monterey, CA: Brooks/Cole.

Corey, M. S. & Corey, G. (2002). *Groups: Process and practice* (6th ed). Monterey, CA: Brooks/Cole.

Corey, M. S. & Corey, G. (2006). *Groups: Process and practice* (7th ed.). Monterey, CA: Brooks/Cole.

Corey, G., Corey, M. S., & Callanan, P. (1990). Role of group leader's values in group counseling. *Journal for Specialists in Group Work, 15*(2), 68–74.

Corey, G., Corey, M. S., & Callanan, P. (1993). *Issues and ethics in the helping professions* (4th ed.). Pacific Grove, CA: Brooks/Cole.

Corey, G., Corey, M. S., Callanan, P., & Russell, J. M. (1982). *Group techniques.* Monterey, CA: Brooks/Cole.

Corey, G., Corey, M. S., Callanan, P., & Russell, J. M. (1992). *Group techniques* (2nd ed.). Pacific Grove, CA: Brooks/Cole.

Corey, G., Corey, M. S., & Callanan, P. (1993). *Issues and ethics in the helping professions* (4th ed.). Pacific Grove, CA: Brooks/Cole.

Cormier, W. H., & Cormier, L. S. (1991). *Interviewing strategies for helpers: Fundamental skills and cognitive behavioral interventions* (3rd ed.). Pacific Grove, CA: Brooks/Cole.

Corsini, R. (1968). Immediate therapy in groups. In G. M. Gazda (Ed.), *Innovations in group psychotherapy* (pp. 15–41). Springfield, IL: Charles C. Thomas.

Cottingham, H. F. (1973). Psychological education, the guidance function and the school counselor. *The School Counselor, 20,* 340–345.

Couch, R. D., & Childers, Jr., J. H. (1989). A discussion of differences between group therapy and family therapy: Implications for counselor training and practice. *Journal for Specialists in Group Work, 14*(4), 226–231.

Council for Accreditation of Counseling and Related Educational Programs (CACREP). (1993). *CACREP accreditation standards and procedures manual.* Alexandria, VA: Author.

Courtois, C. A. (1988). *Healing the incest wound: Adult survivors in therapy*. New York: Norton.

Courtois, C. A., & Leehan, J. (1982). Group treatment for grown-up abused children. *Personnel and Guidance Journal, 60*(9), 564–566.

Covey, S.R. (1989). *The 7 habits of highly effective people: Powerful lessons in personal change*. New York: Simon & Schuster.

Cox, J. A., Banez, L., Hawley, L. D., & Mostade, J. (2003). Use of the reflecting team process in the training of group workers. *Journal for Specialists in Group Work, 28*, 89–105.

Craig, D. P. (1978). *Hip pocket guide to planning and evaluation*. Austin, TX: Learning Concepts.

Cross, W. E., Jr. (1978). Models of psychological nigrescence: A literature review. *Journal of Black Psychology, 5*, 13–31.

Croteau, J. M., Talbot, D. M., Lance, T. S, & Evans, N. J. (2002). A qualitative study of the interplay between privilege and oppression. *Journal of Multicultural Counseling & Development, 30*, 4, 239–258.

Crouch, E., Block, S., & Wanless, J. (1994). Therapeutic factors: Interpersonal and intrapersonal mechanisms. In A. Fuhriman & G. Burlingame (Eds.), *Handbook of group psychotherapy: An empirical and clinical synthesis* (pp. 269–315). New York: Wiley.

Crowley, P. M. (1989). Ask the expert: A group teaching tool. *Journal for Specialists in Group Work, 14*(3), 173–175.

Cummings, A. L. (2001). Teaching group process to counseling students through the exchange of journal letters. *Journal for Specialists in Group Work, 26*, 7–16.

Daignault, S. D. (2000). Body talk: A school-based group intervention for working with disordered eating behaviors. *Journal for Specialists in Group Work, 25*, 191–213.

Dana, R. H. (1993). *Multicultural assessment perspectives for professional psychology*. Boston: Allyn & Bacon.

D'Andrea, M., & Daniels, J. (1997a). Multicultural group counseling. In S. Gladding (Ed.), *New developments in group counseling* (pp. 105–110). Greensboro, NC: ERIC Clearinghouse on Counseling & Student Services.

D'Andrea, M., & Daniels, J. (1997b). RESPECTFUL counseling: A new way of thinking about diversity counseling. *Counseling Today, 40*, 30–31, 34.

Dansby, V. S. (1996). Group work within the school system: Survey of implementation of leadership role issues. *Journal for Specialists in Group Work, 21*(4), 232–242.

Davenport, D. S. (2004). Ethical issues in the teaching of group work. *Journal for Specialists in Group Work, 29*, 43–50.

Davies, D., & Jacobs, A. (1985). "Sandwiching" complex interpersonal feedback. *Small Group Behavior, 16*(3), 387–396.

Davis, L. E. (1979). Racial composition of groups. *Social Work, 24*, 203–218.

Davis, L. E. (1984). *Ethnicity in social group practice*. New York: Haworth.

Davis, L. E., Cheng, L. C., & Strube, M. J. (1996). Differential effects of racial composition on male and female groups: Implications for group work practice. *Social Work Research, 20*, 157–166.

DeLucia, J. L. (1991). An interview with H. Allen Dye: Perspectives on the field of group work. *Journal for Specialists in Group Work, 16*(2), 67–73.

DeLucia, J. L., Coleman, V. L., & Jensen-Scott, R. L. (Eds.). (1992). Counseling with multicultural populations (Special Issue). *Journal for Specialists in Group Work, 17*(4), 235–242.

DeLucia-Waack, J. L. (1996). Multiculturalism is inherent in all group work. *Journal for Specialists in Group Work, 21*(4), 218–223.

DeLucia-Waack, J. L. (1997a). The importance of processing activities, exercises and events to group work practitioners. *Journal for Specialists in Group Work, 22*(2), 82–84.

DeLucia-Waack, J. L. (1997b). Measuring the effectiveness of group work: A review and analysis of process and outcome measures. *Journal for Specialists in Group Work, 22*(4), 277–293.

DeLucia-Waack, J. (2002). A written guide for planning and processing group sessions in anticipation of supervision. *Journal for Specialists in Group Work, 27*, 341–357.

DeLucia-Waack, J. L., & Bridbord, K. H. (2004). Measures of group process dynamics, climate, leadership behaviors, and therapeutic factors. In J. DeLucia-Waack, D. A. Gerrity, C. R. Kalodner, & M. T. Riva *Handbook of group counseling and psychotherapy* (pp. 120–135). Thousand Oaks, CA: Sage.

DeLucia-Waack, J. L., Bridbord, K. H., & Kleiner, J. S. (2002). *Group work experts share their favorite activities: A guide to choosing, planning, conducting and processing.* An Association for Specialists in Group Work Publication.

DeLucia-Waack, J. L., & Donigian, J. (2004). *The practice of multicultural group work: Visions and perspectives from the field.* Belmont, CA: Brooks/Cole

DeLucia-Waack, J., & Fauth, J. (2004). Effective supervision of group leaders: Current theory, research, and implications for practice. In J. DeLucia-Waack, D. Gerrity, C. Kalodner, & M. Riva (Eds.), *Handbook of group counseling and psychotherapy* (pp. 49–62). Thousand Oaks, CA: Sage.

DeLucia-Waack, J. L., Gerrity, D. A., Koldner, C. R., & Riva, M. T. (2004). *Handbook of group counseling and psychotherapy.* Thousand Oaks, CA: Sage.

DePree, M. (1989). *Leadership is an art.* New York: Dell Publishing.

DeRoma, V., Root, L. P., & Battle, J. V. (2003). Pre-training in group process skills: Impact on anger and anxiety in combat veterans. *Journal for Specialists in Group Work, 28,* 339–354.

DeSpelder, L. A., & Strickland, A. L. (2005). *The last dance: Encountering death and dying.* Boston: McGraw Hill.

Dies, R. R. (1983). Bridging the gap between research and practice in group psychotherapy. In R. R. Dies & K. R. MacKensie (Eds.), *Advances in group psychotherapy: Integrating research and practice* (pp. 1–26). New York: International Universities Press.

Dies, R. R. (1985). Research foundation for the future of group work. *Journal for Specialists in Group Work, 10*(2), 68–73.

Dinkmeyer, D. D., & Muro, J. (1971). *Group counseling: Theory and practice.* Itasca, IL: F. E. Peacock.

Dinkmeyer, D. D., & Muro, J. J. (1979). *Group counseling: Theory and practice* (2nd ed.). Itasca, IL: F. E. Peacock.

Donigian, J. (1993). Duality: The issue that won't go away. *Journal for Specialists in Group Work, 18*(3), 137–140.

Donigian, J., & Hulse-Killacky, D. (1999). *Critical incidents in group work* (2nd ed.). Pacific Grove, CA: Brooks/Cole.

Donigian, J., & Malnati, R. (1997). *Systemic group therapy: A triadic model.* Pacific Grove, CA: Brooks/Cole.

Donnelly, T. A. (Producer), & Friedkin, W. (Director). (1997). *12 Angry Men* (Film). (Available from MGM Worldwide Television Productions, Inc., Orion Home Video).

Downing, N. E., and Rousch, K. L. (1984). From passive acceptance to active commitment: A model of feminist identity development. *The Counseling Psychologist, 13,* 695–709.

Dreikurs, R. (1964). *Children: The challenge.* Des Moines, IA: Meredity Press (Duell, Sloan and Pearce.

Drum, D. J., & Knott, J. E. (1977). *Structured groups for facilitating development: Acquiring life skills, resolving life themes and making life transitions.* New York: Human Sciences Press.

Dufrene, P. M., & Coleman, V. D. (1992). Counseling Native Americans: Guidelines for group process. *The Journal for Specialists in Group Work, 17,* 229–234.

Dugo, J. M., & Beck, A. P. (1997). Significance and complexity of early phases in the development of the co-therapy relationship. *Group Dynamics: Theory, Research, and Practice 1,* 294–305.

Dustin, R., & George, R. A. (1973). *Action counseling for behavior change.* New York: Intext Educational Publishers.

Dye, A. (1981). Challenges to ethical behavior in group work. *Counseling and Values, 25,* 227–235.

Dyer, H. S. (1967). *The discovery and development of educational goals.* Princeton, NJ: Educational Testing Service.

Egan, G. (1986). *The skilled helper* (3rd ed.). Pacific Grove, CA: Brooks/Cole.

Ellis, A. (1971). *Growth through reason: Verbatim cases in rational-emotive psychotherapy.* Palo Alto, CA: Science and Behavior Books.

Evans, R. (1972). *Group counseling workshop.* River Falls, WI: University of Wisconsin–River Falls.

Evensen, E. P., & Bednar, R. I. (1978). Effects of specific cognitive and behavioral structure on early group behavior and atmosphere. *Journal of Counseling Psychology, 25*, 66–75.

Everly, G. S., & Mitchell, J. T. (1997). *Critical Incident Stress Management (CISM): A new era and standard of care in crisis intervention.* Ellicot City, MD: Chevron.

Everly, G. S., Lating, J. M., & Mitchell, J. T. (2000). Innovations in group crisis intervention: Critical Incident Stress Debriefing (CISD) and Critical Incident Stress Management (CISM). In A. R. Roberts (Ed.), *Crisis intervention handbook: Assessment, treatment and research.* New York: Oxford Press.

Fairchild, T. N., & Seeley, T. J. (1996). Evaluation of school psychological services: A case illustration. *Psychology in the Schools, 33*, 46–55.

Falco, L. D., & Bauman, S. (2004). The use of process notes in the experiential component of training group workers. *Journal for Specialists in Group Work. 29*, 185–193.

Fall, K. A., & Levitov, J. E. (2002). Using actors in experiential group counseling leadership training. *Journal for Specialists in Group Work, 27*, 122–135.

Faust, V. (1968). *The counselor-consultant in the elementary school.* Boston: Houghton Mifflin.

Feldman, L. B. (1990). Fathers and fathering. In R. L. Meth & R. S. Pasick (Eds.), *Men in therapy* (pp. 88–107). New York: Guilford Press.

Figley, C. R., & Barnes, M. (2005). External trauma and families. In P. C. McKenry & S. J. Price (Eds.). *Families and change: Coping with stressful events and transitions* (pp. 379–402). Thousand Oaks, CA: Sage.

Finkel, M. J., Ragnar, S., Bandele, A., & Schaefer, V. (2003). Diversity training in graduate school: An exploratory evaluation of the safe zone project. *Professional Psychology: Research & Practice, 34*, 555–612.

Fitts, W. H. (1965). *Manual: Tennessee (Department of mental health) self concept scale.* Counselor Recordings and Tests (Box 6184, Nashville, TN 37212).

Fitz-Gibbon, C. T., & Morris, L. L. (1987). *How to design a program evaluation.* Newbury Park, CA: Sage.

Fonda, F. (Producer), & Lumet, S. (Director). (1957). *12 Angry Men* (Film). (Available from MGM Worldwide Television Productions, Inc., United Artists)

Forrester-Miller, H. (1989). Dr. Irving Yalom discusses group psychotherapy. *Journal for Specialists in Group Work, 14*(4), 196–201.

Forester-Miller, H. (Ed.). (1990). Ethical and legal issues in group work (Special issue). *Journal for Specialists in Group Work, 15*(2).

Forrester-Miller, H., & Davis, T. E. (1995). *A practitioner's guide to ethical decision making.* Alexandria, VA: American Counseling Association.

Forrester-Miller, H., & Duncan, J. A. (1990). The effects of dual relationships in the training of group counselors. *Journal for Specialists in Group Work, 15*(2), 88–93.

Forrester-Miller, H., & Rubenstein, R. L. (1992). Group counseling: Ethics and professional issues. In D. Capuzzi & D. R. Gross (Eds.), *Introduction to group counseling* (pp. 307–323). Denver, CO: Love.

Forsyth, D. R. (1990). *Group dynamics.* (2nd ed.). Monterey, CA: Brooks/Cole.

Frankl, V. E. (1984). *Man's search for meaning: An introduction to logotherapy* (3rd ed.). New York: A Touchstone Book, Simon and Schuster.

Fuhriman, A., & Burlingame, G. M. (Eds.). (1994). *Handbook of group psychotherapy: An empirical and clinical synthesis.* New York: Wiley.

Fuhriman, A., & Burlingame, G. (2001). Group psychotherapy training and effectiveness. *International Journal of Group Psychotherapy, 51*, 399–416.

Fukuyama, M. A., & Coleman, N. C. (1992). A model for bicultural assertion training with Asian-Pacific American college students: A pilot study. *Journal for Specialists in Group Work, 17*(4), 210–217.

Fullmer, D. W. (1971). *Counseling: Group theory and system.* New York: Intext Educational Publishers.

Furr, S. R. (2000). Structuring the group experience: A format for designing psychoeducational groups. *Journal for Specialists in Group Work, 25*, 29–49.

Furr, S. R., & Barret, B. (2000). Teaching group counseling skills: Problems and solutions. *Counselor Education and Supervision, 40*, 94–104.

Gardenswartz, L., & Rowe, A. (1993). *Managing Diversity: A complete desk reference and planning guide.* Homewood, IL: Business One Irwin and San Diego, CA: Pfeiffer.

Garrett, M. T., (2004). Sound of the drum: Group counseling with Native Americans. In J. L. DeLucia-Waack, D. Gerrity, C.R. Kalodner, C. R., & M. T. Riva (Eds.), *Handbook of group counseling and psychotherapy* (pp. 169–182). Thousand Oaks, CA: Sage.

Garrett, J. T., & Garrett, M. T. (1994). The path of good medicine: Understanding and counseling Native Americans. *Journal of Multicultural Counseling and Development, 22*, 134–144.

Garrett, M. T., Garrett, J. T., & Brotherton, D. (2001). Inner circle/outer circle: A group technique based on Native American healing circles. *Journal for Specialists in Group Work, 26*, 17–30.

Garrett, M. W., & Osborne, W. L. (1995). The Native American sweat lodge as metaphor for group work. *The Journal for Specialists in Group Work, 20*, 33–39.

Gawrys, J., Jr., & Brown, B. O. (1963). Group counseling: More than a catalyst. *The School Counselor, 12*, 206–213.

Gadza, G. M. (1968). Preface. *Journal of Research and Development in Education, 2*, 1–2.

Gazda, G. M. (1971a). *Group Counseling: A developmental approach.* Boston: Allyn & Bacon.

Gazda, G. M. (1971b). *Human relations development: A manual for educators.* Boston: Allyn & Bacon.

Gazda, G. M. (1984a). *Group counseling: A developmental approach* (3rd ed.). Boston: Allyn & Bacon.

Gazda, G. M. (1984b). Multiple impact training. In D. Larson (Ed.), *Teaching psychology skills: Models for giving psychology away* (pp. 87–101). Monterey, CA: Brooks/Cole.

Gazda, G. M., & Brooks, D. K., Jr. (Eds.), (1985). The development of the social/life skills training (theme issue). *Journal of Group Psychotherapy, Psychodrama and Sociometry, 38*, 1–68.

Gadza, G. M., Duncan, J. A., & Meadows, M. E. (1967). Group counseling and group procedures: Report of a survey. *Counselor Education and Supervision, 6*, 306–310.

Gazda, G. M., & Larson, M. J. (1968). A comprehensive appraisal of group and multiple counseling research. *Journal of Research and Development in Education, 1*(2), 57–132.

Gelso, C. J. (1993). On the making of a scientist-practitioner: A theory of research training in professional psychology. *Professional Psychology: Research and Practice, 24*, 468–476.

Gelso, C. J., Mallinckrodt, B., & Judge, A. B. (1996). Research training environment attitudes toward research, and research self-efficacy: The revised research training environment scale. *The Counseling Psychologist, 24*, 304–322.

Gendlin, E. T., & Beebe. J. (1968). An experimental approach to group therapy. *Journal of Research and Development in Education, 2*(2), 19–29.

Giles, M. W. (1977). Percent black and racial hostility. *Social Science Quarterly, 58*, 412–417.

Gillam, S. L. (2004). Pre-planning considerations in teaching group counseling courses: Applying a general framework for conceptualizing PEDAGOGY. *Journal for Specialists in Group Work, 29*, 75–86.

Gilmer, B. V. H. (1970). *Psychology.* New York: Harper & Row.

Ginott, G. M. (1968). A functional approach to group counseling. In G. M. Gazda (Ed.), *Basic approaches to group psychotherapy and group counseling.* Springfield, IL: Charles C. Thomas.

Gladding, S. T. (1984). The metaphor as a counseling tool in group work. *Journal for Specialists in Group Work, 9*(3), 151–156.

Gladding, S. T. (1990). Coming full circle: Reentry after the group. *Journal for Specialists in Group Work, 15*(2), 130–131.

Gladding, S. T. (1991). *Group work.* New York: Merrill.

Gladding, S. T. (1992a). *Counseling as an art: The creative arts in counseling.* Alexandria, VA: American Counseling Association.

Gladding, S. T. (1992b). *Uses of metaphors and poetry in counseling.* (videotape). Available from American Counseling Association (5999 Stevenson Ave., Alexandria, VA 22304).

Gladding, S. T. (1994). *Group work: A counseling specialty* (2nd ed.). Englewood Cliffs, NJ: Prentice-Hall.

Gladding, S. T. (1999). *Group work: A counseling speciality* (3rd ed.). Englewood Cliffs, NJ: Prentice-Hall.

Gladding, S. T. (2002). *Group work: A counseling specialty* (4th ed.). Upper Saddle River, NJ: Prentice-Hall.

Gladding, S. T. (1997). The creative arts in groups. In H. Forrester-Miller & J. A. Kottler (Eds.), *Issues and challenges for group practitioners* (pp. 81–99). Denver: Love.

Gladding, S. T. (1998). *Counseling as an art: The creative arts in counseling.* Alexandria, VA: American Counseling Association.

Gladding, S. T. (2000). Group work practice ideas: The use of the creative arts in counseling. *The Group Worker, 28*(3), 7–9.

Glass, S. (1978, March). Group work in the 80s: What's next after encounter groups? Luncheon address at the meeting of the Association of Specialists in Group Work, Washington, DC.

Glasser, W. (1965). *Reality therapy.* New York: Harper & Row.

Glasser, W. (1969). *Schools without failure.* New York: Harper & Row.

Glasser, W., & Wubbolding, R. (1995). Reality therapy. In R. Corsini & D. Wedding (Eds.), *Current psychotherapies* (5th ed., pp. 293–321). Itasca, IL: F.E. Peacock.

Goldenberg, I., & Goldenberg, H. (1996). *Family therapy: An overview* (4th ed.). Monterey, CA: Brooks/Cole.

Goldenberg, M. M. (1990). *Pharmacology for the psychotherapist.* Muncie, IN: Accelerated Development.

Goldman, L. (1962). Group guidance: Content and process. *Personnel and Guidance Journal, 39,* 518–522.

Goleman, D. (1995). *Emotional intelligence.* New York: Bantam Books.

Goodman, J. L., & Huether, C. (2004, November). Enhancing teaching effectiveness with the use of the Personal Responder System and small group work. Workshop conducted at the 24th Annual Lilly Conference on College Teaching, "Creating community for teaching and learning," Miami University, Oxford, Ohio.

Gore-Felton, C., & Speigel, D. (1999). Enhancing women's lives: The role of support groups among breast cancer patients. *Journal for Specialists in Group Work, 24,* 274–287.

Gossard, M. H. (August, 19, 2002). Health: How are we doing? *Newsweek,* 53.

Granello, D. H., & Underfer-Babalis, J. (2004). Supervision of group work: A model to increase supervisee cognitive complexity. *Journal for Specialists in Group Work, 29,* 159–174.

Granrose, C. S., & Oskamp, S. (Eds.). (1997). *Cross-cultural work groups.* Thousand Oaks, CA: Sage.

Greeley, A. T., Garcia, V. L., Kessler, B. L., & Gilchrest, G. (1992). Training effective multicultural group counselors: Issues for a group training course. *Journal for Specialists in Group Work, 17*(4), 197–209.

Greenberg, J. A. (1974). *Psychodrama: Theory and therapy.* New York: Behavioral Publications.

Guanipa, C., Talley, W., & Rapagna, S. (1997). Enhancing Latin American women's self-concept: a group intervention. *International Journal of Group Psychotherapy, 47,* 355–372.

Gumaer, J. (1973). Peer-facilitated groups. *Elementary School Guidance and Counseling, 8,* 4–11.

Gumaer, J. (1982). Ethics and the experts: Insight into critical incidents. *Journal for Specialists in Group Work, 7*(3), 154–161.

Guth, L. J. (2001). Getting to know each other. In J. L. DeLucia-Waack, K. H. Bridbord, & J. S. Kleiner (Eds.). *Group work experts share their favorite activities: A guide to choosing, planning, conducting and processing* (pp. 42–44). Alexandria, VA: Association for Specialists in Group Work.

Guth, L. J., & McDonnell, K. A. (2004). Designing class activities to meet specific core training competencies: A developmental approach. *Journal for Specialists in Group Work, 29,* 97–112.

Gutierrez, F. J. (1990). Exploring the macho mystique: Counseling Latino men. In D. Moore & F. Leafgren (Eds.), *Problem solving strategies and interventions for men in conflict*. Alexandria, VA: American Counseling Association.

Guzzo, R., Jett, R., & Katzell, R. (1985). The effects of psychologically-based intervention programs on worker productivity: A meta-analysis. *Personnel Psychology, 38,* 275–291.

Hacker, C. (2001). Counselor, Columbine High School, Certified Trauma Specialist, Jefferson County Schools, Golden, CO (Personal Communication).

Hadley, R. G., & Mitchell, L. K. (1995). *Counseling research and program evaluation*. Pacific Grove, CA: Brooks/Cole.

Hage, S. M., & Nosanow, M. (2000). Becoming stronger at broken places: A model for group work with young adults from divorced families. *Journal for Specialists in Group Work, 25,* 50–66.

Halbur, D. (2002). Ball in play. In J. L. DeLucia-Waack, K. H. Bridbord, & J. S. Kleiner (Eds.) *Group work experts share their favorite activities: A guide to choosing, planning, conducting and processing.* (pp. 45–46). Alexandria, VA: Association for Specialists in Group Worktion.

Haley-Banez, L., & Walden, S. L. (1999). Diversity in Group Work: Using optimal theory to understand group process and dynamics. *Journal for Specialists in Group Work, 24,* 404–422.

Hall, J. (1969). *Decision by consensus*. Teleometrics International.

Hamachek, D. E. (1971). *Encounters with the self*. New York: Holt, Rinehart, and Winston.

Hamachek, D. E. (1978). *Encounters with the self* (2nd ed.). New York: Holt, Rinehart, and Winston.

Hamburg, B. A., & Varenhorst, B. B. (1972). Peer counseling in secondary school: A community mental health project for youth. *American Journal of Orthopsychiatry, 42,* 566–581.

Hansen, J. C., Warner, R. W., & Smith, E. J. (1980). *Group counseling: Theory and process*. Chicago: Rand McNally College Publishing.

Hanson, P. G. (1972). What to look for in groups. In J. W. Pfeiffer & J. E. Jones (Eds.), *1972 Annual handbook for group facilitators* (pp. 21–24). La Jolla, CA: University Associates.

Harman, M. J., & Withers, L. (1992). University students from homes with alcoholic parents: Considerations for therapy groups. *Journal for Specialists in Group Work, 17*(1), 37–41.

Harmin, M., Kirschenbaum, H., & Simon, S. B. (1973). *Clarifying values through subject matter*. Minneapolis: Winston Press.

Havighurst, R. J., & Neugarten, B. L. (1968). *Society and education* (3rd ed.). Boston: Allyn and Bacon.

Hayes, R. I. (1987). A message from the president-elect. *ASGW Newsletter, 15*(3), 1–6.

Helms, J. E. (1990). Generalizing racial identity interaction theory to groups. In J. E. Helms (Ed.), *Black and white racial identity: Theory, research, and practice* (pp. 187–204). Westport, CT: Greenwood Press.

Helms, J. E. (1995). An update of Helm's white and people of color racial identity models. In J. G. Ponterotto, J. M. Casas, L. A. Suzuki, & C. M. Alexander (Eds.), *Handbook of multicultural counseling* (pp. 181–198). Thousand Oaks, CA: Sage.

Hensley, L. G. (2002). Teaching group process and leadership: The two-way fishbowl model. *Journal for Specialists in Group Work, 27,* 273–286.

Herlihy, B., & Corey, G. (1996). *ACA ethical standards casebook* (5th ed.). Alexandria, VA: American Counseling Association.

Hesse, H. (1971). *Siddartha*. New York: Bantam Books.

Hetzel, R. D., Barton, D. A., & Davenport, D. S. (1994). Helping men change: A group counseling model for male clients. *Journal for Specialists in Group Work, 19*(2), 52–64.

Hetzel, R., Stockton, R., & McDonnell, K. (1994). Trends in training group counselors. Paper presented at the American Counseling Association Annual Convention, Minneapolis, MN.

Higgs, J. A. (1992). Dealing with resistance: Strategies for effective groups. *Journal for Specialists in Group Work, 17*(2), 67–73.

Hill, C. E., & Corbett, M. M. (1993). A perspective on the history of process and outcome research in counseling psychology. *Journal of Counseling Psychology, 40,* 3–24.

Hill, S. F. (1969). *Learning thru discussion*. Beverly Hills, CA: Sage.

Hill, W. F. (1966). *Hill interaction matrix (HIM) monograph*. Los Angeles: University of Southern California, Youth Studies Center.

Hinckley, R. G., & Herman, L. (1951). *Group treatment in psychotherapy*. Minneapolis: University of Minnesota Press.

Hines, M. (1988a). Editorial: Introduction to the special issue. *Journal for Specialists in Group Work, 13*, 171–172.

Hines, M. (1988b). Similaritites and differences in group and family therapy. *Journal for Specialists in Group Work, 13*, 173–179.

Hittleman, D. R., & Simon, A. J. (1997). *Interpreting educational research: An introduction for consumers of research*. Upper Saddle River, NJ: Prentice-Hall.

Ho, M. K. (1984). Social group work with Asian/Pacific-Americans. *Social Work With Groups, 7*, 49–61.

Hogan, R., Curphy, G. J., & Hogan J. (1994). What we know about leadership: Effectiveness and personality. *American psychologist, 49*(6), 493–504.

Holcomb-McCoy, C. C. (2005). Empowerment groups for urban African-American girls: A response. *Professional School Counseling, 8*(5), 390–392.

Homans, G. C. (1950). *The human group*. New York: Harcourt, Brace, Jovanovich.

Hoppock, R. (1976). *Occupational information* (4th ed.). New York: McGraw-Hill.

Horne, A. M. (1994). Developing group work for diverse groups. *Journal for Specialists in Group Work, 19*(3), 138–139.

Horne, A. M. (1995). Editorial. *Journal for Specialists in Group Work, 20*(1), 1–2.

Horne, A. M., & Campbell, L. F. (1997). Round pegs in square holes. In H. Forester-Miller & J. A. Kottler, (Eds.), *Issues and challenges for group practitioners* (pp. 57–80). Denver, CO: Love.

Horne, A. M., & Rosenthal, R. (1997). Research in group work: How did we get where we are? *Journal for Specialists in Group Work, 22*(4), 228–240.

Hosie, T. W. (1994). Program evaluation: A potential area of expertise for counselors. *Counselor Education and Supervision, 33*, 349–355.

Housley, P. C. (1996). *The use of qualitative and quantitative measures in program evaluation: A practical example*. Paper presented at the annual meeting of the National Association of School Psychologists, Atlanta, GA.

Hovestadt, A. J., Fennell, D., & Piercy, F. P. (1983). Integrating marriage and family therapy within counselor education: A three level training model. In B. F. Okun & S. T. Gladding (Eds.), *Issues in training marriage and family therapists* (pp. 31–41). Ann Arbor, MI: ERIC/ CAPS.

Howard, J. (1968). Inhibitions thrown to the gentle winds. *Life*, July 12, 48–65.

Hubbard, J., & Miller, K. E. (2004). Evaluating ecological mental health interventions in refugee communities. In K. E. Miller & L. M. Rasco (Eds.). *The mental health of refugees* 337–374. Mahwah, NJ: Lawrence Erlbaum Associates.

Huhn, R. P., Zimpfer, D. G., Waltman, D. E., & Williamson, S. K. (1985). A survey of programs of professional preparation for group counseling. *Journal for Specialists in Group Work, 10*(3), 124–133.

Hulse, D. (1985). Overcoming the social-ecological barriers to group effectiveness: Present and future. *Journal for Specialists in Group Work, 10*(2), 92–97.

Hulse, W. C. (1950). The therapeutic management of group tension. *American Journal of Orthopsychiatry, 20*, 834–838.

Hulse-Killacky, D. (1986). The classroom as a group: How to survive and thrive as leaders and teachers. *Educational Dimensions, 2*(1), 1–2, 8.

Hulse-Killacky, D. (1996). Using the classroom as a group to integrate knowledge, skills and supervised practice. *Journal for Specialists in Group Work, 21*(3), 151–213.

Hulse-Killacky, D., Killacky, J. & Donigian, J. (2001). *Making task groups work in your world*. Upper Saddle River, NJ: Merrill Prentice Hall.

Human potential: The revolution of feeling. (1970). *Time*, November 9, 54–58.

Impara, J. C., & Plake, B. S. (Eds.). (1998). *The thirteenth mental measurements yearbook*. Lincoln, NE: University of Nebraska Press.

Ingersoll, G. M. (1998). Applying experimental methods to diabetes education research and evaluation. *The Diabetes Educator, 24 (6)*, 751–759.

Ipaye, T. (1982). Introducing group counseling into Nigerian secondary schools: Report of a three-year experience. *International Journal for the Advancement of Counseling, 5*, 35–47.

Ivey, A. E., & Alschuler, A. S. (1973). An introduction to the field. *Personnel and Guidance Journal, 51*, 591–597.

Jackson, B. W., & Hardiman, R. (1983). Racial identity development: Implications for managing the workforce. The NTL Manager's Handbook. New York: NTL Institute.

Jacobs, A., & Spradlin, W. W. (1974). *Group as agent of change*. New York: Behavioral Publications.

Jacobs, E. E. (1992). *Creative counseling techniques: An illustrated guide*. Sarasota, FL: Psychological Assessment Resources.

Jacobs, E. E., Harvill, R. L., & Masson, R. L. (1988). *Group counseling: Strategies and skills*. Monterey. CA: Brooks/Cole.

Jacobs, E. E., Harvill, R. L., & Masson, R. L. (1994). *Group counseling: Strategies and skills* (2nd ed.). Monterey, CA: Brooks/Cole.

Jacobs, E. E., Masson, R. L., & Harvill, R. L. (2006). *Group counseling: Strategies and skills* (5th ed.). Australia: Brooks/Cole.

James, W. (1890). *The principles of psychology*. Vol. 1. New York: Holt.

James, L., & Martin, D. (2002). Sand tray and group therapy: Helping parents cope. *Journal for Specialists in Group Work, 27*, 390–405.

Janis, I. L. (1971). Groupthink. *Psychology Today, 6*, 43–46, 74–76.

Janis, I. L. (1972). *Victims of groupthink: A psychological study of foreign policy decisions and fiascos*. Boston: Houghton-Mifflin.

Jimenez, R., Klinger, J., Pugach, M., & Richardson, V. (In press). Qualitative studies in special education.

Johnson, D. W. (1972). *Reaching out: Interpersonal effectiveness and self-actualization*. Englewood Cliffs, NJ: Prentice-Hall.

Johnson, D. W. (1981). *Reaching out: Interpersonal effectiveness and self-actualization* (2nd ed.). Englewood Cliffs, NJ: Prentice-Hall.

Johnson, D. W., & Johnson, F. P. (1979). The use of counseling groups to improve interpersonal skills. *Journal for Specialists in Group Work, 4*(4), 211–215.

Johnson, D. W., & Johnson, F. P. (1982). *Joining together: Group theory and group skills* (2nd ed.). Englewood Cliffs, NJ: Prentice-Hall.

Johnson, D. W., & Johnson, F. P. (1994). *Joining together: Group therapy and group skills* (5th ed.). Englewood Cliffs, NJ: Prentice-Hall.

Johnson, D. W., & Johnson, F. P. (1997). *Joining together: Group theory and group skills* (6th ed.). Englewood Cliffs, NJ: Prentice-Hall.

Johnson, J. A. (1963). *Group therapy: A practical approach*. New York: McGraw-Hill.

Jones, K. D., & Robison, E. H. III. (2000). Psychoeducational groups: A model for choosing topics and exercises appropriate to group stage. *Journal for Specialists in Group Work, 25*, 343–355.

Jordan, K. (2001). The long term effect of September 11th: How family counselors can assist primary trauma victims with PTSD. *The Family Digest. International Association of Marriage and Family Counselors, 15*(1), 1, 3–4, 6–9.

Jordan, K. (2002). Providing crisis counseling to New Yorkers after the terrorist attack on the World Trade Center. *The Family Journal, 10*, 139–144.

Jourard, S. (1968). *Disclosing man to himself*. Princeton, NJ: Van Nostrand.

Journal for Specialists in Group Work. (1979). Special issue: Group counseling and the dynamic of structure. *4*(4), Author.

Journal for Specialists in Group Work. (1985). Special issue: Critical issues in group work: Now and 2001. *10*(2), Author.

Juntunen, C. L., Cohen, B. B., & Wolszon, L. R. (1997). Women and anger: A structured group. *Journal for Specialists in Group Work, 22*(2), 97–110.

Kahn, A. P. (1993). *Encyclopedia of mental health.* New York: Facts on File.

Kalodner, C., & Coughlin, J. (2004). Psychoeducational and counseling groups to prevent and treat eating disorders and disturbances. In J. DeLucia-Waack, D. Gerrity, C. Kalodner, & M. Riva (Eds.), *Handbook of group counseling and psychotherapy* (pp. 481–496). Thousand Oaks, CA: Sage.

Kane, C. (1995). Fishbowl training in group process. *Journal for Specialists in Group Work, 20*(3), 183–188.

Kaneshige, E. (1973). Cultural factors in group counseling and interaction. *Personnel and Guidance Journal, 51,* 407–412.

Kanfer, F. H., & Goldstein, A. P. (Eds.). (1975). *Helping people change.* New York: Pergamon Press.

Kanter, R. M. (1977). Women in organizations: Sex roles, group dynamics, and change strategies. In A. G. Sargent (Ed.), *Beyond sex roles.* St. Paul, MN: West Publishing Co.

Kaplan, H. I., & Saddock, B. J. (1993). *Comprehensive group psychotherapy* (3rd ed.). Baltimore: Williams and Wilkens.

Kassera, W., & Kassera, M. (1979). Energizers as group openers. *Journal for Specialists in Group Work, 4*(4), 201–205.

Katz, A. H. (1981). Self-help and mutual aid: An emerging social movement. *Annual Review of Sociology, 7,* 129–155.

Katz, R. (1973). *Preludes to growth: An experimental approach.* New York: Free Press.

Keel, L. P., & Rapin, L. S. (1997, April). *Bridging with group workers on best practice standards.* Roundtable seminar presented at the annual meeting of the American Counseling Association, Orlando, FL.

Kees, N. L., & Jacobs, E. (1990). Conducting more effective groups: How to select and process group exercises. *Journal for Specialists in Group Work, 15*(1), 21–29.

Kees, N. L., & Leech, N. L. (2002). Using group counseling techniques to clarify and deepen the focus of supervision groups. *Journal for Specialists in Group Work, 27,* 7–15.

Kemp, C. G. (1970). *Group counseling: A foundation for counseling with groups.* Boston: Houghton Mifflin.

Kessler, R. C., Mickelson, K. D., & Zhao, S. (1997). Patterns and correlates of self-help group membership in the United States. *Social Policy, 27,* 27–46.

Killacky, J., & Hulse-Kilacky, D. (2004). Group work is not just for the group class anymore. *Journal for Specialists in Group Work, 29,* 87–96.

Kim, J. (1981). *The process of Asian American identity development: A study of Japanese-American women's perspectives of their struggle to achieve personal identities as Americans of Asian ancestry.* Dissertation Abstracts International, 42, 1551A. (University Microfilms No. 81-18080).

Kim, B. S., & Abreu, J., (2001). Acculturation measurement. In J. G. Ponterotto, J. M. Casas, L. A. Suzuki, & C. M. Alexander (Eds.). *Handbook of multicultural counseling* (2nd ed, pp. 394–424). Thousand Oaks, CA: Sage.

Kirby, J. (1985). *Consultation: Practice and practitioner.* Muncie, IN: Accelerated Development.

Kiresuk, T. J., & Sherman, R. E. (1968). Goal attainment scaling: A general method for evaluating community mental health programs. *Community Mental Health Journal, 4,* 443–453.

Kirschenbaum, H. (1977). *Advanced value clarification.* LaJolla, CA: University Associates.

Kitchener, K. S. (1984). Intuition, critical evaluation and ethical principles: The foundation for ethical decisions in counseling psychology. *The Counseling Psychologist, 12,* 43–55.

Klaw, E., & Humphreys, K. (2004) The role of peer-led mutual help groups in promoting health and well being. In J. L. DeLucia-Waack, D. A. Gerrity, C. R. Kalodnar, & M. T. Riva (Eds.), *Handbook of group counseling and psychotherapy* (pp. 630–640). Thousand Oaks, CA: Sage.

Klein, E. B. (1985). Group work: 1985 and 2001. *Journal for Specialists in Group Work, 10*(2), 108–111.

Kline, W. B. (1990). Responding to "problem" members. *Journal for Specialists in Group Work, 15*(4), 195–200.

Korda, L. J., & Pancrazio, J. J. (1989). Limiting negative outcome in group practice. *Journal for Specialists in Group Work, 14*(2), 112–120.

Koss, M., Goodman, L., Fitzgerald, L., Russo, N. F., Keita, G. P., & Browne, A. (1994). *No safe place: Male violence against women at home, at work and in the community*. Hyattsville, MD: American Psychological Association.

Kottler, J. A. (Ed.). (1982). Ethical issues in group work (Special issue). *Journal for Specialists in Group Work, 7*(3).

Kottler, J. A. (1992). *Compassionate therapy: Working with difficult clients*. San Francisco, CA: Jossey-Bass.

Kottler, J. A. (1994a). *Advanced group leadership*. Pacific Grove, CA: Brooks/Cole.

Kottler, J. A. (1994b). Working with difficult group members. *Journal for Specialists in Group Work, 19*(1), 3–10.

Kottler, J. A. (2001). *Learning group leadership: An experiential approach*. Needham Heights, MA: Allyn/Bacon.

Kottler, J. A. (2004). Realities of group counseling. *Journal for Specialists in Group Work, 29*, 51–54.

Kranzow, G. W. (1973). *Peer counseling handbook*. ESEA Title III. Peer Counseling Project. Special Education District of Lake County (4440 W. Grand Ave., Gurnee, IL 60031).

Kraus, K. L., DeEsch, J. B., & Geroski, A. M. (2001). Stop avoiding challenging situations in group counseling. *Journal for Specialists in Group Work, 26*, 31–47.

Kraus, K., & Hulse-Killacky, D. (1996). Balancing process and content in groups: A metaphor. *Journal for Specialists in Group Work, 21*(2), 90–93.

Krumboltz, J. D., & Thoreson, L. E. (Eds.). (1976). *Counseling methods*. New York: Holt.

Kubie, L. (1958). *Neurotic distortion of the creative process*. Lawrence, KS: University of Kansas Press.

Kulic, K. (2003). An account of group work with family members of 9/11. *Journal for Specialists in Group Work, 28*, 195–198.

Kulic, K. R., Dagley, J. C., & Horne, A. M. (2001). Prevention groups with children and adolescents. *Journal for Specialists in Group Work, 26*, 211–218.

Laird, D. A., & Laird, E. (1967). *Psychology: Human relations and motivation*. New York: McGraw-Hill.

Lakin, M. (n.d.). On the distinctions between group psychotherapy and dyadic psychotherapy, (audio tape). Available from Counselor Recordings and Tests (Box 6184 Acklen Station, Nashville, TN 37212).

Lakin, M. (1969). Some ethical issues in sensitivity training. *American Psychologist, 24*, 923–928.

Lakin, M. (1970). Group sensitivity training and encounter: Uses and abuses of a method. *Counseling Psychologist, 2*(2), 66–70.

Lakin, M. (1979). What's happened to small group research? Epilogue. *Journal of Applied Behavioral Science, 15*, 424–427.

Landis, D., Bennett, J. M., & Bennet, M. J. (Eds.). (2004). *Handbook of Intercultural Learning* (3rd ed). Thousand Oaks, CA: Sage.

Landreth, G. L (1973). Group counseling: To structure or not to structure. *The School Counselor, 20*, 371–374.

Lange, A. J., & Jakubowski, P. (1976). *Responsible assertive behavior: Cognitive/behavioral procedures for trainers*. Champaign, IL: Research Press.

Lawler, E., III, Mohrman, S., & Ledford, G., Jr. (1995). *Creating high performance organizations: Practices and results of employee involvement and total quality management in Fortune 1000 companies*. San Francisco: Jossey-Bass. Cited in Wheelan, S. (2004), *Groups in the workplace*. In J. DeLucia-Waack, D. Gerrity, C. Kalodner, & M. Riva (Eds.), *Handbook of group counseling and psychotherapy* (pp. 401–413). Thousand Oaks, CA: Sage.

Leach, M. M., & Carlton, M. A. (1997). Toward defining a multicultural training philosophy. In D. B. Pope-Davis & H. L. K. Coleman (Eds.), *Multicultural counseling competencies: Assessment, education and training, and supervision* (pp. 184–208). Thousand Oaks: CA: Sage.

Leary, T. (1957). *Interpersonal diagnosis of personality: A functional theory and methodology for personality evaluation*. New York: The Ronald Press.

Lee, C. C., (1987). Black manhood training: Group counseling for male Blacks in grades 7–12. *Journal for Specialists in Group Work, 12,* 18–25.

Lee, C. C., Oh, M.Y., & Mountcastle, A.R. (1992). Indigenous models of helping in non-Western countries: Implications for multicultural counseling. *Journal of Multicultural Counseling and Development, 20,* 1–10.

Lee, C. L., & Armstrong, K. L. (1995). Indigenous models of mental health intervention: Lessons from traditional healers. In J. G. Ponterotto, J. M. Casas, L. A. Suzuki, & C. M. Alexander (Eds.), *Handbook of multicultural counseling* (pp. 441–456). Thousand Oaks, CA: Sage.

Lee, E., Munro, B. H., & McCorkle, R. (1993). A shortened version of an instrument measuring bereavement. *International Journal of Nursing Studies, 30,* 213–226.

Lee, F., & Bednar, R. I. (1977). Effects of group structure and risk-taking disposition on group behavior, attitudes and atmosphere. *Journal of Counseling Psychology, 24,* 191–199.

Leong, F. T. L. (1986). Counseling and psychotherapy with Asian-Americans: Review of the literature. *Journal of Counseling Psychology, 33,* 196–206.

Leong, F. T. L. (1992). Guidelines for minimizing premature termination among Asian American clients in group counseling. *The Journal for Specialists in Group Work, 17,* 218–228.

Leong, F. T. L., Wagner, N. S., & Kim, H. H. (1995). Group counseling expectations among Asian American students: The role of culture-specific factors. *Journal of Counseling Psychology, 42,* 217–222.

Leveton, E. (1977). *Psychodrama for the timid clinician.* New York: Springer.

Lewin, K. (1951). *Field theory in social science.* New York: Harper.

Lieberman, M., Yalom, I., & Miles, M. (1973). *Encounter groups: First facts.* New York: Basic Books.

Lifton, W. (1966). *Working with groups* (2nd ed.). New York: Wiley.

Lindt, H. (1958). The nature of therapeutic interaction of patients in groups. *International Journal of Group Psychotherapy, 8,* 55–69.

Linton, J. M. (2003). A Preliminary qualitative investigation of group processes in group supervision: Perspectives of master's level practicum students. *Journal for Specialists in Group Work, 28,* 215–243.

Littrell, J.M. & Peterson, J.S. (2002). Establishing a comprehensive group work program in an elementary school: An in-depth case study. *Journal for Specialists in Group Work, 27,* 161–172.

Lloyd, A. (1990). Dual relationships in group activities: A counselor education/accreditation dilemma. *Journal for Specialists in Group Work, 15*(2), 83–87.

Loewy, M. I., Williams, D. T., & Keleta, A. (2002). Group counseling with traumatized East African Women in the United States: Using the Kaffa ceremony. *Journal of Specialists in Group Work, 27,* 173–191.

Luft, J. (1963). *Group processes: An introduction to group dynamics.* Palo Alto, CA: National Press Books.

Luft, J. (1970). *Group process: An introduction to group dynamics* (2nd ed.). Palo Alto, CA: National Press Books.

Luft, J. (1984). *Group process: An introduction to group dynamics* (3rd ed.). Palo Alto, CA: Mayfield.

MacDevitt, J. W. (1987). Conceptualizing components of group counseling. *Journal for Specialists in Group Work, 12*(2), 76–84.

MacKenzie, K. R. (1997). Clinical application of group development ideas. *Group dynamics: Theory, research & practice, 1,* 275–287.

Madanes, C. (1981). *Strategic family therapy.* San Francisco: Jossey-Bass.

Mahler, C. A. (1969). *Group counseling in the schools.* Boston: Houghton Mifflin.

Maier, S. F., & Seligman, M. E. P. (1976). Learned helplessness: Theory and evidence. *Journal of Experimental Psychology, 105*(1), 3–46.

Maier, S. F., Seligman, M. E. P., & Solomon, R. L. (1969). Pavlovian fear conditioning and learned helplessness: Effects on escape and avoidance behavior of (a) the CS-US contingency and (b) the independence of the US and voluntary responding. In Campbell & Church (Eds.), *Punishment and adverse behavior.* New York: Appleton.

Makuch, L., Robison, F. F., & Stockton, R. (1998, January). Leadership characteristics inventory: Development and tryout. Presentation at the 6th National ASGW Group Work Conference. Tucson, AZ.

Maples, M. F. (1992). STEAMWORK: An effective approach to team building. *Journal for Specialists in Group Work, 17*(3), 144–150.

Markus, H.R., & Kitayama, S. (1991). Culture and the self: Implications for cognition, emotion, and motivation. *Psychological Review, 98,* 224–253.

Marrotta, S.A., Peters, B. J., & Paliokas, K. L. (2000). Teaching group dynamics: An interdisciplinary model. *Journal for Specialists in Group Work, 25,* 16–28.

Martin, V., & Thomas, M.C. (2000). A model psychoeducation group for shy college students. *Journal of Specialists in Group Work, 57,* 79–88.

Maslow, A. H. (1943). A theory of human motivation. *Psychological Review, 50,* 370–396.

Maslow, A. H. (1954). *Motivation and personality.* New York: Harper.

Maslow, A. H. (1962). *Toward a psychology of being.* Princeton, NJ: Van Nostrand.

Maslow, A. H. (1967). Self actualization and beyond. In J. F. T. Bugenthal (Ed.), *Challenges of humanistic psychology* (pp. 279–286). New York: McGraw-Hill.

Maslow, A. H. (1970). A theory of human motivation. In *Motivation and personality* (2nd ed.). New York: Harper and Row.

Mason, M.A., Skolnick, A., & Sugarman, S.D. (2003). *All our families: New policies for a new century* (2nd ed.). New York: Oxford University Press.

Mathis, R.D. & Tanner, Z. (2000). Structured group activities with family-of-origin themes. *Journal for Specialists in Group Work, 25,* 89–103.

Matthews, C. O. (1992). An application of general systems theory (GST) to group therapy. *Journal for Specialists in Group Work, 17*(3), 161–169.

May, R. (1953). *Man's search for himself.* New York: Norton.

Mayer, G. R., & Baker, P. (1967). Group counseling with elementary school children: A look at group size. *Elementary School Guidance and Counseling, 1,* 140–145.

McBride, M. C., & Emerson, S. (1989). Group work with women who were molested as children. *Journal for Specialists in Group Work, 14*(1), 25–33.

McClure, B. A. (1989). What's a meta-phor? *Journal for Specialists in Group Work, 14*(4), 239–242.

McClure, B. A. (1990). The group mind: Generative and regressive groups. *Journal for Specialists in Group Work, 15*(3), 159–170.

McClure, B. (1998). *Putting a new spin on groups: The science of chaos.* Mahwah, NJ: Lawrence Erlbaum Associates.

McCoy P. C. (1997). Group research: A practitioner's perspective. *Journal for Specialists in Group Work, 22*(4), 294–296.

McCue-Herlihy, B. (1996). A student's perspective on learning to do group work. *Journal for Specialists in Group Work, 21*(3), 169–171.

McDonnell, K. A. (1996). *A qualitative study of beginning therapy group leaders.* Unpublished manuscript, Indiana University at Bloomington.

McGoldrick, M., & Gerson, R. (1985). *Genograms in family assessment.* New York: W.W. Norton.

McGoldrick, M., Giordano, J., & Pearce, J. K. (1996). *Ethnicity and family therapy* (2nd ed.). New York: Guilford Press.

McKay, M., & Paleg, K. (Eds.). (1992). *Focal group psychotherapy.* Oakland, CA: New Harbinger.

McKenry, P.C. & Price, S.J (Eds.). (2005). *Families & change: Coping with stressful events and transitions* (3rd ed.). Thousand Oaks, CA: Sage.

McManus, P. W., Redford, J. L., & Hughes, R. B. (1997). Connecting self to others: A structured group for women. *Journal for Specialists in Group Work, 21*(1), 22–30.

McMillon, H. G. (1994). Developing problem solving and interpersonal communication skills through intentionally structured groups. *Journal for Specialists in Group Work, 19*(1), 43–47.

McRae, M. B. (1994). Interracial group dynamics: A new perspective. *The Journal for Specialists in Group Work, 19,* 168–174.

McRae, M. B., & Johnson, S. D. (1991). Toward training for competence in multicultural counselor education. *Journal of Counseling and Development, 70,* 131–135.

McRoy, C. R., & Brown, B. M. (1996). Effect of conceptual level of group conflict interaction. *Journal for Specialists in Group Work, 21*(1), 11–17.

Meichenbaum, D. (1977). *Cognitive behavior modification: An integrative approach.* New York: Plenum.

Meichenbaum, D. (1985). *Stress inoculation training.* New York: Pergamon Press.

Merchant, N. M. (1991). *Racial identity development: Process and outcome of a racial awareness program.* Unpublished doctoral dissertation. University of Cincinnati, Cincinnati, OH.

Merchant, N. M. & Butler, M. K. (2002). A psychoeducational group for ethnic minority adolescents in a predominantly White treatment setting. *Journal for Specialists in Group Work, 27,* 314–332.

Merchant, N. M., & Dupuy, P. (1996). Multicultural counseling and qualitative research methods: Shared worldview and skills. *Journal of Counseling and Development, 74,* 537–541.

Merta, R. J. (1995). Group work: Multicultural perspectives. In J. G. Ponterotto, J. M. Casas, L. A. Suzuki, & C. M. Alexander (Eds.). *Handbook of multicultural counseling* (pp. 567–585). Thousand Oaks, CA: Sage.

Merta, R. J., Johnson, P., & McNeil, K. (1995).Updated research on group work: Educators, course work, theory and teaching methods. *Journal for Specialists in Group Work, 20,* 132–142.

Merta, R. J., Ponterotto, J. G., & Brown, R. D. (1992). Comparing the effectiveness of two directive styles in academic counseling of foreign students. *Journal of Counseling Psychology, 39,* 214–218.

Merta, R. J., Romero, J., & Bennett, M. (1997, August). *Therapeutic factors in process-oriented multicultural group work.* Poster session presented at the annual conference of the American Psychological Association, Chicago, IL.

Merta, R. J., & Sisson, J. A. (1991). The experiential group: An ethical and professional dilemma. *Journal for Specialists in Group Work, 16*(4), 236–245.

Merta, R. J., Stringham, E. M., & Ponterotto, J. G. (1988). Simulating culture shock in counselor trainees: An experiential exercise for cross-cultural training. *Journal of Counseling and Development, 66,* 242–245.

Merta, R. J., Wolfgang, L., & McNeil, K. (1993). Five models for using the experiential group in the preparation of group counselors. *Journal for Specialists in Group Work, 18*(4), 200–207.

Mikesell, R. H., Lusterman, D-D., & McDaniel, S. H. (1995). *Integrating family therapy: Handbook of psychology and systems theory.* Washington, DC: American Psychological Association.

Miller, M. J. (1993). The lifeline: A qualitative method to promote group dynamics. *Journal for Specialists in Group Work, 18*(2), 51–54.

Miller, P.H. (2002) *Theories of developmental psychology* (4th ed.). New York: Worth Publishers.

Miller, S., Nunnally, E. W., & Wackman, D. B. (1975). *Alive and aware: Improving communication in relationships.* Minneapolis, MN: Interpersonal Communication Programs.

Minuchin, S. (1974). *Families and family therapy.* Cambridge, MA: Harvard University Press.

Miranda, A. O, Molina, B., & MacVane, S. L. (2003). Coping with the murder of a loved one: Counseling survivors of murder victims in groups. *Journal for Specialists in Group Work, 28,* 48–63.

Mitchell, J. T., & Everly, G. S. (1996). *Critical incident stress management: The basic course workbook.* Ellicott City, MD: International Critical Incident Stress Foundation.

Moreno, J. L. (1964). *Psychodrama* (Vols. I–III). New York: Beacon House.

Moreno, Z. (n.d.). *Psychodramatic rules, techniques and adjunctive methods,* (monograph). New York: Beacon House.

Morganette, R. (1990). *Skills for living: Group counseling activities for young adolescents.* Champaign, IL: Research Press.

Morganette, R. (1994). *Skills for living: Group counseling activities for elementary students.* Champaign, IL: Research Press.

Morran, D. K. (1992). An interview with Rex Stockton. *Journal for Specialists in Group Work, 17*(1), 4–9.

Morran, D. K. (2005). An interview with Rex Stockton: Past, present and future reflections. *Journal for Specialists in Group Work, 30,* 209–219.

Morran, D. K., & Stockton, R. (1985). Perspectives on the development of group psychotherapy research programs. *Journal for Specialists in Group Work, 10,* 186–191.

Morran, D. K., Stockton, R., & Harris, M. (1991). Analysis of group leader and member feedback messages. *Journal of Group Psychotherapy, Psychodrama, and Sociometry, 44*(3), 126–135.

Morran, D. K., Stockton, R., & Robison, F. F. (1985). Feedback exchange in counseling groups: An analysis of message content and receiver acceptance as a function of leader versus member delivery, session and valence. *Journal of Counseling Psychology, 32*(1), 57–67.

Morran, D. K., Stockton, R., & Whittingham, M. H. (2004). Effective leader interventions for counseling and psychotherapy groups. In J. DeLucia-Waack, D. A. Gerrity, C. R. Kalodner, & M. T. Riva (Eds.), *Handbook of group counseling and psychotherapy* (pp. 91–103). Thousand Oaks, CA: Sage.

Morran, D. K., Stockton, R., & Teed, C. (1998). Facilitating feedback exchange in groups: Leader interventions. *Journal for Specialists in Group Work, 23,* 257–268.

Moustakas, C. (1972). *Teaching as learning.* New York: Ballantine Books.

Muller, L. E. (2000). A 12-session, European-American-led counseling group for African-American females. *Professional School Counseling, 3,* 264–269.

Muller, L. E. (2002). Group counseling for African American males: When all you have are European American counselors. *Journal For Specialists in Group Work, 27,* 299–313.

Muro, J. J., & Freeman, S. L. (1968). *Readings in group counseling.* Scranton, PA: International Textbook.

Muro, J. J., & Denton, G. (1968). Expressed concerns of teacher-education students in counseling groups. *Journal of Teacher Education, 19,* 465–470.

Myers, L. J., Speight, S. L., Highlen, P. S., Chikako, I. C., Reynolds, A. L., Adams, E. M., & Hanley, C. P. (1991). Identity development and world view: Toward an optimal conceptualization. *Journal of Counseling and Development, 70,* 54–63.

Napier, A. Y., & Whitaker, C. (1978). *The family crucible: The intense experience of family therapy.* New York: Quill, HarperCollins Publishers.

Napier, R. W., & Gershenfeld, M. K. (1993). *Groups: Theory and experience.* (5th ed.). Boston: Houghton Mifflin.

National Association of Social Workers. (1993). *Code of ethics of the National Association of Social Workers.* Washington, D C: Author Retrieved February 9, 2006 from (http://www.naswdc.org/pubs/code/default.asp).

National Board for Certified Counselors. (1989). *Code of ethics.* Greensboro, NC: Author, http://www.nbcc.org.

National Board for Certified Counselors. (2002). Code of ethics. *NBCC News Notes, 14*(2), 3–4, Retrieved February 9, 2006 from http://www.nbcc.org/pdfs/ethics/NBCC-CodeofEthics.pdf

National Board for Certified Counselors. (1997a, Fall). Standards for the ethical practice of web-counseling. *NBCC Newsnotes, 14*(2), 3–4.

National Board for Certified Counselors. (1997b, Fall). State counselor licensure/certification: September 15, 1997. *NBCC NewsNotes, 14*(2). 6b–6e.

National Education Association. (1969). Lost on the moon: A decision making problem. *Today's Education, 58*(2), 55–56.

National Institute of Health (2001). The numbers count: Mental disorders in America (Publication No. 01-4584).

Nelson, R. C. (1971). Organizing for group counseling. *Personnel and Guidance Journal, 50,* 25–28.

Nichols, M. (1984). *Family therapy: Concepts and methods.* New York: Gardner Press.

Odom, S. L., Brantlinger, E., Gersten, R., Horner, R. D., Thompson, B., & Harris, K. (2004, Fall). Quality indicators for research in special education and guidelines for evidence-based practices: Executive summary. *Division of Research, Council for Exceptional Children.*

Ohlsen, M. M. (1970). *Group counseling.* New York: Holt, Rinehart & Winston.

Ohlsen, M. M. (1974). *Guidance services in the modern school* (2nd ed.). New York: Harcourt Brace Jovanovich.

Ohlsen, M. (1977). *Group counseling* (2nd ed.). New York: Holt, Rinehart and Winston.

Ohlsen, M. M. (Ed.) (1979). *Journal for Specialists in Group Work, 4*(2).

Ohlsen, M. M., Horne, A. M., & Lawe, C. F. (1988). *Group counseling* (3rd ed.). New York: Holt, Rinehart and Winston.

Osborne, N. L. (1990). Ben Cohn: Group counseling and the acting-out underachieving adolescent. *Journal for Specialists in Group Work, 15*(1), 2–9.

Otto, H. (1967). *Guide to developing your potential.* New York: Scribners.

Overmeier, J. B., & Seligman, M. E. P. (1967). Effects of unescapable shock upon subsequent escape and avoidance learning. *Journal of Comparative and Physiological Psychology, 63,* 23–33.

Owens, P. C., & Kulic, K. R. (2001). What's needed now: Using groups for prevention. *Journal for Specialists in Group Work, 26,* 205–210.

Pack-Brown, S. P., Lipford-Sanders, J., & Shaw, M. (1995). Kujichagulia-uncovering the secrets of the heart: group work with African American women on predominantly White campuses. *The Journal for Specialists in Group Work, 20,* 151–158.

Pack-Brown, S. P., Whittington-Clark, L. E., & Parker, W. M. (1998). *Images of Me: A guide to group work with African-American women.* Needham, MA: Allyn & Bacon

Page, B. (2004). Online group counseling. In J. DeLucia-Waack, D. Gerrity, C. Kalodner, & M. Riva (Eds.), *Handbook of group counseling and psychotherapy* (pp. 609–620). Thousand Oaks, CA: Sage.

Paritzky, R. S., & Magoon, T. M. (1982). Goal attainment scaling models for assessing group counseling. *Personnel and Guidance Journal, 60,* 381–384.

Pasik, R. S., Gordon, S., & Feldman, L. B. (1990). Fathers and fathering. In R. L. Meth & R. S. Pasick (Eds.), *Men in therapy* (pp. 152–180). New York: Guilford Press.

Patterson, C. H. (1996). Multicultural counseling: From diversity to universality. *Journal of Counseling and Development, 74,* 227–231.

Patton, M. Q. (1997). *Utilization-focused evaluation.* (3rd ed.). Thousand Oaks, CA: Sage.

Pearson, R. E. (1981). Basic skills for leadership of counseling groups. *Counselor Education and Supervision, 21*(1), 30–37.

Pearson, R. E. (1986). Guest editorial. *Journal for Specialists in Group Work, 11*(2), 66.

Pedersen, P. (1988). *A handbook for developing multicultural awareness.* Alexandria, VA: American Association for Counseling and Development.

Pedersen, P. B. (1998). The cultural context of the American counseling association code of ethics. *Journal of Counseling and Development, 76,* 23–28.

Personnel and Guidance Journal. (1972). *50*(4).

Petersen, C., Glover, J. A., Romero, D., & Romero, P. (1978). The effects of a cross-cultural simulation game on participants' personal characteristics. *Social Behavior and Personality, 6*(1), 21–26.

Peterson, J. V., & Nisenholz, B. (1995). *Orientation to counseling* (3rd ed.). Boston: Allyn & Bacon.

Pfeiffer, D. C., & Jones, J. E. (1969–1985). *A handbook of structured experiences for human relations training* (Vols. I–X). San Diego, CA: University Associates.

Phan, L. T., Merchant, N., Salazar, C., Torres-Rivera, E., Banez, L., & Vasquea-Evans, L. M. (2005). Operationalizing ASGW Diversity Competencies. ACA Convention Program #443, Atlanta, GA.

Pierce, K. A., & Baldwin, C. (1990). Participation versus privacy in the training of group counselors. *Journal for Specialists in Group Work, 15*(3), 149–158.

Pistole, M. C. (1997). Attachment theory: Contributions to group work. *Journal for Specialists in Group Work, 22*(1), 7–21.

Platt, J., & Spivak, G. (1976). *Workbook for training in interpersonal problem-solving thinking.* Philadelphia: Department of Mental Health Sciences, Hahnemann Community Mental Retardation Center.

Polcin, D. (1991). Prescriptive group leadership. *Journal for Specialists in Group Work, 16*(1), 8–15.

Polkinghorne, D. E. (1988). *Narrative knowing and the human sciences.* Albany, NY: SUNY Press.

Ponterotto, J. G., Casas, J. M., Suzuki, L. A., & Alexander, C. M. (Eds.). (1995). *Handbook of multicultural counseling.* Thousand Oaks, CA: Sage.

Ponzo, Z. (1991). Critical factors in group work: Clients perceptions. *Journal for Specialists in Group Work, 16*(1), 16–23.

Pope, M. (1999). Applications of group career counseling techniques in Asian cultures. *Journal of Multicultural Counseling and Development, 27,* 18–30.

Pope-Davis, D. B., Breaux, C., & Liu, W. M. (1994). A multicultural immersion experience: Filling a void in multicultural training. In D. B. Pope-Davis, H. L. K. Coleman (Eds.), *Multicultural counseling competencies: Assessment, education and training, and supervision* (pp. 227–241). Thousand Oaks, CA: Sage.

Poppen, W. A., & Thompson, C. L. (1974). *School counseling: Theories and concepts.* Lincoln, NE: Professional Educators Publications.

Portman, T. A. A., & Portman, G. L. (2002). Empowering students for social justice (ES2J): A structured group approach. *Journal of Specialists in Group Work, 27,* 16–31.

Powdermaker, F. B., & Frank, J. D. (1953). *Group psychotherapy.* Cambridge, MA: Harvard University Press.

Powell, J. (1969). *Why am I afraid to tell you who I am?* Niles, IL: Argus Communications.

Price, P. (2004). All about depression. *International Society for Mental Health Online,* http://www.allaboutdepression.com/cau_02.html

Psychotherapy Finances. (1997, May). 1997 fee, practice and managed care survey. *Psychotherapy Finances, 23*(5), 1–12.

Rapin, L. (2004). Guidelines for ethical and legal practice in counseling and psychotherapy groups. In J. DeLucia-Waack, D. Gerrity, C. Kalodner, & M. Riva (Eds.), *Handbook of group counseling and psychotherapy* (pp. 151–166). Thousand Oaks, CA: Sage.

Rapin, L. S., & Keel, L. P. (1996a, January). *Best practice guidelines for group workers: Enhancing ACA's 1995 Code of Ethics.* Seminar presented at the Association for Specialists in Group Work 4th National Group Work Conference, Athens, GA.

Rapin, L. S., & Keel, L. P. (1996b, April). *Best practice guidelines for group workers: Applying ACA 1995 Code of Ethics.* Seminar presented at the annual meeting of the American Counseling Association, Pittsburgh, PA.

Rapin, L. S., & Keel, L. P. (1997, February). *ASGW members' roundtable on group best practice guidelines: Input to Ethics Committee.* Seminar presented at the Association for Specialists in Group Work 5th National Group Work Conference, Athens, GA.

Rapin, L. S., & Keel, L. P. (1998). ASGW best practices in group work. (Adopted by ASGW Executive Board March 29, 1998).

Rapin, L., Wilson, F. R., & Newmeyer, M. (2005). Working with ASGW group work training standards. ACA Convention Program #566. Atlanta, GA.

Raths, L. E., Harmin, M., & Simon, S. B. (1966). *Values and teaching.* Columbus, OH: Charles E. Merrill Publishing.

Reddy, W. B. (1985). The role of change agent in the future of group work. *Journal for Specialists in Group Work, 10*(2), 103–107.

Rencken, R. H. (1989). *Intervention strategies for sexual abuse.* Alexandria, VA: American Counseling Association.

Ridley, C. R., Mendoza, D. W., & Kanitz, B. E. (1994). Multicultural training: Re-examination, operationalization, and integration. *The Counseling Psychologist, 22,* 227–289.

Riordan, R. J. (1996). Scriptotherapy: Therapeutic writing as a counseling adjunct. *Journal for Counseling and Development, 74,* 263–269.

Riordan, R. J., & Matheny, K. B. (1972). Dear diary: Logs in group counseling. *The Personnel and Guidance Journal, 50,* 379–382.

Riordan, R. J., & White, J. (1996). Logs as therapeutic adjuncts in group. *Journal for Specialists in Group Work*, *21*(2), 94–100.

Ritchie, M. H., & Huss, S. N. (2000). Recruitment and screening of minors for group counseling. *Journal for Specialists in Group Work*, *25*, 146–156.

Rittenhouse, J. (1997). Feminist principles in survivors groups: Out-of-group contact. *Journal for Specialists in Group Work*, *22*(2), 111–119.

Ritter, K. Y., West, J. D., & Trotzer, J. P. (1986). Comparing family counseling and group counseling: An interview with George Gazda, James Hansen, and Alan Hovestadt. *Journal of Counseling and Development*, *65*(6), 295–300.

Riva, M. T., & Kalodner, C. R. (1997). Group research: Encouraging a collaboration between practitioners and researchers. *Journal for Specialists in Group Work*, *22*(4), 226–227.

Riva, M. T., & Korinek, L. (2004). Teaching group work: Modeling group leader and member behaviors in the classroom to demonstrate group theory. *Journal for Specialists in Group Work*, *29*, 55–64.

Riva, M. T., Lippert, L., & Tackett, M. J. (2000). Selection practices of group leaders: A national survey. *Journal for Specialists in Group Work*, *25*, 157–169.

Riva, M. T., Wachtel, M., & Lasky, G. B. (2004). Effective leadership in group counseling and psychotherapy. In J. L. DeLucia-Waack,, D. A. Gerrity, C. R. Kalodner, & M. T. Riva (Eds.), *Handbook of group counseling and psychotherapy* (pp. 37–48). Thousand Oaks, CA: Sage.

Rivera, E. T., Wilbur, M., Roberts-Wilbur, J., Phan, L. T., Garrett, M. T., & Betz, R. L. (2004). Supervising and training pschoeducational group leaders. *Journal for Specialists in Group Work*, *29*, 377–394.

Roark, A. E., & Roark, A. B. (1979). Group structure: Components and effects. *Journal for Specialists in Group Work*, *4*(4), 186–192.

Robinson, III, E. H. (Ed.). (1980). Life coping skills through the group medium. *Journal for Specialists in Group Work*, *5*(3).

Robison, F. F., Jones, E. N., & Berglund, K. E. (1996). Research on the preparation of group counselors. *Journal for Specialists in Group Work*, *21*, 172–177.

Rollock, D. A., Westman, J. S., & Johnson, C. (1992). A Black student support group on a predominantly White university campus: Issues for counselors and therapists. *The Journal for Specialists in Group Work*, *17*, 243–252.

Rogers, C. R. (1951). *Client-centered therapy*. Boston: Houghton Mifflin.

Rogers, C. R. (1952). Barriers and gateways to communication. *Harvard Business Review*, *30*(4), 46–52.

Rogers, C. R. (1961). *On becoming a person*. Boston: Houghton Mifflin.

Rogers, C. R. (1962). The interpersonal relationship: The core of guidance. *Harvard Educational Review*, *32*, 416–429.

Rogers, C. R. (1967). The process of the basic encounter group. In J. F. T. Bugental (Ed.), *Challenges of humanistic psychology*. New York: McGraw-Hill.

Rogers, C. R. (1970). *Carl Rogers on encounter groups*. New York: Harper & Row.

Rokeach, M. (1960). *The open and closed mind*. New York: Basic Books.

Rosenhan, D. L., & Seligman, M. E. P. (1989). *Abnormal psychology* (2nd ed.). New York: W.W. Norton.

Rosenthal, H. G. (Ed.) (1998). *Favorite counseling and therapy techniques: 51 therapists share their most creative strategies*. Bristol, PA: Accelerated Development.

Rossel, R. D. (1981). Word play metaphor and humor in the small group. *Small Group Behavior*, *12*(1), 116–136.

Ruevini, U. (1985). The family as a social support group now and 2001. *Journal for Specialists in Group Work*, *10*(2), 88–93.

Rugel, R. P. (1991). Closed and open systems: The tavistock group from a general system perspective. *Journal for Specialists in Group Work*, *16*(2), 74–84.

Ruiz, A. S. (1990). Ethnic Identity: Crisis and resolution. *Journal of Multicultural Counseling & Development*, *18*, 29–40.

Rybak, C. J., & Brown, B. M. (1997). Group conflict: Communication patterns and group development. *Journal for Specialists in Group Work, 22*(1), 31–51.

Sager, C. J., Brown, H. S., Crohn, H., Engel, T., Rothstein, E., & Walker, L. (1983). *Treating the remarried family.* New York: Brunner/Mazel.

Samide, L. I., & Stockton, R. (2002). Letting go of grief: Bereavement groups for children in the school setting. *Journal of Specialists in Group Work, 27,* 192–204.

Satir, V. (1972). *Peoplemaking.* Palo Alto, CA: Science and Behavior Books.

Sayger, T. V. (1996). Creating resilient children and empowering families using a multi-family group process. *Journal for Specialists in Group Work, 21*(2), 8–89.

Schechtman, Z. (2001). Prevention groups for angry and aggressive children. *Journal for Specialists in Group Work, 26,* 228–236.

Schmidt, E. H. (n.d.). Sensitivity training: A report and critique. University of California, Los Angeles. Graduate School of Business.

Schmuck, R. A., & Schmuck, P. A. (1971). *Group processes in the classroom.* Dubuque, IA: William C. Brown.

Schmuck, R. A., & Schmuck, P. A. (1985). *Group processes in the classroom.* Dubuque, IA: William C. Brown.

Schneider-Corey, M., & Corey, G. (2006), Groups: *Process and practice (7th Edition).* Belmont, CA: Thomson, Brooks Cole.

Schutz, W. (1967). *Joy.* New York: Grove Press.

Seigelman, E. (1983). *Personal risk: Mastering change in love and work.* New York: Harper and Row.

Seligman, M. (Ed.). (1982). *Group psychotherapy and counseling with special populations.* Baltimore, MD: University Park Press.

Seligman, M. P. (1995). The effectiveness of psychotherapy: The Consumer Report study. *American Psychologist, 50,* 965–974.

Seligman, M. E. P., & Maier, S. F. (1967). Failure to escape traumatic shock. *Journal of Experimental Psychology, 74,* 1–9.

Sexton, T. L., Whiston, S. C., Bleuer, J. C., & Walz, G. R. (1997). *Integrating outcome research into counseling practice and training.* Alexandria, VA: American Counseling Association.

Shaffer, J., Brown, L. L., & McWhirter, J. J. (1998). Survivors of child sexual abuse and dissociative coping: Relearning in a group context. *Journal for Specialists in Group Work, 23,* 74–94.

Shakor, M., & Fister, D. L. (2000). Finding hope in Bosnia: Fostering resilience through group process intervention. *Journal for Specialists in Group Work, 25,* 269–287.

Shapiro, J. L., & Shapiro, S. B. (1985). Group work to 2001: HAL or haven (from isolation). *Journal for Specialists in Group Work, 10*(2), 83–87.

Sharma, M. (1998, May). Welcoming Remarks. Multicultural and Spiritual Dimensions of Counselor Supervision Workshop. Cambridge College, Boston, MA.

Shavelson, R., & Towne, L. (2002). *Scientific research in education.* Washington, DC: National Academy Press.

Shaw, M. E. (1981). *Group dynamics: The psychology of small group behavior.* New York: McGraw-Hill.

Sheikh, A. A., & Sheikh, K. S. (1989) (Eds.). Eastern and Western approaches to healing. New York: Wiley.

Shirts, R. G. (1969). *Bafa Bafa: A cross culture simulation.* Del Mar, CA: Simulation Training Systems.

Shostrom, E. L. (1967). *Man the manipulator: The inner journey from manipulation to actualization.* New York: Abingdon Press.

Silverman, P. R. (1985). Tertiary/secondary prevention: Preventive intervention—The case for mutual help groups. In R. Conyne (Ed.), *The group worker's handbook: Varieties of group experience* (pp. 237–258). Springfield, IL: Charles C. Thomas.

Simon, A., & Agazarian, Y. (1974). Sequential analysis of verbal interaction (SAVI). In A. Simon & E. G. Boyer (Eds.), *Mirrors for behavior III: An anthology of observation instruments* (pp. 543–564). Wyncote, PA: Communication Materials Center.

Simon, S. B., Howe, L. M., & Kirschenbaum, H. (1972). *Values clarification: A handbook of practical strategies for teachers and students.* New York: Hart Publishing.

Sklare, G., Keener, R., & Mas, C. (1990). Preparing members for "here and now" group counseling. *Journal for Specialists in Group Work, 15*(3), 141–148.

Sklare, G., Thomas, D. V., Williams, E. C., & Powers, K. A. (1996). Ethics and an experiential "here and now" group: A blend that works. *Journal for Specialists in Group Work, 21*(4), 263–273.

Slavson, S. R. (1952). The dynamics of group work. In D. F. Sullivan (Ed.), *Readings in group work.* New York: Associated Press.

Sleek, S. (1995). Group therapy: Tapping the power of team work. *APA Monitor, 26*(7), 1, 38–39.

Smaby, M. H., Maddux, C. D., Torres-Rivera, E., & Zimmick, R. (1999). A study of the effects of a skills-based versus a conventional group counseling training program. *Journal for Specialists in Group Work, 24,* 152–163.

Sodowsky, G., Kwan, K. K, and Pannu, R. (1995). Ethnic identity of Asians in the United States. In J. G.. Ponterotto, J. M. Casas, L. A. Suzuki, & C. M. Alexander (Eds.), *Handbook of multicultural counseling* (pp. 123–153). Thousand Oaks, CA: Sage.

Sommers-Flanagan, R., Barrett-Hakanson, T., & Sommers-Flanagan, J. (2000). A psychoeducational school-based coping and social skills group for depressed students. *Journal of Specialists in Group Work, 25,* 17–190.

Spitz, H. I. (1996). *Group psychotherapy and managed mental health care: A clinical guide for providers.* New York: Brunner/Mazel.

Sprinthall, R. C., Schmutte, G. T., & Sirious, L. (1991). *Understanding educational research.* Englewood Cliffs, NJ: Prentice-Hall.

Stanko, C. A., & Taub, D. J. (2002). A counseling group for children of cancer patients. *Journal for Specialists in Group Work, 27,* 43–58.

Stewart, J. (2002). *Bridges not walls: A book about interpersonal communication* (8th ed.). Boston: McGraw-Hill.

Stevens, J. O. (1971). *Awareness: Exploring, experimenting, experiencing.* Moab, UT: Real People Press.

Stockton, R. (Presenter) (1992). Developmental aspects of counseling: Process, leadership and supervision, I, II, III (videotapes). Alexandria, VA: American Counseling Association.

Stockton, R., & Morran, D. K. (1981). Feedback exchange in personal growth groups: Receiver acceptance as a function of valence, session and order of delivery. *Journal of Counseling Psychology, 28,* 490–497.

Stockton, R., & Morran, D. K. (1982). Review and perspective of critical dimensions in therapeutic small group research. In G. Gazda (Ed.), *Basic approaches to group psychotherapy and group counseling* (pp. 37–83). Springfield, IL: Charles C. Thomas.

Stockton, R., Morran, D. K., & Velkoff, P. (1987). Leadership of therapeutic small groups. *Journal of Group Psychotherapy, Psychodrama, and Sociometry, 38,* 157–165.

Stockton, R., Rohde, R. I., & Haughey, J. (1994). The effects of structured group exercises on cohesion, engagement, avoidance and conflict. *Small Group Research, 23,* 155–168.

Stockton, R., & Toth, P. L. (1996). Teaching group counselors: Recommendations for maximizing pre-service instruction. *Journal for Specialists in Group Work, 21*(4), 274–282.

Stockton, R., & Toth, P. L. (1997). Applying a general research training model to group work. *Journal for Specialists in Group Work, 22*(4), 241–252.

Sue, D. W., Arredondo, P., & McDavis, R. J. (1992). Multicultural counseling competencies and standards: A call to the profession. *Journal of Counseling and Development, 70,* 477–486.

Sue, D. W., & Sue, D. (1990). *Counseling the culturally different: Theory and practice.* New York: Wiley.

Sue, D. W. & Sue, D. (1999). *Counseling the culturally different: Theory and practice* (3rd ed.). New York: Wiley.

Sullivan, H. S. (1953a). *Conception of modern psychiatry* (2nd ed.). New York: W.W. Norton.

Sullivan, H. S. (1953b). *The interpersonal theory of psychiatry.* New York: W.W. Norton.

Sundstrom, E., DeMeuse, K., & Futrell, D. (1990). Work teams: Applications and effectiveness. *American Psychologist, 45,* 120–133.

Tatum, B. D. (1997). *Why are all the black kids sitting together in the cafeteria?* New York: Basic Books.

Taylor, M., Burlingame, G., Fuhriman, A., Kristensen, K., Johansen, J., & Dahl, D. (2001). A survey of mental health care provider and managed care organization attitudes toward, familiarity with, and use of group interventions. *International Journal of Group Psychotherapy, 51*, 243–263.

Tavantzis, T. N., & Tavantzis, M. T. (1985). Boundaries between family and group therapy. Paper presented at American Association for Counseling and Development National Convention. New York.

Teyber, E. (1997). *Interpersonal process in psychotherapy: A relational approach* (3rd ed.). Pacific Grove, CA: Brooks/Cole.

Thomas, M. C., Nelson, C. S., & Sumners, C. M. (1994). From victims to victors: Group process as the path to recovery for males molested as children. *Journal for Specialists in Group Work, 19*(2), 102–111.

Thomas, V., Pender, D., Brock, C, Gambio, B., Morrow, R., & Neill, M. (2005, April). Best Practice Guidelines at a glance: Promoting excellence through planful practice. Program presented at the Annual Convention of the American Counseling Association, Atlanta, GA.

Thompson, C. L., & Poppen, W. A. (1979). *Guidance activities for counselors and teachers.* Monterey, CA: Brooks/Cole.

Tichy, N. M. (1997). *The Leadership Engine: How winning companies build leaders at every level.* New York: HarperCollins Publishers.

Tiedeman, D. V., & Tiedeman, A. L. M. (1973). Guidance in learning: An examination of roles in self-centering during thinking. *The School Counselor, 20*, 334–339.

Tindall, J. A. (1989). *Peer power: Book 2, applying peer helper skills* (2nd ed.). Muncie, IN: Accelerated Development.

Tindall, J. A., & Gray, H. D. (1985). *Peer power: Becoming an effective helper. Book I-Introductory program* (2nd ed.). Muncie, IN: Accelerated Development.

Tindall, J. A., & Gray, H. D. (1989). *Peer counseling: In-depth look at training peer helpers* (3rd ed.). Muncie, IN: Accelerated Development.

Toffler, A. (1970). *Future shock.* New York: Random House.

Toman, W. (1976). *Family constellations* (3rd ed.). New York: Springer.

Toth, P. L. (1997). A short-term grief and loss therapy group: Group members' experience. *Journal of Personal and Interpersonal Loss, 2*, 83–103.

Toth, P. L. (2005). The contributions of Rex Stockton to the field of group work: Implications and applications. *Journal for Specialists in Group Work, 30*, 199–202.

Toth, P. L., & Erwin, W. J. (1998). Applying skill-based curriculum to teach feedback in groups: An evaluation Study. *Journal of Counseling and Development, 76*, 294–301.

Toth, P. L., & Stockton, R. (1996). A skill based approach to teaching group counseling interventions. *Journal for Specialists in Group Work, 21*(2), 101–109.

Toth, P. L., Stockton, R., & Erwin, W. J. (1998). Application of a skill-based training model for group counselors. *Journal for Specialists in Group Work, 23*, 101–109.

Tripany, R. L., White, V. E., & Wilcoxen, S. A. (2004). Preventing vicarious trauma: What counselors should know when working with trauma survivors. *Journal of Counseling and Development, 82*, 31–37.

Trotzer, J. P. (1971). Process comparison of encounter groups and discussion groups using video taped excerpts. *Journal of Counseling Psychology, 18*, 358–361.

Trotzer, J. P. (1972). Group counseling: Process and perspective. *Guidelines for Pupil Services, 10*, 105–110.

Trotzer, J. P. (1973). Using communication exercises in groups. *Personnel and Guidance Journal, 51*, 373–377.

Trotzer, J. P. (1975). The counselor and the group: Differentiating to facilitate practice. *Guidelines for Pupil Services, 14*, 11–16.

Trotzer, J. P. (1977). *The counselor and the group: Integrating theory, training and practice.* Monterey, CA: Brooks/Cole Publishing Company.

Trotzer, J. P. (1979). Developmental tasks in group counseling: The basis for structure. *Journal for Specialists in Group Work*, 4(4), 177–185.

Trotzer, J. P. (1980). Develop your own guidance group: A structural model for planning and practice. *The School Counselor*, 27(5), 341–349.

Trotzer, J. P. (1984). Brief reviews. *Journal of Psychology and Theology*, 12(3), 248.

Trotzer, J. P. (1985). Interpersonal problem solving: The group counseling approach. In R. K. Conyne (Ed.). *The group worker's handbook: Varieties in group experience* (pp. 91–112). Springfield, IL: Charles C. Thomas.

Trotzer, J.P. (1988a). Family theory as a group resource. *Journal for Specialists in Group Work. 13*, 180-185.

Trotzer, J. P. (1988b). Group and family interface. *Together*, 16(2), 6, 8.

Trotzer, J. P. (1997a). Gleanings of a process observer. *Together*, 25(2), 7.

Trotzer, J. P. (1997b). Gleanings of a process observer. *Together*, 25(3), 6.

Trotzer, J. P. (1997c). Gleanings of a process observer. *Together*, 26(1), 6.

Trotzer, J. P. (1997d). Problem-solving (solution focused and brief) group counseling: A working model. Workshop presented at the Association for Specialists in Group Work 5th National Conference, Athens, GA.

Trotzer, J. P. (1997e) Treating violence and conflict in families. ACA Professional Development Workshop. American Counseling Association (5999 Stevenson Avenue, Alexandria, VA).

Trotzer, J. P. (1998a). Draw your family table/family-o-gram. In H. G. Rosenthal (Ed.), *Favorite counseling and therapy techniques: 51 therapists share their most creative strategies* (pp. 179–181). Bristol, PA: Accelerated Development.

Trotzer, J. P. (1998b). Gleanings of a process observer. *Together*, 26(2), 6.

Trotzer, J. P. (1998c). Problem solving (solution-focused and brief) group counseling: A working model. Association for Specialists in Group Work 6th National Group Workers Conference, Tucson, AZ.

Trotzer, J. P. (2000). Group work practice ideas: Problem solving procedures in group work. *The group worker, 29*, 9–12.

Trotzer, J. P. (2001a). Problem solving group therapy. In R. Corsini (Ed.), *Handbook of innovative therapy* (2nd ed., pp. 501–513). New York: Wiley.

Trotzer, J. P. (October, 2001b). Responding to crises caused by natural disasters: Helping children cope and recover from natural disasters (keynote address). National Changhwa University of Education, Changhwa, Taiwan.

Trotzer, J. P. (2004). Conducting a group: Guidelines for choosing and using activities. In J. De-Lucia-Waack, D. A. Gerrity, C. R. Kalodner, & M. T. Riva *Handbook of group counseling and psychotherapy* (pp. 76–90). Thousand Oaks, CA: Sage.

Trotzer, J. P., & Kassera, W. J. (1971). Do counselors do what they're taught? *The school counselor, 18*(5), 335–341.

Trotzer, J. P., & Kassera, W. J. (1972). *Effect of human relations experience on prospective teachers' attitudes and self concept.* River Falls: University of Wisconsin-River Falls.

Trotzer, J. P., & Kassera, W. J. (1973). Guidelines for selecting communication techniques in group counseling. *The School Counselor, 20*(4), 299–301.

Trotzer, J. P., & Sease, W. A. (1971). The effect of group-centered and topic-centered methods on volunteer college students' self concepts. *Journal of College Student Personnel, 12*, 292–296.

Trotzer, J. P., & Trotzer, T. B. (1986). *Marriage and family: Better ready than not.* Muncie, IN: Accelerated Development.

Trotzer, J. P., West, J., Ritter, K., & Malnati, R. (1985). Integrating and differentiating group and family counseling in theory, training and practice. Presentation at the American Association for Counseling and Development National Convention, New York, NY.

Trotzer, J. P., West, J., Ritter, K., Malnati, R., & Hovestadt, A. (1987). Group and family perspectives on a simulated family session. Presentation at the American Association for Counseling and Development National Convention, Chicago, IL.

Truax, C. B., & Carkhuff, R. R. (1967). *Toward effective counseling and psychotherapy: Training and practice*. Chicago: Aldine.

Tubbs, S. L., & Moss, S. (1978). *Interpersonal communication*. New York: Random House.

Tuckman, B. W. (1965). Developmental sequences in small groups. *Psychological Bulletin, 63*(6), 384–399.

Tuckman, B. W., & Jensen, M. C. (1977). Stages of group development revisited. *Group & Organizational Studies, 2*(4), 419–427.

Unger, R. (1989). Selection and composition criteria in group psychotherapy. *Journal for Specialists in Group Work, 14*(3), 151–157.

Vacc, N. A. (1989). Group counseling: C.H. Patterson—A personalized view. *Journal for Specialists in Group Work, 14*(1), 4–15.

Vacc, N. A., DeVaney, S. B., & Willmer, J. (1992). *Experiencing and counseling multicultural and diverse populations* (3rd ed.). Bristol, PA: Accelerated Development.

Vacha-Hasse, T., Ness, C.M., Dannison, L, & Smith, A. (2000). Grandparents raising children: A psychoeducational group approach. *Journal of Specialists in Group Work, 25*, 67–77.

Van Velsor, P. (2004). Training for successful group work with children: What and how to teach. *Journal for Specialists in Group Work, 29*, 127–136.

Verplanck, W. S. (1970). Trainers, trainees and ethics. *Counseling Psychologist, 2*(2), 71–75.

Villalba, J. A. (2003). A psychoeducational group for limited-English proficient Latino/Latina children. *Journal for Specialists in Group Work, 28*, 261–276.

Visher E. B., & Visher, J. S. (1979). *Stepfamilies*. New York: Brunner/Mazel.

Visher, E. B., & Visher, J. S. (1988). *Old loyalties, new ties: Therapeutic strategies with stepfamilies*. New York: Brunner/Mazel.

Vorrath, H. H. (n.d.). *Positive peer culture: Content, structure and process*. Red Wing, MN: Red Wing State Training School.

Vorrath, H., & Brendtro, L. (1974). *Positive peer culture*. Chicago: Aldine.

Vorrath, H., & Brendtro, L. (1985). *Positive peer culture* (2nd ed.). Chicago: Aldine.

Vriend, T. J. (1969). High-performing inner city adolescents assist low-performing peers in counseling groups. *Personnel and Guidance Journal, 47*, 897–904.

Vriend, T. J. (1985). We've come a long way group. *Journal for Specialists in Group Work, 10*(2), 63–67.

Vygotky, L. S. (1978). *Mind in society: The development of higher psychological process*. Cambridge, MA: Harvard University Press.

Waitley, D. E. (1978). *The psychology of winning*. Nightengale-Conant Corporation (7300 North Lehigh Avenue, Chicago, IL 60648).

Waldo, M. (1985). A curative factor framework for conceptualizing group counseling. *Journal of Counseling and Development, 64*, 52–58.

Walsh, F. (Ed.). (1982). *Normal family processes*. New York: Guilford Press.

Wampold, B. E. (1986). Toward quality research in counseling psychology: Curricular recommendation for design and analysis. *The Counseling Psychologist, 14*, 37–48.

Ward, C. (2001). Natural disasters hit all-time high in 2000. *DisasterRelief.org*. Retrieved August 13, 2001 from http://www.disasterrelief.org/Disasters/010109disasters2000/

Ward, D. (1993). An interview with Bob Conyne. *Journal for Specialists in Group Work, 18*(3), 99–108.

Ward, D. E. (2003). Connections: Fundamental elements of a comprehensive approach to group work. *Journal for Specialists in Group Work, 28*, 191–194.

Ward, D. E. (2004) The evidence mounts: Group work is effective. *Journal for Specialists in Group Work, 29*, 155–157.

Ward, D. E. (2005). Introducing a special issue on the contributions of Rex Stockton. *Journal for Specialists in Group Work, 30*, 197–198.

Ward, D. E., & Litchy, M. (2004). The effective use of processing in groups. In J. DeLucia-Waack, D. A. Gerrity, C. R. Kalodner, & M. T. Riva (Eds.), *Handbook of group counseling and psychotherapy* (pp. 104–119). Thousand Oaks, CA: Sage.

Wehrly, B. (1991). Preparing multicultural counselors. *Counseling and Human Development, 24,* 1–24.

Weinstein, M., & Rossini, E. D. (1998). Academic training in group psychotherapy in clinical psychology doctoral programs. *Psychological Reports, 82,* 955–959.

Weisbord, M. R., & Janoff, S. (1995) *Future Search: An Action Guide.* San Francisco: Berrett-Koehler Publishers.

Welfel, E. R., & Kitchener, K. S. (1992). Introduction to the special section: Ethics education—An agenda for the 90s. *Professional psychology: Research and practice, 23*(3), 179–181.

Wenz, K., & McWhirter, J. J. (1990). Enhancing group experience: Creative writing exercises. *Journal for Specialists in Group Work, 15*(1) 37–42.

West, J. D., & Kirby, J. (Eds). (1981). Troubled family interactions and group intervention. *Journal for Specialists in Group Work, 6*(1).

Wheelan, S. A. (1997). Co-therapists and the creation of a functional psychotherapy group: A group dynamics perspective. *Group Dynamics: Theory, Research, and Practice, I,* 306–310.

Wheelan, S. A. (2004). *Groups in the workplace.* In J. DeLucia-Waack, D. Gerrity, C. Kalodner, & M. Riva (Eds.), *Handbook of group counseling and psychotherapy* (pp. 401–413). Thousand Oaks, CA: Sage.

Whitaker, D. S., & Lieberman, M. A. (1964). *Psychotherapy through the group process.* New York: Atherton.

White, R. W. (1966). *Lives in progress.* New York: Holt, Rinehart, & Winston.

Whiteley, J. M. (1970). Special section: Some ethical questions. *Counseling Psychologist, 2*(2).

Whitman, J. S., Morgan, L. B., & Alfred, A. R. (1996). Graduate students as co-leaders of groups: A trainees experience. *Journal for Specialists in Group Work, 21*(3), 187–193.

Wilbur, J. R., Wilbur, M., Garrett, M. T., & Yuhas, M. (2001). Talking circles: Listen or our tongue will make you deaf. *Journal for Specialists in Group Work, 26,* 368–384.

Wilbur, M. P., & Roberts-Wilbur, S. (1994). Group work with men's beliefs. *Journal for Specialists in Group Work, 19*(2), 65–82.

Williams, G. T. (1990). Ethical dilemmas in teaching a group leadership course. *Journal for Specialists in Group Work, 15*(2), 104–113.

Williams, C. B., Frame, M. W., & Green, E. (1999). Counseling groups for African American women: A focus on spirituality. *Journal of Specialists in Group Work, 24,* 260–273.

Wilson, R., Conyne, R., Bardgett, D., & Smith-Hartle, A. (1987). Marketing group counseling services. *Journal for Specialists in Group Work, 12,* 10–17.

Wilson, F. R., Conyne, R. K., & Ward, D. (1994). The general status of group work training in accredited counseling programs. *Journal for Specialists in Group Work, 19,* 140–154.

Wilson, F. R., Rapin, L., & Haley-Banez, L. (2004). How teaching group work can be guided by foundational documents: Best practice guidelines, diversity principles, training standards. *Journal for specialists in Group Work, 29,* 19–30.

Widra, J. M., & Amidon, E. (1987). Improving self-concept through intimacy group training. *Small group behavior, 18,* 269–279.

Wolpe, J. (1990). *The practice of behavior therapy.* Elmsford, NY: Pergamon Press.

Wrenn, C. G. (1962). *The counselor in a changing world.* Washington DC: American Personnel and Guidance Association.

Wrenn, C. G. (1971). The attitude of caring. *Education News,* January.

Wrenn, C. G. (1985). Afterward: The culturally encapsulated counselor revisited. In P. Pedersen (Ed.), *Handbook of cross-cultural counseling and therapy* (pp. 323–330). Westport, CT: Greenwood.

Wright, E. W. (1963). Group procedures. *Review of Educational Research, 33,* 205–213.

Wubbolding, R. (1991). *Understanding reality therapy.* New York: Harper & Row. Retrieved June 2, 2004 from http://www.newyorkmetro.com/news/articles.wtc.1year.numbers.htm

Yalom, I. D. (1970). *The theory and practice of group psychotherapy.* New York: Basic Books.

Yalom, I. D. (1975). *The theory and practice of group psychotherapy* (2nd ed.). New York: Basic Books.

Yalom, I. D. (1983). *Inpatient group psychotherapy.* New York: Basic Books.

Yalom, I. D. (1985). *The theory and practice of group psychotherapy* (3rd ed.). New York: Basic Books.

Yalom, I. D. (1995). *The theory and practice of group psychotherapy* (4th ed.). New York: Basic Books.

Yeh, C. J., Hunter, C. D., Madan-Bahel, A., Chiang, S., & Arora, A. K. (2004). Indigenous and interdependent perspectives of healing: Implications for counseling and research. *Journal of Counseling & Development, 82,* 410–419.

Young, J. L. (1994). Sapphires-in-transition: Enhancing personal development among Black female adolescents. *Journal of Multicultural Counseling and Development, 22,* 86–95.

Young, M. A. (1997). *The community crisis response team training manual* (2nd ed.). Washington DC: National Organization for Victim Assistance.

Young, M. E. (1992). *Counseling methods and techniques: An eclectic approach.* New York: Merrill.

Yu, A., & Gregg, C. H. (1993). Asians in groups: More than a matter of cultural awareness. *The Journal for Specialists in Group Work, 18,* 86–93.

Zimpfer, D. G. (1984). *Group work in the helping professions: A bibliography* (2nd ed.). Muncie, IN: Accelerated Development.

Zimpfer, D. G. (1986). Planning for groups based on their developmental phases. *Journal for Specialists in Group Work, 11*(3), 180–187.

Zimpfer, D. G. (1991). Pre-training for group work: A review. *Journal for Specialists in Group Work, 16*(4), 264–269.

Zimpfer, D. G. (1989–1992). Review of group literature section. *Journal for Specialists in Group Work.*

Zuk G. H. (1971). Family therapy during 1964–1970. *Psychotherapy: Theory, Research and Practice, 8,* 90–97.

Zuk G. H. (1981). *Family therapy: A triadic based approach* (Rev. ed.). New York: Human Sciences Press.

Index

Page numbers in italics refer to Figures or Tables.